P9-BHS-722

Barbara Clark

**CALIFORNIA STATE UNIVERSITY,
LOS ANGELES**

GROWING UP *Gifted*

THIRD EDITION

Developing the Potential of Children at Home and at School

Merrill Publishing Company

A BELL & HOWELL INFORMATION COMPANY

Columbus   Toronto   London   Melbourne

To my beautiful mother, who started it all,
my son, who allowed me to live with giftedness,
my daughter, who taught me the gentleness of special gifts,
my husband, who believes in growing and miracles,
my dearest father, who loves us all,
and Emily, from whom I'm learning all over again.

129934

Cover Photo: © Nicole Arena. Miss Arena, a senior at the Fort Hayes Career Center in Columbus, Ohio, participates in a visual arts program for gifted students. Her instructors are Phil Arena and Ken Valimaki.

Published by Merrill Publishing Company
A Bell and Howell Information Company
Columbus, Ohio 43216

This book was set in Garamond.
Administrative Editor: Vicki Knight
Production Coordinator: Anne Daly
Art Coordinator: Mark Garrett
Cover Designer: Cathy Watterson

Photo credits: All photos copyrighted by individuals or companies listed. Merrill/Andy Brunk: pp. 45, 115, 135, 217, 459, 531; Marc Balay, Wanda Balay, Carmella Brown, Barbara Clark, Barbara Corrales, Toby Manzares, or Barry Ziff, pp. 1, 5, 29, 57, 67, 69, 73, 89, 93, 98, 109, 123, 124, 139, 163, 171, 175, 210, 251, 275, 307, 316, 331, 344, 382, 391, 427, 430, 437, 440, 503, 547, 575, 590, 596.

References for Chapter Opening Quotations: Chapter 1, A. Perone and D. Pulvino; Chapter 2, Harold H. Anderson; Chapter 3, Bob Samples, 1987, p. 106; Chapter 4, Walter B. Barbe; Chapter 5, Sidney Marland, 1972, p. 23; Chapter 6, Elizabeth Monroe Drews, 1976, pp. 27–28; Chapter 7, Alfred North Whitehead; Chapter 8, Carl Sagan, 1977; Chapter 9, J. Krishnamurti, 1964; Chapter 10, Anonymous; Chapter 11, Kahlil Gibran, *The Prophet* (New York: Alfred A. Knopf, 1960 [© 1923], p. 62); Chapter 12, James Fadiman, 1976.

Library of Congress Catalog Card Number: 87–062849
International Standard Book Number: 0–675–20832–7
Printed in the United States of America

2 3 4 5 6 7 8 9 — 92 91 90 89

PREFACE

As I offer this third edition to you who are interested in the optimal education of gifted learners, I note how much things have changed since the last revision. My thinking has changed, the field has changed, and even the children seem to have changed. We are surrounded by more knowledge, more challenges to old ideas, and more depth and breadth to our understandings. Many of the ideas and suggestions in the last edition remain to be used as they are, for they are not yet commonly available to children; some needed to be reorganized, some to be clarified, and some to be expanded. Thoughts, ideas, and strategies from more scholars, more educators, more students, and more parents needed inclusion. It has been a most productive and exciting period for gifted education and for those interested in gifted individuals. You will find much of that productivity and excitement in this new edition. Hopefully, it has grown just as you have grown, and it will be of greater use to you than before. The changes are presented with a belief in their value to you and to the gifted students you serve whether in the home or at school.

The Contents will show you some of the new organization and the new areas of focus. The first chapter is still concerned with discovering who the gifted are and just what giftedness means. As the inquiry into the structure and meaning of intelligence has been enhanced by new work, so has our discussion. With a better understanding of the functioning of the brain has come exciting information regarding the implications of this field of research for learning and teaching. At the request of our students, a lesson outline for teaching an understanding of giftedness has been included. Too often gifted learners do not really understand what we mean by the term *gifted*, nor do they comprehend the implications and expectations that level of development may have for their lives. Parents and other staff members as well as students will benefit from the implementation of this new unit of study.

The emphasis on creativity as both an integral part of giftedness and an integrative structure required a separate chapter. There is so much yet to be done to assure students of opportunities for growth in this area that the discussion of the concept of creativity is presented in Chapter 2, while strategies to be used in the classroom are offered as part of the intuitive process in Chapter 8.

New information on becoming gifted and growing up gifted enhances Chapters 3 and 4. To understand the characteristics of gifted learners makes differentiation of the curriculum possible; to understand their social-emotional development allows us to meet their needs and extend their visions in a balanced, meaningful way.

There are many alternative program structures available that can be used to build an appropriate continuum of services for gifted learners. Chapter 5 presents a number of these options and outlines how each may be used. Of course only you, the professional, will be able to decide how this information can fit into a program to meet the needs of your students, your school, and your community. Writing a plan for your district or school will be simplified by the use of the outline provided in this chapter.

Procedures for finding gifted learners for your program and a chart of tests that can be used to screen and identify these students can be found in Chapter 6. The overview of an identification procedure being used successfully to identify culturally diverse students will be especially useful for those who are seeking answers to problems in this area. Screening, identifying, and assessing students are three important steps to truly differentiated and individualized programs for gifted learners.

Chapters 7 and 8 have been reorganized and expanded to support teachers who want to provide their students with differentiated and individualized curriculum. Beginning in Chapter 7, an overview is presented of organizational patterns and strategies for gifted programs that are developed from the characteristics and needs of gifted learners. A variety of curriculum models that can be used in developing differentiated curriculum is offered, with a special focus on the Integrative Education Model as a way of structuring the use of the new brain/mind data in the classroom.

Chapter 8 presents a classroom environment and strategies to aid in individualizing and implementing the differentiated curriculum developed in Chapter 7. In addition to techniques for individualizing the program, teachers will find help in developing a responsive learning environment, extending the learning into the community and surrounding natural learning settings, and establishing an integrative learning approach. Strategies are presented for developing the content of specific subject matter; cognitive, affective, physical/sensing, and intuitive processes; and the products necessary for a differentiated, integrative curriculum.

Chapter 9 allows us to focus specifically on how the curriculum can be developed and gifted needs can be met at the middle and secondary school levels.

Adolescence is a special time, and we must understand how these transitions affect gifted students if we are to be effective in helping them learn. Of special help will be the outline of how to share the responsibility for learning with secondary students.

Research continues to give us ideas for how many of the special concerns in gifted education can be met. While questions still confront us in many areas, the review in Chapter 10 of the work that has been done will at least give us some understanding of the problems and a starting point as we explore each area further.

Teachers, administrators, counselors, and parents all provide important support roles for gifted children. As a team they can assure effective, appropriate learning experiences. Information and guides to further the work of these important team members is provided in Chapter 11.

Finally, we look at the possibilities that show promise of significantly affecting the future of our children and through them all of us. We continue to live in times of great change, times of beckoning promise, times that challenge us to be the most of who we can be, to take joy in the human possibilities. If anything, the ideas and challenges are more amazing, more profound than ever before.

At the end of each chapter you will find questions that I have often been asked by teachers and parents around the country and in other countries. The responses are mine. While I believe they are informed responses and reflect much of the thinking in the field, I do not represent them as the only responses that would be appropriate. Others may believe differently; some may have more or less to say about each question. I can only offer my response as the data and my experience allow me to understand. It is my hope that they will provide clarification and a better understanding of those areas that at least some people thought to question.

ACKNOWLEDGMENTS

The acknowledgments for this edition of *Growing Up Gifted* must include appreciation for all of the teachers and gifted students I continue to learn from throughout these years. A very special thanks to Lynn Copley-Graves who was the editor on the first edition and returns with her caring and competence to this third edition, and to Vicki Knight, a joy as administrative editor. Also, thanks to Patricia C. Westhafer, Mary Baldwin College; Maurice Miller, Indiana State University; John M. McLoughlin, Bloomsburg University; Jim Van Tassel, Ball State University; and Julia Roberts, Western Kentucky University, who reviewed the manuscript and provided thoughtful suggestions for strengthening the third edition. But most of all I must include my husband, Terry, who has been and continues to be there for me in so many supportive and loving ways.

In this book it is my hope that all of you who care about gifted individuals will find much that will aid you to discover the excitement and pleasure of being with these special children as they share the process of *growing up gifted*.

CONTENTS

7. Developing a Differentiated Curriculum: Gifted Needs and Curriculum Models 251

8. Implementing a Differentiated Integrative Curriculum: Strategies for Meeting Gifted Needs 307

9. Secondary Schools and the Gifted Adolescent 427

10. Areas of Concern in Gifted Education 459

11. Teachers of the Gifted at School and at Home 531

12. The Amazing Possibilities Ahead 575

I. Understanding the Gifted Individual

ASSESSMENT INSTRUMENT

Before you begin reading this text, you may find it helpful to try the following questionnaire. These questions allow you to look at your beliefs and understandings regarding gifted children. Before each statement place the number that you feel most closely represents your present position. At the end of this exercise the results are discussed. Be as open as you can. You may discover some new insights about yourself.

1—I strongly agree
2—I agree
3—I have no opinion
4—I disagree
5—I strongly disagree

_____ **1** The term *gifted* can mean different things to different people and often causes much confusion and miscommunication.

_____ **2** Intelligence can be developed and must be nurtured if giftedness is to occur.

_____ **3** We seldom find very highly gifted children or children we could call *geniuses;* therefore, we know comparatively little about them.

_____ **4** Thinking of, or speaking of, gifted children as superior people is inaccurate and misleading.

_____ **5** As schools are currently organized, it is not always possible for gifted children to receive appropriate educational experiences without special programs.

_____ **6** Equal opportunity in education does not mean having the same program for everyone, but rather programs adapted to the specific needs of each child.

_____ **7** Gifted children, while interested in many things, usually are not gifted in everything.

_____ **8** Difficulty conforming to group tasks is often the result of the unusually varied interests and curiosity of a gifted child.

_____ **9** Because gifted children have the ability to think in diverse ways, teachers often see them as challenging their authority, disrespectful, and disruptive.

_____ **10** Some gifted chilren have been found to use their high level of verbal skill to avoid difficult thinking tasks.

_____ **11** The demand for products or meeting of deadlines can inhibit the development of a gifted child's ability to integrate new ideas.

_____ 12 Work that is too easy or boring frustrates a gifted child just as work that is too difficult frustrates an average learner.

_____ 13 Most gifted children in our present school system are under-achievers.

_____ 14 Commonly used sequences of learning are often inappropriate and can be damaging to gifted learners.

_____ 15 Gifted children, often very critical of themselves, tend to hold lower than average self-concepts.

_____ 16 Gifted children often expect others to live up to standards they have set for themselves, with resulting problems in interpersonal relations.

_____ 17 Gifted children are more challenged and more motivated when they work with students at their level of ability.

_____ 18 Some gifted children may perform poorly or even fail subjects in which they are bored or unmotivated.

_____ 19 The ability of gifted learners to generalize, synthesize, solve problems, engage in abstract and complex thought patterns, and think at an accelerated pace most commonly differentiates gifted from average learners; therefore, programs for gifted students should stress using these abilities.

_____ 20 The persistent goal-directed behavior of gifted children can result in others perceiving them as stubborn, willful, and uncooperative.

_____ 21 If not challenged, gifted children can waste their ability and become mediocre, average learners.

_____ 22 Gifted children often express their idealism and sense of justice at a very early age.

_____ 23 Not all gifted children show creativity, leadership, or physical expertise.

_____ 24 People who work with, study, and try to understand gifted children have more success educating the gifted than those who have limited contact and have not educated themselves as to the unique needs of these children.

_____ 25 I would be pleased to be considered gifted, and I enjoy people who are.

The questionnaire you have just completed should give you some indication of opinions of gifted children that are supportive to their educational growth. The more "1—I strongly agree" answers you were able to give, the more closely your opinions match those who have devoted their energy to understanding gifted children. In the pages to follow, we examine these issues and others that augment our understanding and ability to better educate gifted children.

1. Who Are the Gifted?

The information in this chapter provides for the reader

- An assessment of beliefs and understandings of gifted children.
- A rationale for a definition of the term *gifted*.
- A discussion of interactive intelligence and its relationship to giftedness.
- An awareness of the nature and the limitations of measuring intelligence.
- An overview of the historical development of the concept of intelligence.
- A discussion of the importance of brain function to the concept of intelligence.
- A lesson for students on understanding giftedness.

The key to understanding how people interact in their environment may be in knowing how the brain works, what behavioral actions are coupled with specific brain functions and how brain processes can be assessed in educational institutions.

—PERONE AND PULVINO

WHO ARE THE GIFTED? A DEFINITION

The question "Who are the gifted?" has been answered in many ways. Some have chosen to say they are the two percent who score highest on a test of intelligence (Terman, 1925); some equate them with creative/productive accomplishments and speak of the necessary clusters of characteristics that define them, i.e., above-average ability, creativity, and task commitment (Renzulli, 1978). Definitions range from general ones, such as the definition postulated by Witty (1940) describing them as children "whose performance is consistently remarkable in any potentially valuable area" (p. 516), to the specific though broad definition used in Public Law (PL) 97–35, the Education Consolidation and Improvement Act, passed by Congress in 1981:

> Gifted and talented children are now referred to as, "children who give evidence of high performance capability in areas such as intellectual, creative, artistic, leadership capacity, or specific academic fields, and who require services or activities not ordinarily provided by the school in order to fully develop such capabilities." (Sec. 582)

With the new research in brain/mind function, a different definition for giftedness becomes possible. The research data give us a much better understanding of the brain processes involved in learning and in the development of high levels of intelligence. Intelligence can no longer be confined to cognitive function, but clearly must include all of the functions of the brain and their efficient and integrated use. Intelligence is defined in this text as total and integrated brain functioning, which includes cognition, emotion, intuition, and physical sensing. We now have a better idea of the biological differences that will be found in very intelligent or gifted learners. It is now possible to speak of the gifted as having at least three areas of advanced or increased brain growth: the growth of dendritic spines, increases in the complexity of networks of synaptic connections among neurons, and the division of neuroglial cells (Wittrock, 1980a).

Such brain development may partially manifest itself in outstanding cognitive ability, academic aptitude, creative behavior, leadership ability, or ability in visual and performing arts. How giftedness will be expressed depends on the genetic patterns and anatomical structure of the individual and the support and opportunities provided by that individual's environment. As we will see, it is not only genetic endowment that results in giftedness; it is also the opportunities the environment provides to develop these genetic programs that will allow some children to enhance their abilities to the point of giftedness while others will be inhibited in their development, some even to the level of retardation. The growth of intelligence depends on the interaction between our biological inheritance and our environmental opportunities to use that inheritance. High levels of intelligence or giftedness are, therefore, the result of a dynamic, interactive process.

Such advanced brain growth, regardless of how it is expressed, will manifest itself in more effective and efficient use of brain function. This may be seen as accelerated thought processing, complex problem identification and solution, use of abstract thought that is often unusual and diverse, and insights of a useful and profound nature. Intellectual development will include the possibility for advanced and integrated growth of all the basic human functions identified by Jung (1964): cognitive, affective, intuitive, and physical sensory.

Given the advance in brain research and our understanding of the learning process, we can now discuss with more precision the nature and development of intelligence and, therefore, of giftedness. The following definition of giftedness encompasses this knowledge and provides an integration of earlier definitions:

> Giftedness is a biologically rooted concept, a label for a high level of intelligence that results from the advanced and accelerated integration of functions within the brain, including physical sensing, emotions, cognition, and intuition. Such advanced and accelerated function may be expressed through abilities such as those involved in cognition, creativity, academic aptitude, leadership, or the visual and performing arts. Therefore, with this definition of intelligence, gifted individuals are those who are performing, or who show promise of performing, at high levels of intelligence. Because of such advanced or accelerated development, these individuals require services or activities not ordinarily provided by the schools in order to develop their capability more fully.

This definition of giftedness relies on evidence of advanced or accelerated development of brain function. Such development can be considered synonymous with high levels of intelligence when intelligence is seen as whole brain function. When understood in this way, the term *gifted* refers to those persons who have developed high levels of intelligence or who show promise of such development.

Giftedness may be identified through many channels: (a) observation of processes used in learning in any content area, in or out of the classroom; (b) observation of performance or products from content or from any problem-solving encounter; (c) results of a wide array of psychometric instruments including tests of intelligence, achievement, and creativity; and (d) self-reporting and reporting from others such as parents, teachers, and peers. Truly, any data that give evidence of accelerated or advanced brain development should be considered.

In the discussion of giftedness, let us distinguish between the typical or most commonly found person we call gifted and the rare genius, sometimes labeled *highly gifted.* Most of our discussion relates to the typically gifted, for these persons are as different from the more highly gifted as they are from the average learner. The highly gifted seem to have different value structures, which usually allow them to cope with the dissonance they find between their perception of life and the average person's. They tend to be more isolated by choice, more invested in concerns of a metanature. They seldom seek popularity or social acclaim. Typically, schools offer these children little; some educators suggest that tutoring with eminent authorities would be far more productive as an educational plan. For further insight into this group, the reader may consult Hollingworth (1942), keeping in mind that we need new data in this area.

One further clarification would aid our definition of *giftedness.* Human beings differ in ability in all human traits. Each of us, in numerous ways, is totally unique, and in no way are we identical. Admission of difference need not, however, necessarily imply superiority. Only the history of our culture can indicate which traits are requisites for human survival and actualization. People of high intelligence do cope better with the demands of today's society. Rather than consider possession of the attribute as superior, wouldn't it be more profitable in the long run to view it as being farther along the way to being all a human can be? If a person on a trip is only 40 miles from the destination while another person on the same trip is 60 miles away, is the first person superior to the second? Admittedly, they see different things, they discuss with a different perspective, and depending on their capability, they may even end their journey at entirely different points. Superiority does not adequately differentiate their experience. So it is with this discussion of giftedness. The gifted person does display many differences compared to others not so developed. While this analogy breaks down quickly when we examine complex relationships, it still allows us to see difference without claiming superiority.

THE CONCEPT OF INTELLIGENCE

The terms *intelligence* and *intellectual ability* express many different ideas. In our discussion we will acknowledge intelligence as the result of the development of all functions of the human brain. To communicate the complexity of this development, we will use the definition developed by Cattell. *Intelligence* is a composite or combination of human traits, which includes a capacity for insight into complex relationships, all of the processes involved in abstract thinking, "adaptability in problem solving, and capacity to acquire new capacity" (Cattell, 1971, p. 8). This last phrase brings out the marvelous ability human beings have to actually change, in this case to increase, their own capacity. We can become more than we were at birth—not more in the sense of exceeding the limits of our inborn characteristics or physical structure, but most certainly more in our ability to use those characteristics and that structure. In some cases we may modify the total to become more efficient, more powerful than these limits seemingly dictated. We have not properly appreciated the ability of our organism to expand or contract as it interacts with the environment.

High intelligence, advanced or accelerated brain function—whether in cognitive abilities such as the capacity to generalize, to conceptualize, or to reason abstractly, or in specific academic ability, leadership, creative behavior expressed through visual and performing arts—results from the interaction between inherited and acquired characteristics. This interaction encompasses all of the physical, mental, and emotional characteristics of the person and all of the people, events, and objects entering the person's awareness. As no two people have identical physical, mental, and emotional properties, neither do they have the same environment. Our reality is unique to each of us. Even so simple a perception as color vastly differs between individuals. We view color differently because our eye structures differ; we respond to color uniquely because our own emotional pattern causes us to develop a personal meaning for each color as our experiences with objects of each color give us additional information. The wonder is not that we all experience our environment so differently, but that we can communicate our experience to each other at all.

We could not from this interactive point of view say which is more important: the inherited abilities or the environmental opportunities to develop them. A restriction on either would inhibit high levels of actualized intellectual ability. As Dobzhansky states, "The genotype and the environment are equally important, because they are indispensable. There is no organism without genes, and any genotype can act only in some environment" (Dobzhansky, 1964, p. 63). *Genotype* means any constellation of genes that an organism receives from its ancestors. *Phenotype* means any combination of characteristics of an organism that can be observed and measured at any point in its development. A phenotype is always in the state of becoming. Prescott (1979) calls this interaction *ecobiology*, explaining it in this way, "The influence of the environment seems to be imprinted on the structure of the brain, which in turn, shapes the environment" (p. 124).

Genes cannot be thought of as causing particular attributes; rather, they have a wide range of effects in different environments. Vernon (1979) considers the nature-nurture controversy sterile and insoluble, since neither heredity nor environment can be held constant in order to discover its effects in isolation.

Harvard biologist Stephen Jay Gould (1981) contends that although some genes may well determine variations in human intelligence, hereditarians err by equating "heritable" with "inevitable."

> Genes do not make specific bits and pieces of a body; they code for a range of forms under an array of environmental conditions. Moreover, even when a trait has been built and set, environmental intervention may still modify inherited defects. The claim that IQ is so many per cent "heritable" does not conflict with the belief that enriched education can increase what we call "intelligence." (p. 156)

An error that Gould (1981) sees in the claims of heritability of intelligence quotient

(IQ) is the confusion of within-group and between-group behaviors. All studies of heritable IQ are within a single population; however, variations among individuals within a group and differences in mean values between groups are entirely separate phenomena. As Gould states, "One item provides no license for speculation about the other" (p. 156).

Slavkin (1987) warns us that even our beliefs about the absolute stability of genes must be reexamined. He states, "We now know that we can rearrange all of the genetic material in the course of expression. The genes are not stable. The transcription of genes from DNA to RNA can actually be rearranged." Genes provide us with a structure or pattern, but are dependent upon the environment for the particular characteristic that they will express. A signal from the environment impacts on a somatic cell and activates a regulatory gene that codes for proteins that trigger or turn on a specific somatic expression within the system. While genes provide us with our own unique menu, the environment makes the actual selection within that range of choice.

Cancro (1971) comments that it is misleading to think of either genes or the environment as being more important: genes can only express themselves in an environment, and an environment has no effect except by evoking genotypes already present. Any reference to "high-IQ genes" must be seen as a misnomer because the nature of the phenotype always depends on the particular environmental history (Rose, 1972). It would be equally incorrect to regard genetic endowment as "setting the limits" (Lerner & Libby, 1976). As Elizabeth Hagen, Emeritus Professor at Teachers College, Columbia University, commented, "I don't think there's enough evidence to distinguish the contribution of genetics from the contribution of experience—they interact" (cited in Silverman, 1986, p. 169).

As seen in the preceding paragraphs, the interaction between genetic and environmental contributions is complex and interdependent. Although all of the results are not yet understood, our exploration of this interaction will focus on the environment. We proceed with the knowledge that a one-sided focus reflects our ability as educators to influence growth and development only in the environmental realm. We fully recognize the importance of the genetic endowment and leave it to others to pursue the advancement of human intelligence by interventions from that side. Further, it must be noted that as we change the environment, we affect the genetic or biological structure of the organism. Education deals with using environments for learning; we must be aware that the decisions for environmental intervention do, in fact, change the neurological and biological structure of the living organism (Rosenzweig, 1966). The only way not to become involved in this dramatic interaction is to disavow being an educator in any form. Those of us who choose to remain in this profession or who parent children must be aware of the total impact of our decision. We investigate this concept further in the next chapter as we discuss early stimulation.

Environmental interaction with the genetic program of the individual occurs whether planned or left to occur by chance. By conservative estimates, this interaction can result in a 20-point difference in measured intelligence; some allow for a 40-point variation or even more (Bloom, 1964; Skeels & Dye, 1959; Hunt, cited in Pines, 1979b). For example, as seen in Figures 1.1a and 1.1b, two individuals with approximately the same genetic capacity for developing intelligence, as a result of the environment with which they interact, could be regarded as high achieving, as potentially gifted, or as educably retarded. Mild retardation, constituting one of the largest catagories of handicapping conditions found among children and adults, stems in large part from deprived environments (Tarjan, 1970). Such environments are apparently caused by far less than optimal prenatal and perinatal conditions in interaction with deleterious factors after birth (Birch & Gussow, 1970).

McCandless (1964), among others, concludes that at least 85 percent of those now functioning as educably retarded do so as a result of deprived, nonsupportive environments. We already know enough about supportive environments to prevent this type of retardation from occurring, enough to assure most of our children a level of functioning that would actualize far higher levels of intellectual ability. Yet, because of society's priorities, social dilemmas, and lack of parental training, we do not use what we know.

Those who work with gifted children must acquire an understanding of the power of this interaction. What we believe about how people become intelligent will very much influence the way we plan for their educational development. If we believe that individuals come to us already gifted, that they were born that way, we will probably feel that we can do little to influence their development. We may believe enrichment will be sufficient for people at this ability to "get by on their own." If, however, we consider giftedness as a dynamic process in which a person's innate ability is in constant and continuous interaction with the environment, and if we believe that the strength of that interaction will determine just how much ability this person will be able to develop, we will accomplish far more. We will become highly sensitive to the person's level, to the needs he or she expresses, and we will know how to support and challenge this developing intellect throughout the entire growth period. Without such efforts, intellectual abilities will be wasted and untold potential will never be realized. A discussion of how intelligence develops is far

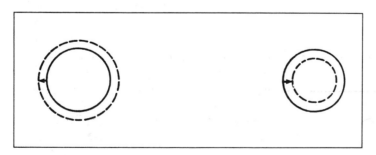

Figure 1.1a *Expanded Potential.*   **Figure 1.1b** *Restricted Potential.*

more than an academic pursuit. For our children, it is a matter of who they are and who they may become.

Measuring Intelligence

Measuring intelligence, up to now, has been dependent mostly on paper and pencil tests. The limited tasks of performance tests narrowly reflect few of the possibilities for human growth. Some of our leading researchers (Hunt & Kirk, 1971; Sternberg, 1981, 1985) perceive a need for a different way of assessing intellectual development. They feel that our reliance on tests comparing people against a standard or norm (decided upon by taking the average of what many people can do and assigning a score to it) prevents us from developing more useful measures. We must discover which activities and skills include both cognition (thinking ability) and motivational development and in what sequence these activities or skills usually appear. From that information, we could set up criterion measures that would tell us not only the present level of a child's development, but also which experiences would best challenge further growth. Sternberg (1981) states that the tests used today are little better than tests used three decades ago and are, in many cases, the same tests. He believes that the weakness of these tests is not the kind of items they contain, but rather their lack of a viable theory base.

Sternberg and several others at Yale University are working on a theoretical base for intelligence. Setting their work in an information-processing framework, these researchers believe that such a theory base will prove more useful than has the factor-analytic, psychometric base previously used for measuring, understanding, and nurturing intelligence. By delineating the components of giftedness and their functions, all of which point to specific abilities found in learners with high levels of intelligence, we may better understand how to program for the development of advanced and accelerated brain development, that is, giftedness.

At present the conventional standardized tests measure analytic abilities fairly well but fail to measure synthetic abilities—those allowing for invention, creativity, and personal contribution (Sternberg, 1986). Sternberg feels that traditional tests benefit students who can solve problems quickly in the intermediate range of difficulty and penalize those who can solve very difficult problems, for such problems have been eliminated. Further he feels that the kind of planning and evaluating needed for good performance in everyday life differs from the kind of planning and evaluating assessed by these traditional tests. Sternberg and other investigators such as Howard Gardner, a Harvard psychologist, and David Feldman, from Tufts University, are currently developing tests that they believe will be more sensitive to varying kinds of intelligence.

From Bar-Ilan University in Israel another psychologist/researcher, Reuven Feuerstein (cited in Mohs, 1982), sees an entirely different problem. Feuerstein believes that the conventional IQ test measures what people already know, which is not as important as what they can learn or where their cognitive deficiencies lie.

Feuerstein believes that such additional information allows learners to overcome their deficiencies, e.g., impulsiveness, lack of precision, and failure to discriminate the important from the unimportant. The real task is to effect change. "We are not interested in providing the child with information or specific skills. We are interested in endowing the child with capacities to benefit from his encounters" (Mohs, 1982, p. 24).

Until more productive measures of intelligence are developed, we will continue to use available measures but would be well advised to supplement their use with other evaluative tools such as observation of the processes, performance, or products of learning; the results from a variety of measures of achievement and creativity; and self-reporting and reports from parents, teachers, and peers.

The most commonly used test of intelligence is the Stanford-Binet Intelligence Scale. This scale was developed to test general intellectual ability, including verbal adroitness, ability to perceive analogies and abstractions, capacity for problem solving, ability to find causal relationships, and classification aptitude. It gained wide acceptance because it did just what was expected of it. Those judged intuitively to be highly intelligent did well on the test, while those who exhibited subnormal ability, in fact, did poorly on the test. The test was never based on an exact definition of intelligence, nor did it reflect any commitment to a rationale for how we develop intelligence. It was based, rather, on relative performance. Large numbers of people have taken the test, lending stability to it, but its predictive nature is limited to performance in similar activities. The predictive validity of such tests ranks highest on performance of school-related tasks, especially for those tested after the age of 5 years. Some claim the reliable prediction of adult occupational status from test data obtained after the age of 9 years (Jensen, 1969).

A person's score on intelligence tests is usually given as the IQ. In developing the intelligence test, variations in test performance caused by age differences were taken into account. This adjustment led to the idea of IQ, which is computed by dividing the mental age by the chronological age times 100. Standardized on the general population, the test evolved to set the average IQ at any age at 100. The middle 50% of the population falls between 90 and 110 IQ. On the Stanford-Binet, an IQ of 132 reflects the beginning of the upper 2% of the population, and a score of 68 IQ reaches the top of the lower 2%.

Borland (1986) cautions against using IQs derived from group tests to make discrete decisions. The difference between scores of 128 and 132 may be a function of the test rather than an accurate representation of the child's ability. When used for screening, as commonly done, the test can lead to unfortunate distinctions. Because of such representation, the common practice of using a group IQ test as a screen for identifying gifted students must be done with an attitude of inclusion, not exclusion. As Borland states, "The danger of false negatives is a real one; . . . the danger of false positives is not" (p. 167).

Many believe there is much to be gained from the judicious use of standardized intelligence tests. In discussing the fourth revision of the Stanford-Binet which she coauthored, Hagen (cited in Silverman, 1986) suggests that the Stanford-Binet be used to identify gifted children between the ages of 4 and 9 from a wide range of backgrounds. She believes that intelligence tests assess different types of reasoning using information collected through different kinds of experience. She developed the newest Stanford-Binet revision to include a wide scope of items that would allow assessment of different types of informational backgrounds. She feels that the instrument becomes more of a verbal test after the age of 9, and that it may hinder appraisal of children whose verbal backgrounds have been limited. For that reason she recommends her Cognitive Abilities Test (Thordike Hagen, 1983) as an alternative. While other tests of intelligence, such as the Wechsler Intelligence Scale for Children (WISC), are used, they tend to measure the same general abilities with the same limitations on predictability.

Another possible explanation may exist for the high correlation among intelligence test stores, academic success or failure, and later occupational status. McClelland (1974) suggests that high correlation may show that only those who control economic and social opportunities, the standards for values and language by which all are judged, are also those who can assure their offspring educational advantages. By knowing the right people, they can influence job selection. McClelland claims that there is no direct evidence to prove that higher test scores can guarantee any person the ability to do the higher status job. While that may be so, the predictive validity, for whatever reason, does exist as society now functions.

Regardless of the "fairness" of intelligence testing, according to the interactive concept of intelligence, any subculture or family pattern that does not support but, in fact, restricts the growth of intelligence will cause its members to receive low test scores (IQs). We could then find fault not with the test, but rather with the subculture or family patterns that brought about such low performance. The environment was unfair, not the test. Scarr-Salapatek (1974b) reports this interesting finding: genetic differences account for almost half of the IQ differences among middle-class children, but for practically none of the IQ differences among lower-class children. We must provide poor children who are truly disadvantaged by their family pattern and members of various subcultures who are limited by the values and opportunities available within their culture with more growth-producing alternatives. In so doing, we must guard against changing cultural and family patterns just because they are different. Diversity is the cornerstone of developing potential, and only patterns that inhibit the development of that potential need modification.

Today these tests of intelligence are being looked at very critically; at the same time, tests sampling other human abilities are being developed. We may soon have a way of knowing more about how a person develops and be able to apply these measures appropriately to a wider range of our human population, but until then we must be cautious about how we use current tests. If added as only one bit of information to many other observations and types of data (e.g., case studies, peer reports, and parent interviews), intelligence tests have value. By themselves, as a sole criterion for selecting educational experiences for children, they are unnecessarily damaging.

Unfortunately many people, including too many educators, believe that the IQ score gives an accurate description of a person's capacity. It does not. We currently have no tests of capacity. The most any test will tell us is how well a person can handle certain problems on the test. Because the tests resemble the material covered in formal schooling, performance on these tests will very likely predict how well the child will do in school-related activities. We must be sure to understand the strengths and weaknesses of each test before making any inferences or predictions about any person's innate abilities or potentials. Much more must be known before any decisions can be made about the person's future.

There is another way to discover growing ability. If from the beginning of their educational experience children were allowed to learn at their own rates, to pursue ideas and activities to whatever depth possible for their ability, and if they were encouraged to be curious in a rich, responsive environment, those children with special needs would begin to emerge very early. An educational program designed to meet each person's needs from the beginning of school can better show us those children with high intellectual ability than any single test instrument Such a program could also be advantageous in building on these strengths continuously. Thus, the problems usually encountered in traditional group-oriented progams would be less inhibiting to the child's development. Later we discuss in detail programming for the gifted, but we might think about this possibility now as it relates to identification of gifted children.

At this time, with so many of our schools moving in lock-step, using only a group approach to instruction and authoritarian modes of organization, we could not possibly rely on this approach for identification. However, I do believe that it has many advantages and that the possibility of moving in this direction exists. We can begin to encourage those involved in education for the gifted to consider approaches and programs that will allow for this type of natural selection.

An Historical Overview

Although the concept of intelligence as interactive has gained wide acceptance, many still either are unaware of recent data or are convinced of another view. Let us look back at how the concept of intelligence has developed over the past century.

Over 100 years ago, Charles Darwin (1859) began his investigation of the origin of the species. His cousin, Francis Galton (1869), had great interest in the hereditary factors that Darwin was investigating, and Galton began asking important questions regarding the heritability of human intelligence. The importance of his investigation into intellectual differences must not be minimized for, prior to Galton, no one had investigated the individual differences of human beings. The very success of this investigation, however, locked us into a limited concept of intellectual development for nearly a century. Because Galton, influenced by Darwin, admired and pursued the heritability issue to the exclusion of environmental effects, he established a pattern that remains a part of the inquiry into intelligence to this day. This resulted in the theory of fixed intelligence. People believed that the amount of intelligence at birth would remain intact until the day the person died. Nothing could add to or subtract from or in any way change this amount. Galton was the first to attempt an intelligence test based on scientific data. His test assumed a relationship between sensory acuity and general intelligence. Though this later proved an inadequate base for such testing, his efforts nevertheless initiated the search for functional intelligence testing. As testing for intelligence became popular, the belief prevailed that if we could find a test powerful enough, we could predict from infancy exactly what the individual would become. The seeming unreliability of infant testing was thought to be a problem of the testing procedure, not of any change in the actual intelligence.

During this period of belief in fixed intelligence, many significant events occurred. In France, in 1905, the government asked Alfred Binet to develop a way to separate a group of slow learners from other school children in order to create a special curriculum and methodology that would aid in their learning. Unlike those who later utilized his intelligence scales and concept of mental age, Binet did not agree with the theory of fixed intelligence or with the unitary factor of intelligence. He believed intelligence to be educable, a belief not again heard until the 1960s. The articles and speeches of Binet would be considered quite radical even today. Many of the educational problems he spoke out against during his day still need change (Binet, 1969). Today in our country, Binet is best known through a revision of his intelligence scale, originally devised by Lewis Terman of Stanford in 1921. This test, the Stanford-Binet Intelligence Scale, originated when no one questioned the belief in fixed intelligence. Later revisions are still based on this assumption.

Testing became very popular during the 1930s and 1940s. For a time in the United States we tested everyone for everything. There were tests for career placement, for various kinds of aptitude, for scholastic ability, for personality factors, and even for predicting success with a future marriage partner. Armies of men and thousands of school children were tested. During this period the test became the ultimate authority. Intelligence testing went to the extreme that a test score placed on a school cumulative record could be used for educational decision making without stating the availability of the protocol or even the name of the test. Parents were not permitted to know the IQ of their children, as the belief prevailed that this number gave evidence of capacity for mental development. So powerful a piece of information could not be trusted to the lay public. Some school districts and classrooms still are reluctant to share this information.

During this period of belief in fixed intelligence, the most extensive study of the characteristics and behaviors of gifted individuals was undertaken. Lewis Terman at Stanford University, working under a grant from the Commonwealth Fund of New York City, began in 1921 by choosing over 1,500 students with an average age of 11 years and IQs over 140, the average being 150. He collected extensive personal and educational data on them. The stereotype of a gifted person at that time pictured a bespectacled, frail youngster, ill at ease socially, lost in a world of books and lofty thoughts, usually isolated in some corner tenuously holding onto sanity. "Early ripe, early rot," the motto of the day, described the gifted person. No clear-thinking parent would ever desire to have such a child. Any attempt to encourage this type of development would be unthinkable. Terman's data went far to dispel these myths. Although his sample was limited culturally, socioeconomically, and racially, his findings were significant in influencing those who held extreme ideas about gifted individuals. His data allow a more realistic opinion and a more accepting view of the gifted. While conceived and mostly conducted during a period of belief in fixed intelligence, Terman's longitudinal work (lasting 30 years during his life and recently updated by some of his colleagues) added to the data disputing fixed intelligence as a viable concept (Terman, 1925).

In the first half of the twentieth century, a student of Galton, G. Stanley Hall, introduced another idea about human development that was a logical outgrowth of the concept of fixed intelligence. This view of development as predetermined was made popular largely by the work of Arnold Gesell (Gesell et al., 1940), a disciple of Hall. Again, a man who made many valuable contributions to our understanding of children became instrumental in solidifying misconceptions about how children grow and develop. Predeterminism assumes that the human organism is programmed in a sequentially time-controlled way, and that regardless of events or environments the program will prevail. Maturation and learning were seen as distinct and separate processes, with maturation controlled by heredity, and learning controlled by the environmental conditions. Maturation was thought to lead necessarily to learning. This idea was carried to such an extreme that avant-garde schools saw any attempt to guide the growth of youngsters as a grievous fault. The abuses that followed inevitably limited growth and demeaned the human beings involved. Parents were advised to allow each child to "flower" unrestrained. Permissive patterns were extolled.

Into this climate of nonintervention and nonstimulation some dissonant information began to appear. At first, any ideas that varied from the norm were disputed, rationalized away, or simply ignored. The work of Maria Montessori exemplifies the reception offered educational methodology based on opposing ideas (Standing, 1966). Although Montessori's work was highly successful, it assumed the educability of intelligence and therefore the inconstancy of the IQ. Not until decades later could the techniques and ideas of Montessori be incorporated into our educational practices. Such ideas were lost until years of evidence began to accumulate. Determined and courageous researchers and practitioners in education and psychology risked their professional reputations to share findings in direct conflict with the concept of intelligence as "fixed." Even today some consider this area of inquiry controversial.

Beth Wellman and her colleagues at Iowa University began to question the premise of fixed intelligence. In 1938, this group began an experiment that later caused them to become part of a professional controversy (Skeels et al., 1938; Skodak & Skeels, 1949; Wellman, 1940). The group established a model nursery school on the grounds of an orphanage. The operation of the orphanage was efficient in that the basic needs of the children were provided, but little time was spent in stimulation or educational activities. The nursery school was highly successful. In fact it seemed to change the intellectual behavior exhibited by the children in attendance. After measuring their progress on achievement and intelligence tests, Wellman reported her findings to the academic community in what must have been a mood of optimistic enthusiasm. In a time when information such as changes in intelligence scores and environmental intervention could be received only with suspicion, when women professors were themselves not taken seriously, small wonder that the following storm of protest became a humiliating experience for the educator.

Not until years later did another team, some of whom had worked on the original project, conduct a similar study after carefully redesigning their approach to meet the criticisms leveled at the Wellman data. This study and subsequent follow-up studies finally made an impact on the academic community. Their findings were intriguing. Children removed from the orphanage to a more stimulating environment (an institution for retarded girls where they received much attention, stimulation, and affection) gained over 20 IQ points when retested, while the control group left at the orphanage lost between 13 and 45 IQ points (Skeels & Dye, 1959). A follow-up study (Skeels, 1966) further dramatized the findings by reporting that the experimental group had become productive, functioning adults, while the control group, for the most part, had been institutionalized as mentally retarded. Few of the latter group were productive adults. Whatever one might think of the research design or sampling methods used, the results were, at the very least, provocative.

In 1960, another event occurred that again raised questions that the prevailing theory of intelligence could not answer. Dennis (1960), while observing deprived conditions in Teheran, Iran, orphanages, found 12-month-old babies who could not sit by themselves (although maturational theories assured this behavior by eight months at the latest). Other 4-year-olds were unable to walk alone, although development scales showed 1 year of age to be the appropriate time schedule. Why? How could the maturational development of these children be so far off the norm? Do environments affect maturation after all? To answer these questions, Dennis conducted a series of experiments. The resulting data, combined with earlier data, showed the concept of fixed intelligence and its natural extension, predeterminism, to be untenable (Dennis & Dennis, 1935; Dennis & Najarian, 1957).

Data such as those produced by the researchers Wellman, Skodak, Skeels, and Dennis made the formulation of a new theory for looking at intelligence necessary. An important new concept of the structure of the intellect now appeared with the factor-analytic work of J. P. Guilford (1956). Guilford felt that psychology had overly restricted its view of human intelligence. His model expanded the factors seen as part of human intelligence and showed their interrelatedness. Guilford, too, discussed intelligence as educable. He drew attention to creativity as an important function of the human mental process.

Not until well into the 1960s did the challenge against fixed intelligence reach significant proportions. A veritable cadre of intelligent men and women now faced the issue. Armed with data resulting from their work, they proceeded from an examination of the dissonance between accumulating information and the old theoretic framework, through the postulation of a new theory of intelligence, to the collection of evidence to support the new hypothesis. The sequence, difficult to assess, affected the literature and theory. Let us mention only a few of the milestone events, knowing that sheer quantity of activity makes the delineation of a chronology of importance impossible.

Work done in the 1920s in Russia had just begun to reach the American academic community. The work of the Russian researcher Vygotsky, which was suppressed during his lifetime, finally became known and discussed. With data received in Europe and finally translated for use in the United States, educators could no longer deny the possibility that learning might lead and direct the quality and speed of maturation. Vygotsky's contributions provided data for the areas of language development, educational remediation, early stimulation, and remediation of physical disability (Vygotsky, 1962).

Also from Europe, in varying quality of translation, came the work of Jean Piaget (1952). This man influenced educational theory and practice to an unprecedented degree. He began his inquiry in a most unscientific manner, one that no scientist would consider sound as a research design. Without objectivity, he selected only three subjects to observe and no control group. The subjects were his own children. However, he described so clearly and in such detail what he observed that his evidence enabled him to evolve principles of growth and development. Later examination of data from a multitude of studies testing respectable numbers verified his principles as viable and useful.

Piaget was among the first to ask about intellectual development during the first few years of human life. Drawn from his background in marine biology, his work emphasized the principles of assimilation and accommodative interaction. He believed that intellectual growth resulted from the learners' active participation in the learning process, invariably sequenced into stages. Although he set no strict time lines on the stages of development, he considered the order unalterable, with mastery of the lower stages preceding learning in the higher stages of cognition. Piaget stated that the age at which a child passes from one stage to another depends upon both the genetic endowment and the quality of the environment. He espoused one of the first interactive theories of intelligence. Researchers around the world later honored him with awards.

The work of Benjamin Bloom (1964) made another important contribution to educational practice, particularly to the growing concern for the years of early intellectual development. A reexamination of previously published data allowed Bloom to suggest a startling hypothesis. People had long assumed (and intelligence testing norms complied with the assumption) that between birth and 18 years of age humans learn in a regularly ascending line. At age 18 they level off to a plateau effect until around 45, the age when a gradual decline to senility begins. Bloom used the reassessed data to show a very different pattern. Although he looked at many human characteristics, just the findings from the area of intelligence will receive comment here. Between birth and 4 years of age children accomplish 50% of the deviation in IQ that they will acquire by 18 years of age. By 6 years of age another 30% will have been added. With the data showing 80% of the deviation in adult IQ actualized by age 6, educators developed a new awareness of preschool years as an essential time for learning. As society's concern for compensatory education also gained a following, many programs were then established to take advantage of the important early years.

The educational community began to focus on the early years of development as educators became aware of the limitations and deceptions caused by the theories of fixed intelligence and predeterminism. Reliance on these older concepts had left us with a near void in understanding how infants and young children develop intellectually. In Chapter 3 we look at the amazing and exciting knowledge that begins to fill this void. Bloom made an important contribution to classroom organization for learning with the publication of his *Taxonomy of Educational Objectives, Handbook I: Cognitive Domain* (Bloom, 1956) and his work with Krathwohl and Masia (1964) in the *Taxonomy of Educational Objectives, Handbook II: Affective Domain.*

For readers nearing or past the magic age of 45, let me hasten to add that subsequent studies done by the Fels Foundation (Kagan & Moss, 1962), the Berkeley Growth Studies (Bayley, 1968; Bayley & Schaefer, 1964), and the Terman data itself (Terman & Oden, 1947) give us a very different view of the "off to senility" phenomenon. Those studies indicate that we do *not* plateau intellectually at 18 years of age; we continue to move either upward or gradually downward depending on the intellectual challenges we engage in and largely upon our personality characteristics. Aggressive, inquiring, active, independent, sensitive people who seek new ideas and adapt comfortably to change tend to continue upward; passive, docile, dependent people who follow set patterns and seek security and repetition gradually lose intellectual facility. Data collected from the Terman studies show that growth patterns continue as people reach their 60s and 70s. Data on aging further support these possibilities.

While we had previously believed that the plasticity of the brain was only available to the very young, Buell and Coleman (1981) have made a remarkable discovery. In their study comparing a normal aged population (ages 68 to 92) with adults (ages 44 to 55) and a population showing senile dementia (SD) (ages 70 to 81), they found that the normal aged persons had longer and more branched dendrites than did either the adults or the SD group. These data suggest a model in which the aging cortex contains both regressing, dying neurons and surviving, growing neurons. This was the first demonstration of plasticity in the adult human brain.

As further support for Buell and Coleman's view, Diamond (1986) has shown that stimulation affects not only young rats but old as well to create a thickening of the thinking part of the brain. A lifetime of curiosity and activity and a love of life are important ingredients if we are to continue the stimulation of neural tissue. As Diamond states, "I found that the people who use their brains don't lose them . . . other denominators were activity, and love of life, and love of others and being loved. Love is very basic" (cited in Hopson, 1984, p. 70). Schai (cited as Ferguson, 1986a) also points to continued activity as necessary to take advantage of the plasticity of the brain. "People who led active lives when they were middle-aged remained stable or showed improvement in mental abilities after age 60. Those who didn't show marked decline" (p. 2).

The constancy of the IQ received a final blow from the work of Sontag, Baker, and Nelson (1958) and Kagan and Moss (1962). Their longitudinal studies followed 300 children from prenatal development through adulthood, with data collected at regular intervals. The results showed consistent change in IQ scores, especially at the extreme ends, with more variation evident for boys than for girls.

Jerome Bruner, J. McV. Hunt, Nancy Bayley, and many others began the task of establishing and supporting a new theory of intelligence. Bruner hypothesized that the young deal with information in three ways: action, imagery, and symbols. He believed that the preschool experience should work toward translating one into the other. Bruner (1964) stated, "The significance about the growth of the mind in the child is to what degree it depends not upon capacity but upon the unlocking of capacity" (p. 14). He saw that the process of translating or unlocking depends upon interaction with the environment of the culture. He attempted to give us a method of implementation as he set forth his new theories on instruction (Bruner, 1960, 1968).

Hunt (1961) brought out the problem of the match, that is, finding the most stimulating circumstances for children at each point in their development. To him, the major challenge of our time was to discover a way to govern the encounters children have with their environment, especially during the early years of their development. With such a match of ability and experience, children could be expected to achieve a substantially higher adult level of intellectual capacity.

Nancy Bayley (Bayley & Schaefer, 1964; Bayley, 1968) gave us a look at the behavioral correlates of mental growth during a 36-year period. Here we get more information on genetic and environmental interaction in the growth of intelligence.

Further support for this new interaction theory of intelligence must be noted in the recent renorming of the Stanford-Binet Intelligence Scale. An analysis of the standardization results showed a dramatic rise in the IQ level, especially among the preschool population. We might assume that the higher education of parents and richer earlier environments—television, higher mobility, wider use of educational toys and books, better nutrition—have helped foster this change. Later studies indicate that the observed change is a genuine phenomenon and not a research error (Thorndike, 1975). This information is even more impelling as evidence when one considers that the new standardization population purposefully included minority representation that had been omitted from the previous samplings.

During the 1980s an expanded concept of intelligence, first suggested by Guilford in a somewhat different form, has been the concern of a number of researchers and scholars, some of whom we will discuss. Each has added a dimension to consider in our understanding of intelligence.

Sternberg (1985) theorizes a triarchic concept of intelligence. To understand intelligence he believes that we must view its development from three aspects: the internal world of the individual, the external world of the individual, and the interaction between these two worlds on the individual's experience. The aspects of the internal world can be exemplified by analytical thinking; the external by contextual thinking or strategies predicated on environmental circumstances; and the interactive by the experiential that synthesizes disparate experiences in insightful ways. According to the triarchic theory, three kinds of mental processes operate: (a) metaprocesses, used to plan, monitor, and evaluate one's problem solving; (b) performance processes, used to carry out the instructions of the metaprocesses; and (c) knowledge-acquisition processes, used to figure out how to solve problems. It is in the area of the experience of the individual that Sternberg feels we fail most notably to identify or support intelligence. Referred to as *synthetic intelligence,* it is this experiential expression of giftedness that most impacts the world. Sternberg believes that augmenting our understanding of this area will permit us to develop a more complete theory of intelligence to provide us with a base for a more useful assessment of intelligence. Such advances may further lead to more effective educational strategies.

From a somewhat different point of view Howard Gardner (1983), a Harvard University psychologist, proposes a theory of multiple intelligences that includes seven relatively independent intelligences—linguistic, musical, logical-mathematical, spatial, bodily-kinesthetic, interpersonal, and intrapersonal. He believes that "Only if we expand and reformulate our view of what counts as human intellect will we be able to devise more appropriate ways of assessing it and more effective ways of educating it" (p. 4).

In the process of formulating this theory Gardner drew from a wide range of studies on subjects including prodigies, gifted individuals, brain-damaged patients, normal children and adults, and individuals of diverse cultures. As an additional basis for this expanded view Gardner is interested in the influence of the current neurobiological data on our understanding of intelligence and its development. From these data Gardner presents evidence supporting the following conclusions: (a) there is considerable plasticity and flexibility in human growth, especially during the early months of life; (b) plasticity is modulated by genetic constraints that operate from the beginning and guide development; (c) human beings are predisposed to carry out certain specific intellectual operations whose nature can be inferred from careful observation; and (d) educational efforts must build upon a knowledge of these intellectual proclivities and their points of maximum flexibility and adaptability.

Gardner's theory addresses many areas that have not previously been seen as a part of intelligence, and he brings additional clarity to the critical importance of both genetics and environment to its development. He does, however, insist that each of his intelligences be essentially independent in function and in doing so sets up a number of questionable dichotomies. He suggests that discovery learning should be preferred over explicit instruction for young children and that explicit instruction is better than discovery learning for older learners. It must be considered, however, that a balance of both experiences could be most effective for any age of learner.

Throughout the discussion of the seven intelligences, Gardner discusses the power of using one of the intelligences that is well developed as an alternative learning mode for others not as developed. This use of the multiple intelligences supporting one another to create powerful learning comes very close to the view of integrative education developed in this text. Gardner shows a deep concern for optimal learning in his theoretic framework.

The interactive theory of intelligence seems now to best describe the data available. For the development of giftedness this theory brings into question a new area of inquiry: How do humans become gifted? In Chapter 3 we examine the evidence in that area.

INTELLIGENCE: THE IMPORTANCE OF BRAIN FUNCTION

In our definition of giftedness, a high level of intelligence is viewed as advanced and accelerated brain function. The data allowing this relationship make an exciting addition to our understanding of the development of giftedness.

Neurobiologist T. Teyler (1977) explains,

> The fabric of the brain is set down as a result of the interaction of genetic blueprints and environmental influences. While the basic features of brain organization are present at birth (cell division is essentially complete), the brain experiences tremendous growth in neural processes, synapse formation, and myelin sheath formation, declining around puberty. These processes can be profoundly altered by the organism's environment. Furthermore, it has been shown that brain processes present at birth will degenerate if the environmental stimulation necessary to activate them is withheld. It appears that the genetic contribution provides a framework which, if not used, will disappear, but which is capable of further development given the optimal environmental stimulation. (pp. 31, 32)

To understand how some individuals become gifted and others do not, we need to become familiar with the basic structure and function of the human brain (see Figure 1.2). As we seek to understand how we might nurture giftedness, such knowledge will prove invaluable.

At birth the human brain contains some 100 to 200 billion brain cells (Teyler, 1977). Each neutral cell is in place and ready to be developed, ready to be used for actualizing the highest levels of human potential. With a very small number of exceptions, all human infants come equipped with this marvelous, complex heritage. While we never develop more, it is hardly necessary, as those we have, if used, would allow us to process several trillion bits of information in our lifetime (Sagan, 1977). At present it is estimated that we actually use less than 5% of this capability (Ferguson, 1973). How this complex system is used becomes critical to

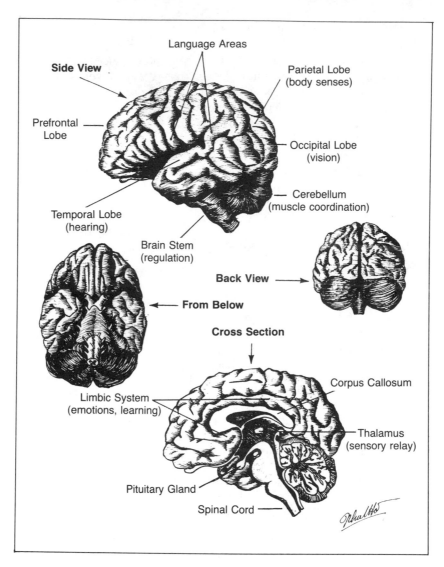

Figure 1.2   The Human Brain.

the development of intelligence and personality, and to the very quality of life experienced by the growing individual.

The Neuron

The nerve cell, or neuron, is the basic unit of the brain. The approximately 100 billion neurons within the brain are so small that 100,000 of them can fit into a

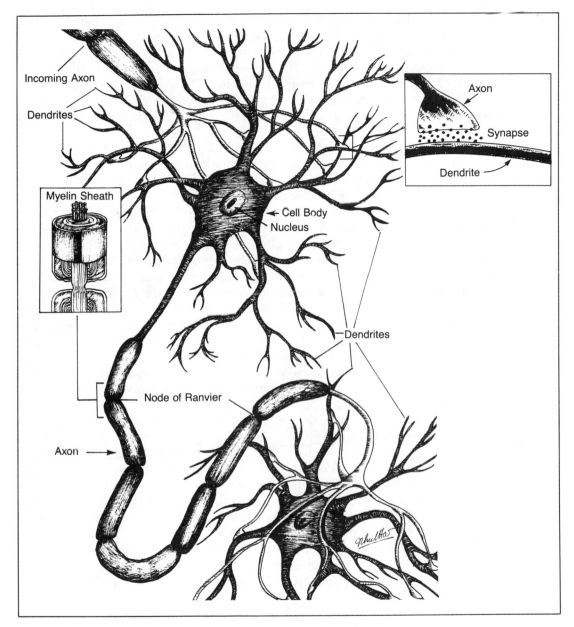

Figure 1.3 *Three Interconnected Neurons.*

space the size of a pinhead. Connections between neurons in the top layer of the brain (cortex) measure 10,000 miles per cubic inch. A neuron is composed of the cell body, the dendrites, and an axon (Figure 1.3). If you open your hand to the fullest extent possible you will have a good representation of the nerve cell. The palm of the hand is the cell body with an indentation at the center that can represent the nucleus of the cell. The extended fingers are located in the appropriate place for the dendrites and would more closely resemble dendrites if branches grew from each finger. The arm extending below the hand makes a good model of the axon that, in fact, extends from the cell body in much the same way. It is possible to use both hands as models of neurons to show the exchange of information as it occurs in the learning process and which is described in the following pages.

Inside the cell body are the nucleus and the biochemical processes that maintain the life of the cell. The neuron is a tiny system for information processing that receives and sends thousands of signals. No two cells are exactly alike nor are any two brains alike. We are as different from one another as snowflakes. The dendrites are short fibers that extend from the cell body, branching out to form the pathways for receiving information from nearby nerve cells. The axon is one long nerve fiber that extends from the cell body and serves as a transmitter, sending signals that are picked up by the branches of the neighboring dendrites. The activity between neurons is carried out by the dendrites of one cell in contact with the axon of another. The end of the axon does not actually touch the dendrite of the other cell but transmits the information chemically across a region where the cells are particularly close. This junction across which impulses travel from one nerve cell to another is called the *synapse*. The transmission of a nerve impulse is an electro-chemical process. At the synapse, the electrical impulses that travel through the cell convert into chemical signals, then back to the electrical impulses. It is this synapse that is thought to be the most likely site for neural mechanisms of learning and memory (Thompson, Berger, & Berry, 1980).

Surrounding the neurons are special cells known as *glia*. These cells outnumber the neural cells ten to one and can be increased by stimulation from the environment (Rosenzweig, 1966). The glial cells provide the brain with nourishment, consume waste products, and serve as packing material actually gluing the brain together. They also insulate the nerve cell, creating a myelin sheath (Figure 1.3, left) a special coating that protects the axon and amplifies the signal leaving the cell. Myelin has an important function, in that it allows the coated axon to conduct information away from the neuron at a much faster rate than unmyelinated axons (Thompson et al., 1980). As we increase the glial cells in the brain, we accelerate the speed of learning. It is rather like the difference that can be seen between electrical conduction through insulated and noninsulated wiring: The speed and power of the charge increase by the use of insulation.

We influence the rate of glial cell production by the richness of the environment we provide (Rosenzweig, 1966). The more glia, the more accelerated will be the synaptic activity and the more powerful will be the impulse exchange from one cell to the next, allowing for faster and more complex patterns of thinking, two characteristics we find in gifted children. The speed of thought is amazing. If a nerve pathway is used often, the threshold of the synapse falls, so that the pathway operates more readily. A wave front is started that may sweep over at least 100,000 neurons a second (Brierley, 1976).

Another way of increasing synaptic activity is by strengthening the neuron's cell body. While we cannot increase the quantity of neural cells, we can increase the quality (Rosenzweig, 1966; Krech, 1969, 1970). This quality enhancement allows again for information to be processed more quickly and for more power to be conducted, resulting in the availability of more complex neural networks. Interaction in an enriched environment changes the chemical structure of the nerve cell, thereby strengthening the cell body.

The human brain begins its development about three weeks after conception with thousands of new cells developing each minute, especially between 8 and 13 weeks. Of the approximately 3 pounds that the brain will weigh in the adult, a second pound is added during the first year after birth, mostly in the cerebellum. The third pound develops between the ages of 2 to 16. "In most normal children, growth occurs rapidly during perhaps a six-month period sometime between the ages of 2 and 4, 6 and 8, 10, and 12, and 14 and 16. Girls' growth tends to occur earlier than boys' within the two-year periods. Furthermore, girls' growth in the 10 to 12 year period is about three times that of boys' growth, and the situation reverses during the 14 to 16 year period" (Sylwester, 1982a, p. 91).

Citing Epstein's (1978) work, Sylwester (1982b) suggests that nongrowth periods might be viewed as important times of cognitive integration, during which children could engage in a wide variety of more relaxed, nonevaluative experiences that make use of the new neural connections just developed, experiences that enlarge their view of nature, society, and work. It may be a time to mature new skills and explore their broad applications, although more evidence is needed to support this theory.

The brain weighs 2% of an adult's body weight and uses 20% of all the body's energy. Our brain generates 25 watts of power when a person is awake, not much less when asleep. Information travels through the brain at 250 miles per hour with several billion bits of information passing through the corpus callosum (Figure 1.2) every second. The cortex is a $2' \times 2' \times \frac{1}{4}''$ six-layer sheet of neurons making up 85 percent of the brain mass and acts on the basis of models and problem-solving techniques it develops. The prefrontal lobe integrates information from other parts of the brain and synthesizes complex responses (Struss & Benson, 1984).

It is by increasing the strength and the speed of transmission or synaptic activity that we can affect the process of learning. We can, through changes in teaching and learning procedures, affect the growth of dendritic branching and increase both the complexity of the network of connections among neurons and the quantity of glial cells. These are the differences we see in brains that show advanced and accelerated development. By the environment we provide, we change not just the behavior of children, we change them at the cellular level. In this way gifted children become biologically different from average learners, not at birth, but as a result of using and developing the wondrous, complex structure with which they were born. At birth nearly everyone is programmed to be phenomenal.

As an aid to understanding the organization and structure of the brain I would like to borrow from Paul MacLean (1978) an analogy he used that has helped me in my thinking and teaching. Would you make a fist with each of your hands so that you can see the fingernails and then place your hands together with the fingernails touching? As you look down at your hands they now form a very respectable model of the human brain. Wiggle your little fingers and you have identified the area through which vision enters the brain. Move your middle finger and you have located the motor area. The language area is just below the middle knuckle on the right hand (left hemisphere), though please note that it is connected to the right hemisphere (left hand) by way of the touching fingernails, which now represent the corpus callosum. This connector has within it more neural connections joining the right and left hemispheres of the brain than there are in any other part of the body. Clearly the interconnection or integration of the right and left hemisphere specializations is biologically intended. With this model we can explore the organization and structure of what MacLean (1978) and others refer to as our *triune brain.*

The Organization of the Brain

The human brain is organized into three formations or three systems with radically different structures and chemistry. This hierarchy of three brains in one may be called the *triune brain* (MacLean, 1978). Educationally this organization presents some important considerations. Two of the three brains have no system for verbal communication. Because the integration of total brain function gives us intelligence, a test that measures primarily verbal communication as its sampling of intelligence may be seen as limited.

Again using our hand/brain analogy, look at just one hand/hemisphere. We will begin with the arm-wrist area, which represents the most primitive, or what MacLean (1978) refers to as the *reptilian brain.* Here we have the simplest and oldest system that we share with many life forms. In the lower brain stem and the innermost areas of the cerebrum we find the seat of autonomic (i.e., automatic) function. It is this system that relieves us of consciously processing each breath and each beat of our heart. Within recent years those working in the area of biofeedback have shown us that while most autonomic functions remain just that, we can, if we choose, bring the awareness of these functions to consciousness, allowing us to monitor or change the process if it has become destructive or inefficient. For example, those with high blood pressure can use biofeedback techniques to monitor and change the inappropriate rate of distribution of blood, consciously helping the body to better regulate this usually automatic function (Taylor & Bongar, 1976; Taylor, Tom, & Ayers, 1981). Here we find the neural pathways for many higher brain centers. Here too are nuclei concerned with motor control and the communication link between the rest of the brain and the cerebellum located at the very base of the brain. The reticular formation is located in this area. It is, in essence, the physical basis for consciousness and plays a major role in keeping us awake and alert.

The second system of the triune brain is known variously as the *old*

Learning about the brain is awesome.

mammalian brain, the *limbic system* (Figure 1.2) and the *emotional mind.* It is located at midbrain and contributes significantly to the learning process. It can be symbolically viewed by partially unclenching your fist and looking at the palm of the hand. One can see the ventricles of the brain that hold the cerebrospinal fluid, as well as the mounds and depressions of the limbic system itself. Here are the biochemical systems that are activated by the emotions of the learner. Here too are the interactions that enhance or inhibit memory. This area affects such diverse functions as anxiety, rage, sentimentality, and attention span. In addition, our feelings of personal identity and uniqueness depend on this area of the brain to combine internal and external experience. It is in this limbic area that the affective feelings provide the connecting bridge between our inner and outer worlds and provide us with our construct of reality, our model of a possible world. This system is often referred to as the *gateway to higher thought,* to the cortical and neocortical functions. It is in this regard that it is of such importance to educators, especially to those who would understand gifted development. By the release of neurotransmitters from the limbic system, the cells of the cortex are either facilitated or inhibited in their functioning. One of the activators for growth of function in this area is novelty (Restak, 1979). Feelings of pleasure and joy have been noted for their increased stimulation to this area (Sagan, 1977). Levels of touch and movement that are too low profoundly affect this area and may result in an increase in violent behavior (Prescott, 1979).

The exposed surface of the fingers and thumbs of both hands held together represents the third system of the triune brain, the convoluted mass known as the *new mammalian brain,* the *cortex,* or the *cerebrum* (Figure 1.2). It is the largest brain, comprising five-sixths of the total, and envelops the two previously mentioned, the lower brain stem and the midbrain, or limbic system. It is here that sensory data are processed, decisions made, and action initiated. The neocortex is necessary for language and speech. Its most overriding functions involve the reception, storage, and retrieval of information.

Luria (in Wittrock, 1980a) also organizes the brain in three functioning units somewhat differently than MacLean (1978). Luria believes that the integration of the whole brain is most important for effective brain function. His units consist of (a) the brain stem and thalamus that regulate the waking state of the brain; (b) the occipital, temporal, and parietal lobes that are responsible for reception, analysis, and storage of information; and (c) the frontal lobes that are responsible for planning, organizing, and creating behavior.

The most recently evolved section of the neocortex, the prefrontal cortex, which is represented by the thumbs in our analogy, provides for behaviors associated with planning, insight, empathy, introspection, and other bases of intuitive thought (MacLean, 1978). It is engaged in firming up intention, deciding on action, and regulating our most complex behaviors (Restak, 1979). It is, in fact, the area that energizes and regulates all other parts: It houses our purpose.

Goodman (1978) more specifically places the following functions in the area of the prefrontal cortex, which he believes develops most fully between 12 and 16 years of age:

1 *Foresight:* ability to see patterns of change, to extrapolate from present trends to future possibilities. This process uses imagination, prediction, and behavioral planning.
2 *Self-regulation:* of bodily processes through insight, internal commands, and generation of visual images. This is the basis for meditation and biofeedback strategies.
3 *Analytic systems thinking:* high form of creativity, complex analysis of input requiring formal logic and metaphor.
4 *Holos:* social sense, rational and emotional; the foundation of altruism.

From these perspectives we do have three somewhat different brains in one: the smallest and oldest, the brain stem; surrounded by the larger, newer brain, the limbic system; and above and around it, the cerebrum or neocortex, the largest brain, consisting of the newest, most sophisticated structures. Under stress this largest, most complex system begins shutting down, turning over more and more functions to the lower, limbic system brain. While rote learning can be continued, higher and more complex learning is inhibited (Hart, 1981). Creating opportunities for the effective operation of this total triune brain is our responsibility as educators and parents. A program model and curricular approach for the development of these total brain processes will be discussed later in this text in the sections on the Integrative Education Model in Chapter 7 and strategies for an integrative curriculum in Chapter 8.

The Hemispheres of the Brain

Another way of looking at the organization of the brain that is productive to understanding learning and the development of intelligence is to become aware of the asymmetry of the brain hemispheres. An investigative area already proving useful in understanding learning explores the idea that each hemisphere of the brain specializes in a particular type of function. This identification of specialized functioning points to the necessity for different types of educational experience if we are to use the potential each of us possesses. Schools have concentrated their focus on the analytic cognitive, left-brain-type of learning while devaluing and, in some cases, actually suppressing any use of the more holistic cognitive, right-brain specialization.

The cerebral cortex of the brain is divided into two hemispheres joined by a large bundle of interconnecting fibers called the *corpus callosum* (Figure 1.2). The right side of the cortex primarily controls the left side of the body, and the left side of the cortex largely controls the right side of the body. While much is yet to be learned, many now feel that the left and right hemispheres of our brain are responsive to different types of experience and respond in unique ways. While it seems that the entire brain is capable of performing all the activities exhibited by any of its divisions, each does, under normal conditions, assume specific duties.

Wittrock (1980a) states that the hemispheres may specialize in the strategy of coding they use rather than in the type of information they code. According to this theory the left brain is most responsible for linear, sequential, analytic, rational thinking. Thought of a metaphoric, spatial, holistic nature is the province of the right hemisphere. The right brain seems better at passive comprehension, the left at active articulation.

Sergent (1983) of McGill University has offered another explanation of the differences of function between the two hemispheres. According to her findings the left hemisphere is better at detailed processing and specializes in high-frequency information. The right hemisphere specializes in larger, nondetailed processing and is better at interpreting low-frequency information.

The right hemisphere seems to be more accurate and faster than the left when time is brief or image quality is poor. The left attends better to detail when it has enough time. Her findings suggest that both hemispheres can analyze and both can process holistically; the difference seems to be in the frequency of the information processed. When viewed in this way it becomes even more necessary to use both hemispheres cooperatively, as such a view points to the complementary capacities the hemispheres possess in processing information.

A possible synthesis of these ideas might be to view the left hemisphere as analyzing incoming data sequentially and naming the details it identifies. In contrast, the right hemisphere focuses on how things are related to a particular phenomenon more than on details, and it processes incoming sensory data simultaneously and spatially in terms of complex wholes.

Ubel (1986) reports that scientists have found each hemisphere controlling the other. The left side prevents the right side from overwhelming us with our emotions. If damage is sustained to the left, the inhibition is removed and depression can follow. What was before thought to be a psychological problem is now understood to be a biochemical problem within the brain.

Emotions of affect are found in both halves of the brain. This description of left/right brain function is true of all right-handed people and over 60% of those who are left-handed. In fewer than 40% of left-handers, the positions appear to be reversed.

Doktor and Bloom (1977) believe that the right/left brain specialization concept may explain the apparent lack of understanding between people in business and academicians. They found that top executives tend to use intuitive, right-brain processing for tasks, while academicians use left-brain analytic processing. Consequently, executives pay little attention to the complex mathematical problem-solving models created by the researchers.

Samples (1975) has shown that when the processes and functions of the right brain are facilitated, the self-esteem increases, the performance of skills typical of left-brain functioning is enhanced, and the students choose to explore greater numbers of content areas in greater depths.

Sex Differences in Brain Lateralization

The lateral organization of the brain seems to develop differently for girls than it does for boys. Greater lateralization or specialized activation of spatial function to the right hemisphere seems to give males superior ability on tests of spatial skills. However, male lateralization of language to the left hemisphere seems to work against them and result in a more narrow though precise ability in language (Witelson, 1976). More important functionally seems to be not the rate of lateral differentiation but how soon the strategies particular to each hemisphere become mature and competent to integrate function. Maturation of the left hemisphere seems to occur earlier and to be more pronounced in girls, which may allow their apparent superiority in verbal learning (Kimura, 1976; Bryden, 1970; Pizzamiglio & Cecchini, 1971; Van Duyne & D'Alonzo, 1976; Reid, 1980). Boys surpass girls on tests of spatial function by 4 years of age (Levy, 1980) and maintain this superiority at least through middle age (Porteus, 1965; Davies, 1965). Language develops earlier in girls than in boys (T. Moore, 1967; Clarke-Stewart, 1973) and it remains into middle age as a superior function (Stevenson et al., 1968; Rosenberg & Sutton-Smith, 1969; Backman, 1972). These tendencies seem to hold across cultures (Porteus, 1965). It seems then to be a function of the brain that the left hemisphere of girls and the right hemisphere of boys mature earlier and that biological differences are largely responsible (Levy, 1980).

It should not be concluded that hemisphere specialization, though it exists, is a simple issue. The following review of data from University of Chicago psychologist Jerre Levy (1980) and Stanford neuropsychologists Diane McGuinness and Karl Pribram (1979) may give us clues as to how we may best develop optimal learning experiences for our children. These differences are not specific to use of just one hemisphere and could not occur without both hemispheres functional and working in integration.

Females excel in

- perception of fine visual detail;
- understanding the meaning of facial expression, face recognition, and identifying the affective implications of tone of voice;
- reading affective and motivational states of others;
- night vision;
- perceiving subliminal messages;
- verbal skills of fluency, grammar, reading (language consists of total meaning including tone, context, expression, etc.);
- sensitivity to odor, taste, touch, and the presence and variation of sound, particularly in high ranges;
- manual dexterity and fine muscle coordination;
- speed of processing information, especially in tasks that require rapid choices;
- interest in people, social responsiveness, and empathy.

Males excel in

- using maps and solving mazes;
- spatial skills, perception of depth in space, perception of three-dimensional objects in two-dimensional representations;
- daylight vision;
- gross motor movements;
- exploratory behavior;
- math, especially geometry and trigonometry;
- observation of objects;
- use of language as a tool for logic and mathematical reasoning (the denotative meaning of language overrides all other information);

- mastering the underlying principles, which are retained and applied in a tightly organized conceptual system;
- independence of situational variables.

The cognitive differences cited in these lists suggest that the organization within hemispheres of the brain is significantly different between males and females, with diffuse organization within and between hemispheres more typical of females and strongly lateralized organization more typical for males. Kimura (1985), however, points out that biological sex is much more variable and dynamic than was ever before imagined. From her work she has found that brain organization is variable from person to person and within the same person at different times, and that on most tests of cognitive ability there is enormous overlap of males and females. She believes that sex differences in brain organization are dynamically affected by the environment rather than a crystallized pattern laid down entirely by the genes. As she says, "There may be no inherent characteristics unique to the brain of either sex that necessarily limit the intellectual achievements of individual men or women" (p. 58).

We need to consider the implications of these data to the curriculum offered and the timing of its offering. In our former reliance on contingencies as the basis for learning it was assumed that learning proceeded in an evenly timed pace that was the same for girls and boys. This lack of planning for individual needs must now be reconsidered. While all learning blends biological and environmental factors, these biological data do suggest that our previous practices may not have been as efficient or effective as they might have been. It is not to be assumed that such biological differences rule out effects of the environment. The environment reinforces and magnifies those aptitudes considered sex-appropriate by our society. Nor do all males or females fit these data. As with any generalized data, we have only the dominant trend. Tradition and stereotypic roles defined by our culture of what masculine and feminine behaviors are still serve to limit a full range of function for both boys and girls.

While the hemispheres of the brain do show specialization, the entire brain is capable of performing all the activities exhibited by any of its divisions (Pribram, 1977). It would therefore be more accurate to speak of one hemisphere leading the other during certain tasks rather than viewing a person as right-brained or left-brained. The goal would be to have available leadership from the hemisphere whose processes would be most appropriate to the effective solution in any situation. The ability to use the strategies from either hemisphere would be ideal.

Most of us do have a dominant style that we are most comfortable in using. Herrmann (1981) has developed an instrument for assessing these preferences. Some of his results indicate that when we use our left-brain mode we show preference for written directions, structured places, organized tasks, lists that can be crossed off when things are accomplished, successful results, control, and closure. When we are using our right-brain mode we more easily tolerate a lack of closure and large amounts of ambiguity, desire lots of space, see the whole problem or situation, appreciate an artistic and aesthetic focus, and enjoy spontaneity. Herrmann believes that we can teach our whole brain to work together and that we must do so if we are to have the advantage of our full ability and creativity. If we are concerned about the optimal growth of intelligence, we must provide within the environment the opportunities for the use of both right- and left-brain processes. As Wittrock (1980a) explains, "It seems clear that the sophistication and variety of cortical brain function cannot be reduced to any single dichotomy. The cortex of the brain performs a myriad of different functions within and across its hemispheres" (p. 393).

It is most important that we recognize not only the specialization of the hemisphere but also the evidence of the need for interaction and intersupport between the hemispheres. For example, trained musicians listen to music with both left and right brain. More nerve connections exist between the halves of the brain than from the brain to the rest of the body. To actualize the potential we possess, we must develop both types of function and integrate our learning experiences. If we continue to focus all our attention on the rational cognitive functions of our brain, we will paradoxically limit these very functions. Without the support of a well-developed right hemisphere, such left-brain growth will be inhibited. For years, good teachers and parents have intuitively used both right- and left-brain functions in their teaching. The evidence for specialization now validates their teaching ideas. The teacher or parent who has been unaware of the need for such integration and who has felt that the only valid learning comes from rational inquiry will consider this information new and perhaps even controversial. Levy (cited in Ferguson, 1983) contends that normal brains are built to be challenged and operate at optimal levels only when cognitive processing requirements are complex enough to engage both hemispheres. In a later discussion of the most appropriate environment for learning we will discuss the need for a safe environment, one that is nonthreatening. However, Levy warns that *nonthreatening* must not be mistaken for *nonchallenging*. She believes that challenges are what engage the whole brain and allow for optimal learning.

As mentioned, the specialization of the hemispheres is not absolute. All parts of the brain are interdependent and support all functioning. Such an investigation does allow us to view from another perspective the human qualities we have often overlooked and undervalued. Those of us who work with gifted children can find exciting implications for our learning and that of our students in this area of inquiry. As Nebes (1975) comments,

> If there is any truth in the assertion that our culture stresses left hemispheric skills, this is especially true of the school systems. . . . If the right hemisphere does indeed process data in a manner different from the left, perhaps we are shortchanging ourselves when we educate only left-sided talents in basic schooling. . . . Many problems can be solved either by analysis or synthesis, but if people are taught habitually to examine only one approach their ability to choose the most effective and efficient answer is diminished. (p. 16)

It is important, therefore, that we do not overemphasize the separate functions of the hemispheres. For most activities, both mental and physical, the human requires both hemispheres to function in close integration, allowing thereby the understanding of both the computation and the conceptualization of mathematics, the structure and the melody of music, the syntax and the poetry of language. "The existence of so complex a cabling system as the corpus callosum must mean, it is important to stress again, that the interaction of the hemispheres is a vital human function" (Sagan, 1977, p. 175).

Brain Waves

An activity of the brain that seems to have important implications for learning is the production of different brain wave frequencies. Through measurement we learn that a variety of activity levels can be correlated with the various frequencies. Some data also indicate that the coherence of these frequencies in various parts of the brain facilitates different types of learning. Houston (1977b) introduced the idea of coherence of brain waves as a force in maximizing the use of human energy. The ability to focus energy from the entire brain is seen to result in accelerated learning, healing, and higher levels of consciousness.

The value and implications of brain wave training are still being investigated, with many findings and claims being openly disputed. One such debate centers on the "alpha state." People can slow the rhythm of the brain down to 8 to 12 cycles per second, as compared to the 12 to 28 cycles per second common to beta wave production. Some have claimed that by slowing down the brain waves, a pleasant floating state of consciousness, similar to the relaxed states that allow mind/body integration and heighten the ability to focus brain energy, occurs. The even slower 4 to 7 cycles per second of theta waves was claimed to allow deeper relaxation and a state conducive to creative thought and use of psi abilities (see p. 267) and 1 to 3 cycles per second typifies the slowest wave, delta, that infrequently occurs and barely maintains body functioning. This issue remains under controversy due to the extremely complex nature of the brain. Even the alpha state is not a single phenomenon, but a conglomerate of perhaps some 600 phenomena, with equally numerous correlated characteristics that are dependent on the location, form, appearance, and movement pattern of the alpha wave. Also involved in the complexity may be the influence of the body's circadian rhythms, the changes in the atmospheric environment, or even the rhythmic activities of the universe (Brown, 1974).

British physicist Maxwell Cade is conducting a very interesting exploration of the differing states and correlated behaviors of alpha. For several years, Cade has been developing instrumentation that will identify and illustrate complex electroencephalograph (EEG) patterns and their related hierarchy of subjective physical states. His "Mind Mirror" shows the left-right symmetry and the relative amounts of beta, alpha, theta, and delta rhythms operating. He has identified and described five, possibly six, major states and their "shapes," which he reports in the *Brain/Mind Bulletin* (Ferguson, 1977c):

1 The unilateral pattern of an untrained individual.
2 Alpha rhythms bilateral; calm, detached alertness; no thinking, no images.
3 Alpha blocking; passive awareness; symmetrical beta and theta.
4 "Meditation"; calm detached; inward and outward awareness.
5 Lucid awareness; higher amplitude alpha than in State 4; invariably symmetrical. Subjects can open eyes, converse, move around, solve problems, read and comprehend, all without disturbing this state. Healers have been observed in this state when "sending healing energy."

The possible sixth pattern, appearing egg-shaped, seems to be associated with the subjective impression that one is creating one's own reality.

Research in the area of brain waves and their meaning is the least easily validated of the areas of brain research, due to inadequate data from as yet limited tools of measurement such as those used to record the EEG patterns. As our skills of investigation increase, the possibilities for learning about ourselves and our relationship to our world should prove very exciting.

The Brain as a Hologram: A Holographic Model of Reality

Pribram (1971, 1977) postulates a holographic theory of the mind and believes that the brain is a hologram that stores all information in each part. A hologram is a record of optical information processing that stores light from every point in the scene that is distributed or scattered throughout the hologram's surface. When placed in a coherent light source, the hologram can regenerate the original wave pattern from any point on its surface, resulting in what appears to be a three-dimensional object. The hologram has a fantastic capability to retrievably store information.

To produce a hologram, the single wavelength light of a laser beam is split with a mirror. Half of the beam is aimed directly at the photographic plate; the other half rebounds from the object to hit the plate. Instead of recording an image, the plate records interference patterns of the colliding light waves. To reconstruct the image, a laser is directed at the plate at the same angle as the original laser. The hologram appears as a three-dimensional image that can be turned and studied from different angles (Fincher, 1981).

Pribram was attracted to the holographic theory of the brain because the hologram is a unique storage device in which every bit of information is distributed over the entire surface and the retrieval process is reconstructive, two properties he believed could be found in the brain. Pribram also believes that the hologram is a model for consciousness. A brain stores information in a variety of ways, can use either linear or spatial modes, and projects space and time, qualities of the holographic process. Pribram agrees with Bohm (Ferguson, 1977a) that reality is the result of our own construction that we make by interpreting frequencies from another dimension, a universe that itself is holographic and transcends time and space. The implications of such a theory change the concept of reality and affect every aspect of our lives. Our potential for affecting our own life is infinite, and the importance of our perception of reality is awesome. Further possibilities of this theory are discussed in Chapter 12. For educators, acceptance of such a theory will lead to teaching methods that seek to reduce anxiety and foster activities that create harmony, coherence, connectedness, and recognition of individual differences in learning styles.

GIFTEDNESS: A BIOLOGICAL DIFFERENCE

From animal and human brain/mind research, we can now postulate that individuals with high levels of intelligence, gifted individuals, show the following measurable biological differences:

1 There is an increase in neuroglial cell production allowing more nourishment and support for the neurons (Rosenzweig, 1984; Thompson, Berger, & Berry, 1980).
2 The neurons become biochemically richer, allowing for more complex patterns of thought (Rosenzweig, 1966; Krech, 1969).
3 There is an increase in the amount of dendritic branching and the number of dendritic spines, thus increasing the potential for interconnections between neurons (Hutchinson, 1986).
4 There is an increase in the number of synapses and in the size of the synaptic contact, allowing more complex communication within the system (Hutchinson, 1986; Thompson, Berger, & Berry, 1980).
5 More use is made of the activity of the prefrontal cortex of the brain. This allows more future planning, insightful thinking, and intuitive experiences (Restak, 1979; MacLean, 1978).
6 More use is made of alpha wave activity within more areas of the brain. The gifted individual can move into this state more quickly and stay in it longer than average learners. Such a state allows more relaxed and concentrated learning, higher levels of retention, and more integration of hemispheric modalities (Lozanov, 1977; Martindale, 1975).
7 There is more coherence and synchronicity of brain rhythms more often, allowing heightened concentration, focused attention, and in-depth probing and inquiry (Millay, 1981b).

For further information in the area of brain/mind research, see Asimov (1965), Bogen (1975), Chall and Mirsky (1978); Eccles (1973), Ferguson (1973), Fincher (1981), Hart (1975), Isaacson (1974), Koestler (1968), Krashen (1975), Levy and Reid (1975), Ornstein (1973a, b), Ornstein and Oyle (1975), Pietsch (1981), Pribram (1971, 1977), Restak (1979), Sagan (1974, 1977), Samples (1976), Samples, Charles, and Barnhart (1977), Scientific American (1979), Springer and Deutsch (1981), Wittrock (1980a, b), and Wittrock et al. (1977).

IMPLICATIONS OF BRAIN RESEARCH FOR CLASSROOM EDUCATION

In Chapters 8 and 9, we will discuss ways of providing environments and strategies for optimizing development that are the result of the new discoveries in brain research. The following are just a few of the findings that directly affect learning:

1 Optimal development requires the active involvement of the learner:
   —Concrete experiences and stimulation are needed.
   —Written material (texts and workbooks) are not appropriate to teach abstract concepts.
   —Active sensory stimulation is needed at elementary *and secondary* levels.
2 Attention and concentration rely on the impact of the environment on the brain:
   —The reticular formation, limbic system, and thalamus actively select stimuli.
   —The brain responds to novelty, to the unexpected, and to discrepant information; novelty registers information independent of rewards or punishment and is more effective (Restak, 1979).
   —When asked to repeat, drill, or do reinforced repetitive activities the brain habituates, i.e., responds automatically without thought and may be counterproductive to learning a concept (Johnson, 1982).
3 Right/left hemispheres show specialization:
   —When not actively involved the right hemisphere switches and generates thought not related to the external input.
   —The processes and content of both specializations need to be included in curriculum planning to take advantage of their complementary nature.
   —Opportunities must be given for alternative modes so that we teach to the whole cortex; thus we must integrate rather than teach as if each specialization were a separate subject.
4 The brain is a model builder generating models of reality:
   —Individualized instructional planning is strongly indicated as each person responds uniquely to the environment (Wittrock, 1980a,b).

A LESSON ON UNDERSTANDING
GIFTEDNESS

While it is very important for teachers at home and at school to understand what is known about the brain, how it functions, and how its functioning relates to intelligence and to giftedness, it is even more important that the child understands. By presenting the information on how intelligence develops, what it means to be gifted, and how that level of development affects a person's life, the child can become a part of that development. Such understanding can empower children and allow them to become partners in their own education. Besides, they find it fascinating.

The following series of steps is one way to accomplish sharing information on giftedness:

Step 1 Using the hand model of the brain outlined in this chapter explain the function of the brain and its integrative nature (see pp. 27–31).

Step 2 Using your hands as models of neurons (see pp. 25, 26), explain how learning occurs in the brain.

Step 3 After introducing some of the known information about the brain, ask the children to choose groups of five to seven, give each group a large sheet of paper and markers, and ask the children to write down everything they know about the brain. Allow enough time for them to complete the task, approximately 20 minutes. You will be the best judge of when most have recorded all they can remember.

Step 4 Using a spokesperson from each group, have the children report back to the total group. After each report clarify any information that is unclear, extend any information that you can, and be sure to correct any information that is faulty by giving more current research. You need not say their ideas are wrong; instead say, "We now know . . ." or "Later research has found that . . . ."

Step 5 Use models, slides, pictures, film, video, or any other support materials to help the students develop the concepts further. An extremely powerful tool is the use of actual brains preserved for display. We found in working with children of all ages that they were very interested in seeing the brains of various animals, comparing them, and discussing the limits each size or organization presented. The most impactful way to present such information is to allow the students to learn to dissect the material. Later, a visit from a neurobiologist or neurosurgeon can be arranged for the purpose of allowing the children to watch an actual human brain dissection. It is a most memorable experience.

Step 6 Discuss how the brain changes when it is stimulated appropriately (see p. 38). Discuss high levels of intelligence as the result of these changes and the kinds of behavior we can observe that tells us a person is intelligent (see pp. 126–132).

Step 7 Discuss the label we have used to identify people who exhibit high levels of intelligence (i.e., gifted). Be sure to help the children understand the dynamic nature of intelligence, i.e., that we must challenge ourselves or we can lose brain power.

Step 8 Ask the children to identify some of the problems people who are "gifted" might face in our society. Look at possible solutions or alternative ways these problems can be handled. Identify and discuss some of the advantages a "gifted" person might have.

Step 9 Share with the children tools and ideas for nurturing their intelligence.

All of the above steps can be used with any age child at home or at school with modifications. Parents will find such discussions a good base for open communication and later consideration of problems that arise from the child's experiences as a gifted child.

In summary, we have begun our exploration of gifted individuals by establishing a common base of understanding of the terms and concepts that we will use throughout our discussion. The term *gifted* refers to individuals who are functioning at, or who show promise of functioning at, high levels of intelligence. *Intelligence* is defined as advanced or accelerated development of brain function. It is a composite of the human functions of cognition, emotion, intuition, and physical sensing and can be expressed in a variety of ways including outstanding cognitive ability, academic aptitude, creative behavior, leadership, or ability in visual and performing arts. Intelligence includes the capacity for insight into complex relationships and for the processes of abstract thinking, adaptability in problem solving, and capacity to acquire new capacity.

The concept of intelligence used is based on the principle of interaction, considering both heredity and environment as necessary components of the concept. The interactive concept of intelligence is seen as critical to an understanding of the development of gifted individuals, and an overview of the evolution of the concept was presented to aid in this understanding. A look at current research seems to indicate that the interactive concept best explains the known data. *Interactionism* regards the fertilized ovum as an organism in adaptive interaction with its environment and states the belief that physical conditions surrounding the embryo may alter the direction of development. The genotype appears to provide controlling directives for development and set limits for the range of phenotypic variation, but we are unable to know the full range possible. While genes provide programs for individual potential, they do not guarantee this potential will be achieved.

Questions Often Asked

1. What do you mean by intelligence? giftedness? creativity? Are they the same?

When we speak of *intelligence* it is important that we do not just think of school activities or rational thinking. The more we know about the human brain the more we notice that intelligence must include our physical ability; our emotional health; and our creative, insightful intuition along with our verbal and visual thinking. Intelligence results from the development of *all* of our brain functions.

Giftedness is a label we give to children who are performing or give evidence of performing at high levels of intelligence, i.e., advanced, accelerated, integrated, full-brain functioning.

Creativity is a high form of intelligence and results from the synthesis of all of our brain's functions, the knowing that is processed internally and that which comes to us from outside our system. At least four areas of creativity are being studied: creativity as rational thought, as unique products, as high levels of mental health, and as an intuitive spark. We must understand all of these areas if we are to understand creativity, for it is the integration of all of these abilities that allows us to create. Creativity is a very holistic concept.

When intelligence, giftedness, and creativity are all related, they are synonymous. I believe that high levels of intelligence are labeled *giftedness* and that creativity is the highest expression of giftedness.

2. Can all children become gifted?

From the data neurobiology is providing it is evident that nearly are children are born with very complex and unique brain structures. While each child will be different, they all seem to have extraordinary potential. It is my belief that, if given the opportunity to develop optimally, most children could perform at the level we now call *gifted* and that it is probably more natural that they do so.

3. Should children know that they have been identified as gifted?

Not only should they be told, it is most important that they understand what *giftedness* means. Children who are intelligent know they are different, and it is important that they understand what their differences mean and how they became gifted. The lesson on giftedness in this chapter would be a good starting place.

4. Which is most important for the development of intelligence, heredity or environment?

Both are important, and current research recognizes that the interaction between them is complex and interdependent. At this time few knowledgeable scientists even try to speak of one as being more important than the other.

5. When does development of intelligence begin?

The unique genetic program of the individual begins to show the impact of the environment from conception on. The brain cells begin their development about 3 weeks after conception. From this we can see that the development of intelligence and our involvement in that development begin very early in utero.

6. Is IQ a measure of a person's intellectual capacity?

No. We have no measure of intellectual capacity. Such a measure would be possible only if intelligence did not change and were fixed from birth instead of dynamic as we now know it to be. IQ is the score given for a measure of our performance on specific tasks, many of which we use in school-related activities. Our capacity will change depending on the opportunities we are given to develop. To get a reasonably adequate idea of our intellectual ability at any stage of development we will need as many different kinds of measures and observations as possible.

7. How does knowing about the brain help us to understand and better educate gifted learners?

The more we know about how we learn, the better we will be in creating opportunities for learning. If we know that stimulation from the environment increases our brain's ability to function, then we will be concerned about providing appropriate stimulation. As we learn what activities and circumstances allow for optimal brain development we will become far better at educating all children.

8. Why is your definition of intelligence important to how you educate a child?

If you believe that a child is born with a set amount of intelligence, you will not be concerned with providing opportunities for optimal development; you will only be interested in providing information and content. You will believe that gifted children can get by on their own. If you believe that intelligence is dynamic and dependent on the environment interacting with what is inherited, you will be concerned about the environment you provide; you will not leave education to chance.

2. Creativity: The Highest Expression of Giftedness

In this chapter the reader will discover

- A model of creativity showing the integration of the four major areas of human function:
    Thinking—cognitive
    Feeling—affective
    Physical/sensing
    Intuitive.
- Information on each category of creativity as identified in the literature and its definition, characteristic population, and conditions for development.

Creativity as process is important not because the product of each moment is such a gem, but because the process is the essence of life itself.

—HAROLD H. ANDERSON

Creativity is a very special condition, attitude, or state of being that nearly defies definition. Over the years, scholars and researchers, artists and musicians, and philosophers and educators have tried to use words to communicate this amazing phenomenon. Probably the most unexplainable part of creativity lies in the fact that, even though few agree on a definition, when we say the word, everyone senses a similar feeling. We may not be able to explain what it is rationally, but we know it just the same. When we are being creative, we are aware of its special excitement.

Over and over in discussions of creativity, we find statements to the effect that everyone has a great deal of creativity as a child, but that very few retain it as adults. My favorite expression of this idea can be found in a flier advertising a creativity training program, *New Directions in Creativity* by Renzulli (1973b). He says, "Creativity is as common in small children as runny noses and yet is quite rare in adults." All who comment on this state of affairs go on to ask, "Why must it be so? How does it happen?"

Inside of me I believe that everyone who has defined or discussed creativity is right, though their positions sound disparate. And at the same time, they are wrong because they speak of only the part of creativity that they see or that fits their belief system. Such a limited view of creativity has caused us to recognize only a portion, an isolated part of what, in fact, is a far more complex, more integrated, whole. It is as though we have viewed and discussed only a small, exposed segment, the rational part, while we have only hinted at the most important part.

Some have used creativity synonymously with giftedness; some have limited it to feelings and affective development. It seems incorrect to use it in either of those ways, as it has none of the limitations of those concepts; creativity includes far more. It is the highest expression of giftedness.

AN INTEGRATED CONCEPT OF CREATIVITY

Looking again at the basic functions of thinking, feeling, sensing, and intuiting (Jung, 1964), we find that we must now develop another dimension, for the integration of these functions releases creativity (see Figure 2.1). Restrict any one of the functions and you reduce creativity. Creativity involves the synthesis of all functioning, and yet it is still more. It includes a spark from another dimension.

Previous reviews of creativity delineated various categories to organize the

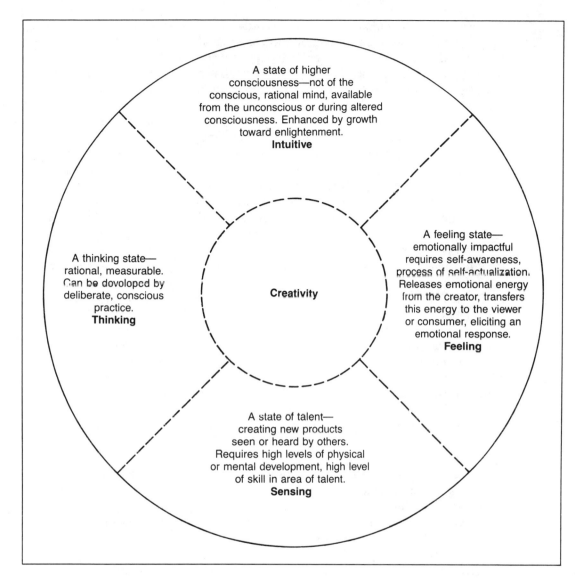

A state of higher consciousness—not of the conscious, rational mind, available from the unconscious or during altered consciousness. Enhanced by growth toward enlightenment.
Intuitive

A thinking state— rational, measurable. Can be developed by deliberate, conscious practice.
Thinking

Creativity

A feeling state— emotionally impactful requires self-awareness, process of self-actualization. Releases emotional energy from the creator, transfers this energy to the viewer or consumer, eliciting an emotional response.
Feeling

A state of talent— creating new products seen or heard by others. Requires high levels of physical or mental development, high level of skill in area of talent.
Sensing

Figure 2.1   Creativity Circle.

information known and the diverse points of view. They seem to lack a common base in the organizations used. When one categorizes with areas as diverse as curiosity, measurements, relationship to intelligence, personality, and motivation as components of the same system, no base remains for comparing the results of research or the differing viewpoints. To provide a common system of categorizing that results in clearer understanding of the information about creativity, the material could be organized according to human function. All research, characteristics, discussions of enhancing practices, and so on are grouped in one of four areas, depending on the definition the author or researcher gives creativity and which function that definition uses. In some cases, the confusion in the literature results directly from the fact that the author neglects to state a point of view on creativity and uses the term as though everyone agrees on a single definition. This is the source of contradictory research results.

The following model coincides well with the Integrative Education Model described in Chapters 7 and 8, not by coincidence. The categories of creativity incorporate these functions: (a) rational thinking; (b) high levels of emotional development or feeling; (c) talent and high levels of mental and physical development; and (d) higher levels of consciousness, resulting in use of imagery, fantasy, and breakthroughs to the preconscious or unconscious states.

When viewed from this common base, instead of describing different phenomena or even different types of creativity, all of these perceptions may be only fragments of the total; creativity includes all of these ideas and more. Thinking, feeling, sensing, and intuiting unify to become creativity. With only one function operating alone a person could not create.

The definition of giftedness used earlier in this chapter now aids in our understanding of creativity. As giftedness is the result of total integrated functioning of the human brain, so creativity, the highest expression of giftedness, can be viewed from the biological brain/mind base. All of the functions of the human brain/mind system are involved at higher and higher levels when creativity occurs. Gowan (1981) discussed the relationship between giftedness and creativity by first distinguishing between personal and cultural creativity. He believed that anyone could be taught personal creativity, but that giftedness is necessary for cultural creativity, the form that produces major discoveries and ideas which significantly add to and inevitably change the future of humankind. He saw giftedness only as the potential for creativity.

It is my belief that only as the functions combine and interact, drawing from and giving to each other, can creativity occur. A belief in this unity underlies this discussion of the different perceptions of creativity. Although researchers and authors may define creativity from a one-function viewpoint, they draw from other functions to discuss or develop it; for example, although a population may be identified by tests of fluency or flexibility, they may use self-awareness to increase creativity. A few authors do acknowledge the holistic nature of their work, but nearly all treat creativity more holistically than they define it.

CREATIVITY: A RATIONAL THINKING FUNCTION

The rational view of creativity has accumulated the most literature and nearly all of the testing. To get an idea of how researchers view this aspect of creativity, look at a few definitions proposed by advocates of the rational thinking position:

- Torrance (1962): "the process of sensing gaps or disturbing missing elements; forming new hypotheses and communicating the results, possibly modifying and retesting the hypotheses" (p. 16).
- Parnes (1967): "Creativity is a function of knowledge, imagination, and evaluation" (p. 6). He sees the processes involved as fact finding, problem finding, idea finding, solution finding, and acceptance finding.
- Williams (1968): An act of creativity is a conscious act of human intelligence. Operationally, he defines it as including knowledge, mental processes based on cognition, divergent-productive and associative thinking, evaluative behaviors, and communicative skills.
- Guilford (1959): "aptitude traits that belong most clearly logically in the area of creativity . . . fluency of thinking and flexibility of thinking, as well as originality, sensitivity to problems, redefinition and elaboration . . . classifiable in a group of divergent thinking abilities" (p. 160).
- Taylor (1959): Interested most in scientific creative ability, he discusses five levels of creativity: expressive, productive, inventive, innovative, and emergenative. He views the steps in the process as mental labor, incubation, illumination, and deliberate effort.

The criterion for selecting and evaluating creative students from the view of creativity as rational is usually a high score on a test designated as a creativity measure, such as the Minnesota Test of Creative Thinking (MTCT) (Torrance, 1962); Torrance Tests of Creative Thinking (TTCT) (Torrance, 1966); and Remote Associates Test (RAT) (Mednick & Mednick, 1967). In fact, most instruments for measuring creativity come from this rational approach. Other ways to select and evaluate creative students congruent with this point of view have been tried:

- Honor point ratios and achievement test scores: Results are quite poor (Yamamoto, 1964).
- Teacher nomination: Also found to be quite inaccurate, identifying less than one-third (Ellinger, 1964; Holland, 1959).
- Peer nomination: Results unproductive (Torrance, 1962).
- Intelligence tests: Torrance (1962) shows that if you use only an intelligence test and identify the upper 20% as gifted, you will miss 70% of those who would fall into the upper 20% of a test of creative thinking ability.

Tests of creativity (defined as a rational function), such as the MTCT, may test some of the same abilities as intelligence tests (Wodtke, 1964; Yamamoto, 1965). However, Torrance (1962) found a low correlation between the two types of measures in unselected populations. He found practically no correlation in high-ability populations. He reports correlations that are slightly higher for girls than for boys and that high scores on the MTCT were usually obtained by children with IQ scores of at least 115.

Guilford (1967) found the relationship between divergent-production test scores and IQ scores generally low; he suggested that, although a high IQ did not guarantee doing well, being above average in IQ was almost a necessity. Others have found the same relationship. However, an IQ of 120 is often mentioned as the lowest score possible to establish a base of knowledge broad enough to use the analytic, synthetic, and evaluative thinking necessary for rational creative production (Getzels & Jackson, 1962; Smith, 1965). When production of associations (naming instances, alternative uses, similarities, pattern meanings, and line meanings) is used as the criterion for creativity, the correlation with intelligence measures is even lower (Wallach & Kogan, 1965).

Criticisms of tests of creativity range from Yamamoto's challenge to their validity to Barron's report of the viewpoint of creative individuals. Yamamoto (1964) warns us against assuming that the factor-analytic model of creative thinking abilities satisfactorily explains high scores (or even low) on these traits and thinking of the test items as representative samples of these traits. He believes we need more evidence for these assumptions.

Barron (1969) presents an interesting view by suggesting that highly creative individuals become very annoyed with the above types of tests. These individuals reportedly consider the tests too superficial, for they fail to engage the deeper levels of a person involved in creative work. Further, the fragmentation of the factor-analytic model provides no opportunity for the more holistic quality of creativity. Finally, the tested students felt that "short and closely timed tests do violence to the very essence of the creative process" (p. 37).

Thorndike (1963b) finds that tests of creativity lack internal consistency and that they do not seem to test any common characteristic. He believes it essential that measured creativity, potential creativity, and achieved creativity show an approximate relationship.

With a belief system that assumes creativity to be measurable, educators and researchers who adhere to the rational definition of creativity continue to look for adequate tests to identify and evaluate creative individuals. Part of the problem may be that the contributions of the sensing, feeling, and intuitive functioning of these individuals, although probably far more important, are less easy to measure.

Characteristics of the Rationally Thinking Creative Individual

Those who subscribe to the rational viewpoint of creativity (Hughes, 1969; Kurtzman, 1967; Stein, 1962) find the following attributes common to those they designate as creative:

- Self-disciplined, independent, often antiauthoritarian
- Zany sense of humor

- Able to resist group pressure, a strategy developed early
- More adaptable
- More adventurous
- Greater tolerance for ambiguity and discomfort
- Little tolerance for boredom
- Preference for complexity, asymmetry, open-endedness
- High in divergent thinking ability
- High in memory, good attention to detail
- Broad knowledge background
- Need think periods
- Need supportive climate, sensitive to environment
- Need recognition, opportunity to share
- High aesthetic values, good aesthetic judgment
- Freer in developing sex role integration; lack of stereotypical male, female identification.

In a study with creative adolescents, Halpin, Payne, and Ellett (1973) found significant differences between females and males, as shown in Table 2.1.

The business community is quite involved in the study of and training for creativity. They, too, see the process as holistic, drawing on everything from knowledge, logic, imagination, and intuition to the ability to see connections and

Table 2.1 *Differences Between Creative Females and Males.*

Females	Males
Liked school, especially courses in sciences, music, and art	Disliked school
Liked their teachers	Disliked their teachers and thought they were uninteresting
Regularly read news magazines and other nonrequired reading and special reports	Did little homework
Were active in dramatics and musical productions	Disliked physical education and seldom engaged in team sports
Did not go out on dates as often	Were regarded as radical or unconventional
Were daydreamers	Often wanted to be alone to pursue their own thoughts and interests

distinctions between ideas and things (*Business Week,* 1985). They are most interested in the concept of using the whole brain, including the medical viewpoint enhanced by technology that enables scientists to see both sides of the brain flickering on and off when a person is engaged in creative thought.

A great deal of corporate money is going into training top executives and research-and-development (R&D) laboratory employees to become more creative. The training proceeds from a set of assumptions that includes the educability of creativity. Herrmann (1981), one of the most popular consultants, was one of the first to promote creativity as a combination of different types of thinking— analytical, verbal, intuitive, and emotional—and to connect learning creativity to whole brain function. Herrmann has shown that only 5 percent of the business people he surveyed naturally show equal development in the various types of thinking; these are the ones most endowed with creativity. He is, therefore, focusing on aiding others to use the whole brain more effectively.

The business community operates on other assumptions drawn from the research about creative people (*Business Week,* 1985):

- Creative types are independent, persistent, highly motivated risk takers who are generally hard to get along with. Hunches, instincts, and emotions play an important part in their decision making. They prefer the complex and asymmetrical, and disorder is not a source for anxiety.
- Their childhood was marked with exposure to diversity and unusual freedom in exploring and making decisions.
- They are gadabouts constantly exchanging ideas with colleagues at the cutting edge of their fields.
- Formal education does not enhance creativity, but rather tends to stifle it.
- The IQ threshold for creative production is approximately 130.
- Creators spend years mastering their field.

Amabile (1986) has found in her research that in the arenas of business and science, creative production takes more than talent, personality, and cognitive ability. The most important factor seems to be the creator's love of creating. She found that the most creative individuals do it for the fun and satisfaction they personally receive. They find their opportunities for creativity are reduced with supervisory restrictions, deadlines, and reward structures. With the help of observation from famous creators, controlled experiments, and interviews with R&D scientists, Amabile has discovered six factors that undermine creativity and interest in the creative task:

1 Expected evaluation—People who are concentrating on how their work will be evaluated are less creative than people who do not have to worry about such reviews.
2 Surveillance—People who are conscious of being watched as they are working will be less creative than people who are not aware of being monitored.

3 Reward—People who perform a task primarily to gain a tangible reward will be less creative than those who are not working principally for recognition or payment.

4 Competition—People who feel direct, threatening competition with others in their work will be less creative than those not focusing on rivalry.

5 Restricted choice—People who must perform their tasks in accordance with designated restrictions will be less creative than people given a freer choice. In R&D interviews, freedom of choice in how to approach work was the most potent feature leading to creativity.

6 Extrinsic orientation—People who are led to concentrate on all the extrinsic reasons for doing a task will be less creative than those thinking about all the intrinsic reasons. (pp. 13, 14)

While Amabile considers intrinsic motivation necessary for creativity, her research has led her to believe that there are two additional necessary components: (a) domain-relevant skills, i.e., skills in a specific field that were learned through formal education and experience; and (b) creativity-relevant skills, i.e., ways of thinking and working that are conducive to creativity. These skills, along with task motivation that is intrinsic, are more conducive to creativity than any reward system or external pressure.

Intrinsic motivation can be taught or at least modeled in such a way that children show higher levels of intrinsic motivation after training than untrained children. Amabile (1986) and her colleagues Hennessey and Grossman used videotapes showing children being interviewed by an adult, sharing statements of interest, excitement, and deep involvement in some aspect of their studies. The children also talked about how they felt that high marks and teacher approval were nice but not as important to them as enjoying their work. In addition to changing the level of intrinsic motivation for the viewers, the videotapes "immunized" the students against the negative effects of extrinsic constraints on their creativity. This work seems very promising and provides us with a simple and realistic way to accomplish an important goal—increasing intrinsic motivation within our students.

Development of Creativity—The Rational Thinking Aspect

Most writers and researchers agree that all people have the ability to be creative, at least while they are young. However, the growth of creativity defined by test performance is not continuous, but rather increases from three to four and one-half years of age and then takes a small drop. It begins to rise again, making a sharp drop at the fourth grade. The scores in fluency, flexibility, originality, and elaboration drop so significantly that some students have lower scores in the fifth grade than they had in the third grade. The scores begin to rise again and continue through the junior year except for a slight drop at seventh grade (Torrance, 1962, 1968). These studies showed that as early as third grade, girls were more reluctant to think creatively than were boys. Torrance believes girls have, by this time, been conditioned to be more passive and accept things as they are, rather than try to manipulate or change things. He also found that contributions made by boys were more highly valued by their peers.

What conditions can facilitate development of this aspect of creativity? The following compilation comes from the research of Anderson and Anderson (1965); Domino (1969); Drevdahl (1956); Eisenman and Schussel (1970); Gowan (1981); Landry (1968); MacKinnon (1964); Nichols (1964); and Torrance (1962, 1966). These factors facilitate development:

- Situations that present incompleteness, openness
- Allowing and encouraging lots of questions
- Producing something, then doing something with it
- Granting responsibility and independence
- Emphasizing self-initiated exploring, observing, questioning, feeling, classifying, recording, translating, inferring, testing inferences, and communicating
- Bilingual experiences resulting in development of greater potential creativity due to the more varied view of the world, a more flexible approach to problems, and the ability to express self in different ways that arise from these experiences
- Birth order (first-born males more creative [on tests of creativity] than males born later)
- Predisposing and focusing of the child's interests and attention by parents, by the stimulation of the school environment, and by self-motivation.

These factors inhibit development:

- Need for success, limiting risk taking or pursuit of unknown
- Conformity to peer group and social pressure
- Discouragement of exploration, using imagination, inquiry
- Sex role stereotyping
- Differentiation between work and play (e.g., learning is hard work)
- Adherence to "readiness" viewpoint for learning
- Authoritarianism
- Disrespect for fantasy, daydreams.

New ideas are not easy to come by, and once they arrive it is not easy to keep them alive and growing. Tucker (1986) has 10 strategies he believes will allow us to better generate and develop new ideas:

1 Allow yourself relaxation time, or as Tucker calls it "dream space." If you want a creative mind you must allow time for it to develop.

2 Discover your best time and your best space for generating ideas. Your environment can support your creativity.

3 Find other creative people to be with, people who excite you and stimulate your creativity.

4 Once you are with these people draw them out; ask questions about their interests and enthusiasms.

5 Break out of old routines and patterns; try things you thought you didn't like or haven't tried.

6 Generate a plan or deadline that you tell to someone else, then work toward meeting your own plan.

7 Develop a high level of expertise in your area of innovation. Use information from diverse resources—books, magazines, and people, including other innovators.

8 Discover other people's sources of inspiration.

9 Study problems as opportunities for novel solutions.

10 Try your ideas out on others, first with safe people, later with those who will be more critical.

The schools could make important contributions toward advancing creativity, for this aspect of development is considered learned behavior and, therefore, is capable of improvement through instruction. Skills such as those measured on the MTCT have significantly increased through special programs (Crutchfield, 1969; Davis, Manske, & Train, 1967; Parnes, 1963; Torrance, 1960). If schools are to do this job, there must be a change in their focus. Cole (1969) makes the point in an interesting analogy: If people were computers, schools would be "programming" to receive, store, retrieve, and reproduce information only. We must also "program" other processes involved in the processing, organization, efficient utilization, and application of information. Williams (1968) believes that all learning involves creative organization of the culture's knowledge with the individual's experience. This creativity will then produce new and unique perceptions of the culture. While the process may differ slightly from program to program, most agree with Wallas (1926) that it must include preparation, incubation, illumination, and verification.

Treffinger (1986) proposes a model that can be used to organize the fast-growing field of strategies to improve students' creative-thinking and problem-solving abilities. The model has three levels: I, Learning Basic Thinking Tools; II, Learning and Practicing Problem-Solving Models; and III, Dealing with Real Problems and Challenges. At Level I students learn tools for generating and analyzing ideas, both divergently (brainstorming, attribute listing, etc.) and convergently (making inferences, thinking with analogies, categorizing, etc.). While all gifted programs should include this level of learning, all students would benefit from this opportunity.

Level II gives students the opportunity to apply the basic thinking tools in complex and systematic structures. Odyssey of the Mind and Future Problem

Solving exercises are examples of Level II activities. Students must have participative experiences included in learning about and practicing these models.

Solving real problems is the focus of Level III. It is suggested that students have experience with the other levels before becoming involved in this level if they are to be successful.

This three-level model of creative learning allows us to monitor the kinds of activities presented to develop creativity and to be sure that the necessary experiences are a part of our curriculum. Treffinger and others envision the teacher as becoming the facilitator, the arranger of appropriate experiences, the encourager, the skill builder. Effective teachers tend to have common behaviors. Anderson (1968); Cole (1969); Ellinger (1964); Hughes (1969); Kneller (1965); Parnes (1963); Torrance (1962); and Williams (1968) describe activities of teachers who successfully develop creativity:

- They do more thinking activities (convergent, divergent, evaluative).
- They use fewer memory activities.
- They use evaluation for diagnosis, not judgment; rewarding correctness of spelling, punctuation, grammar, neatness, handwriting, or quantity inhibits the production of original ideas.
- They give opportunities to use knowledge creatively.
- They encourage spontaneous expression.
- They provide an atmosphere of acceptance.
- They provide a wealth of stimulation from a rich and varied environment.
- They ask provocative questions.
- They value originality.
- They encourage students to examine new ideas on their merit and not dismiss them as fanciful.
- They provide for unevaluated practice and experimentation.
- They teach skills of creative thinking, such as originality, fluency, flexibility and elaboration, deliberate idea finding, deferred judgment, forced relationships, alternative thinking, hypothesis setting.
- They teach skills of researching, such as self-initiated exploring, observing, classifying, questioning, arranging and using information, recording, translating, inferring, testing inferences, representing experience and observations, communicating, generalizing, and simplifying.

Another clue: Creative teachers have proved more effective at teaching creativity than those who are not themselves creative.

Frierson (1965) raises an interesting question: Do students who improve on problem-solving skills become more effective in their pursuit of personal and occupational goals than noncreative problem solvers, or do they merely learn strategies that enhance scores on these types of creativity tests? Longitudinal research with students in programs for developing productive and creative thinking

Creative teachers encourage creativity in their students.

skills will need to answer this query; however, if this is only one aspect of the total phenomenon of creativity, there will be other important factors to consider.

With so much research energy focused on this aspect of creativity, a picture emerges of the antecedents incorporating data about parent and peer relationships of students included in this population.

In line with the facilitating conditions already mentioned, parents of creative children tend to be less authoritarian. The entire family stresses openness and expresses an enthusiasm for life. Parents value the expression of feelings and individual divergence. Permissive parents have more spontaneous, original, self-initiating, and independent children. These children also seem less hostile, more outgoing and friendly. Their parents allow them more freedom in decision making and in exploring the environment. Their parents read more to them and often take them to the library. The parents prefer guidance over punishment and seldom use physical punishment.

The parents are themselves creative and show self-assurance and initiative. Comfortable with change, they prefer unstructured demands. They value their own autonomy and independence but are conscientious and dependable toward their children. Clearly, they serve as role models for their children (Domino, 1969; Drevdahl, 1964; Dreyer & Wells, 1966; Ellinger, 1964; Getzels & Jackson, 1961; Gowan, 1965; Holland, 1961; MacKinnon, 1964; Nichols, 1964; and Watson, 1957).

Torrance (1981) reported interesting results from an investigation of the patterns of various cultural groups in an attempt to understand the universality of the slump in creative development at the fourth-grade level. Looking at seven different cultural groups—advantaged U.S.; disadvantaged, minority U.S. (black); primitive, Western Samoa; West German; Western Australian; East Indian; and Norwegian—he came to the following conclusions:

- Cultural factors strongly influence the course of creative development, the level of creative functioning, and the type of creativity that is most evident.
- In most cultures there are discontinuities in creative development, in some around the fourth grade, in some not until the sixth grade.
- Such discontinuities occur whenever the children of that culture are confronted with new stresses and demands.
- General rankings can be made among cultures of the level of creative functioning, with the children within the advantaged cultures showing a higher creativity index than children of less advantaged cultures.

Peers in the school climate influence learning; in the case of creative students, their peer interactions do not seem to facilitate creative growth. In grades two through six, peer sanctions operate against the most creative children, and few are credited for their contributions to the group. They develop, therefore, a tendency to work alone. In the sixth grade, highly creative children encounter open hostility, aggression, criticism, and rejection. Their peers use organized efforts to limit their scope of operation and to impose sanctions. By junior high school, creative students who are not intellectually gifted are discounted, with their ideas being considered wild and their behavior deviant and wrong. Creative boys gain more acceptance from their peers when engaging in divergent behavior than creative girls. Is it any wonder that the more creative the students, the less they like school (Kurtzman, 1967; Liberty, Jones, & McGurie, 1963; Torrance, 1963)?

For those who develop this aspect of creativity, we can picture a warm, affectionate family background with stimulation and encouragement to be unique and to value that uniqueness. Creative individuals who have learned independence of thought and deed can become intrinsically motivated and set their own standards. Placing such people in the traditionally oriented, conformist setting of school leads to growth inhibition, frustration, and often the denial and abandonment of creative potential. Creative students fare somewhat better with creative teachers. Consider this: We have just looked at those who are creative thinkers, those who are creative in the one function our schools value most. How then do those creative in other aspects fare?

CREATIVITY: A FUNCTION OF FEELING

Those who view creativity from the feeling perspective focus on the emotional well-being and self-actualizing qualities of the human being. For them, creativity forms more of an attitude or belief system that permeates all the life choices and activities of the creative person. It is a concept of health, naturalness, intunedness, and development of unique potentials. Here are some definitions of this aspect of creativity:

- Maslow (1959): "Self-actualizing creativeness . . . sprang directly from the personality, which showed itself widely in ordinary affairs of life and which showed itself not only in great and obvious products but also in many other ways (p. 85) . . . a tendency to do anything creatively . . . expressive of being quality . . . rather than its problem-solving or product-making quality . . . a defining characteristic of essential human-ness" (p. 94).
- Fromm (1959): "Creativity is the ability to see (or to be aware) and to respond" (p. 44). He views it as an attitude for living.
- Anderson (1959): Creativity in human relations; "relating to others which admits one's own uniqueness and dignity and at the same time respects a uniqueness and dignity in others" (p. 120).
- Moustakas (1967): "To be creative means to experience life in one's own way, to perceive from one's own person, to draw upon one's own re-sources, capacities, roots. . . . Only from the search into oneself can the creative emerge" (p. 27). He believes that in true experience every expression is creative, the creation of the person one is and is becoming.
- Rogers (1959): "The mainspring of creativity . . . man's tendency to actu-alize himself, to become his potentialities" (p. 72).
- Krishnamurti (1964): "Creativeness has its roots in the initiative which comes into being only when there is deep discontent . . . One must be wholly discontented, not complainingly, but with joy, with gaiety, with love" (pp. 47, 48).
- May (1959): "Creativity is the encounter of an intensively conscious human being with his world" (p. 68).
- Taylor (1976): Transactional motivation (the person shapes the environ-ment rather than being shaped by the environment) and environmental stimulation (behavior is initiated toward unpredictable but creative out-comes) combine to form a system he calls creative transactualization that is in continuity with self-actualization.
- Hallman (1963): "Creativity is defined as a way of conducting one's life rather than in terms of the number and kinds of objects which one may have produced" (p. 132).

According to this view, a measure of self-actualization is the criterion for selecting and evaluating creative students. The Personal Orientation Inventory (POI) (Shostrom, 1964) has been developed as such a measure. The relationship between measures of creativity defined as a thinking function (e.g., TTCT) and self-actualization measures is seen only in the elaboration trait. Murphy, Dauw, Horton, and Friedian (1976) speculate that "self-actualization may be a larger, global concept whereas creativity measured by the TTCT may be a more clearly defined trait in the realm of intellectual abilities" (p. 43). In Damm's (1970) study, the groups of students who obtained high scores on both intelligence (as measured by the California Test of Mental Maturity) and creativity (as measured by the Remote Associates Test) were superior in self-actualization (as measured by the POI) to those who had obtained a high score in only intelligence or creativity or low scores on both.

Other ways of selecting and evaluating self-actualizing creative persons are limited. Maslow, from as early as 1950, studied people who were self-actualizing. He began by choosing people who, in his opinion, were the most healthy and the most self-fulfilling. He felt they were motivated by growth needs (trends toward self-actualization, i.e., ongoing actualization of potentials, such as the fulfillment of mission, a fuller knowledge and acceptance of one's own intrinsic nature, an unceasing trend toward unity, integration, or synergy from within), rather than by the basic needs of safety, belongingness, love, respect, and self-esteem. Maslow (1959) reports these common attributes in his population of self-actualizers:

- A special kind of perception
- More spontaneous and expressive
- Unfrightened by the unknown, the mysterious, the puzzling; often attracted to it
- Resolution of dichotomies: selfish and unselfish; duty and pleasure; work and play; strong ego and egolessness
- Able to integrate
- More self-accepting, less afraid of what others would say, less need for other people, lack of fear of own emotions, impulses, and thoughts
- Have more of themselves available for use, for enjoyment, for creative purposes; they waste less of their time and energy protecting themselves against themselves
- Involved in more peak experiences, integration within the person and between the person and the world, transcendence.

Fromm (1959) believes the following characteristics are necessary for creativity to occur:

- Capacity to be puzzled
- Ability to concentrate
- Ability to experience self as creative, as the originator of one's acts

- Willingness to be born every day
- Ability to accept conflict and tension from polarity rather than avoiding them
- Courage to let go of certainties, to be different, to be concerned with truth, to be certain of one's own feelings and thoughts and trust them.

Others have found that creative persons have the ability to identify closely with the feelings and expectations of others (Taylor & Williams, 1966).

To develop creativity from the feeling aspect, the following conditions have been suggested (Anderson, 1968; Drews, 1965; Fromm, 1959):

- Provide an environment rich and varied in stimulation.
- Teach with materials and methods harmonious with each other and with the teacher.
- Delineate clearly and repeatedly the aims of this type of program.
- Allow free interplay of differences.
- Make environment and materials friendly, nonthreatening, thereby allowing disagreement and controversy without hostility (this allows children to engage freely in behavior underlying creativity).
- Reduce anxiety in classroom, especially that created by the teacher.
- Handle differences as confrontations, not as conflicts.
- Find integrative elements in differences.
- Emerge unifying concepts.
- Allow individuation and differentiation within the unity.
- Foster positive change in directions congruent with student's predilections in cognitive and affective areas.

Drews (1964–1966) successfully used 10 half-hour films (*The Being and Becoming Series,* Drews & Knowlton, 1963) dealing with the life-styles and value systems of creative and socially concerned adults. By presenting an anthology of heroic characters, ideas, and issues, she was able to make significant changes in the direction of greater motivation to learn, openness, and the valuing of self-actualization.

A very provocative finding by Anderson (1959) indicates that "socially integrative behavior in one person tends to induce socially integrative behavior in others" (p. 130). This says a lot to teachers and parents about their techniques and modeling behaviors.

Although in the past people assumed that those who are highly creative are less emotionally stable, less mature, and more childlike, the data seem to counterindicate such an assumption. High creativity does not seem to result in neuroticism; in fact, no relationship was found (Feldhusen, Denny, & Condon, 1965; Flescher, 1963; Ohnmacht, 1966). Gowan (1981) observed that creative people have a great fund of free energy that seems to result from a high degree of psychological health.

In addition to creating the conditions and allowing the freedom to develop the feeling aspect of creativity, no one set of skills can be taught. Unlike the rational aspect of creativity, this area does not develop by asking the learner to try consciously to be more creative. Creativity, in this respect, is enhanced by the absence of trying. The more one strives to succeed, the more anxious or competitive one feels and the more out of tune and insensitive one becomes. Feelings of self-confidence, self-acceptance, and self-esteem provide the basis for growth in this area of creativity. Creativity as a feeling function interrelates and supports all of the other aspects. Rational functioning alone produces predictable associations. However, add emotions, and the original associations increase. Emotions are also inseparably involved in creative activity, inspiration, and intuition.

Fearn (1976) has developed a very interesting and useful model for teaching the feeling aspect of creativity. He suggests that creativity is the process of persons, limited and confined by what is known in their cultural space and time, reaching out beyond their limits to grasp ideas or concepts that already exist, but that are not presently known. His model, Individual Development: Creativity, is concerned with two basic processes, involvement with data and involvement with self. Data involvement includes collecting necessary knowledge and follows the assumption that creativity does not occur in a vacuum. Awareness, fluency, and flexibility are parts of the collection process that then depends upon self-discipline, elaboration, and complexity preferences for further development. At this point, the personal ability to risk, question, imagine, and perform originally become important. He sums up the model, which has been used successfully in inservice teacher workshops, with this statement of the final process:

> Individual reaching out is the process whereby the person who is (a) sufficiently aware of the task and its parameters, (b) willing to risk the known and unknown consequences of stepping beyond the established, and (c) sufficiently disciplined to see a task through to self-satisfaction and who arranges creative behaviors appropriately manages to bring into his or her space (and perhaps the spaces of millions of others) an arrangement or a definition that increases consciousness by contributing to a total collection of possibilities. (p. 62)

Simonov (1970) discusses the relationship of emotions to creativity. He believes positive emotions are far more productive than negative ones. To develop creativity from this view requires more than "the simple elimination of unpleasant feelings" (p. 54). Without stimulation, positive emotions do not arise. Increasing the amount of information available to a person enriches positive emotions. How emotions interrelate with rationality is shown in Simonov's statement: "Strengthening of rationality in a modern person leads not to weak emotions, but rather to richer and more complicated emotions" (p. 55). Positive emotions, rationality, and intuition all seem to lead to creative actions, the talent aspect.

CREATIVITY: THE TALENT ASPECT

The talent aspect of creativity includes the product, the art form, and the realm of the talented creator:

- Maslow (1959) calls this aspect special talent creativeness; he defines it as a production that results from activity, control, and hard work.
- Rogers (1959) in recognizing this type of creativity describes, "emergence in action of a novel rational product, growing out of the uniqueness of the individual on the one hand and the materials, events, people or circumstances of his life on the other." (p. 71)
- May (1959) also sees this area when he says, "Creativity is bringing something new into birth . . . the expression of the normal man in the act of actualizing himself . . . as the representation of the highest degree of emotional health." (pp. 57, 58)
- Simonov (1970) sees the product the artist has created as "a model of the artist's attitude toward a phenomenon He creates the model with the aim of getting to know, checking and specifying his attitudes." (p. 55)
- Rhodes (1961) — "the birth of an idea and its embodiment in form recognizable by someone or society as valuable." (p. 305)

The criterion for evaluating creativity in this aspect is how original, inventive, or imaginative the product is. Simonov (1970) sees the criterion as that of social consumption. He believes that the longer a work survives, the closer the creator has come to "perceiving and presenting an essential truth of human existence" (p. 77).

How can this aspect of creativity be developed? Many of the conditions for facilitating growth of the talent aspect are the same as we found necessary for the rational thinking and the feeling aspects. Furthermore, Cole (1969) has found that "the creative process is very similar among different people regardless of the diverse nature of the products" (p. 247). The creator has these inner conditions or characteristics (May, 1959; Maynard, 1970; Rogers, 1959):

- Openness to experience, new ideas
- An internal locus of evaluation
- An ability to toy with elements and concepts
- Perceiving freshly
- Concern with outside and inside worlds
- Ability to defer closure and judgment
- Ability to accept conflict and tension
- Skilled performance of the traditional arts
- High theoretical and aesthetic values.

To facilitate creative and artistic production externally,

- Treat the child with respect and allow freedom to explore the universe.
- Create an atmosphere with really good music, books, and pictures as a natural part of the child's world.
- Treat ideas and questions respectfully.
- Respect the child's privacy.
- Value the unusual, the divergent.
- Help the child learn by mistakes.
- Avoid sex role stereotyping.
- Encourage self-expression.
- Teach the child to look and really see.
- Help the child learn to trust the senses.
- Permit the child's own creativity to emerge.

Rogers (1959) writes of the psychological safety and freedom needed to carry out a creative act. Psychological safety can be created by "accepting the individual as of unconditional worth . . . providing a climate in which external evaluation is absent . . . and by understanding empathetically" (pp. 78–80). By *psychological freedom,* he means the complete freedom of *symbolic* expression with responsibility only to one's self.

In Schaefer's (1970) study, the parents of creative (as defined by number and quality of creative products) adolescent girls were well educated, and most mothers worked outside the home. Both parents had more interest in cultural-intellectual pursuits than in social-civic organizations or sports. The parents read far more than average, engaged in creative hobbies, and played musical instruments. They provided their children with role models for creative people.

When one is involved in a creative act, there is likely to be first the "Aha!" or "Eureka!" feeling, then an anxiety of separateness, and finally a strong desire to communicate. At this point the product begins to emerge (Rogers, 1959).

Again, we see the interdependence of the different views of creativity. No one view fully explains either the process or the emerging product. The area least explored and yet probably most indispensable to the act or attitude of creativity is our next area for discussion, the higher levels of consciousness, the intuitive aspect.

CREATIVITY: A FUNCTION OF HIGHER LEVELS OF CONSCIOUSNESS

Our society places so much value on the rational, analytic type of thinking that recent researchers of the human brain claim an unbalanced focus on one half, the dominant left hemisphere.[1] Although both sides seem to receive similar informa-

---

[1] The left hemisphere dominates in nearly all right-handed people and in all except approximately one-third of the left-handed people. For them, the location of functions seems to be reserved.

tion, they process the information differently. The left side concerns itself more with verbal forms and uses logical, analytic processing, while the right side reacts more nonverbally and uses more of a holistic synthesis in its operations.

Differentiation and emphasis on left-hemisphere functions have led many researchers to look toward the right side of the brain as a pathway to creativity. It may be that through our contact with the right hemisphere, we will find ways to understand the unconscious or preconscious state, believed by some to contain the roots of creative acts. Researchers have begun to explore altered states of consciousness as possible areas of information on creativity. They examine the use of drugs, trances, hypnotism, meditation, chanting, dreams, fantasies, and daydreams for clues to lead us to the intuitive, creative spark (Bogen, 1975; Ferguson, 1973; Krashen, 1975; Krippner, 1968; Nebes, 1975; Ornstein, 1972, 1973a; Oyle, 1975).

As we examine creativity from the higher levels of consciousness aspect, we must be aware that much of what happens can only be understood experientially and that rational, verbal explanations dilute the events, for the essence of the experience may be changed by its description. With this difficulty in mind, let us look at yet another view of the meaning of creativity:

- Anderson (1962) indicates that a creative product is never completely a product of one's rational, everyday state of mind.
- Taylor (1963): "There is reason to think that much of the creative process is intuitive in nature and that it entails a work of the mind prior to its arising to the conscious level and certainly also prior to its being in expressible form. It is most likely preconscious, nonverbal or preverbal, and it may involve a large sweeping, scanning, deep, diffused, free and powerful action of almost the whole mind" (p. 4).
- Krippner (1968): "Without access to alternative levels of awareness, creative behavior may be stifled or blocked" (p. 149). He further indicates that it is "essential to the individual's well-being and creative development."
- Koestler (1964): "The temporary relinquishing of conscious controls liberates the mind from certain constraints which are necessary to maintain the disciplined routines of thought but which may become an impediment to the creative leap. . . . The creative act, in so far as it depends on unconscious resources, presupposes a relaxing of controls and a regression to modes of ideation which are indifferent to the rules of verbal logic, unperturbed by contradiction, untouched by the dogmas and taboos of so-called common sense. At the decisive stage of discovery the codes of disciplined reasoning are suspended (p. 178). . . . Language can become a screen which stands between the thinker and reality. This is the reason why true creativity often starts where language ends" (p. 177).
- MacKinnon (1965) gives being more intuitively perceptive as one of the major conditions for creativity.

Characteristically, those who would be identified as creative from this view (Koestler, 1964; Krippner, 1968; Martindale, 1975; Schaefer, 1970) would

- Have their energy field accessible
- Have ability to tap and release unconscious and preconscious thought
- Be able to withstand being thought of as abnormal or eccentric
- Be more sensitive
- Have a richer fantasy life and greater involvement in daydreaming
- Be more enthusiastic and impulsive
- Often show abilities of synesthesia (e.g., tasting color, seeing sound, hearing smells)
- Show different brain wave patterns than the less creative, especially during creative activity
- When confronted with novelty of design, music, or ideas, get excited and involved (less creative people get suspicious and hostile)
- When given a new solution to a problem, get enthused, suggest other ideas; overlook details and problems (less creative students analyze the defect rather than explore potentials).

In an interesting study, Martindale (1975) found that creative people show a pattern of brain wave production during creative activity and creativity testing that is the reverse of those less creative. Most people produce alpha waves (slower than average brain waves) while relaxing and reduce alpha production while working on a problem. Creative people produce fewer alpha waves when relaxing and increase them when working on an imaginative problem. The creative seem to have higher resting levels of brain wave activity, resulting in fewer alpha waves than average people. "Creativity and intellectual ability require two different thought processes: the former calls for low cortical arousal and defusing one's powers of concentration, the latter calls for higher cortical arousal and focused attention" (pp. 48–50). Martindale concludes that the creative do not consciously control their alpha; they view the world differently because they process information differently and have different brain wave patterns.

When discussing how to develop creativity as a function of consciousness, several components need to be mentioned. The ability to relax is the first skill needed. The skills of imagery and imagination also facilitate creativity and the development of higher levels of consciousness. We discuss strategies for acquiring these skills in Chapter 8.

Griffiths (1945) defines *imagination* as a mode of thinking concerned with fantasy and daydreams. *Imagery* is defined as a type of sensory experience in which images arise independent of external stimulation. Eidetic imagery, a type of three-dimensional imagery, often occurs in children, but tends to disappear as we get older. It persists in only a few highly imaginative adults and is associated with the sudden flash of insight. The decline with age is due to the predominance of verbalism and conscious control, claims Rugg (1963). While one is very young, linguistic vocabulary increases, verbalizing is limited, and concept formation takes

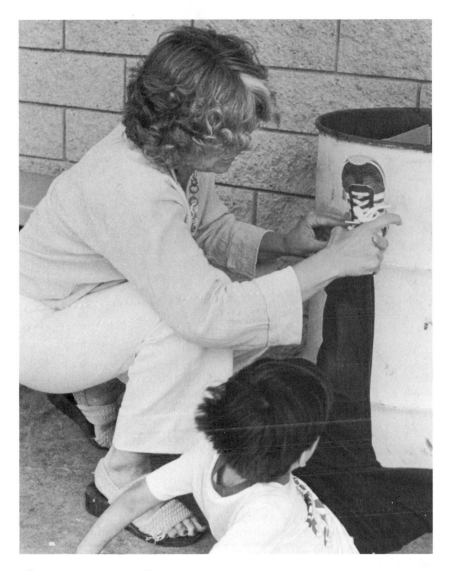

There are many creative ways to learn.

place slowly. In adulthood, if home and school have been "successful," the reality-mind has taken over. Andrews (1930) reports that the more uncommon types of imagination (personification, fantastic stories, etc.) were found to be most prevalent at age 3 and one-half, although they occur in few children. By 5 years of age, they were on the wane. Girls seem to peak 1 year before boys.

Society, and schools in particular, have expectations that block creativity. Krippner (1967) lists 10 assumptions guaranteed to stop creativity in all but the hardiest:

1 Everything must be useful.
2 Everything must be successful.
3 Everything must be perfect.
4 Everyone must like you.
5 You shall not prefer solitude to togetherness.
6 You must have concentrated attention.
7 You must not diverge from culturally imposed sex norms.
8 Do not express excessive emotional feeling.
9 Do not be ambiguous.
10 Do not rock the cultural boat.

Griffiths (1945) found that a limited environment also restricts the level of creative performance.

The criterion for evaluation in creativity's higher level of consciousness aspect is the availability of the preconscious or unconscious state to the person. Krippner (1968) asserts that the ability to operate simultaneously at different levels of consciousness is characteristic of this type of creative person and those "individuals who spend all their waking hours in rational, everyday consciousness are functioning below their optimal level and perhaps demonstrating signs of emotional disturbance" (p. 148).

As of now, with the exception of the researchers mentioned, few have looked at consciousness and its relationship to creativity. It seems clear from the recent data coming to us from neurophysiology, brain research, dream research, anthropology, drug therapy, and other fields that such investigation is necessary and would prove to be quite productive in helping us to understand the total meaning of creativity.

CREATIVITY: AN INTEGRATIVE APPROACH

A number of individuals have recognized the limitations of focusing on only one aspect of creativity and have combined several of these areas in their work. They view creativity from process and product, from skill development and use of intuition. Personality, verbal skill, and talent expressed through achievement are the elements of a study by Callaway (1969), who concludes,

The complete creative act, as depicted by those who have probed its process as well as by the subjective analysis of the creators, themselves, is seen to involve much more than "divergent thinking." Socially useful creativity demands the synergistic cooperation of the entire personality, including all physical mechanisms and modes of thought. Affective and conative dimensions are as essential as the cognitive ones. (pp. 240–241)

Gowan (1972) also pointed out the holistic nature of creativity. In his discussion, he grouped the investigations of creativity into the areas of (a)

A holistic concept of creativity allows us to discover the many ways each of us can express ourselves creatively.

cognitive, rational, and semantic; (b) personal and environmental; (c) mental health and openness; (d) Freudian and neo-Freudian; and (e) psychedelic, existential, and irrational. He viewed these subdivisions on a continuum. He presented helpful overviews of all of the areas and of their relationship to the total concept. Later work expanded his involvement with the irrational aspect (Gowan, 1974, 1975). He stated,

> Creativity is a characteristic not only of individual human behavior, but also of the species in general. What is true of the development of the superior individual is also true of the developing aspects of mankind. The emergence of creative abilities is a triumph not only of individual development, but as Bucke (1929) points out, the harbinger of evolutionary progress for all men. (Gowan, 1972, p. 70)

Others who view creativity from this integrated vantage point are Leonard (cited in Ferguson, 1973):

> A brain composed of such neurons obviously can never be "filled up." Perhaps the more it knows the more it can know and create. Perhaps, in fact, we can now propose an incredible hypothesis: *The ultimate creative capacity of the brain may be, for all practical purposes, infinite.* (p. 288)

and Ferguson (1973):

There is a strong likelihood that creativity does not need to be developed in man but simply liberated (p. 289). . . . The view of creativity as a nonintellectual activity fails to take into account the dynamic, unitary and coherent nature of the brain. Emotion and intellect, freedom and discipline, reason and intuition, the precise and the gossamer, primary and secondary processes, chaos and order—all of these apparent opposites can exist in creative harmony in the human brain. (p. 295)

Earlier in this chapter we discussed the holographic functions of the brain. The brain may indeed be a hologram interpreting a holographic universe. Viewing this possibility, with its exciting implications for expanding our view of the reality in which we live, which we may even create, Gowan (1981) suggested that far more attention must be paid to the development of our creative abilities. At the very least he believed we should (a) study creativity directly in high school and university classes; (b) help young children learn techniques of relaxation, stress reduction, and the incubation of creative thought; (c) help children practice use of imagination and imagery; and (d) encourage creative production appropriate to their developmental phase.

Trowbridge (1978) discusses creativity in terms of a dynamic balance between the processes associated with the three substrates of the brain, the primary reticular brain stem (action), the limbic system (affect), and the cortical areas (cognition). Creativity depends on the balance between action, emotion, and cognition with the addition of insight or intuition, the ability to synthesize the components of a situation into a meaningful whole.

Harrington (1980) argues for the inclusion of kinesthetic and muscular modes of representation and expression in the creative process. He believes that such involvement facilitates creativity by encouraging the analogical and metaphorical transformation of information.

Herrmann (1981) suggests a view of creativity that allows for the synthesis by comparing the steps of creativity directly to brain function. The first step he suggests is using the learner's interest, which he believes to be whole-brain derived. At the preparation stage, the left-brain would take the leadership position. During the incubation and illumination stages, the right-brain processes would be dominant as the "Aha!" experience occurs. The critical left-brain analytic process of verification follows. Finally the emerging product or solution is put into use, and the application again requires the whole brain to act in synthesis. Creativity must include feelings, rational thinking, intuitive thinking, and physical actions. It is the extension of giftedness, a truly integrative function of our efficient, effective human brain. The art of creating allows us to become more than we could have imagined.

Andrews (1975), in a study involving scientists who had been project directors, found the following:

1 A lack of relationship between creative ability and innovativeness.
2 A lack of relationship between verbal intelligence and either innovativeness or productiveness.

3 Creative ability accomplished more when the scientist had

   a A perception of self-initiation of the activity

   b Substantial power and influence in decision making

   c A feeling of professional security

   d Freedom to conduct the activity without inhibiting administrative supervision

   e A project small in scope, time, and personnel requirement

   f Other activities to engage in

   g High motivation.

Under favorable conditions high creative ability correlates with innovativeness of output. In unfavorable conditions the reverse is true. It was strongly urged that the social and psychological setting of the creative process be considered most seriously. The impact of the above-mentioned factors was cumulative, and only with several factors evident did positive correlation occur.

Barron (1969) has been one of the researchers to look at the creative person for answers to the creative process. To use data from this source effectively requires an integrative approach. Even among those who identify themselves primarily with one aspect of creativity, there is considerable overlap with other aspects. It is hoped that this trend will continue as we learn more about creativity as the synthesis of all human functions.

In this chapter, we have looked at the concept of creativity from a holistic point of view. A model was presented using the four human functions as a base and synthesizing the important aspects of creativity: the rational, the emotional, talent, and higher consciousness. While the research is often unclear as to the area of creativity it is investigating, this model and the accompanying definitions and population characteristics should allow us to draw more useful comparisons with other areas of creativity or with less creative individuals. The conditions favoring development of each aspect should allow teachers and parents to provide better for creative individuals and encourage a more complete and balanced experience in developing creativity.

Questions Often Asked

1. Why should we consider a holistic concept of creativity?

If we continue to look at only the rational aspect of creativity, or to believe that only the products of creative acts define creativity, we will limit our understanding of the role creativity can play in our lives. If we include both the affective and the intuitive aspects of creativity we will discover the amazing range of ways each of us is able to express ourself creatively. We will appreciate our capability to create and be closer to realizing our unique human potential.

2. Is everyone creative?

Everyone has the potential for the development of creativity, just as we each have as yet unknown potential for developing all aspects of our intelligence.

3. How can creativity be measured?

The rational aspect of creativity can be measured by the current creativity tests. The products or physical aspects can be measured by highly proficient performers and artists through a jurying process. In either case the standards will be those agreed to by that society judging. The emotional and intuitive aspects may result in a breakthrough that can be communicated and change the culture and thereby be judged. Our daily creative behaviors are more likely to be appreciated by those close to us or more importantly by ourselves. Experiencing ourselves as creative beings is a joy in itself.

4. Why can't more people be creative?

They probably can but choose not to for fear of being thought different, strange, unusual, silly, dumb. . . . Unfortunately being creative in a society that values rational, material gains requires taking risks. Some may not realize how creative they could really be if given the opportunity and the belief in themselves. A safe place to be creative is sorely needed, both at school and at home.

5. Can we really teach people to be creative?

We can teach some of the aspects and skills of creative behavior. We can model creative acts and attitudes. We can provide safe places for creativity to be expressed, and we can value its expression. We can take the risk of sharing our creativity. I doubt that we can teach someone else all there is to know about being creative, but maybe being willing to share all we know about it will be enough.

3. Becoming Gifted

The purpose of this chapter is to provide the reader with

- An understanding of the importance of early learning to the development of giftedness.
- An awareness of some of the environmental influences on cognitive development during prenatal, perinatal, infancy, and early childhood periods.
- An awareness of the concept of sensitive periods and their importance to optimal development.
- Specific suggestions for developing a nurturing environment for optimal intellectual growth from birth through 3 months; 4 through 10 months; 10 months through 2 years; and 2 through 5 years of age.
- Many of the characteristics that are unique to gifted learners, the needs that these characteristics may cause, and some of the concomitant problems.

Children never give a wrong answer ... They merely answer a different question. It is our job to find out which one they answered correctly and honor what they know.

—BOB SAMPLES

We now begin our inquiry into an area that has been omitted in the literature of gifted education. As a student and now with my students, I found it necessary to study the fields of biology, psychobiology, neurobiology, medicine, and linguistics to bring together data that are crucial to the understanding of how giftedness occurs. Though we have begun to collect data on the origin of giftedness, we know little of the phenomenon we call *highly gifted* or *genius*. However, as information becomes available at a geometrically progressive rate, the excitement of events to come can surely be glimpsed.

As early as 1955, Pressey admonished educators and parents to create genius. Pressey's plan for developing genius is still thought-provoking today (Pressey, 1964). He studied the careers of eminent European musicians in the past century and American athletes in the 1950s. He suggested that the following factors are important to their development and possibly to the development of all special talent or ability: (a) excellent early opportunities for ability to develop with encouragement from family and friends; (b) superior early and continuing guidance and instruction; (c) frequent and continuous opportunity to practice and extend their special abilities and to progress as they are able; (d) close association with others of similar ability; (e) opportunities for real accomplishment within their capabilities, but with increasing challenge; and (f) provision for strong success experiences and recognition of these successes. While genius may not result, we have every reason to believe that a level of giftedness may be attainable for a great many children. Although Pressey's comments grew from logical theorizing, we now have evidence to support his conclusions. The new knowledge comes (a) from data showing us the responsiveness of the central nervous system (CNS), including the brain, to environmental demands, and (b) from new discoveries concerning the sensitivities and propensities inherent in the CNS.

As the brain researcher Elio Maggio (1971) writes, "Experience, in other words, molds neurophysiological mechanisms, even those which appear more stable and closely depending upon genetic and biochemical factors" (p. 81). McCall (1979) believes that the potential for change remains, "although naturalistic circumstances typically conspire to favor stability" (p. 189). He notes that experience is cumulative and that children are a dynamic force in the selection and creation of their own environments. This ability to create their own environment promotes a degree of stability. By living in the same family until adulthood and as adults selecting experiences that are similar to the intellectual environment we experienced in childhood, we further contribute to the stability of the environment on our intellectual growth. The evidence tends to support the possibility of change in such growth, however, if circumstances and environments are changed. For that reason, McCall believes that although naturalistic circumstances favor environmental stability, mental capability is not essentially imprinted by age 6. The plasticity of the system responds to the impact of the environmental experience.

Even before data supported these theories, clues to the importance of the earliest years as the nurturing point for eminence had been found. Goertzel and Goertzel (1962) reported on the lives of a host of eminent people and found that, without exception, these individuals had grown up in early stimulating environments. Colvin (1915) states that all the prodigies he studied were educated from the first months of their lives. Fowler (1962a, b), Hollingworth (1942), and Terman (1925) reported no subjects of high ability who had not been exposed to early stimulation. Ausubel (1967) even contended that failure to stimulate in the early years was irreversible. Young genes display more plasticity than adult genes. Educators have long believed in early achievement, especially in speech and reading, as a sure sign of giftedness. Let us now ask a question that I find as optimistic as it is fascinating: Can early opportunity for achievement and early stimulation create giftedness? More accurately, can such opportunity allow the developing child to actualize more of the potential available that may well fall within the range of performance we call *gifted?*

EARLY LEARNING: THE IMPORTANCE OF DEVELOPING POTENTIAL

Lipsitt, Mustaine, and Zeigler (1976) compare the findings of infant studies to the phenomena now being observed in athletics: Increased knowledge of human systems and their nurture, human aspirations and motivations, and opportunities for individual performance combine to bring out higher levels of excellence year after year. The first four years of life are the most critical for human development. Not only is physical survival tenuous, but patterns for both the personality and the actualization of learning ability have begun. The personality established and the type of learning opportunities available will facilitate or inhibit the development of inherited intellectual capacity. Again we have the choice. We may either plan to provide the most nourishing environment that is possible within our current knowledge, or we may allow this important interaction to occur by chance. Regardless of how we choose to approach these formative years, interaction will occur and intelligence will develop. Whether that development leads to actualization or loss of human potential depends on us.

Prior to the 1960s, relatively few studies viewed the developing infant as more than a biological entity. The earlier picture of the infant showed a reflexive organism unable to see or hear, who was only partially aware of being alive. People believed that pain, pleasure, and perception came about much later, as the neural structure completed its development. No logical person would have spoken of stimulation. For that reason parents, mostly mothers, were given instructions on bathing, feeding, and other physical concerns related to infant care. Motherhood became very clean, sterile, and convenient, as disposable bottles, disposable diapers, and ever-increasing amounts of expensive equipment made mother and child more safe and hygienic. Classes on child rearing were held, again largely for mothers, but no one considered the mental development of the new person.

Then a few researchers began to observe and publish what many intuitive mothers already knew. Infants were far more capable than anyone had believed. From the moment of birth their world was available to them. Some researchers even began looking at the prenatal and perinatal periods of development. The findings are exciting! From 1960 until today we have witnessed an explosion of information about these periods and about the early childhood years that follow. We can no longer "just let children be children" without our awareness that we are inducing events that will have permanent effects on their lives. Many of our children have been fortunate; many others have not. We can do something about ameliorating development. We now have the knowledge that will allow more potentially gifted children to actualize their potential. We may find that most children could be functioning at the level we now called *gifted;* for some there will be further reaches of development as yet unknown. Let us look at some discoveries we have made about our own human infants. We have only begun to understand; there is still much to learn.

Animal studies provide answers to some very important questions. At the level of gene action and cell development, it is possible to generalize animal results to humans. Comparison is less useful at the level of behavior. In the first instance, the patterns of action are the same. At their brain research laboratories at the University of California at Berkeley, Krech (1969), Rosenzweig (1966), and their colleagues sought to discover the effect experience has on learning. Specifically, they questioned whether differential experience could modify the brain in measurable anatomical and chemical terms. Their initial study involved two groups of rats from the same genetic strain. One group was reared in a nonstimulating environment. They placed each animal in solitary confinement in a small cage situated in a dimly lighted, quiet room. These rats received no attention, but they had unlimited access to the same standard food provided both groups. The other group was environmentally enriched by living together in large, wire mesh cages in a well-lighted, noisy, busy laboratory. The cages were equipped with toys, and the rats were allowed to explore freely the environment outside of the cage thirty minutes each day. Upon later examination of these rats, the researchers found that the brain cortexes of those rats had significantly expanded and had grown thicker and heavier than those of the deprived group!

Of greater importance, the researchers found an increase in the number of glial cells (which seem to play a vital function in the nutrition of the neurons and in the learning capability of the animal), an increase in the size of the neuronal cell bodies and their nuclei, and an increase in diameter of the blood cells supplying the cortex. Chemical changes had also occurred. Enriched brains showed more acetylcholinesterase, the enzyme involved in the transsynaptic conduction of neural impulses, and cholinesterase, the enzyme found in glial cells (see Chapter 1).

Later experiments showed that, in the brains of rats sacrificed after stimulation had ceased for a period of time, the weight and size changes were no longer apparent, but the chemical changes remained. These changes correlate with changes in problem-solving ability; stimulated rats rank as superior problem solvers. A later experiment will prove quite thought-provoking for anyone concerned with disability. In this experiment they blinded two groups of rats and studied them along with two groups of sighted rats. They stimulated one group of sighted and one group of blind rats, and they left the other two groups unstimulated. The results showed that in learning ability the sighted, stimulated rats were, of course, significantly more capable. Interestingly, they found that the blind, stimulated rats were significantly better learners than either the sighted or blind nonstimulated groups. It would seem from these results that stimulation is critical even to damaged organisms (Rosenzweig, 1966).

As a result of other experiments conducted to examine the effect of early stimulation on animals, Seymour Levine of Stanford University declared: "Minimal changes in the early environment have proved to have profound effects on the subsequent performance of the developing organism" (1957, p. 405). He discovered that other very significant effects were derived from lack of stimulation. Being undisturbed, even in a warm, sheltered environment with a nourishing mother, could not provide the experience needed for later coping and learning behavior. Animals provided with early experience that was stimulating, even at times traumatic, seemed to be more emotionally stable, more curious, and more able to learn and to display appropriate coping behavior; however, too much aversive stimulation reverses the effects; anxiety can be debilitating (Levine, 1957, 1960).

In work done to learn more about the functioning of the human brain, Scheibel and Scheibel (1964b) found far more complexity than previously supposed. In addition to the millions of cells found in the human brain, each individual cell has hundreds of branches called dendrites. The dendrite, the structure that forms part of the connection (called a synapse) with another nerve cell, makes possible the transmission of impulses from one cell to another. The Scheibels discovered that each dendrite seems to have a different function. To complicate the picture further, each dendrite has thousands of spines that may further differentiate functions. The number of possibilities of individual learning differences and levels of intelligence could be enormous. Early environmental experiences appear to be the key determinants to the density and quantity of spines.

Cooper and Zubek (cited in Bodmer & Cavalli-Sforza, 1970) at the University of Manitoba found that when rats from "bright" and "dull" strains had been raised for one generation in a restricted environment, a difference in learning ability could no longer be perceived. When raised in a stimulating environment, they did almost equally well. Another researcher, James L. McGaugh (cited in Krech, 1969) of the University of California at Irvine, tested chemical stimulation of mice. He found that mice showing hereditarily superior learning ability can be surpassed by mice who are hereditarily dull, but chemically enriched. Krech (1970) suggests that chemical changes from rich environmental interaction have a similar effect.

Along with these research trends came research directed at exploring the specific factors within the environment that interact with the characteristics of human infants to promote or facilitate development, such as home qualities, patterns of mother-child or father-child interaction, forms of communication, and others (Beckwith, 1971; Clarke-Stewart, 1973; Lewis & Rosenblum, 1974; White & Watts, 1973; Yarrow et al., 1973). While there are still many unanswered questions, a substantial amount is known on the cognitive-affective-social capabilities of infants and the mechanisms that contribute to their development.

One question continued to concern early childhood educators: Can learning, or rather the benchmarks for development, be accelerated, or is it dependent solely on maturation? Among types of learning, physical control seems most clearly affected by maturation. Haynes, White, and Held (1965) conducted an experiment on newborns in a nursery to answer the above question. The researchers placed mobiles in the babies' cribs, replaced plain sheets and bumpers with patterned ones, changed positions of the infants, and provided other forms of sensory enrichment. When compared with other babies, the enriched group accelerated the first major event in the developmental motor sequence, fisted swiping, by several weeks. More importantly, Haynes et al. concluded that once children operate at a higher level, they assimilate more information to allow their cognitive development to proceed even more rapidly. Techniques to accelerate infant development include those that make available more color, more complex patterns, and more accessibility to the world around them. Dr. Hunt (Pines, 1979b) tells us that development does not come just from exposure to stimulating environments. The child must be allowed to cope, to interact with the environment. Acting on things, interacting with people, and having the people and the environment be responsive are critical.

These studies and other similar findings mean to the educator that by early stimulation we may reverse the effects of deprivation that have occurred over past generations. Of course, we could equally restrict an environment to the degree that a leveling effect takes place regardless of the genetic advantage enjoyed at birth. We can no longer leave early stimulation to chance. While genetic differences among human beings do exist, such differences are insufficient to explain different intellectual abilities. Early experience can validate or invalidate the genetic contribution to our intellectual growth.

"Long-lasting effects occur as a result of experience. The more complex the experience, 'the richer' the environment, the more complex the brain" (Restak, 1986, p. 91). To use the environment as a powerful interacting agent, we must know more about our children and their capabilities. Environmentally produced individual differences begin at birth, possibly before. We must provide an environment rich in opportunities and responsive to each individual. We must also allow ourselves to be effective observers in order to assure optimal growth. If even such less complex animals as rodents show individual differences and require differential treatment and programming, and if such programming can make such critical differences, what must infants require? Can we dare to neglect the implications of these findings?

Prenatal and Perinatal Interaction

Interaction with the environment begins to affect the infant significantly during the prenatal period. Some researchers investigating this area of growth warn that the history of the mother governs occurrences during this period. Drugs, alcohol, and cigarettes used prior to conception by the mother will affect her ability to conceive a healthy fetus. Her diet and health habits, her anxiety and mental health will all be reflected in the child she bears. Even more dramatic effects can be noted during the fetal period. Researchers have shown a cause-and-effect relationship between diseases, malnutrition, and drug use by the mother and the damage to the growing fetus.

Factors affecting the health of the mother and, therefore, the child she is carrying were found by the Preschool Nutrition Survey (Owen et al., 1974). Very young mothers have less adequate nutritional reserves, as they are still growing themselves. Further, teen-age mothers are less likely to have adequate diets during gestation. Lower-class mothers tend to have far more first-time pregnancies before they are seventeen (42%) than do upper-class mothers (4%). The nutrition and overall health of the mother directly affect intellectual growth as well as the more obvious physical growth of her infant. We are also aware of genetic problems that can now be detected in utero. There are, however, very few acceleration studies available to show the same causal relationship in humans.

Ockert S. Heyns (1963), of the University of Witwatersrand in Johannesburg, South Africa, conducted one study that raises some interesting speculation. Heyns became aware of a vast number of children born with brain damage presumably because of forced passage through the bony pelvic area of the mother during birth. In 1954, Heyns devised a vacuum chamber to fit over the abdomen. He believed the device would relax the uterus and the abdominal muscles during labor, thus reducing the pain of childbirth and allowing for easier delivery. Pregnant patients used the chamber for 30-minute periods the last 10 days prior to and throughout delivery. Heyns was very pleased with the results, finding deliveries easier and of shorter duration. He could bring the women into the final stages of birth in a more relaxed and vigorous state.

Some months later Heyns began receiving reports of unusually advanced behavior and growth in the infants of mothers he had used in his experiment. After many favorable reports, Heyns decided to test these infants against physical and mental norms. What he found caused him to bring his procedure to the attention of the London University Hospital for verification. Infants using the decompression chamber scored 18% higher than norms on tests of the landmarks of infant development; 16% scored 48% higher. Children at 12 months appeared as physically and behaviorally developed as normal 2-year-olds.

After replication and study, the hospital researchers made an announcement about the advanced mental and physical development. Use of the vacuum chamber seemed to allow for an increase in oxygen available to the fetus at a decisive point in the physiological and neural development of the infants. While many countries have since used this delivery method, doctors in the United States have not adapted its use on any wide scale. It is still considered experimental. Along this same line, however, natural childbirth and many techniques for relaxation during fetal development and birth are becoming quite widespread today. Concern has even been raised over birth trauma; procedures for ensuring the infant a less painful and shocking beginning are being used more commonly (Lamaze, 1970; LeBoyer, 1975). Verny (1981) gives evidence to show that how children are born, how painful, smooth, or violent, will largely determine who they become and how they will view the world around them. The only reason we may not consciously recall our birth experience may be the effect of the hormone oxytocin, which is secreted by the mother during labor and birth and which has an amnesic effect. We can be deeply affected by the experience without consciously remembering it.

Quoting research from many sources, Verny (1981) has shown the fetus to be a hearing, sensing, feeling being. By the fourth month the unborn child can frown, squint, and grimace. By the fifth month the child is sensitive to touch. At 4 or 5 months the unborn child reacts to sounds and melodies; Vivaldi and Mozart cause the child to relax, Beethoven and Brahms stimulate movement. It has been reported that the fetus hears clearly from the sixth month in utero and can be seen to move in rhythm to the mother's speech. In 1980, for the first time, scientists managed to record sounds from within the amniotic sac of a mammal. Using a sheep embryo, the experiment showed that external sounds, including conversation, are clearly audible. From these and other results on fetal hearing, it is now concluded that the auditory experience of the unborn child is more significant than was previously thought (Armitage, 1980).

By five months the fetus is very sensitive to light. If a light is shone on the mother's stomach, the child will look the other way or show a startled reaction, reports Verny. By the seventh or eighth month the neural circuits of the fetus are as advanced as a newborn's, and the cerebral cortex is mature enough to support consciousness. Memory may begin somewhere between the sixth and the eighth month.

An area of concern to many of the prenatal researchers influences the self-esteem and security feelings of the infant. Attitudes of the mother seem to be picked up clearly by the infant in utero by the sixth or seventh month. Some researchers feel that the mother's attitude toward the child has the single greatest effect on the well-being and future welfare of the unborn. Even when the mother pretends to be pleased with the pregnancy, but deeply resents or rejects the baby, the baby knows the true feelings and reacts to them. Intense stress or prolonged discomfort in the life of the mother is deeply felt by the infant she is carrying. Studies indicate that anxious and troubled children result from unrelieved anxiety experienced by the mother during the pregnancy (Stott, 1973, 1977; Huttunen & Niskanes, 1978; Verny, 1981).

Bonding

An issue that may affect our ability to optimize human development is that of bonding, the intimate, emotional attachment between mother and infant. Poor bonding may contribute to psychological and social disorders throughout childhood and shows a high correlation with unsocial, unproductive adult behavior, even violence. The quality of the bonding may be determined by at least three variables: hormones, physical contact, and timing. The increase in estrogen levels experienced by the mother just prior to birth provides a triggering for the bonding response but is not sufficient to establish it; physical contact within moments of the birth experience seems to be required (Kennell & Klaus, 1979). Says Dr. Kennell, "The hours after birth seem to comprise a sensitive period for maternal-infant attachment" (Marano, 1981, p. 66). In ways that are physiologically measurable, bonding buffers both mother and child from the effects of stress. Breast feeding, frequent verbalizing with the infant, holding, and rocking all are factors in good bonding.

The results of 10 studies (Kennell et al., 1974) show a significant difference between the behavior of mothers who had early contact with their babies (i.e., those who had their baby with them for 1 hour during the first 2 hours after delivery and for an extra 5 hours on each of the next 3 days) and those who followed the usual hospital routine (i.e., a brief glimpse of the baby at birth and visits of 20 to 30 minutes for feeding every 4 hours). At 1 month the babies of early-contact mothers handled stress more easily and received more support from their mothers. Their relationship with the mother evidenced more intimacy and more eye contact. At 1 year the early-contact mothers spent more time supporting and caring for their babies. At 2 years the linguistic patterns of the early-contact mothers were more supportive of the development of complex linguistic skills. Desmond, Rudolph, and Phitaksphraiwan (1966) observed that the newborn is in a very alert and active state for approximately 1 hour immediately after birth. Infants have their eyes wide open, and are able to follow objects with their eyes and head. After this period the infant falls deeply asleep for 3 to 4 hours. The early responsiveness of infants to their environment and their ability to interact with their parents makes this an optimal period for the formation of affectional bonds. Verny (1981) contends that children who learn most quickly and seem happiest have bonded with their mothers after birth. "By joining mother and child, bonding supplies not only someone who understands and loves the baby but also an ally who can provide the infant with the stimulation he needs to expand emotionally and intellectually" (p. 153).

Bonding after birth seems to be a continuation of the bonding process begun in the womb. The last 2 or 3 months before birth are important for establishing affectional ties that can be carried into the hours and days immediately after birth. Study after study shows that happy, content women are far more likely to have bright, outgoing infants. The when and the how of optimal development, the beginning of giftedness, must be seen as occurring prior to birth. Intelligence is partially dependent on the life of the unborn child.

Genetic-Environmental Interaction During Infancy (Birth Through 2 Years)

Much of the research with humans has attempted to discover all that infants are capable of doing. We will not be able to make decisions about what children should do until we know what they *can* do. We have only begun to explore this period of growth. Already many different experiences can be suggested to allow infants to explore their world more easily and facilitate their opportunities for interaction. We now know that infants from birth are active, perceiving, learning, and information-organizing individuals. With our present knowledge, we could best provide the optimal interactive environment by relying on the human resources of the infant to select, from the large quantity of activities available, only those events or experiences that are stimulating. This would provide the best match for the infants' point in development. As we understand the period of infancy with greater clarity, we will have clues available to aid us in providing the proper stimulation at the proper time for each infant. Making optimal use of this important learning period may not be too far beyond us.

The Preschool Nutrition Survey (Owen et al., 1974) produced some interesting clues to early facilitation or inhibition of growth in infants. Reported by socioeconomic class, the survey discovered that food was used as an extrinsic motivator (reward) for children of all classes, but while 54% of the lower-class parents used food in this way with their children, only 23% of the upper-class did so. Nearly one-fourth of the lower-class parents used the withholding of food as a punishment, but only 4% of the upper-class parents did so. Such practices do not encourage good nutritional habits in children. Nor do they contribute to the balance of nutrients needed to support the growing intellect, i.e., advanced and accelerated brain development.

Brazelton (1979) has shown that at birth babies orient themselves to sound and prefer the human voice, especially the high pitch of the female voice. They can imitate facial gestures and synchronize their body movements to rhythm. In addition to hearing very early Restak (1985) notes that babies seem to have an inborn genetic ability to elicit and respond to the meaning that is expressed through inflections in meaningful conversation. When the talk becomes gibberish or is just the recitation of the alphabet, the response does not occur.

Klaus (cited in Marano, 1981) finds that newborns born to unmedicated mothers spend nearly 40 minutes of their first hour in a state of rapt attention, eyes bright, wide open, capable of focusing and fixating on objects. Restak (1986) summarizes by saying that, "the neonate is a storer of information, can transform aspects of his world into representations, manipulate these representations, and infer that something felt in the mouth looks a certain way and no other" (p. 195).

Four-month-old babies have been shown to detect sight/sound correlations. In one experiment two films were presented to the babies, one of a woman playing peek-a-boo to the camera and the other a musical showing musical instruments. Each had an appropriate accompanying sound track. The films were presented side-by-side in front of the infants with the sound tracks played one at a time. The infants watched the film that was appropriate to the sound track being played at each moment. Another experiment had a mother and father sitting side-by-side while one or the other of their voices played between them and their baby at 3½ months of age. Again the baby could easily identify which parent was talking and turned her attention to the appropriate parent.

Touch is important in the development of the infant. It is indispensable for establishing normal feelings of affection and care, attachment, the maintenance of optimal physiologic function, and for preventing physiological imbalances, behavioral peculiarities, hostilities, and suppressed anger and rage. It is as necessary to normal infant development as food and oxygen (Restak, 1986).

A number of studies in the past decade have shown abilities of infants that are at variance with models of development previously accepted, such as that of Piaget (1954). Meltzoff and Moore (1977) have found that infants as young as 12 to 21 days old can imitate movements that they cannot see themselves perform, such as sticking out the tongue, grimacing, and opening their mouths. Infants can not only copy the behavior of others selectively, but seem to have a means of referring the conduct of others to things they can do without visible knowledge. Bower et al. (1970) and Gardner (1971) report that by 5 months of age infants are able to track moving objects visually in the sense of object permanence. Not only do they anticipate the reappearance of an object that moves behind a screen, but, if a different object emerges, they will look back to the screen to find the missing object. Such evidence indicates that infants are far more capable than we have assumed.

The classic study conducted by Fantz in 1961 added much to our knowledge of the learning capability of human infants. By using measures of attention, he established a fact unknown to science: Babies see from the moment of birth. They seem to have an innate ability to perceive patterns, thereby facilitating the development of form perception. They develop their ability for perceiving complex forms to a high level of discrimination by two months. When given opportunities to interact with patterns of varying degrees of complexity, infants seem to prefer more complex designs. In their order of preference, the complexity of printed matter is second only to a preference for the human face. This information allowed the first sensitive period for learning to be delineated from birth to two months as the time when the human infant can most easily acquire form perception. It is critical that the environment provide patterns to be viewed during this sensitive learning period if the ability is to be optimally used (Fantz, 1961).

When we consider the amount of stimulation usually available to the infant, we recognize that far more could be done to take advantage of this sensitive learning period. Most infants kept in a basket or enclosed crib are provided with only occasional changes in their field of vision. If interaction with the environment occurs from birth, repetition of this limited view must indeed be boring. For the infant reaching out visually without the ability to change body positions, the world of ruffled canopies, ceilings, pastel sheets, and occasional mobiles must be quite limiting. Fortunate is the child who during this period experiences different areas of the home, the out-of-doors, and various objects and people. The utilization of complexity seems to become cumulative with early experience because form and complex patterns result in a preference by the infant for more and more complex forms and patterns (Fantz, 1965). We must note that if this period is not used, the infant will still need to develop these visual skills. A delay will only retard development and may result in less than optimal use of the child's potential. Ideas for more adequate cultivation of this period will be given at the end of this chapter.

We can already by 3 months of age begin to see evidence of the limitations the environment may be creating on intellectual growth. Researchers have observed that tests administered during this period can predict to a certain extent future language development, quality of interaction with the environment, and personality characteristics that help determine future learning patterns. One researcher calls this first 3-month period a deprivation period for many children. The growing child cannot possibly assume responsibility for the quality of environmental interaction during this time. The infant depends almost totally on others for any intellectual stimulation that occurs.

The quantity of stimulation seems to influence not only intellectual development, but the quality of interaction as well. Children from homes crowded with other children and/or an abundance of sights and sounds often exhibit deprived growth patterns (Kagan, 1968; Murphy, 1972; Wachs, 1969). Differentiated, meaningful interaction is necessary. The infant must be responded to directly; what the baby does must be the cause of the resulting action. Not only is cognitive stimulation necessary, but emotional involvement is shown to be predictive of later intellectual development. Birns and Golden (1972) found pleasure in the task to predict later cognitive performance better than early cognitive measures. Early laughter at complex events is probably one of the best predictors because it taps the motivational, attentional, affective, and cognitive ability of the infant. Sroufe (1979) contends that emotion is necessarily integrative. It is as accurate to say that emotional experience and expression facilitate cognitive growth as it is to say that cognitive factors are involved in emotional development.

Further, adults must get involved. In an interesting study, Carew (1976) reported that children prior to 2 years of age require demonstrations and modeling behaviors on the part of the caregiver. The person in charge of the infant needs to provide a variety of language patterns, visual encounters, and other sensory opportunities for the growing infant. However, such interaction must be responsive to the child. Fear of overstimulation is unnecessary if you center the learning plan on responses to the infant and the expressed needs of the infant. Simply stopping an activity if the child shows discomfort or in any way indicates a dislike for it benefits the child. In a study conducted at the Harvard Pre-School Project, too much stimulation (in this case pinwheels spinning while mobiles jumped overhead) made the infants cry. I doubt if infants will allow themselves to be overstimulated without giving some indication to the offending adult. In this context, consider the response some thoughtless parents get when they take tired infants into restaurants or public meetings. We can all vouch for the unmistakable messages the infant is sending

In the study reporting the need for demonstration prior to 2 years of age, Carew (1976) indicated that a change occurs at this age. The nurturing caregiver must then pull back, allowing discovery behavior to become the dominant mode of operation for the child. To be most facilitative in developing a child's potential, direct guidance is advisable and necessary prior to 2 years of age, while opportunities for discovery and encounters within a rich environment are preferred after that age. Guidance will, of course, still be necessary.

Sensitive and Critical Periods for Learning

Some researchers have labeled the first 24 hours after birth a sensitive period for the normal maternal reaction to the newborn (Salk, 1973). There is evidence of qualitative and quantitative differences in later maternal behavior dependent on the amount of contact during this period (Kennell & Klaus, 1979). Visual complexity is best learned during the intellectually sensitive period from birth to 2 months. Discovery of other sensitive periods is necessary for optimal development to be realized. Bloom's major hypothesis proposed that the environment in which the individual develops will have the greatest effect on a specific characteristic in its most rapid period of change (Bloom, 1964). The definition of the *sensitive period* reflects this hypothesis. During this period all systems—visual, mental, and motor—are ready to be used. If activated by the environment, they will be used together at peak efficiency. The time when an organizational process accelerates most rapidly is a *critical period* for the resulting organization, if failure to use a process during this time results in loss of the process or function (Vygotsky, 1974). Epstein (1978) comments,

> The role of intellectual experience or learning is to select among existing networks created by the genetic apparatus during brain development. If the complete spectrum of needed experience is not available to the organism, it loses forever the possibility of having those functions that are operated by the lost networks. (p. 354)

He shows evidence that human brain growth occurs primarily during age intervals of 3 to 10 months, 2 to 4 years, 6 to 8 years, 10 to 12 or 13 years, and 14 to 16 or 17 years. The sensitive period concept tells us that intensive and novel intellectual inputs to children may be most effective during these brain growth stages.

The field of biology has long accepted the theory of sensitive periods. The first trimester of fetal growth is seen as a critical period for physical growth. Now milestone events are just beginning to be uncovered for sensitive or critical periods in mental development. Animal studies of the imprinting phenomenon hint that such mental developmental periods do exist, but only a few as yet have been documented in humans (Lorenz, 1969; Scott, 1962).

Creating a Responsive Environment for Early Learning (Birth Through 2 Years)

In the process of developing intelligence, young children have a great need for a responsive environment. Both people and objects in the environment can be growth-producing only if they have some meaning or use for the child. Jeffrey (1980) reminds us that it is not the stages or sequence of development that is our most important focus, but rather the individual differences that appear with that development, differences in the ability to perform and to profit from the experiences provided. Age is an inadequate index of neurological and physical maturation, as both are changed by the environment of the child and by that child's genetic program.

Earlier theories on how children develop suggested that both parents and teachers should wait until the children ask for an activity. In that way we could be sure that children were ready to learn. Now this seems far too wasteful of their resources, an unnecessary barrier to their developing potential. As we become aware of children's ability to choose only those activities or objects for which they are ready among a variety of activities or objects, our skill in structuring a rich environment becomes more necessary. The better we know a child, the less difficult is our task. However, we do not have to wait until we know what children need. We need only make available a large variety of objects and activities and then observe and respond as the children interact. The availability of many resources, including the parent and teacher, will allow children to stretch beyond known areas, to experiment with new materials and ideas, and to develop at their own pace and in their own style. Dubos (1969) states that human potential has a better chance of developing when the social environment is sufficiently diversified to provide a variety of stimulating experiences. He comments,

> The total environment affects individuality through the influences it exerts on the organism during the crucial phases of development, including the intrauterine phase. These early influences affect lastingly and often irreversibly practically all anatomical, physiological, and behavioral characteristics throughout the whole life span. (p. 6)

It is true, as Krech reminds us, that "each species has species-specific experiences that are maximally enriching and maximally efficient in developing its brain"

(Krech, 1969, p. 373). The most effective way to create a learning environment for the young child would be to take advantage of those experiences that most enrich human growth. Unfortunately at this point in time we do not yet know enough about the timing or detail of these experiences. We must continue to explore this area and develop this all-important learning curriculum. Until this is done, and probably even then, responsiveness to the child interacting with a rich and varied environment will be our best guide to optimal development. Parents have for years approached the cognitive areas of learning cautiously for fear of harming their child or teaching something in the ''wrong'' way that would need to be unlearned at a later time. With a responsive-environment approach, there can be no wrong way of learning. In a situation where the child and the parent or teacher respond sensitively to each other, only growth and pleasure in learning can be the outcome. Sroufe (1979) comments that ''caregivers may be so effective in promoting development because they help create the appropriate affective climate and tune their behaviors to the infant's tension level, catching it at the peak of organized engagement, rather than simply because they respond to its behavior in a reliable, mechanical fashion'' (p. 507).

From Birth Through 3 Months

The optimal environment for an infant must include attention, from the moment of birth, to all of the basic needs, both physical and psychological. The needs for security, safety, nutrition, belonging, and love are basic to all infants. Only as these needs are met, can the infant give any attention to self-concept and intellectual development at optimal levels. Indeed, how the basic needs are met will critically influence how self-concept and intellectual ability develop. According to reports, infants who are gratified much of the time and who experience tension infrequently show more capacity for handling stress than infants more often subjected to frustration. Infants in an environment characterized by frequent and exuberant expressions of positive feelings tend to develop a high degree of initiative (Yarrow, 1968). Other books deal in detail with how to provide for the basic needs. While they cannot in reality be separated from intellectual growth, we artificially make that separation. Here we assume that attention to the basic needs is given, as we explore means of optimizing the growth of intellectual ability.

During the first 2 months infants are referred to as *newborns* and, though they are responsive to external stimuli and able to learn from the environment, they are dependent on biological states and inborn dispositions (Karmel & Maisel, 1975; Emde & Robinson, 1976; Parmelee & Sigman, 1976). Some researchers (Meltzoff & Moore, 1977) have found that newborns, some only 1 hour old, can mimic or imitate the behavior of adults with whom they are interacting. Such studies convince Verny (1981) that ''the presence of well developed thinking, including handling of abstract ideas, is found in the newborn'' (p. 171).

The first 3 months of postnatal life may be the most critical for the infant's developing brain since the first trimester of intrauterine fetal life. During this period the infant has no mobility and must depend upon the caregiver for all intellectual stimulation. We have a baby who we now know can see, hear, and smell, and who can do all these things with discrimination. Here is a baby ready to interact with the environment, ready to learn. In too many cases this interaction is severely limited—so much so that some researchers have called this period the greatest deprivation period for human infants. Little is known about how we may best enrich this period. Some clues do exist about activities that have proven enriching for some infants. They could, in a responsive environment, be made available to all newborns.

From birth, innate programming seems to facilitate the use of language, hands, eyes, etc. by the human infant. Unlike any other animal, the human infant has the ability to pick up logical rules. This important competency is basic and available from birth. Bruner (1964) found that not only do infants notice more detail in the environment than we believed, but they actively invent rules or theories to explain what they observe. Even at 3 weeks, an infant will have complex hypotheses about the world and will react if proven wrong. One experiment supporting this observation used the baby's caregiver and a stereo sound system. The baby responded happily to the caregiver standing by when the sound of the caregiver's voice came from the same location. However, when the caregiver's voice came from a part of the room different from the location of the caregiver, the baby became solemn and then upset.

The best rule for stimulating an infant during this period is to maintain a responsive environment. Over and over in the literature on development of intellectual capacity we find reference, usually emphasized, to the importance of responding to an infant's cues or signals of distress. In times past it was thought that picking up babies when they cried would "spoil" growing children. The results of not attending to, ignoring, or allowing infants to "cry it out" are now viewed as far more damaging. One of the differences between institutionalized infants and home-reared infants is that institutions do not attend to crying behavior. The results indicate that institutionalized infants lose their sense of control over the environment and become passive, externally motivated children. This does not produce optimal intellectual growth (Provence & Lipton, 1962). The quantity, timing, and degree of consistency of the caregiver's responses to the infant play important roles in developing and reinforcing the infant's belief that his or her behavior can affect the environment (Lewis, 1972). This belief regarding inner locus of control seems to be learned early in life.

Parents should be advised to respond to infants when they cry and to look for what might be causing the discomfort. If nothing appears wrong, consider the cry a call for loving attention. Rocking and cuddling infants will reassure them and allow them to feel wanted and loved. Parents should also respond to babies' coos and giggles. In this way, infants learn that they can influence the world and that they really matter. The infant will learn that actions other than crying bring attention. However, you need not wait for these signals. Playing regularly with babies, enjoying them, and displaying spontaneity and affection will establish a basis for loving that will last a lifetime. Such care will allow infants to develop into trusting, loving, warm human beings. White (1975) believes that infants fail to learn not because they are not bright enough but rather because they have not been properly shown. Parents can provide all the right things but they must do so with their child's rhythms and abilities in mind if they are to succeed. There is an almost geometric progression between the amount of meaningful time spent with a child and that child's intellectual growth. Ainsworth (1974) asks that caregivers see the world from the baby's point of view. It is then not possible to be rejecting, interfering, or ignoring because all responses, even refusals, acknowledge the baby and provide specifically for that baby's needs.

It is important to know that, for a few days after birth, an infant seems able to cope with only one activity at a time. Between 3 and 5 weeks, the infant can do one thing, such as nurse, while looking at another source of interest. However, when the viewed activity becomes more interesting, the first activity stops. Between 2 and 4 months an infant will continue the first activity while involved in the second, but with less intensity, almost as though the shift can more easily be made between the two if participation in the first activity is at least superficially maintained.

Early exploration is important to later development.

Table 3.1 *Birth Through 3 Months.*

Caregiver Activities	Because
Respond to infant's activity and signals, e.g., awakening and looking; offer objects for baby to look at.	This establishes feeling of inner locus of control, ability of child to affect the environment.
Respond to distress signals (crying) and give attention to cause. Crying it out is definitely *not* recommended.	This establishes a code of mutual expectancy.
Breastfeed if possible, for both the infant and the mother. If you must bottle feed, change positions for each feeding, e.g., right arm holding baby, then left. This happens naturally when breastfeeding.	This encourages development and coordination of both eyes.
Change position of crib in room.	This increases visual stimulation.
Place mobiles over crib, patterned with a variety of shapes, colors (make your own); use patterned sheets, clear bumpers; change position and surroundings of infant.	This develops visual complexity skills, nourishes growth of intelligence through heightened interaction with the environment, stimulates curiosity.
Rock infant while holding next to chest for 10-minute periods; pick up infant and place on the shoulder. Rocking chairs are most useful at this age.	Infants handled in this manner show more visual attention than other infants (White & Castle, 1964; Korner & Grobstein, 1966).
Allow bare-skin cuddling, yours and baby's; rub baby's skin with nubby towel when drying; tickle, squeeze, and pinch a little in games; give baby "feely" objects, put them in hand, e.g., velvet, silk, sponge.	This stimulates sensory development; baby learns about feeling.
Turn lights on and off for visual stimulation.	Infants are normally overly sensitive to bright sunlight; care must be taken not to create discomfort.

The infant under 3 months does not have to touch or manipulate in order to learn something about structure; the infant's attention suffices. Probably the infant learns much about the environment through merely attending to it. Although action is not necessary, it can facilitate learning because activity is accompanied by an

Table 3.1 *Birth Through 3 Months. (continued)*

Caregiver Activities	Because
Provide a variety of sounds and speech patterns (music box, radio, variety of rhythms, voices).	These are important prelanguage experiences.
Play vocal games, imitate baby's cooing, introduce real words by naming body parts and toys.	Familiar sounds are of high interest to infants; builds vocabulary, initiates conversation, establishes babies' perceived control of their lives (Hunt, cited in Pines, 1979b).
Allow lots of different smells.	This stimulates olfactory sense.
Introduce the playpen, or a hard, broad surface, not carpeted. It allows baby to move from room to room with you. Cover the floor with a plastic mat and turn baby loose on tummy. Keep temperature up so that baby can play without restrictive clothing (85° F). Play on floor with baby, be near; encourage movement, e.g., rolling over, creeping.	This allows intellectual stimulation.
Provide toys that are patterned, manipulative, textured (rattles are not very interesting toys).	This stimulates self-initiated activities.
Toward the end of this period, use crib devices the baby can bat and play with. They should be brightly colored, have complex shapes, and be strong enough to take abuse. The parts should be hung with semirigid attachment (not string) so that motion can occur, but not too much motion; no sharp or loud sounds or any abrupt changes in stimulation such as flashing lights.	This develops hand-eye coordination.

increased alertness and, therefore, a greater likelihood of noting differentiating attributes of an object. However, active involvement is clearly an effective aid to acquiring cognitive structures (Kagan, 1971).

This period of the infant's development is important because it holds an initiating place in the child's learning system. What first goes into the system in the way of skills, beliefs, and ideas will set up a resistance to future dissimilar patterns of learning. Initial learning is far more difficult to unlearn. In the activities outlined in Table 3.1, it must be stressed that the caregiver is the most critical factor in the child's learning.

A responsive environment can occur only through an aware adult who responds to signals initiated by the child. Stimulation and demonstration of language and skills are available only if the adult provides them.

Be aware that 90% of all social interaction with a child from birth to 18 months occurs during caregiving activities such as changing diapers, dressing, bathing, and feeding. These activities should be treated not as chores to get out of the way as quickly as possible but as learning opportunities and as times to communicate with the child. Parents must be encouraged to smile and talk a lot even if they feel the baby cannot understand. These are the most important moments of the baby's life. A major factor to the success of parents of competent infants is the parents' belief that they can influence their child's mental development (Kagan, 1971). Table 3.1 gives specific suggestions to parents for activities most appropriate to this age group.

From 4 Through 10 Months

Much physical activity begins from 4 through 10 months that will remain a dominant factor through all of infancy. Societies that value and use physical affection and bodily contact in rearing their young produce relatively nonviolent adults (Restak, 1979). Among the most productive methods of providing such contact are holding, carrying, rocking, and cuddling the child. Restak considers movement and physical closeness absolute requirements for normal brain development and believes that immobility alone can create abnormal mental experiences and disturbed behavior. Understimulation can result in later hyperactivity.

During this period, interest in active exploration will also be noticeable: exploring with touch, by mouthing; with sounds, by reaching; and always visually. The amount of visual experience, the decor and colorfulness of the home, the presence of a variety of responsive play objects, and the freedom to explore the environment were seen to have a significant relationship with performance on infant testing from 5 to 36 months (Bradley & Caldwell, 1976; Wachs, 1976; Yarrow et al., 1972). The infant enjoys people now more than before and develops obviously affectionate ties. This can be a delightful period for both child and caregiver (Table 3.2).

From 10 Months Through 2 Years

During the 10-month to 2-year period, the baby experiences real mobility. The major driving force seems to be curiosity. At this stage, the infant's curious nature establishes roots and begins to flower into what will later be experienced by the learning child as motivation. Unreasonably applied limits and controls can cause frustration, leaving an aimless, internally unmotivated child as a result. Let us stress that allowing a baby to freely explore the environment (made safe by having dangerous items placed out of reach) is the single most important action to ensure intellectual growth. The environment need not be filled with expensive toys. Any

Books can be fascinating to early learners.

small, manipulatable, visually detailed articles, objects to climb on, objects to move on, all easily accessible, will provide much stimulation. As the baby increasingly experiments and interacts with the environment, guidance, of course, is necessary. Whenever possible, the natural environment should be used to provide correction for the baby's misjudgments. In this way natural consequences can themselves become teachers, and the baby can learn to change or adapt in his or her own way.

A toddler I observed waiting for a plane with his mother was engaged in

Table 3.2 *From 4 Through 10 Months.*

Caregiver Activities	Because
Use playpen only until baby becomes mobile, if used later only for very short periods (5 to 10 minutes).	The playpen restricts environmental interaction, creates limit to intellectual development.
Provide toys of interest, e.g., mirrors (very appealing to baby now; be sure they are safe, unbreakable); stacking toys; moderately small objects for dropping, throwing, banging; moving and pop-up toys are interesting late in this period. Be cautious about expensive "eduational toys"; it is not necessary to buy toys; homemade toys, designed to your baby's needs, are often far better.	These provide intellectual stimulation.
Play games with fingers and toes, stroke legs, pat back; talking and identifying parts of baby can also be added. Encourage baby to pat caregiver, touch fingers, play pat-a-cake; allow to play unrestrained by clothing.	These activities contribute to the baby's perception of self and the beginnings of cognitive experience (Murphy, 1972).
Play peek-a-boo games.	These provide visual, auditory, problem-solving stimulation; encourage cognitive anticipation.
Play, talk, interact with infant during all caregiving activities.	This is the most important for language development and motivation.

exploration of the airport environment. Suddenly, as the baby was walking along a railing, he came to a hinged gate that opened into the area behind the counter. The hinge was fairly strong, but the child could swing the gate open a short way before it returned to a closed position on its own. The toddler pushed open the gate over and over, intent upon watching the hinge and the automatic return of the gate. He was hurting no one nor was he bothering anyone. Even if the gate had closed on his hand it would have caused little discomfort and would have provided a lesson the child would likely have incorporated into his schema for swinging doors. However, his mother saw him moving the gate and rushed to scold and spank, hurting him far more than the gate would have. Noisy crying followed, accompanied by more spanking. What should have been a useful learning experience became a power struggle ending with a frustrated, sobbing little boy commanded to sit in an overly large adult chair until his mother felt he could "behave himself."

Table 3.2 *From 4 Through 10 Months. (continued)*

Caregiver Activities	Because
Encourage new games invented by baby such as drop toy—caregiver picks it up—baby drops toy.	Baby develops beginnings of inner locus of control, senses an active influence on environment, increases motivation.
Play games using eyes and language in games, e.g., "Look at Daddy, look at Mommy, look at baby's foot, look at kitty, look at . . ."(include things above, below, to right, to left).	This promotes eye coordination and focus, language experience, coordinating sight and sound, words with things.
Take trips to the grocery store, drug store, department store (only when baby is rested, *not* during usual nap time). On trips talk about what is being seen.	These alert attention to varied environments, allow enrichment of sensory experience.
Cook and talk to baby, talk at meals, encourage baby to use words (infant seats are useful on trips or to have baby nearby as you work).	This is an important language experience.
Look at books and talk, read to baby.	Symbols of language become familiar, important, a source of fun and pleasure.

This happened in contrast to a mother I observed on a ferry one afternoon cautiously monitoring her toddler's actions while appearing unconcerned. Only when the child approached a dangerous situation, such as an open ventilation duct, did the mother move up to him to distract him to some new interest. She never interfered with his dignity nor attempted to be overly controlling. Both the mother and the little boy were enjoying the trip.

Babies are remarkably curious from 10 months to 2 years about things adults would find totally uninteresting, such as hinged doors, cellophane wrappers, tiny pieces of dust, and plant leaves. Parents should expect fascinated repetitions and allow for them. They should be extra alert to remove dangerous items from the environment. In this way children can begin their own self-initiated, autonomous learning.

White (1975), in his work at the Harvard Pre-School Project, has established this period as the most decisive for intellectual development. White thinks it essential to nurture balanced development in many areas, including children's interests, people (noticeably the primary *caregiver*), exploration of the world, and use of their own bodies (for instance, motor skills). This period will bring essential

Table 3.3 *From 10 Months Through 2 Years.*

Caregiver Activities	Because
Organize and design a safe physical environment that allows for a variety of sensory experiences; family living areas and outdoor areas should be available for exploration of the senses: • Visual: plants, fish in bowls, pictures, patterned objects, mirrors • Auditory: exposure to many types of music, voices, rhythms, singing, bells, drums, shakers, music boxes, animal sounds • Tactile: a variety of textures to feel (soft, hard, rough, smooth), sculpture, finger food, mud play, finger paints, painting with jello • Olfactory: bakery smells, flower smells, farm and field smells • Gustatory: snacks of differing tastes and textures.	Toddlers spend most of their time gaining information, building concepts, and observing.
Provide a variety of toys and household objects to play with: for stringing, nesting, digging, pounding, screwing; construction toys (pieces not too small), peg boards, record players, magnets, magnetic letters, alphabet blocks, prisms, water toys, flashlights, spin tops, jigsaw puzzles, magnifying glasses, dolls, collections of small objects, toy animals, various household tools, books, and art materials.	This gives intellectual stimulation, supports later learning, strengthens perception and problem-solving abilities.
Play games like hide-'n-seek, treasure hunts, guessing games, matching and sorting, finger games, circle games; encourage and provide materials for imitative play, such as "I do what you do."	This facilitates concept development, practice in planning and carrying out complicated projects, anticipating consequences, developing skills of problem solving.

development in language, curiosity (leading to motivation), social development, and intelligence (Table 3.3).

In order to develop the goal-directed behavior so important to learning activity, children from ten months through two years of age must experience satisfaction from their efforts, response to their actions, support for reaching out, safety, acceptance, and trust. Only as these are made a part of children's life will they begin to explore and move cognitively toward mastery of more complex skills. If deprived of these experiences, their motivation for learning and potential for wonder and discovery is stunted. Creativity as well as competence will suffer.

Table 3.3 *From 10 Months Through 2 Years. (continued)*

Caregiver Activities	Because
Teach child to be aware of and name objects in the environment (including baby's own body parts). This can be done by playing games with the caregiver, giving names to objects as they are used.	This provides language experience.
Look at scrapbooks with child, read books to child, make books familiar.	This provides symbolic language experiences.
Make scrapbooks with the child of pictures of animals, cars, trips. These can become the child's own books.	This gives language experience.
Talk to baby during all caregiving activities: bathing, dressing, eating, use patterns of speech with baby that you use with other members of the family; short 20- to 30-second "conversations" are important.[a]	This helps baby to understand more complicated sentences, increases language background and experience.
Take neighborhood walks to library, stores, playgrounds, on collection excursions, out to feed birds; always discuss what is seen and experienced.	This provides a background of experiences for future concept building.

[a]Note: When engaging children in "conversation" try to talk about what they are doing from their perspective. Try to understand their meaning for the activity and what they may be learning from it. Then try to give them something new and interesting to think about along the same lines. Allow children to initiate the activity and then respond enthusiastically, but be careful not to insist on doing it only your way.

Also use language to heighten curiosity and develop interest. Teach children vocabulary words to express their interests by engaging them at the point of interest. This will further help children see adults as valuable resources. Talk to your child even before you are sure the child understands what you are saying. It is important to use a variety of speech patterns and normal conversational intonations. Remember, you are the model. While the act of repeating sounds the baby makes is fun and can be enjoyed by both adult and baby, the child needs good speech models and language patterns. Babytalk does not provide a useful model for children to emulate. Children do create unusual patterns for their own use. However, repetition of these patterns by the adult limits children to those unique patterns.

During this period children become more mobile. Children need most to interact with the environment for optimal intellectual development to occur. Accessibility to the living area and outdoor areas enhances discovery and self-initiated activities by children. The caregiver must carefully prepare these areas to make them safe and rich in sensory experiences. Lots of objects and materials, not only toys but common household items and junk, all help to construct responsive learning environments. Overuse of playpens and walkers at this stage can be detrimental to intellectual development. The caregiver should continue with trips, reading, and other activities enjoyed by the child in earlier stages. Now more

Introducing a preschool child to the larger community is exciting.

activities of a physical, manipulative nature should be included. Demonstration and modeling behavior by the caregiver are still important.

During this period of beginning mobility the pattern for discipline will be established. While each child responds differently to various methods of discipline, keep in mind that your actions teach far more than your words and that each action has long-term as well as short-term consequences.

In the past, punishment was seen as necessary to teach children proper behavior. Power and Chapieski (1986) report that physical discipline proved to be unsuccessful and limiting to the growth of cognitive ability in 14-month-old babies in both the short and long terms. In their study babies who were physically punished were more likely to willfully grasp forbidden objects and were least likely to obey restrictions. When tested 7 months later these babies scored lower on measures of infant development than children who received no physical discipline. Making a variety of safe objects and toys available for exploration and play lowers the need for discipline and provides opportunities for the development of visual/spatial skills and problem-solving ability.

Positive guidance has proved far more productive of good behavior than punishment. Misbehavior should indicate to the caregiver that some guidance is needed. If at all possible, find out what preceded the incident. Preventing the next problem may be as simple as changing the cause. For example, when a child begins crying and throwing things out of the shopping basket, everything within reach of the child's seat is fair game. In retrospect, the caregiver had taken the child out during the morning and had stopped to do shopping on the way home. The child had not eaten lunch. Nap time had been invaded by the shopping trip. Rather than punishment, acknowledgment of the child's discomfort and an attempt to remedy the situation as soon as possible would be appropriate. These considerations may be more productive of good behavior than reprimands and physical abuse. Meanwhile, make the child as comfortable as possible by picking him or her up and talking soothingly. After all, the caregiver is at fault. We must guide children in finding better solutions to frustration, but timing is important. Choose a time when they are not tired or hungry.

When we hit a child we are conveying the rule that this behavior solves problems. When we yell at a child we teach that yelling is an appropriate way of interacting to gain attention. While at times a slap on the hand or bottom most effectively halts further misbehavior, physical punishment should be used only as a very temporary solution with a verbal follow-up as soon as possible. Exploration of the cause of misbehavior and explanation of the rules violated and consequences of the action will clarify the need for punishment. Rather than watch children make an error and then punish them, try to anticipate the error and warn them that they are approaching a decision point. We can prepare the child to look ahead. We should encourage reflection, give practice in alternative thinking, and share our knowledge of the consequences.

Children must also have some alternative coping techniques. If screaming is all we know how to do when our wishes are frustrated or we need attention, then we'll scream. If we can be assured of getting notice by spitting our food or throwing toys, then we will continue these behaviors. Helping children find better techniques for releasing frustration and getting attention works far better. This requires effective guidance, not punishment. We will produce the same type of behavior we model. The golden rule of "do unto others" never fit better. We should point out that children may encounter damaging behaviors much worse than physical abuse. Lack of acceptance, disregard, and the worthlessness children feel from being ignored by those important to them have far more devastating and long-lasting effects.

Research in child development, especially relating to the area of atypical children, often uses statistics from socioeconomic groups or social classes to explain acceleration or limitations. With increasing evidence we know that we must look beyond the group or class and into the family pattern for our data. In the area of cognitive development, knowledge of the family pattern has proven most beneficial. The answer to how children can develop the ability to think in consequences and alternatives, to build rationales, and to become good problem solvers and good choosers can be found within the family experience (Hoffman & Hoffman, 1964, 1966; Stone, Smith, & Murphy, 1973). The following characteristics are commonly found in families that produce children with highly actualized potential and self-esteem.

- Parents accept their children as individuals, are loyal sources of support, openly express acceptance.
- Parents set clear limits based on each child's ability to understand consequences; goals are clear; success is expected as a right of the child, not of the parent.
- Parental guidance is reasonable, realistic, and appropriate to each child.
- The family tends to be liberal and flexible, but not permissive.
- The family is aware of the environment and relates to the environment in a caring, protective way. Children are helped to see their part in the natural order and to respect this unity.
- Parents are relatively self-assured, are on good terms with one another; they accept the responsibility for their own actions.
- Parents lead active lives outside of the family and do not rely on their families as the sole or necessarily major source of gratification and esteem.

Children with high self-esteem more often acquire a sense of independence, exhibit exploratory behavior, assert their own rights, develop a strong inner locus of control, and express more self-trust. These traits lead them to personal happiness and more effective functioning.

Low self-esteem results in higher levels of anxiety, more frequent psychosomatic symptoms, less effectiveness, and more destructive behavior. Children with low self-esteem find it hard to believe that any personal action can have favorable outcomes. Instead, they believe themselves powerless and unworthy of love or attention.

Money, education, social class, time spent with the child (quality, not quantity), physical attractiveness, and socioeconomic group identification will influence how society treats a child. However, family acceptance and the child's response to that acceptance are critical factors in developing self-esteem and intellectual potential during this period (Coopersmith, 1967).

An environment controlled by rules rather than by attention to individual characteristics of a specific situation produces children who relate to authority rather than to rationality. Although often compliant, these children have never learned to find appropriate solutions to problems. The consequences of their actions are regarded in terms of immediate reward or punishment rather than future effects and long-range goals (Hess & Shipman, 1965).

As much as we want to provide an environment where our children can actualize their intellectual capacity, our society wants and needs good, fully human beings. These persons can establish a more nurturing, good society. While each of us would add our own criteria to the term *good,* I believe we would agree on all factors that allow humans to be more caring, responsible, and growth-producing for both themselves and others. With these ultimate goals in mind, we must foresee the relationship between what occurs in the home, reflecting on the child, and the adult the child will become. Children become what they live. If fear is used for control, the child will learn fear and the use of fear as a controlling technique. Violence fosters violence; abuse teaches abuse; disrespect brings forth disrespect. Mature, loving people must be the responsible caregivers for our future generations. Our homes must establish an environment of trust by providing respect and trust for each family member from the oldest to the youngest. We can generate trust by using affirming behavior, as opposed to judgmental behavior, as follows:

Child: Cries (He broke his toy.)
Caregiver: I can see you're really unhappy. What can we do?

Rather than:

Caregiver: Stop that crying! You did it yourself and you know boys don't cry. Crybaby! Now you'll be more careful. Go play and leave me alone!

Caregivers must guide children to see both the strengths and the weaknesses in their personalities. A growing, sincere person who can say "I was wrong" or "I'm sorry" to a little child, who can admit hurt or anger as well as joy and affection, makes the best teacher for someone learning to be human. Empathic understanding is valuable and should be used often, but probably the most critical behavior a child can experience is total acceptance as a person. The behavior of the child may not be acceptable. Ways may be sought to change that behavior. Always accepting the child and letting the child know of that acceptance is the most growth-producing gift the child can receive. Effective guidance and personal acceptance are essential to the development of a child's potential.

Intellectual Development During Early Childhood (2 Through 5 Years)

Another sensitive period, in addition to the one mentioned for visual (form) complexity, exists for language development. Linguists have theorized that between 18 months and 4 years of age every human has available an innate ordering device for learning language, referred to as the Language Acquisition Device (LAD) (Chomsky, 1966; McNeill, 1966). During this LAD period, the environment of the child must be rich in language experience. Never again will the child have the ability to learn language-related activities with such ease. Learning is cumulative. If we are to optimize the learning opportunities of our children, we must take advantage of those periods when learning proceeds most rapidly and efficiently (Lenneberg, 1967). Young children will acquire language effortlessly if language is around them, but the kind of language they acquire, whether an instrument of clarity, precision, and imagination or only a tool to handle biological and social exchanges, will depend on the linguistic environment supplied by adults (McKenna, 1978).

Reading as a visual language experience is analogous to speech as an auditory language experience. Both represent receptive language, and both may present similar cognitive problems to the learner. Possibly the LAD period presents the child with an advantage in organizing visual language input (reading), as it does for other language experiences (Moore, 1961, 1967; Chukovsky, 1966). Callaway (1970) presents a further conjecture that reading experiences could enhance cognitive performance through physiological changes in brain cells.

In an attempt to understand better how the LAD period affects young children, I conducted an early reading experiment with children 2 through 4 years of age (Dunn, 1969). My goal was to discover the effectiveness of teaching 2-through 4-year-olds several basic reading skills, names of letters, letter sounds, and a few basic words by televised presentations. This was prior to *Sesame Street.* From my background in preschool television programming, I was convinced that this medium could give large numbers of children the opportunity to explore the world of symbolic language.

For 15 minutes once a week for 16 weeks, 45 mothers brought their children to the campus to watch in small groups the televised antics of a feline puppet and me. Using songs, games, and stories, we involved the children in basic reading experiences. Our 2- to 4-year-old boys and girls had IQs ranging from 74 to 134 and represented several racial and ethnic groups and socioeconomic levels.

I found the results exciting yet frustrating. All children reached mastery on all items tested. Their growth was statistically significant at the .001 level over the growth of the control group. Neither IQ, age, nor any other variable we looked at seemed to influence the results except for a slight time advantage evidenced by those children whose parents read to them. This was exciting, as it supported results of other early childhood reading experiments. The frustration came from the low expectation level that I had set as the researcher. Halfway through the experiment my concern regarding too much material presented too quickly became instead too little presented too slowly. Children began leaping ahead, and by the end of the 4-month period, over half had taken the tools offered by the program and had begun to read. I had not pretested for reading, so I could comment only briefly on this fact in the results. A follow-up study a year later showed that, of those children responding, all had continued to develop their reading skill; several had been accelerated in school placement and identified as gifted children.

Before leaving this study I would like to mention one unplanned event. Several of the mothers were unable to locate baby-sitters for their younger children and were allowed to bring them to the campus. One younger brother, who at the end of the experiment was 1 year, 6 months old, came every week. While the student watched the televised presentation, his younger brother could be seen through the one-way glass of the observation booth wandering about the room, sometimes watching, sometimes participating, and often seeming to be interested in play of his own design. During the posttesting he again accompanied the family and, just out of curiosity, I asked if he would like to be tested too. He joined in with gusto. At his own private testing session I found that this child, whose chin could barely clear the table to see the cards and test items, knew several letters, could identify several letter sounds, and had a reading vocabulary of five words.

While not reported with the experimental group, this finding made me wonder just how capable our young children are. How much could they learn if the opportunities were presented? With our group of 45 I had the pleasure of sharing a whole new world of activities. Some obtained library cards, although mother had to sign for them. One young man discovered that writing could be a useful tool and used his basic skills to print a note declaring his annoyance with the behavior of his little friend next door. Billboards became wonderful adventures. As one 3-year-old informed me, when she couldn't find anything else fun to do, she could read her baby a book.

I found with my group the same confidence and joy Fowler (1962a, b) expresses in his research on the outcome of early reading activity. I am convinced that reading is a natural, happy event if introduced during this LAD period. What we do at 6 years of age may be remedial reading. If you were to force someone to remain immobilized during the 9- through 12-month period and only allow walking activity later, around 3 or 4 years of age, you would find it necessary to teach balance, left-right sequencing, how to place one foot in front of the other, shifting weight, and other incremental skills. Let us make an analogy to our approach to reading. Children I have known and those reported in the literature (Durkin, 1966; Fowler, 1962a, b) learn with ease and pleasure during the LAD period. At 6 years of age learning to read becomes quite a different matter. We must later deliberately teach what is incidentally learned during the earlier period. Few children are allowed the opportunity to interact with symbolic language during this early period. Professional education has done an excellent job of convincing parents that they cannot teach reading. And yet, if allowed the opportunity to play with words, if read to or shown any of the ways letters can be used to represent sound, children find their own way to learn. In an environment that responds as the children direct, that is rich in good language experiences, children enjoy learning in their own way. Learning to read is no exception.

Some years ago educators informed parents that early learning was a waste of time. People accepted the notion that children who learned later would catch up anyway. Too many people, without looking at new data, still believe this to be true. The work of Durkin (1966) has given us a different view of children who read early. Her research shows that children who enter school already reading have a learning advantage that continues to accelerate during the school years. By sixth grade, far from "catching up," the late readers (those learning in first grade) were increasingly outdistanced by the performance of the early readers. Fowler (1963) found much the same to be true and linked the results of early reading to the higher intellectual development of his children. He found reading not only easily accomplished by younger children, but felt that it enriched their play life and resulted in happier, more well-rounded children.

My interest in the benefits of early reading was piqued when I first met Ragan Callaway at UCLA in 1968. I had been working in a clinic for problem learners, trying to develop a remedial program for four nonreaders who were 11 years old and possessed measured intelligence of over 130 IQ on the Binet. As I wondered how such a problem could have occurred, I began a search for prevention. At that point I met Dr. Callaway. He came from a background in biology, having studied to the doctoral level, when he noted occurrences that seemed even more interesting than his studies in biology. His first child began to show a great interest in symbolic language. As Callaway followed and abetted that interest, he found his son was capable of learning to a degree traditionally held as impossible.

Pursuing his son's experiences in learning convinced Callaway of the fallacies to traditional thought. After another young son also read prior to his second birthday, Callaway's interest in education grew. He became principal of a school where he initiated a program of preschool reading that resulted in all of the children reading prior to school entry. Ultimately, he made a change in curriculum for the primary grades. After completing a doctorate with Elizabeth Drews at the University of Michigan, Callaway came to UCLA and conducted research in early reading in the Los Angeles area.

All of this experience and vast exploration of literature led to the publication of his monograph Modes of Biological Adaptation and Their Role in Intellectual Development (1970). This work links the biological aspects of growth to learning and intellectual development. He brought out in the monograph the ideas of general plasticity of the human genetic and cellular structure and the special sensitivity of the organism to early experience. These ideas underscore the sensitive or critical period concept.

Callaway's work, having drawn praise from geneticists, educators, and psychologists all over the world, provides guidelines and a solid rationale for educational programs that could take advantage of these important learning periods. He sees reading activity with the young as a triggering device, perhaps the best available, that turns on the genetic potential of the child. "There is very little of the brain not finally involved in the relatively simple act of seeing a letter and pronouncing its label" (Jeffrey, 1980, p. 350).

We have long known that gifted children read early. Could it be true that children are gifted because they read early? Could this activity and other types of stimulation set into motion structural changes in the organism that result in high-level intellectual development? The data now available support this possibility.

To understand how a person's capacity for learning is affected by the early environment, especially during critical or sensitive periods, we must return to the principles of interaction. Experience affects gene production by making demands on the cell's metabolic resources in such a way that the organism is able to meet similar learning demands in the future more easily. If these demands are made early and repeated, they make lasting changes in the neural structure of the organism. Increased activity increases the amount of transmitter fluid produced at a synapse, the point where there is firing from one brain cell to another during thinking. Nerve cells and fibers become larger through use as does the capillary network. As we saw in Chapter 1, the thickness and weight of the entire cortex increase by environmental enrichment. There is evidence that experience does lead to maturation. Callaway (1970) points out that we have had evidence available for over 35 years that myelinization of the optic tracts is accelerated by stimulation. He points out that the assumption that genetic material is completely prepro- grammed, and therefore contributes to a stable, inheritable mental capacity, cannot be supported in light of more recent evidence.

Creating the Responsive Environment (2 Through 5 Years)

We now have a child who is interested in the world and other children. This child has outgrown the baby stage. During the 2- through 5-year period the child's mental powers show rapid growth. Speech, mobility, and increasing social involvement all add to the fast-paced intellectual development.

Two-year-olds may seem inflexible and are often very vocal about their demands. Their energy is abundant and their curiosity is high. Children at this age enjoy routine, as they have difficulty making up their minds. Three-year-olds seem to feel much more secure about their world. As language and motor abilities rapidly develop and social skills increase, this age group needs caregivers to explain and model behaviors such as generosity, altruism, and care for others (Owen, 1984; Stollak, 1978). Stollak suggests that affection and responsiveness to the child's needs, a stimulating and varied environment, encouragement of exploration and independence, and fair discipline all show a high correlation with positive child development. The play materials from previous periods are useful, but in different ways. Three-year-olds create, draw, pretend, and imagine, but only if allowed to and if provisions for these activities have been made. Space to explore their own way and time to "do it myself" are needed. Children at this age are now thinkers. Cognitive psychologists such as Jean Piaget (1952) and Jerome Bruner (1960, 1964, 1968) have helped us to understand how thinking develops.

Development of the Rational Mind.   Piaget (1952, 1954, 1965), an eminent Swiss psychologist honored by educational groups throughout the world, believed that there were qualitative as well as quantitative differences between the thinking of adults and children. It was not only how much they knew, but the way they knew. The mind, he believed, is always trying to balance between assimilation, bringing in new information that fits our belief system and accommodating our belief system or thought structure to allow for new information, for change. As we grow, ever more complex structures are needed to understand our world and we require more elaborate schemes.

Development of the thought processes involved in such schemes was thought by Piaget to occur in four discrete and qualitatively different stages. The first stage relies primarily on the senses and bodily motion to develop a few simple schemes. This stage is, therefore, called the *sensorimotor stage* and includes the period of infant development (birth to 18 months). The second stage, called *preoperational,* includes the years from about 2 to 7. Children now begin to develop an understanding that symbols can represent objects, words can replace and communicate reality. At stage three, children can classify things and think with some logic; they are aware of and can formulate laws of logic. This is the stage of *concrete operations,* occurring around 7 to 11 years of age. Finally somewhere around 12 years of age, a person reaches the stage of *formal operations.* Now we find future thinking, critical and alternative thinking, creative problem solving, idealism, and comprehension of metaphors.

While Piaget's theory uses age only as a guide, not as immutable delineations of norms of behavior, it should be noted that he was not interested in accelerated development. Others were. While not disputing the sequential nature of the stage theory, Webb (1974) concluded that the rate of maturation to a new stage depended on IQ. High-IQ children between 6 and 11 achieved maturation in a few months while normal-IQ children took a year or two. Piaget felt that the stages were developmental, not bound to age limits, proceeding sequentially one after the other. His framework allows for an understanding of the variability of learners, as it shows the differences in the structure of thought and does not view levels of intelligence as just acquisitions of new knowledge. He looked at what was observable with the children he studied, not what was possible or even preferable. Podgoretskaya (1979) believes that what was observed did not reflect age-linked characteristics, but rather gave evidence for the types of problems that occur in the thinking process when its development is left to chance. His thesis is that such defects can occur at any age if thinking is allowed to develop spontaneously and unsupported by a responsive environment.

Flavell (cited in Chance & Fischman, 1987) finds a problem with Piaget's stage-dependent theory. While stages imply long periods of stability followed by abrupt change, what actually happens is that important changes occur gradually, often imperceptibly, over months or even years. Chance and Fischman also point out that by focusing on children's use of logical thought and deductive reasoning, Piaget ignored areas of thought such as creativity—a most important growth area that influences the quality of all thought and reasoning.

Clearly human growth is far more complex than can be accounted for by the concept of broad developmental stages. Not only age but the quality of the environment affects this schedule (Chance & Fischman, 1987). For example, researchers have found that memory ability grows rapidly from birth through age 5 with its progress determined by the number of memory strategies learned by children. One such strategy is rehearsal. When trying to remember a list of items to buy at their play store children who repeat the items and rehearse what they are to purchase remember more items than those who do not, regardless of age. Such strategies are not learned naturally as children grow. Sophisticated strategies, such as categorizing, are learned through experience, often by imitating older children or adults. It would be well to teach mnemonic strategies both at home and at school.

Young children can also learn systematic hypothesis testing if taught some simple skills of logic. While Piaget (1952) believed that only children over 14 could solve scientific problems, this is true only if the children have no opportunity to play with such ideas earlier.

One of the most important skills children can learn regarding problem solving is how to be systematic and organized. Even impulsive children can be helped to be better problem solvers by instruction and encouragement in organizing their actions (Chance & Fischman, 1987).

Development of the Metaphoric Mind.   It has been pointed out that what Piaget is really describing is the development of only one of our mind styles, the linear-logical style of the left hemisphere (Samples, 1977). Also, the descriptors Piaget uses are valid only in cultures that have placed their emphasis on linear-logical thought processes. What about our other mind, the metaphoric, intuitive, holistic mind valued by Einstein, Bruner, da Vinci, Salk, and a myriad of other creative thinkers who have changed our culture? Samples (1977) suggests a hierarchy of metaphoric modes within which students at any age have the ability to perform. Through use of these modes students were found to develop more comfort and ability in exploring concepts, ideas, and processes in rational ways. The first, the Symbolic Metaphoric Mode, exists when either an abstract or a visual symbol is substituted for an object, process, or condition. By making the visual symbolism available, understanding can be achieved even by those who are not as adept at deriving meaning from abstract symbolism; that is, by drawing or sculpting an idea, one may understand the meaning and express it through the written word.

Next, the Synergic Comparative Mode occurs when "two or more objects, processes or conditions are compared in such a way that the both are synthesized into a greater whole as a result of the comparison" (Samples, 1977, p. 690). Here lie the roots of holistic cyclic thought, the true beginnings of the power of the other mind. While the linear-logical mind would view by seeing the differences, the holistic mind views by seeing the connections allowing an extension or expansion of the original idea. "The petal of the flower looked like white velvet" gives you two unlike objects that serve, by the connection, to extend and enhance your view of the flower.

The Integrative Metaphoric Mode exists when people experience objects, processes, or conditions directly with all of their physical and psychic being. This would require the involvement of all of the functions of the human being—feelings, rational thinking, intuitive thinking, and physical sensing in the learning process. This mode is what we later will refer to as Integrative Education (Chapters 7 and 8), engaging total brain function as we learn.

Finally, the Inventive Metaphoric Mode begins at any time an individual creates a new level of awareness or knowing through a self-initiated exploration of objects, processes, or conditions. Samples (1977) emphasizes the process of creating, which is to the metaphoric modes of intelligence what discovering is to the linear-logical modes.

While the growth of the metaphoric, holistic mind is available throughout our life—and, when used, can be shown to result in higher feelings of self-confidence, self-esteem, and compassion; a wider exploration of traditional content and skills; and higher levels of creative invention—current teaching strategies, environments, and curriculum neglect its use. Allowed at the beginning stages of the young child's learning experiences, the acceptance of this mind style disappears as we progress in school. Samples (1977) assures us that, though his data show this disappearance, he and his colleagues have found that the metaphoric mind does not disappear. In my work I too have found that children understand and respond to any encourage- ment to use the other way of knowing. Both parents and teachers can, by valuing this equally important part of each of us and by accepting, encouraging, and creating spaces for its use, allow the development of both mind styles, optimizing the actualization of our fullest potential.

The Preschool Experience—For the Toddler (18 Months to 3 Years)

During this time of rapid growth for the young child it is important that all modes of learning be nurtured. Many of the characteristics of giftedness may already be evident and should be supported. Throughout this chapter we have looked at how we might optimize growth for our children, and the results of that rich interaction now begin to be evident. Rather than just identifying giftedness, the activities of the years prior to and including this period can be said to produce giftedness.

Scarr (cited in Hall, 1984) reports that until children are 2 years old they need a lot of warm, loving care from adults, though the caregiver need not be the parent. In a day-care situation at this age there should be no more than 4 children to each adult. When a child receives enough attention from adults, a child left in day care before age 2 does just as well as children who are home with their mothers. When placed in programs with many other children before age 2, a child does not do as well intellectually as other children, either as a preschooler or later as an 8-year-old. Scarr found that there was also something lacking in the emotional development that causes the child to be considered less cooperative and more aggressive than other children. After 3 years of age an educational program with other children becomes important. The child will actually do better than children who stay at home with their mothers. The more planned educational experiences a child over 3 has, the better that child does in intellectual, language, personal, and social development—significantly better than children placed in programs focused on free play.

Curriculum for preschool must be rich in variety and stimulating in process.

Hayward (1985, pp. 16–18) makes the following suggestions for the toddler's learning environment, whether at home or at school:

1 *Make use of famous works of art.* Change the pictures in the child's room once a month. Have available varied pictures, posters, charts, etc. Traditional children's pictures can be mixed with reproductions of famous works of art (usually available on loan from libraries, museums, or universities). Hang some of the reproductions at the child's eye level. Hayward states, "A two-year-old child I knew would often get out of her bed at nap time and sleep on the floor underneath a picture that she adored which was taped about two and one-half feet above the floor" (p. 17).
2 *Have a surprise bag.* Change the object once or twice a week. Without looking inside the bag the child puts his or her hand inside, then feels

the surprise and tries to guess what it is. Begin with objects that are easy to identify and, as the child's ability to observe and analyze increases, use objects that are less readily distinguishable. Treat the child's mistakes as helpful clues and encourage risktaking.

3 *Hang educational charts.* Have charts of the alphabet, animals, the development of a seed into a plant, etc., on the wall for the child to observe and discuss. (These charts are available at educational supply stores.) Clear contact paper extends the life expectancy of pictures or paper materials that children will be handling.

4 *Use child-sized bookshelves.* Place the bookshelves low enough to allow children to reach books, magazines, catalogs, department store fliers, and other reading materials that are an important part of the child's environment.

5 *Use the yard as a laboratory.* The yard can be a marvelous laboratory wherein the child can observe and experiment. Such things as where puddles go, why shadows change their size and shape, how rocks can be so many different colors, etc., can be fascinating. Do some of the experiments listed in children's science books.

6 *Use the community for learning.* Libraries, museums, children's theaters, concerts, tide pools, markets, and businesses all enrich the child's experience. Prepare for the "field trip" by discussing and reading about the whats and whys of the place you will be visiting. Have the child ready to look for some specific item or event when you go. Be sure to discuss the trip when you return, and allow the child to do something to record or remember the important things that were observed. An increasing number of resources and classes to help children develop important skills are now available for the toddler.

Remember that the most important thing in early learning is not the information taught, but the processes learned and the attitudes developed. Developing the intellectual ability of children truly means helping them to develop physically, emotionally, socially, cognitively, and intuitively. By their own experiences or through playing imaginative roles children can learn the appropriate social skills for many situations. Learning how to behave in school, at restaurants, in the dentist's office, or at parties can be the result of play that includes these imagined social exchanges (Chance & Fischman, 1987).

Gardner (cited in Chance & Fischman, 1987) reports that creativity develops rapidly in early childhood, peaking at about 7 years of age. Schools create a climate that suppresses creativity and, through its emphasis on right answers and correct procedures, causes what will be seen as a decline of growth in this area that may not rise again until the teens. While such suppression of creativity and decline in growth need not happen, until schools share more concern for the growth of creativity, it is likely to be stifled unless appropriate experiences are provided.

The Preschool Experience—
For Early Age Learners (4 to 5)

By age 4 children are very verbal, and teachers use high levels of this ability to identify very able children. In addition, 4-year-olds are alert, curious, attentive, active, and characteristically, of great joy to their teachers, can easily be engaged in the excitement of learning. At this age children show emotions that make it relatively easy for an observant teacher to provide an appropriate learning environment responsive to the child's needs and interests. Each 4-year-old seems to be a bundle of sensory-motor energy.

Four-year-olds are still living in a "me first" world. As with the younger children, discovering how and at what level these children function and then challenging and supporting their growth is the primary job of their teachers both at home and at school. According to Christine Cenci, team leader for the Early Age Program at our summer demonstration school, this Herculean task begins by simply watching the children. They will let you know everything you need to know in order to enhance and educate them.

Cenci shares some suggestions for creating a productive, healthy social-emotional climate in the learning setting (Clark, 1986):

1 Share much of the decision making by placing more of it in the hands of the children.

2 Include the children in resolving their arguments and differences. One procedure is to take both children aside and follow this plan:

Step 1—*Child A* is allowed to tell what happened without being interrupted. *Child B* is allowed to tell what happened without being interrupted. *Child A* responds to *B,* then *child B* responds to *A* until what has happened has been exhausted. (Remember: they are discussing *just what happened,* not what will or what might have happened.)

Step 2—*Child A* tells what he or she wants (example: no more being hit in the shoulder by *child B*); *child B* tells what he or she wants (example: *child A* must stop pulling the ball out of *child B's* hands).

Step 3—The teacher asks *A* if *A* can agree to what *B* wants, then asks *B* if *B* can agree to what *A* wants.

Step 4—At agreement, the teacher excuses both children. Most often an agreement is reached, but when one isn't, the teacher reconvenes the meeting to determine upon what they can agree.

3 Work to extinguish or incorporate "off-the-wall" comments made by the children. For example, if there is a discussion of the Mobius strip going on and someone shouts, *"John's peepee is blue,"* there are many viable responses the teacher can make. Smiling and saying, "Peepee or urine is not blue but in a moment you will use blue paint to . . . ," is one alternative response, or "Peepee or urine could change color to show us illness but in this Mobius you could use dark blue to show one-sidedness. . . ." The

teacher might even say, "Joey is really feeling funny today so I'm eager to see how he uses any color, even blue, to color his Mobius pathway."

Another way of using seemingly irrelevant comments is to turn the comment into a useful question. For example, if while discussing machines one child says, "I love whales. I saw lots of whales once," the teacher might say, "Whales are quite interesting and so very big. It is fun to watch big whales move. Do you know how these big machines move?"

Always take the children from where their minds are and lovingly pull them beyond. In these examples the children were not denied their observations and their outbursts were made useful.

4 Use questions as a tool for growth. For example, if a child who has a cut hears the teacher say, "How can I help?" the child then must decide if a hug, a bandage, an ice cube, etc., is needed. The teacher then moves to help. When a child says, "I can't find anything to do," the teacher can respond with, "What have you missed here today? Let's look. Do you see a center that you've forgotten? How about trying that one? How long would you say is fair? Will you let me know how it works out?"

On occasion, however, questions have a deleterious effect and must be redirected. Often when a child is revealing something sensitive in a trust group, expressing a loss or a joy, or needing to relate an experience, the child's intense look should remind the teacher *No questions, this child needs to unload this.* Patient, eye-to-eye contact helps teachers know when to ask questions.

5 Watch the child's body posture. The body can provide valuable assessment data. Small children's bodies will often reflect what is in their thoughts. Watch for slumping, skipping, head down, eyes away, a red face, quietness, fast talking, or bubbly actions. Small children turn away from an activity if they are losing interest, and just as a child is turning to grab another child the teacher can say, "Gentle hands, use gentle hands." Recognizing these and other body actions can allow the teacher to approach the next learning opportunity better informed, and can in many cases provide an early warning system.

6 Use *I* statements. As with children and adults of all ages, *I* statements empower both the teacher and the learner. When a teacher says, "You need to help me, You need to try harder," or "You need to go out now," the statements are not only misleading, but also may be untrue. What is actually being revealed is the teacher's need, and statements such as "I need you to help me, I need you to try harder," and "I need you to go out now" set an honest emotional climate, inviting much more cooperation.

7 Promote the spontaneous spark. As the child rushes to the board with "I can do it!" do not insist on a raised hand or a *wait-your-turn* lesson. Listen, evaluate, approve, encourage, and then invite the child to carry the idea further *after* sitting back down. For example, a lecture/demonstration of the instruments of a symphony orchestra is given by a guest speaker, and then the children are invited to experience the instruments at centers around the room. Roger walks thoughtfully to the center where the drums, cymbals, bells, and baton have been placed. He picks up the baton and with great authority raps for attention from all the "musicians" in the room.

He then carefully conducts a symphony of his own for the next 10 minutes. The rules of rotation and taking turns can be suspended for those 10 minutes with a nonverbal understanding between the teacher and the children. (pp. 55–56)

For information on how to set up and schedule either the toddler classroom or early-age classroom as they were developed for the summer demonstration project which we called the New Age School, see *Optimizing Learning: Using the Integrative Education Model in the Classroom* (Clark, 1986).

The curriculum for all preschool children must be rich in variety and stimulating in process. For those who are developing faster and who show higher levels of intelligence, such variety and stimulation are even more necessary. In their experiences we can include more activities allowing self-direction, exposure to more abstract concepts, and more involvement with the tools and skills for operating in the areas of reading, mathematics, science, research, art, music, and writing, and the world in which they live. A home or classroom that seeks to optimize growth in young children will incorporate the same elements found in Chapter 8 for organizing responsive, individualized learning environments. The differences will be in timing, strategies, and the amount of support needed. Decentralization is appropriate with centers or areas for academic and artistic activities. Choice making can be developed and used by children as young as 2 and gives the children a sense of competency and achievement, as it does to children further along in their learning. Even very young children can learn to manage their own choice of centers or areas in which to participate, their use of time, and other experiences leading them toward becoming independent learners—such as voluntary adherence to limits on numbers of children who can participate in a given center at a certain time and signals as to when and where activities are most appropriate. It takes more complex planning and structuring to allow the necessary freedom and independence that develop high levels of interaction for young children and ultimately produce higher levels of intelligence. However, the results are so valuable and so important to the future of the child that any parent or teacher would be well advised to expend this extra effort.

Language patterns and vocabulary can be very important teaching tools. The choice of words can make a child feel either suppressed and helpless or supported and competent. For instance, in situations where the child is involved in an activity that is not allowed, the parent or teacher could use language allowing an alternative choice, e.g., "You can't do this, but you can do this," directing the child to a more appropriate activity. This language produces choice and allows the child to begin to develop alternative thinking skills. Set up situations where the child can be invited to explore and test hypotheses. When a child encounters an obstacle, ask "How can we do that?" If the child encounters something too risky or too scary, suggest "I'll go with you and then you can go all the way through that tunnel. Next time you can do it yourself if you want to." Be sure to use lots of verbal reminders of the child's worth just for being who he or she is, not just when something is done well. As you pass by, say briefly "I really like you." Do be sure that you also share your negative human feelings clearly. Children notice when things are unpleasant. It would be better to state your feeling, such as "What you are doing makes me angry," rather than leaving to chance the interpretation of what is happening. You then have given the child the opportunity to change, and he or she need not misinterpret your feelings in a negative self-concept. Always with gifted children use lots of humor; they delight in it.

The curriculum for gifted young children must play to the ages and stages of growth by always stretching just a bit beyond the normative expectations. Viewing each stage of development as an exciting opportunity for growth will allow a far more appropriate learning situation. For example, the "terrible twos" are seen as a time for testing the limits, for risk taking; the threes begin real involvement with opportunities to build social skills; during the fours the child moves from "me" to others; and the fives give endless possibilities for developing independence. A responsive environment allows the organic needs of the child to be met.

When selecting a preschool for their gifted children, parents can improve the possibility of choosing an appropriate program by carefully observing the following:

1 *The teachers:* How do the teachers interact with the children? Do the teachers genuinely like children? Are they being authentic, showing their real feelings, letting the children know them as people? The research on programs for young children indicates that no one program can be shown to be the best. All models investigated were effective when teachers were committed to the model and dedicated to the children (Roedell, Jackson, & Robinson, 1980).

2 *The environment:* Is it nourishing for children? Is it pretty, colorful, thoughtfully organized? Is it flexible, pleasant, and inviting? Does the environment change to stay interesting? The involved, caring parents or teachers who provide ways for children to learn things that both they and the children find interesting produce the most effective environment for learning.

3 *The activities:* Are there lots of different activities at different levels of difficulty? Are there activities to challenge and stretch the children's thinking? feelings? intuition? physical sensing? Can the children go as far as they want with an activity? Are there lots of skills for the children to master creatively?

In a study conducted by the High/Scope Educational Research Foundation (Bridgman, 1986), the role of teachers and their organization of the preschool classroom was found to be critical to the long-term effects of such educational experiences. Youth who had taken part in highly academic, teacher-controlled preschool programs were found to have twice as many instances of drug abuse and juvenile delinquency and up to five times as much involvement in property

Gifted children are often unusually curious.

destruction and other violent acts as those who had attended programs stressing child-initiated activities. The latter group were also found generally to be more well adjusted, participating more in sports and other extracurricular activities, and having better relations with their families. David Weikart, lead researcher on the project, comments that all three models (using teacher-controlled; child-initiated, cognitively oriented; and child-initiated, free-play activities) gave the children involved an intellectual head start in school; however, the social consequences for the child seemed to be very different. "Apparently, a preschool curriculum that emphasizes direct transmission of knowledge is less successful in helping children adapt to the interpersonal realities of rules and conventions" (Bridgman, 1986, p. 15).

Academic subjects can be introduced in an integrative way, that is by combining cognition with feeling, physical sensing, and intuition, as will be described for older children in Chapter 8. The following two exercises (Integrative Lessons 3.1 and 3.2 from Clark, 1986, pp. 186, 187, and 190) and the preschool curriculum presented in Table 3.4 provide examples of activities to enhance integrative education.

At the Science Center
Integrative Lesson 3.1   Touch Color (Chromatography)*
Purpose:

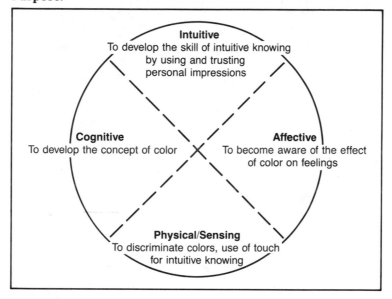

Time involved: Approximately 45 minutes.

Materials needed: Plastic water glasses, round paper towel disks with strips cut out of each, set of disks with a color in the middle and no strip cut out, felt tip pens of various colors.

Organization preferred: Small group of children around table with teacher.

Teacher role: Demonstrator, facilitator, questioner.

Procedure:

1 Demonstrate how color placed on a paper towel disk separates into different designs as water is absorbed into the disk. The color will separate into its color components as this absorption takes place. Fill a clear plastic glass two-thirds full of water. Place a disk of paper toweling cut as indicated below and slightly larger than the top rim of the plastic glass flat across the top of the glass. Allow the tab attached to the disk to fall into the water. As the tab absorbs the water the color will begin to separate into lighter and lighter elements. In the discussion of this demonstration introduce color words and discuss descriptors (blue—cool; red —hot, etc.).

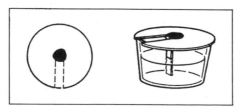

*Taken from a lesson by Chris Cenci.

2 Ask the children to experiment with various colors on paper towel disks. Encourage the children to make different mixtures of color with different felt tip pens, as well as different designs at different points on the disk's surface.

3 After each child has had an opportunity to create several disks with various designs say, "Some of the papers give you certain feelings. How do you feel when you see this color? This design?"

4 "Is there something in one of the designs specifically about you? Find it and outline it in black pen."

5 Set up a chart rack. Put slits in the form of an *x* on a tagboard hanging from the rack, then have the children relax and reach through. Ask them to determine the color of the disk on the other side.

On a different day:

6 Each of us has a special, lovely color that gives us a special feeling. Look around the room. "If you see that color move to it."

On a different day:

7 Put an item of one color in a bag. When the children are in their circle show them the bag and ask them to close their eyes and imagine something there. Ask them to open their eyes and pass the bag around the circle. Then ask them what color is the item in the bag. You may give them several color words from which to choose. Discuss and then show. Be sure to acknowledge the idea of "on target" and "off target" rather than saying the child is right or wrong.

At the Reading Center
Integrative Lesson 3.2 *My Own Alphabet/Picture Cards*
Purpose:

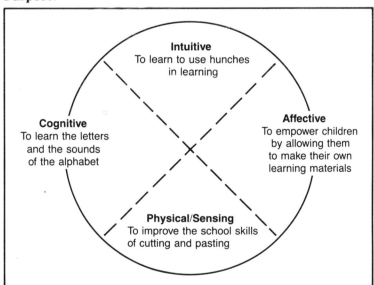

Time involved: 10 to 15 minutes or as long as the children are interested.
Materials needed: Old magazines, scissors, paste, file cards with letters at the top (e.g. "A, a," "B, b," etc.).
Organization preferred: Individual activity or small group.
Teacher role: Facilitator.
Procedure:

1 Sit with the children and look through old magazines for small pictures of objects with a beginning sound like the letter at the top of the card. Invite them to guess when they are not sure.
2 Cut out the picture (or allow the children to do so under your supervision) and help them paste it on the card.
3 Ask the children to say the names of the objects as they paste them onto the card.
4 Invite a child to choose from the cards a picture that she or he really likes. Have the child think of that picture, seeing it in his or her mind. The other children are invited to guess what picture the child is seeing. Save the cards for other games.

Evaluation: Check for accuracy of letter names and sounds when playing with the cards later.

Games to play with alphabet/picture cards:

• Scramble: Mix up all the cards and ask the child to sort them into piles or by rows.
• Matching Letters: Use a large chart with the letters printed on one side. Ask the child to match the card to the letter on the chart. (Variation: place on the table two cards which have the same letter and one with a different letter. Ask the children which doesn't match.)
• Alphabet Dominoes: Use alphabet cards to play dominoes.
• Take Away: Place several alphabet/picture cards on a rack or table. Have the children close their eyes while you take away one card. Ask the children to open their eyes and identify which card is missing.
• Guess My Card: Have one child choose one card and be sure no one else can see it. Invite the older children to guess which card the child is holding. Use "on target" or "off target" to indicate the accuracy of the guess.

Table 3.4 Preschool Curriculum

Caregiver Activities	Because
Organize an environment that allows choice and a high degree of variety and novelty. Organize so that the child can follow through on an activity to its conclusion, e.g., when writing a story, illustrate it and bind into a book; when planting seeds, water and care for plant as it grows.	It helps develop an independent, autonomous learner; inner locus of control; intellectual stimulation; sense of responsibility.
Centers or areas where children can discover basic concepts, e.g., in math or science; specific school skills, e.g., writing, hole punching, use of ruler; and develop awareness of themselves.	They provide intellectual stimulation, cognitive skills, problem-solving abilities.
Provide inspiration and materials for children to write their own books and poems, with the help of an encouraging adult who will write as the story/poem is dictated.	This is useful in developing creativity, basic reading skills, language experience, intuitive skills.
Provide a variety of art materials, e.g., glue, colored paper, scissors, beans, bits of yarn, ribbon, scraps of wood, crayons, large-sized paper, marking pens, water paints, clay; materials that will stretch them beyond where they have gone, e.g., "Find something inside the clay and let it come out with your hands."	This facilitates developing creativity, sensory skills, artistic and intuitive abilities.
Provide sharing times and social outings with other children; organize group games and cooperative activities; allow opportunities to settle differences with other children, guiding only when necessary.	Research shows that young children can increase their cooperative social interactions, ability to overcome obstacles and to talk with peers, and decrease negative behavior (Roedell, Jackson, & Robinson, 1980). This allows children to grow in social problem solving.
Make use of the community and the surrounding areas for field trips and exploration.	This develops a sense of competency, autonomy, deeper understanding and appreciation of nature.
Provide opportunities to establish a relationship with a significant adult friend.	This allows children to get another point of view on issues; acquaints them with other interests, language patterns, and vocabulary; allows them to be guided and listened to when they feel parents cannot.

Development of Giftedness and Talents

From an important study Bloom (1982; Pines, 1982) reports results that validate and extend the thesis of Pressey (1964) mentioned at the beginning of this chapter, that giftedness and high levels of talent are created. By interviewing individuals who had attained "world class" status in a variety of fields, their parents, and their teachers, the conditions and determinants of their success were elicited.

Just as Pressey suggested, these gifts and talents could not have been actualized without the encouragement, support, and environmental opportunities provided by the parents and teachers. Genius indeed cannot "will out" in spite of circumstances, but must be developed, perhaps even created. Whatever the original "gifts," Without extremely favorable supporting and teaching circumstances over more than a decade they would not have been likely to reach the levels of attainment for which they were selected. . . . The most striking finding in talent development is the very active role of the family, selected teachers, and sometimes the peer group in supporting, encouraging, teaching, and training the individual at each of the major stages in his or her development. (Bloom, 1982, p. 511)

As we have seen, and Bloom confirms, data show that most human beings are born with enormous potential. However, three characteristics seem to be necessary to achieve at high levels: unusual willingness to do great amounts of work, a determination to do one's best at all cost, and the ability to learn rapidly. These traits appear to emerge from the early socialization and attitudes in the home and the early training provided by teachers. The evidence that learning rates can be altered by appropriate educational and environmental conditions suggests that very favorable learning conditions provided in the early years can markedly influence learning rate. As the rate of learning is an expression of advanced and accelerated brain development, this evidence relates to our discussion of developing intelligence.

Of major interest is the power of the parents' belief in the child. If the parents believe that a particular child has special ability they will hold different expectancies, allow more opportunities to develop the ability, and treat this child differently. Even if, in fact, the child was not significantly more able than others in the family, these beliefs and expectations and what they caused parents, teachers, and the child to do, Bloom found, seem most important to the early and resulting later development of the given ability in reaching an outstanding level. Only one child in each family tended to be chosen for exceptional development in a given ability—not necessarily the most able, but the one with the greatest desire to excel.

It was further discovered that it is "the values and interests of the parents that will determine which traits and qualities will be given great encouragement and further cultivation and which traits and qualities will be ignored" (Bloom, 1982, p. 520). Contrary to previously held belief, Bloom found that the children received opportunities and encouragement first and only later were seen to possess special ability. The following factors seem to be most important in the identification and development of special ability:

- Parents who greatly value and enjoy either music, arts, sports, or intellectual activity and view it as a natural part of life so that the child learns to speak its language;
- Parents who believe in the work ethic;
- A first teacher who is warm and loving, who makes lessons seem like games, instructs on a one-to-one basis, and includes parental interest;
- A second teacher who emphasizes skills and self-discipline and continues to individualize instruction;
- Access to a master teacher who opens doors.

From this study we find more evidence for the importance of early learning, for opportunities and encouragement to be available. It seems even more evident that children develop their ability because of instruction and attention, not the other way around.

It should be noted that parents are natural teachers. No one else can equal their knowledge of the child, their concerns and responsiveness. With a few learning tools at their disposal, parents can play a major part in their child's early education. Attitude lends the most important ingredient to any learning situation. The child must approach learning with a spirit of adventure and playfulness. Learning should be a joy, not a punishment; a favor, not a duty. Parents can ensure this attitude if they allow the child's natural curiosity to guide the task. Falbo and Cooper (1980) found that the amount of time parents spend playing with their preschoolers is directly related to an increase in verbal intelligence test scores.

Karnes, Shwedel, and Steinberg (1984) conducted a study comparing the attitudes, values, and behavior of parents of young gifted and nongifted children in the hope that the information would help them develop an effective parent component for their preschool program for gifted learners. While many similarities were found to exist between the groups, the parents of the gifted children did report some interesting differences. Parents of the gifted engaged in school-related activities six times more frequently than the parents of the nongifted, e.g., they read to their child three times as long each day, encouraged language development, encouraged freedom, and exposed their children to a variety of experiences including museums, nature walks, and natural history museums.

In a later pilot study conducted by Karnes and Shwedel (1987) some interesting differences in attitude and practices between fathers of young gifted children and fathers of young nongifted children were reported. Fathers of gifted children were found to have longer and more frequent instances of involvement with their children, including reading to their children three times as long and sharing activities such as trips and movies. More emphasis was placed by these fathers on reading, oral language, and development of their children's fine motor skills. Fathers of nongifted children emphasized physical activities. Fathers of the gifted were more concerned about how their actions affected their child's self-esteem and reported avoiding negativistic turns of phrase, holding unconditional positive regard for their children, and encouraging their children's unusual questions. Finally, fathers of the young gifted children in the study valued and encouraged independence in their children while most fathers of the nongifted felt that their children were already too independent. These are interesting areas of emphasis that teachers of children at home and at school may want to investigate regarding their own beliefs and practices.

A report on parental style warns that children of authoritarian parents who "attempt to shape, control, and evaluate the behaviors and attitudes of their children in accord with an absolute set of standards" are not as successful in school as are the children of parents who use a more authoritative style, i.e., setting clear standards while recognizing children's rights, expecting mature behavior, and fostering a healthy share of verbal exchange (Stanford study, 1986, p. 3). The study shows that the correlation between parenting style and success in school crosses ethnic boundaries. Another finding of the study was that placing too much emphasis on either punishing or rewarding children for grades results in lower performance and less internal motivation for the student.

Parents should view teaching as a pleasure to be shared with their child. Parents need not worry if their child seems reluctant to learn at any given moment. Given opportunities by parents flexible to a variety of responses, chances are that the child will learn faster than expected. If not, the child must be allowed to set the learning pace. Most importantly, remember to foster the excitement of learning. Parents can be assured that

- Young children are capable of a great deal of learning.
- Their children will enjoy learning.
- They can be their child's most responsive teacher.
- They will enjoy sharing this experience with their child.

Among the many books to guide parents toward more specific activities to stimulate and enrich their child's environment, I would suggest Beadle, 1970; Beck, 1967; Cass-Beggs, 1978; Doman, 1964; Ellis and Scholtz, 1978; Engelmann and Engelmann, 1966; Fine, 1964; Goldstein-Jackson, 1978; Gordon, 1970; Hendricks, 1979; Lehane, 1976, 1979; Levy, 1975; Marzollo and Lloyd, 1972; Painter, 1971; Weiss, 1972; White, 1975; White and Watts, 1973; and Yarrow, Rubenstein, and Pedersen, 1973.

CHARACTERISTICS OF GIFTED LEARNERS

Now that we have discussed giftedness and intelligence and how the interaction of heredity, environment, and the uniqueness of the child develop such high levels of ability, let us look at the demands such development may make on the gifted learner.

As a human being develops higher levels of functioning, many unique patterns and traits emerge. For that reason, the education of groups of gifted individuals is not an easy task. They are not a homogeneous group. The more gifted a person becomes, the more unique that person may appear. There are, however, many characteristics that often recur in groups of gifted individuals. While an individual may not exhibit all of these characteristics, knowledge of all the characteristics may avail our attempts to optimize learning environments and understand the demands higher levels of intelligence make on individuals within our society. To show more clearly examples of these characteristics, their resulting needs, and concomitant problems, we borrow from an organization developed by Hagen and Clark (1977).

While many of these characteristics that are typical of highly gifted learners are also found with the moderately gifted, we would find them with a higher degree of intensity and energy involved in the former. The desire to know and the capacity to create structure and organize data are noticeably greater and more efficient in the

Parents should encourage gifted children to engage in and enjoy non-competitive physical activities.

The gifted are more autonomous, self-directed, and intrinsically motivated.

highly gifted population, although their overly demanding view of self may result in even more difficulty developing a realistic self-concept and lead to an unreasonably low self-esteem (Powell & Haden, 1987). Even more than with other children we must rely on the highly gifted child to guide us in our parenting and teaching to approaches appropriate for them. Their unique needs leave us with no norms to follow.

As we look more closely at the characteristics and needs of gifted learners, we should mention a common problem in identifying these children. Teachers often attribute a high achiever with giftedness. While there can be no certainty as to clear distinction in every instance, gifted children usually exhibit the ability to generalize, to work comfortably with abstract ideas, and to synthesize diverse relationships to a far higher degree. The high achiever generally functions better with knowledge and comprehension-level learning. While high achievers get good grades and accomplish much, they lack the range and diversity of the gifted. Some need only increased opportunity; others become frustrated by more complex opportunities. The responsive environment is the teacher's best guide. This chapter has discussed in detail the responsive environment. Briefly, it is environment rich in opportunities for interaction where children can participate in their own learning, select the types of inquiry most appropriate for their learning style and pace, and have access to additional experiences ahead of their observed need.

Tables 3.5 to 3.9 are organized into cognitive (thinking, Table 3.5), affective (feeling, Table 3.6), physical (sensation, Table 3.7), intuitive (Table 3.8), and societal (Table 3.9), closely approximating the functions available in the human brain. With each characteristic, there is a delineation of possible concomitant problems. This format is an extension of the work of Scagoe (1974) and incorporates her suggestions.

Throughout this chapter we have seen evidence of the importance of optimizing the early learning periods if we are to actualize a child's potential. It seems increasingly clear that the roots of intelligence can be found not only in the genetic endowment of the individual but also within the earlier experiences the individual has with the environment. It is doubtful that even the finest, most richly endowed brain can function at its optimum without an equally enriched environment.

Researchers are finding clues to competent functioning in the prenatal, perinatal, and postnatal periods of human development. Some feel parenting for optimal development must include the health and living habits of the mother-to-be even prior to conception. We can no longer ignore the critical periods for development through the fetal period and the early years of life. The use of critical and sensitive periods for learning may make the difference between average and gifted performance. At the very least, we can use current information to guide our children toward becoming healthier, more intellectually able, more sensitive, and more motivated, self-directed learners. If each parent of each child were to use even what is now known about nurturing human bodies and minds, how very different our world would be. As a result of advanced and accelerated brain function, gifted individuals often exhibit many similar characteristics. Although no one individual would exhibit all or even the same cluster of these characteristics, they help us to understand gifted individuals and the demands high levels of intelligence make upon them better. There is much yet to learn. Many questions remain unanswered, but already we can change our world; we can create a miracle. The amazing thing is we need not wait—we already know how.

Text continues on page 133.

Table 3.5 *Differential Cognitive (Thinking) Characteristics of the Gifted.*

Cognitive development rests on the understanding and integration of a vast quantity of experiences of the environment. Educational programs should provide for an array of such experiences and encourage the processes of analyzing, organizing, and evaluating, as well as those processes of a more visual, rhythmic, and holistic nature that seem to coexist within our cognitive functioning. Differentiation for gifted learners requires assessment of and planning for each child's unique characteristics, some of which may be found below.

Differentiating Characteristics	Examples of Related Needs	Possible Concomitant Problems
Extraordinary quantity of information, unusual retentiveness	To be exposed to new and challenging information of the environment and the culture, including aesthetic, economic, political, educational, and social aspects; to acquire early mastery of foundation skills	Boredom with regular curriculum; impatience with "waiting for the group"
Advanced comprehension	Access to challenging curriculum and intellectual peers	Poor interpersonal relationships with less able children of the same age; adults considering children "sassy" or "smart aleck"; a dislike of repetition of already understood concepts
Unusually varied interests and curiosity	To be exposed to varied subjects and concerns; to be allowed to pursue individual ideas as far as interest takes them	Difficulty in conforming to group tasks; overextending energy levels, taking on too many projects at one time.
High level of language development	To encounter uses for increasingly difficult vocabulary and concepts	Perceived as a "show off" by children of the same age.
High level of verbal ability	To share ideas verbally in depth	Dominates discussions with information and questions deemed negative by teachers and fellow students; use of verbalism to avoid difficult thinking tasks
Unusual capacity for processing information	To be exposed to ideas at many levels and in large variety	Resents being interrupted; perceived as too serious; dislikes routine and drill
Accelerated pace of thought processes	To be exposed to ideas at rates appropriate to individual pace of learning	Frustration with inactivity and absence of progress
Flexible thought processes	To be allowed to solve problems in diverse ways	Seen as disruptive and disrespectful to authority and tradition

Comprehensive synthesis	To be allowed a longer incubation time for ideas	Frustration with demands for deadlines and for completion of each level prior to starting new inquiry
Early ability to delay closure	To be allowed to pursue ideas and integrate new ideas without forced closure or products demanded	If products are demanded as proof of learning, will refuse to pursue an otherwise interesting subject or line of inquiry
Heightened capacity for seeing unusual and diverse relationships, integration of ideas and disciplines	To mess around with varieties of materials, ideas, opportunities for multidisciplinary learning	Frustration at being considered "off the subject" or irrelevant in pursuing inquiry in areas other than subject being considered; considered odd or weird by others
Ability to generate original ideas and solutions	To build skills in problem solving and productive thinking; opportunity to contribute to solution to meaningful problems	Difficulty with rigid conformity; may be penalized for not following directions; may deal with rejection by becoming rebellious
Early differential patterns for thought processing (e.g., thinking in alternatives, abstract terms; sensing consequences; making generalizations; visual thinking; use of metaphors and analogies)	To be exposed to alternatives, abstractions, consequences of choices, opportunities for drawing generalizations and testing them, and solving problems by use of visual or metaphoric strategies	Rejection or omission of detail; questions generalizations of others, which may be perceived as disrespectful behavior; considers linear tasks incomplete and boring
Early ability to use and form conceptual frameworks	To use and design conceptual frameworks in information gathering and problem solving; to seek order and consistency; to develop a tolerance for ambiguity	Frustration with inability of others to understand or appreciate original organizations or insights; personally devised systems or structure may conflict with procedures of systems later taught
An evaluative approach toward self and others	To be exposed to individuals of varying ability and talent, and to varying ways of seeing and solving problems; to set realistic, achievable short-term goals; to develop skills in data evaluation and decision making	Perceived by others as elitist, conceited, superior, too critical; may become discouraged from self-criticism; can inhibit attempting new areas if fear of failure is too great; seen by others as too demanding, compulsive; can affect interpersonal relationships as others fail to live up to standards set by gifted individual; intolerant of stupidity
Unusual intensity; persistent, goal-directed behavior	To pursue inquiries beyond allotted time spans; to set and evaluate priorities	Perceived as stubborn, willful, uncooperative

Table 3.6 *Differential Affective (Feeling) Characteristics of the Gifted.*

High levels of cognitive development do not necessarily imply high levels of affective development. The same heightened sensitivities that underlie gifted intelligence can contribute to an accumulation of information about emotions that the student needs to process. The affect-based information comes from sources within and outside of the child. Gifted children need to learn that their cognitive powers applied to this material will help them to make sense of their world. Their educational program must provide opportunities to bring emotional knowledge and assumptions to awareness, and to apply verbal ability and inquiry skills in the service of affective development.

The early appearance of social conscience that often characterizes gifted children signals an earlier need for development of a value structure and for the opportunity to translate values into social action. This can occur in the context of the society of the classroom and should then be extended into the larger world, as appropriate to the child's increasing competence and widening concerns.

Differentiating Characteristics	Examples of Related Needs	Possible Concomitant Problems
Large accumulation of information about emotions that has not been brought to awareness	To process cognitively the emotional meaning of experience; to name one's own emotions; to identify one's own and others' perceptual filters and defense systems; to expand and clarify awareness of the physical environment; to clarify awareness of the needs and feelings of others	Information misinterpreted affecting the individual negatively
Unusual sensitivity to the expectations and feelings of others	To learn to clarify the feelings and expectations of others	Unusually vulnerable to criticism of others; high level of need for success and recognition
Keen sense of humor—may be gentle or hostile	To learn how behaviors affect the feelings and behaviors of others	Use of humor for critical attack upon others resulting in damage to interpersonal relationships

128

Characteristic	Goal / Need	Possible Concomitant Problem
Heightened self-awareness, accompanied by feelings of being different	To learn to assert own needs and feelings nondefensively; to share self with others, for self-clarification	Isolates self, resulting in being considered aloof, feeling rejected; perceives difference as a negative attribute resulting in low self-esteem and inhibited growth emotionally and socially
Idealism and sense of justice, which appear at an early age	To transcend negative reactions by finding values to which he or she can be committed	Attempts unrealistic reforms and goals with resulting intense frustration (suicides result from intense depression over issues of this nature)
Earlier development of an inner locus of control and satisfaction	To clarify personal priorities among conflicting values; to confront and interact with the value system of others	Has difficulty conforming; rejects external validation and chooses to live by personal values that may be seen as a challenge to authority or tradition
Unusual emotional depth and intensity	To find purpose and direction from personal value system; to translate commitment into action in daily life	Unusual vulnerability; has problems focusing on realistic goals for life's work
High expectations of self and others, often leading to high levels of frustration with self, others, and situations; perfectionism	To learn to set realistic goals and to accept setbacks as part of the learning process; to hear others express their growth in acceptance of self	Discouragement and frustration from high levels of self-criticism; has problems maintaining good interpersonal relations as others fail to maintain high standards imposed by gifted individual; immobilization of action due to high levels of frustration resulting from situations that do not meet expectations of excellence
Strong need for consistency between abstract values and personal actions	To find a vocation that provides opportunity for actualization of student's personal value system, as well as an avenue for his or her talents and abilities	Frustration with self and others leading to inhibited actualization of self and interpersonal relationships
Advanced levels of moral judgment	To receive validation for nonaverage morality	Intolerance of and lack of understanding from peer group, leading to rejection and possible isolation

Table 3.7 *Differential Physical (Sensation) Characteristics of the Gifted.*

People of highly developed intellectual ability may be unusually vulnerable to a characteristic "Cartesian split" between thinking and being: a lack of integration between mind and body. During school years, when the gifted student is experiencing large discrepancies between physical and intellectual development, the school may be unintentionally encouraging the student to avoid physical activity. If a child's intellectual peers are physically more advanced so as to make him or her feel physically inadequate, while physical peers are less intellectually stimulating and not within his or her friendship group, the usual competitive playground games may be neither inviting nor satisfying to the gifted child. If the physical development of the gifted child is to be encouraged, programs should provide experiences that develop integration between mind and body in children with nonnormative development patterns.

Differentiating Characteristics	Examples of Related Needs	Possible Concomitant Problems
Unusual quantity of input from the environment through a heightened sensory awareness	To engage in activities that will allow integration and assimilation of sensory data	Attention moving diffusely toward many areas of interest; overexpenditure of energy due to lack of integration; seeming disconnectedness
Unusual discrepancy between physical and intellectual development	To appreciate their physical capacities	Results in gifted adults who function with a mind/body dichotomy; gifted children who are only comfortable expressing themselves in mental activity, resulting in limited development both physically and mentally
Low tolerance for the lag between their standards and their athletic skills	To discover physical activities as a source of pleasure; to find satisfaction in small increments of improvement; to engage in noncompetitive physical activities	Refuse to take part in any activities where they do not excel; limiting their experience with otherwise pleasurable, constructive physical activities
"Cartesian split"—can include neglect of physical well-being and avoidance of physical activity	To engage in activities leading to mind/body integration; to develop a commitment to own physical well-being; to extend this concern to the social and political realm	Detrimental to full mental and physical health; inhibiting to the development of potential for the individual

Table 3.8 *Differential Intuitive Characteristics of the Gifted.*

This area of the human experience is involved in initiating or insightful acts and in creative activity. While this is the least well-defined area of human endeavor, it is probably the area that promises the most for the continuance and fulfillment of humankind. All other areas provide support for and are supported by this area of function. As each area evolves to high levels, more of the intuitive and creative are available.

Differentiating Characteristics	Examples of Related Needs	Possible Concomitant Problems
Early involvement and concern for intuitive knowing and metaphysical ideas and phenomena	Opportunities to engage in meaningful dialogue with philosophers and others concerned with these ideas, to become aware of own intuitive energy and ability; guidance in developing and using intuitive energy and ability	Ridiculed by peers; not taken seriously by elders; considered weird or strange
Open to experiences in this area; will experiment with psychic and metaphysical phenomena	Guidance in becoming familiar with, analyzing, and evaluating such phenomena; should be provided a historical approach	Can become narrowly focused toward ungrounded belief systems
Creativity apparent in all areas of endeavor	Guidance in evaluating appropriate uses of creative efforts; encouragement for continued development of creative abilities	Seen as deviant; becomes bored with more mundane tasks; may be viewed as troublemaker
Ability to predict; interest in future	Opportunities for exploration of "what if" questions, activities of probability and prediction	Loss of highly valuable human ability

131

Table 3.9 *Differential Societal Characteristics of the Gifted.*

Society has unique needs for the services of unique individuals. While we would not wish that education for the gifted focus on societal needs at the expense of the needs of these individuals, neither can education of the gifted disregard the importance of their mature social roles. Gifted students need direction in exploring all the opportunities society has to offer them and the ways of contributing what they have to offer to society. They need conceptual frameworks to organize their experience of society (e.g., Maslow's [1968] hierarchy of needs), and they need opportunities to develop those skills that will make it possible for them to affect society. Educational programs should provide for the options, conceptual frameworks, and skills that will underlie effective social involvement of gifted students.

Differentiating Characteristics	Examples of Related Needs	Possible Concomitant Problems
Strongly motivated by self-actualization needs	Opportunities to follow divergent paths, pursue strong interests, help in understanding the demands of self-actualization	Frustration of not feeling challenged; loss of unrealized talents
Advanced cognitive and affective capacity for conceptualizing and solving societal problems	Encounters with social problems, awareness of the complexity of problems facing society, conceptual frameworks for problem-solving procedures	Tendency for "quick" solutions not taking into account the complexity of the problem; young age of gifted person often makes usable alternatives suspect; older, more experienced decision makers may not take the gifted person seriously.
Leadership	Understanding of various leadership steps and practice in leadership skills	Lack of opportunity to use this ability constructively may result in its disappearance from child's repertoire or its being turned into a negative characteristic, e.g., gang leadership.
Solutions to social and environmental problems	Meaningful involvement in real problems	Loss to society if these traits are not allowed to develop with guidance and opportunity for meaningful involvement
Involvement with the metaneeds of society (e.g., justice, beauty, truth)	Exploration of the highest levels of human thought; application of this knowledge to today's problems	Involvement in obscure groups with narrow, perfectionistic beliefs

132

Questions Often Asked

1. Can early learning create giftedness?

It would probably be more accurate to say "nurture giftedness," but yes, early learning is very important to developing high levels of intelligence.

2. How early can a baby learn?

Many researchers have reported evidence of memory being developed during the sixth and seventh month in utero. At birth most of an infant's sensory system is operable and showing levels of discrimination, e.g., responding to music heard prior to birth, mother's rhythms, and the sound of her voice. Most researchers believe that babies are aware and processing information and experiences long before they can control their body movements to let us know that they are learning.

3. Can you overstimulate a baby?

Yes, but not without knowing about it. Babies share readily and loudly when they are uncomfortable with their environment. They give many subtle cues even before that. It is important that caregivers pay attention to their babies for cues and follow their lead as each child is unique. The baby will let you know quite dependably when you have gone too far. Unfortunately, the most serious problem most babies have is understimulation or stimulation that is not directed specifically to them. That is extremely wasteful of their potential.

4. What are sensitive and critical periods for learning?

Sensitive periods are periods of growth that occur when all systems—sensory, mental, and motor—are ready to be used. If activated by the environment, they will be used together at peak efficiency, e.g., visual complexity from birth to 2 months, language acquisition between 18 months and 3 years. The time when an organizational process proceeds most rapidly is a critical period for the resulting organization. Failure to use a process during this time results in loss of the process or function, e.g., the first trimester of fetal life for physical growth and the first few months of life for the development of depth perception. If you miss a sensitive period you miss the time for optimal learning, but if you miss a critical period the result will be loss of function.

5. How do you discipline a gifted child?

All children respond best to guidance; however, for the gifted child it is essential. These children can be reasoned with and learn from the process quite readily. Remember that we teach mostly by our actions. If we want to teach someone how best to solve a problem we would model the solution we want them to use in the future. That is the best reason to think carefully about rewards and punishments before using them. Limits and boundaries are essential but they should be fair. As soon as the child can understand the consequences of any action, use natural consequences and alternative coping behavior as guidance. The successful parent assumes the child had good intentions but didn't know the most appropriate way to carry them out. (Please reread pp. 92 to 101 for a more detailed discussion.)

6. How early should children be taught academic subjects such as reading and math?

Reading to children can begin before they are 1 year old. It is a most effective way to begin the development of the skills and positive attitudes needed for successful, lifelong reading. Math begins with counting—toes, fingers, buttons on mommy's dress, etc. Alphabet and number songs and rhymes add to the beginning of "academic" learning as well. If you mean when should a child be sat down and forced to learn skills and drills I would have to respond "never!" Learning can be such fun for everyone, I'll never understand why we have made it such a chore at school.

7. Don't children who learn later in school catch up to early learners?

No, they do not. Many researchers have shown that instead of "catching up" the distance between early and late learners continues to grow throughout the grades until by sixth grade the late learner is at an incredible disadvantage. Parents are the best teachers when they allow their young children to be their guides; they have the best teacher-to-child ratio, the best overall knowledge of their child's needs, and they can allow continuous progress. Besides it's great fun!

8. Do all gifted children have similar characteristics?

Some do; however, as we develop more of our intelligence we become more unique. The lists of characteristics only give you some of the behaviors that have been commonly observed among many, many gifted youngsters over a long period of time. No child will have them all, but by knowing how some bright children express themselves you may understand more about the children with whom you live.

4. Growing Up Gifted

Within this chapter the reader can find

- A discussion of social-emotional development and its relationship to the gifted.
- A view of the importance of self-concept.
- A discussion of moral development and the developing personality.
- A discussion of attitudes as they relate to the growth of gifted children.
- Ideas for encouraging integrative growth of gifted individuals in the home and in the school and for providing for the cooperative involvement of both.

The characteristic most readily identifiable in gifted children, varying both in kind and degree, is sensitivity. Whether the sensitivity is to one or more particular areas of learning, sensitivity to discovering or solving problems, or sensitivity to the feelings of one's fellow man, it is so much a characteristic of giftedness that it can almost be said that the two terms are synonymous.

—WALTER B. BARBE

In order to develop our potential intellectual abilities, we must understand and nurture our cognitive, social-emotional, physical, and intuitive selves. A limit to any one function limits all functioning. To approach maximum intellectual capacity, one's cognitive, social-emotional, physical, and intuitive development must be highly operable and well integrated.

SOCIAL-EMOTIONAL DEVELOPMENT AND GIFTEDNESS

Children who, by fortunate circumstances, develop more of their potential seem to meet a different set of social and emotional consequences than will the more typical child. In the 1920s, people assumed that these children were emotionally borderline neurotics or even psychotics (Terman, 1925). Their advanced performance was viewed with great suspicion. A child prodigy was thought to become an adult imbecile. Parents who found their preschoolers reading would discourage such activities and encourage "playing with little friends" as an antidote. The fear that a neighbor, or worse yet a teacher, would discover precocious behavior in their child led many parents to adopt drastic and punitive actions when they observed any advanced behavior. Although attitudes have changed, some of these types of responses to advanced development still linger.

In that climate of suspicion and rejection of advanced development, Terman (1925) began his study at Stanford mentioned in Chapter 1. Terman collected data for 35 years on the emotional and social characteristics of children he identified as gifted. They are now adults, and researchers still collect data on them. What Terman found did not support the prevalent view of his day. The majority of children in his 140+ IQ group were physically more attractive than the more typical children. Later studies have linked this finding to better nutrition among children of his population and to the early experiences of most optimally developing children (Laycock & Caylor, 1964). Far from being the misfits and drudges people called them, the gifted youngsters in his population became leaders, organizers, football captains, and class officers. They enjoyed a significantly greater popularity, and their classmates viewed them positively. They showed marked superiority in moral attitudes, as measured by tests of character. Terman found that their moral judgment developed earlier than that of the average population. These children seemed well rounded and achieved well in most school subjects. Later data showed this population to be socially more able to adjust. They suffered less as adults from social problems such as divorce, alcoholism, and suicide than the average population. This group also had less ill health, less insanity, and a lower mortality rate than the average population (Terman & Oden, 1947).

Terman's subjects not only completed higher levels of schooling in larger numbers than the typical population, they also received more honors and awards while doing so. Professional accomplishments were measured only among the men, as women of that time period were not encouraged to seek careers. This gifted group had an outstanding record of achievement and made a far higher than average number of contributions to society. While the limitations of this study must be noted as we view the accomplishments of the group (e.g., the overloading of participants from higher socioeconomic levels), we must recognize it as a major accomplishment in the field of gifted education. As Terman himself remarked, "I take some pride in the fact that not one of the major conclusions we drew in the early 1920s regarding the traits that are typical of gifted children has been overthrown in the three decades since then" (Terman, 1954, p. 223). While his profile of the gifted child has been expanded as we study broader based populations, his statement remains essentially true.

It is as difficult to speak of the social-emotional characteristics of gifted individuals as of any other of the characteristics we have looked at before. Discussions of generalizations will bring out characteristics often found in the population, but all are seldom applicable to any one gifted individual. For the most part, given the opportunity for healthy development, the social-emotional adjustment of gifted children tends to proceed better than among the more typical population. Hollingworth (1926) found a strong positive correlation between intelligence and the desirable traits of character and temperament. Boehm's (1962) study of the development of moral judgment shows that brighter middle- and working-class children make moral judgments earlier; bright middle-class children show the most advanced development. Newland (1976) warns us to assure the gifted that we are concerned with their social interaction *with* others, not just their social adjustment *to* others.

In compiling the studies of the social-emotional characteristics of gifted children, a very positive profile emerges:

- Young gifted children, when compared with chronological peers, feel more comfortable with themselves and with their interpersonal relationships. They perceive themselves to have greater personal freedom than do their average classmates. They value cooperative and democratic forms of interaction though they are less willing to compromise. They report more positive feelings regarding themselves and others (Lehman & Erdwins, 1981).

- Gifted children undergo better emotional adjustment than average children (Lightfoot, 1951; Mensch, 1950; Ramaseshan, 1957), although some studies indicate a closer relationship to socioeconomic differences than to intellectual differences.
- Bright children tend to be more independent and less conforming to peer opinions, more dominant, more forceful, and more competitive than typical learners (Lucito, 1964; Smith, 1965).
- The gifted often show leadership ability and become involved in community projects and concerns. Concern for universal problems and the welfare of others begins much earlier than with more typically developing children. The gifted also become aware of issues of morality and justice very early (Cox, 1926; Martinson, 1961). When involved in group leadership, they emphasize parliamentary procedure and minimize the use of more autocratic or laissez-faire approaches to governance (Cassel & Haddox, 1959).
- Gifted children seem to prefer their intellectual peers to their chronological age peers, resulting in a social preference for older children and adults. They lack interest in children of lower mental age, and they choose friends among children like themselves (Barbe, 1965; Mann, 1957).
- Studies repeatedly show that the social status of bright children is high, and their classmates prefer them as companions. This factor seems to diminish at the secondary level, especially if other preferred factors of popularity, e.g., athletic ability, are not also evidenced (Coleman, 1962; Gallagher, 1958; Grace & Booth, 1958; Johnson & Kirk, 1950; Martyn, 1957; Miller, 1956; Purkey, 1966; Tannenbaum, 1962).

Although the very nature of being different in a society that does not value difference, even positive difference, brings more adjustment problems to the individual who is gifted, the very ability that creates the problem can supply the solution. A direct relationship between educational opportunities and adjustment does exist for the gifted (Martinson, 1972). Hunt (Pines, 1979b) believes that when parents place demands on their children without giving them the means to meet such demands and when they fail to respect the child's intrinsic motivation, their children can grow up to be very unhappy people. The gifted need help in learning to accept themselves as they are, to appreciate the ways in which they are both similar to and different from others. We must create opportunities for them to experience and value themselves as unique persons.

For the highly gifted child, the question of social adjustment takes on an added dimension. These few children have even more problems finding other children to whom they can relate. They become bored with school work, and they find fewer mental challenges within the school setting. Among groups of fellow

Social skills are learned very early.

students and teachers alike, those of lesser ability often display mediocrity and poor decision making. The highly gifted child ends up feeling disrespect for the judgment and actions of those in authority (Hollingworth, 1942).

In a study conducted in the Chicago public schools (Leaverton & Herzog, 1979) regarding the overall adjustment of highly gifted children, it was found that those tested scored in the twenty-fifth percentile on Social Confidence and the thirty-second percentile on Self-Acceptance subtests of the Self-Observation Scales. The conclusion from this study was that these children are in need of counseling to help them reach an adequate social and emotional adjustment. It was noted that very low priority had been given to the problems of this group, only 13 of the 113 tested had been seen by the school psychologist, and that referral was essentially for the purpose of testing only.

The more highly gifted the child, the more the risk of social maladjustment and unhappiness increases (Hollingworth, 1942; Tannenbaum, 1983). Roedell (1984) has identified eight areas of vulnerability of which we must be aware if we are to minimize these risks: uneven development, perfectionism, adult expectations, intense sensitivity, self-definition, alienation, inappropriate environments, and role conflicts. She finds that the most frequent symptom among this population is lack of confidence and a helpless orientation toward perceived failure. When this interacts with their heightened perfectionism we find ineffective problem solving and increasingly lowered self-concept. These problems can be alleviated. Gallagher and Crowder (1957) found that in special schools, highly gifted children experience fewer problems of adjustment by working with mental age peers. For further discussion of the highly gifted, see Question #1 in Questions Often Asked at the end of this chapter.

Origins of Social-Emotional Development

One of the first people to look at the healthy emotional development of human beings was the psychologist Abraham Maslow. Neither satisfied with the view that humans need control, nor content with the focus of most psychologists on pathology and remediation, Maslow (1971) believed that "well" individuals could become even healthier. He called the pursuit toward developing one's potential *self-actualization*. Maslow identified a group of people whom he felt exhibited outstanding health, both physically and emotionally. He then collected data coalescing the characteristics they had in common. While the concept of *self* was far from new (in fact, many psychologists, philosophers, and researchers had referred to it), Maslow first listed identifying characteristics that could indicate a high level of development in the social-emotional domain. From his work, Maslow (1971) identified the following traits among his examples of self-actualizers:

1 More aware, more in touch, more perceptive, more realistically oriented.
2 More accepting of self, others, and the natural world.
3 Spontaneous, natural, authentic.
4 More autonomous and self-directed; largely free of the need to impress others or to be liked by everyone; resistant to conformity.
5 Intrinsically motivated; having metamotivations (e.g., actualization of potentials, capacities, and talents; fulfillment of their life's mission or purpose; self-knowledge; self-acceptance; growth toward unity and synergy).
6 Seeking unity, oneness, integration, increased identification with humanity.
7 Working for a cause, devoted to a task or calling, viewing work and play as one.
8 Holding universal values (beauty, justice, truth) that are important to well-being. Working toward fulfillment of metaneeds (see #5, metamotivations).
9 Capable of rich emotional reaction and freshness of appreciation.

10 Enjoying a high frequency of peak experiences (moments of highest happiness or fulfillment) and frequent mystic, natural, or cosmic experiences.

11 Capable of deep empathy and profound relationships with others; great ability to love and to enjoy sexuality.

12 Seeking privacy on occasion for periods of intense concentration.

13 Creative, less constricted in thought processes; using a sense of humor that is not hostile.

14 More democratic in character structure.

15 Continually wondering about life; treating each day as new.

Remarkably, many of these characteristics can be identified in gifted children.

THE SELF-CONCEPT

As work in the area of understanding and facilitating emotional growth developed, it soon became apparent that the concept of *self* was central. Researchers and practitioners such as Allport, Aspy, Brookover, Combs and Snygg, Coopersmith, Jersild, Jourard, May, Maslow, Purkey, and Rogers, to name but a few, have, within recent years, brought the concept of self back to psychology and education after abandonment for years by the behaviorists. (Contributions made by each person named are cited in the references at the end of this book.) As interest in the concept of self increased, researchers found that the view of self determines achievement and enhances or limits the development of a person's potential.

The *self* may be defined as a complex and dynamic system of beliefs that individuals hold to be true about themselves. The concept is organized and can be modified (Purkey, 1970). It is, in part, constructed by us as a result of the interactions we have with others. The beliefs we have about ourselves literally determine our actions and our perceptions of the world and other people. We construct our own reality from these beliefs and often operate as though our view is the only view possible (Combs & Snygg, 1959; May, 1967; Rogers, 1961). Growth of self-esteem makes the self-actualizing, integrated person possible. With that in mind, let us look at one especially unexpected finding. Gifted individuals often have lower self-concepts than their more typical peers (Trotter, 1971). One reason for this could be associated with the unusually high expectations the gifted have for themselves. Parents of gifted children, sometimes accused of "pushing" their children, are actually more concerned because their children seem to push themselves unrealistically. This pressure can be far more demanding than any external pressure. Parents and teachers need to be aware of self-expectation so that they can provide help for the gifted child in acquiring more realistic goals and more adequate coping behavior. The frustration of never living up to your own standards and expectations can be very self-defeating and interfere with mental and emotional growth.

Perfectionism, common among the gifted, can become compulsive behavior. At least as painful for the gifted individual is the way this characteristic may be used against others. Not only must gifted persons meet high standards and attain specified levels of performance, but often their acceptance of other people is based on the other person's ability to meet these standards. These expectations of others can seriously interfere with interpersonal relationships, the view the gifted have of their world, and, certainly, how other people view them. Unfortunately, unless someone helps gifted children to understand the dynamics of this problem and provides some alternative behaviors, it can continue throughout their lives.

If the quality of our life depends on our level of self-esteem, why do we find so many who lack adequate levels? As we have seen, the concept of self develops quite early. The following story will illustrate how information from the environment begins to affect the development of self-esteem.

A small boy about 2 years of age was sitting in a garden watching a little "bug" move slowly across the ground. The child was fascinated by the fact that the little thing had so many legs yet still was able to move without falling down. It wasn't long ago since he had a lot of trouble just managing to move around on his own two legs. He still got them mixed up occasionally. Now as he looked closely at the "bug," he noticed other strange things. There was hair all over its legs. And when he looked really closely, the "bug" really wasn't black. There were some purple and green and even some red and orange colorings on its body. The funny things that came out of its head were really neat, too.

Just then an amazing thing happened. The bug jumped. It jumped up onto a nearby leaf and, of all things, it spit threads out of its back end. The child had seen people spit, but never had he seen anything spit out of its back end. He watched this happen again and again. Then, to his disbelief, the thing walked on its *own spit!* Well, this was getting to be too much. Someone in the house was missing all of this. She was such a nice, fun person, and he loved her very much; yet she couldn't see and share it all with him. He knew she wouldn't be able to come out there into the garden because, actually, that was why he was there. Earlier she had suggested that he spend the morning outside because she had so much work to do. But, maybe . . . if he was very careful . . . he could get his hands together like a little cup and very carefully lift the bug up and carry it into the house. Oh, he wouldn't leave it there. He would bring it right back. And he wouldn't hurt it. He just wanted her to see it, just for a minute. Happily, he picked it up and started toward the house. The door to the kitchen was pretty hard to maneuver, especially when he had to use both hands to keep the bug safe, but he managed. As soon as he was inside he went right to his mother and held his treasure up high for her to see. What followed was not at all what he expected! As he left the house to return the "nasty, dirty, horrible, ugly spider" to its place in the garden, he thought about what she had just said. She must be right, she was always right; he knew that. Well if she was right, then he must be wrong.

Situations such as this give little people messages about their ideas, their competence, and their image of who they are very early in life. Even children from very nurturing homes find their lives filled with individuals, groups of people, and institutions ready and very willing to show them how they are wrong—to acquaint them, often forcibly, with the "right way."

Experiences such as this begin the formation of the concept of self. We are born with a center core—our essence—that is unique to us and is our real self. Tiny babies have no problem communicating to us the real needs or desires they feel. Expressing the real self is never a problem at the beginning. But, as the child in the garden discovered, it does not take long before other information causes us to doubt the messages from our center core. After enough dissonant information enters our awareness, a shell begins to build around this lovely, real center, and it is made up of all the "crummy" stuff we feel and believe about ourselves after encounters such as these.

At some point, however, it becomes far too difficult to present ourselves to the world as the "crummy" person this shell leads us to believe we are. So at around 10 to 13 years of age, we begin to look around for another image to adopt. Often we completely forget the inner core of our real self and remember only the "crummy" shell as the definition of who we are. This second shell is formed from all of the nice and enjoyable things we find in other people. "There is someone who smiles a lot," we say. "People seem to like that so I'll smile a lot." "That person wears clothes a certain way that others find attractive; I can do that!" And the second shell builds. Soon we have an image to present to the world that is really great; our image is filled with nice ways of doing things and an agreeable appearance. Unfortunately this image of self is phony, and we know it. Now we must spend time and energy to keep other people far enough away that they do not see through our image. We are sure that if we let them in too close they will find out about the "real" person we are—the crummy, inept, incompetent person we know we really are—the person we know from the first shell. We now accept this shell as us. We have forgotten the beautiful, unique center core, our essence, our real self.

No matter how loving or how caring our family is, we all experience this shell-building phenomenon. Parents must find ways to recognize, accept, and support the center core. Educators can establish classrooms that allow self-discovery and support for individual and unique development. As growing people, we must keep in touch with this essence, accepting ourselves and allowing others to know us as the unique people we are. Work in this area shows us that, from the earliest days of our lives and as long as we live, our awareness and understanding of who we are will have the most effect on determining the quality and direction of our existence (Briggs, 1970; Satir, 1972).

A young woman around 20 years of age, who was in one of my first classes at the university, came up to me after we have been discussing the common characteristics and problems associated with being gifted. Hesitantly and with much confusion, she began to relate how she personally identified with the concepts we had been discussing. She stated that she knew she could not have been gifted because she remembered always having questions when everyone else had been satisfied with the information given. She was often told that she spent too

---

much time investigating a subject when the class needed to move on. Other students often groaned audibly at her remarks or shared insights, a happening that she interpreted as proof of her stupidity. She had, since junior high school, changed most of these "bad" habits and had withdrawn into her own world of interests, accepting some B's, mostly C's, and occasional D's as appropriate representation of her ability as a student. She was, however, intrigued by a number of ideas we discussed that seemed personally applicable. After sharing her bewilderment later that evening, she decided to call her parents in Pennsylvania. At our next class session she shared the news that her parents had been told when she was in the third

grade that she was highly gifted, around 165 IQ, but did not mention it to her on the advice of the school personnel. What started as the natural curiosity and expectations of a very bright mind, because of inadequate information about the reasons for her differences, turned into self-doubt and self-criticism to the point that her actual performance was inhibited and her growth arrested. She later used this information to reexamine the attitudes she had developed about herself and her abilities. She began to take more risks, to become more aggressive in pursuing academic and personal knowledge. She will never compensate for the lost years, but she made remarkable progress.

The first step toward intervening in low self-esteem is to acknowledge and clearly affirm what appears to be occurring. For example, the response to a frustrated attempt to complete perfectly a project still beyond the skill of the child would be simply, "You really would like that to be finished perfectly, wouldn't you?" or "It just isn't quite the way you want it yet, is it?" From statements such as these, if open communication exists with the child, a discussion of this need will usually follow.

Unrealistic self-expectations can result in another way of behaving. When others know that children are gifted, they may expect their work to have the aura of quality. Sometimes this results from a heterogeneously grouped regular classroom environment where, indeed, the work of the gifted child is outstanding compared to that of others in the room. In such cases, gifted children become used to being "best." They begin to consider everything they attempt to be exemplary. They may put forth small amounts of effort to achieve success. Many gifted children under these circumstances learn poor study habits, develop disrespect for efforts of others, and bluff their way through educational experiences using their advanced verbal ability or their facile and nimble brain for guessing answers and outcomes. They may seldom need to develop their skills or integrate their abilities. When finally challenged to academic thought or called upon for synthesis and evaluative processing, they become lost. Such sudden loss of power may cause them anger or frustration. Again, good communication of realistic expectations based on the assessed needs and abilities of the child can prevent this situation.

Children do not need to know their IQ score, but they must understand the behaviors associated with a high level of development. Becoming aware of the needs and responsibilities of giftedness will allow gifted children to examine their actions and the expectations they have of themselves and others. They will view their own progress more realistically and be able to clarify their beliefs and motives (Dubrowsky, 1968). These children must have adequate feedback on how others feel when their expectations are placed on them. Experience with the outcomes resulting from nonacceptance of those who do not meet personal standards is necessary for more effective and fulfilling interpersonal relations between the child and others.

Another contributor to the self-doubt often felt by the gifted individual is the lack of recognition from others. Parents and teachers often praise and show appreciation for the performance of those who are obviously just gaining skills, while they expect such performance from the gifted person. Because a person seems to accomplish a difficult task with ease or is able to do many things very well, the others in the environment soon come to expect such behavior and seldom show any appreciation for the quality of performance or effort involved. Without appropriate comments, it becomes difficult for gifted persons to develop a realistic idea of the quality of their contributions. The parent or teacher who only communicates constructive criticism can damage the child's developing self-concept. Sharing genuine appreciation or admiration for excellence is never inappropriate.

For gifted people, the pattern of shell building described earlier is intensified. Both self-imposed and external expectations are so much greater that the gifted often develop and maintain the second shell in desperation. Focus on the second shell may result in children who try to meet everyone's expectations and become perfect children, never allowing themselves to disappoint parents, teachers, or any other significant person knowingly. These children have an impossible task. They may try to meet their parents' needs and find that these differ from the teacher's needs; both may conflict with peer ideals and pressures. The gifted often attempt a trade-off with varying degrees of satisfaction for themselves. Barbe (1954) found that, in a society such as ours that does not value mental precocity, gifted children tend to take one of three patterns for adjusting to their world. They may choose to withdraw, to isolate themselves from the group. This occurs most often when the situation offers no challenge. Or they may become the class clown, showing off in an effort to be accepted and to gain favorable attention. This behavior may be carried to the point that teachers and peer group alike reject their attempts as being inappropriate or silly, or they may view the child as a nuisance. Finally, they may seek conformity through pleasing others or by pretending not to know answers in an effort to seem like everyone else, to hide a superior intellect. This dangerous game of nonuse may result in loss of function; growth cannot be nurtured through this subterfuge. In this way, gifted children may find themselves becoming role players or what our educational system calls "underachievers." Chapter 10 delves into this problem further.

A child may choose to become what the parents value, then shift to perceived teacher values. How closely these are aligned will determine the energy expended. Then the child discovers peer values. A girl from a middle-class family may discover that, if she wishes to be considered feminine and gain acceptance, the perfect papers required by parents and teachers become a liability. The challenge of inquiry into unusual subjects "for girls" becomes less rewarding. For boys, the masculine ideal of athletic competence may dictate refocus in that direction. Again, peer values may cause reordering of accepted parental and teacher values. In either case children may discover the use of giftedness to appear not at all gifted. As we have seen from the dynamic nature of intelligence, such denial and disuse can have the long-lasting consequences of diminished intellectual development.

In an attempt to provide some clearly differentiated measures of self-concept with gifted children and to look at gender as a variable, Loeb and Jay (1987) conducted a study using a multimethod approach. Their results showed that teachers and mothers of gifted students generally rated them as having fewer problems in almost all areas than did the teachers and mothers of the control students. They also found that girls differ from boys on their perceptions of themselves as gifted. Girls were more likely to find achievement through conformity, as demanded in elementary school, congruent with a positive self-image and feelings of control over their lives. Boys, however, define their ideal male as aggressive, self-reliant, and individualistic, a pattern that does not seem to fit well into this conformity learning pattern. Later, during adolescence, the learning demands seem to reverse and the girls' pattern of "learned femininity" is not as supported by high school achievement styles. Loeb and Jay suggest defeminization of early education and redefinition of gender roles as possible modifications to aid in growth of self-esteem among both gifted girls and boys.

MORAL DEVELOPMENT

For those who want to guide the development of the gifted child, moral development is another important concern. The level of intellectual power indicated by giftedness could be used against the person or society in general just as it could be used toward positive goals. Even if not used negatively, inadequate moral development would allow intellectual power to be inhibited by external validators, keeping gifted individuals from contributing their innovation and re-creation needed by society.

For over 20 years Lawrence Kohlberg of Harvard studied, hypothesized, and tested his theories that sought to explain how we acquire moral character. His work is very important to gifted education, for he believed, as did Piaget (1932), that maturity in the intellectual realm influences a person's maturity in moral development (Kohlberg, 1964, 1972; Lickona, 1977).

Kohlberg used the term *moral development* to indicate the level of internalization of principles that regulate one's conduct in human relations. The data that he had amassed came from longitudinal studies following 50 individuals for some 20 years. These studies of many cultures and countries are designed to show how moral development can be stimulated. He believed that all humans must pass through five stages sequentially, though not necessarily at the same age. He believed that the majority of adults in our culture never reach the fifth stage of principled morality. He clearly believed that we can establish moral climates and that these climates will most benefit development in the moral area. While some short-term benefits may arise from direct teaching of moral principles, the overall environment and interactions of the child within that environment have far more significance in later life.

Let us look briefly at the stages of moral development as Kohlberg identified them. At Stage 1 authority figures dictate the child's actions. Children follow moral rules to avoid punishment. During the first 5 to 8 years of life, most children find this belief reinforced regularly.

At Stage 2 the child gradually becomes aware of the idea of reciprocity: "If I do something for you, you will do something for me." There is a concern for rewards: "What's in it for me?" Throughout both these stages, which generally continue through the primary grades, the emphasis is on external control and on concrete consequences.

Stage 3 finds the child seeking to meet the expectations of others, being a "good" child. Being "nice" is now seen in a broader context. The ability to see situations from the position of other persons helps determine the action a child will take.

At Stage 4, this concern for others now encompasses more of society. The law, rules of the social system, and a desire to do one's duty gain consideration. Avoidance of guilt and social disapproval motivate the child. These last two stages bring us through adolescence. Kohlberg estimated that only 10% of the adult population goes beyond this externally controlled level of development. With Stage 5 comes the maturity of internal commitment to principles of one's own conscience. At this stage, responsibility, the rights of others, and human dignity are also truly understood. Avoidance of self-condemnation is now important. Notice the reminiscence of Maslow's self-actualized person at this level.

Kohlberg (1964, 1972; Muson, 1979) offered a very interesting conclusion resulting from his studies with members of differing cultures, social classes, races, socioeconomic groups, and both sexes. He believed that the differences in moral development between groups are not related to any cultural values or beliefs, but to the amount of social participation and responsibility they have been allowed. The more interaction, the more maturity. The sense of participation and involvement in an overall moral environment heightens the growth of moral conduct much more than direct teaching from the family or other institutions. Kohlberg had some specific suggestions for heightening that involvement.

Favored as a way of fostering progress through the stages is the provision of opportunities for "role taking." This technique allows the child to assume the viewpoint of others or to act out a situation, taking the part of one of the other participants. This can be used in the family or in the classroom. The situations can be real or imagined problems. Acting on the basis of moral reasoning is an important step for children. The sharing of responsibility for decision making and the evaluation of that decision allow moral growth. Adults who use only authority unilaterally teach a child that morality is not for everyone, thereby retarding the youth's movement to higher levels of development.

Throughout his work, Kohlberg often mentioned the establishment of a moral climate or environment. This could be the most critical factor to the child both in the home and in school. By establishing a just environment, one can teach justice. A child who experiences moral, humane behavior from others progresses in moral development. One component of this environment is discipline.

In a review of the literature on outcomes of styles of discipline, Becker (1964) supports Kohlberg's position that the actions of adults and their chosen method of discipline greatly influence moral behavior. The goal is to help children take responsibility for their own behavior. Again, authoritarian or power-assertive techniques fall short of the goal and can create uncooperative, aggressive behaviors. Warm, love-oriented discipline, making use of acceptance, understanding, frequent explanations, and reasoning, results in internalization of moral concepts and cooperative, nonaggressive behavior. Even when authoritarian discipline through fear of physical punishment succeeds in squelching overt hostility, the child's anger remains and is only suppressed temporarily. In establishing a moral environment, adults do not give up their authority; rather, they change it. Instead of authority based on fear, threat, punishment, or rewards, the basis becomes the ability to mediate conflict fairly, to guide and facilitate successful solutions to problems, and to help discover alternatives for evaluation.

Vare (1979) cites unique emotional needs and cognitive developmental potential as the rationale for developing a program of moral education for the gifted. By including both cognitive goals (logical, rational evaluation; critical, analytical thinking) and affective goals (empathy, openness and trust, tolerance or acceptance), Vare builds a confluent model that she believes to be more appropriate to the gifted than other previously used programs. She includes a variety of discussion, action, and investigative strategies and sets them in the classroom, which itself must be a model of a democratic atmosphere of openness, tolerance, and concern for others. The goal of such a program is the development of morally autonomous individuals who will not show the discrepancy between intellectual ability and developed moral reasoning found by Tan-Willman and Gutteridge (1981) in their study of academically gifted adolescents.

Another element important to producing a moral climate is good, open communication. Children can be taught to communicate respectfully and clearly with others. Again, the example of the adults in their environment will have most impact, but there are games and strategies that can be directly taught (see Chapter 8, the section called Strategies for the Feeling or Affective Domain). The family or class meeting described later in this chapter (p. 165) can give interactive opportunities for all group or family members.

Recent findings by Yarrow and Zahn-Waxler (Pines, 1979a) indicate that with the appropriate environment and experiences children as young as 1 year can exhibit behaviors that show concern and empathy for others. Yarrow refers to the behaviors she is researching as altruistic. According to the data, all children seem to have the capacity for early development of altruism, but there are enormous individual differences in their development that increase between 18 and 24 months of age. The most powerful factor in producing altruistic behavior was the intensity with which mothers conveyed the message that their children must not hurt others. Physical restraint or punishment without an explanation of how the children had hurt another did not lead to altruism and was actually counterproductive. The other factor that was related to development of this trait was the mother's altruistic behavior toward the child and others in the family. In a later study it was noted that the patterns of altruism set in this early period remained consistent at least through the age of 7.

Paul MacLean (1978), the brain researcher whose work we reviewed in Chapter 1, believes that altruism and empathy are related to the function of the prefrontal cortex, the newest part of the human brain. He states that if these neural circuits are not brought into play at the critical time of development they may never function properly. Providing a responsive learning environment for our children can now be seen as important to their biological, mental, and emotional growth.

Webb, Meckstroth, and Tolan (1982) point out that one of the most serious problems in gifted children's early concern for moral issues is that their ability to understand the issues cognitively is often far beyond their ability to cope with the issues emotionally. Being told that you are the hope for the world, they comment, puts an awesome burden on a child. We must be aware of their limits in understanding as well as delight in their idealism.

Though Kohlberg and other affective educators have much more to say about creating such an environment, one more element must be included here. Children grow morally only as much as their self-esteem allows. Earlier, this chapter considered the importance of self-esteem. Low self-esteem seems to limit growth in moral development, which in turn affects the child's view and treatment of others (Briggs, 1970; Lickona, 1977; Purkey, 1970; Satir, 1972). The social-emotional growth of our gifted children must be considered by every parent and teacher not only because such growth can sharpen intellect, but even more importantly because such growth becomes the basis for use of that intelligence.

THE DEVELOPING PERSONALITY

Another important theorist in the area of social-emotional development is Erik Erikson. Erikson (1950, 1968) also delineates stages or periods of life to express his view of a growing personality. His eight stages encompass all ages of human life and represent periods during which experiences dictate major adjustments to the social environment and the self. The way each adjustment is handled will affect the way the person adjusts to or handles the next stage of development. While these experiences may be present during most of a person's life, the focus or critical stage is believed to proceed in the following order (Erikson, 1950):

1 *Trust vs. mistrust:* Here we find the roots of inner and outer locus of control. If as infants children experience affection and consistency, they form the belief in a secure world wherein they are effective, they matter. If instead their experience is threatening, unpredictable, stressful, or apathetic, they will believe their world to be untrustworthy, unmanageable, one in which they have no control.

2 *Autonomy vs. shame or doubt:* Toddlers who are allowed to feel pride and success in their experiences of learning to care for themselves gain a sense of self-confidence and self-control. If they are continually limited, criticized, or punished they will believe themselves to be inadequate or bad and experience shame and self-doubt.

3 *Initiative vs. guilt:* As 4- or 5-year-olds begin to explore the world beyond themselves, they discover how the world works and how they affect it. If this exploration is challenging and effective, they learn to deal with people and things in positive ways and gain a strong sense of initiative. If, however, their efforts are always criticized and punished they will feel guilty for self-initiated actions.

4 *Industry vs. inferiority:* From 6 to 11 years of age, children develop numerous skills at home, at school, and in the outside world. An evaluation of competence when compared with peers is important at this time. Mistakes must be viewed as growth experiences if further inquiry and exploration are not to be limited.

5 *Ego identity vs. ego diffusion:* The adolescent explores and affirms belief systems and basic values. If all the roles and beliefs found in their lives cannot be resolved into an integrated identity, the result is what Erikson calls ego diffusion.

6 *Intimacy vs. isolation:* In late adolescence and young adulthood the focus is on developing the ability to share one's self with another and still retain the essential self. The success one has in doing this reflects the success of the previous 5 areas of experience.

7 *Generativity vs. self-absorption:* As adults with the problems of earlier stages at least partially resolved, individuals can now direct their focus toward assisting others, one's own children, social issues, etc. Unsuccessful resolution of earlier issues can result in overconcern for one's health, comfort, and psychological needs.

8 *Integrity vs. despair:* As one views one's life from the perspective of age, the evaluation may reflect meaning, purpose, and satisfaction or a series of bungled attempts, unresolved efforts, and lost opportunities. The attitude of worth will be affected by this evaluation.

Erikson has given us a map of clues we might look to as we work to understand our gifted children. While the intensity with which they approach each of these stages and the resources they bring to bear on meeting the conflicts presented in each developmental period may be of a larger scope, the focus remains. If we are to optimize their development, we must become aware of these points of focus.

In reporting on the relationships between family patterns and development of personality factors in gifted children, Cornell and Grossberg (1987) found that family cohesion, expressiveness, and lower family conflict are associated with better overall adjustment and more favorable cognitive development and school achievement. Cohesion is also highly correlated to fewer problems with discipline or self-control, and, along with family expressiveness, is associated with high self-esteem and lower anxiety as assessed by child self-report and with higher academic self-esteem as assessed by classroom teachers. Cornell and Grossberg point out that, from their data, neither the subject matter of family activities nor the degree of structure imposed on family members is as critical to the child's adjustment as the quality of family interaction. "It would seem more important to the child's adjustment that family members interact cooperatively, with minimal conflict and maximum freedom for personal expression" (p. 64).

ATTITUDES

The gifted individual faces another problem while growing up in the area of attitudes. This is a little like discussing the age-old problem of the chicken and the egg: Which came first? Do the attitudes of others result from the actions of the gifted person, or is the gifted individual's behavior the result of other people's attitudes and prejudices? A little of both is probably true.

The moral teachings of nearly all cultures contain the idea that what you give forth will be returned to you in like kind: Those who view life positively will have positive experiences; those who give generously will receive generously from others; love begets love. This seems to be quite true of attitudes of groups toward each other. Since the literature on attitudes tends to agree that attitudes are learned and therefore educable, we need to be more aware of the attitudes that we and others communicate toward the gifted.

In a thought-provoking article, Margaret Mead (1954) reveals the plight of the gifted child in the American culture of 1954. Her observations are, unfortunately, just as applicable to American culture of today. She observes that Americans have a narrow competitive range; like must compete with like; all success, to be approved, must result from effort, abstinence, and suffering. The very term used to label children who exhibit high intellectual ability, *the gifted,* indicates that their success has been given, not earned. Therefore, giftedness is to be viewed with suspicion, if not outright hostility.

American society also tends to grade or rate attributes rather than allow uniqueness and incomparability. Therefore, we reduce giftedness to an IQ score. By our refusal to recognize special ability in intellectual areas, we waste the ability of uncounted numbers of gifted children (Mead, 1954):

If they learn easily, they are penalized for being bored when they have nothing to do; if they excel in some outstanding way, they are penalized as being conspicuously better than the peer group . . . .The culture tries to make the child with a gift into a one-sided person, to penalize him at every turn, to cause him trouble in making friends and to create conditions conducive to the development of a neurosis. Neither teachers, the parents of other children, nor the child's peers will tolerate a Wunderkind. (p. 213)

As a remedy for such outcomes Mead suggests,

The more diversified, the more complex the activities within which children are encouraged to play a role the better the chance for . . . the gifted child to exercise his special talent . . . much more than rewards and praise, the gifted child needs scope, material on which his imagination can feed, and opportunities to exercise it. He needs inconspicuous access to books, museums, instruments, paints, ideas, a chance to feed himself with the accumulated heritage from the genius of other ages. He needs a chance for contact, however fleeting, perhaps only on television or in a special movie, with those who are masters in the abilities with which he has been specially endowed. And within our sternly Puritan tradition, he may well need also a special sense of stewardship for the talents which he has been given, and explicit moral sanction against selling his birthright for a mess of pottage. (p. 214)

Newland (1976) points out that sensitivity to the educational needs of the gifted is at a disturbingly low level among educators in general. The Advocate Survey appended to the Marland (1972) Report to Congress described pupil personnel workers as apathetic to hostile in their attitudes toward gifted students. Lack of preparation for working with or understanding the needs of this population may account, in part, for this attitude. The negative attitudes of this group must be changed because of their influence on the attitudes of administrators and teachers through inservice and counseling contacts (Martinson, 1972). Through concerned educators at the state and local level dedicated to developing awareness of gifted needs this seems to be changing.

Attitudes of Teachers

The work of Rosenthal (1968) and others gives us a clear picture of how important the teacher's attitude is to the performance of the student. The level of expectation communicated by the teacher can so easily lead to self-fulfilling prophesies. David Aspy's results readily show the power of the teacher to affect the achievement and growth of the child. He found that the perception teachers have of their own ability and worth most significantly relates to the success of their students (Aspy & Bahler, 1975). As an example of the impact of attitude, I relate the following personal experience.

To emphasize the importance of teacher attitude to the achievement and well-being of gifted students, we might share the experience of a very bright young man I have known for several years. After about 4 years of participation in an excellent gifted program modeled after the cooperative learning environment, the young man began a new experience as a high school student. The "program for the gifted" at this high school provided enrichment whenever the teacher found it possible within the context of the regular class. This student found little enriching, but he tried to cope with the new situation as well as he could. Rare were his challenges; he made his grades without much effort. In one course insisting on the memorization of many details, he had to spend extra time prior to any exam so that the details could be reproduced accurately and in proper order.

After one particular exam in which the student felt he had done well, his exam was returned with the failing grade, F. Not used to such outcomes and feeling that something had to be wrong, as he still believed his answers were correct, he approached the teacher. There followed a rather one-sided inquiry into the reasons for the failing mark, and the student became increasingly frustrated and upset as the teacher sat smiling at his discomfort. Finally, the young man demanded to know why he had failed, and the teacher's response was, "Oh, you didn't really get an F." At this point he showed the student an A+ recorded in his grade book—the highest mark in the class. "I just wanted to see how you would take it if you got an F," the teacher commented. The response he got from his student was sharp and alienating. The boy began looking for other ways to meet his needs from that moment on His high school experience had become, with this last indignity, disappointing to say the least. He completed high school by attending university classes arranged for him by the teacher of his former gifted class.

If perception or attitude so powerfully affects students, it would be fruitful to examine the data on attitudes of school personnel toward the gifted. In general, the attitudes held by the majority of school personnel toward gifted individuals are not positive. Although early entry to school is often sought as a solution for precocious children and such early entrants have a record of performing well academically, this practice is favored neither by school administrators nor by teachers (Braga, 1971; Hobson, 1979). In a study to assess the attitudes of kindergarten and first-grade teachers toward academically talented early entrants it was found that these children were assigned the lowest ranks of all candidates to be considered for these classrooms (Jackson, Famiglietti, & Robinson, 1981).

The perception improves, however, among those who have more direct experience and among those who have had courses aimed at understanding and educating gifted children (Justman & Wrightstone, 1956). The Pegnato and Birch study (1959) shows the inability of teachers to identify gifted children accurately. The School Staffing Survey (1969–70) done by the U.S. Office of Education reveals that 57.5% of school administrators in American schools stated that they had no gifted children. These three studies indicate a lack of awareness toward the needs of the gifted and suggest a need for a greater availability of gifted education courses.

Attitudes of teachers toward gifted students affect not only the students and their performance but also the acceptance and effectiveness of the gifted program and the morale of the school as a whole. Dettmer (1985) looked at the attitude differences between regular classroom teachers, teachers of the gifted (who had received training), building principals, and school psychologists on a number of questions concerning gifted students and their education. These were among the statistically significant findings:

- Gifted students were perceived as presenting a threat to teachers by the teachers of the gifted but not by the regular classroom teacher.
- All groups perceived that "gifted youngsters are influenced greatly by the emotional climate in the home or schoolroom" was true, except for the regular classroom whose agreement was significantly less strong.
- The level of agreement differed between teachers of the gifted (strongly agreed) and the regular classroom teacher and principals (agree to uncertain) on the statement, "If tests indicate that a gifted student has acquired the basic skills, it is acceptable to omit usual assignments and alter the requirements."
- Principals believed that gifted children should remain with their age peers for better social adjustment, but teachers of the gifted disagreed.

Dettmer suggests that as unsupportive attitudes or misinformation among the school staff can result in the debilitation of the education of gifted students, school districts would do well to prepare all staff members through inservice in gifted education.

Specifically, Weiner and O'Shea (1963) found that the higher the level of education attained by university students, teachers, or administrators, the more accepting they were of the gifted individual. Attitudes of teachers who work with the gifted are more favorable than those who do not. Also, university students who had attended lectures on the gifted displayed more favorable attitudes. In another study, Weiner (1968) reported that school psychologists and psychometrists experienced with the gifted favored them significantly more than those with no experience. An attitude survey administered to faculty of five major universities indicated a strong positive attitude toward gifted education, with those identifying themselves as previous participants in programs for the gifted being the most positive (Weiss & Gallagher, 1980).

Attitudes of Peers

While the attitudes of peers, at least during elementary school, are usually positive, teachers, parents, and administrators fear elitism and snobbishness. In a study by Mills (1973), experience with the gifted and a background in gifted education again related to attitudes of acceptance. Younger respondents from 10 to 29 years of age were less sympathetic than those 30 to 39 years old. Blacks and Chicanos were less favorable than Caucasians. The higher people rated themselves in mental ability, the more favorable they tended to be toward gifted children. Teachers of regular classes, education administrators, community leaders, and lay public all showed significantly unfavorable attitudes toward the gifted. Instruction and experience seem to be the most successful ways to improve attitudes. The impact these attitudes have on gifted individuals makes it necessary to consider these results seriously.

Newland (1976) feels that the gifted need to be taught attitudes of commitment, service, continuous learning, and discovery or truth seeking. He believes that these attitudes come naturally to the gifted, but that they have been inhibited or actually blocked by the structure of the schools toward conformity and their toleration of underachievement.

It seems, then, that the power of attitudes in society and specifically within the educational community may be a prime force in furthering or denying educational opportunities for our gifted children.

INTEGRATING COGNITIVE, SOCIAL-EMOTIONAL, PHYSICAL, AND INTUITIVE GROWTH

While we cannot be assured that persons with high levels of cognitive development develop equally well socially, emotionally, physically, and intuitively, we can make use of their cognitive ability to facilitate the other skills and thereby strengthen their intellect. The degree to which the other abilities have been nurtured determines the ability to think at high levels. The integration of these functions is necessary to actualize the potential of any one function.

Brain researchers recognize hemispheric specialization. That is to say, the left side of the brain is primarily responsible for logical, analytic, linear thought including language, while the right side is primarily involved in spatial, holistic, more analogous, or intuitive types of functions, as described in Chapter 1. If necessary, each hemisphere could replicate the functions of the opposite side. But unless such a need exists, and retraining occurs, the specialization pattern will be followed. Although the majority of the population has left-right brain functioning operable as cited, in some cases, as evidenced by left-handedness or ambidexterity, the reverse may be true. In all cases, when the brain functions normally regardless of the side of functioning, specialization does occur (Bogen, 1975; Gazzanega, 1975; Krashen, 1975; Nebes, 1975; Ornstein, 1972).

This apparent separation is the strongest argument for integration of the cognitive/physical and the affective/intuitive functions. For, while specialization exists, there are more connectors between brain hemispheres than from the brain to any other part of the human body. The obvious need for integration is apparent even in the structure of the brain itself. According to brain research, mammalian sensory systems must be used in facilitating environments if normal development is to occur (Blakemore, 1974). Haggard (1957) found that early exclusive emphasis or focus on cognitive (left brain) performance can have noticeable attitudinal consequences as well. Such children developed competitive, hostile attitudes toward their peers and disdain for adults in order to maintain their position of intellectual superiority.

In order to optimize the development of all individuals, that they might truly realize their potential and discover their authentic selves, we must look for an integrated approach both at home and at school.

Assuring Integrated Growth

The family plays an important role in creating integrated growth. Newland (1976) comments that all social traits reflect family patterns. Satir (1972) found that, as problem children come from problem families, healthy, open, growing children come from nurturing families. While her work began with therapeutic counseling for problem families, she has developed a framework to guide families who seek to develop family structures that can enhance the growth of each family member. Such families are productive of highly functional, well-integrated children. In her ideal family, Satir summarizes,

> We have adults who clearly show their own uniqueness, who demonstrate their power, who clearly show their sexuality, who demonstrate their ability to share through understanding, kindness and affection, who use their common sense, who are realistic and responsible. (p. 228)

She believes such a family is an open system. This is in opposition to a closed system where self-worth is secondary to power and performance, where rules are created and enforced by the boss (usually father), who knows what is best for all, and where change is resisted for there is only one way to do things—the right way. Satir believes that human beings cannot flourish in a closed system; they may barely exist. We are concerned with more than just existing. We are discussing optimizing human potential to help our children become self-actualizing.

In his study of self-actualizing people, Maslow (1968) conceptualized a hierarchy of human needs that he used to explain how emotional development is facilitated or inhibited. According to this hierarchy, human energy is used to provide for needs at six levels: basic physical needs, safety needs, love and belonging needs, needs for self-esteem, self-actualization, and transcendence. If needs at any one level remain unmet, energies will be drained off at that level, inhibiting further progress and causing overemphasis on that need level. Such limitation would make attainment of the integrated person difficult. Awareness of need levels can provide parents with a model for directing family and home efforts toward healthy, integrated development. It is important to note that as growth occurs individuals may be operating on several levels at the same time with more or less emphasis. Under certain circumstances and under differing conditions, one may regress or progress through the various levels of need.

As the six need levels identified by Maslow may provide a framework for working with integrated development in the home, they should also be introduced into classrooms. While the goal of self-actualization has not been actively sought in most school systems, it has for decades been a declared goal in most public schools' philosophical statements of purpose. Through the work of educators such as George Brown (1971) at the University of California at Santa Barbara, the implementation of such goals becomes a reality.

Using Maslow's hierarchy as a framework, let us look at how such a program might be structured to assure integrated growth for gifted individuals. As their ability in cognitive areas develops to higher levels, the potential for development of feeling and intuitive areas also grows.

Level 1—Basic Physical Needs

At Home.   The first level provides for the basic physical necessities to support life. Human survival depends primarily on food, clothing, and shelter. Most families clearly provide for these necessities, and modern societies attempt to subsidize those who cannot. During inadequate provision for survival, energies focus totally at this level until such needs are at least minimally met.

Of less intensity than the needs for food and shelter, but typical of gifted children and of concern to their parents, is the high energy level and the need for less sleep these children exhibit. Parents may find it helpful to engage their child in more complex activities earlier, e.g., household responsibilities, organized play groups, and sports.

At School.   These basic physical needs are usually met, at least minimally, by the home. In some low socioeconomic areas, however, such provisions for basic needs may not be available. In these cases the school, as an agent of society, has instituted free lunch programs and subsidized nutrition periods. Although not always successful or sensitive to the population they seek to serve, such programs aim to meet needs at this primary level.

Teachers may wish to examine their classrooms for opportunities to meet needs at this level. Some children have more energy to spend on learning when provided additional nourishment. There are those in every classroom who can accomplish more, with a higher level of concentration, if they can munch on a handful of raisins or a few carrot sticks in the process. Such additions to classrooms need not be treated as rewards or wasted by misuse if children have proper explanations of purpose and need. When classrooms model respect for individual needs and concern for growth, proper use of healthy treats can be self-directed.

For those students exhibiting high energy as part of their physical characteristics the classroom must provide additional stimulation as an outlet. Active learning, rather than the traditional tools for learning such as demonstrations and paperwork, will be the rule for these children.

Level 2—Safety Needs

At Home.   The second level does not so clearly concern all families. At this level we find provisions for safety needs. By this we mean physical as well as psychological or emotional safety. Most will agree on the need for physical safety in a family. When this is missing, the results are obvious, and intervention is seen as desirable. However, the lack of emotional safety for a family or family member is not so clearly recognizable. Some families use threat and fear as control strategies. They regulate behavior by such tactics. In some cases the "different" member of the family becomes the scapegoat, and the safety needs of this individual go unfulfilled. Unless this deficit results in physical problems (e.g., psychosomatic illness) or in acting out or antisocial behavior, modern society does not allow intervention. A significant number of people find it necessary to focus an unproductive quantity of their energy on the safety-needs level.

At School.   Classrooms most often offend the safety-needs level. The reward-punishment-competition model used by so many educators to elicit student motivation toward school-related tasks forces children to spend a great deal of energy ensuring their own psychological safety. According to the work of Feldhusen and Klausmeier (1962), superior mental ability may make it possible for a child to assess more adequately the real danger in any threatening object, situation, or person. Children of low or average IQ may show greater anxiety and generalized fear because of their limited intellectual capacity to evaluate the threat or danger. Possibly a more anxious low or average IQ child is less free to respond to the teacher, the learning material, and the learning situation. Whether the child is bright or less able, this study shows that, rather than providing drive or motivation to learn, anxiety in the classroom is debilitating and interferes with the learning process.

Add to these factors the attitudes previously discussed that educators often hold toward gifted children. Include the sensitivity of these atypical learners to their environment, and we have a picture that points clearly to an expenditure of energy at this level that gifted children can ill afford.

To ensure your program against such wasteful and unnecessary practices, consider these steps that can be taken: Provide inservice on educating the gifted child for *all* teachers within your school setting. The more teachers or administrators know about gifted children and their special needs, the more favorable will be the attitudes and actions directed toward them. Provide accessible information on alternatives for classroom organization and management. It is likely that we will continue to teach as we have been taught unless we become familiar with other approaches. We have now developed strategies and patterns of organization that are exciting and nurturing for human growth that were not available 10 years ago. As these ideas are perfected, they must be made known to classroom teachers and building administrators.

Climates that promote psychological safety must also consider the characteristic of perfectionism often exhibited by gifted children. Psychological safety requires reduced tension and stress, if children are to perform to their own satisfaction. For the gifted, external or self-imposed pressure for achievement can become unreasonable. Webb, Meckstroth, and Tolan (1982) feel that such pressure may be one of the major causes of depression among gifted youngsters. An environment where risk taking is valued, in which trust is developed, and where mistakes are seen as cues to aid learning relieves students of the need to be perfect.

All educators in decision-making positions must seek out information to aid in the establishment of more powerful, more humane learning environments to fulfill these safety needs. We look at some of these strategies in Chapter 8.

Level 3—Love and Belonging Needs

Human beings need to love and to feel loved, to be in physical contact with one another, to associate with others, and to participate in groups and organizations.

At Home.   This level establishes a foundation of love and caring that influences how each family member views the others and operates in the world. Feeling affection is important: Affection felt and shared is even more fulfilling for human needs. Boys and girls will benefit from learning about themselves and others as loving beings. Families model this love and caring. While gifted children may be able to analyze the problems within family patterns lacking strong love relationships, they, as much as the more typical individual, still establish patterns for themselves similar to those the family displays. Families must provide sufficient opportunities for development of this level. Nurturing families fit quite naturally into this area. All humans must feel that they matter, that there is a group or a person with whom they can identify. Belonging is a reciprocal arrangement. It does not occur simply by proximity. There must be give and take, respect, and appreciation, as well as some degree of opportunity to share in movement toward a common goal. Many families fail to give adequate time or concern toward providing experiences for all members to meet their needs at this level. Group activities, as well as respect for individual pursuits, must be provided. On occasion, individuals attempt to meet belonging needs outside the family. This can be a positive growth process if not used just to compensate for family deficits. Some ways of ensuring growth beyond this level would include

- Involvement in planning and carrying out family trips or activities.
- Accepting each person as worthy, listening to each, responding to each.

- Expressing pleasure for accomplishments of each member without comparison.
- Cooperative planning and decision making in so far as each member is able.
- Open communication between family members.
- Cooperative action with each person's contribution seen as valuable to the whole family.
- Allowance of time to develop understanding and empathy among family members.

At School.   Here again schools can contribute significantly to meeting human belonging needs. Every classroom would certainly benefit through establishment of a wealth of various resources. What better resource than the children themselves? Gifted children often bring to the learning situation a vast quantity and diversity of knowledge and comprehension. They can often contribute highly creative ways to apply such knowledge. The teacher loses out as much as the children if these resources remain untapped.

To assure a rich learning environment, teachers should establish a climate of trust within the classroom that allows each child to see each other child as a person instead of the object a stranger becomes. Where such a climate exists, learners can learn from each other and from the environment as well as from the teacher.

Often gifted children see themselves as different, alien, not belonging to the group. The label itself may create problems between these children and others in the classroom. By identifying with the label these children may feel isolated and unnoticed for any reason other than their ability level. Teachers must make sure that they relate to these children in other ways, rather than through their level of achievement. They must feel they are valuable in ways other than just their giftedness.

Another way teachers may promote belonging needs among gifted students is to ensure that, for at least part of the school experience, the gifted spend time with their intellectual peer group. While there often has been resistance to such placement, especially when it means leaving the age-alike group, a study by Colangelo and Kelly (1983) advised schools to place less concern on age-peer rejection when gifted programs are implemented and more focus on acceptance by intellectual peers. When we ask gifted students to remain with their age peers as academic models in the classroom, are we so sure they wish to always be models? Wouldn't they rather belong?

Belonging does not just occur. Children, as adults, easily establish categories for people. "He is my friend," "They are different than we are," "She is stuck-up," "They're just too stupid," "She thinks she's so smart" represent some of the unfortunate labeling activities that form categories. People then become objects within the category, and they lose their uniqueness. Newland (1976) comments that when gifted and nongifted children are taught together, we cannot expect grouping alone to ensure knowledge and understanding of each for the other. There must be interpersonal interaction. And this must be a priority for the teacher. It becomes as important to acknowledge and respect the differences between these groups as it does to look at the similarities. Newland urges that democracy not be seen as egalitarian conformity. To counter a movement toward exclusion or conformity, the teacher must take deliberate action to set up situations in which children can experience each other as unique individuals and as contributing, valuable people. When teachers do not value these activities enough to include them in their daily classroom routine, children will spend a great deal of unnecessary energy seeking fulfillment of Level 3 needs.

Level 4—Needs for Self-Esteem

At Home and at School.   Children need positive responses from others to provide a sense of well-being and self-satisfaction. Responses received by gifted children are often less than positive and can lower their view of themselves. Statements such as, "If you are so gifted figure it out," "Of course you don't need any help, you know everything," or "You're capable of better work than that" are unlikely to support a positive view of self.

Acknowledgment is another response often missing for the gifted child. They are expected to accomplish the task, create a solution, or come up with a new idea. It is too easy to take their achievements for granted. Personal, individual recognition of their work, their originality, and their efforts is essential and should be shared by teachers and students on a regular basis.

When the three lower level needs are met, the child can deal with more abstract thinking skills, release more creativity, and become more self-directed. While this area will require an ongoing expenditure of energy, attention to needs in this area makes the cognitive activities of learning and the affective activities of healthy living possible. Classrooms do not play the same role as the home in this need area. At this level different facets of the child will be revealed and perfected. With gifted children this can be critical. Forced to restrict their inquiry and experiences to already known areas of competence for fear of loss of esteem or even love, their wasted potential will be extensive. By encouraging diverse pursuits, internal validation, and the idea that mistakes provide learning experiences, teachers will furnish the opportunity for fulfillment at this need level.

At this level energy can also be released to engage in the risktaking required for learning. Teachers and parents alike expect children to enter classrooms ready to learn. Only if the needs at the previous three levels have been adequately met will this be possible. Energy too heavily focused in survival, safety, or belonging areas will make energy for learning or creative activity at this fourth level unavailable.

Level 5—Needs for Self-Actualization

At Home and at School.   The fifth level relates to the self-actualization needs of humans. At this level Maslow's research makes its greatest contribution. While we may work in several levels simultaneously or focus on different levels at different times, we ultimately reach our highest potential development at this level. Gifted children have tremendous potential toward self-actualization. Our society benefits from their progress toward self-actualization as do they themselves. The greatest contributions to our culture have come from individuals who developed their potential at all levels of functioning, allowing them to integrate all ways of knowing, to risk taking unknown or unpopular stands, and to implement the insights their expanding beliefs made possible. The classroom that values, encourages, and provides opportunity for diversity, self-exploration, introspection, interaction, and quiet contemplation is the classroom where self-actualization will likely occur.

In addition to the characteristics of the self-actualizing person from Maslow's (1971) work mentioned at the beginning of this chapter, the concept expands with Morris's (1966) description of *awareness of self:* (a) self as a choosing agent, unable to avoid choosing his or her way through life; (b) self as a free agent, free to set the goals for his or her own life; (c) self as a responsible agent, accountable for the choices made and how he or she lives those choices. Communicating these propositions becomes the major task of educators if they desire to nurture self-actualization. Teachers must arrange learning situations so that the truth of these ideas is experienced by each individual. For gifted individuals with heightened awareness and greater capacity for growth, this educational opportunity becomes critical.

Maslow (1971) suggests these clues for developing self-actualization:

1 Experience each moment fully, vividly, and with full concentration.
2 Think of life as a process of choices, your choices.
3 Listen to your Self; trust your inner voice.
4 Take responsibility for yourself.
5 Dare to be different, nonconforming, real.
6 Do what you do with joy, and do it well.
7 Set up conditions that will allow more peak experiences; perceive the world and life positively.
8 Open up to yourself, identify your defenses, and find the courage to give them up.

The goal is to have access to all of your life, all of your potential, to be who you are.

Transcendence: a joyous process.

Level 6—Needs for Transcendence

Had Maslow lived another decade, he would have added a sixth level. He had already begun an inquiry into the need and meaning of this next level, which he called *transcendence*. He saw it as "the very highest and most inclusive or holistic level of human consciousness, behaving and relating, as ends, rather than as means, to oneself, to significant others, to human beings in general, to other species, to nature, and to the cosmos" (Maslow, 1971, p. 279). While Maslow could not complete his work at the sixth level, many others have now begun to explore this apex—possibly the level that reflects the true meaning of human existence.

The transcendence level includes the nurture of intuitive abilities. To create a world where the oneness of all being is understood and practiced, where the unity with and interdependence of all parts of the cosmos are valued and provide the basis for action, is a noble undertaking. We can live most effectively if we transcend the self by becoming the most each of us can be and recognizing and valuing this in others while, underlying the uniqueness, we experience the connectedness.

At Home. From the clues we have, families in which individual members seek growth toward transcendence provide the most impact on the development of this level of growth. Allowing the expression of ideas and observations of unusual physical or psychic nature is important. Providing an open forum for discussion and experience with such events will nurture the transcendence level.

In working in the area of transcendence, each family member will likely have a personal commitment toward a particular path, but some areas available for group exploration might be concentration exercises, meditation, and biofeedback training. Any family activities that put the child in close communication with nature, such as sailing, hiking, or camping, can be used as experiences leading to transcendence. While in the peaceful beauty of nature, we should take time to sit quietly, observe, appreciate, and sense the unity with all life that such places and moments can bring. Leading children to discover their transcendence level can be a joyous process, beginning with the attitudes the parent shares.

High levels of developed cognitive ability do not guarantee high levels of affective or emotional development. While the capabilities exist, opportunities to develop them must be made part of the child's experience. One very early trait in the emotional growth of gifted children is their intense sense of justice and unwavering idealism. The parent of a gifted child will soon experience the futile effort of explaining why injustice so often exists. In attempting to convince my children that "the world just isn't fair," I had limited success. "If it isn't, it should be, and why aren't you (the adult) doing something about it?" they responded. To try to discuss with a 3-year-old how one person could affect only a limited amount of inequity was frustrating for both of us. My reasons were not acceptable to my son's world view. The sense of justice is tremendously valuable to society and beautiful in its motivating power for humanistic action. We must guide the idealism of children so that they do not become so frustrated that they lose it early and replace it with cynicism or the sense of being powerless. Parents need to be alert in seeking alternatives with the child when solutions that seem inequitable are posed. A real sharing of problem solving at the child's level of understanding cannot begin too early. Hollingworth (1926) points out that gifted children may be readily disciplined by appeals to reason, presentation of alternative views, modeling, and consistency of expressed values. With this approach, gifted children may keep their sense of justice intact.

Some families have a trying situation to overcome in order to maintain family unity. This situation occurs when one sibling is identified as gifted while another is not. It may be very difficult for the more typical child to understand the difference, and special consideration of the needs of both should prevail. The situation is analogous to having one child recognized for athletic ability or artistic talent while the other child is seen as only average in these abilties. The family must clearly recognize the ability of the identified child and just as clearly recognize whatever abilities the other child shows in other areas. A family that values intellectual functions over other human abilities will communicate that bias to less able children. The human and interpersonal consequences will be difficult for all concerned. Give all family members a chance to be respected and valued for their own unique abilities.

In our family, we organized family councils to provide the arena for exposing perceived inequities perpetrated by either parents or siblings. There we sought alternative solutions that could better meet the needs of all concerned. At first, we held council once a week, but later we found that calling council on demand of any family member better served all our needs. I often went to our meetings, at the beginning, with the solution to a problem I planned to clear up already thought out. My goal was to convince the others, my son, my daughter, and my husband, that I was right. This approach was not useful. I soon became aware that the others often had better solutions that were far easier to carry out because all felt committed toward the plan they had helped design. All kinds of problems came before our group, from mother's need for neat and tidy rooms to sister's perceived harassment at the hands of an unaware brother. Questions of allowance, homework, bedtime, house chores, teacher attitudes, and comfort of visiting relatives all were handled with serious and cooperative planning. Through the years the council served to lessen the powerlessness, to increase the comfort level of family members, and generally to provide us all with excellent practice in developing our problem-solving skills, creative thinking abilities, and feelings of caring. Family councils became a meaningful way to communicate and share within the family. I highly recommend them, especially for families who live with gifted children.

At School. Establishing this sense of unity in a classroom begins with what Weinhold (1976) calls *transpersonal communication.*

> Transpersonal communication is designed to help people to trust the validity of their personal experiences and accept what they learn from these experiences as their best source of wisdom and truth. This includes both thinking and feeling processes. It teaches people to play hunches, use their intuition and follow their thoughts and feelings rather than direct them in predetermined ways. (p. 124)

Any of the strategies for open communication offered in Chapter 8 (p. 382) can begin this process. Remember that the attitudes and beliefs a teacher has about teaching and learning have even more effect than the techniques used. A teacher must first believe in self-evolving education—that the process of self-discovery is central to any learning. As is true for parents, teachers teach more from who they are and what actions stem from their beliefs than from what they know. Combs (1969) finds that certain belief systems relate to effective teachers. Among these are beliefs about the nature of people, themselves and their ability, what their purposes are, their area of knowledge, and their approaches to teaching. We discuss this information in Chapter 11 (p. 534), Teachers of the Gifted—At School. The teacher has the most influence on creating the climate in the classroom, and a favorable climate must exist for growth toward transcendence to occur.

The development of an integrated person is clearly a complex process. In cases where home and school lend support in the same areas, growth will be significant. To ensure that the parent and teacher do support similar areas, each must be conscious of the environment the other creates for the child. With this knowledge, they will both be able to provide support and experiences when they are needed. A teacher can initiate this type of communication more easily than a parent. Providing deliberate contact points, meetings, and conferences for parental involvement in the school program assures both the teacher and the parent that the child's development will proceed effectively. The extra effort made to encourage parent involvement or at least the opportunity for contact will pay off handsomely from the educational standpoint. Many gifted programs have survived only because of adamant parent support. Many are dramatically enriched by parent participation.

A parent who does not receive communication from the school has ways to seek involvement. Becoming informed about the community, the district, and gifted education in general could be the first step. Seeking other parents for support and for sharing resources will be valuable to both the parent and the children. Offering informed support to the children's program can do more to improve the quality of their experience than any criticism the parent may offer. Most school personnel have the same goals for the children as the parents. A cooperative effort may help both succeed in providing the quality educational program all desire.

This chapter has focused primarily on the social-emotional and integrative growth of gifted children. The origins of social-emotional development are to be found very early in the child's interaction with the world. The child's evolving self-concept critically influences social-emotional development. We found that both the concept of self and moral development can facilitate or inhibit intellectual growth. For gifted children, the social-emotional aspects of growth present special problems.

Our concern for optimal development and appropriate educational opportunities for gifted children requires that we consider the effect of attitudes on this process. The attitudes of both gifted people and those who work and live with them were seen to affect their development significantly. It is important to integrate growth in all of the human functions if we are to optimize the development of intelligence. Even cognitive function is limited if integration of the other areas is left to chance. Both homes and schools have an important part to play in this integration. Later chapters will present strategies to aid in making this process more effective.

In Part II, the concerns and involvement of schools in educating gifted children become the major focus. Although the information will be most useful in the classroom, administrative offices, and by those educators who are concerned about educational services for gifted individuals, the parent as a cooperative, supportive resource remains a critical factor in the process of growing up gifted.

Questions Often Asked

1. How do you identify highly gifted children, and how do they differ from less gifted children?

The highly gifted are usually identified by exceptionally high levels of performance on school work, intelligence tests, or achievement tests. Different districts have different criteria for their identification and even the IQ score used may range from 140 to 165, or even 180. The highly gifted seem to have intense and abundant energy, high levels of curiosity, advanced concept development, and a large vocabulary that seems to develop very early. They can appear very mature at one moment and typically childlike the next. They differ from less gifted children every bit as much as they differ from average learners. They have many of the same characteristics and problems of gifted children but to a higher degree. For example, gifted children have difficulty finding peers who think as they do and often choose to be with older children; highly gifted children have even more difficulty and may find even older children unable to understand their concerns.

2. Are gifted children as advanced emotionally as they are cognitively?

Sometimes, but often the development pattern will allow one area to advance and then the other. There is no guarantee that a very bright child will be socially or emotionally mature. However, gifted children can develop emotional levels rapidly, for they can understand, empathize with others, and express their own feelings well when given any opportunity and a little guidance.

3. Why would gifted children have low self-concepts? They seem to have everything.

Not all do; however, it is not uncommon for gifted children to have an ideal of what they think they should be that does not match what they think they are. Often their physical ability has not caught up with their mental ability, and they cannot accomplish the things they want to in the way they want. Sometimes the signals they receive from others add to this lower self-image. When they still have questions to ask and other children do not, they can interpret that to mean that they do not understand as well as others. When they say something and other children groan or say "Not that again," they may believe they have said something dumb or inappropriate. Others, assuming that gifted children know how exceptional an idea or product they are working on is, will criticize the idea or product when meaning to be helpful. Part of the low self-concept of gifted children is from just feeling different; constantly feeling different can make people doubt themselves after a while. There are many reasons, some involving outside pressure, some involving the child's pressure internally, but the result can be never meeting one's own standards, never being good enough. It is all too common among gifted children that what they see and what others see are just not the same.

4. Why do some teachers, principals, and other school personnel seem to have negative attitudes toward gifted students?

Unfortunately studies show that this is too often true. Gifted children do not fit easily into the structure of most schools and classrooms. Because they can be 2 to 8 years ahead of the curriculum offered at any grade level, they make it very hard for a teacher of 20 to 30 other children to find appropriate curricular experiences for them. They often question and seek more information about ideas than the teacher is prepared to give. This can be seen as a challenge to the teacher's authority. They may refuse to do work that they consider boring or to repeat or practice lessons if they already understand the material. In classrooms where everyone is expected to do much the same work and cover the same material, this can be seen as a real problem. Gifted children can be demanding, challenging, intense, critical, oversensitive, highly verbal, and physically active, and they can devour material rapidly. None of these traits are in and of themselves problems, but they can present real problems for teachers who are not prepared to meet these needs. Some teachers do not know what to do with these youngsters and feel incompetent and threatened by them. For administrators gifted children present needs for special services. This may be perceived as pressure on an already tight budget or cause special arrangements to be made that seem unnecessary. Fortunately, these attitudes can be changed with inservice in gifted education.

5. Are most gifted children hyperactive?

Most gifted children have high levels of energy; they require less sleep, and they are very, very curious. These traits can look like hyperactivity, but there is a difference. The energy of a gifted child is focused, directed, and intense. The energy of a hyperactive child is diffuse, random, and sporadic. Gifted children can attend to an activity of their interest for long periods of time; hyperactive children cannot. The brighter the child, the more the energy may look excessive.

6. Is it alright for a gifted child to be a loner?

Gifted children commonly seek times to be alone. Maslow gives the need for times of isolation as one to the characteristics of self-actualizing people. If, however, the child is seeking isolation as an escape from teasing, criticism, or unfair treatment, that can be a problem. Gifted children need to be taught skills of communicating with others and need help in understanding how to be accepting toward and accepted by others. Choosing to be alone is different from being alone because of being rejected. A consistent pattern of isolation should be questioned. All human beings need love, affection, and belonging.

7. *What can I do for a child who is too much of a perfectionist?*

The first thing is to acknowlege that whatever perfectionistic children perceive to be inadequate is truly their perception. My experience has been that children do not benefit from being told that something they think is awful actually is very good, even if I think it is. Instead of,

Child: "This is just dumb. I made a mess of it."
Parent/Teacher: "Oh no, it really is quite good,"

which results in the child believing that you either do not see the problem, you are insincere, or you have very low standards try,

Child: "This is just dumb. I made a mess of it."
Parent/Teacher: "I can see you are not satisfied with the way that turned out. What would you like it to be that it isn't?"

This gives you a chance of understanding what the child sees as a problem and perhaps providing additional resources or direction.

One of the best ways to aid a child to handle perfectionism is to discuss some of the problems you have faced and the strategies you have used to work on your own perfectionist need. Most parents of gifted children and teachers attracted to working with them have had or are having similar problems. Children like to hear how we solve problems we have that are similar to theirs.

II. The School and the Gifted Individual

A RATIONALE FOR GIFTED EDUCATION

So many times those who believe that gifted children do not need special provisions confront those of us who are concerned about the education of the gifted. Many sincerely feel that truly gifted children will remain gifted and fulfill their educational needs on their own. Others feel that if teachers are doing their job, the gifted should be able to get by without the special attention that other atypical learners need. How do we answer those people who refuse to consider special education for the gifted, who block any attempt to provide programs as undemocratic, elitist, or wasteful? There are several ideas we must ask them to consider:

1 Giftedness arises from an interactive process that involves challenges from the environment stimulating and bringing forth innate capabilities and processes. Although they are most easily affected during the early years, these innate mechanisms require challenge throughout the individual's lifetime for high levels of actualization to result. As we saw in Chapter 3, we either progress or regress; stability is not possible. Just to retain giftedness, not to mention furthering the potential, gifted children must participate in programs appropriate to their level of development.

2 Jefferson once said, "There is nothing more unequal than equal treatment of unequal people." Our political and social system is based on democratic principles. The school, as an extension of those principles, purports to provide an equal educational opportunity for all children to develop to their fullest potential. It is then undemocratic to refuse to allow gifted children the right to educational experiences appropriate to their level of development. We do not ask retarded children to work in the same programs and to progress through the same curricula as the more typical learners. How, then, can we justify holding back the gifted student? It would be unjust to require all individuals to perform the same tasks at the same level. Offering all individuals opportunities at only one level with the assumption that this level will meet the needs of all is just as unfair. For truly equal opportunity, a variety of learning experiences must be available at many levels so that all youths can develop those skills and abilities they choose to their level of ability.

We would not ask children who are not yet advanced to the normative level to work there, limiting their growth by creating a situation from which they cannot gain understanding or advance educationally. Neither should we ask advanced students to bide their time and limit their growth by working at a normative level. Each person has the right to learn and to be provided opportunities and challenges for learning at the most appropriate level where growth proceeds most efficiently.

3 When human beings are limited and restricted in their development, when they are not allowed to move, or to reach beyond, they often

become bored, frustrated, and angry. There is physical and psychological pain in being thwarted, discouraged, and diminished as a person. To have ability, to feel power you are never allowed to use, can become traumatic if continued. Terman (1925) viewed the gifted as the largest group of underachievers in education; subsequent research shows that gifted children still lack educational care. At present, slightly over one-half of the possible gifted learners in the United States are reported to be receiving education appropriate to their needs (Sisk, 1987).

4 In the past there has been much reference to the term *elitism* when referring to education for gifted individuals, but I believe the problem lies in the meaning of the word. If one means "the chosen ones or the select group," as though the existence of giftedness came only as a bestowing of riches or honor from a higher authority, we might justifiably treat such individuals as an already accomplished population who need only try and their every wish or thought will be fulfilled. Such individuals would, of course, need no help. They could get along quite well with their already fully functioning gift.

However, if we mean "a group chosen because of some special skill or ability, which, if fostered, could become truly outstanding (such as athletic prowess, musical talent, or business acumen)," I believe elitism to be entirely justifiable and proper for the benefit of society as a whole. To be superior to others in physical abilities (e.g., boxers, runners, skaters, tennis players) or artistic abilities (e.g., pianists, photographers, conductors, actors) is valued and rewarded in our society. Everyone accepts the idea that such athletes and artists work or train continuously; they, therefore, earn their prestige and status. Not so with intellectual ability. Often viewed with suspicion, considered by some a threat, assumed by many to derive ability from mystical sources, those who possess giftedness are accused of trying to develop elitism even when appropriate educational opportunity is all they seek. Society does not feel personal threat from those accomplished in physical or artistic areas, but often exhibits this reaction in the presence of intellectual ability. Can we continue to justify elitism for some as beneficial to our society, while we fear it in others? Does our society have more need for physical and artistic ability than for intellectual ability? Curiously, the establishment of adequate programs for the gifted results not in the type of snobbishness feared, but in improved social relations and better attitudes of the gifted toward themselves and others (Gallagher, 1966).

Society gains from the advancement of all abilities and from the highest development of all of its members, whatever their strengths. That which nurtures and actualizes each individual nourishes us as a society.

5 Gifted youngsters very soon discover that their ideas and interests are quite different from those of their age-mates. They usually enter school having already developed many of their basic skills. Almost from the day

they start school they begin to sense isolation, for others consider them different. As the roots of a poor self-concept become established, the school often does nothing, for its curriculum and organization are not sufficiently individualized. Most schools seek to develop skills that allow participation in society, not the re-creation of that society. Traditional education must be modified. A colleague once said, "Intellectually, they need someone to play chess with, while emotionally they may need someone with whom they can climb trees."

6 When the needs of the gifted are considered and the educational program is designed to meet these needs, these students make significant gains in achievement, and their sense of competence and well-being return. Gifted children in special programs learn to work more efficiently; they develop good problem-solving skills and see solutions from many viewpoints. They experience concepts and materials in a dynamic relationship, and they can use their vast amount of knowledge to serve as a background for unlimited learning.

7 Contributions to society in all areas of human endeavor come in over-weighted proportions from this population of individuals. Society will need the gifted adult to play a far more demanding and innovative role than that required of the more typical learner. We need enough integrated, highly functioning persons to carry out those tasks that will lead us to a satisfying, fulfilling future. Part II proceeds from this view of individual and societal needs.

5. Programs for the Gifted

This chapter will provide the reader with

- Information on the status of gifted programs and the support they receive.
- A discussion of the organization of programs for gifted learners.
- Goals of a gifted program.
- The role of the administrator/coordinator.
- Information of the advantages and disadvantages of types of structures for programs for the gifted.
- A presentation of some of the program models now being used.
- A matrix to help guide you in the selection of program alternatives.
- Resources and ideas for using the community in a program for gifted learners.
- A discussion and planning guide for evaluating gifted programs.
- A guide for a written plan.

The relatively few gifted students who have had the advantage of special programs have shown remarkable improvements in self-understanding and in ability to relate well to others, as well as in improved academic and creative performance. The programs have not produced arrogant, selfish snobs; special programs have extended a sense of reality, wholesome humility, self-respect and respect for others. A good program for the gifted increases their involvement and interest in learning through the reduction of the irrelevant and redundant.

—SIDNEY P. MARLAND

GIFTED PROGRAMS YESTERDAY AND TODAY

Organizing a program that will deliver educational services to gifted learners is one of the most complex, most researched, and least clarified areas of gifted education. The administrative structure is critical to the success of the gifted program. It will reflect the commitment of the school to either expand or inhibit the opportunities for learning experienced by the gifted individual.

We have seen the importance of continuous stimulation to optimal development and have discussed some of the unique learning needs of this population. Let us look at how the school program deals with these needs.

In most traditional classrooms, the teacher groups the students into several ability groups. The educational achievement of any normal, chronologically age-grouped class ranges over 4 to 8 years, depending on the grade level. The range broadens as children progress from kindergarten to sixth grade. Because the range of achievement can be so vast, the teacher plans the instructional program for the average, at-grade-level learner. Some modification is made for the bottom group and for the top group, but most instruction falls within the normal range. For the very slow learners remediation programs, often mandated by the state and well financed, are available in most schools. Classes for the learner found at the bottom 2% of the intelligence scale will provide special educational modifications for those students whose needs for a different learning program are obvious. This provision is accepted and expected by both parent and educator alike.

For the slow student, part-time resource rooms will be available, as well as special tutors or special classrooms where these students receive appropriate educational programs until they are able to keep pace with the average learner. The time spent in the special educational facility is dependent on the level of need the student exhibits. In either case, the regular classroom is expected to provide for only part of the program this atypical learner needs.

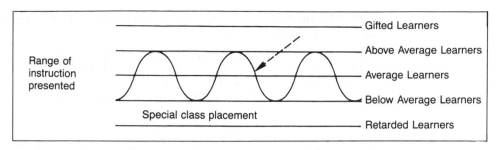

Figure 5.1 *Range of Traditional Classroom Instruction.*

On the other end of the scale, the school's organization may be quite different. The learners in the upper 2% of the intelligence scale need as much special instruction to continue their growth as the students at the lower end. Yet seldom are special classes provided or resource personnel made available. Because all students must adjust to the average classroom program, the gifted student loses most (Figure 5.1).

This situation leads to loss of ability, especially among girls and minority students, as regression toward a more average ability level is the observed outcome. This loss can be prevented.

Education of the Gifted

During several periods of recent American history, programs for educating gifted learners were encouraged. Terman's study during the 1920s brought on one such period. The dramatic accomplishments of the Russian space program in the late 1950s and early 1960s, which became a concern for the United States with the public launching of Sputnik, heralded another. We are now again involved in a revaluing of our educational system in general with more than usual national attention being directed toward education of the gifted.

The current focus on education of the gifted was heightened by the 1971 report to the Congress by the then U.S. Commissioner of Education, S. P. Marland, Jr., on the status of education for the gifted and talented in the United States (Marland, 1972). The report brought to light the inadequate provisions and widespread misunderstandings found in this area. Some of the findings were the following:

1 There are at least 2.5 million students in the elementary and secondary school population who may be considered gifted and/or talented.
2 Only a small percentage of this population is receiving any special education services.
3 Differential education for the gifted and talented receives very low priori-

ty at the federal, the state, and most local levels of government and educational administration.

4 The cost, both individual and social, is enormous when this population goes unserved, for these students cannot excel without assistance.

5 The apathy and even hostility among teachers, administrators, guidance counselors, and psychologists make even identification of these students difficult.

6 While programs can provide significant outcomes, lack of services results in psychological damage and permanent impairment of the ability of gifted and talented students.

The report also called attention to the fact that, at that time, the federal government had no role in the leadership or delivery of services for gifted and talented individuals.

The data comprising the report were collected from four major sources: the Advocate Survey, a questionnaire designed to elicit responses to major issues in gifted education from 239 experts in the field; the School Staffing Survey, in which school principals reported data concerning staffing and services to elementary and secondary gifted and talented students in their schools; Project Talent, a longitudinal study of 400,000 gifted and talented students made in 1960; and the State Survey, designed to be used by the 50 State Departments of Education as a part of the 10 regional hearing procedures. All of these documents, results of which are appended to the Report to Congress, make interesting, though rather less than encouraging, reading for all persons involved in education for the gifted. Some information gathered from these sources follows:

1 Of all schools surveyed, 57.5% reported no gifted individuals among their students.

2 What services exist are located mostly in the cities and suburbs, although even these programs are generally isolated, experimental, and temporary.

3 One-third or more of the known gifted receive no special instruction.

4 Fewer than 2% of the known gifted at the high school level are given opportunities to work with specialists or in other school settings. These students are at a level of knowledge that requires such opportunities if they are to learn.

5 No gifted students are served in 21 states.

6 At least 500,000 gifted students in the United States receive no special instruction.

With these facts making the needs of gifted and talented (G/T) students so apparent, the report put forth several recommendations and, through them, put into motion the first federally supported effort to improve education for the "most neglected and potentially productive groups of students" (Marland, 1972, p. ix).

One outcome to the Marland report was to name 1 Office of Education staff member in each of the 10 Regional Offices of Education throughout the United States as an advocate for education of the gifted. Another was the creation of an Office of Gifted and Talented, housed under the jurisdiction of the Bureau of Education for the Handicapped. This office and its staff were an important force in developing state and national programs for the gifted and talented. In 1974, another step forward was taken when federal funds were allocated under the Special Projects Section of PL 93–380 to state departments of education and local districts. During the first year, 1975, the government allocated approximately 2.5 million dollars to spend on improvement of programs for the gifted population. Also from the Office of Education has come the Presidential Scholars Program in which 121 gifted and talented students, at least 2 from each state, are to be chosen each year to receive a medal presented in Washington, D.C., by the President of the United States. In the third year, the amount of federal support rose to 6.4 million dollars. In 1976 the Office of Gifted and Talented awarded a contract to the Council of Exceptional Children to conduct a national survey to identify current policies, resources, and services for the education of gifted and talented children in the United States and its territories (Mitchell & Erickson, 1978). From the report it was evident that the status of G/T education had improved since the Marland report in 1972. The findings were reported in five major categories:

1 *Gifted and Talented Children.* Using the Office of Education definition, it was estimated that 3% of the school-aged population could be gifted and talented, some 1,352,915 children and youth. The survey found that in the 32 states reporting, 437,618 gifted and talented children were provided some type of special educational service in 1976–77: It showed a range of 0.06% to 4.5% per state served, with 23 states identifying and providing service to 1% or less of their school population, and only 2 states providing for more than 3% of their school-aged population.

2 *State Policy.* Some type of written policy providing for service to G/T children was reported in 43 of 51 states (84%); a definition of G/T was included in the policies of 38 states; identification procedures were described in 30 state policies; and guidelines for service were described in 27 states. Only 18 states had an officially approved state plan.

3 *State Personnel.* At least 1 full-time person was assigned to G/T education in 27 states, while 14 others had at least 1 part-time person; 10 states had less than a half-time position assigned, and 4 states had no one at all. In all, 48.18 positions had been allotted to persons assigned to G/T programs.

4 *Federal and State Funding.* Federal and state appropriations totaling $27,384,316 were reported by 14 states; 93.1% of this amount came from the state funds. Federal funds totaling $3,219,162 were utilized by 19 states, and 23 states utilized state funds totaling $47,076,154. State funds

accounted for 95% of the total amount expended on programs for G/T education, with 8 of the 30 states reporting responsible for 91.8% of this expenditure.

5 *Preparation of Personnel.* One or more courses in G/T education were offered by 177 institutions of higher education in 45 states. State-sponsored inservice training in G/T education was reported by 42 states.

The conditions identified in the Marland Report as deterrents to development of programs for G/T were still operative in 1977, including lack of adequate funding, trained personnel, and training opportunities; problems in identification; and lack of evaluative data on program effectiveness, especially with special subpopulations. In 1978, Congress passed the Gifted and Talented Children's Act (Public Law 95–561, Part A, Title IX of the Elementary and Secondary Education Act) allowing state educative agencies to distribute 75% of the funds with 25% distributed by the Office of Gifted and Talented as discretionary grants. With a change of administration at the federal level, a new philosophy regarding federal support of education began to take form, and during 1981, PL 97–35, the Education Consolidation and Improvement Act, was passed by Congress. This act placed programs for gifted and talented into a block grant with 32 other programs and projects, with appropriations for the block to be sent directly to the states for administration. As a result of this block funding, the Office of Gifted and Talented was removed from the Division of Special Education and Rehabilitative Services, whose programs were not in the block, and placed in the Division of Elementary and Secondary Education, where it was then reduced to the position of consultant. The future of the federal involvement remains in question, though paradoxically the interest in and commitment to education of gifted and talented children throughout the nation have never been higher. Many of those concerned are turning to the private sector for possible support.

An update of the 1978 study (Mitchell, 1982) showed that by then only two states reported no programs for G/T learners. Total state department funding rose to $126,530,674. The problems most frequently mentioned by the state directors surveyed were lack of adequate funding, the need for training qualified teachers, and development of a comprehensive K–12 program.

The Commerce Technical Advisory Board of the U.S. Department of Commerce expressed in its report and recommendations, Learning Environments for Innovation (Branscomb, 1980), concerns shared by many educators of the gifted:

> What we fear is that the basic educational philosophy is far too biased in the direction of remedial learning and fails to identify, much less foster the development of special talents or unique skills. The United States educational system is better at preserving convention than sparking invention, developing logical rather than conceptual thinking, promoting risk aversion rather than acceptance of change, specialization rather than multiple skills, conformity rather than distinctive talents, independent rather than joint responsibility (pp. 23, 24). Moreover, we are concerned that the present trends of back to basics and dispense with the frills more and more eliminate

the "hands on" experience which may be necessary to develop right brained skills which we believe are essential to innovative technologists and managers as well as creative artists (pp. 24, 25).

A gifted child has only one chance in twenty to be identified by the school system; for the gifted disadvantaged child the chances are a factor of ten worse—less than one chance in 200.

Even if the unusually talented are lucky enough to be identified, the amount of money available to enrich their academic programs can only be described as shocking (p. 25).

Therefore, one of the major recommendations in this report was "that immediate steps be taken by federal, state, and local officials to give programs for the identification and training of gifted students their immediate attention and priority"(p. 37).

A survey conducted for 1986–87 by the State Directors of Gifted and Talented Programs (State of the States: Gifted and Talented Education, 1987), with 42 states responding, reported that 23 states mandate gifted and talented education for the public schools in their states. All states reporting had at least some permissive legislation addressing service to this population. Only three states reported having no personnel assigned to gifted and talented programs at the state level. Approximately 1.5 million students were reported receiving gifted and talented services in the nation's public schools.

Sisk (1987) reports that the states in 1985 were spending approximately $175 million on gifted education, with only a small percentage of this amount coming from the block grant made possible from the Education Consolidation and Improvement Act of 1981. Sisk concluded from her survey that where there is a full-time state consultant for the gifted, and where state funds are available for gifted programs, viable programs for the gifted do exist. Sisk believes that considerable growth has been made in the past decade in total numbers of dollars expended and numbers of gifted students being served, though a gap still exists between the goal of providing for all gifted students in the public system and the current offerings.

While in the 1980s the United States federal government all but abolished its role in supporting or even encouraging the appropriate education of its most able children, advocacy groups, including national organizations for the gifted, began to form in an attempt to meet some of these needs. Because of this advocacy legislation is now being considered to once again allow the federal government a small but important leadership role in education of the gifted. The success of such groups and the continued support of state and local educational agencies are crucial to the future of gifted education in this country.

Worldwide, interest in the education of the gifted and talented is steadily growing. In 1975, the World Council for Gifted Children was formed and through its international conferences and newsletters is attempting to develop a worldwide network and support system that can benefit gifted children and those who work with them.

As the movement continues to make more and more people aware of the needs of gifted children and to find ways to meet those needs more appropriately, let us now look specifically at your community and how it may best serve the gifted in your local area.

Programming by Level of Involvement

Using the atypical learning model in the same way at the upper end of the intelligence scale as at the lower end may provide a solution to the problem of serving the gifted. Could we not consider three types of gifted learners as we already consider three levels of handicapped learners? These would be the mildly gifted, the moderately gifted, and the highly gifted. The educational modifications could then be provided partially on the basis of how much need the student has for a differential program. The focus here is on the different needs of gifted learners, not on IQ scores.

The mildly and moderately gifted student could be provided with a cluster of at least five gifted students in a regular, heterogeneously grouped classroom with a teacher skilled in assessment and individualized instruction and willing to flexibly group by need. A resource room for the gifted and a resource teacher to supplement the experiences provided by the regular classroom would add strength to this program. Mentorships or special core-subject placement might be additional program options.

In the fall of 1985 the results of a 4-year study sponsored by the Sid W. Richardson Foundation were published (Cox, Daniel, & Boston, 1985). The study sought to respond to three issues: (1) What programs for able learners exist? (2) Which programs are most effective and offer the best chance for adaptation to many environments? and (3) What recommendations would assist schools in serving able learners? The results of the study support the concept of programming by levels of involvement. The Pyramid Project, an outgrowth of the study and an attempt to implement its recommendations, has provided special 5-year funding for a pilot program in four school districts in the Dallas-Fort Worth area. The structure used by the pilot districts starts with a broad base of able students whose individual needs are met by acceleration and enrichment in the regular classroom. The second level of the pyramid represents fewer students who have more specialized needs and who require special classes. At the third level, or peak, even fewer exceptionally gifted students are represented who may have special interests or talents and who would find their needs best met in special schools.

The recommendations resulting from the Richardson study are summarized for the areas of administration, discovering talent, program, staff development and teacher support, and evaluation (Cox, Daniel, & Boston, 1985):[1]

[1]From *Educating Able Learners: Programs and Promising Practices* by Jim Cox, Neil Daniel, and Bruce O. Boston (A National Study conducted by the Sid W. Richardson Foundation). Copyright © 1985 by The University of Texas Press. Reprinted by permission of the publisher.

Administration

- Develop a written philosophy for the education of able learners that is consistent with the goals and values of the school district and community. This fundamental first step should include a careful consideration of all the recommendations that follow.
- Select a coordinator or coordinators during the early planning stages. As the person responsible for the success of the program, the coordinator should participate in the planning.
- Assess the current program for able learners. Those elements that serve their needs well may be retained and expanded as other options are added.
- Adopt flexible pacing at all levels. Recognizing that not all students learn at the same rate, allow students to advance as they master content and skills, at whatever pace is most natural and offers the steadiest challenge for each.

Discovering Talent

- Broaden the process for assessing student abilities. This recommendation is implicit in our adoption of the term "able learners," intended to include a larger population than those customarily identified as "gifted students."
- Assess the abilities of all students, and use the results as a basis for appropriate programming decisions.
- Recognize that there is neither a single kind of intelligence nor a single instrument for measuring intelligence. Rather there are multiple intelligences and multiple measures.
- Encourage parents, primary teachers, and others responsible for the supervision of children to note their abilities and interests early and to provide appropriate stimulation. Remember that discovering and nurturing talent are inter-dependent.
- Observe the ability of children to solve problems or fashion products over an extended period as an indicator of interest and ability.
- Use puzzles and games that young children find motivating to discover their talents. A child's ability to recognize patterns in a given intellectual realm will indicate potential in that intelligence and aid in developing an intellectual profile. Pay close attention to the child's ability to use other symbol systems as well as the verbal.
- Give thoughtful attention to special groups such as minorities. Avoid tests that are dependent on English vocabulary or comprehension. Supplement testing with checklists of characteristics valued by the subcultures. The screener should understand and respect each population and, if possible, speak the child's native language.
- Use a wide range of testing strategies, including out-of-level testing. If students' abilities are to be assessed with standardized instruments, be sure they have a good congruence or "match" with the objectives of the curriculum and programming.
- Throw a wide net, keeping entrance requirements fairly modest and tentative. Avoid arbitrary cut-offs. The goal is to include all students who can benefit from enriched programming rather than exclude any who are mar-

ginal. Monitor regularly and let those with talent and motivation move ahead.

- Avoid labeling any group of children as *the* gifted. To do so implies that some children are gifted in every area, and other children are gifted in none.
- Provide a psychologically safe environment. Teach students to value their abilities and to use their individual strengths.

Program

- Recognize the importance of counselors in several capacities: participating in student assessment, ministering to the affective needs of students, guiding program selection of students, and counseling in career and college choices.
- Build a comprehensive program as you would piece together a mosaic. Do not expect all elements to be in place at once.
- Take care that programs are sequential, carefully integrated, and articulated throughout the system.
- Offer program options that reach through and beyond the normal institutional boundaries: across disciplines, across grade levels, and across levels of intelligence.
- Encourage independence through projects that culminate in real products and employ the methods of inquiry used by real scholars.
- Develop specific plans for concurrent enrollment at all levels—elementary, middle, middle/high school, and high school/college.
- Recognize that a few students will benefit from the opportunity to leave school and enter college early.
- Make use of community resources, including the private sector. For example, include one-to-one mentoring relationships between students and business and professional leaders, or offer internships at the secondary level so that students can examine one or more career interests as an aid to informed academic and career choices.
- Cooperate with area museums, arts organizations, and civic groups to increase educational options available outside the school walls.
- Encourage students to participate in some of the fine educational programs available after school, on Saturdays, and during the summer.
- Consider specialized schools if the population of the community and the district's resources will support them. Although an ambitious undertaking, a residential school can serve a wider area than a single school district, and the school can be a laboratory for teaching strategies and curriculum content.
- Recognize that racing through the curriculum is not the primary goal of a well-conceived educational program. Balance acceleration with enrichment activities for diverse types and degrees of intelligence.

Staff Development and Teacher Support

- Consider staff development a continuous process for teachers, consultants, and administrators.

- Develop teaching strategies that are appropriate to the learning styles of able students, and encourage a wide range of thinking and questioning skills.
- Arrange for joint planning among teachers at different levels with careful attention to the K–12 sequence in each content area.
- Help teachers develop a manageable record-keeping system that allows them to monitor student progress without undue loss of instructional time.
- Provide the regular classroom teacher adequate support services—clerical support, for example, or a resource teacher—so that enrichment is available to able learners in the regular classroom.
- Use nearby colleges or universities as a resource for ongoing staff development and for innovations in curriculum as well as for educational research.

Evaluation

- Plan the evaluation design as the program is being developed. It is necessary, for example, to establish base line data in order to monitor progress.
- Conduct comprehensive and regular program evaluation to assure accountability. The evaluation design must answer questions about the success of individual program elements and about their impact on student growth and achievement.
- Employ an external evaluator or team of evaluators to reinforce internal evaluation, to assure objectivity, and to add credibility. (pp.153–156)

As we have seen, highly gifted students are found far less often and many educators have suggested that schools, as they are now organized, have little to offer these individuals. In addition to special schools suggested by the Richardson study, magnet programs, mentor programs, radical acceleration, and private tutoring may provide other appropriate programming options.

While the idea of differentiating within the gifted population following the model used by other atypical learning populations may not solve our problem for providing appropriate experiences for these students, it does suggest a more thoughtful approach. Differentiation quite clearly points to the parallel need these students have with other atypical learners for modifications in educational programs that will allow them to optimize their potential.

PLANNING THE GIFTED PROGRAM

The planning necessary to develop a gifted program that will provide the best match for the needs of your students, the expectations of the parents, the philosophy of the school administration, the resources of the community, and the resources and commitment of the school staff is a bit like orchestrating a symphony. There are the homework to do and skills to perfect, there are personnel and materials to collect, beliefs and abilities to assess, cooperation to solicit. To put it all together the timing is crucial.

Components of a Gifted Program

Renzulli (1975a) identified seven key features that experts in the field of gifted education agreed were basic to a successful program: (1) the selection and training of teachers; (2) a curriculum designed to evoke and develop superior behavioral potentialities in academic areas and the arts that is both systematic and comprehensive; (3) multiple appropriate screening and identification procedures; (4) a statement of philosophy and objectives that support differential education for the gifted; (5) staff orientation to promote a knowledgeable and cooperative attitude; (6) a plan of evaluation; and (7) a delineation of administrative responsibility.

With these elements in mind, let us look at the steps we may take and the information we must have to make the program a reality. A rationale for the need to educate gifted individuals has already been discussed. A planning committee composed of teachers, administrators, parents, community representatives, and gifted students should be asked to develop the philosophy statement and goals for the program.

Goals of a Gifted Program

What do you want schools—even families—to accomplish? Do you want to shape adults who will simply repeat what has been done by previous generations? Or do you want individuals who are capable of invention? Those are the real questions. If you want to produce conformists, then the traditional school is perfect. But, if you want original thinkers, you need methods that will permit invention, not simply external reinforcements. (Piaget in Weinheimer, 1972, pp. 118, 120)

The primary goal of the gifted program is to provide opportunities for gifted learners to meet the needs that cannot be met in a regular classroom program, whether those needs are found in content, process, enrichment, or in all three. With these provisions gifted students will be enabled to grow as integrated people toward their full potential. What is done specifically for each child will depend on assessment data. Programs for the gifted do not begin with different curricula or different structures for learning, but with the distinct needs of each gifted learner taken into consideration. The gifted program is different only because, and in the same way that, the gifted learner's needs are different. With this understanding, we may say that, generally, a gifted program should

- Provide opportunities and experiences particularly suited to the needs of the gifted learners and through which they can continue developing potential.
- Establish an environment that values and enhances intelligence, talent, affective growth, and intuitive ability.
- Allow active and cooperative participation by the gifted students and their parents.

- Provide time, space, and encouragement for gifted students to discover themselves, their powers, and their abilities, and to become all that they can be.
- Provide opportunities for gifted students to interact with children and adults of various abilities, including the bright and talented, to be challenged to know and revere humanity for its uniqueness and its connectedness.
- Encourage gifted students to find their place in human evolution by discovering what abilities and in what areas they wish to contribute.

Educational programs for gifted students cannot just be different, they must be qualitatively different. These programs must have the same goals for gathering knowledge and developing skills as we find in regular programs. Programs for the gifted share many of the same strategies and concerns as the regular programs. But unless the gifted program goes beyond fact gathering and process development, toward providing opportunities for gifted students to find their own areas of interest and ability, to experience the problems of their chosen areas, and, through personal effort, to develop real solutions that affect others, we do not have a program for the qualitatively different learner we call *gifted*.

The next step will be to assess the resources and needs of the school, the staff, the parents, and the community. Knowledge of the discrepancy between what you want to have happen ideally and what is available and actually exists will allow you to plan more realistically what you may accomplish now and what you must develop for future implementation.

It would be well at this point to establish the role of the administrator in designing and maintaining varied and appropriate programs for the gifted in your community. The committee will need to assemble all policy materials that affect the implementation of the program.

THE PROGRAM COORDINATOR

Once we have decided on the type of program we want for our gifted students, how do we organize to provide it? Some districts give the responsibility to the school principal, others to the special education director. Some add it to the responsibilities of the school counselor, and some hire a part-time teacher for the assignment. In all of these cases, the most well-meaning people will find it difficult to succeed. Adding such a program to an already overloaded administrator or counselor merely admits its low priority in the district and ensures both the organizer and the program of inadequate energy for the job. The teacher will find the part-time status detrimental to any relationship with full-time personnel, with parents, and with the students. There is not enough time to develop the personal contacts, the assessment materials, and the type of continuous program that is necessary. In many cases, teachers in this position find themselves working full time for part-time pay. While such a situation is common in this profession because lack of closure is inherent in any work with growing people, it should not be encouraged. Planning a program based on this type of professional commitment is unfair and can lead to an inadequate program.

It has been found that in states where the total time of at least one person is devoted to gifted education, far more students have been adequately served. What is true for state levels can be also said for local levels. Whatever monies are allotted to educating the gifted students in your district would be best spent on a full-time person. If your district is small, cooperate with other surrounding districts to establish the position of Coordinator of Gifted Programs. I have heard some people, especially parents, say that the money should not be spent on administering the program; it should be spent on the kids. Ultimately, the gifted students will gain more in educational services with a full-time coordinator. When monies are "given to the kids," they are usually spent on materials or experiences that may or may not fit into a planned program. Sometimes undirected money ends up buying library books or reading kits or sometimes laboratory equipment or computers. None of these does any harm in itself, but do any of them bring the gifted students closer to meeting their needs? How do these materials or experiences provide a continuing program? Who decides which materials or experiences are appropriate? Again, the full-time coordinator seems the best buy. The Coordinator of Gifted Programs in your district would do the following:

1 Plan the overall structure of the district gifted program in consultation with teachers, administrators, and parents.
2 Take care of all administrative paperwork inherent in the district program (such as writing proposals for funding, evaluating data, etc.).
3 Interview and recommend teachers for the program for either integrated classes or special classes.
4 Conduct teacher inservice in gifted education for identification and implementation of programs.
5 Arrange meetings of teachers responsible for education of the gifted in the district.
6 Conduct parent meetings for inservice in gifted education and encourage active participation in the district program.
7 Establish case studies on all students who have been screened for gifted identification.
8 Conduct assessments of all students identified as gifted and establish profiles.
9 Chair the selection committee for identification of students for the gifted program.
10 Organize a mentor program as a part of the opportunities available to the gifted in the district.
11 Arrange for field trips that are needed for the gifted program.

12 Contact local colleges, universities, and museums for educational experiences available to gifted students who are advanced in areas not taught within the local school.

13 Provide support and resources for teachers with gifted students in their classrooms.

14 Teach special classes for gifted students in small districts or occasionally in large districts.

15 Evaluate the district program and individual school programs to strengthen service to gifted students by obtaining data from teachers, students, and parents.

16 Provide a liaison between parents and the school; regular teachers and special teachers; and the administration, the program personnel, and the community at large. Communicate regularly with the school board.

17 Serve on administrative committees with general education responsibilities to provide advocacy for the gifted learner (textbook selection committee, etc.).

18 Attend workshops and meetings to stay informed about current ideas and practices in gifted education.

As you can see, anything less than a full-time position would restrict the program. There are many opportunities appropriate to gifted students throughout the community that cost very little, but which require someone to ferret them out and make them available. A good coordinator can ensure a successful program for the gifted. Of course, the selection of the coordinator is critical. Choosing a person with teaching or counseling experience who is open, is excited about learning, enjoys gifted individuals, and has a very positive view of life would be wise. Additional training in gifted education would greatly benefit the position. An experienced educator from the same district would provide a lot of support for the program, although certainly that criterion is not as important as the person's attitudes and background. Having a full-time coordinator for delivery of services in educating the gifted provides many advantages. Potential contributions to the entire district's educational system are endless.

You are now ready to consider the many options for the structure you will use for the delivery of service to the gifted individuals who are selected for your program.

PROGRAM ORGANIZATIONS FOR EDUCATING THE GIFTED

There are many options for organizing programs for gifted learners. How much progress gifted individuals make in learning and how successful they are in fulfilling their unique potential will depend on how many of their needs can be met by the program in which they participate and how much time they are allowed

Table 5.1 *Gifted Programming Alternatives.*

Gifted Needs Met by Program	Abstract concepts	Accelerated pace	Advanced content	Complex processes	Continuity	Continuous progress	Flexible grouping	Flexible time
Programs For Delivery of Services								
Regular Classroom								
with cluster								
with pullout	✓			✓	✓			
with cluster and pullout	✓			✓	✓			
Individualized Classroom								
with cluster	✓	✓	✓	✓	✓	✓	✓	✓
with cluster and pullout	✓	✓	✓	✓	✓	✓	✓	✓
with cross-grading	✓	✓	✓✓	✓	✓✓	✓✓	✓✓	✓
Adjunct Programs								
Mentors, tutorials, and internships	✓	✓	✓	✓				
Independent study	✓	✓	✓	✓				✓
Resource rooms	✓	✓	✓	✓			✓	
Special Class Scheduled With Some Heterogeneous Classes	✓✓	✓✓	✓✓	✓✓	✓	✓	✓	✓
Special Classes	✓✓	✓✓	✓✓	✓✓	✓✓	✓✓	✓✓	✓✓
Special Schools	✓✓	✓✓	✓✓	✓✓	✓✓	✓✓	✓✓	✓✓

Levels of Involvement

Level 1 Mildly Gifted
Level 2 Moderately Gifted
Level 3 Highly Gifted

Independence	Individualization	Interdisciplinary	Peer interaction	Varied products	Variety of material	Examples of Program Models
			√			
√			√	√	√	Revolving Door Identification Model (Renzulli, 1977; Renzulli, Reis, & Smith, 1981)
√			√√	√	√	
√	√	√	√√	√	√	
√	√	√	√√	√	√	
√√	√√	√	√√	√	√√	
√	√		√	√		Autonomous Learner Model (Betts, 1985)
√√	√			√	√	Autonomous Learner Model (Betts, 1985)
√	√	√	√	√	√	Revolving Door Identification Model (Renzulli, 1977; Renzulli, Reis, & Smith, 1981)
√	√	√	√	√	√√	International Baccalaureate Program[a] (Nicol, 1985) Autonomous Learner Model (Betts, 1985) Purdue Secondary Model (Feldhusen & Robinson, 1986)[a]
√√	√√	√√	√√	√√	√√	Purdue Three-Stage Model (Feldhusen & Kolloff, 1986) Hopkins Acceleration Model (Stanley, 1979)[a]
√√	√√	√√	√√	√√	√√	

[a]Secondary only.

to meet those needs in the program. Table 5.1 provides an overview of some of the program options and which needs of gifted learners each particular program choice may fulfill. The choice of organization will not assure that the needs indicated *will* be met, only that within the particular structure those needs *could* be met. Factors other than structure, such as teacher skill, administrative support, etc., will determine the quality of the program; however, adoption of some structures will actually limit your ability to meet some of the needs gifted learners may have. Each district would be advised to have a wide variety of programs available for the range of services needed. Because no one structure can meet the needs of all the gifted learners in any district, providing a continuum of planned services would be the best practice.

Meeting the needs of gifted learners will be discussed in more detail in Chapters 7 through 9; for now, only an outline of some of those needs will be presented for use as criteria for program selection. The criteria for meeting the needs of gifted learners will be determined by whether the structure provides the possibility for (1) continuity of appropriate learning experiences; (2) continuous progress, accelerated pacing, and advanced content; (3) flexibility of grouping and pacing; (4) variety of materials and levels of complexity; (5) intellectual peer interaction; (6) complex processes; (7) varied products and outcomes; (8) interdisciplinarity; and (9) varied grouping, including independent study, small groups, teams, and committees.

Delivery of Services

The program for the gifted can deliver these services through a variety of structures, some more successful than others. The choice of structure will depend on several considerations:

1 *The level of involvement of the population to be served.* As we discussed earlier, the level of giftedness in which the child is involved should be considered in program planning. A special class may be most appropriate for a highly gifted learner, but unnecessary and socially limiting for less gifted students; an individualized, cross-graded classroom that both clusters gifted learners and pulls them out for special classes may be the best possible choice for the great majority of youngsters, but be totally unsuitable and limiting for a highly gifted learner.

2 *The training and skills of the teacher.* While an individualized classroom may best meet learner needs, if the teacher does not have management skills for this degree of complexity such a structure will have a very limited chance for success.

3 *The educational philosophy of the administration.* It is difficult at best to develop and deliver appropriate services for the highly unique learners

we call *gifted.* If there is little support from the administration it can be impossible. Work carefully to get the support needed physically, financially, and most of all philosophically from those who make decisions for your program. A team effort is important for the success of the program and the growth of the learners within it.

4 *The cooperation of the parents and the community at large.* Building parent and community support are mentioned in detail in Chapter 11; their importance is all that will be mentioned here. As part of the team, parents can bring a wealth of resources and information to the program. Without their support, or worse, with their opposition, the program has a limited chance of delivering the best service.

Types of Structures

In planning the gifted program, you must consider the limitations as well as the strengths of your particular setting. The attitudes and beliefs of the school administration and the community, as well as the skills of the teacher, will shape your program. Let us look at several ways of grouping with the idea that you would use the one most suited to your particular situation. By being aware of the difficulties that the model could present because of its structure, you will try to prevent as many of the problems as possible. The continuum will range from ability grouping in regular classrooms to special schools.

Regular Classrooms

The regular classroom when traditionally organized (see p. 177) is not adequate for gifted education. Such classrooms rely on group instruction and a set curriculum. The instruction is usually by subject, with similar experiences for everyone. Whitmore (1980) comments, "It seems likely that future research could prove that the regular classroom is the most restrictive environment for the gifted child. . . . This finding will be most probable if teachers are not helped to become more able to effectively individualize instruction" (p. 68).

With Cluster. Clustering gifted students could meet their needs for peer interaction, but usually group teaching does not provide for appropriately differentiated curriculum. Having at least five gifted students clustered in the regular classroom can make it a more appropriate environment in which they can learn, but only if the teacher is aware of and tries to meet their differentiated needs.

With Pullout. In a pullout class students leave the regular class for a specified amount of time for special instruction and then return to spend most of their time in the regular program.

ADVANTAGES. Gifted students may have an opportunity to work at their level of ability and in their area of interest and to interact with other gifted students for at least part of their school time. Upon leaving the regular program, the student may experience seminars, specialized resource rooms, special classes, field trips, or other unique learning situations.

DISADVANTAGES. The major part of the school week is still not an appropriate learning experience for meeting the needs of gifted students. Often gifted students are asked to do the regular classroom work missed when pulled out, in addition to the special class work. Furthermore, the special class has little time for meeting all of the gifted needs, teachers may resent interruption of their program, and other students in the regular classroom may envy and isolate the gifted child because of the special class. Teachers in pullout programs must establish good working relations with the regular class teachers if this plan is to benefit the gifted learner.

As a result of data collection over a 4-year period, the Richardson study (Cox, Daniel, & Boston, 1985) recommended against the use of the pullout structure for delivery of services to the gifted student. Viewing pullout as a part-time solution to a full-time problem, the researchers suggest a more comprehensive program structure.

With Cluster and Pullout. Combining clustering and pullout has the same advantages and disadvantages as each alone, except for the additional advantage of the possibility for more interaction with gifted peers and better follow-through with the gifted program. The quality of this program will depend on the pullout teacher and class.

The moderately gifted and the mildly gifted would need less specialized grouping if classrooms could be individualized. In cross-graded, individualized classrooms, a cluster group of five to seven gifted students would be adequate to meet the needs of each for peer challenge. When this type of clustering is done in a classroom that is not organized to meet individual needs, when flexible grouping cannot occur, or when different types of ability are not valued and nurtured, the gifted student cannot flourish.

Individualized Classrooms

By individualizing a classroom we can make use of individual, team, and flexible small-group instruction. Assessments are used to determine the curriculum and materials for each student. The classroom is decentralized and gives access to many types of learning. In most cases such classes are cross-graded, with students from several age levels. Learning centers are often found in these classrooms.

ADVANTAGES. The advantages of this setting are that gifted students are more likely to work at their own level and pace and the learning experience is continuous.

DISADVANTAGES. If there are only one or two gifted students, they may feel isolated and have no one with whom to share ideas. This type of classroom requires a highly competent teacher, or it can become unstructured or only partially individualized. The teacher may not have enough resources available to keep up with a gifted learner and 35 others.

With Cluster. Clustered individualized classrooms have the same advantages and disadvantages as individualized classrooms without the disadvantage of the isolation of being the only gifted learner.

With Cluster and Pullout. Individualized classrooms with cluster and pullout have the same advantages as individualized classrooms, with the additional advantage of more resources available to both the gifted learner and the teacher. In this situation, the problems created by the pullout program will not be evidenced. If all students are valued and allowed to meet their needs, no students will feel that they must do what every other person does. The gifted can meet their needs without envy from others. Such a program has continuity and allows each student's needs to be met all through the week.

With Cross-Grading. Cross-grading (combining several age-graded classes into one group, e.g., first through third grade) has all of the previous advantages with even easier access to materials and a pace appropriate to the gifted students' level of development. By cross-grading we can move away from the age-in-grade lockstep that has for years been so limiting to all students.

Adjunct Programs

In addition to many of the structures previously mentioned, adjunct programs give additional service to students with special needs. These often are planned at times that provide minimal services for gifted students, such as after school, on Saturdays, or during the summer. Only when they are planned as a part of a well-integrated, full-time program can adjunct programs provide the full value of which they are capable.

Mentors, Tutorials, Internships. One adjunct program option you can make available for enrichment, which often provides acceleration, is a mentors' program that includes tutorials and internships. Mentors are people who share their expertise with gifted learners interested in their field and at a point of development in that field where they can benefit from involvement with an expert. Mentors can be found in many places. Older students can become mentors for younger students, especially if a structure is provided for their contact and some prior training in interpersonal relations is made available. Retirement communities provide an excellent resource for mentors, as many retired persons have the experience and record of achievement to share and the time to share it. Parents of gifted students may provide mentorship for other students. Also, don't overlook the practicing professionals in your community. Though their time may be at a premium, they will often make time for that one bright, inquiring student who finds their field fascinating.

Mentors should not be considered the same as other traditional teachers who need to evaluate, report, and record the progress of the student. In this relationship there is a more equal partnership involved, with more emphasis on the guidance aspect of learning. Mentors provide a social contact, a sponsorship into the world of the profession being shared. Mutual interest and trust will be necessary components of successful mentorships. As you organize to provide the mentors' program, you may want to review programs such as the Mentor Academy Model (Runions, 1980), which has developed a procedure for implementing this valuable alternative for enrichment.

Another unique mentors' program, the Art Partnership Networks, involves the artistically gifted child (Szekely, 1981). This program enlists college students, majors in every field of art, as mentors to elementary school children who show interest and ability in art. The college artists are introduced as visiting artists after completing a series of workshops designed to acquaint them with a philosophy of giftedness. The college artists then come into elementary classrooms to work with one child or a small group who have expressed and demonstrated interest. The results of the program are encouraging and have gained the support of teachers, parents, the PTO, and school personnel.

As part of the report on the Richardson study (Cox & Daniel, 1983) the following mentor and internship programs were described: the Illinois Governmental Internship Program, the Executive High School Internship Association (a national organization), the Executive Assistant and the Creative and Performing Arts Programs (a Dallas-based program), Texas A&M University's Career Education Model, and other programs found in Texas. Betts (1985) has a strong component of mentorship in his Autonomous Learner Model.

Independent Study. Although independent study can include acceleration of material and concepts and can be carried out in a variety of settings, it is most often used to provide enrichment. The outcome of independent study should be a self-directed learner who can investigate real problems; but too often teachers expect students, because they are gifted, to be self-directed learners from the start. They often have the curiosity, the interest, and the motivation to pursue a study of their own choosing; but all too often they do not have the skills, such as how to search for primary sources, use professional methods of inquiry, collect and organize raw data, analyze and evaluate data, and form conclusions. These skills often need to be taught if the student is to be successful. Doherty and Evans (1981) suggest a three-phase process for using independent study. Phase 1 is teacher led and incorporates learning centers, experimentation, and simulation as the student explores the depth and breadth of the academic area. Phase 2 is the independent study and involves a nine-step process of locating and using data, producing new ideas, and developing a product that is examined by experts:

Step 1—The student selects a topic that is issue-oriented.

Step 2—The student establishes a schedule.

Step 3—The student develops five or more questions (first objectives) to direct the research.

Step 4—The student secures references and seeks sources or raw data.

Step 5—The student researches the topic, collects raw data, and takes notes.

Step 6—The student develops five final objectives using Bloom's taxonomy.

Step 7—The student has a conference with the teacher, who evaluates the depth of knowledge and the idea production.

Step 8—The student makes a product showing some of his or her new ideas.

Step 9—The student's product is displayed, evaluated with a friend, and examined by an expert. (p. 109)

The final phase is a culminating seminar. This process allows students to build the skills necessary to carry out an investigation that will satisfy their intellectual curiosity and truly enrich their academic lives.

The use of independent study for gifted learners is supported by the findings of a study by Stewart (1981): When compared to learning styles of more average students, there was an apparent preference among the gifted students for instructional methods emphasizing independence, i.e., independent study and discussion. The general population within the study preferred more structured methods, i.e., lectures and projects. For a selection of enrichment activities to be used at home and at school you may want to consult Kanigher's book on everyday enrichment (1977).

All of these provisions have been and are currently being used in various combinations and with varying degrees of success. Research shows that none is without merit, nor does any one answer all the needs of gifted students. In light of the extensive literature, further research and modification of these programs would seem unnecessary. Adherence to only these models for so long may have held schools back in their abilty to fully meet the needs of the gifted individual.

In using any of the traditional program models, as we have in the past, we are left with some uncomfortable problems. Programs often exist for minimal periods of time throughout the gifted students' educational experience, resulting in little continuity of learning experiences. Often gifted students are faced with having their needs met only during the allotted special program time (e.g., one half-day a week, a few weeks a year, or a 6-week summer program). Not only are they asked to give up their free time so that their special learning needs can be attended to, but there is an assumption that, during the rest of their school time, these needs do not exist, or if they do, they can be sublimated until the allotted period arrives.

Other problems, such as labeling and lack of skills in social integration and interpersonal relationships, often result from these part-time provisions. It therefore becomes important to find a way to individualize school learning experiences so that gifted individuals can have their atypical needs met continuously throughout their school career. Their differences must become strengths, not the handicaps they often are in a traditional setting. The gifted have a right to pursue learning at their own pace to their own level of capability, with challenges available on a full-time basis and progress encouraged by their learning environment.

Resource Rooms.   The provision of resource rooms can be a part of many types of programs. Usually resource rooms are used to enrich the regular school program, and a minimum amount of time is allowed for participation after which the student returns to the regular classroom. If the only provision for meeting the needs of the gifted is through a resource room, the result may be a partial experience lacking continuity and seldom meeting their full range of needs. If resource rooms are available as part of a well-planned and well-integrated program, they can be a source of enriching experiences and add to the options available to teachers seeking to provide for special interests and special talents.

Special Class Scheduled With Some Heterogeneous Classes

Providing a special class scheduled with heterogeneous classes is especially appropriate for intermediate, middle, and secondary schools organized by subject. Some examples might be concurrent enrollment at colleges and high schools, and interdisciplinary academic core classes with electives.

ADVANTAGES.   Programs and environments can be designed in the special class to meet the needs of the gifted. By moving into classes for subjects that stress talent rather than giftedness, the students can learn to appreciate other students for their abilities. The mildly and moderately gifted would find this helpful.

DISADVANTAGES.   A special class requires a specially trained teacher, or it can be just as inhibiting as no program. Often these classes are different only in the population attending them and in the added quantity of assignments. It is important to individualize in this setting, for the gifted are quite different from each other. Although gifted students are not highly advanced in every discipline, many secondary schools use tracking across all areas.

Special Class

The special class structure can provide for all of the gifted needs and can be used at any level. It is most appropriate for the moderately to highly gifted student. It has the advantages and disadvantages of the previous mixed structure without the involvement with other groups that may be talented in other areas. In the special class gifted students can be challenged to their full potential in every area. They are stimulated and not tempted to hide their gifts in order to be accepted. Teachers specially trained to work with gifted learners are essential for these classes to be effective.

Special Schools

The special school structure is recommended most often for highly gifted or talented students and has the advantages and disadvantages of special classes in a more intensified form. Governor's schools, high schools for the performing arts, and residential schools for math and sciences are some of the types of schools that one can find under this category. When considering total separation, we might look at the level of the students' involvement in giftedness. All gifted students need to interact with those who can challenge them. For the highly gifted, ability grouping would justifiably comprise the major part of their educational experience.

Educational decision makers are often concerned that removing gifted students from the regular classroom will be detrimental to the other students left behind. Teachers are sometimes concerned that their slower children will have no incentive, that the "spark" will be gone. In an attempt to measure the effects of ability grouping on gifted and nongifted learners, Goldberg and Passow (Passow, 1980) conducted a study in which they compared achievement gains between classes heterogeneously grouped with gifted students and classes comprised of nongifted students only. In science there were small differences evident, with the presence of gifted students contributing an upgrading effect. However, in social studies only the very bright students gained from their presence and then only if less able students were involved also. When the class had only bright and above-average students, the attendance of the gifted had an inhibiting effect. In math there was found to be a downgrading effect when nongifted and gifted were grouped together, and in all other areas there seemed to be no consistent or significant trend. In this study as in others, we find that grouping in and of itself is insufficient to have significant effects on achievement among the gifted: The curriculum content and processes must change to become more appropriate to the gifted learners. When this is the case, the longer the gifted are allowed to be in special programs, the greater will be *their* gain (Martinson, 1972).

General Administrative Provisions

The evidence is clear that neither ability grouping, enrichment, nor acceleration should be used alone in programming for the gifted, as each provides for a different need exhibited by this population. It should also be noted that each provision requires the presence of the others if it is to be effective and bring about the desired outcome. We will, however, discuss each separately with the research that has focused on that particular administrative provision.

Ability Grouping

Ability grouping is a provision that allows some students to be separated from the more typical students by some given criterion, in this case, the level of measured intelligence or achievement. Ability grouping may be implemented as special classes or schools, magnet programs, special groups meeting prior to or after school, pullout programs during school hours where gifted students are separated for a given period of time and then returned to the regular program, or summer workshops. At the secondary level, a tracking system is often used to group students into classes based on academic ability.

Flexible ability grouping has many advantages. In the 1971 hearings held by the U.S. Department of Health, Education, and Welfare, gifted students expressed preference for programs where they are separated for part of the day, but not totally segregated from other students. They asked for flexibility in their program and in their curriculum (Marland, 1972).

A summary of research on ability grouping with gifted students presents a contradictory picture. The following conclusions recur in several of the studies (Barbe, 1955; Borg, 1964; Breidenstine, 1936; Findley & Bryan, 1971; Goldberg et al., 1965; Justman, 1954; Kulik & Kulik, 1982; Simpson & Martinson, 1961; Sumption, 1941):

1 Significant academic gains result when programs are adjusted to student abilities. Grouping alone is insufficient to show differences in achievement of grouped over nongrouped gifted students.
2 Attitudes of parents, teachers, and gifted students are generally favorable toward special groups or classes, especially if such grouping is flexible and not totally segregated.
3 Positive development in self-concept and a sense of well-being result from special group placement.
4 The amount of time spent in special groups or classes relates positively to achievement gains of gifted students.
5 Attitudes of other parents and teachers are reported as more negative toward grouped learners.
6 There is more opportunity for individual expression, in-depth study, acceleration, and freedom from regimentation in ability-grouped classes.
7 There are more high achievers and fewer underachievers reported in ability-grouped classes.

While ability grouping may provide a partial answer to the question of appropriate education for the gifted, other modifications must be made for the program to succeed. When ability grouping is used, the research recommends the following:

1 Recognize that there will still be individual differences. There is a tremendous range found within the gifted group; they are not homogeneous. Assess and plan for individualized instruction.
2 Avoid complete segregation.
3 Select secure, specially trained teachers.

4 Encourage growth in all functions, not just the intellectual.

5 Communicate with all teachers and parents.

6 Be informed on research, evaluation, and curriculum for this population.

Ability Grouping for Elementary Students. All of the nine models mentioned could be used with gifted elementary students. One example of the use of ability grouping in elementary gifted programming can be seen in Renzulli's Revolving Door Identification Model (RDIM), shown in Table 5.1 (Renzulli, 1977; Renzulli, Reis, & Smith, 1981). Supporting the recommended use of multiple criteria for identification, the model uses standardized tests and subjective evaluation of student performance and potential through teacher, peer, parent, and self-nomination. RDIM allows a rather large group of children who meet the criteria of above-average academic ability, creativity, and task commitment to receive special enrichment opportunities on a rotating basis. Underlying this model is the belief that this type of "giftedness" is shown only at certain times, in certain areas of study, and under certain circumstances. When behavior showing evidence of such creative, productive accommplishment becomes apparent, the student is allowed to pursue such accomplishment in a resource room setting through independent or small-group work. Those using the model like its inclusion of larger numbers of children, its provision for individualized education while the child is in the resource room, and its emphasis on practical application of products (Delisle, Reis, & Gubbins, 1981).

Ability Grouping for Secondary Students. Once the organization of the school moves to departmentalization, the flexibility of ability grouping available to the elementary teachers disappears. It is far more common to find provision for gifted made (if indeed any is made) in the form of special classes, as described on p. 198. These might be formed through tracking gifted students into designated classes in a few or all of their academic subjects: advanced placement classes, academic core classes, independent study groups, or group seminars. Some special schools have been formed at the secondary, such as the governor's schools and the special talent schools in Los Angeles and New York City. For more detailed information on programs at the secondary level see Chapter 9.

Not included in the continuum for ability grouping are the special groups the student may experience as adjunct programs. These would meet before or after school or during the summer. The student experience can range from special interest groups or classes with a single subject content to an open, varied approach. Disadvantages special groups have, if used as the total gifted program, are that they do nothing about the student's gifted needs during the entire day and they usually lack continuity. If used only as enrichment experiences with appropriate planning during the regular school day, these adjunct experiences can provide a joyful, worthwhile part of the program for student and teacher alike.

Enrichment

Enrichment is usually the addition of disciplines or areas of learning not normally found in the regular curriculum and is used at both the elementary and the secondary levels. One may also find more difficult or in-depth material available on the typical curricular subjects. While enrichment is feasible at any time in any organization model, it is generally used in a traditional classroom to meet the needs of advanced learners without having to separate them from the typical learners at their grade level.

If enrichment is to be done in regular classrooms without individualized instruction, the following minimum requirements help make the program effective:

1 The teacher must be able to identify and list the students who are gifted.
2 The teacher must be able to show the specific curriculum modifications being made for the gifted learners.
3 There must be one person with supervisory responsibility over the entire program (such as the Coordinator of Gifted Programs) to help provide resources for the regular teacher. (Kough, 1960, p. 147)

Enrichment, the administrative provision most used in programs for gifted, must be well planned and enhanced by other modifications or it will meet few of the gifted student's needs. By a total focus on enrichment, growth in content and process needs may be overlooked. From the research, we find that this idea has seldom been carefully implemented, and it causes the least change in the opportunities provided for the gifted learner. Enrichment in many classrooms often means just more work, sometimes more of the same work.

When enrichment is used, Gallagher (1964) recommends including activities that develop

- the ability to associate and interrelate concepts;
- the ability to evaluate facts and arguments critically;
- the ability to create new ideas and originate new lines of thought;
- the ability to reason through complex problems;
- the ability to understand other situations, other times, and other people; to be less bound by one's own peculiar environmental surroundings. (p. 80)

Enrichment may appeal to district administration and school boards as the most inexpensive way to meet gifted needs. If the problems of limited teacher time, lack of teacher knowledge in every area, limited availability of resources, and individualized planning are not met, this provision may be, by far, the most expensive in waste of human potential. Enrichment is most effective when combined with other provisions and modifications.

Acceleration

Acceleration can take many forms. It can mean early entrance to formal schooling, moving through a primary area in 2 rather than 3 years, grade skipping, advanced placement, or moving through material at an accelerated rate. However it is implemented, it will result in student completion of formal schooling in less time than is usually required.

Research reported on acceleration is almost uniformly positive in its results (Alexander & Skinner, 1980; Anderson, 1960; Bish & Fliegler, 1959; Braga, 1969; Fund for the Advancement of Education, 1957; Gallagher, 1966; Justman, 1953; Lehman, 1953; Lucito, 1964; Morgan, Tennant, & Gold, 1980; Plowman & Rice, 1967; Pressey, 1955; Reynolds, 1962; Terman & Oden, 1947; Worcester, 1955). Some of the rationales and advantages reported are as follows:

1 Gifted students are inclined to select older companions because their levels of maturity are often more similar. Neither the method nor the age of acceleration appears to be of consequence.
2 Acceleration can be used in any school.
3 Acceleration allows capable students to enter their careers sooner, resulting in more productivity.
4 Because of their spending less time in school, the gifted students' educational costs are lowered.
5 Accelerated students do as well as or often better than the older students in their classes.
6 There is less boredom and dissatisfaction for the bright student.
7 Social and emotional adjustment are generally high, in most reports above average, when accelerated.
8 In general, teachers and administrators are opposed to acceleration, while parents and students, especially those who have experienced acceleration, are for it. Some possible reasons given for the negative attitudes of some educators are the convenience of lockstep, chronological grade placement, ignorance of research, discredited belief in social maladjustment, and state laws preventing early admission.
9 To be successful, acceleration must be continuous and coordinated.

In an attempt to clarify the research findings on acceleration, Kulik and Kulik (1984) performed a meta-analysis of 26 studies of acceleration effects concluding that gifted and talented students are able to handle the academic challenge that accelerated programs provide. In support of this finding they reported that,

> First, talented youngsters who were accelerated into higher grades performed as well as the talented, older pupils already in those grades. Second, in the subjects in which they were accelerated, talented accelerates showed almost a year's advancement over talented same-age nonaccelerates. (p. 421) [Author's note: In this study talented is used interchangeably with gifted, and gifted and talented.]

While acceleration should not be used as the total plan for a gifted program, the literature shows very few disadvantages to this provision when used on an individual basis. For the highly gifted, opportunities for acceleration are essential. The work of Stanley of Johns Hopkins University (Nevin, 1977) validates its importance. In a project begun in 1971, Stanley gave students highly gifted in mathematics an opportunity to develop their ability at an accelerated pace. Not only has his program met with success among the students, but the results—their contributions to our society—have already been evidenced.

PROGRAM MODELS

There are several well-developed program models you may wish to consult as you structure the continuum of services in your district. Each can provide for a part of your population, and each has procedures you can adapt for developing that specific structure. The following review will give you some information on each of several well-known models. If any particular model seems appropriate to meet a portion of the needs on your continuum of services, you are advised to take advantage of the detailed planning available with the model that can be obtained by contacting the originator. Keep in mind that the best use of any model is as it is adapted to your specific needs. These are intended to be organizational takeoff points. You are the professional, and you must decide how and when to use the structure and its procedures. Although none of these models used alone will provide a total gifted program, each may provide for a part of your continuum of service plan.

The Autonomous Learner Model for the Gifted and Talented

Developed in the late 1970s as a way to meet both the social-emotional and cognitive needs of high school gifted youngsters, the Autonomous Learner Model (ALM), developed by Betts (1985) (Table 5.1), is presented in a special class setting generally using one period at specified times throughout the week. The ALM is developed for a 3-year timeline, and it is expected that the gifted high school or junior high student will progress through the five major dimensions in that period of time. The ALM is divided into five dimensions:

1 Orientation, which, as the name implies, acquaints the students and their parents with the model and its expectations.
2 Individual Development, which stresses the attitudes and concepts necessary to support lifelong learning.
3 Enrichment Activities, which allow students to explore content that is generally not a part of the regular curriculum and to become aware of resources available to them for their use.

4 Seminars, which allow groups of students to pursue topics of their choice through research, then to present their results to a larger group for their own growth through self-evaluation.

5 In-Depth Study, which presents students with long-term opportunities to pursue their own areas of interest with small groups or alone.

At this point in the ALM the learners determine what will be learned, how it will be presented, what will be necessary for their data collection or presentation, what the final product will be, and how the learning will be evaluated.

Although ALM is not a total program for gifted learners, it is especially appropriate for the departmentalized structure of secondary schools. The model addresses itself to more than just the cognitive needs of the student and encourages independence in the learning setting.

The Purdue Three-Stage Enrichment Model for Gifted Education at the Elementary Level

This model, developed by Feldhusen and Kolloff (1986), has been planned for implementation in a pullout enrichment program at the elementary level. As the name suggests, it is presented in three stages:

I Divergent and Convergent Thinking Abilities, which gives students the opportunity to experience problem solving, decision making, and forecasting that will require the use of fluency, flexibility, originality, and elaboration.

II Development of Creative Problem-Solving Abilities, which offers techniques and strategies that may be applied in a creative problem-solving process to real problems.

III Development of Independent Learning Abilities, which requires the student to share with an audience a product developed from personal interest and investigation.

Again, though this model is designed to meet the needs of gifted students for only a part of their program, it does provide skills and strategies that can be carried into any part of the learning experience.

The Purdue Secondary Model for Gifted and Talented Youth

Discussed as a comprehensive model of service for secondary departmentalized schools the Purdue Secondary Model, developed by Feldhusen and Robinson (1986), offers a potpourri of choices and possible structures to meet the diverse cognitive and affective needs of gifted, talented, and high-ability students (Table 5.1). Within the model are provisions for counseling services, seminars, advanced placement or honors classes, acceleration, enrichment, cultural experiences, and career education. Saturday school, summer classes, correspondence study, and college classes are seen as viable alternatives for delivery of services in addition to regular classroom instruction.

By use of this comprehensive programming plan, gifted students have many options for meeting their unique needs. The model provides both accelerated and enriched learning experiences as it addresses the broader issue of curriculum development in a secondary setting.

The Enrichment Triad/Revolving Door Model and the Secondary Triad Model

Although the Enrichment Triad/Revolving Door Model (Renzulli, 1977; Renzulli & Reis, 1986), along with the Secondary Triad Model (Reis & Renzulli, 1986), is in part a curricular model, the delivery-of-services component should be examined as an often-used program model. The Revolving Door Model (Table 5.1) is essentially a pullout program utilizing a resource room for the presentation of enrichment to meet the unique needs of gifted students. From this basis a wide array of goals, services, strategies, and procedures are offered to provide services for elementary and secondary gifted students. The Enrichment Triad/Revolving Door Model operated from a unique set of assumptions regarding the definition and identification of giftedness. Rather than seeing any individual as gifted or potentially gifted, the model assumes that the concept of giftedness reflects behavior resulting from an interaction among three basic clusters of human traits, i.e., above-average general and/or specific abilities, high levels of task commitment, and high levels of creativity. The model further assumes that gifted behaviors can be developed, that they are not always present, and that service should be provided only when such behaviors are exhibited.

Students are identified for a Talent Pool that should comprise 15 to 20% of the school population by use of psychometric, developmental, sociometric, and performance information. A step-by-step decision-making format is described for forming the Talent Pool (Renzulli, Reis, & Smith, 1981). This detailed formatting of procedures is one of the strengths of the model; because of these well-thought-out formats, most of the program and curricular operations can be easily followed and adapted to any setting.

It is basic to the operation of the Revolving Door Model that the Talent Pool students be provided with performance-based learning situations in the regular classroom that will help teachers identify which individuals and small groups should revolve into advanced-level experiences based on their interest in particular topics or problem areas. More detail regarding these learning experiences is presented in Chapter 7 in the discussion of curricular models. Once a student or group of students has given evidence of interest, need, and commitment to the degree that a special project should be initiated, the students will be revolved into the resource room following the appropriate steps and support procedures. The extent to which the student or students will remain in the resource room will be individually assessed and planned. A large part of the success of such a pullout program depends on the cooperation and training of the regular classroom teacher. The originators of the model hope that all teachers and students at all levels can benefit from this structure and the detailed procedures that have been worked out to support it.

The Hopkins Acceleration Model—Study of Mathematically Precocious Youth (SMPY)

For over a decade the Study of Mathematically Precocious Youth (SMPY) has developed educational opportunities in several areas of radical acceleration (Stanley, 1979) (see Table 5.1). An 8-week, fast-paced accelerated mathematics program was begun in 1977 for seventh graders (Fox, 1981). Algebra II and plane geometry were offered. These classes differed from most homogeneously grouped programs for the gifted in several ways: Students were selected from measures of specific aptitude in mathematics; they were allowed to self-select into the program after being told that the work load was heavy; there was maximum use of academic learning time, that is, the real time in which a student is actually engaged in learning (Berliner, 1979); the material was fast paced and used a high level of abstraction and complexity; no class time was spent on drill or practice; and activities were kept to a minimum. The program was not individualized and demanded intensive self-study.

In addition to the fast-paced math, a program for accelerated language arts was begun in 1978 at Johns Hopkins University (Durden, 1980), and a tutorial program based on diagnostic testing, followed by prescriptive instruction in math and verbal ability, was piloted in the summers of 1979 and 1980. Stanley (1979) admits that these programs are designed to serve highly able, achieving, and motivated students:

> With more than 2,000 mathematically able boys and girls already identified, we do not have time and facilities to look for latent talent or potential achievers, worthy though that pursuit surely is. We leave that to the many persons who prefer to specialize in identification and facilitation of underachievers, "late bloomers," and the "disadvantaged gifted." Aside from some concern about sex differences in mathematical precocity, we have not tried to screen in a set percent of any group. From socioeconomic and ethnic standpoints, however, the high scorers have been a varied lot. (p. 101)

The SMPY program, its principles, and its procedures have been replicated in several other states at other universities and provide one alternative for a specific population of highly gifted learners.

Because one of the most commonly found characteristics of gifted individuals is their ability to learn at a faster rate than more typical learners, acceleration in some form should be available in every gifted program, at both the elementary and secondary levels.

USING THE COMMUNITY

Many gifted programs have stretched their resources by using community facilities and people as part of the teaching process. Using the Coordinator of Gifted Programs as the organizer, have you thought of

1 Equipping a van or bus as a mobile laboratory to take your students into the field for an integrated experience in science, geography, social science, language, mathematics, and interpersonal relations?
2 Contacting your nearest retirement community for experts who could serve as mentors to students who are ready for advanced challenges? Some people who would be uncomfortable teaching in a larger group may be willing to work with one or two youngsters.
3 Contacting parents to give lessons on their area of interest at their place of business or before groups in your classroom?
4 Using the business facilities close to your school (stock exchanges, real estate offices, stores, hospitals, pharmacies, insurance companies, etc.) for learning opportunities? These facilities are not to be used for one-time-only field trips, but as ongoing or more in-depth contacts. These visits would be especially meaningful to the few students who have special interest in a related field.
5 Using tape recorders to direct teams of students on independent searches or explorations of the surrounding area (its history, its geography, its climate, its economic or cultural nature, etc.)?

The community can also be an amazing source of free materials for the asking. Have you tried contacting

1 The telephone company? They have old telephone poles, used equipment, cable spools, and storage containers; some will even set up a communication system in your room as a public relations service.
2 Electronic companies? They have obsolete electronic parts that can be used for great experiments.
3 Construction projects, lumber and hardware stores? Besides the obvious, in their scrap bin they may have old fencing, paint, rope, bricks, and other treasures.

4 Billboard companies? Their throwaways are great for signs and displays.
5 Rug stores or rug cleaners? If they know it's for kids at school, they often have odds and ends to make a van or classroom really livable.
6 Nurseries, agricultural schools, park departments? They may have plants to donate to science projects and botany buffs.
7 Meat packers or meat markets? Check for spare parts the biologists and anatomists could use.

The list is endless; once you and your students start thinking this way, you will add many, many more. Be sure to check your district or state surplus warehouse. For very little money, you can get a lot of useful items—everything from typewriters and computers to paper cups and newsprint. Check your local community college or university warehouse. Don't forget your school's storage room. Hidden treasures are everywhere. If the school will value the items and write a letter specifying that any materials contributed were donated, the donor can use this as a tax deduction. This practice tends to encourage contributions.

Commitment and Community Involvement

Community involvement does not just happen by chance. A person has to believe that effort spent in community-related activities will indeed make some difference. Gifted students often have a high degree of idealism, and if allowed to use their abilities to make needed changes in the school or community, such activity will foster future commitment to societal goals. Here are some possible activities:

1 Conduct a survey in the school or community that will provide information needed to change something. Then use it.
2 Make a place in the school or community more beautiful. Be sure to obtain agreement on what you consider more beautiful.
3 Work with community groups or organizations for civic improvement.
4 Plan a money-raising project for a worthy charity or to buy needed materials for the school.

Class projects can often be made more meaningful by involving students in the larger community.

Rural Programs

In addition to the possibilities for programming for gifted learners already mentioned, those planning for rural areas may want to consider mobile enrichment vans, independent study "hot lines" (access to mentors through a telephone

Using the community for learning enhances any gifted program.

system), itinerant teachers, correspondence courses, summer seminars followed by monthly meetings, and residential summer institutes (Silverman, 1980). Witters and Vasa (1981) consider the most important task in the provision of educational opportunities for rural gifted to be the selection and training of teachers who work with these students.

Birnbaum (1977) also emphasizes the teacher need and adds others to be considered. Problems with access to resources, from transportation to materials, are seen as inhibiting to cultural and intellectual development. Continuous and assertive leadership is necessary to change a number of other factors inhibiting to the development of quality gifted programs: poor general community understanding, teacher/administrator hostility, and logistical and organizational problems. Cooperatives, consortia of districts, summer programs, and mobile services are suggested by Freehill (1977) as possible solutions.

Pitts (1986) makes seven suggestions about developing a gifted program for administrators of rural schools. He believes that advanced planning is a necessary first step that might not be given proper emphasis. He suggests that, at a minimum, *giftedness* as it will be used must be defined by teachers and administrators, general goals should be set, the program's content should be decided, and an identification procedure should be selected. Because the best teachers are often called upon for any new project and undoubtedly will be asked to participate in this program, Pitts believes that, as a second step, it is important for these teachers to understand the amount of time and energy the planning process will take and to express willingness to take on this new commitment. Third, he cautions those planning the program to be aware that identification procedures are particularly delicate and critical in a small town. He suggests a blind review of the screening data that involves members of the local Board of Education. Fourth, he feels it is important to start small, and fifth, to use existing resources as much as possible. Sixth, program planners must consider the need for adequate transportation, and finally, they must remember that a local program is to meet local needs to the extent allowed by local resources and not attempt to duplicate programs designed for other larger or more affluent communities. Even though planning and implementing a gifted program in a rural community may need extra care to succeed, Pitts believes that such a program "can produce a sense of community pride, can open doors of career opportunity and greater academic success for students, and can stimulate enthusiasm and renewed commitment on the part of the teaching staff which make the hours of planning and program development worthwhile" (p. 25).

EVALUATING THE PROGRAM

The word *evaluation* is, for many people, anxiety producing. It has come to mean a judgment: the act of validating or invalidating a person or thing. Often the word is mistakenly used to mean examination or testing. If used properly, it would mean "to ascertain the value of or to get to know about someone or something." Evaluation goes far deeper than testing, although tests may be used as part of the data collection process. In this discussion, we will consider evaluation as the process of collecting a variety of data to help us understand the student or the program—data that can be used to improve program planning and implementation.

When planning your program evaluation, the first question should be, "Who needs to know what?" What persons are interested in, involved in, or responsible for the gifted program? Included in this group should be, at least, the student, the teacher, the administrator(s), the board members, and the parents. Find out what each of these persons or groups needs or expects to learn from an evaluation. They will all want some information (e.g., data on academic progress and social-emotional growth, gains in decision-making ability and leadership). Some of the groups will need information not required by the others. For example, parents would want information on the effects of home involvement, and the board members would need data on finances.

Make a list of what each group wants to know. Don't assume you know what they want; ask them orally or in writing. Then you are ready to put together the tools and instruments that will give you the data. You might choose to use standardized or specially constructed tests, rating scales, questionnaires, interview schedules, or observation techniques. Look at the program goals; these are expectations that, ideally, the teacher, the student, the administration, and the parents cooperatively delineated. To discover which of these goals have been reached, you might include the student's file of work completed, teacher observations, parent questionnaires, and the student's self-reports and testing records. Have some of the interested groups visit the program to report their impressions. After reviewing the information, you may wish to develop new procedures for meeting your goals, or you may find that rethinking and changing the goals would be desirable.

If your assessment procedures (discussed in Chapter 6, p. 243) are used regularly, data collection becomes relatively easy. Assessment should be ongoing throughout the year. When you find additionally needed data that your assessment overlooks, expand the assessment procedure to include such information. When used properly, evaluation data become part of the total assessment package.

In addition to information about pupil progress, be sure to evaluate the learning situation. Are the structure, the time allowed, and the classroom atmosphere conducive to meeting the needs of the gifted students and the goals of the program? Collecting this kind of information will tell you not only if the program is working, but why. An interesting instrument to use for this purpose is the Class Activities Questionnaire (Steele, 1969). It assesses five areas of the learning environment: *lower and higher thought processes* (based on Bloom's [1956] taxonomy); *classroom focus* (the role of the teacher and whether the students play a passive or active role); *the classroom climate* (attitudes and feelings); and *student opinions* (about class, about things to change, etc.). Others are useful, such as the interaction analysis procedures developed by Flanders (1960), or you could devise a questionnaire specifically to meet your needs.

Be careful in your evaluation to view the students' growth individually, in comparison with their own past achievements and developed criteria only. The student and the teacher could decide together what form the evaluations should take to show achievement when the learning goal has been completed most effectively. Gifted students do not necessarily show growth against group norms because they are already near the ceiling of many tests. To expect gifted students to raise their test scores or percentile ranks is not appropriate to measuring their progress.

To make the program evaluation as effective and efficient as possible, set out a plan that allows you to cycle information throughout the year. Make sure you

1 Know clearly what each person or group involved in your program needs to know.

2 Choose instruments and tools to give you that information.

3 Set up collection points throughout the year in addition to your assessment procedure.

4 Collect only useful data. If you find state or district forms or procedures that require the collection of irrelevant data, discuss them with people at that level. Tell them what data you have, and inquire into their need for the data they are requesting. You may find that they will be willing to change their procedures into a more meaningful model. Sometimes procedures become institutionalized and continue as they always have only because no one questions their purpose.

5 Communicate your information to all concerned persons and groups. It is impossible to get the kind of support your program needs if key people remain unaware of what you are doing. From the student to the board member, keep all persons informed.

6 Use your evaluation data to produce growth in the program and with the gifted students. If done properly, evaluation will never be a final judgment.

For information on specific program evaluations and sample evaluation designs, you may wish to consult the Association for the Gifted's booklet on sample instruments (Renzulli, 1979b), the National/State Leadership Training Institute on Gifted/Talented *Guidebook for Evaluating Programs* (Renzulli, 1975b), the *Diagnostic and Evaluative Scales for Differential Education for the Gifted* (Renzulli & Ward, 1969), and the *Administrator's Handbook on Designing Programs for the Gifted and Talented* from CEC/ERIC (Van Tassel, 1980, Chapter 11).

THE WRITTEN PLAN

We have discussed the rationale for gifted programs, the selection of a planning committee, the philosophy and goals of a gifted program, the assessment of resources needed, the role of the administrator and the coordinator, a variety of traditional and exemplary program structures for the delivery of services to the gifted learner, and the importance of evaluation on these programs. We are now ready to develop a written plan. Kaplan (1974) suggests that the written plan must communicate the program clearly and be able to serve as a reference for any questions regarding its implementation and what it is intended to accomplish. It should also be a guide for evaluating the program goals. In the case of a change of personnel, the plan should be detailed enough to provide for continuity for the new staff. The following are 11 elements that Kaplan considers essential to a written plan:

1 Population, enrollment
2 Descriptive summary
3 Philosophy, goals, and objectives
4 Identification procedures
5 Organization patterns: prototypes, facilities, time allocation
6 Curricular opportunities: activities, techniques, materials
7 Differentiation from regular school program
8 Accountability of personnel
9 Supportive services: inservice, consultants, auxiliary personnel
10 Budgetary allocations
11 Evaluation processes. (p. 199)

We have discussed many of these elements. We will look at the strategies for a differentiated curriculum in the pages to follow.

In summary, if we are to meet the needs of gifted learners, we must have a planned, coordinated, continuous program. This program must be open and responsive to the changing individual, while providing continuous challenge and an adequate diversity of content and process. While we may draw from more traditional gifted education models, our own community, our parents, students, and staff must make the decisions of structure and intent. While some goals can be generalized, others must be specifically set by the teacher, the student, and the parent in a cooperative effort.

A gifted program is difficult to implement without a person who will be responsible, one who will give it full-time support. Money spent on a qualified enthusiastic coordinator will be wisely spent, for the returns are abundant. Continuous evaluation to adjust the gifted program is only one of the tasks involved in assuring its effectiveness. Society needs the establishment and maintenance of challenging programs for gifted students. Our job is not easy. As Drews (1976) comments,

Clearly, we shall never meet the needs of the gifted by systems of prescribed programming, by behavioral objectives and accountability. The prime characteristic of the gifted is their individuality. The precondition of creativity is spontaneity. The creative moment is an intuitive flash. Those of our students who have this potentiality cannot be made to fit into neat sequences of stages of development, whether of intellect or character, as Piaget or Kohlberg suggests. (p. 27)

But be of courage. Important things are seldom easy.

Questions Often Asked

1. Which is better for a gifted learner, acceleration or enrichment?

Gifted students need both acceleration and enrichment, and any gifted program should be designed to provide both. When to use each will depend on the student's needs.

2. Will grouping by ability result in elitist groups of gifted students?

If you mean "Will they feel superior?" No, not usually. In fact, research shows that students who are grouped with their age peers are more likely to feel superior than those who are grouped with their intellectual peers. We must be sure what we mean when we use that term, however. The word *elite* actually means "a group chosen because of some special skill or ability." Perhaps we should ask why it is alright to be chosen for a special group for athletics or the arts, but it is not alright to have an advanced group in academics, and especially not to show higher levels of intelligence.

3. Which program structure is best for educating gifted learners?

That will depend on which gifted learners are being served and where they live. The needs of the student and the resources of the school and the community should be considered when deciding what program structure to use. A wide range or continuum of services is best as has been pointed out by the Richardson study and its Pyramid Project (Cox, Daniel, & Boston, 1985). Of course some structures allow more service than others. If you consult Figure 5.1 you will see that an individualized classroom, cross-graded and with cluster and pullout possibilities, provides far more continuity and service than a regular classroom with a pullout program that provides minimum service for only part of the time. It might also be interesting to note that the Richardson study reports that the pullout format is the least effective and the most expensive option we can use.

4. Shouldn't we spend the funds for the gifted on the children instead of on an administrator?

In programs that have a full-time coordinator to administer the planning and implementation, the quality of the program and the range of services to the students have been found to be far better. When each classroom teacher is responsible for the expenditure of the funds, that teacher's training and knowledge of the needs of the gifted will determine how well the funds will be spent to meet those needs. When you consider that fewer than one out of six teachers who work with gifted students has any training regarding education for the gifted, the likelihood of that arrangement being productive is minimal. In addition to all the other services coordinators provide, they can arrange for many learning experiences for the youngsters that are free or very inexpensive. Teachers may not have the time or knowledge of resources to make this happen.

5. If you live in a small district with few gifted learners, how can you provide a continuum of services?

While your ability to provide a wide range of services may be less, your ability to involve the community is much greater than would be possible in a large, more impersonal area. By working for continuity, continuous progress, challenge, and personal involvement you will be able to meet the individual needs of each gifted learner and at the same time provide an enriched experience for all of the students in your area.

6. Should we identify the children first and then plan a program to meet their needs, or plan a program first and then identify students to fit it?

This is a bit like the chicken and the egg; both have advantages. This is also one of the reasons for having as wide a continuum of services as possible. Remember, the only reason you are identifying children as gifted is to find appropriate placement and educational experiences for them. If your community has limited resources, for example, no resources for performing arts programs, it would be inappropriate to identify students with performing arts talent as part of your program. Know your resources first; then plan your basic program structure. By allowing flexibility within the structure you will be able to serve most of the students in need of special service.

6. Finding the Gifted Within the School Setting

This chapter provides for the reader

- Information on the need for identifying gifted individuals in schools.
- Methods and uses of screening for gifted students.
- A tool for identification of gifted students by teachers.
- Procedures for identification of cognitive, academic, creative, leadership, and arts abilities.
- A discussion of identifying the culturally different, handicapped, or educationally atypical gifted individual.
- Ideas for assessment of individual needs in content, process, and enrichment.

The creative and gifted students reach out beyond the amassing and recall of facts. They are at home with the overarching concepts involving the great unitive themes. They strive for a coherent view of themselves, of the world, and of human destiny. Indeed it is by this quality, more than by standardized tests, that we can identify them, for they are ever seeking the interrelations that lead to a higher synthesis.

—ELIZABETH MONROE DREWS

To provide educational experiences that lead a child to the next level of development, we must be aware of what that learner has already accomplished. In schools that provide individualized learning opportunities, that observe, evaluate, and assess as a part of the growth experience, and that make available access to many levels and types of learning simultaneously, identification is not viewed in the same way that it must be viewed in the more traditional school organization. In schools that use discrete grade placement, primarily determined by chronological age, and that use group instruction almost totally, it may even be necessary to label and isolate atypical learners for at least part of the time. In secondary schools where departmentalization by subject is the most common way to present the world to a learner, this will certainly be necessary. Advanced placement classes and honors sections are often used to meet this need. Such provisions do not take the place of individual assessment, and planning for appropriate experiences for each learner is still necessary.

When public education began in our country, years before testing became available, students often moved through their educational program as their ability allowed. Fewer pupils studied in smaller, multigraded classrooms. Bright children in classrooms where materials were available over a range of grade levels, often as many as eight, could easily learn from older children and become involved in work beyond their own age groups. The early system not only made it possible for students to complete eight grades of schoolwork in a shorter time period, but encouraged them to do so. The ability to pursue any higher levels of education depended on the financial support available to the student. Only bright students had these opportunities, as most families could not economically support the less able students. This was a time when much education stemmed from the home, and experience was viewed as a good teacher. It was possible for eminent people such as Thomas Edison, Jessie Benton, and Albert Einstein to be educated by their families when they, for one reason or another, could not remain in the public educational system.

There are numerous advantages to a more integrated approach to education. For now, let us look at those that affect the educational experience of the gifted child today. Some years ago I taught a cross-graded class of gifted youngsters in a rural area of one of the Great Plains states. The children were all gifted learners, and the school was committed to providing any resources necessary to further their educational growth. It was possible to develop a program that allowed the children to work at their own level of ability and interest. The program used group instruction, individual conferencing, contracts, and group projects. It made much use of peer and cross-grade tutoring and small-group projects. Students worked with a variety of levels of materials; at times, second graders worked in eighth-grade material for some subject areas and in third-grade materials for others. This was true of the third graders and the fourth graders as well. They soon lost sight of what "grade" they were in and dealt with material as they were ready for it. Those exceptionally accomplished in one area dealt with very advanced materials in that area while they worked at less advanced levels in other areas of learning. Some recreation or project work included the entire class, for learning many skills was a joint venture. We had an exciting time.

As a child became ready or approached a new level or interest area, appropriate learning opportunities were available. Their abilities did not need to be identified; they could just "bubble up." We could use materials and school and community resources, including a variety of people, to ensure continued growth. Later, in a similar plan in Illinois, classes of kindergarten children were observed, and those who showed ability in any particular area were given the opportunity to expand their skills and talents as they "bubbled up." Provisions for advanced learning became a normal part of these classroom situations. In both cases, the schools were committed to providing for individual needs and encouraging unique growth. Identification was a continuous occurrence. Special grouping and specialized instruction were normal parts of the classroom routine.

A few years later, working in another area of the country, I experienced a different and, unfortunately, more common way of instructional organization. This classroom had children all at one grade with a range of ages not more than 2 years apart. However, their learning abilities were extremely divergent. The IQs ranged from 80 to 180, with only three children above 130. Several spoke only Spanish. It seemed obvious that this would have to be a very individualized program that would need a wide variety of experiences and an even broader range of materials and learning opportunities. To my dismay, I was expected to teach third-grade reading, to use the state-adopted text at grade level, and to give standardized tests at regular intervals. Using any of the tests to diagnose was not allowed. Whether appropriate to the learner or not, they had to be administered and turned in for scoring. Just a printout of the stanines achieved by the students was returned for classroom use. The administration then used the results to compare schools within the district and to make decisions on these comparisons. The room was regularly visited to see that the furniture was in place (fire rules) and that the children were seated and quiet. My final defeat came with the declaration that teachers in first through third grade (this was a third-grade room) would be prohibited from using materials from the upper grade bookroom, and that it would be locked with keys issued only to eligible staff members. This was to prevent children from going ahead of their grades so that they would not be bored when they were given material the following year.

In educational settings such as this, identifying atypical learners becomes a concern. In such rigid situations, the energy to meet the needs of the school administration and still provide meaningful individualized learning for such diverse students becomes too overwhelming. Of course one can try, against all odds, to enrich the learning of children such as the three with bright minds. More likely, the push for conformity will prevail, and any extra energy will be spent trying to bring the slow children up to the pace and norms the school expects. One way to ensure a gifted learner's growth in this situation is by identification and at least partial segregation. We discussed the possibilities of programming for the gifted in Chapter 5.

Because not all children and teachers find themselves in situations where the "bubble-up" method can work and because, even in ideal situations, assessment, profiles, and case studies are extremely valuable, let us look at alternative procedures for finding gifted children.

SCREENING AND IDENTIFICATION PROCEDURES

What do we know about discovering the gifted in large populations of students? This is indeed a difficult task, for although one can generalize certain characteristics within this population, individuals may not possess the same characteristics as other gifted individuals or exhibit them in quite the same way. They may not appear to have any physically observable differences. The gleam in their eye and that extra energy level they seem to possess does not show in many educational situations. Depending on how their previous life experiences have dealt with their giftedness, they may even actively attempt to appear quite "ungifted." They may, too willingly, go along with the classroom program.

To confound the issue, not all gifted children cooperate in a classroom. Many resist routine, exhibit nonconformist behavior, and may be classified as behavior problems. Others may be labeled slow learners because they are bored, uninterested in material learned long ago, and nonresponsive to classroom activities. Unless observation of activities of their own choosing is involved, they may even appear to be educationally retarded or emotionally disturbed. Many gifted youngsters are discovered only after their frustration leads them, by teacher request, to the office of a counselor for testing for a learning-handicapped program. They are just as likely to withdraw into the "good" child syndrome, passively doing only what is required and drawing attention to themselves only for excessive participation in school-approved activities such as reading. This is especially common among girls. Because the very qualities that cause a person to be gifted can be successfully used to hide giftedness, we need to be aware of some identification procedures.

Let us look again at our definition. Gifted children are those who have developed or show evidence of developing high levels of intelligence, with *intelligence* being defined as advanced or accelerated whole brain function. Such children may exhibit any of the characteristic behaviors we discussed in Chapter 3. We will be especially concerned about gifted children who show their intelligence through high performance in abilities in the cognitive, specific academic, creative, leadership areas, or ability in the visual and performing arts, when such ability cannot be furthered in the program ordinarily provided by the schools. We will further concern ourselves with children who show the potential for high performance.

Were it not so expensive, the quickest way to find a large percentage of cognitively gifted youngsters would be the administration of individual intelligence tests. If you have access to the protocol, the original copy of the test with the actual responses recorded, you have a good diagnostic tool. If tests are used properly, they provide much information. Test scores alone give very limited data; without a protocol they can be nearly valueless. On some groups of children, the more commonly given intelligence tests may not provide enough information. For some, the child-rearing practices of their parents, the language they use most, and their past experiences are not reflected in these tests. The scores may give a false picture of their abilities. Although Binet (Binet & Simon, 1973), in originating the intelligence scales in 1906, and Terman (1916), in revising and popularizing these scales, both warned that they were to be used as only one piece of datum along with other important information about the student in any process of educational decision making, such was seldom the case. Even now, the intelligence test looms very large as a selection tool for gifted individuals. Earlier we discussed some of the limits of the intelligence test, but even the weaknesses mentioned are not the main reason that individual intelligence tests are not used as screening devices. The expense of having such a test administered by a licensed school psychologist is prohibitive. Only after the school has some assurance that the child will perform successfully on such tests can they be scheduled. How, then, can we provide that assurance?

For children who express their intelligence through creative thinking, other tests and activities will be indicated. To identify leadership or arts abilities will take observation and judgment of products or events. What procedure can be devised to find those who are ready to advance in all these areas?

It should be evident that to find and serve children from each of the areas of ability will take varied and numerous resources. It would be well for a school advisory committee to make some initial recommendations prior to the implementation of any identification procedures:

1 What resources (material and personnel) does the school or community have for providing programs for advanced learners?
2 Are they adequate to provide for all five areas of ability?
3 If not, which areas should be included?

It will be assumed that the cognitive and specific academic ability areas would be included, for these are usually the primary focus of the school. Very probably creative ability should also be included, as abilities in these areas are supportive to the cognitive functions and are not totally separable. Leadership may become an important subcomponent of the gifted program in which the learners could choose to participate. Visual and performing arts talent take very special resources significantly different from those for the other ability areas. The school may need to enlist professional artists, musicians, actors, and dancers from the community to supplement the program in this area.

Dirks and Quarfoth (1981) compared two multiple criteria models for identifying gifted children, one developed for depth (scoring well on one area) and the other for breadth (scoring well on several areas). Children selected for breadth had high classroom grades and were well thought of by their teachers. Those selected for depth included more children and more promising underachievers than the breadth model. The authors of this study believe the depth model to be more valuable in identification.

Screening

Identification begins by screening for children who show need for a different quality of educational experience. As shown in Figure 6.1, screens that could be used for all areas of ability include

- Nomination forms—from teachers, principal, counselor, psychologist, and others
- Teacher reports of student functioning—including intellectual, physical, social, and emotional functioning; learning style and motivation
- Family history and student background—provided by parents—including historical and developmental data on the student, health and medical records of student and family, educational and occupational background of parents, description of family unit, anecdotes of the student in the home that indicate unusual capacity and early development, family activities and interests, and the child's out-of-school activities and interests
- Peer identification
- Student inventory—of self, values, interests, and attitudes toward school and out-of-school activities
- Student work and achievements
- Multidimensional screen tests.

For best results, none of the above should be used alone; instead, all should be used in combination for screening, and later as part of the data in the identification

Figure 6.1 Identification Procedure.

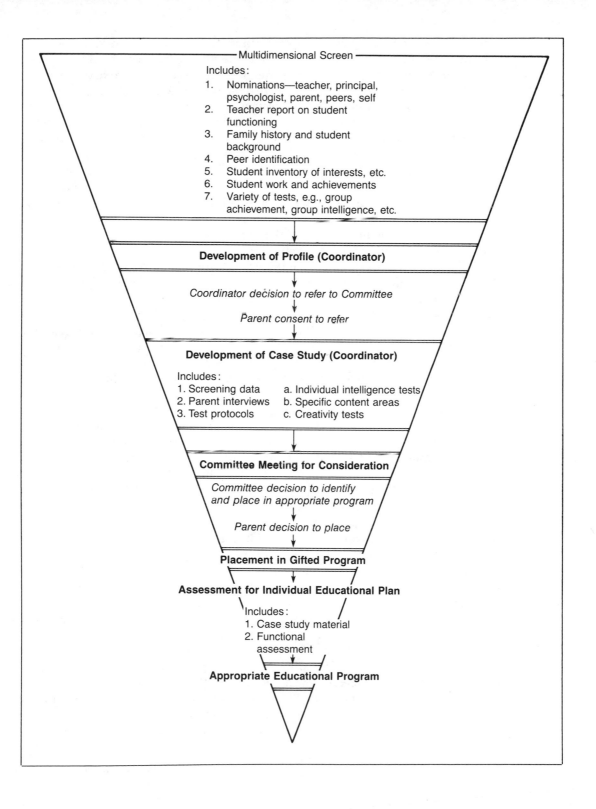

Multidimensional Screen

Includes:
1. Nominations—teacher, principal, psychologist, parent, peers, self
2. Teacher report on student functioning
3. Family history and student background
4. Peer identification
5. Student inventory of interests, etc.
6. Student work and achievements
7. Variety of tests, e.g., group achievement, group intelligence, etc.

Development of Profile (Coordinator)

Coordinator decision to refer to Committee

Parent consent to refer

Development of Case Study (Coordinator)

Includes:
1. Screening data   a. Individual intelligence tests
2. Parent interviews   b. Specific content areas
3. Test protocols   c. Creativity tests

Committee Meeting for Consideration

Committee decision to identify and place in appropriate program

Parent decision to place

Placement in Gifted Program

Assessment for Individual Educational Plan

Includes:
1. Case study material
2. Functional assessment

Appropriate Educational Program

process. The actual identification of a child as gifted requires the judgment of a selection committee. Screening should be done as early as possible in the child's school career. Identification at kindergarten level allows the child to have appropriate education throughout the school experience. Early screening can prevent the waste of talent we now find all too prevalent.

The most commonly used screen is teacher observation and selection of those nominated for testing. Logically we would believe the teacher to be the one most familiar with the child and best qualified to make such a recommendation. But let us look at the usual situation. One teacher works with 35 to 45 children during the day; at secondary level the number can be six times greater. The curriculum aimed at the norm may not challenge any obviously brilliant performance. Depending on how many years the child has been in the system, the child may have developed adaptive skills to "fit in." We know that much of this "adjustment" has already occurred by the third grade, especially among gifted girls.

We must consider the particular beliefs and attitudes of the teacher. How does the teacher imagine a gifted child? In a study by Pegnato and Birch (1959) done at the junior high school level, they found that teachers most often choose children like themselves as gifted. Whatever the teacher values will be the criterion for selection. That is understandable. How can we select those aspects that we do not experience as valuable or good? Often the quiet, well-behaved, well-dressed youngster who gets good grades is a prime target for teacher selection. In their study, Pegnato and Birch found that teachers identified only 45% of the children in their classes who were cognitively gifted, actually missing 55%. Further, of the children they named, only 26% actually tested high enough to qualify; 74% of the students selected for testing did not. This problem exists to an even greater extent in lower grades. According to Jacobs (1971), the effectiveness of teacher identification drops from the 45% identified at junior high to 10% in kindergarten.

We cannot assume that even the highly gifted are easily identified. Barbe (1965) reports that, through teacher selection, 25% of the most gifted students went undetected. Unawareness of the gifted causes this problem: If teachers cannot recognize enough of the gifted in their classes, there may be waste of human potential. However, administering individual intelligence tests is expensive; if teachers select too many students who do not qualify as gifted when tested, the teachers' errors can waste the often limited monetary resources designated for the gifted. The dilemma is then to select enough students not to miss those who are gifted, and yet not to select too many who will not test as gifted. Teachers must be both effective (correctly nominating a high percentage of children who are the gifted in their class, that is, not missing a lot who are gifted) and efficient (having a high percentage of those they nominate identified for the gifted program, that is, not nominating a lot of children who are not gifted). Gear (1978) found that the effectiveness of teacher selection was improved without any loss in efficiency by a five-session training program. The teachers completing the program were, in fact, twice as effective as were untrained teachers. A study by Borland (1978) showed that teachers can improve their efficiency in selecting cognitively gifted students when they are given a list of specific behaviors to rate. Their ability to predict academic achievement was quite high.

Unfortunately, too few teachers know how to identify the characteristics of gifted learners. One way does exist to help those who are screening to improve their accuracy in selecting children who do, in fact, have unusual ability. By distributing a list of common characteristics found among gifted children, we can encourage people to look for those they might otherwise miss.

Looking for Children Who May Be Gifted

If you observe a child showing some of the following behaviors, you may want to look more closely. That child could be gifted.

In the classroom does the child

- Ask a lot of questions?
- Show a lot of interest in progress?
- Have lots of information on many things?
- Want to know why or how something is so?
- Become unusually upset at injustices?
- Seem interested and concerned about social or political problems?
- Often have a better reason than you do for not doing what you want done?
- Refuse to drill on spelling, math facts, flash cards, or handwriting?
- Criticize others for dumb ideas?
- Become impatient if work is not "perfect"?
- Seem to be a loner?
- Seem bored and often have nothing to do?
- Complete only part of an assignment or project and then take off in a new direction?
- Stick to a subject long after the class has gone on to other things?
- Seem restless, out of seat often?
- Daydream?
- Seem to understand easily?
- Like solving puzzles and problems?
- Have his or her own idea about how something should be done? And stay with it?
- Talk a lot?
- Love metaphors and abstract ideas?
- Love debating issues?

This child may be showing giftedness cognitively.

Does the child

- Show unusual ability in some area? Maybe reading or math?
- Show fascination with one field of interest? And manage to include this interest in all discussion topics?
- Enjoy meeting or talking with experts in this field?
- Get math answers correct, but find it difficult to tell you how?
- Enjoy graphing everything? Seem obsessed with probabilities?
- Invent new obscure systems and codes?

This child may be showing giftedness academically.

Does the child

- Try to do things in different, unusual, imaginative ways?
- Have a really zany sense of humor?
- Enjoy new routines or spontaneous activities?
- Love variety and novelty?
- Create problems with no apparent solutions? And enjoy asking you to solve them?
- Love controversial and unusual questions?
- Have a vivid imagination?
- Seem never to proceed sequentially?

This child may be showing giftedness creatively.

Does the child

- Organize and lead group activities? Sometimes take over?
- Enjoy taking risks?
- Seem cocky, self-assured?
- Enjoy decision making? Stay with that decision?
- Synthesize ideas and information from a lot of different sources?

This child may be showing giftedness through leadership ability.

Does the child

- Seem to pick up skills in the arts (music, dance, drama, painting, etc.) without instruction?
- Invent new techniques? Experiment?
- See minute detail in products or performances?
- Have high sensory sensitivity?

This child may be showing giftedness through visual or performing arts ability.

It is important for teachers to be a part of the selection process. First, they have data to offer that are not available to other members of the identification team. Second, they need to become aware of, understand, and support the program for the gifted if it is to succeed. Without some involvement in the selection process, they would be unlikely to cooperate or contribute to any further planning.

Two other screening procedures have yielded results. Interviews with parents of young children reveal a great deal. Parents are very aware of the behavior of their child. When asked relevant questions, they can provide information that is clearly indicative of potential giftedness. In a study, Jacobs (1971) discovered that parents could identify 76% of the gifted children in a kindergarten classroom. This was significantly higher than the teacher's ability at that level—4.3%.

Peers have been extremely helpful in identifying other potentially gifted children for screening. Questions such as "Whom would you choose to help you if you were having difficulty with your arithmetic?" or "If you were planning a learning center on (subject), whom would you choose to be in your group?" or "Who is the smartest person in our room?" form part of a list of identifying questions that can produce important, and often otherwise unnoticed, information about the students in a class. Gold (1965) suggests sociograms for peer screening. A similar device was used at fourth-grade level with success by Granzin and Granzin (1969).

The work of a student can be very useful in the screening process. Both school and extracurricular activities should be considered. Often the work done on a hobby or toward solving a unique problem at home will indicate advanced thinking and creative ability. The more information that can be obtained, the more chance that the screening will be effective in locating gifted students.

Some of the screening tools (Table 6.1) that have been used successfully by districts for some of the areas they wish to serve are the Bella Kranz Multidimensional Screening Device (Kranz, 1978); the Baldwin Identification Matrix (Baldwin, 1980); and the scale developed by Renzulli and Hartman (1971). Perrone and Male (1981) have developed the GIFTS Talent Identification Procedures, which consist of one or more behavior rating sheets plus scoring and interpretation materials. Raters are asked to rate the child only in the areas of talent that they have had the opportunity to observe. Some of the areas that could be assessed are mathematics, English, music, science, reading, interpersonal relations, art, etc. Whitmore (1980) reminds us that "The effective use of behavioral characteristics in the identification process is dependent upon an appropriate environment for observation of superior mental abilities and awareness that a gifted child may excel only in very specific areas or may be underachieving in one or more of the basic skills" (p. 67).

Cognitive

To the Generic screen add group intelligence tests (for examples see Table 6.1). Group intelligence testing may be useful as part of the screening procedure;

Table 6.1 *Suggestions for Screening and Identifying Gifted Learners.*

Expression of Giftedness	Screening	Identification
Generic	Nomination forms Reports of student functioning Family history and student background Peer identification Student inventories Student work and achievements Multidimensional screen tests, e.g., Kranz; Baldwin; Renzulli and Hartman; Perrone and Male	
Cognitive	Group intelligence tests, e.g., California Test of Mental Maturity; Lorge-Thorndike Intelligence Test; Henmon-Nelson Tests of Mental Ability; Otis-Lennon Mental Ability Test; Pinter General Ability Tests; Primary Mental Abilities Test; Kuhlmann-Anderson Individual intelligence tests, e.g., Peabody Picture Vocabulary Test; Slosson Intelligence Test; SOI Screening Tests for Gifted and Talented Children	Stanford-Binet Intelligence Scale Wechsler Intelligence Scales for Children Cognitive Abilities Tests Differential Aptitude Tests Kaufman Assessment Battery for Children
Specific Academic	Student's work Functional assessment of content areas Group achievement tests, e.g., California Achievement Tests; Metropolitan Achievement Tests; Stanford Achievement Test; Iowa Tests of Basic Skills	Test in specific areas of content

Table 6.1 *Suggestions for Screening and Identifying Gifted Learners. (continued)*

Expression of Giftedness	Screening	Identification
Creative	Personality inventories, e.g., Alpha Biographical Inventory; Adjective Check List; Group Inventory for Finding Creative Talent; Khatena and Torrance Creative Perception Inventory; Torrance Tests of Creative Thinking Observation of problem solving	Creativity Tests for Children Creativity Assessment Creativity Perception Inventory Something About Myself
Leadership	Observation in and out of the classroom Scales on leadership from Kranz; Renzulli and Hartman; Perrone and Male	No formal standardized tests available
Visual and Performing Arts	Observation and recommendations from professional artists Peer nominations	Seashore's Measures of Musical Talents Standardized Tests of Musical Intelligence Horn Art Aptitude Inventory Meier Art Tests On-site task completion Juried student work

however, a cutoff score of 115 IQ should be used. A higher cutoff will result in many gifted students' being missed. By using this cutoff, Pegnato and Birch (1959) found that 92% of the gifted, who then scored 135 IQ on an individually given test of intelligence, could be located.

Martinson (1974) suggested the possibility of mutliple, abbreviated tests as a possible screen. Such testing seems to reduce the cost of identification, can be administered by untrained examiners, and lacks cultural bias. The pupils also enjoy the tests. While having advantages as a screen, this abbreviated testing approach should not replace individual testing for identification.

Specific Academic

To the Generic screen add group achievement tests. Functional assessment of just what the child can do would also be most useful here. Often knowledge of achievement in subject matter areas is limited within a curricular range deemed appropriate for a particular grade level. If the child has never had an opportunity to show you how high he or she can achieve in reading or math, planning for continuous progress becomes impossible.

Creative

To the Generic screen you may wish to add a personality inventory such as the Alpha Biographical Inventory (Institute for Behavioral Research in Creativity, 1968) or the Adjective Check List (Gough, 1960), either of which would be appropriate for high school students, and the Group Inventory for Finding Creative Talent (Rimm & Davis, 1976). For all students the Torrance Tests of Creative Thinking (Torrance, 1966) would be appropriate. Observation of the child in an open-ended problem-solving situation should provide useful anecdotal material. For other examples of screening see Table 6.1.

Leadership

Observation of leadership skills in and out of the classroom will provide anecdotal material for screening in this area. The multidimensional scales mentioned in the generic area include sections related to leadership abilities.

Visual and Performing Arts

Observation and recommendations from professional artists would provide excellent additional screening material. Peer nominations have been highly reliable in this area (Kavett & Smith, 1980).

Identification

Actual identification for the purpose of placement in a gifted program is best done by a group of professionals representing a variety of areas of expertise, such as the principal, a teacher, a counselor or psychologist, and the program coordinator. They should develop a case study or profile to aid in the identification decision and also later in program planning for the individual. One of the major purposes of identification is to obtain information that will help educators provide the program that will be best suited to the development of the gifted student's potential. The report should provide enough information to make good educational planning and placement possible.

All of the materials developed for the screening process now become a part of the data that provide a background for the identification decision. In addition you will need data that discriminate in the areas you have chosen to serve. Care must be taken to use tests and procedures that are valid measures of the skills you are seeking and for the population you are testing. In a survey of identification practices now used in gifted and talented education, the National Report on Identification, Assessment, and Recommendations for Comprehensive Identification of Gifted and Talented Youth (Alvino, McDonnel, & Richert, 1981), it was noted that "many tests/instruments are being used for purposes and populations completely antithetical to those for which they are intended and were designed" (p. 128). Such data may only serve to confuse the identification process and the program planning to follow. As Richert (1985) notes, some of the other problems in identification they found were that education equity is being violated in the identification of significant subpopulations; multiple criteria are being combined inappropriately; and instruments and procedures are being used at inappropriate stages of identification, i.e., diagnostic tests used as part of screening.

The panel members for the National Report on Identification, Assessment, and Recommendations for Comprehensive Identification of Gifted and Talented Youth offered the following six principles which they felt should underlie all identification procedures:

1 *Advocacy.* Identification should be designed in the best interests of all students.
2 *Defensibility.* Procedures should be based on the best available research and recommendations.
3 *Equity.* Procedures should guarantee that no one is overlooked. The civil rights of students should be protected. Strategies should be outlined for identifying the disadvantaged gifted.
4 *Pluralism.* The broadest defensible definition of giftedness should be used.
5 *Comprehensiveness.* As many as possible gifted learners should be identified and served.
6 *Pragmatism.* Whenever possible, procedures should allow for the modification and use of tools and resources on hand. (Richert, 1985, pp. 68, 69).

Cognitive Ability

Hagen (1980) states, "The standardized tests for individual administration that are most useful in identifying the potentially gifted are those that appraise scholastic aptitude of general cognitive development, such as *The Revised Stanford-Binet Tests of Intelligence* and the *Wechsler Intelligence Scales for Children—Revised*" (p. 18). Shortened versions of individual intelligence tests have been published; while they may be useful for screening, Hagen warns that they are not suitable for identifying gifted or potentially gifted individuals. She believes that by changing the time limits, content, or directions of the test the data on reliability, validity, and norms for that test are no longer applicable. The number and variety of cognitive skills appraised by the shortened test are limited also.

Two tests suggested for inclusion in the identification process are the Cognitive Abilities Tests (Thorndike & Hagen, 1983) and the Differential Aptitude Tests (Bennett, Seashore, & Wesman, 1963), as shown in Table 6.1. These tests give scores on verbal, quantitative, and nonverbal reasoning. The Otis-Lennon Mental

Ability Test gives but one score, cannot be differentiated, and does not appraise high-level thinking skills well (Hagen, 1980).

A test of fairly recent origin, the Kaufman Assessment Battery for Children (K-ABC), is an individually administered measure of intelligence and achievement (Table 6.1) intended for children from 2½ to 12½ years old (Kaufman, 1984). Taking its basis from the current work in cerebral specialization, the test focuses on the processes of the brain, especially in regard to Sequential Processing, Simultaneous Processing, and a combination of the two, the Mental Processing Composite. The designer believes that this focus on process rather than content and de-emphasis on factual knowledge and applied school-related skills make the test useful in assessing the intelligence and achievement of all children, especially gifted children, gifted minority children, and gifted children with learning problems.

Specific Academic Ability

The best single indicator of future academic achievement is the present level of achievement in the area of interest; therefore, data should be obtained on

> (1) the level of achievement in general academic skills; (2) the level of achievement in skills and knowledge related to a specific academic area; (3) the level of development of general verbal, quantitative, nonverbal and spatio-visual problem-solving skills; (4) originality; (5) persistent long-term interests; (6) out-of-school time spent on activities related to an academic area; and (7) the trend in complexity of activities that an individual undertakes on his or her own initiative. (Hagen, 1980, p. 10)

Some tests suggested are the Iowa Tests of Basic Skills (Linquist & Hierony, 1979) and the Stanford Achievement Test (Kelley et al., 1965).

Creativity

Measures of creativity (Table 6.1) that emphasize divergent thinking, e.g., the Creativity Tests for Children (Guilford, 1973), correlate very modestly with tests of intelligence, and most creativity tests correlate just as little with each other. While tests of creativity may be only assessing a small part of what creativity is about (see Chapter 1), some you may find helpful in addition to those used for screening are the Creativity Perception Inventory (Khatena & Torrance, 1976); and the Creativity Assessment (Williams, 1979).

Leadership

According to Alvino et al. (1981), the most significant identification deficiency of gifted individuals is in the area of leadership. Informal, subjective measures are most commonly used. The sections of the Kranz and Renzulli/Hartman scales mentioned in the discussion of screening tools provide data in this area.

Friedman, Friedman, and Van Dyke (1984) found that a combination of nominations from self, peers, and teachers could be used as a predictor of leadership ability. Of the three, self-nomination was the most powerful predictor leading the researchers to suggest that a simple, straightforward "volunteer" approach should be tried and its power tested. The relationship between these findings and other measures of leadership was not established.

Visual and Performing Arts

We know very little about the early indicators of gifted performance in the areas of visual and performing arts. At present the best indicator of giftedness in these areas is the ability to perform in the specific area chosen. A panel of experts should be assembled to judge such performances. It is believed that the general level of cognitive skills and achievement in the academic areas should receive no weight in these decisions, as there is no evidence that such measures are predictive of artistic achievement (Rubenzer, 1979; Hagen, 1980). Even tests of creativity have no demonstrated and proven validity as measures of artistic and musical talent (Hagen, 1980), although Torrance has found that those students who major in speech, drama, and art attain higher scores on these tests than do other students (Barbe & Renzulli, 1975).

When used with other data, the Seashore's Measures of Musical Talents has been found useful (Kavett & Smith, 1980; Rubenzer, 1979), as has the Horn Art Aptitude Inventory and the Meier Art Tests (Rubenzer, 1979). While Saunders (1982) indicates that the Meier Art Tests can be used to determine levels of aesthetic awareness, he reports that Alexander (1981) has found the Meier Art Tests to be culture bound and of doubtful value for children under 12 years of age. Saunders (1982) suggests several ways to secure artistic screening and identification data, including the process of assigning a variety of tasks to 25 to 30 applicants at a time and asking them to complete the tasks on site in one sitting. The tasks tested were two-dimensional and three-dimensional organization and art problem-solving abilities. Other means for gathering data were suggested:

> Take a number from 0 to 9, make an art work from it. Think of as many ideas as possible, save them, and bring all notes and sketches (to the interview).
>
> Record a dream you remember that had great impact. It does not have to be a recent dream. Draw it in a cartoon form. Include as many elements of the dream as possible, but do not use words.
>
> Using six to ten different found objects (such as screws, a broken wheel, a soda can), construct a three-dimensional portrait of yourself at age 85. Try to use the materials in unusual ways. Try to show not only how you look at that age, but how you might feel. Don't worry about the details, but instead try to suggest the general characteristics, use

glue, string, or wire to hold your piece together. The whole piece should be no bigger than 1½ feet by 1½ feet.

Fold a large piece of paper in half. Using a pencil, charcoal or crayons do a drawing of the sun on one half, and do a drawing of the moon on the other. Think carefully about their differences and similarities. (p. 9)

Ellison et al. (1976) has researched and developed a procedure for using biographical information as a predictor of artistic talent and claims it to be superior to more traditional measures.

The Case Study

Once the data on a child who is being considered for the gifted program have been collected, they must be put into a usable form for the selection committee. A number of plans have been suggested for ranking or quantifying the results of the screening and identification process. For examples of such plans see Gowan, Demos, and Torrance (1967), Hagen (1980), Baldwin (1980), and Vermilyea (1981). Information to include in the data for the committee that will comprise the student's case study should incorporate the following, much of which has been already developed for screening.

1 *Family History and Student Background.* Provided by parents, this will include historical and developmental data on the student; health and medical records of student and family; educational and occupational background of parents; description of family unit; anecdotes of the student in the home that indicate unusual capacity and early development; family activities and interests; and the child's out-of-school activities and interests.

2 *Teacher Report of Student Functioning.* This report includes observations of intellectual, physical, social, and emotional functioning; learning style; and motivation.

3 *Nomination Forms.* These are collected from teachers, principal, counselor, psychologist, and others.

4 *Student Inventory.* The student provides an inventory of self, values, interests, and attitudes toward school and out-of-school activities.

5 *Test Protocols.* These individual and group tests include scores and the psychologist's interpretation. If other criteria are to be used in lieu of scores, they should be included. For students of separate criteria such as special populations (e.g., disadvantaged gifted, handicapped gifted), include all data necessary for decision making regarding selection and placement.

6 *Student's Work or Achievement Awards.*

After the student has been identified, the parents must be informed of the decision and asked for permission to place their child in whatever program the school provides. The signed permission form will then be place in the permanent case study file. Administrators should explain to the parents the concept of giftedness and the purpose of the program and then ask for any suggestions they may have, clearly inviting their participation.

PROBLEMS OF IDENTIFYING THE CULTURALLY DIVERSE, HANDICAPPED, OR EDUCATIONALLY ATYPICAL GIFTED INDIVIDUAL

As we saw in Chapter 3, giftedness results partially from an early interaction with a stimulating environment. Family patterns or persons who provide such stimulating interaction can be found in any culture, at any socioeconomic level, and in spite of many disabling conditions. Such differences, however, may make traditional identification procedures ineffective for discovering such ability.

Problems of Traditional Intelligence Tests for Culturally Diverse Learners

The way IQ tests are constructed has built-in limitations and assumptions that can be unfair to groups who are not closely identified with the dominant culture. First, one assumption of most intelligence tests is that intelligence is a single, unvariable factor. More current data indicate that intelligence is neither a single factor nor is it a constant one (see Chapter 1). Although our belief about the reality of intelligence has changed, our measuring tools still proceed from our previous beliefs.

Another problem results from the choice of items on the tests. Out of an infinite number of human accomplishments and interests, the items have been restricted to concepts and skills found in school curricula, especially the more basic abilities: reading, language arts, and arithmetic. For this reason, IQ tests tend to be good predictors of success within the school environment. A wide variety of other human activities and abilities that could be well developed in our atypical learners (e.g., fluency, originality, problem solving in other than academic areas) are not even represented. To make sure the variation of the growing intellect from younger to older children would not disturb the IQ scores, all items that did not fit the smooth growth pattern that the tests assumed were deleted. Items that displayed any bias for either sex were also deleted. By such limited selection procedures, the tests become very narrow in their focus.

The population modeled for standardization of any test is important to measure its usefulness. The standardization of most commonly used IQ tests has been done within the major culture. For example, the Stanford-Binet was standardized and its scores for success established on white children of English-speaking parents. It has become known as the "Anglo test." Many believe that such bias makes this test inappropriate as a measure of ability for children outside the Anglo culture.

These restrictions have led many educators and psychologists to call for the construction of "culture free" tests. Although many have tried (Cattell, 1949; Davis & Eells, 1953; Leiter, 1951), the results have been disappointing. Jensen (1969) found that blacks not only score higher on conventional tests such as the Stanford-Binet and Wechsler than they do on "culture free" tests, but that they also score higher on verbal than on nonverbal subtests. In fact, Jerison (1977) contends that a nonverbal test of intelligence may be a contradiction in terms because, even if words are avoided, the language and language-related functions of the brain are inevitably dominant in most human performance.

In studies reported by Christiansen and Livermore (1970), Holland (1960), Johnson (1962), and Mercer and Smith (1972), Mexican-American children performed significantly better on nonverbal than on verbal intelligence tests. The higher performance more adequately reflected the school grade point average of these children than did the scores received on verbal scales.

Another possible problem of obtaining valid test results seems to be in the test administration. Katz, Robinson, Epps, and Wally (1964) and Katz, Roberts, and Robinson (1965) report that, in several experiments, the race of the test administrator had an effect on the test results of black students. They believe that the white environment in general may be stressful and threatening to black children. It can create a situation that predicates against accurate test results. The effect of examiner variables (bilingualism, ethnic group membership, and style of test administration) on the test performance of Spanish speaking children was reported by Bordie (1970), Palomares and Johnson (1966), and Thomas, Hertzig, and Fernandez (1971). In a review of experimenter effects in bicultural testing, Sattler (1970) concludes that they play a critical role in any cognitive performance.

Torrance (1969) believes that testing culturally diverse children should include a concern for mood setting or for providing activities that will awaken the creative processes. He states that they should not have imposed time limits, and that ways should be provided for the examiner to record the children's responses. He found these procedures quite effective in eliciting hidden verbal abilities.

In considering the problem of finding hidden ability in the culturally diverse population, Renzulli (1973c) suggests that we need to develop non-language-dependent identification strategies that do not require written production. He believes it important to make the identification process a continuous one among the culturally diverse.

In a comprehensive article on the identification of gifted black students, Frasier (1987) makes several suggestions for improving the process. She believes the nomination or screening phase would be more successful if it included nominations from more people in addition to the teacher, e.g., community leaders, peers, and self. A checklist of learning styles for black populations would be informative. She cites Hilliard (1976) as an example of the learning style one might find with Afro-American people:

1—Tend to view things in their entirety and not in isolated parts.
2—Seem to prefer inferential reasoning to deductive or inductive reasoning;
3—Appear to focus on people and their acitivities rather than objects;
4—Tend to prefer novelty, personal freedom, and distinctiveness;
5—Tend to approximate space, number, and time instead of aiming for complete accuracy;
6—Have a keen sense of justice and quickly perceive injustice; and
7—In general tend not to be "word" dependent, but are proficient in non-verbal as well as verbal communication. (p. 35)

Such checklists may alert teachers to behaviors that are unique to the specific culture and allow them to look for giftedness from a new perspective. Frasier (1987) closes her discussion of identification with the following guidelines:

1 Focus on the diversity within the black population.
2 Gather data from multiple sources, objective and subjective.
3 Use professionals and nonprofessionals who represent various areas of expertise relevant to your program.
4 Plan identification procedures that occur as early as is possible and that are continuous.
5 Pay special attention to the different ways in which children from different cultures manifest behavioral indicators of giftedness. (pp. 174, 175)

These are good guidelines for all of us to follow regardless of the population we are seeking and wish to serve.

Multidimensional assessment again becomes the theme as Tonemah (1987) discusses the identification of American Indians for the gifted program. In an effort to develop effective leadership within the American Indian community, a group known as the American Indian Research and Development, Inc. (AIRD) was formed. Because the group has concerns that standardized test scores by themselves cannot measure total achievement, they suggest that the scores not be used as the sole source of evaluation of student performance. In addition, the group recommends that professionally trained psychometrists (preferably American Indian) administer the evaluation to American Indian students, and that group achievement and intelligence tests be developed and normed with American Indian student populations. In an effort to gain a tribal perspective of giftedness and talent, AIRD surveyed tribal people asking them to list the characteristics of their tribe's gifted and talented students. The results are being used as part of the gifted student identification and selection process and will form the basis for a critical look at the curriculum. The goals of AIRD are receiving support from the tribal people, and the hope is that their efforts may eventually lead to an American Indian Gifted and Talented Academy.

Alternative Identification Procedures
for Culturally Diverse Learners

Many suggestions for finding ability in culturally diverse people lean heavily toward the identification of noncognitive skills. Much of the investigation has centered on creative abilities, with discussion under the label of gifted and talented—*talented* here designating creative abililty. This practice needs close examination. We do not for the most part use tests of creativity to identify the major population of cognitively gifted children. How, then, can we use such identifiers for other children we include in this population? Some data indicated that children with creative ability may be a different population, that they may or may not be gifted cognitively. In an attempt to find tests that would discover intellectual promise among minority children, Hilliard (1976) used several types of testing. While additional students were discovered, those who excelled in creativity were not the same students who showed cognitive promise. If we are including the gifted and the talented in all of our identification and programming procedures, this seems a justifiable practice; however, if we are using only measures of cognitive intelligence on the majority, while including tests of creativity for only a few, we may be developing an unfair situation. Programs developed for highly cognitive students may not meet the needs of the creative student.

There are, however, many alternatives that you may find useful. Bruch (1971) has been concerned with the problem of finding members of subcultures, primarily southeastern black students, who have potential not evidenced on traditional tests. She hypothesized that, by looking at patterns of strength other than those required for the usual IQ test, we can find otherwise untapped black, disadvantaged, gifted children. Some areas of strength she feels need to be considered are visual and auditory figural content (e.g., art and music), memory, convergent production in practical problem-solving situations, awareness of details in descriptions, fluency of ideas, spontaneous categorization and classification of spatial items, and awareness of natural relationships or systems. Her work has led her to the development of a form of the Binet that she feels favors southeastern black students and allows the gifted among them to be identified. Her instrument, an abbreviated version of the Stanford-Binet, is known as the Abbreviated Binet for Disadvantaged (ABDA).

Another test that has been developed to correct the problems found in traditional testing is the System of Multicultural Pluralistic Assessment (SOMPA). The SOMPA uses three assessment models: (1) the medical model, a deficit model that focuses on pathology; (2) the social system model, which compares the behaviors of the child to the behaviors of those in the social system to which he or she belongs; and (3) the pluralistic model, which assumes that only if factors such as exposure to skills and materials, motivation, and learning experiences, etc. are held constant, can learning potential be assessed. This use of adaptive behavior and estimated learning potential to identify gifted children from culturally diverse or disadvantaged backgrounds is a new approach that shows promise but has not yet been validated (Mercer & Lewis, 1978).

Bernal (1978) suggests three techniques for identifying gifted Hispanic students: (1) culturally pluralistic assessments such as Mercer discusses above; (2) Piagetian measures for K–3, that is, looking for advanced schema used in problem solving on a test such as the Cartoon Conversation Scales, which are available in English or Spanish; and (3) bilingual language proficiency scales where rapid and advanced growth in language would provide a good indicator of high intelligence. The Raven's Progressive Matrices Test (Raven, 1947) has been helpful for mass screening (Wescott & Woodward, 1981).

In 1985 a school district within the greater metropolitan area of Los Angeles, the Montebello Unified School District, began a program of special identification of bilingual, bicultural students for their gifted program. This program was designed to meet the needs of a district that had a large Hispanic population (84%) that had been underrepresented in the gifted program. The procedures for identification, though multidimensional in nature, had not been successful in producing balanced identification of bilingual, bicultural students. From the beginning the task of designing and implementing such a program fell to Patricia Almada, Bicultural, Bilingual Coordinator for the district, and Kazuko Tanaka, the district's Gifted Coordinator. A grant was written and monies from Federal Chapter II funds provided for time and personnel to implement the program.

A committee was formed to consider the characteristics of the gifted and to search the literature for other models and best practices used to identify bilingual, bicultural gifted students. Though they found few models, they found several ideas that had not been a part of their multidimensional screen; among them, peer nomination had been found to be very valid, and parent interviews were found to be very important. The literature suggested that administrative support was necessary for the success of any new program, so they decided to place the new identification projects only at sites with large bilingual, bicultural populations and a principal who considered the project important. Because of the time involved, some of the funds were allocated to pay a project facilitator at each site. The assigned sites served primarily Hispanic populations, many of whom spoke Spanish as their first language, so all materials were developed in both Spanish and English.

The project began at each site with an inservice of the total staff to acquaint them with the characteristics of the gifted and the purposes of the project. Teacher nomination forms were developed and distributed to all project site teachers and their aides. To nominate a child, the forms required the teachers only to check any of 25 characteristics, arranged in question form, that they had observed with the children in their classrooms, e.g., "Who in your room is especially curious?" The procedure was planned to take less than 20 minutes to complete. The teachers were then asked to choose five children at random from the class and ask them in Spanish or English the questions on the characteristics form. The teachers' and children's completed forms were sorted by category, and children who received three or more nominations (checks) in any category were referred for further study. The project leaders found that this procedure worked well with children in second, third, and fourth grade. It did not produce good results with K–1 children who wanted to talk only about their friends.

With the compiled list of teacher and student nominations the site facilitators then went to the cumulative records file for more information on each child. High average group test scores were noted with knowledge that, among low-achieving peers, many students would seem high achievers even though they were really not in need of special services. Only evidence of able performance was considered.

After the substantiating data had been assembled the parents were called in for additional verification. When the parents were told of the purpose of the interview, the facilitator received interesting reactions. One mother said, "Out of my four children I knew he was different." Another commented, "It's about time you found him," showing no surprise at the school's inquiry. Still another cried when told of the possible placement for, as she noted, she had never had any positive experiences with being called to school. Her child seemed always to be in trouble.

With the data accumulated, the site facilitator chose the most qualified students and referred them to a Selection Committee composed of the Bilingual Facilitator, or the Coordinator for Gifted Programs, the child's regular teacher, the site administrator, the site facilitator, and the school psychologist. This committee chose the students who in their judgment would most profit from the gifted program and sent a letter to the parents inviting them to a meeting to explain the district's gifted program and the experiences their child would have. Only after the parents had agreed to the placement and signed the forms for participation was the child officially considered placed. Children who were not selected received a personal notification from the site facilitator letting them know that they would not be receiving the services at this time, but would be noted for consideration should they need the services in the future.

The identification program is now in its third year and is considered very promising by the district. Over 350 bilingual, bicultural students that would otherwise have been missed have been placed in the district's gifted program. These had been chosen from nominations of over 1,200 bilingual, bicultural students, demonstrating the efficacy and efficiency of this procedure. For more information you may wish to write to Kazuko Tanaka, Coordinator for Gifted and Talented Education, Montebello USD, 123 S. Montebello Blvd., Montebello, California 90640.

Another alternative, behavioral identification, is being used with success by Malone (1974) and Malone and Moonan (1975). Their results indicate that selected combinations of behavioral characteristics can be made to categorize gifted and nongifted kindergarten children correctly. They find that this procedure in no way restricts inclusion of culturally diverse children.

Another way of using behavior as an indentifier was reported by Childs

(1981). This is the use of the Adaptive Behavior Inventory for Children (ABIC) (Mercer & Lewis, 1977). The ABIC is a structured parent interview covering family, community, peer relations, nonacademic school roles, earner/consumer, and self-maintenance. The study found that gifted chilren do more activities related to independence and social responsibility and do them earlier than their chronological peers. Childs found the gifted children consistently superior to normal children in adaptive behavior, as measured by the ABIC, and feels that adaptive behavior can and should be used as part of the identification process. Childs points out that the ABIC showed no significant differences among races or cultures in its standardization sample. Torrance (1977) believes that by use of his "creative positives," more talent can be discovered and developed among the culturally diverse and economically disadvantaged. He has developed a system for using his data for nontest ways of identifying the creative among the gifted in these populations.

Other means of identification have been used. Some teachers have found that the math concept scores of disadvantaged students on standardized tests are good predictors of the ability to succeed in gifted programs. Gear (1976) has successfully used a training program she designed, Identification of the Potentially Gifted, to improve the teacher's effectiveness in identifying intellectually gifted students.

There are many new directions now being explored to make identification fairer and more useful. The decade of interest in the work of Jean Piaget has begun to stimulate researchers to move in the direction of developing tests based on his theories. The current interest in brain research evokes numerous attempts to use the new knowledge of brain function as a measure for intelligence. Ertl (1968) has designed a comparison measure of the relationship between the electrical activity of the human brain and intellectual measurement in psychological testing. Results of his experiment show a strong relationship between superior intelligence and response time to sensory stimulation. The use of Ertl's Brain Wave Analyzer has been shown to discriminate more accurately between academically gifted and academically handicapped students (ages 12 through 14) in combination with the Primary Mental Abilities tests or the Sequential Tests of Educational Progress (STEP) than do these tests when used alone. While Ertl's brain wave analyzer cannot substitute for paper and pencil tests, it can make a valuable contribution to the understanding of learning potential (Fischer, Hunt, & Randhawa, 1978).

Also of interest is the work of Schaefer and Marcus at Sonoma State Hospital (1973) on measuring the electrical discharge from a person's brain when a stimulus is presented unexpectedly. They believe that the difference between the electrocortical response of a surprised brain and a prepared brain may be related to intelligence. Much interest has also been shown in the work of E. Roy John and his team at New York Medical College's Brain Research Laboratory. Their test of brain function, the Quantitative Electrophysiological Battery (QB), is both quick and sensitive, and it presents a more accurate picture of learning than a battery of traditional tests (Goleman, 1976). Such techniques may aid in the identification not only of culturally diverse children but of the handicapped gifted as well.

Identifying the Handicapped Gifted

One of the major problems in finding the gifted among the handicapped is a function of the expectation that is the result of labeling. Because most special education programs in schools have far more fiscal and human resources at the disposal of the handicapped child, identification will usually be for that program. Once labeled, teachers expect the child's needs and behavior to fall within those normally found in the identified group. Needs for these children are so often deficit needs that remediation will be the primary concern. In this climate, evidence of giftedness is often missed. So few teachers in the handicapped setting have been exposed to the characteristic behaviors of gifted children that they may interpret any observed deviations from the norm as being unique to the handicapping condition. Even when giftedness is suspected, it is often difficult for a child receiving special services to find a place in a gifted program. The disability teacher may not wish to disrupt the program in the primary area. The teacher in the gifted program may be so limited in time and resources that finding a place for the child may be too difficult. The administration may be under restrictions as to financial and program qualifications. A child who is gifted and also blind, deaf, or physically disabled may find it almost impossible to experience any opportunities for enhancing that ability at school.

The child labeled learning or educationally handicapped has an even more complex problem. Often such a child has extreme ability in one or two areas and remedial needs in others. Such a child may also have a behavioral problem and find working with groups difficult. The tests given because of hyperactivity, disruptive classroom conduct, or extreme withdrawal are often the very tests that spot gifted ability. The excessive energy that creates problems may also be behind the student's achievement in a few areas of interest. Unfortunately, it is not rare to find children in a learning handicapped class who were only unable to cope with the structures of a rigid regular classroom. We have previously discussed the importance of self-concept to the success of the student. You can clearly see the results of a negative view in this situation.

Suter and Wolf (1987) have identified several characteristics of this population, including impaired long- and short-term memory, visual or auditory processing difficulties, visual motor integration problems, poor self-concept, high levels of self-criticism, withdrawal or aggression, short attention span, difficulty following directions, and poor peer relations. Suter and Wolf warn that the giftedness of these children often goes unnoticed, because they may use it to mask their learning difficulties or they may be identified with learning disability children and their giftedness be totally overlooked. Several common findings from Suter and Wolf's research with the WISC-R may help to detect these children: Large verbal-performance discrepancies are frequently seen; subscales that assess verbal reasoning abilities tend to show high scores; and scores on Digit Span, Arithmetic, and Coding tend to be low. These researchers again ask for a multidimensional approach as necessary to appropriate identification of the handicapped gifted.

A study of WISC-R profiles by Schiff, Kaufman, and Kaufman (1981) found that a large discrepancy in scores between the verbal section and the performance section indicated a child with learning disability who might also have a high level of intelligence. In the majority of their sample (87%) the verbal scores were higher.

Recognizing these special problems, in 1975 the Bureau of Education for the Handicapped (BEH) funded two projects whose goals were to develop and demonstrate models for identifying and programming for young gifted and talented children. One project is located in the public schools of Chapel Hill, North Carolina. The Chapel Hill project has developed a package for training teachers in the identification of very young potential candidates for the handicapped gifted program. The techniques suggested for identification are structured and unstructured observations, checklists, and sociometric measures (Blancher-Dixon & Turnbull, 1978).

The other project is located at the Institute for Child Behavior and Development at the University of Illinois, Champaign-Urbana campus. In a report of this project, Karnes and Bertschi (1978) found two levels of identification to be necessary: Some children could be identified during program placement procedures; others required some remediation of the handicapping conditions before their talents emerged.

The training program of all special educators should include some information regarding gifted children. A credential requirement in California provides all special education trainees with a generic core of experience that allows them to learn about and be involved with all types of exceptional learners. The students at our university now have an increased awareness of the needs of gifted children and a growing interest in course work that will provide them with more information on how to identify and serve handicapped gifted children.

Most of the identification strategies for culturally diverse, disadvantaged, and handicapped gifted individuals have focused on the cognitive abilities; a few have considered the creative behaviors. Is there a need for measures of academic, leadership, or arts abilities that take into consideration the effects of being atypical? Is leadership expressed differently in disadvantaged or culturally diverse surroundings? Would an arts audition be different if the artist were culturally diverse or handicapped? Perhaps these special talents can be seen when skills of creativity, leadership, and the arts are evaluated; perhaps there is no need for special measures—only a change of attitude and more open-minded observation. While these are not easy questions to answer, the answers will help us include in our identification all the ways giftedness can be expressed. This area definitely bears investigation.

ASSESSMENT

Having identified those children who require differential education, we must now discover what each child's individual needs are. In the area of education for the gifted, a strange phenomenon occurs. Usually the major part of the differential experiences offered to gifted individuals is provided within a minimum amount of time, often outside the classroom. The advisability of such programming was examined in Chapter 5, but the existence of such practices presents us with a dilemma.

In most special education settings, the word *need* has a connotation of deficiency. In gifted education it means quite the opposite. When gifted individuals are assessed for "needs" for special provisions, these denote areas of strength that cannot be properly nurtured in a regular classroom setting. This is not to say that gifted students would have no need for remedial help in some academic areas, nor does it imply that the gifted individual is equally gifted in all areas. Such is just not the case. However, where special attention or funding is found to meet gifted needs, it is the nurture of advanced ability that is intended and not the remediation of deficits. If attention must be given to deficit needs, the regular school program assumes the role. Remediation becomes part of a gifted program only if such a program comprises the major portion of the student's educational experience, such as full-day special class placement. When limited part-time programs are used for remediation, children have no opportunity to grow in their areas of gifted need. These are the areas for which no provisions are made in the regular classroom setting and for which these children have been identified. Programs for the gifted learner must focus on these areas. With this in mind, let us look at the problem of assessing these needs.

The needs of the gifted may be found in areas of content, process, and enrichment. Once such needs are identified, appropriate programs can be planned. Assessment is not, however, only a beginning to the year's activity. To be effective, assessment must continue throughout the year. While some assessment tools have infrequent use, others should be continuous with the student's program as it changes, to reflect the growth such assessment procedures bring to light.

In developing any assessment package, information from both students and parents needs inclusion. Both have unique contributions that will add to the data bank from which good educational decisions can be made. It is inadequate to get such information only once or even yearly. Frequent planning and reporting conferences that include parents and students will additionally aid in establishing communication, gaining support for the program, and ensuring the success of the student's educational goals.

Content Assessment

There are at least three major ways to assess the student's level of capability in content areas:

1 *Norm Referenced Tests.* These tests include standardized or specially constructed, intelligence or achievement, and individual or group measures. Norm referenced measures use the performance of other individuals as the standard by which the student is compared.

2 *Criterion Referenced Tests.* These include tests of specific content skills, either teacher written or published. These measures have a predetermined standard or criterion of performance against which the student is compared.

3 *Functional Assessment.* This measure involves observing a student working to determine his or her level of functioning.

Information on standardized tests should be found in the child's case study and should include the test protocol or booklet and the report from the psychologist with an interpretation of the test results. When the score alone is recorded without interpretation, the specific areas of strength and weakness shown on each test disappear. Two children scoring exactly alike could have very different areas of strengths. They would therefore require quite different provisions in their educational programs. Meeker (1969) devised a technique for teachers using templates to analyze the Stanford-Binet in areas designated by the Guilford Structure of Intellect (Guilford, 1967). The resulting information may be synthesized into a profile of strengths and weaknesses for a program of specific skill-building activities developed and researched by Meeker. Without the protocol information, the diagnostic value of the test is wasted, eliminating the value of the test score when recorded alone.

Both criterion referenced and norm referenced assessments may be functionally and informally given. Classrooms that use centers or learning activity packages as part of their program can use these approaches to gain assessment information. Allowing students to correct criterion referenced tests as pretests for skill areas and then providing self-instructional materials for areas not yet understood allow the teacher a greater amount of time to direct higher level learning. Parents in the classroom can act as monitors for final posttest recording that will give additional useful data to the assessment procedure. Users of these assessments should be sure that all content ratings are based on age or grade expectations and not on class norms or the achievement of other gifted children.

Process Assessment

How the student learns is as important as what the student learns. Once we know what content should be available, we must discover the ways in which our students process information. What learning styles or sensory modalities do they use? How independent or self-directed are they? What skills of leadership or initiative do they possess? What research or learning-how-to-learn skills have they already developed? How much of their creativity do they use? We need to ask questions such as these.

There are a number of tests available to help you develop a profile of the major affective characteristics of your learners, such as their values, interests, locus of control, anxiety levels, and self-esteem. Detailed information on conducting affective assessment has been compiled by Anderson (1981).

In addition to the information available from published tests of creativity (e.g., Torrance, 1966), the *Taxonomy of Educational Objectives* (Bloom, 1956) can be used to examine which process skills gifted students have developed and which need further development. The processes of analysis, synthesis, and evaluation are all within the capability of gifted students, but they do not reach their most effective level without provision of opportunities for development. Again, it should be noted that these students possess the ability to work with abstracts, concepts, and diverse and integrative thought patterns. The students will need to be familiar with conceptual frameworks such as Bloom's (1956) taxonomy or Suchman's Inquiry Model (Suchman, 1962) in order to meet this differential need. These models are discussed in Chapter 8.

One important way to assess process skills is to observe a student's involvement in problem-solving situations. This can be done individually or even quite successfully in groups. The Inquiry Training sessions discussed by Suchman (1962) can provide these group situations. Approximately 10 students are presented a dissonant event by verbal or visual means. They are asked to inquire into the circumstances of the event to discover what caused the results they observed. In a formal inquiry session (described in Chapter 8, p. 345), students begin to ask questions, formulate hypotheses, test their hypotheses, and evaluate their ideas. Through observation of such sessions, teachers may become aware of the mental processes their students use to solve problems and the effectiveness of such techniques. Teachers can learn a great deal by careful observation.

Another observational technique to provide process assessment is the contrived problem for group focus. For example, a small group could be given a simulated plot of land to develop as a community. The community should become the place where they would most like to live. Given a house, a business of their choice, and a vote on all development within the community, they must first place their house and business to everyone's satisfaction and then provide for any other facilities they feel necessary to the welfare of the community. With few rules and only the physical materials to manipulate (e.g., simulated lakes, trees, hills, houses, stores, roads) the group must organize, provide its own leadership, develop group communication, and set its own limits. All of these processes can be observed, and the "game" becomes a rich source for assessing process skills.

Gorman (1974) provides formats for student inventories of study habits and skills, personal profiles, learning styles, leadership abilities, and other areas that can add significant data to your process assessment.

Assessing for Enrichment Needs

Enrichment needs, probably the easiest to gain information about, are the most commonly assessed. For the gifted learner, the world seems filled with an overwhelming abundance of exciting things to learn about. Most gifted individuals will be pursuing interests in a large variety of subjects at any given time. The educator will need to learn what those interests are and may ask both the student and the parents for that information. In addition to the interests already being investigated by the student, opportunities should be provided to open up new areas not yet known. Not all gifted students will be interested in all areas; assessing the level of interest after exposure to new experiences will be important.

Once assessments have begun to give information on the gifted student, a profile should be developed and the case study file updated. We can now include recommendations for programming and placement on both content and process and suggest some areas for enrichment. This will allow the teacher to develop a far more effective and meaningful gifted program. Regardless of the model or program followed for delivery of educational services, assessment is essential to meet the needs of gifted students successfully. The profile of gifted learners usually shows areas of relative strength and weakness. Most gifted students show at least average ability in all school-related activities. It is important, however, to assess the strong areas carefully and not to assume strength and ability in all areas. Some educators plan programs for the gifted on the assumption that these learners are gifted in everything. This is not the case. Of all the atypical populations of learners, this group will show the highest degree of uniqueness and a definite need for individual planning.

Within this chapter we have looked at the rationales and procedures for selecting gifted children who need special educational provisions to continue their growth. We have discussed screening procedures and the problems of screening; we have viewed identification from a variety of perspectives, including the importance of assessment and case studies; and we have looked at the special problems encountered in identifying the atypical, the handicapped, and the culturally diverse gifted learner. But all of this would be meaningless if we did not then look at programming to meet these special needs. The main purpose for identification is to provide special educational experiences that can enhance the continuous growth of every gifted child.

Questions Often Asked

1. Why identify gifted children at all? Wouldn't it be better just to improve education for everyone?

Improving education for everyone is the goal for which we all strive; however, while we are doing that we must also make sure the needs of these underserved children are met. Most school systems do not individualize their instruction to the degree that children with special needs can receive an appropriate educational experience. Remember, brain researchers tell us we must use and challenge our brain or we will lose ability. Unless specially planned, school experiences seldom challenge bright students. As schools are now organized and run, identifying children with special needs is the only way to ensure that these needs will be met. Gifted children are among that special needs group that must be identified and served.

2. Should we identify preschool gifted children?

Many of the characteristics and behaviors typical of gifted learners can be observed very early. The only reason to identify them is for appropriate placement and educational planning. As we saw in previous chapters the early years are the most plastic and should be enriched if we are to allow children to be all that they can be. At present there are few early learning programs available that provide well-rounded, integrated, and enriched programs; there are even fewer that provide appropriately for young gifted children. With this in mind I would be more concerned about challenging all children from where they are, allowing continuous progress and enriching experiences, and letting the children guide us to their next steps than I would be about formal identification. Appropriate, stimulating experiences are our best way to nurture giftedness.

3. If a child has high IQ scores but is not highly creative is this child gifted?

Such a child can be; however, one score is never enough to know if a child has special needs. Certainly a high IQ score is one piece of datum that indicates a need for more information. The biological changes that result in gifted behavior may be expressed in many ways. Creativity may not be the way a particular child expresses his or her giftedness.

4. Should we use the same tests for low-socioeconomic-level students as we do for the others?

Yes, if you are using a wide variety of tests and demonstrations of ability. Where we once got into trouble in this regard was when we gave only the standardized intelligence tests to children and then to be more "fair" gave creativity tests to "special criteria" children from very poor communities. We then placed those who scored high in both groups together and gave them the same learning experiences. As a result we penalized the low-socioeconomic-level children by placing them in an academic setting for which they had no skills. Hopefully, we have learned from our past errors and now offer both groups a wide range of data collection and multidimensional testing for identification and a continuum of services for programs.

5. Aren't "culture free" tests best for identifying culturally diverse students?

Although some tests may be more "culture bound" than others, none are "culture free." While there is still controversy regarding which tests are best for whom, our safest avenue is to provide multidimensional testing and develop a good profile of the child from which we can make sound educational decisions. Because children will be asked to perform in the mainstream culture, I doubt that we would be doing them a service by providing "culture free" experiences. Sensitivity to their cultural experiences and provision for further opportunities enhancing wider cultural understanding would be more helpful.

6. What is the best identification procedure?

Generally, nominations are requested at the beginning and then multidimensional screening is done, resulting in an educational profile that can be used to decide if further identification is appropriate. If it is, the profile material is developed into a case study with a variety of more specific and individualized information added. This material then goes before a committee of school personnel for the decision regarding placement. Next, assessment of specific needs is done, using the case study information and any additional functional assessments needed. An individual educational plan can be developed from this information.

7. Isn't the case study approach too expensive to be practical?

Much of the information used for the case study is available for every child from the school's cumulative records. The additional data will be needed only if the child passes the initial screen. The most expensive parts of the process are the coordinator's time spent collecting the data and the committee's time for considering identification and appropriate placement. Other approaches may be more expensive in that they are inefficient if the methods allow too few to be found or ineffective if the screen allows too many needing further identification. The most expensive would be to lose human potential by inappropriate, narrow procedures that leave gifted children unserved.

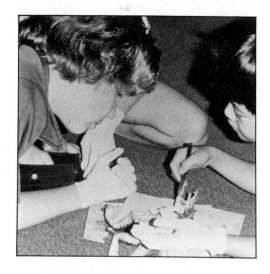

7.

Developing a Differentiated Curriculum
Gifted Needs and Curriculum Models

Presented in the chapter for the reader are

- An overview of the relevant characteristics and needs of gifted learners, accompanied by suggested organizational patterns and examples of strategies for meeting these needs.
- A discussion of differentiating curriculum and its importance in gifted education.
- A curriculum criteria checklist.
- A discussion of several curriculum models used with gifted learners.
- An introduction to the Integrative Education Model (IEM).
- Steps to a differentiated curriculum.

After you understand about the sun and the stars and the rotation of the earth, you may still miss the radiance of the sunset.

—ALFRED NORTH WHITEHEAD

You have organized and established a program that will allow your gifted learners to continue to develop their abilities and interests. You have identified the ways in which your gifted learners express their giftedness. Now we will look again at giftedness as a total brain function, as a level of advanced and accelerated development causing special needs that are seldom met in the regular school program. High levels of intelligence make demands on the gifted learner that can be seen in characteristic behaviors. These demands create special needs. In this chapter we will look again at an overview of characteristics commonly found among gifted learners, examples of related needs, organizational patterns that facilitate meeting these needs, and examples of strategies and program provisions for use in the classroom. There are several current, recognized models that can provide educators with ways to develop a curriculum that is appropriate and challenging for gifted students. Some of these models will be discussed. Finally we will explore the Integrative Education Model and its promise for developing a more holistic view of gifted education, where through individualization and differentiation all expressions of giftedness may be served and nurtured.

AN OVERVIEW OF ORGANIZATIONAL PATTERNS AND STRATEGIES FOR GIFTED PROGRAMS: AN INTEGRATIVE APPROACH

As an overview of organizational patterns and examples of strategies showing their relationship to the characteristics and needs of gifted individuals in each of our four areas of brain function, we will examine a model that was developed for gifted programming. In the original development of the model by Hagen and Clark (1977), the intuitive function was omitted. This area of function has been added to the original that included a societal component. The overview now discusses the Cognitive Domain, the Affective Domain, the Physical Domain, the Intuitive Domain, and the Societal Domain and becomes the basis for integrative education for the gifted and its implementation within society.

The special educational needs of gifted pupils result from characteristics in those domains that differentiate them from typical learners. An analysis of those characteristics can provide us with a model for organizing educational programs. Programs that relate clearly to the differentiating characteristics of this population can most effectively meet the educational needs and nurture the high-level abilities of gifted pupils.

While all students have unique needs, some generalizations about needs that result from highly developed intelligence can be made. These generalizations can serve as a starting point for program planning.

The model presented here extends earlier work of Ward (1961) and others by organizing the characteristics and needs of the gifted into each of the five domains. Organizational patterns and classroom teaching strategies are suggested for each identified need. Each domain is divided into a hierarchy, with examples provided for appropriate program provisions at each level.

The Cognitive Domain

Cognitive development rests in part on the analysis, integration, and evaluation of a vast quantity of experiences of the environment and on an understanding of those experiences. Educational programs should provide an array of experiences and encourage development of the processes of understanding, analyzing, organizing, integrating, and evaluating. It is now known that cognition can also be spatial and visual in its processing. The effectiveness of cognitive processing is enhanced when both these modes are available to the learner. Qualitatively different planning for the gifted implies recognition of the ways in which their differential cognitive characteristics affect these processes.

Differential Cognitive Characteristics of the Gifted

The following differential cognitive characteristics have been identified in the gifted:

- Extraordinary quantity of information; unusual retentiveness
- Advanced comprehension
- Unusually varied interests and curiosity
- High level of language development
- High level of verbal ability
- High level of visual and spatial ability
- Unusual capacity for processing information
- Accelerated pace of thought processes
- Flexible thought processes
- Comprehensive synthesis
- Early ability to delay closure
- Heightened capacity for seeing unusual and diverse relationships and overall gestalts
- Ability to generate original ideas and solutions

- Early differential patterns for thought processing (e.g., thinking in alternatives and abstract terms, sensing consequences, making generalizations, visualizing solutions)
- Early ability to use and form conceptual frameworks
- An evaluative approach toward oneself and others
- Persistent goal-directed behavior.

Each of these characteristics creates related educational needs that make demands upon school programs in terms of modifications in classroom organization and methodology. Table 7.1 presents some examples of appropriate modifications related to the cognitive characteristics and needs of gifted pupils. The examples given are only representative of possible patterns and strategies. Addition of alternative organizations and materials is encouraged.

Program Provisions in the Cognitive Domain

Program provisions responsive to the special characteristics and needs of gifted pupils can also be thought of in terms of the categories of a taxonomy of cognitive objectives. Bloom (1956) and his colleagues have classified educational objectives in the cognitive domain into a hierarchy, using the categories of knowledge, comprehension, application, analysis, synthesis, and evaluation. The educational planner who wishes to emphasize a particular category of objectives will need to provide for appropriate educational experiences. The needs of the gifted might be met by such provisions as the following:

A *Knowledge*
  1 Exposure to the environment and the culture, including esthetic, economic, political, educational, and social aspects
  2 Exposure to peers, adults, and other students with expertise in the student's interest areas
  3 Advanced and/or unusual subject matter
  4 Experience in identifying data needs and establishing data organization
B *Comprehension*
  1 Opportunities to communicate and exchange ideas, information, and opinions in a variety of ways
  2 Experience in data collection
C *Application*
  1 Opportunities to work with peers, adults, and students who have expertise in student's interest areas
  2 Instruction in developing original applications of knowledge and understandings, including hypothesizing and hypothesis testing

Table 7.1 *The Cognitive Domain.*

Differentiating Characteristics	*Examples of Related Needs*	*Organizational Patterns*	*Examples of Classroom Strategies*
Extraordinary quantity of information, unusual retentiveness	To be exposed to new and challenging information about the environment and the culture: aesthetic, economic, political, social aspects To acquire early mastery of basic skills	Individualized learning: out-of-classroom experiences	Information organized at levels of difficulty with self-checking pretests and posttests available, and a variety of methods for learning available at each level
Advanced comprehension	Access to challenging curriculum and intellectual peers	Self-selected flexible groupings; opportunity to enroll in advanced classes on other campuses, if appropriate ones can be found	Group discussion on mutually selected topics; work on advanced topics of interests; advanced materials available
Unusual curiosity and variety of interests	To be exposed to varied subjects and concerns To be allowed to pursue ideas as far as their interests take them	Integrated curriculum Flexible scheduling	Mentor program; simulations
High level of language development	Opportunity to encounter and use increasingly difficult vocabulary and concepts	Work with academic peers	Edit and publish a book, journal, play, or TV script

Table 7.1 The Cognitive Domain. *(continued)*

Differentiating Characteristics	Examples of Related Needs	Organizational Patterns	Examples of Classroom Strategies
High level of verbal ability	To share ideas verbally and in depth	Self-selected flexible grouping	Work on projects of student's choosing that involve communication and exchange of opinions in a variety of ways
High level of visual and spatial ability	Opportunities to express ideas visually; to learn integratively	Individualized learning; integrated curriculum	Incorporate visual mode in products
Unusual capacity for processing information	To be exposed to a large variety of ideas at many levels	Learning centers available at many levels in a variety of subjects	Projects involving hypothesizing and hypothesis testing, for development of research skills
Accelerated pace of thought processes	To be exposed to ideas at rates appropriate to individual pace of learning	Individualized curriculum, advanced placement	Brainstorming; speed reading; opportunities for acceleration of content; self-paced instructional materials
Flexible thought processes	To be allowed to solve problems in diverse ways	Cooperative student-teacher-parent planning for learning objectives and experiences	Teacher acceptance of unusual products; open-ended assignments; opportunities to examine and/or alter existing patterns physically and mentally

Comprehensive synthesis	To be allowed a longer incubation time for ideas	Flexibility in assignment of deadlines; cooperative instructional planning; individual conferences	Continuous assessment of progress; individualized deadlines for products
Early ability to delay closure	To be allowed to pursue ideas and integrate new ideas without forced closure or products demanded	Integrated curriculum and activities for which no product or judgment is required over a large block of time, mutually agreed upon	Presentation of dissonant events for solution; classroom creating climate of respect for ideas; opportunities for reflection
Heightened capacity for seeing unusual and diverse relationships and overall gestalts	To "mess around" with varieties of materials and ideas	Integrated curriculum	Unstructured periods of time for exploring materials; teacher acceptance of unusual approaches
Ability to generate original ideas and solutions	To build skills in problem solving and productive thinking; to contribute to the solution of meaningful problems	Small group experiences; access to data throughout the community; opportunity to move out into the community for information	Planning and implementing solutions to community problems
Early differential patterns for thought processing: thinking in alternatives and abstract terms, sensing consequences, making generalizations, and visualizing solutions	To be exposed to alternatives, abstractions, the consequences of choices, and opportunities for drawing generalizations and testing them	Small group activities; opportunities to interact with adult experts in areas of the students' interests	Activities promoting the development of inquiry skills; instruction in and opportunities to analyze their own learning processes, communication, and decision making, and to compare them with the processes used by peers and adults

Table 7.1 *The Cognitive Domain. (continued)*

Differentiating Characteristics	Examples of Related Needs	Organizational Patterns	Examples of Classroom Strategies
Early ability to use and form conceptual frameworks	To use and design conceptual frameworks in information gathering and problem solving To seek order and consistency To develop a tolerance for ambiguity	Individual contracts; learning centers; access to the community	Individualized projects integrating knowledge from various areas of life into new divergent, and/or convergent physical and mental structures; designing learning experiences for others Simulations and other activities that emphasize the social cost of various solutions
An evaluative approach toward self and others	To be exposed to people of varying ability and talent and to varying ways of seeing and solving problems To set realistic, achievable short-term goals To develop skills in data evaluation and decision making	Flexible groupings with individualized learning available	Self-evaluation and cooperative evaluation experiences Instruction and practice in goal setting, goal evaluation Introduction to models of decision making and practice in their use on real problems
Persistent, goal-directed behavior	To pursue inquiries beyond allotted time spans To set and evaluate priorities	Flexible time modules, individualized instruction, small support groups	Value clarification exercises (see Simon, Howe, & Kirschenbaum, 1972); self-chosen projects

D *Analysis*
   1 Opportunities to examine and/or to change or alter existing patterns physically and mentally
   2 Instruction in, and opportunities to analyze, their own processes of learning, decision making, and communication, and then to compare these processes with the processes used by others
E *Synthesis*
   1 Opportunities to integrate knowledge from various areas of their lives into new, divergent, and/or convergent physical and mental structures
F *Evaluation*
   1 Opportunities to identify and clarify standards of comparison and evaluation
   2 Instruction in, and opportunities to develop, data evaluation skills
   3 Instruction in, and opportunities to develop, decision-making skills
   4 Opportunities to evaluate personal choices in terms of available data, individual needs and goals, and choice consequences.

The Affective Domain

High levels of cognitive development do not necessarily imply high levels of affective development. The same heightened sensitivities that underlie gifted intelligence can contribute to an accumulation of more information relating to emotions than the student can process. This affect-based information comes from sources both within and outside of the child. Gifted children need to learn that applying their cognitive powers to this material will help them to make sense of their emotional world. The educational program must provide them with opportunities to bring emotional knowledge and assumptions to awareness, and to apply verbal ability and inquiry skills in the service of affective development.

The early appearance of social conscience that often characterizes gifted children signals an earlier need for development of a value structure and for the opportunity to translate values into social action. This can begin in the society of the classroom and should then be extended into the larger world, as appropriate to the child's increasing competence and widening concerns.

Examples of classroom strategies suggested here have a heavy cognitive component. The discussion of each activity is essential in helping the students to process the personal meaning of their experiences cognitively. The teacher can be alert for opportunities to focus the discussion in ways that will draw upon higher cognitive processes, and thereby assist the children to a fuller integration of cognition and affect.

Educational planning for the affective development of gifted pupils, like the planning for cognitive development, must stem from the characteristics of the children to be served, and the special needs implied by those characteristics.

Differential Affective Characteristics of the Gifted

The following differential affective characteristics have been identified in the gifted:

- Large accumulation of information about emotions that have not been brought to awareness
- Unusual sensitivity to the expectations and feelings of others
- Keen sense of humor—may be gentle or hostile
- Heightened self-awareness, accompanied by feelings of being "different"
- Idealism and a sense of justice that appear at an early age
- Earlier development of an inner locus of control and satisfaction
- Advanced levels of moral judgment
- High expectations of self and others, which often lead to high levels of frustration with self, others, and situations
- Unusual emotional depth and intensity
- Sensitivity to inconsistency between ideals and behavior.

Table 7.2 gives some examples of ways in which classroom organization and teaching strategies can relate to the affective characteristics and needs of gifted pupils.

Program Provisions in the Affective Domain

Behavioral objectives in the affective domain have been organized by Krathwohl, Bloom, and Masia (1964) into the following hierarchy: awareness, receiving, responding, valuing, integration into a value structure, and characterization by a value. Program objectives appropriate to the affective characteristics and needs of gifted pupils may be thought of in the same conceptual framework.

A *Awareness*
1 Opportunities to identify and name one's own emotions
2 Opportunities to identify one's own perceptual filters and defense systems and those of others
3 Opportunities to expand and to clarify awareness of the physical, social, and emotional environment

B *Receiving*
1 Experiences and instruction in attitudes of receptivity and suspended judgment
2 Opportunities and support for actively seeking ideas and feelings from others

C *Responding*
1 Opportunities and support for communicating personal expressions in a variety of ways
2 Opportunities to identify, establish, and participate in environments in which personal responses are invited, encouraged, and valued

Table 7.2 The Affective Domain.

Differentiating Characteristics	Examples of Related Needs	Organizational Patterns	Examples of Classroom Strategies
Large accumulation of information about emotions that have not been brought to awareness	To process the emotional meaning of experience cognitively	Individual learning center activities and small discussion groups	Task cards and group discussions based on *Feelings* by Polland (1975)
	To name one's own emotions		
	To identify one's own and others' perceptual filters and defense systems	Large and small discussion groups	Awareness exercises in the first chapter of *Awareness* by Stevens (1971). After the teacher has led a sample activity or two, others can be put on task cards for student-led small group activity, in upper elementary or secondary groups.
	To expand and clarify awareness of the physical, social, and emotional environment	Large or small group or individual learning center activity	Physical environment: an exercise in finding your "spot" as in Castaneda (1972, pp. 18–25). After reading the pages, students try to find their spot, then write about or discuss their own process, how it felt to be in the different places they tried, the attributes of the place they selected, etc.
			Social environment: One-way glasses as in *Toward Humanistic Education* (Weinstein & Fantini, 1970, pp. 71–79)

Table 7.2 *The Affective Domain. (continued)*

Differentiating Characteristics	Examples of Related Needs	Organizational Patterns	Examples of Classroom Strategies
Large accumulation of information about emotions that have not been brought to awareness (continued)			Emotional environment: Magic Circle method from the *Human Development Program* by Bessell and Palomares (1970)
	To clarify awareness of the needs and feelings of others	Can be a total class activity; requires a safe climate emphasizing respect for individuality	Magic Circle discussion about the magic box that has something in it to make every person happy. Children imagine what might be in the box for them and guess about what might be in the box for other children in the group, telling why they think that would make that particular child happy (Bessell & Palomares, 1970).
Unusual sensitivity to the expectations and feelings of others	To learn to clarify the expectations of others	Large and small task-oriented groups	Out-of-focus slides, as described by Sonntag (1972, p. 6)
Keen sense of humor—may be gentle or hostile	To learn how behaviors affect the feelings and behavior of others	Group discussion in a climate that supports caring and honest exchange of feelings and ideas	Silent Partners in Sonntag (1972, p. 27)
Heightened self-awareness accompanied by feelings of being "different"	To learn to assert own needs and feelings nondefensively; to share self with others, for self-clarification	Large and small communications-oriented groups	See Sonntag (1972), particularly Teacher Intervention, pp. 31–35

Characteristic	Objective	Grouping	Activities
Idealism and a sense of justice, which appear at an early age	To transcend negative reactions by finding values to which student can be committed	Small group discussions, grouping gifted students together	Activities drawn from *Values Clarification* by Simon, Howe, and Kirschenbaum (1972)
Earlier development of an inner locus of control and satisfaction	To clarify personal priorities among conflicting values To confront and interact with the value systems of others	Small group discussions; self-chosen groups	*Values Clarification*, Simon, Howe, and Kirschenbaum (1972)
Advanced levels of moral judgment	To receive validation for nonaverage morality	Discussion groups with adults or intellectual peers	Exercises in resolving moral dilemmas by Kohlberg (1972, 1974, 1976a, 1976b, 1977)
High expectations of self and others, which often lead to high levels of frustration with self, others, and situations	To learn to set realistic goals and to accept setbacks as part of the learning process	Small groups specifically organized to develop realistic goal setting and reality-based self-concept	Self-esteem activities developed by Coopersmith (1975)
Unusual emotional depth and intensity	To find purpose and direction from personal value system To translate commitment into action in daily life	Participation in community social-action groups	Classroom examination of the opportunities for involvement offered by various community groups Out-of-classroom opportunity to work with group selected by the individual student
Sensitivity to inconsistency between ideals and behavior	To find a vocation that provides opportunity for actualization of student's personal value system, as well as an avenue for his or her talents and abilities	Out-of-classroom opportunity to interview persons in various careers about the opportunities for actualization of value systems offered by their career	Classroom discussion on ethical questions faced by persons in selected careers, and resolutions consistent with the student's value system

D *Valuing*
   1 Opportunities and instruction in constructing and clarifying personal values
   2 Opportunities and support for expressing personal values including caring, caring for, and caring about
E *Integration into a value structure*
   1 Opportunities to identify a variety of value systems
   2 Opportunities to clarify short-term goals and examine them in relation to personal values and to achievability
   3 Support for making a personal value system the foundation for career choice, including encouragement for discovering the student's own *vocation,* in the sense of *that which one is called to do.*
F *Characterization by a value*
   1 Opportunities to examine how values and belief systems affect decisions in world events.
   2 Opportunities to evaluate outcomes of a variety of value decisions.
   3 Support for examining outcomes of life events based on personal value structure.

The Physical Domain

People of highly developed intellectual ability may be unusually vulnerable to a characteristic "Cartesian split" between thinking and being, a lack of integration between mind and body. During school years, when the gifted student experiences large discrepancies between physical and intellectual development, the school may unintentionally encourage the student to avoid physical activity. If a child's intellectual peers are physically more advanced so as to make him or her feel physically inadequate, but the physical peers are less intellectually stimulating and not within the child's friendship group, the usual competitive playground games may be neither inviting nor satisfying to the gifted student. If the physical development of gifted students is to be encouraged, programs should provide experiences that develop integration between mind and body in students with nonnormative developmental patterns (Table 7.3).

Differential Physical Characteristics of the Gifted

The following differential physical characteristics have been identified in the gifted:

- Unusual discrepancy between physical and intellectual development
- Low tolerance for the lag between their standards and their physical capacity
- Cartesian split—can include neglect of physical well-being and avoidance of physical activity.

Table 7.3 The Physical Domain.

Differentiating Characteristics	Examples of Related Needs	Organizational Patterns	Examples of Classroom Strategies
Unusual discrepancy between physical and intellectual development	To appreciate their physical capacities	Cluster groups of gifted pupils	Sensory awareness activities from *Sense Relaxation* by Gunther (1966) Body awareness activity, Chapter 2, Communications Skills, Sonntag (1972) Activities to heighten awareness of the pleasures of having a healthy body, and of the means for health maintenance; *The Well Body Book* (Samuels & Bennett, 1973).
Low tolerance for the lag between their standards and their athletic skills	To discover physical activity as a source of pleasure	Physical education offered in a variety of structured, nonstructured, competitive, cooperative, and individual processes	*Sense Relaxation*, Gunther (1966)
	To find satisfaction in small increments of improvement	Small groups organized to learn and teach new physical activities	*Awareness Through Movement*, Feldenkrais (1972)
	To engage in noncompetitive physical activities or activities in which they compete against themselves	Individual and group opportunities for self-expression (through dance, movement, pantomime, etc.) in various areas of the curriculum	*Improvisation for the Theatre*, Spolin (1963) *Music*, Wampler (1973)

Table 7.3   The Physical Domain. (continued)

Differentiating Characteristics	Examples of Related Needs	Organizational Patterns	Examples of Classroom Strategies
"Cartesian Split" can include neglect of physical well-being and avoidance of physical activity	To engage in activities leading to mind/body integration	Out of class time provided to explore the disciplines devoted to mind/body integration (Yoga, Judo, T'ai-chi Ch'uan, etc.)	Invite teachers or advanced students of these physical/philosophical disciplines to visit class and hold demonstrations Instruction in techniques of relaxation and tension reduction; *Sense Relaxation,* Gunther (1966)
	To develop a commitment to one's own physical well-being	Individual, small group, or large group	Develop a personal plan for meeting nutritional and activity needs; follow it, note effects, modify it, etc.
	To extend this concern to the social and political realm	Out-of-class time provided for community involvement	Identify current health needs of the community; examine the implications of current social and political policies for the health of the people in the community.

Program Provisions in the Physical Domain

Program provisions for gifted pupils to meet the needs of the physical domain can also be organized according to the following taxonomy:

A *Awareness*
1 Experiences designed to heighten and clarify sensory awareness
2 Experiences designed to promote awareness of the student's own body and the creation of a positive body image
3 Experiences and information to heighten awareness of the pleasures of having a healthy body, and of the means for health maintenance and growth
4 Information and opportunities for inquiry into the clarification of physical responses to emotions

B *Involvement*
1 Instruction and practice in techniques of relaxation and tension reduction
2 Opportunities for self-expression through movement, pantomime, dance, etc.
3 Opportunities to develop individual physical competence and experience the satisfaction of physical activity in ways chosen by the student from a wide range of structured and nonstructured, competitive, cooperative, and individual processes

C *Integration*
1 Exposure to, and opportunities to learn, one of the disciplines devoted to mind/body integration: Yoga, Judo, T'ai-chi Ch'uan, etc.
2 Support for, and assistance in making, the care and development of one's own body a part of an individual life-style
3 Opportunities to examine the implications of current social and political policies for the health of people in the community.

The Intuitive Domain

The intuitive function is involved in initiating or insightful acts and in creative activity. While this is the least defined area of human endeavor, it is probably the area that promises the most for the continuance and fulfillment of humankind. All other areas provide support for, and are supported by, this area of function. As each area evolves to higher levels, more of the intuitive and creative functions become available. One of the most interesting yet least understood areas of intuitive functioning is the phenomenon called *psi,* which incorporates such experiences as déjà vu that occur in the nonphysical realm of our existence. Bowles and Hynds (1978) describe psi in this way:

Since the beginning of recorded history, people have been perplexed by personal experiences in which they dream about events that later occur, know what another person is thinking without being told, perceive events that happen too far away to be seen, or influence something solely by an exercise of their minds. Experimental investigation of these unusual occurrences leads the scientists who study them to hypothesize an unknown factor underlying all of them. They call this factor *psi*.

Psi, the twenty-third letter of the Greek alphabet, is often used in scientific equations to stand for the unknown. When used in connection with psychic occurrences, psi represents a mystery that, after fifty years of laboratory study, one hundred years of scientific investigation, and centuries of great popular interest, remains unsolved. (p. 1)

Table 7.4 presents some examples of strategies to enhance development of the intuitive domain.

Differentiating Intuitive Characteristics of the Gifted

The following differentiating intuitive characteristics have been identified in the gifted:

- Early involvement and concern for intuitive knowing, psi and metaphysical ideas, and phenomena
- Open to experiences in this area; will experiment with psi and metaphysical phenomena
- Creativity apparent in all areas of endeavor
- Acceptance and expression of a high level of intuitive ability, especially with the highly gifted.

The Societal Domain

Society has unique needs for the services of unique individuals. While we would not wish that gifted education focus on societal needs at the expense of individual actualization, neither can education for the gifted disregard the importance of their social roles at maturity. Gifted students need direction in exploring the variety of opportunities for contributing what they have to offer society. They need conceptual frameworks to organize their experience of society (cf., Maslow's [1968] hierarchy of needs); and they need opportunities to develop those skills that will make it possible for them to have an effect on society. Educational programs should provide for the options, conceptual frameworks, and skills that underlie the effective social involvement of gifted students.

Table 7.4 The Intuitive Domain.

Differentiating Characteristics	Examples of Related Needs	Organizational Patterns	Examples of Classroom Strategies
Early involvement and concern for intuitive knowing, psi and metaphysical ideas, and phenomena	Opportunities to converse meaningfully with philosophers and others on these ideas	An environment of trust and acceptance; independent study; mentors, guest experts, group experiences, and discussions	Small group meetings with experts to discuss and explore phenomena
			Exercises on centering, and relaxation (Hendricks & Fadiman, 1975; Hendricks & Wills, 1975; Hendricks & Roberts, 1977)
	To recognize own intuitive energy and ability		
	Guidance to develop and use intuitive energy and ability		Use of imagery, fantasy, and dreams
Open to experiences in this area; will experiment with psi and metaphysical phenomena	Guidance in becoming familiar with, analyzing, and evaluating such phenomena	An environment where these ideas are valued	Lessons directed to use of psi and intuitive energy

Table 7.4 *The Intuitive Domain. (continued)*

Differentiating Characteristics	*Examples of Related Needs*	*Organizational Patterns*	*Examples of Classroom Strategies*
	Should be provided a historical approach	Access to resources discussing phenomena throughout history	Controlled experiments investigating such phenomena Discussions of nonscientific evidence Independent study of brain research and psi research relationship
Creativity apparent in all areas of endeavor	Guidance in evaluating appropriate uses of creative efforts Encouraging ongoing development of creative abilities	Flexible, open classroom; teacher acceptance of unusual products or ideas Integrative learning	Valuing activities dealing with results of the creative process Creativity exercises are in Beechhold (1971), DeMille (1973), Massialas and Zevin (1967), and Parnes (1967).
Acceptance and expression of a high level of intuitive ability, especially with the highly gifted understanding and accepting this ability		A safe, accepting environment	Opportunities to use and develop abilities in a variety of subject areas (see activities on p. 400)

Differential Societal Characteristics and Social Expectations of the Gifted

The following differential societal characteristics have been identified in the gifted:

- Strongly motivated by self-actualization needs
- Advanced cognitive and affective capacity for conceptualizing and solving societal problems.

These differential social expectations have been identified for the gifted:

- Leadership
- Solutions to social and environmental problems
- Involvement with the metaneeds of society (e.g., justice, beauty, truth).

Table 7.5 gives some examples of ways in which classroom organization and teaching strategies can relate to the societal characteristics and social expectations of the gifted.

Program Provisions in the Societal Domain

The needs of gifted pupils in the societal domain fall mainly into four categories: the need to be an effective member of a group; the need to understand what is going on in a group and to be able to influence the group process; the need to extend one's feeling of membership from family and small group to the community at large; and the need to extend identification with one's community to identification with the human community. Program provisions in the societal domain can be organized according to this hierarchy:

A *Membership*
  1 Opportunities to participate in activities with a variety of groups (e.g., intellectual peers, varying age levels, varying ability levels, handicapped and nonhandicapped combinations)
  2 Opportunities to identify and examine roles in group membership and their effect on this group
  3 Opportunities to become aware of and practice methods and results of open communication
  4 Opportunities to see the self in relation to others and the effect each has upon the other
  5 Opportunities to examine and understand their own functioning within a group and to receive instruction in and opportunity to improve that function
B *Group process*
  1 Opportunities to identify and examine a variety of leadership styles and their consequences

Table 7.5 *The Societal Domain.*

Differentiating Characteristics	*Examples of Related Needs*	*Organizational Patterns*	*Examples of Classroom Strategies*
Strongly motivated by self-actualization needs	Opportunities to follow divergent paths and pursue strong interests	A trusting environment where self-esteem is supported and self-exploration valued and actively facilitated	Values clarification exercises (Kohlberg, 1972, 1974, 1976a, 1976b, 1977); Magic Circle activities (Bessell & Palomares, 1970); self-esteem activities (Coopersmith, 1975)
	Help in understanding the demands of self-actualization		
Advanced cognitive and affective capacity for conceptualizing and solving societal problems	Encounters with social problems	Access to the community	Visiting experts and community workers; small group field trips for information
	Awareness of the complexity of problems facing society	Flexible grouping allowing gifted to work together during part of the program	Debates, simulations, analysis of real problems
	Conceptual frameworks for problem-solving procedures	Small group work	Simulations; problem-solving models (Gallagher, 1975)

Leadership	Understanding of various leadership styles and practice in leadership skills	Integrated age and ability levels; cooperative planning and implementation of program	Leadership training groups; creating a government for the group; organizing and implementing social, cultural, or curricular programs
Solutions to social and environmental problems	Meaningful involvement in real problems	An environment where concern with social problems is valued; flexible programs permitting off-site involvement	Simulations; planning and implementing programs benefiting segments of the school community or the community at large
Involvement with the metaneeds of society, e.g., justice, beauty, truth	Exploration of the highest levels of human thought; application of this knowledge to today's problems	Independent study; flexible groupings; access to community	Great Books program; visiting experts; future studies

    2 Opportunities to learn and apply leadership skills, including solicitation and use of counsel, advice, and criticism

    3 Opportunities to develop, demonstrate, and communicate expertise in some field to colleagues

    4 Opportunities to be sensitized to power issues and to explore the exercise and distribution of power

C *Extended membership*

    1 Opportunities to identify the problems of one's own social community—problem finding

    2 Opportunities to develop possible and/or innovative solutions to community problems

    3 Opportunities to function in cooperation with others in the community to implement solutions

    4 Opportunities for recognition and respect of parent and community values

D *Identification with humankind*

    1 Opportunities for recognition of commonalities among human beings transcending natural or created boundaries

    2 Opportunities for cognitive and affective understanding of human interdependence

    3 Opportunities to mesh individual goals and needs with group and societal goals and needs

    4 Opportunities for recognition of the possibility of conflict between the needs and goals of humanity and the personal and group needs and goals

    5 Opportunities to develop a value system in which the long-term needs of humanity have priority.

The intellectually gifted child characteristically differs from the average child in cognitive, affective, physical, intuitive, and societal behavior. These characteristic differences are the source of the special educational needs of gifted children. Methods, materials, and organizational patterns for educational programs should be clearly related to the needs and characteristics of the children in all five aspects of human development. The framework presented here is far from complete, and is offered in the hope that caring parents and educators will find it valuable as they seek to develop "qualitatively different" educational programs and experiences that will help to actualize the abilities of pupils with unusual capacities and unusual needs.

DIFFERENTIATING CURRICULUM

As Kaplan (1986) reminds us, "The ultimate goal of a differentiated curriculum is that it recognizes the characteristics of the gifted, provides reinforcement or practice for the development of these characteristics, and extends the recognized characteristics to further levels of development'' (p. 182). In addition to beginning with the assessed needs of each gifted learner as discussed earlier in this chapter, and because those differentiated needs can commonly be found among many of the gifted, some general elements that help to define a differentiated curriculum can be discussed. The principles of a differentiated curriculum for the gifted/talented as developed by the Curriculum Council of the National/State Leadership Training

Differentiating the curriculum must allow transfer of learning, generating new information.

Developing a Differentiated Curriculum

Institute on the Gifted and the Talented (cited in Kaplan, 1986) provide this framework for appropriately differentiating curriculum for this population:

- Present content that is related to broad-based issues, themes or problems.
- Integrate multiple disciplines into the area of study.
- Present comprehensive, related and mutually reinforcing experiences within an area of study.
- Allow for the in-depth learning of a self-selected topic within the area of study.
- Develop independent or self-directed study skills.
- Develop productive, complex, abstract and/or higher level thinking skills.
- Focus on open-ended tasks.
- Develop research skills and methods.
- Integrate basic skills and higher level thinking skills into the curriculum.
- Encourage the development of products that challenge existing ideas and produce "new" ideas.
- Encourage the development of products that use techniques, materials and forms.
- Encourage the development of self-understanding, i.e., recognizing and using one's abilities, becoming self-directed, appreciating likenesses and differences between oneself and others.
- Evaluate student outcomes by using appropriate and specific criteria through self-appraisal, criterion referenced and/or standardized instruments. (p. 183)

There has been much discussion to the effect that a differentiated curriculum cannot really be planned until the needs of each student are known. However, as Kaplan points out, defining the curriculum and outlining what is to be taught and general ideas about the processes to be used are not the same as implementing the curriculum. After the needs of the students are known, implementation will occur and the ways in which the curriculum will be modified to meet each student's needs will be decided. Kaplan's Grid Model, discussed later in this chapter, will provide an excellent guide for these decisions.

The Shoulds and Should Nots of an Appropriately Designed Differentiated Curriculum

The following list (Clark & Kaplan, 1981) specifies what an effective curriculum should and should not include:

1 The curriculum *should* be planned and sequentially organized to include specific expectations for the acquisition of subject matter, mastery of skills, creation of products, and development of attitudes and apprecia-tions related to self, others, and the environment.

The curriculum *should not* be a potpourri of learning activities that are disjointed and haphazardly selected without reference to specified criteria.

2 The curriculum *should* place emphasis on the interdependence of subject matter, skills, products, and self-understanding within the *same* curricular structure.

The curriculum *should not* focus on the attainment of cognitive competencies in isolation from the development of affective competencies. Nor should the curriculum focus on affective development without concern for cognitive growth.

3 The curriculum *should* include provisions to meet the need for some type of instructional pacing by any or all of the following means:

a Making it possible to accomplish a range of learning experiences in a shorter span of time using a continuous progress curriculum

b Assigning students to curricula at levels beyond those expected at the students' age/grade level

c Eliminating from the curricula what is already learned and substituting curricula more appropriate to student interest, abilities, and needs.

The curriculum *should not* penalize students for being gifted or talented, through restricting their opportunities to learn by ignoring those characteristics that define their giftedness.

4 The curriculum *should* allow for the expression of some aspect of the individual's interests, needs, abilities, and learning preferences. The curriculum *should* be organized to allow for some individualization and self-selection.

The curriculum *should not* be without defined expectations and clearly expressed opportunities for teacher-directed as well as student-selected learning activities.

5 The curriculum *should* provide opportunities to learn to reconceptualize existing knowledge, to perceive things from various points of view, and to use information for new purposes or in new ways.

The curriculum *should not* stress the accumulation of knowledge or reinforce mastery without simultaneously encouraging students to be productive thinkers.

6 The curriculum *should* provide learning experiences for students to address the unresolved issues and problems of society and apply personal and social data to analyze, clarify, and respond to such issues and problems.

The curriculum *should not* focus only on knowledge of the world as it is, but should encourage the development of perceptions of the need to invent in order to restructure the world into what it ideally could be.

7 The curriculum *should* incorporate learning experiences that foster the development of the complex thought processes that encourage the cre-

ation of unique products and develop strategies of productive thought. The curriculum *should* teach both fundamental and higher level thinking skills as integral parts of every learning experience.

The curriculum *should not* overemphasize mastery of fundamental basic skills, nor should it exonerate gifted/talented students from mastering these. The curriculum *should not* ignore the development of fundamental or basic skills for the mastery of higher level thinking skills.

8 The curriculum *should* provide opportunities for students to practice leadership and followership skills and appropriate and varied forms of communication skills and strategies.

The curriculum *should not* be based on the assumption that gifted/talented students can assume positions of leadership without the development of skills and understandings that promote this end.

While this is a useful guide, you will always need to assess your gifted learners for their particular needs. They are your very best guide to an appropriate curriculum.

A Curriculum Criteria Checklist

The following criteria (Clark & Kaplan, 1981) are appropriate for all good educational experiences; however, the characteristics found among gifted learners make them especially necessary to a differentiated curriculum. To be sure your curriculum is appropriate for gifted learners check to see if it includes provisions for all of these criteria:

_____ **1** *Continuity.* A comprehensive set of learning experiences is provided that reinforces specific curricular objectives.

_____ **2** *Flexibility.* The scope and sequence of the curriculum are modified to accommodate emerging student and teacher needs.

_____ **3** *Responsiveness to learner needs.* Definition of the curriculum is based on an assessment of individual/group abilities, interests, needs, and learning styles.

_____ **4** *Diversity.* Alternative means are provided to attain determined ends within a specified curricular framework.

_____ **5** *Integration.* The integrative use of all abilities, including cognition, emotion, intuition, and mind/body, is provided in a single curriculum.

_____ **6** *Openness.* Preset expectations are eliminated that might limit the learnings within the curricular framework.

_____ **7** *Independence.* Some type(s) of self-directed learnings are provided.

_____ **8** *Increasing levels of advanced abstraction and difficulty.* Acceptance of the student's readiness to learn beyond traditional age/grade expectations and provisions for stimulating such readiness are present.

_____ **9** *Substantive learning.* Significant subject matter, skills, products, and awarenesses that are of consequence or of importance to the learner and the disciplines are included.

_____ **10** *Decision making.* Students are able to make some appropriate/relevant decisions regarding what is to be learned and how it can be learned.

_____ **11** *Principles of learning.* Teaching practices that allow for motivation, practice, transfer of training, and feedback are included.

_____ **12** *Creation/re-creation.* The creative process is applied to improve, modify, etc. one's creations to challenge prevailing thought and offer more appropriate solutions.

_____ **13** *Interaction with peers and variety of significant others.* Students can learn about and meet with individuals who share the same and different gifts/talents.

_____ **14** *Value system.* Consistent opportunities are available to develop and examine personal and societal values and to establish a personal value system.

_____ **15** *Communication skills.* Verbal and nonverbal systems and skills are developed to dialogue, share, and exchange ideas.

_____ **16** *Commitment to society.* Provisions are made to understand and relate to the society in which one lives and to find one's place in it.

The Grid

Other models presented in this section give us a structure for developing just parts of a curriculum, because most of them are models for defining and developing the individual processes used in learning. However Kaplan's (1986) model, which she calls the *Grid* (see Figure 7.1) is the only model described herein that includes and organizes all the components of a differentiated curriculum.

The components of Kaplan's Grid are the theme; content; processes, e.g., productive thinking skills, research skills, and basic skills; and products. Affective concerns, descriptions of learning experiences, and activities are also important parts of her model.

The Theme

Kaplan suggests that we start to plan a differentiated curriculum with a theme, rather than a topic, as the organizing element. When we select only a topic, we may be limiting the learning possibilities of gifted students. While topics will incorpo-

Figure 7.1 The Grid: An Example.[1]

Theme—POWER				
Content	Productive Thinking Skills	Research Skills	Basic Skills	Products
Relationship between economic, social, personal displays of power to needs and interests of individuals, groups, and societies	differentiate between fact and opinion	use a retrieval system	identify the main idea	develop an oral presentation
Significance of personmade and natural sources of power to changes in beliefs, life-style and communication	prove or disprove	take notes	write a paragraph	make a graphic representation
Conditions which promote the exercise of power by individuals, organizations, and countries	establish criteria to judge	use fiction and nonfiction	sequence	write an editorial
Value of social forms of power to human rights and environmental usage	substantiate with evidence	use newspapers and journals	classify	debate

[1]By Kaplan (1986) from *Systems and Models for Developing Programs for the Gifted and Talented*, Mansfield, CT: Creative Learning Press Inc. Used by permission. p. 184.

rate parts of the theme's overall interest, a wide variety of interests and the ability to generalize and see relationships are more available to the learner when the larger units of themes are used. Examples of themes are Extinction, Effects of Systems, Knowledge as Power, and Leadership and Followership.

The Content

Kaplan refers to *content* as "the knowledge and information defined as useful, important, timely, and interesting for gifted students to acquire as a consequence of their matriculation through an educational program" (p. 185). She believes that the development of skills and the assimilation of content are interactive, and both must therefore be of importance to the planning. She lists some rules to consider in selecting content:

1 It should be referenced to the theme.
2 It should be multidisiciplinary.
3 It should embody information that all students are expected to learn, and it should be consonant with the needs, interests, and abilities of the gifted students, and of particular importance or interest to individual students or groups of students.
4 It should allow for the integration of subject areas.
5 It should allow a time perspective that includes and relates past, present, and future.

The Process

Some of the processes mentioned by Kaplan to be considered are productive thinking skills, basic research skills, learning-to-learn skills, life skills, and the skills of technology. Rather than choose one set of skills Kaplan suggests the integration of various categories of processes into the curriculum planning and implementation.

The Product

Both as a tool for learning and as a verification of learning, the product communicates the synthesis and assimilation of both knowledge (content) and skills (processes). Products must be allowed to be communicated in visual, oral, and written formats and result from a variety of production skills such as varied technology and materials, self-determined criteria for evaluation, and identification of formal and informal outlets to share the products.

Kaplan's work is clear and concise, giving many examples to clarify each component. Any of the process models mentioned in this book can be used to develop the process section of the Grid. As a closing comment on planning differentiated curriculum Kaplan states, "Once the curriculum is differentiated, it

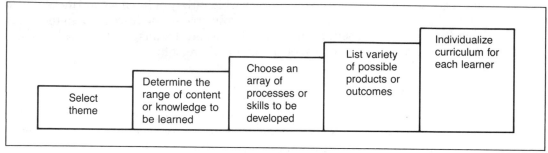

Figure 7.2 *Steps to a Differentiated Curriculum*

Source: Based on the work of Kaplan (1986).

needs to be individualized for students" (p. 192). Figure 7.2 shows Kaplan's steps leading up to the final step of individualizing the curriculum.

Maker (1986) suggests procedures for placing themes, content, processes, and products into a scope and sequence. This will allow us to know how such curriculum plans fit together, and to assure both that the important skills and concepts for personal and career growth are developed and that continuity of the program is maintained over time.

MODELS OF LEARNING AND TEACHING OFTEN USED IN DEVELOPING CURRICULUM FOR THE GIFTED LEARNER

A number of conceptualizations of the learning process have influenced the development of curriculum in gifted education. They have provided structures that allow careful consideration of how learning may occur and how experiences may be designed to enhance growth in skills related to thinking and learning.

The Taxonomy of Educational Objectives: Cognitive Domain

One of the conceptualizations most often used is the *Taxonomy of Educational Objectives: Handbook I: Cognitive Domain,* edited by Bloom (1956). Table 7.6 presents and clarifies the taxonomy in ways that have been found useful in curriculum planning. Bloom presents and clarifies a taxonomy of learning that illustrates the importance of presenting learning at many levels to meet the needs of a variety of learners. Average and more able students need to have learning

Table 7.6 *Taxonomy of Educational Objectives: Cognitive Domain.*

Area of Taxonomy	Definition	What Teacher Does	What Student Does	Process Verbs	
Knowledge	Recall or recognition of specific information	Directs Tells Shows Examines	Responds Absorbs Remembers Recognizes	define repeat list name label	memorize record recall relate
Comprehension	Understanding of information given	Demonstrates Listens Questions Compares Contrasts Examines	Explains Translates Demonstrates Interprets	restate describe explain identify report tell	discuss recognize express locate review
Application	Using methods, concepts, principles, and theories in new situations	Shows Facilitates Observes Criticizes	Solves problems Demonstrates use of knowledge Constructs	translate apply employ use practice shop	interpret demonstrate dramatize illustrate operate schedule

Table 7.6 *Taxonomy of Educational Objectives: Cognitive Domain. (continued)*

Area of Taxonomy	Definition	What Teacher Does	What Student Does	Process Verbs	
Analysis	Breaking information down into its constitutent elements	Probes Guides Observes Acts as a resource	Discusses Uncovers Lists Dissects	distinguish calculate test contract criticize debate question solve analyze	appraise differentiate experiment compare diagram inspect inventory relate examine
Synthesis	Putting together constituent elements or parts to form a whole requiring original, creative thinking	Reflects Extends Analyzes Evaluates	Discusses Generalizes Relates Compares Contrasts Abstracts	compose propose formulate assemble construct set up manage	plan design arrange collect create organize prepare
Evaluation	Judging the values of ideas, materials, and methods by developing and applying standards and criteria	Clarifies Accepts Harmonizes Guides	Judges Disputes Develops criteria	judge evaluate compare score choose estimate predict	appraise rate value select assess measure

presented at the levels of knowledge, comprehension, application, analysis, synthesis, and evaluation. Opportunities to work at more advanced levels are crucial for the more able student. Because the brain must continue to be stimulated or lose its capability, the fact that the majority of classrooms have been found to present learning experiences only at the lower levels is of concern to all teachers who wish to optimize learning.

The Taxonomy of Educational Objectives: Affective Domain

Bloom was also involved in a second organization delineating a hierarchy of learning, the *Taxonomy of Educational Objectives: Handbook II: Affective Domain* (Krathwohl, Bloom, & Masia, 1964). The purpose of this list of objectives was to sequence behaviors that would indicate growth in the emotional area of function. As we see in Table 7.7 these levels are receiving, responding, valuing, organization of a value structure, and characterization by a value.

One of the best things about working with gifted learners is that they enjoy these types of organizers. Not only can the teacher find them helpful in curriculum development, but the students can, after becoming familiar with the taxonomic structure, actually analyze and create experiences at each level themselves. While the taxonomy is often used as a linear model, it can also be viewed as cyclic, with

Table 7.7 *Taxonomy of Educational Objectives: Affective Domain.*

Category	Subdivisions	Student Behavior to Be Attained (Educational Objectives)
1.0 Receiving Attending	1.1 Awareness	Observes: recognizes, is aware of; develops sensitivity to
	1.2 Willingness to	Accepts others; develops a tolerance for. Listens carefully: recognizes persons as individuals
	1.3 Controlled and selected attention	Discriminates; appreciates alertness to values; selects reading materials

Table 7.7 *Taxonomy of Educational Objectives: Affective Domain.* (continued)

Category	Subdivisions	Student Behavior to Be Attained (Educational Objectives)
2.0 Responding	2.1 Acquiescence in responding	Willing to comply; observes rules and regulations
	2.2 Willingness to respond	Voluntarily seeks information, engages in variety of activities. Responds to intellectual stimuli; engages in research
	2.3 Satisfactory in response	Finds pleasure in reading, listening, conversing, art, participation in groups
3.0 Valuing	3.1 Accepting a value	Develops a sense of responsibility, of kinship, of need for worship
	3.2 Preference for a value	Interest in enabling others; examines a variety of viewpoints; assumes active role in politics, literary organizations
	3.3 Commitment	Displays a high degree of certainty, loyalty, faith in the power of reason
4.0 Organization	4.1 Conceptualization of a value	Establishes a conscious base for making choices. Identifies admired characteristics. Analyzes basic assumptions underlying codes of ethics and faith. Forms judgment as to responsibility of society to the individual and environment. Develops personal goals.

Table 7.7 *Taxonomy of Educational Objectives: Affective Domain. (continued)*

Category	Subdivisions	Student Behavior to Be Attained (Educational Objectives)
4.0 Organization	4.2 Organization of a value system According to Edward Spranger values may be organized around the following: 1. Theoretical 2. Economic 3. Aesthetic 4. Social 5. Political 6. Religious	Examines role of democracy in conserving human and natural resources; accepts own potentialities and limitations realistically; views people as individuals, without prejudice; develops techniques for conflict management. Accepts responsibility for the future.
5.0 Characterization of a Value	5.1 Generalized set—the basic orientation which enables the individual to act consistently and effectively in a complex world	Readiness to reverse judgments or change behavior in light of evidence; to change one's mind and face facts: confidence in ability to succeed; solves problems in terms of what is rather than wishful thinking
	5.2 Characterization—one's personal philosophy of life demonstrated in behavior	Develops a code of behavior based on ethical principles consistent with democratic ideals: behavior which is consistent with beliefs

Source: From *Taxonomy of Educational Objectives: Handbook II: Affective Domain* by David R. Krathwohl et al. Copyright © 1964 by Longman Inc. Reprinted by permission of Longman Inc., New York.

the highest level, evaluation, seen as producing new information that becomes knowledge and then moves through the entire process (Figure 7.3).

Although one often hears that gifted learners should be working at the top levels of the taxonomy, such a statement can be quite misleading. It would not be possible for gifted students to analyze information that they do not understand. All students need to be exposed to experiences at all levels of the taxonomy. The emphasis in instruction makes the difference, as gifted students often bring a large amount of knowledge to class with them (see Figure 7.4).

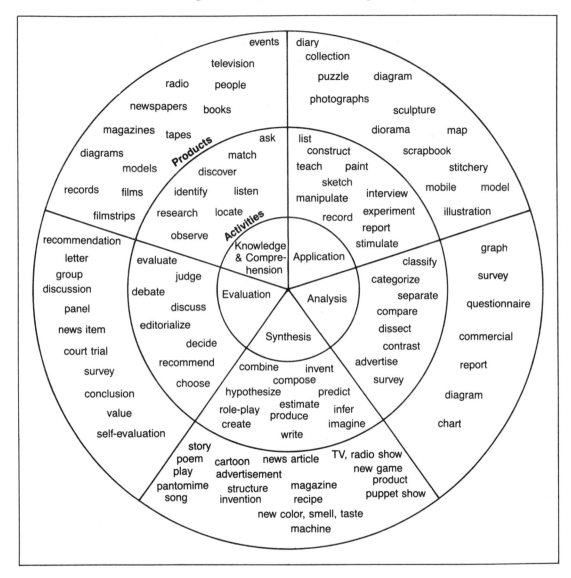

Figure 7.3   Taxonomy Circle.[2]

[2]The wheel in Figure 7.3 was developed by my colleague, Barry Ziff, and a class of teachers of the gifted. They found it very useful in curriculum building.

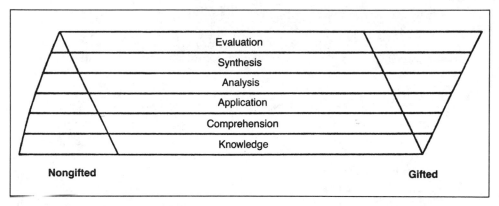

Figure 7.4   Taxonomy Ladder.

The Structure of Intellect Model

Another major organizer used for development of curriculum in gifted education is the Structure of Intellect (SOI) Model (Guilford, 1967). The model (Figure 7.5)

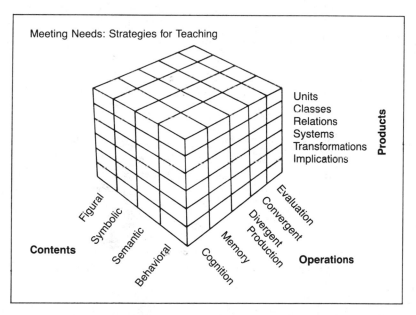

Figure 7.5   Theoretical Model for Guilford's Structure of Intellect.[3]

[3]By J. P. Guilford, from *The Nature of Human Intelligence.* New York: McGraw-Hill, 1967. Reprinted by permission.

---

provided psychology with a multifactor view of intelligence to replace the single-factor view previously used.

The factor analysis of numerous aptitude and ability tests provided the basis for Guilford's SOI Model. The division of intellectual abilities into three dimensions—contents, operations, and products—and their subdivisions gives this model the means to show interrelationships between human abilities (Guilford, 1967). Some educators, especially Meeker (1969), extend the use of the SOI Model to serve as a basis for a diagnostic-prescriptive tool in the teaching of thinking skills.

Meeker asserts that the use of the SOI Model provides a theory of intelligence for education, where previously one had not existed. She believes that, by using the model for curriculum development, we can meet the educational needs of each child more adequately. Meeker has, therefore, developed assessment techniques that make use of the major tests of intelligence, the Stanford-Binet and the Wechsler. These tests can delineate the student's areas of strength and weakness that correspond with specific abilities on the SOI. The resulting profile of the student provides the basis for a curricular plan that may then be implemented by the use of materials developed by Meeker for classroom use.

While Meeker has made the SOI much more available to the classroom, the very success of her efforts may cause some teachers to restrict their planning to use of just these materials. We must be sure to include more than just activities of a cognitive nature in our total educational program. After all, the SOI is a theoretical model of intellectual abilities that, at best, only partially explains human functioning. While Meeker has made a valuable contribution, the SOI materials must be carefully integrated into a comprehensive educational plan that views intellectual ability as only one area of human functioning.

The Three-Dimensional Model

An adaptation of the Guilford SOI Model was developed by Williams (1979) to combine cognitive and affective factors. The resulting three-dimensional model looks similar to the SOI cube and incorporates curriculum, teacher behaviors, and pupil behaviors. By use of these dimensions Williams believes that teachers can construct curriculum that can effectively cause pupils to think and feel creatively in any subject area. Figure 7.6 shows the three-dimensional model developed by Williams.

The Inquiry Model

That any discipline could be taught at any age if the basic structure of the discipline were communicated in ways the child could understand was strongly believed by Bruner (1960). He urged educators to address themselves to the process of

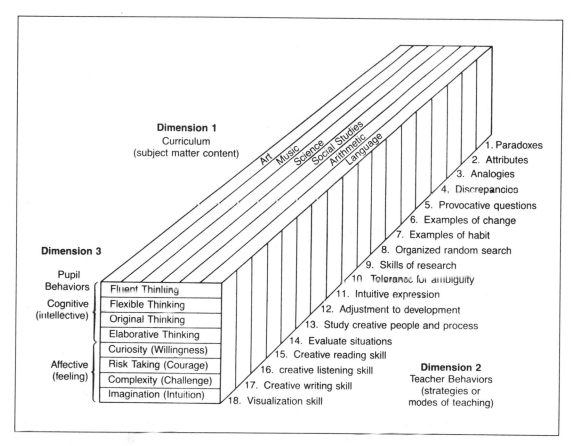

Dimension 1
Curriculum
(subject matter content)

Art, Music, Science, Social Studies, Arithmetic, Language

1. Paradoxes
2. Attributes
3. Analogies
4. Discrepancies
5. Provocative questions
6. Examples of change
7. Examples of habit
8. Organized random search
9. Skills of research
10. Tolerance for ambiguity
11. Intuitive expression
12. Adjustment to development
13. Study creative people and process
14. Evaluate situations
15. Creative reading skill
16. creative listening skill
17. Creative writing skill
18. Visualization skill

Dimension 3

Pupil Behaviors

Cognitive (intellective)
- Fluent Thinking
- Flexible Thinking
- Original Thinking
- Elaborative Thinking

Affective (feeling)
- Curiosity (Willingness)
- Risk Taking (Courage)
- Complexity (Challenge)
- Imagination (Intuition)

Dimension 2
Teacher Behaviors
(strategies or
modes of teaching)

Figure 7.6   Three-Dimensional Model for Constructing Curriculum by Williams.[4]

learning, to present science as the scientist would learn it. One educator who developed a strategy for doing just that was Richard Suchman.

Suchman (1961, 1962) developed the Inquiry Model from his understanding of the scientific model of thinking (Figure 7.7). While it may oversimplify human thought by leaving out important areas, it is quite useful in teaching many important processes. Suchman's program gives students practice in solving problems, by establishing the properties of all objects or systems involved in the problem, finding which objects or systems are relevant to the problem, and discovering how they function in the solution. Sessions are designed to help students learn to formulate and test their own theories and to become aware of their own learning processes. The outcomes lead not so much to new answers, and never to right or wrong answers, but to new and more productive questions.

[4]By Williams. Used by permission.

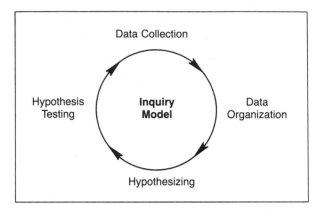

Figure 7.7   A Visualization of the Inquiry Model.

The Enrichment Triad Model

The Enrichment Triad Model (Renzulli, 1977) is a process model that supplements the Revolving Door Model's concept of pullout and resource room structure dicussed in Chapter 5. This model began as an answer to criticism regarding enrichment programs that were not differentiated but seemed to provide good education for all students. The model has two stated objectives.

> Program Objective No. 1—For the majority of time spent in the gifted programs, students will have complete freedom to pursue topics of their own choosing to whatever depth and extent they so desire; and they will be allowed to pursue these topics in a manner that is consistent with their own preferred style of learning. (p. 307)

> Program Objective No. 2—The primary role of each teacher in the program for gifted and talented students will be to provide each student with assistance in (1) identifying and structuring realistic solvable problems that are consistent with the student's interests, and (2) acquiring the methodological resources and investigative skills that are necessary for solving these particular problems. (p. 312)

As implied in its name, the Enrichment Triad Model identifies the three types of enrichment, shown in Figure 7.8.[5] The first two types, General Exploratory Activities and Group Training Activities, are considered appropriate for all learners and provide the basis for the overall enrichment of gifted and talented students. They are intended to provide strategies for expanding student interests and developing the thinking and feeling processes. Type III enrichment, Individual and Small Group Investigations of Real Problems, is the only one appropriate mainly for gifted students. In Type III enrichment, the student is to focus on real work methods of inquiry to provide first-hand experience in a particular field of interest.

[5]By J. Renzulli (1986) from *Systems and Models for Developing Programs for the Gifted and Talented.* Mansfield, CT: Creative Learning Press, Inc. Used by permission.

The School and the Gifted Individual

The first two types of enrichment are to be provided by regular classroom teachers, who are given inservice to acquaint them with the methods and strategies identified as part of the model. Some of these will be discussed in more detail in Chapter 8. At these levels four services may be provided: (1) interest and learning style assessment, (2) curriculum compacting, (3) general exploratory experiences, and (4) group training activities. At the third level, Type III, a specialist provides service for the student or group of students who have been identified as ready to pursue an independent project of their interest.

The model is well thought out and extensively used, and it has a large variety of support materials and forms to aid its step-by-step delivery of service at the elementary and secondary levels. It is now available for a schoolwide enrichment program (Renzulli & Reis, 1986).

Other Theories and Models

An interesting theory that seeks to identify the components of cognitive giftedness for the purpose of improving differentiated curricular planning has been advanced

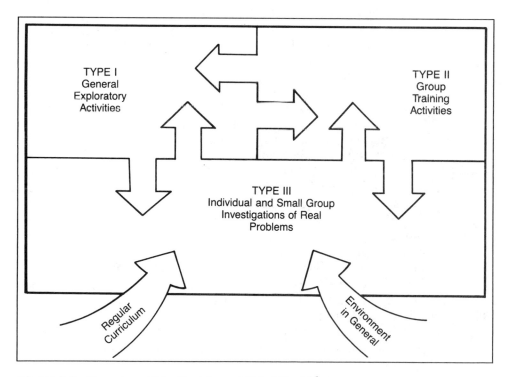

Figure 7.8 *Overview of the Enrichment Triad Model.*[5]

by Sternberg (1981). He believes that gifted learners tend to excel in their access to and implementation of the following:

- Decision as to just what the problems are that need solving
- Selection of appropriate components and steps leading to problem solution. Research indicates that when intuitive leaps are necessary for problem solution, most individuals have available in their heads all of the elements necessary for solution, but what distinguishes problem solvers is the ability to retrieve these elements.
- Selection of strategies to evolve a plan of action for solving problems
- Learning ways within a discipline to represent information to be built up to use in problem solving
- Decision regarding allocation of resources
- Ability to monitor solutions, being flexible in changing plans as needs dictate. This was seen as one of the most important differences between gifted and nongifted learners.

Sternberg believes that giftedness can be understood in terms of superior functioning, activation of, and feedback from information processing components of various kinds, and that it may be trainable if that training emphasizes the development of such functioning.

Other models currently used in the development of curriculum for the gifted include Treffinger's (1975) model, which delineates a step-by-step approach for teachers to guide students toward becoming self-directed learners; and Taba's (1966) strategies, which lead students through sequential cognitive tasks to a resolution of conflict that includes the understanding of feelings, attitudes, and values. A rather complex, open-ended structure, Taba's give evidence of producing growth in abstract reasoning (often declared as a goal in gifted programming).

During the past two decades a number of models have been developed that focus on the thinking process and its place in curriculum planning and implementation. This brief review of some of these models reveals an immersion in the linear, rational aspects of the brain's function. While these models remain excellent educational tools for teachers to use as part of their planning for gifted learners, other brain functions need to be incorporated into the learning experience. Integrating the emotional, physical, and intuitive functions, and more of the spatial, gestalt specialization of the cortex will make these models even more effective. The following Integrative Education Model was designed to address all the major processes of learning and to integrate them into the curriculum. It will be discussed in detail and will be used as the organizer for the presentation of strategies in Chapter 8.

The School and the Gifted Individual

THE INTEGRATIVE EDUCATION MODEL: USING BRAIN/MIND RESEARCH IN THE CLASSROOM

Rationale

The Integrative Education Model (IEM) (Clark, 1983, 1986) was developed to synthesize the current findings from brain research, the new physics, general systems theory, and psychology as they relate to education, and to show the application of these data to optimal teaching and learning. From all of these disciplines comes the concern for connectedness and wholeness.

Brain researchers indicate that the complex human brain operates best when all of its functions are integrated. Learning is optimal when thinking (both linear and spatial), feeling, physical/sensing, and intuition are all a part of the learning experience. Such experiences must be novel, complex, pleasurable, relatively free of tension, and challenging if they are to be brain compatible. If not appropriately stimulated to take advantage of each unique genetic program, the individual learner will be unable to actualize the full extent of his or her potential. The often repeated maxim based on the dynamic nature of brain function is "use it or lose it."

For many physicists the view of reality that holds the most promise is the integrated, holistic view. They, along with general system theorists, hold that the human is but one system of energy in a vast complex of interrelated systems. What each of us does affects all of us, each thought adding to or detracting from the total power of thought. When viewed from this perspective, all learning is connected and the learner must be allowed to participate in this interdisciplinary nature of knowledge if optimal understanding is to become possible.

The investigations of psychology continue to support these notions of integration and to bring to us patterns of human behavior that allow more effective teaching and learning. Studies of the self-concepts of teachers and learners add to our knowledge of how to best develop environments to support optimal learning. Data on the role of choice and perceived control on the part of the learner add to our ability to structure the learning experience to ensure success. These and other areas of inquiry lead to the need for important changes to be made in the structures and methods used in teaching and learning.

The Integrative Education Model is a model of learning and teaching that has a highly complex, flexible structure, is decentralized, and is individualized. It allows variations in pace, level, and grouping. The IEM encourages student choice, participation, and involvement. By better meeting the needs of each learner, the IEM can be used in the regular classroom where it allows for giftedness. It optimizes learning by offering brain-compatible teaching experiences.

As we have seen in Chapters 1 and 3, within the past two decades findings have been reported from a variety of disciplines that dramatically affect our

---

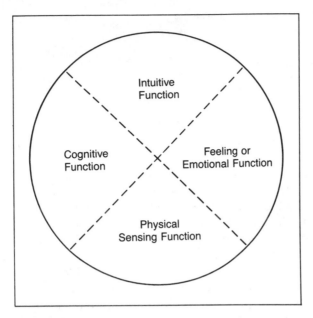

Figure 7.9 *Integrative Education: A Model for Developing Human Potential*

concepts of teaching and learning. Intelligence can no longer be defined as only a rational process. For over thirty years we have known intelligence to be interactive (Hunt, 1961); now we find it to be integrative (Chapter 1). It requires not just the use of the rational cognitive function, but depends on the integration of the spatial cognitive function, the feeling or emotional function, the physical or sensing function, and the intuitive thinking function as well. While we can speak of and experience these functions separately, it is the integration of these functions that creates high levels of intelligence and optimal development of human potential. Figure 7.9 shows the integration of these functions in the Integrative Education Model.

In every subject area, the IEM combines thinking with feeling, intuition, and physical sensing. Through this model each function of the brain is allowed to support the others, resulting in a very coherent, powerful learning experience.

The Functions of the Brain

The Thinking Function (Cognitive)

The thinking, or cognitive function includes the analytic, problem-solving, sequential, evaluative specialization of the left cortical hemisphere of the brain as well as the more spatially oriented gestalt specialization of the right cortical hemisphere.

Higher intelligence requires accelerated synaptic activity and an increased density of the dendrites (Chapter 1), which allows the establishment of complex networks of thought. Stimulating environments promote the advanced capacity to generalize, conceptualize, and reason abstractly.

The Feeling or Emotional Function (Affective)

This is the function that is expressed in emotions and feelings and, while affecting every part of the brain/mind system, it is primarily regulated from the limbic area by biochemical mechanisms housed there. This function more than supports thinking processes; it does, in fact, provide the gateway to enhance or limit higher cognitive function. Worthwhile academic programs integrate emotional growth.

The Physical or Sensing Function

This function includes the entire sensorium: sight, hearing, smell, taste, and touch. The access to our world is through the physical senses; our level of intellectual ability, even our view of reality, will depend on how our brain organizes and processes this information. We know that gifted learners have a heightened ability to bring in information from their environment and process this information in ways that expand their view of reality. They do, however, often define themselves by their cognitive ability. They may recognize their value through this ability alone, and they may focus more and more energy toward the pursuit of cognitive excellence. They may ignore their physical growth and development. Although we are aware of the above-average physical development of many gifted children, we must also notice how they value and share physical pursuits far less than cognitive endeavors. It is common for gifted learners to develop a Cartesian split, which, if unrecognized and left to intensify, can limit the cognitive growth they so value. Integration of the body and the mind becomes an essential part of an integrated program.

The Intuitive Function

According to Jung, intuition "does not denote something contrary to reason, but something outside the province of reason" (Jung, 1933, p. 454). He considered intuition vital to understanding. This function, which we all have but use in varying degrees, represents a different way of knowing. We use this ability when we feel that we know, but we cannot tell how we know. It is a sense of total understanding, of directly and immediately gaining a concept in its whole, living existence. People often repress and devaluate it because it does not operate in the rational manner our western mind has been taught to expect. Activating intuition gives a person a sense of completeness, of true integration. This powerful tool leads to the understanding of concepts and people and to an expansion of the human reach.

The physicist, Capra (1975), tells us that rational knowing is useless if not accompanied and enhanced by intuitive knowing. He equates intuition with new creative insights, and he states,

> These insights tend to come suddenly and, characteristically, not when sitting at a desk working out the equations, but when relaxing in the bath, during a walk in the woods, on the beach, etc. During these periods of relaxation after concentrated intellectual activity, the intuitive mind seems to take over and can produce the sudden clarifying insights which give so much joy and delight to scientific research. (p. 31)

Many of those working to include the development of intuition in the educational setting believe that the ability to concentrate, to work at complex tasks with unusual clarity, results from the intuitive function. Identified now as a part of the function of the prefrontal cortex, intuition becomes a part of the planning, future thinking, and insight so necessary to the intelligent person.

Integrating the Functions

By the use of integrative education and strategies incorporating this construct, students can expect to make impressive gains in areas of cognition, self-concept, and social-emotional development. Among the cognitive gains will be accelerated learning, higher levels of retention and recall, and higher interest in content. In other areas improvement will be seen in how competent the student feels, pleasure derived from learning, interpersonal relations, and teacher-student rapport (Bordan & Schuster, 1976; Galyean, 1977–1980, 1978–1981; 1979; Lozanov, 1977; Prichard & Taylor, 1980; Samples, 1975).

The Integrative Education Model uses all of the modifications previously mentioned including ability grouping, acceleration, and enrichment. The strategies for implementing integrative practices will be discussed in Chapter 8. In its ability to use more of the brain/mind system, focusing narrowly on neither the cognitive nor any other single component, the IEM presents a truly supportive, powerful learning model. By combining previously used structures with the new brain/mind information, we can come far closer to the optimal learning experience we all desire.

Within the structure of the IEM, learners of all levels of ability and interest can be served. Because of its decentralized and personalized organization and its concern for total brain function, giftedness, regardless of how it is expressed, can be nurtured and enhanced. The IEM has been successfully implemented in a variety of settings, including self-contained classes both homogeneously and heterogeneously grouped at elementary and secondary levels; resource room settings; and a special-school setting.

Components of the Integrative Education Model

The IEM can be organized into seven major components:

I. The Responsive Learning Environment

This component requires that the environment be viewed as a support for optimizing learning. Within this component is a concern for both the social-emotional environment and the physical environment. The teacher, the parent, and the student are seen to be a team in achieving effective learning. The following can be used as a guide to developing this component:

1 There is an open, respectful, and cooperative relationship among teachers, students, and parents that includes planning, implementing, and evaluating the learning experience.
2 The environment is more like a laboratory or workshop, rich in materials, with simultaneous access to many learning activities. The emphasis is on experimentation and involvement. Centers may be present.
3 The curriculum is responsive, flexible, and integrative. The needs and interests of the students provide the base from which the curriculum develops.
4 There is a minimum of total group lessons. Most instruction is in small groups between individuals.
5 The student is an active participant in the learning process. Movement, decision making, self-directed learning, invention, and inquiry are encouraged.
6 Assessment, contracting, and evaluation are all used as tools to aid in the growth of the student.
7 Cognitive, affective, physical/sensing, and intuitive activities are all valued parts of the classroom experience.
8 The atmosphere is one of trust, acceptance, and respect.
9 The environment is highly structured and presents a complex, flexible organization to meet the needs of each student. There is evidence of individualized activities.
10 Materials are accessible to the students.
11 The ambience is productive, supportive, and positive.
12 Color, sound, and other sensory stimuli are used to support learning.
13 The physical placement of the furniture, seating of the students, and traffic patterns are planned to support learning.
14 There is evidence of student work and input in the physical appearance of the room.

II. Relaxation and Tension Reduction

The human brain processes more and retains information longer when tension is reduced. Strategies for reducing tension are important tools for both teachers and learners. The following can be used as a guide for developing this component:

1 The ambience of the classroom, including teacher attitude, is calming and stimulating, and has a minimum of stress.
2 Relaxation techniques are used to support learning, including to develop coherence, before testing, and in transitions.
3 The teacher models a relaxed, centered, calm manner.

III. Movement and Physical Encoding

Because using the physical/sensing function of the brain provides support for learning by increasing understanding and retention of concepts, movement and physical encoding strategies are considered an important part of the teaching process. The following can be used as a guide for developing this component:

1 Movement in the room is purposeful.
2 Physical sensing, e.g., touch, smell, taste, is used to support learning.
3 Movement of the body is used to support the development of concepts, i.e., physical encoding.

IV. Empowering Language and Behavior

The brain uses emotions to trigger the production of biochemicals to enhance or inhibit the thinking functions. IEM encourages the use of language and behavior that empowers learners, both between the teacher and the learner and among learners. This component includes strategies to build community and positive interpersonal and intrapersonal communication. The following can be used as a guide for this component:

1 The teacher's language creates for the students a sense of competence, support, closeness, ability, and caring.
2 The teacher uses physical and verbal affirmation, humor, constructive feedback, and "I" messages rather than "You" messages with the students.
3 The teacher uses questions to empower the students and to share the responsibility for learning.
4 The teacher avoids the use of should, shouldn't, must, must not, always, and never and phrases things positively.
5 The teacher uses body language that empowers the learner.

6 The teacher gives opportunities for self-evaluation.

7 The teacher gives students opportunities to share ideas and strategies with each other.

8 The teacher helps students gain control over debilitating speech, both inner and oral in nature.

V. Choice and Perceived Control

Choice and perceived control play an important part in the success and continued achievement of the learner. Strategies that build skills of decision making, ability to align personal and school goals, and foster alternative thinking and self-evaluation are encouraged. The teacher must include choice in the environment and in the learning experiences if optimal learning is to be achieved. The following can be used as a guide for this component:

1 There are choices of activities, timing, and/or ways to learn. Nonnegotiables are known and choices given as to how these can be accomplished.

2 The teacher incorporates lessons in decision making and gives opportunities to practice these skills.

3 The choices given are real with no hidden preference on the part of the teacher.

4 Students are given the opportunity to develop alternatives, help plan learning experiences, and develop structures and organizations for their learning.

5 The teacher avoids giving excessive help and praise or sympathy for easy work that is poorly done.

6 The teacher shares the scope and sequence of the content and skills with the students and individually discusses their growth with them.

7 The teacher models alternative thinking.

8 The teacher values mistakes as learning experiences.

9 The students are involved in establishing agreements for appropriate behavior rather than having the teacher impose rules of behavior.

10 The teacher gives the students opportunities to align their goals with the school goals.

11 Students are given many alternative coping strategies for solving problems.

VI. Complex and Challenging Cognitive Activities

Because there are at least two ways to process thinking, opportunities must be provided for learning that allows use of both rational linear and spatial gestalt processing. By providing novelty, complexity, variety, and challenge in the classroom as the standard for each lesson, the educational process becomes more brain compatible. The following can be used as a guide for this component:

1 Pretesting and posttesting are used, and continuous assessment is evident.
2 Lessons are developed at the level of the learner and paced to meet each individual's needs.
3 Tasks used to develop learning are interesting, integrative, and challenging.
4 Students are engaged and motivated to learn.
5 Both rational linear and spatial gestalt processes are used in the learning experience.
6 Variety and novelty are a part of the learning experience.
7 The student is given choices and shares the responsibility of planning the learning experience.

VII. Intuition and Integration

Because intuition, future planning, and creativity are brain processes thought to be unique to human beings and may be their most powerful brain functions, inclusion of activities that allow use of these processes is considered essential to optimizing learning. These are highly synthetic functions and require teaching opportunities that are multisensory, multidisciplinary, and integrative. The following can be used as a guide for this component:

1 The teacher provides experiences in which the child can demonstrate evidence of intuitive processing at three levels.
  Level 1—use of minimum of known information to reorganize, hypothesize, suggest solutions
  Level 2—use of known information plus hunches to establish probabilities
  Level 3—synthesis of many known and unknown sources to create new information, artistic products, etc.
2 The teacher uses imagery, fantasy, and/or visualization to support the learning experience.
3 The teacher uses "what if" and open-ended, future-thinking strategies.
4 The teacher uses intuitive stretches, e.g., Lady Bug (see Chapter 8, p. 398).
5 The teacher uses integrative lessons.
6 The teacher encourages creativity.

Results

Students who are taught in this way have been found to be

- More relaxed, more at ease with themselves and others
- More positive, caring, and respectful of each other and their teachers
- More creative, try more unusual solutions and engage in more alternative and higher level cognitive activities
- Initiating more learning activities
- More positive and enthusiastic about their learning, more highly motivated
- More independent and responsible.

It is important to note that the Integrative Education Model is inclusive not exclusive in nature. It forms a framework that asks that all content, all process, and all products integrate the four major functions of the brain. Whichever curriculum or program model you choose, integrative education can be a part of it. In view of the excitement and success this integrative approach has been seen to bring to gifted students of all ages it deserves to be considered the beginning step in your planning.

Van Tassel-Baska (1986a) organizes the models presently used into three categories: content, process/product, and concept, and helps us to see the value and limitations of each.

1 *Content Models.* These tend to emphasize the importance of subject areas and domains of inquiry. They are often used with an individualized, diagnostic-prescriptive instructional approach. They accommodate the gifted student's need for acceleration and subject mastery. The SMPY program at Johns Hopkins University (Stanley, Keating, & Fox, 1974) uses such a curriculum model (see p. 207).

2 *Process/Product Models.* These emphasize scientific and social investigatory skills that result in high quality products. They serve the needs for independent inquiry and guidance by a mentor. The Type III of the Renzulli's (1977) Enrichment Triad Model exemplifies this category (see p. 206).

3 *Epistemological Concept Models.* These focus on systems of knowledge and expose students to key ideas, themes, and principles within and across disciplines. They meet the needs for complex and abstract thought and ability to see relationships with the understanding and appreciation of powerful ideas as their goal. The Junior Great Books Program is an example of the use of this type of curriculum model.

Table 7.8 *Categorization of Models by Van Tassel-Baska.*[6]

Model Type	Preferred Content Match	Salient Student Characteristics
A. Content	Mathematics (traditional) Foreign language English grammar Reading	Independent learner High achievement motivation

B. Process/Product	Science
	Mathematics
	   (problem-solving
	   orientation)
	Writing
		High interest in single topic
		Task commitment

C. Concept	Humanities
	Social studies (e.g., history,
	   economics)
	Literature
		High-level verbal reasoning
		   skills
		Broad-based interests and
		   reading behavior

Van Tassel-Baska (1986) suggests that there are variables to consider when choosing the type of curriculum model you will implement. She mentions considering such factors as curriculum areas that lend themselves more readily to one model than another, the preferences and needs of the learner (some prefer acceleration of content while others want the stimulating group interaction of challenging concepts), and motivational considerations. She believes that using models from each category is the best approach for implementing a balanced program. Her categorization (see Table 7.8) clearly shows the content area and the gifted characteristics that each category best represents.

In this chapter an overview of the characteristics and needs of gifted learners was presented, accompanied by suggestions for organizational patterns and sample strategies for meeting these needs. Models for developing differentiated curriculum were reviewed with an overview developed by the author of how they fit into a framework for differentiating curriculum provided by Kaplan (1986). The Integrative Education Model was presented with a rationale, a definition of brain functions, and a discussion of its major components. In the next chapter examples of strategies and lessons will be given to individualize and implement differentiated curriculum.

[6]Van Tassel-Baska (1986) from *Effective curriculum and instructional models for talented students* (p. 168). *Gifted Child Quarterly, 30* (4) used by permission.

Questions Often Asked

1. Why is knowing characteristics of gifted learners important?

It is from the characteristics of gifted learners that we can get a general idea of what their needs may be. As we plan to meet those needs this knowledge will give us a way to prepare and a place to start. If we know that certain behaviors are characteristic of gifted children we will not be surprised or concerned when some of those behaviors are expressed. Many times teachers and parents who have heard these characteristics for the first time comment, "Oh, that's why he does that!" or "I thought she was just being weird."

2. What is the difference between differentiation and individualization?

Differentiation is the preparation that is made for the curriculum to respond to the characteristic needs of gifted children, e.g., allowing for a faster pace of learning and choosing themes and content that allow for more complex investigation. *Individualization* is the process of adapting that curriculum to the needs and interests of a particular gifted student. A program will need both to be really successful.

3. If I have content that is required by the district, how can I differentiate the curriculum for the gifted students in my classroom?

Content or skills that are required for all children can be put into the context of a more complex theme or can be enriched by broader questions. For example, a study of prehistoric times can be included in the theme of Effects of Change or the question of the relationship of past to present to future. It is also possible to include a range of different processes and products in your planning that will allow the gifted learners in your classroom to make choices and to meet their needs more appropriately while meeting the district requirements. It is also possible to consider compacting, a strategy that Renzulli (1977) has detailed with procedures and forms in his Enrichment Triad Model (see Chapter 8). As long as the student can show evidence of having learned the required content, the time can be then planned more appropriately.

4. How can I decide which processes are most important to teach?

This is when you want the process assessment data from your children we discussed in Chapter 6. Generally you would choose a range of processes that are appropriate to your theme, stated by your district as necessary, and interest-

---

ing to the students in your class. From those the students can choose the
processes most necessary for them.

5. Should the students decide which products they will use to show what they have learned?

You may have some products that you feel are necessary to require of all the
students. These become nonnegotiable. In addition to those, allowing students
to offer suggestions about how they can show what they have learned is very
motivating and empowering. The research indicates that it is this type of choice
that produces more quality and retention. Be sure to invite them to develop a
criteria for the evaluation of their self-selected products.

6. Does every learning experience have to have a product?

If you mean a physical product, no. There are many outcomes that can share
learning that need not be physical products, e.g., a student teaching a concept
successfully to the class, using an activity to build upon for a later product, or
showing a change of attitude after a learning experience.

7. If your district is using one model of curriculum development is it all right to include some ideas from a different model?

You are the professional and know best what will work for you and your
students. Most model developers would hope that you will adapt their work so
that it is most useful for you. One caution, be sure the strategies from the
second or third model fit your philosophy just as you made sure the original
model did. If you are using an overall framework, e.g., Kaplan's Grid, it will be
easier to make the appropriate choices and present a unified plan using the
ideas from many sources.

8. Implementing a Differentiated Integrative Curriculum
Strategies for Meeting Gifted Needs

Within this chapter the reader will find

- A plan for individualizing a differentiated program.
- Suggestions for establishing a responsive learning environment as a setting for optimal learning.
- Strategies to enhance the content areas of the curriculum, including language arts, science, mathematics, social sciences, and visual and performing arts.
- Strategies to integrate the process areas of the curriculum, including cognitive process, affective process, physical process, and intuitive and creative process.
- Formats for expanding the products available to learners.

Mere critical thinking, without creative and intuitive insights, without the search for new patterns, is sterile and doomed. To solve complex problems in changing circumstances requires the activity of both cerebral hemispheres; the path to the future lies through the corpus callosum.

—CARL SAGAN

From an understanding of the characteristics and needs of the gifted learner we have discussed how a program can be planned and how a differentiated curriculum can be developed. To implement that curriculum we now discuss individualizing it, developing strategies for it, and creating a climate in which it can function. This chapter uses Kaplan's (1986) framework of content, process, and product from Chapter 7 to provide a structure for presenting strategies that have been found to work effectively with gifted students. Content strategies cover the areas of language arts, science, math, social science, and the visual and performing arts. The categories of the Integrative Education Model (see Chapter 7) are used to discuss process strategies in the areas of cognitive, affective, physical/sensing, and intuitive functions. Product suggestions follow naturally from these discussions. All of these suggestions may be adapted to any age group and must be a comfortable part of your teaching if they are to be effective. Use what you find valuable, and include all of the tools you have found successful. You are the expert; you know your children.

INDIVIDUALIZING THE PROGRAM

In Chapter 5, and again throughout the Hagen and Clark (1977) model in Chapter 7, we have emphasized the importance of individualized instruction. Because many things have been called individualized learning, not all of which are effective, what is meant by individualized learning in the context of this book needs now to be discussed. Unless you understand not only what it is, but how it is begun, an individualized program will be impossible to implement.

One way to understand the importance of individualizing the curriculum for each learner would be through the eyes of a child in a classroom where everyone learns in the same way, with the same material, at the same time. Keeping in mind what brain researchers tell us about the need gifted children have for high levels of stimulation, which if not supplied results in self-generated stimulation blocking all external input, Arden G. Thompson's (1987) remembrance has poignant insight:

I'm a night
exploding
fireflowers;
rockets and
shrieking shimmers
split my sky!
Now a giant
clam on a reef
with showers
of fishes
rainbowing by.
A hungry, hungry
polar bear on a
slippery, tippy
chunk of ice.
Who? Me?
No, teacher;
I'm not bored.
I think
your class
is nice.

In a study directed by Bloom and Sosniak (1981), it was found that of those persons studied who achieved exceptional accomplishment of international note, their early instruction and a large part of their later instruction in their field of accomplishment had been individualized. This was one of the differences identified between the instruction offered to the exceptionally accomplished and the traditional schooling experience.

Individualization can be defined as a way of organizing learning experiences so that the rate, content, schedule, experiences, and depth of exploration available to all students stem from their assessed achievement and interests. Varying degrees, or levels, of individualization are possible:

- *Level 1*—The teacher assesses each student's needs, resulting in an individualized level and pace of instruction.
- *Level 2*—The instruction becomes more personalized when in addition to individualized level and pace the student becomes involved in the selection of goals.
- *Level 3*—Once Levels 1 and 2 have been achieved, the student can begin to incorporate self-directed or independent study skills, as well as the responsibility to self-select learning activities and materials.
- *Level 4*—Total individualization allows teacher and student to cooperatively assess and select goals, learning materials, activities, and instructional techniques. This also allows the student to self-pace, self-level, and self-evaluate, using the teacher as a consultant and resource.

Optimum learning will occur when the environment allows students to

- Assume some responsibility for their own learning
- Become independent learners
- Learn at their own pace
- Learn via material related to their own style
- Learn on a level appropriate to their abilities
- Be graded in terms of their own achievement
- Experience a sense of perceived control, achievement, and self-esteem.

There are a number of strategies that can help you to individualize. Programmed learning offers students a way to move at their own pace through skill-level learning. It includes individual assessment and allows students continuous feedback on work that is done at their own level. Programmed learning can free the teacher from much unnecessary drill work and allow the student to learn materials basic to higher learning or research by a self-checking procedure.

Instructional packages provide an excellent way for students to work individually or in small groups and be in charge of their learning. A learning activity or instructional package includes an assessment or pretest procedure that permits students to discover their own level of need, multisensory resources and activities, and a self-evaluation or posttest component. The package gives students an excellent way to move through basic materials and new information. It should be self-paced and allow students to correct all their own mistakes prior to the teacher's evaluation of the learned information or skill.

Another structure often used to aid students in developing the skills for individualizing is the learning contract. It can be as simple as a statement of need or intent by the student, a description of what will be needed for accomplishing such a goal, and the agreed-upon evaluation procedures or criteria for deciding when the project or learning goal has been completed. Or it can be very complex, depending on its use and the student's ability to be self-directed. Usually the teacher and the learner cooperate in negotiating the learning contract; negotiation may even include the parents. Contractual decisions should be made after substantial assessment has been completed and its results have been discussed with the student. Cooperatively the teacher and the student (and sometimes the parent) must decide on the objectives, resources to be used, possible activities, reporting alternatives, and evaluation procedures for both self-assessment and teacher assessment. While contracts give a mutually agreed-upon base for beginning, they must always remain negotiable. Many factors, such as detours and side investigations, can cause the original plan to need modification.

In developing an individualized program, remember that one of the most critical areas of concern in cognitive development is motivation. We have found that a very important way to bring out the motivation of students is to make them aware of their own power and to allow them to exercise it. Any way that a program or course can be structured to give more choice to the student uses that power. So often schools have rules that create the opposite effect.

Not all gifted students make choices easily. Structuring the choices will be necessary for those who have difficulty in order to guide them gradually into their own power. Others will be ready for responsible freedom. They should be given independence immediately. The following ideas have been found to work in allowing responsible choice:

1 Whatever the nonnegotiables are, whether mandated by the state, the district, or the school, let them be known. Discuss with the students the real consequences to you and to themselves of choice related to these nonnegotiables (for example, if the state requires the completion of a certain course of study, discuss how that can be accomplished and what will happen if it is not). If certain books are to be covered, discuss the time span necessary. Give students the information and choices in whatever areas are possible. One teacher found that by telling the students what the class requirements were and what other things could be done when they had finished, she and the students were able to work out a time span that got the required work completed in time to pursue the other material and projects. Before, students in her classes had moved slowly and unwillingly through only the required work.

2 If tests must be used for evaluation, give a choice between objective and subjective examination, between teacher-written or student-written tests. Often, even though you offer the same tests you have previously used, the element of choice creates more willing, more motivated students.

3 If tests are not required, contract with students to make a choice over a wide range of possible criteria to be used for evaluation. They can contract for a particular level of performance if grades are to be given.

4 Set up many ways of reaching the same learning goal. At the secondary level, classrooms in English can become learning labs just as well as classrooms in chemistry. In the elementary class, the possibilities are limited only by the teacher's creativity.

5 Cross-grading can be accomplished even in traditionally structured schools by developing a relationship between different age classes or nearby schools and allowing students extended passes to work with these other students in their classrooms.

6 Make available off-school sites for those interested in working independently.

7 Make public and accessible the requirements for entry into the colleges and universities that your students will likely attend. Let students make choices about which of these sets of requirements best meets their needs.

Implementing a Differentiated Integrative Curriculum   **311**

Gifted students are interested in current topics that involve them and their personal welfare. Any new information, such as discoveries in brain research or physics, that can be shown to affect them and their world is of great interest, especially if presented with all the unanswered questions and future challenges.

Interdisciplinary presentations are most requested by gifted students. One teacher with the proper background or a team from differing disciplines can make this approach available. Be aware that what the students are asking for is not tandem teaching, one instructor then the other, but a real team situation where the students can be a part of an interaction between disciplines.

Secondary departments might consider using an open, individualized approach that would allow more subject areas to be taught at higher levels. One school with a small faculty can offer 5 years of all basic languages plus Latin, Russian, and Greek by teaching in an individualized pattern. Students can sign up for the language of their choice at their appropriate level. By the individualization model, they can receive instruction while others pursue their own choices during the same period. One period of typing could be individualized to accommodate many levels and instructional goals. A business teacher in my class recently developed a programmed typing manual to help her individualize such a class. This method of presenting instruction would work for all subject areas.

Dunn and Dunn (1975) present one of the best approaches to individualizing I have yet discovered. They provide a step-by-step approach to individualize a classroom successfully. Briefly, they suggest that you do the following:

1 Give students opportunities to build the skills needed for participation in individualized learning:
   a to make choices (choosing wisely leaves many options; choosing less wisely leaves fewer options, and only consequences can determine the value of the choice)
   b to self-evaluate
   c to share.
2 Teach students the skills of learning in small groups:
   a role playing
   b peer teaching
   c group analysis
   d discussion.
3 Establish instructional areas that will support individualized learning:
   a interest centers
   b learning stations
   c media center
   d game area
   e quiet reading and study area
   f assessment center.
4 Develop student independence:

    a knowledge of resources, location, and use

    b alternative thinking in activities and in reporting.

5 Carefully assess students, curriculum, and resources.

6 Help class learn skills of cooperative assessment, goal setting, evaluation.

7 Let class assume more responsibility for planning and implementing the program.[1]

These steps are not easy. They require time and effort to be used successfully. However, if your goal is for independent, stimulated learners, you will find your efforts well rewarded.

Developing the Individual Educational Plan for Gifted Students

One way some states have chosen to assure that their gifted students' needs for individualized planning are met is to modify the federal law requiring that all handicapped students receive an annual Individual Educational Plan (IEP) specified by the 1975 Education for All Handicapped Children Act (PL 94–142). By legislative action several states have included the gifted learner in with the handicapped as children with special needs. As a result, individualized planning has been mandated for gifted learners in those states.

An IEP is easy to plan from the profile we have developed using the assessments we discussed. In addition to the profile data, we must identify objectives that will reflect the needs the profile shows; plan activities to meet them, including a timeline for implementation; and develop an evaluation of the child's progress toward these objectives. It is important to be realistic but not adhere to minimum limits when planning these objectives. One advantage of the IEP system is the planning conference at which the parents, the teacher, the gifted specialist, and the school psychologist and other appropriate school personnel meet to discuss the educational plan and its implementation. If done in a cooperative spirit, this team effort can have very positive outcomes for all concerned, especially the child.

THE RESPONSIVE LEARNING ENVIRONMENT

An important part of the Integrative Education Model, the responsive learning environment requires educators and parents to develop attitudes toward learning and views of gifted education that support optimal, integrated human growth. Skills

---

[1]From the book *EDUCATOR'S SELF-TEACHING GUIDE TO INDIVIDUALIZING INSTRUCTIONAL PROGRAMS* by Rita Dunn and Kenneth Dunn. © 1975 by Parker Publishing Company, Inc., West Nyack, New York 10994. Published by Parker Publishing Company, Inc., West Nyack, New York 10994.

of assessing, planning, and implementing individualized programs become important. The environment expands in meaning and usefulness. This type of structure has many titles and identifers, such as informal learning, natural learning, integrated day, and open education. The responsive learning environment seems to describe the educational structure best.

The roots of this organizational plan are buried deeply in the work of Plato, Socrates, Froebel, Pestalozzi, Dewey, Montessori, Piaget, and numerous other innovative educators. Basically, it strives toward a unique learning experience for each individual. Participation is seen as necessary to learning, and involvement is encouraged to ensure the assimilation of concepts. While the responsive learning environment has a different format for each group of learners, there are some basic characteristics:

1 There is an open, respectful, and cooperative relationship among teachers, students, and parents that includes planning, implementing, and evaluating the learning experience.
2 The environment is more like a laboratory or workshop, rich in materials, with simultaneous access to many learning activities. The emphasis is on experimentation and involvement.
3 The curriculum is flexible and integrative. The needs and interests of the student provide the base from which the curriculum develops.
4 There is a minimum of total group lessons. Most instruction occurs in small groups or between individuals. Groups can be formed by teachers or students and will center around needs or interests.
5 The student is an active participant in the learning process. Movement, decision making, self-directed learning, invention, and inquiry are encouraged both inside and outside the classroom. Students may work alone, with a partner, or in groups. Peer teaching is important.
6 Assessment, contracting, and evaluation are all used as tools to aid in the growth of the student. Frequent conferences keep student, teacher, and parents informed of progress and provide guidance for future planning.
7 Cognitive, affective, physical, and intuitive activities are all valued parts of the classroom experience.
8 The atmosphere is one of trust, acceptance, and respect.

The responsive learning environment is flexibly structured and presents a complex learning organization for the student. This environment has the ability to meet all learners at their present level of cognitive, emotional, social, physical, and intuitive development and to help them to move from that point. In this learning environment, gifted students can pursue interests in depth with a minimum of time limitations. They are no longer singled out, but they can be grouped flexibly with other students as their learning needs demand, or they can work individually whenever it is more appropriate. The gifted learner can function as a teacher, a challenged student, a researcher, an apprentice, a resident expert, or a learning manager. The classroom becomes more of a laboratory for learning and is more closely related to the real world. In fact, the student may often more profitably engage in projects and inquiries outside of the classroom in the larger community. To help you understand the format and structure of this type of organization, I refer you to the detailing of one such program reported in *Optimizing Learning* (Clark, 1986). Now let us look at this structure as it affects gifted individuals.

The Social-Emotional Environment

In an environment where each student is considered a unique individual, the atypical needs of the gifted student cause no one to feel out of place. Self-concept can be developed in a realistic perspective with every person valued for those qualities he or she possesses. Accomplishments can be shared, and the value of the contributions of others can be experienced. Labels become unnecessary and identification inappropriate as a result of the system's continuous assessment

Gifted students can gain recognition without seeming to dominate. They learn responsibility through the many opportunities provided for accepting responsibility for personal goals. Gifted students strengthen the inner locus of control by continuous encounters with the intrinsic values in learning from their own interest or from real need.

In a traditional classroom, the gifted student must often contend with the isolation that results from labeling. In a responsive learning environment where labeling is unnecessary, such isolation occurs less frequently. Gifted youngsters have a need to seek out their intellectual peer group. They accomplish this easily when older and younger children can work together in a cross-graded classroom with flexible grouping and freedom of movement. Any problems encountered in living together as a group can be resolved by the group to give a natural setting for the development of leadership skills.

Building Trust

The first step in developing an environment that can promote social-emotional growth is the establishment of trust. A trusting environment does not just happen; it is deliberately planned. Classrooms that have used the Integrative Education Model have included use of language and behavior that allows students to feel competent, activities that are more cooperative than competitive, and time for building positive interpersonal interactions. Only when there is trust within the class can students feel safe to take the risk of learning. Trying things you don't know and things at which you may not succeed, making mistakes, and noticing that you learn differently from others all require a safe environment. It may take a long time to build the trust needed to enhance a learning experience, but the time and effort taken to establish such an environment are well spent. Here are some suggested strategies for building a trusting environment.

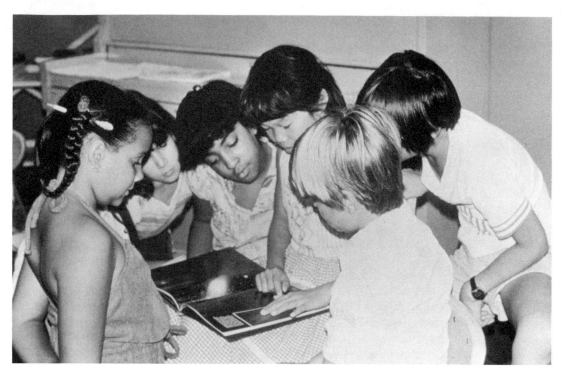

A responsive environment encourages cooperative learning.

Appreciation Circle.   An appreciation circle can be used to end a class session or as a morale builder. There are many variations, but the idea is to give students the opportunity to tell what they appreciate about each other. One structure would be to divide into groups of five and have one person remain silent as the others tell that person one thing they like or appreciate. Continue having a different person remain silent until all have participated. This is very powerful when larger groups or the whole class speak to one person at a time.

Name Game.   At the beginning of the year, let the class become acquainted by ending a session with this game. All students sit in a circle. Beginning with the teacher, say your name and turn to the student on your right (or left). That student says his or her name and your name, the next student says his or her name, the second student's name, and your name. Continue around the circle. Even with 35 children participating, this works surprisingly well. Assure the children that they can ask a name if they forget. Few will need to.

Trust Circles and Lines.   End a class session with a trust-building activity. Have students sit on the floor, shoes off, shoulder-to-shoulder in a circle. One person stands in the center and all the others place their feet on this person's feet and ankles. Those in the circle now raise their hands and arms in front of them, ready to catch and pass the center person around the circle. When all in the circle are ready, the center person falls back into the circle with feet on the floor securely supported by all the other feet. By bending only at the knees and relaxing, the center person can be passed from hand to hand around the circle easily. Be sure students are close enough so that several will be supporting the center person at all times.

Another trust activity involves forming parallel lines so that one person can be passed down the row and back, shoulder high, very easily. The weight or height of the person is unimportant, as at least four pairs of hands will support him or her at all times. Both exercises provide the passed person with a sense of well-being and trust for the others. Try it yourself. Your students will enjoy your trust.

As resources for group interaction strategies, see Galloway (1970), Gorman (1974), Johnson (1972), Otto (1973), Reihart (1970), and Schmuck and Schmuck (1971).

Choice and Perceived Control

During the past few years an impressive number of researchers in projects throughout the country have found that choice and the resulting perception of control are motivational variables that significantly affect children's academic achievement as well as their self-concept (Arlin & Whitley, 1978; Barnett & Kaiser, 1978; Calsyn, 1973; Matheny & Edwards, 1974; Stipek & Weisz, 1981; Thomas, 1980; Wang & Stiles, 1976). Interestingly it is not just the choice or control that is allowed children that makes the difference, but their perception of that choice. The possibilities for choice may be in the program, but unless children clearly see those alternatives and believe that they can really make a choice that will be acceptable, the positive effect will be missing.

One of the attributes of gifted learners is their early development of an internal locus of control. This means that they often do things for the pure pleasure of it. They can get very excited about learning new information, and they derive much satisfaction from discovering the solution to a problem. The term *locus of control* is used to express the idea that the perceived control can be located either within the child (as when a choice is made from the child's interest) or externally (as when a reward is given for making the choice). This is where gifted children show themselves to be characteristically different from the average learner. Gifted children are found to have more inner locus of control at a younger age than do average learners. It is one of the notable differences that needs to be considered when educational experiences are planned for the gifted. It is important to note that success in later life is in direct correlation to how much inner locus of control the individual has developed. This perception of responsibility for and control over one's life is the single most important condition for success, achievement, and a sense of well-being (Allen et al., 1974; Bar-Tal et al., 1980; Dweck & Goetz, 1978; Lao, 1970; Morrison & McIntyre, 1971; Phares, 1975).

Schools use external rewards, such as grades, prizes, gold stars, special privileges, threats, and punishments, without considering whether the child is intrinsically motivated or not. It has been established that the more the environment, either home or school, provides external controls, the greater will be the loss of the inner locus (Deci, 1975). Source of motivation is just what we who work with the gifted must notice. Greene (1974), Lepper, Greene, and Nisbett (1973), and others have found that, for children who have intrinsic motivation, an external reward system can be devastating. The child will no longer work for the joy or notice the satisfaction of accomplishment, but will focus on the learning task as a means to a different goal, the reward. Once the reward stops being offered, the task ceases to be worthwhile. For gifted learners this is most important. Not only do they have more inner control available earlier, they are more sensitive to the demands of the environment. They can, in fact, lose more of their perceived power faster than will the average learner. It then becomes important to plan an environment that builds inner locus and heightens the perception of choice. Development of intrinsic motivation and internal locus of control are important goals for gifted students to help them function positively in society and find personal satisfaction in whatever they choose to do. Be careful that unexamined practices of using rewards do not undermine this development.

Deci (1985) believes that unless the environment interferes, both teaching and learning are intrinsically motivating for most people. His research shows that both activities are performed most effectively when they are intrinsically motivated. The social environment has an important effect on which type of motivation people will use. Deci states,

> Extrinsic motivation predominates in environments that are controlling, while intrinsic motivation is fostered by environments that support autonomy. Changing the environment can alter the motivational patterns and the results they foster. (p. 52)

Deci and his colleagues found that even modest reminders about standards and accountability can set up controlling patterns within teachers. They tended to talk more, direct more, control more, evaluate more, and to criticize more. They did not allow students to experiment with the task and gain a conceptual grasp of the problem. The result was that students who were in freer classes solved 80% more of the problems given than did the controlled students. Deci comments, "When teachers are pressured and controlled to provide results, they respond with rigid, controlling behavior" (p. 53).

In another study of children's perceived competence and feelings of self-worth, as well as their level of intrinsic motivation, Deci found that children in classrooms of controlling teachers showed less intrinsic motivation, perceived themselves to be less competent, and felt less good about themselves, while students in freer classes displayed greater intrinsic motivation and greater conceptual learning; both groups did equally well on rote memory tasks.

Deci suggests that teachers establish "autonomy-oriented limits" in the classroom by these methods:

1 Use minimal pressure and make limits as wide as possible so that within them, children have real choices about how to behave. Deci comments, "Both limits and consequences for overstepping them must be stated clearly, and the consequences should be appropriate for the severity of the transgression" (p. 53).

2 Set limits so that children can monitor their own behavior and receive relevant feedback about the effectiveness of their performance.

3 Help children understand that all of their feelings are legitimate even when their actions are not.

Challenging widely held assumptions on competition and its productivity, University of Texas psychologist Robert Helmreich (cited in Kohn, 1986) reported that after seven different studies with vastly different groups and measures of success, competitiveness is associated with poorer performance. It is not only competitiveness of an individual that he found to undermine achievement; even a structure that demands competition tends to have the same effect. His findings have been strengthened by the work of Johnson and Johnson (cited in Kohn, 1986) who reviewed 122 studies done on achievement or performance in competitive, cooperative, and/or individualistic classrooms between 1924 and 1981. They found 65 studies showing that higher achievement was promoted by cooperation, 8 studies where the findings were reversed, and 36 studies that showed no significant difference between competitive and cooperative classrooms. According to the Johnsons, the advantage of cooperation holds for all subjects and age groups, and even promotes higher achievement than independent work. It appears from the research that, though competition may seem to make teaching easier by use of games that attract and hold the students' attention, this strategy only makes teaching easier, not more effective. It is the gaming that catches the attention, not the competition; cooperative games are preferred by children even more than competitive games. Children simply do not learn better when competition is introduced into the classroom.

Kohn's (1986) review of the evidence found some interesting additional reasons for competition's failure. Success depends on the ability to utilize resources efficiently, and competition makes sharing of resources and skills impossible as people have to work against each other, resulting in hostility and suspicion. Competition fails to promote excellence because of the emphasis on trying to beat others. Extrinsic motivators, such as competition, are simply not as rewarding, nor do they call forth the level of excellence as do our own intrinsic structures. As Kohn comments, "Years of research have shown that extrinsic motivators not only fail to spur people on to higher achievement but actually undermine intrinsic motivation, the sort that produces better results" (p. 28).

Successful experiences are not enough. If children succeed, but believe that you gave them that success, it does not add to the perceived power. Likewise, failure can be viewed as positive if children believe by their own effort success would be possible. The world must be seen as able to be acted upon; it must not be viewed as a place where one is helpless and everything just happens to you. This perception is established very early, within the first 2 months. It is this perception that is one of the triggering mechanisms for developing higher levels of intelligence (deCharms, 1976; Gordon, 1977; Andrews & Debus, 1978).

How then can we plan an environment that works for the gifted child and increases a sense of perceived control? Here are some suggestions:

1 One critical factor is the structure of the program. It must be a complex structure that attempts to give every child alternatives at an appropriate level of choice. A flexible, responsive structure is important at home as well.

2 Incorporate lessons in making good choices and how to develop responsible choices. Children need a lot of practice in choosing.

3 The choices must be real; that is, any that are presented are equally acceptable to the teacher (or parent), and there is no hidden preference.

4 The situations for choice must come with a procedure for child-developed alternatives to be considered whenever possible. "If you don't find what you want within what we suggest, what do you suggest?" becomes the question.

5 Teachers must believe that children can and should make the major part of the decisions about their learning experience. We are there to provide the organizers, the resources, and the structure to help the child be effective. Assignments can be given by teachers or parents, but the order and timing of the completion can be left to the child. It has been found that with even this much control children complete a significantly higher percentage of their assignments (Wang & Stiles, 1976). Children who participate in discussion groups, family councils, planning sessions for trips, committees, etc. show far more satisfaction and responsible participation in the class or family (Sharan, 1980; Stipek & Weisz, 1981; Thomas, 1980).

6 Children need specific skills to make good choices. Some of these are development of alternative thinking patterns, ability to build personal power through relaxation and tension reduction, imagery, intuitive strategies, and the ability to see and evaluate consequences.

7 Each child has irreducible dignity and can be helped to see that in self and others. Such experiences must be built into a home or school day. Demonstrations of caring cannot be left to chance.

8 One of the primary responsibilities of a faculty is to model effective interpersonal relationships and personal power. "If you want to see how it looks to be working toward effective growth," we must say to the child by our actions, "look at us, talk to us, we're trying too."

Homes and schools must be organized with flexibility and a structure that provides alternatives. Parents and teachers need to see themselves as the resources for ever-widening, child-initiated choices. That children feel comfortable with ambiguity and in novel and open-ended situations is tremendously important. The behavior of all children is significantly influenced by their perceived locus of control. Success, achievement, and well-being come with personal power and the perception of inner control. Helping children develop their power is up to each of us, parents and teachers alike. For gifted children it is a matter of survival.

Empowering Language

Empowering language allows the student to hear what is being said. Gibb (1961) asks us to consider language a "people process." He suggests that if we want our students to hear our message, we must be aware of the need to reduce defensive listening. Worse than nonlistening, defensive listening reduces the ability of the student to engage in a task either alone or in a group, causes distortion of what is heard, and affects the climate of the classroom by creating more defensiveness among those present. Gibb believes that defensive climates differ from supportive climates in the following ways:

1 A defensive listener perceives the sender to be judging, while a supportive listener perceives the sender to be requesting information, or sharing feelings, ideas, or perceptions.

2 A defensive listener perceives the sender to be attempting to change or control the listener, while a supportive listener recognizes attempts to define a mutual problem for which no solution is now known.

3 A defensive listener perceives the speaker as having a hidden agenda, being dishonest or devious, while the supportive listener perceives the speaker as being honest and straightforward.

4 A defensive listener perceives the speaker as being inconsiderate, seeing the listener as worthless and inferior, while the supportive listener recognizes attempts to identify with and be concerned about the listener.

5 A defensive listener perceives the speaker as having all the answers, as being inflexible, and as being opinionated, while the supportive listener perceives the speaker's open-minded, honest opinion and willingness to consider the opinions of others.

If students spend their time and energy on defensiveness and resistance there will be little energy or time for learning. One way to contribute to a supportive climate in your classroom would be to affirm your students rather than judge them. Show them that their behavior is the problem, not who they are as people.

Example: Larry noisily enters the room, throws a book on his desk, kicks the chair, and passes loud and profane judgement on the day, the school, and everyone in it.

Affirming response: *Larry, I can see you are really upset. Would you like to step outside and talk about it or would you rather work a while now and discuss it later?*

Judging response: *Larry, you know that kind of behavior is not permitted in this room! What is the matter with you? Can't you grow up? Now sit down and get to work.* (Clark, 1986, p. 129)

Shared Responsibility Model

The Shared Responsibility Model (SRM) by Saundra Sparling (cited in Clark, 1986) was first developed for low-socioeconomic-level students in an urban school setting. Over the past 6 years it has been used with students from age 2 to 50, of ability levels from the learning handicapped to the gifted, and in groups numbering from 5 to 50.

The SRM is focused on two goals. One is to provide educators with a way to gradually share with students more of the responsibility for their behavior and learning achievements. The second is to relieve some of the teacher's burden of managing and controlling student behavior. The philosophy of the SRM considers the control of student behavior to be the student's responsibility.

The strategies employed by the model can be easily modified for the teacher's and the student's level of skill and need for structure. In the SRM responsible behavior is conceptualized as falling on a continuum between being totally teacher controlled and totally student controlled. What works best is a shared responsibility producing optimum levels of freedom and structure for both (deCharms, 1984).

In the SRM it is recognized that teachers may lack skills for sharing responsibility just as students may lack skills for accepting it. Therefore, all activities are designed to help students learn to take responsibility and to help teachers learn to give it away. For further information on the SRM, please write to Saundra Sparling, 6126 Condon Ave., Los Angeles, California 90056.

The Physical Environment

Gifted individuals often have the ability to integrate and synthesize information from many disciplines to develop new concepts or to enhance their understanding. In an open environment, the opportunity for this type of synthesis is available and even encouraged. Imagine this classroom: It has many activity areas and quiet, comfortable reading and study areas. Also, discussion areas are available to students and teacher/student groups. It has conference areas as well as large group spaces. Individual carrels are numerous. Space is provided by a greater use of floor and table surfaces, with movement facilitated by a minimum of desks and chairs. The walls display alternative activities and materials for self-directed study. Closets and cupboard doors provide media centers, and the use of many ways of learning is evident. At the beginning of the year, teacher-initiated activities and materials dominate; but by the end of the year, the environment will be representative of all the learners within. Gifted learners can structure this type of physical space to meet their unique abilities and levels of inquiry.

Movement in and out of the classroom to the library or other learning centers is not inhibited, and special grouping for specific interests is not uncommon. Pursuing any interest, however unusual, is not seen as odd by the other learners in this individualized setting. No one is asked to wait for the group to catch up or to do busy work to pass the time. Individual contracts and projects make it possible for each student to learn at his or her own pace. The need the gifted learners often feel to pursue a subject in depth, to branch out into other related fields, or to stay with one inquiry for long periods of time is met without inhibiting the needs of others. There is adequate opportunity for the gifted to share their accomplishments by constructing a learning center to instruct others, conducting a seminar of other interested students, or meeting with a mentor for the challenge of expert advice and criticism. If the gifted student's needs cannot be met within the classroom, outside resources can be made available and arrangements made for field trips or apprenticeship programs. While these may also be arranged in a traditional classroom, the novelty of such arrangements and the exit from the classroom make reentry a social problem for the gifted student. The richness of materials and opportunities makes the responsive learning environment a place where gifted individuals can meet their unique needs on a full-time basis.

Structuring the Classroom Environment

The learning setting can facilitate or inhibit the learning program. The environment has far more impact than we previously assumed; it affects even the energy the student has to expend on learning goals. Although many factors could be stated as being part of the learning environment, this discussion will concern itself primarily with the physical setting.

Space.   In an individualized program, the teacher must first develop a classroom with sufficient "people space." So many educational settings are overfilled with desks, tables, chairs, and equipment; space for people to move about, to group flexibly, to manipulate materials, and to actively participate in their own learning is restricted. People space can be obtained in a number of ways:

1 Take out furniture. In most learning environments, students do not need individual desks. If students are engaged in a variety of activities, rarely will everyone need to be sitting and writing at the same time. Writing can be done on the remaining tables, at centers, or on portable clip-boards. Each student's materials can be stored by use of racks, boxes or carton walls, or hall lockers.

2 Carpet some areas. Carpeted areas provide good group spaces and can be used for seating people quite flexibly. Carpet also reduces the noise

of movement. Carpeting causes a room's atmosphere to become more interactive, less tense, and more pleasant. Students seem to show more pride in their surroundings and exercise care in the use of a carpeted facility. At the university, I teach a class that has several sections. I have noted with interest that when class takes place in the usual classroom of desks, board flooring, and sterile surroundings, there is far less discussion and interaction among the students than in the carpeted room that has pillows and floor spaces for seating. A different quality of learning occurs.

3 Use walls, windows, closets, and drawers for teaching areas. For example, a reclaimed teacher's desk makes a fine media center. The drawers provide space for storing projectors, films, slides, and filmstrips. The knee well makes a good projection area as it is somewhat protected from light. By sitting on the floor, a small group can participate quite effectively in a self-directed media presentation. Don't overlook the backs and insides of drawers, and the bottoms of tables for use as learning center areas. Can you imagine how much more interesting number facts become when third-grade students must work them lying on the floor with a flashlight, reading them off the bottom of a table? Even in secondary and university settings, more flexible use of space would be beneficial.

4 Bring in comfortable, movable furniture. A few comfortable pieces such as a couch or overstuffed chairs can provide reading and meeting spaces that will attract students. Floor pillows or small padded stools can provide highly flexible seating spaces also. In our university classroom these have made a significant instructional difference.

At first, the children may find it difficult to imagine how a classroom can be different. Let them help improve the learning environment by giving them a few options for changing their space. They will be more responsible and involved in using the classroom if they have a part in creating it.

Light and Color.   Now that we have begun to look at the space in the classroom, let us think a moment about light and color. In Ismael's book (1973) on the effects of the environment, she suggests that soft lighting makes people less self-conscious and more receptive. When she tried it, she found interaction and cooperation among students increased. She felt a new sense of ease in teaching and communicating. Ott (1973) has found that natural light or full spectrum light is important to the proper use of human energy. Fluorescent light omits the needed ultraviolet rays, and pink fluorescent light increases irritability, hyperaggressiveness, and negative feelings.

Meer reports that increasingly, researchers are finding that the components of light are necessary to our mental and physical well-being. Some of their conclusions include,

1 The brighter the room (short of the level that produces glare), the better the performance.
2 Lighting that is appropriate at age 25 may have too much glare for the same person at age 45.
3 People show a great preference for natural lighting; sunlight makes people feel good.
4 Having windows facilitates the opportunity to observe variety, change, and nature's rhythm, all of which contribute to positive feelings.
5 In subdued light people feel closer to each other, speak more softly, and make less noise.
6 People tend to sit facing the light.
7 How much control people have over the lighting system affects how they feel about the system.

There has begun to be an interest in the relationship between light and health. Gerard (cited in Meer, 1985) believes that light and color in visualizations can have a dramatic impact upon health and well-being. He finds that it is more reliable to use visualizations of color than to use the actual color.

Color can be used for a variety of purposes. Heline (1969) gives the following information on our response to color.

1 Reds stimulate and invigorate the physical body.
2 Oranges energize.
3 Yellows vitalize and accelerate mental activities.
4 Greens are restful and soothing to the nervous system.
5 Blues are inspirational, calming.

By using color in relationship to the activity you are desirous of implementing, you may enhance the result.

Not all students have the same light and color preferences, so you may wish to vary the light intensity and color opportunities available and invite the students to use the environment as they feel best.

Sound. What about sound? Each of us has a differing need for silence and sound. Noise can be quite distracting; "busy people sound" is less so. Because the type of exciting, involved learning that we are discussing requires movement, we must consider the sound that this produces. Carpets help, easy flowing movement patterns within the room help, less furniture to move around helps. Sometimes, when students are not used to moving around and working on their own, they will need direction and advice from the teacher. This can create a source of noise if not handled well. Try creating a sign-up space such as an "I need you" list on the chalkboard where students can list their names when they need help in a project or lesson. Check the board and go to each individual, in order, as soon as possible. It works very well and reduces noise, frustration, and interruptions measurably.

The use of listening posts for films, slides, filmstrips, and video and audiotape systems is excellent to reduce noise. If students are to have free access to a lot of learning centers and media simultaneously, listening posts are essential. Not only should lessons be recorded on tape for student growth, natural sounds such as water running in brooks, birds, ocean sounds, and wind in trees can be excellent contributions to the learning environment. Music can create different moods, can calm or inspire; some claim it heals. Whether played or heard, music has an important place in the learning environment. As you provided spaces for differing intensities of light, so too, must you provide for quiet, thoughtful activities and louder, busy learning.

Shapes. Have you considered the structural designs with which you surround yourself and your students? The pyramid has intrigued humans for centuries. Its shape seems to have some effect on the environment. A great deal of literature discusses the properties of the pyramid. What about other shapes? The geodesic dome created by Buckminster Fuller, the spirals used by Frank Lloyd Wright, and all of the hexagons, pentagons, trapezoids, and spheres are claimed to affect those who live within them. We have lived so long in square and rectangular boxes; what effect would changing our space have? You may wish to explore this information with your class. There may be significant benefits to being more aware of the shape of our environment.

Climate. Temperature, quality of air, and odors all change the responses of learners. People differ in their needs along these dimensions. Plants and animals create a different climate in a classroom. In creating a learning environment, we might well be more aware of these factors.

Nourishment. The body has needs that, if met, can improve the entire learning ability of the student. Some people work well only when they have sufficient energy, and they need added fuel to maintain that level. Nuts, raisins, and vegetable sticks in bowls placed around the room can supply needed fuel. If you explain the purpose and allow students to be responsible for meeting their needs, you will find little misuse. Remembering Maslow's hierarchy of needs (see Chapter 4), we can understand why, if students do not fulfill their body needs, little energy is available for complex, higher level learning activities.

Sharing the Classroom. Teachers in classrooms that must be shared with other classes have a different and more difficult problem. For some elementary teachers, the environment belongs to them only part of the day; another teacher and another class move into the space regularly. In many departmentalized secondary schools, teachers change rooms each period. Many itinerant teachers of the gifted have no space that is really their own. While these situations create more difficulties, they can be worked out. Design boxes that have all the props you will need for a center and create portable environments. We have developed very attractive "learning boxes" that visually add to the interest of the contents and can be used as part of the learning center itself. I have found that when I have to use a room for only certain periods, I need a good deal of portable equipment.

Look for storage room in closets or nearby offices to house your media equipment and materials. Try to get at least basic flexibility built in the rooms that you use, such as moveable tables and chairs, carpeted flooring, and attractive wall display areas. You may be able to share these areas with the other classes, although I have found that if my students and I are willing to arrange the displays, the other teachers are more than happy to let us. Let me inject one other small but important suggestion: After your class is over, return the furniture to its usual arrangement. I discovered that I could do anything in my classroom as long as the teacher following me did not have to put it back in its "proper" order. Oh yes, and while you are working out your way of sharing, start working toward changing the need to work this way. Convince scheduling or the administration of the importance of the environment to creating effective learning; keep trying to get your own space.

There is far more to consider in creating an environment for learning. It is beyond the scope of this book to do so. As you investigate your classroom, the following observations may be helpful. When you come into the classroom, do you feel good about being there? Does the environment seem pleasant, inviting, purposeful? Would you like to spend time there, given a choice? Try to see it from the student's viewpoint—does it still seem a good place to be? If you enjoy being there, you can be pretty sure the students will also. Of course, you could ask them.

Learning Centers. Another aid in structuring the environment for individualization is the use of learning centers, for they can serve many purposes. They can be set up as learning stations, assessment centers, game areas, media centers, or interest centers. They can be teacher created, student created, or the result of a cooperative venture. They may have a specific purpose or may be for exploration and discovery. They may develop content knowledge or process skills, or enrich either. They can be located anywhere in the room, using tables, desks, walls, doors, drawers, or whatever is available for their function.

Pflum and Waterman (1974) conclude that every learning center, regardless of its purpose, must have the following components:

1 *Directions.* Make them simple and clearly stated; they may be written or taped.
2 *Purpose.* As soon as the child gets to the center this should be obvious; not only must the children understand what the center is for, but also what is expected of them in it.
3 *Content.* This is why the center exists; the center can use manipulative materials, media, books, other people, etc., to communicate the content.

4 *Activities.* Provide a variety of ways the children can apply what they have learned.

5 *Evaluation.* This is the way the children let you know what they learned; it can be very simple or an involved project; don't limit the evaluation procedures to testing alone; some centers do not require any evaluation other than the child's reaction to working there.

Some books to investigate for ideas and purposes for learning centers are Allen (1968); Christianson (1969); Kahl and Gas (1974); Kaplan, Kaplan, Madsen, and Gould (1975); Kaplan, Kaplan, Madsen, and Taylor (1973); and Voight (1971). Books for changing the educational environment and learning spaces in secondary schools include Beach (1977); James (1968); Mason (1972); and Truesdell and Newman (1975).

The obvious benefits of a more flexible, open approach to learning have been verified (Bremer & Bremer, 1972; Hassett & Weisberg, 1972; Silberman, 1971; Stephens, 1974; and many others). The importance of this type of experience to the gifted is even more apparent. When offered alternative models, the gifted students and their parents overwhelmingly choose this model.

They encounter problems, however, in the transition from current programs for gifted education to the more extensive models. During transition, students, parents, teachers, and administrators need to work together to establish the kind of educational experience needed and most appropriate to the situation. Most parents of gifted students have successfully promoted a flexible, open learning environment with their own child for at least 5 years before the professional educator arrives. They have much information and ability to offer to the further educational program for their child through their familiarity with the open, individualized approach. The educator has alternatives and organizers to offer, as well as opportunities to broaden and deepen the student's experiences with living. The educator must direct the efforts and organize the opportunities for learning. This expertise will then bring focus and meaning to the experience in order to create a climate conducive to risk taking, exploration, and growth. The student offers unique information to the educational planning. Interest, level of skill, preferred methods, and style of learning are some of the necessary pieces of information that can be offered only by the student. Working together with the support of a capable administrator, this group can bring about a unique and useful educational program.

Too often, without proper planning, an organization that is called "open education" or "individualized learning" produces more chaos than openness or individualization. To ensure against this, the transition should be treated as a slowly evolving process. Because most teachers, students, parents, and administrators have experienced learning in schools organized in the traditional way, some of their expectations may be hard to give up. They may believe that learning occurs only in quiet rooms; everyone must learn from one book the same things at approximately the same time; and grading is the only way to show progress. Only as the skill of the

---

teacher progresses can the organization of an individualized environment progress. It will always be growing and becoming, as are the learners within.

Currently, this model takes many forms. School-within-a-school and alternative open schools draw gifted students and can be used to provide for their needs. They usually consist of four or more faculty members, drawn from different disciplines, who cooperatively team and integrate their disciplines in an open structure. Such programs are individualized, involving both students and parents in the educational decision making. Wherever found, open schools usually have a waiting list for entrance, for they are viewed favorably by gifted students and their parents alike. In some areas, entire schools use the open structure, while in others, only a resource room is presently available for this type of learning. Begin where you can, move slowly and knowledgeably. Your goal is to organize for learning that will better meet the atypical needs of gifted individuals. By individualizing education, we can better meet the needs of every learner.

Opening Classrooms for Growth: Eight Steps to the Responsive Learning Environment

As you begin to open your classroom for growth, consider these eight steps:

1 Find out what provisions your district has made for meeting the needs of gifted learners.
2 Look at the needs gifted learners characteristically evidence (see Chapter 3), and discover how many your current district program strives to meet.
3 Do background reading, attend workshops, and/or take courses on gifted education and individualized education.
4 Develop a plan to change your present district program into what you would like it to be. Single out the steps you feel are necessary to expand or change your gifted program.
5 Discuss your plan with other parents, teachers, and administrators, and your peer group. Modify your plans if needed.
6 Present your plan to another group—if you are a parent, to your principal; if you are a teacher, to parents; to whoever might be interested. Modify your plan if necessary.
7 Plan to inform all interested groups and solicit their cooperation and assistance.
8 You are now ready to begin the change. Move only as fast as you feel comfortable. Remember, this is a long-term plan, and you are providing a starting point for years of growth.

These eight steps sound deceptively simple. They are not. Each step may take months to accomplish. Change is very difficult to bring about. Be satisfied with small increments that move in the planned direction. For some people, change is very threatening and for some, almost impossible. Seek out those who understand what you intend to do and its importance. You will need them for your own emotional support, as well as for aids to make the change happen. Only our efforts can better the education for gifted learners. If establishing good programs were easy, it would have been done by everyone long ago.

Extending Learning Beyond the Classroom

When learning is extended beyond the classroom into the community or nearby nature areas, integrative education becomes very natural and effective. The Learning Expedition, which is a step beyond the standard field trip, can yield enormous educational benefits. By planning and participating in such overnights or extended field trips the class becomes a cooperative unit and gains experiences not available in a classroom setting.

Allowing students to plan the Learning Expedition from beginning to end gives them an opportunity to experience the natural consequences of their planning and organization. This is learning at its best. Students are also provided with endless opportunities for leadership at all levels and gain self-esteem from having taken responsibilities and personal risks. The success of this endeavor is made possible by allowing students to operate within a high level of trust, interacting openly and honestly. In such an environment it is possible to accomplish rather impressive goals. There are four broad objectives for organizing Learning Expeditions:

1 To support cognitive growth in the content area(s).
2 To further develop and reinforce throughout the experience student thinking skills such as inferring, analyzing, hypothesizing, predicting, verifying, and integrating.
3 To develop an environment wherein the discussion of values and attitudes is natural and productive.
4 To provide experiential activities that support personal growth, trust, openness, responsibility, independence, interdependence, honesty, integrity, self-confidence, and the personal commitment to excellence.

Pages 83 to 108 of *Optimizing Learning* (Clark, 1986) will give you a detailed procedure for developing your own Learning Expedition. Designed by Tobias Manzanares, a science teacher at Schurr High School, Montebello, California, this program is complete with forms used and directions given for a successful experience.

Journal writing allows expression and clarifies learning on an expedition. →

Implementing a Differentiated Integrative Curriculum   331

The Responsive Learning Environment:
A Checklist

You know your classroom is becoming more responsive when any of the following begin to happen:

_____ 1 The emotional climate is warm and accepting.

_____ 2 The class operates within clear guidelines decided upon cooperatively.

_____ 3 The students are deeply involved in what they are doing.

_____ 4 Student activities, products, and ideas are reflected abundantly around the classroom.

_____ 5 There is cooperative planning between teacher, student, and parents.

_____ 6 The teacher bases instruction on each individual student and his or her interaction with the materials and equipment.

_____ 7 For assessment purposes the teacher closely observes specific work or concerns of the student and asks immediate questions.

_____ 8 The teacher keeps notes and histories of each student's intellectual, emotional, physical, and intuitive development.

_____ 9 The teacher keeps a collection of the student's work for use in evaluating development.

_____ 10 The teacher uses evaluation as information for the student and to guide the student's instruction.

_____ 11 The teaching day is divided into large blocks of time within which students and teacher cooperatively determine their own routine.

_____ 12 Students work at various activities both individually and in small groups.

_____ 13 Many activities go on simultaneously.

_____ 14 The teacher groups students for lessons directed at specific needs.

_____ 15 Students voluntarily group and regroup themselves.

_____ 16 There is a diversity of materials, including many levels and manipulatives (concrete materials that can, by the student's handling, create a clearer understanding of abstract ideas, e.g., objects to be grouped to clarify set theory).

_____ 17 Materials are readily accessible to the students.

_____ 18 Students work directly with manipulative materials.

_____ 19 The environment includes materials developed by the teacher.

_____ 20 The environment includes materials developed and supplied by the students.

___ **21** Books are supplied in diversity and profusion.

___ **22** Students use "books" written by classmates.

___ **23** All students have their own personal storage space (not necessarily their own desks).

___ **24** Students can use other areas of the building, the yard, and the community for learning.

___ **25** The teacher expects students to use time productively and expects that their work and learning will be of value.

The teacher is central to creating the environment, not only by setting the tone but also by establishing the organization, the sense of coherency, and the attitude toward learning. The teacher helps define personal and class goals and helps students find motivation for learning. Aspy and Bahler (1975) have found that it is the teacher's concept of self that affects the achievement of students even more than their own concept of self. The teacher who wishes to establish a responsive learning environment must be able to

- Assess the level of ability, interests, and needs of the students.
- Develop the scope and sequence of what is to be taught.
- Plan a variety of materials and levels of content.
- Plan with choice.
- Plan with students.
- Present a variety of levels and activities using strategies for facilitating learning.
- Evaluate a variety of levels and activities.
- Share responsibility for learning with the students.

Students taking part in the responsive learning environment will also need skills if optimal learning is to take place. These students must demonstrate an ability to

- Plan learning experiences, both independently and with the teacher or peer.
- Work in a decentralized environment.
- Learn in small groups.
- Learn independently.
- Use resources and appropriate equipment.
- Make choices.
- Self-assess and evaluate.
- Conference with the teacher.
- Share the responsibility for learning.
- Use the tools of the Integrative Education Model.

In summary, the emotional-social environment must provide the students with the support and safety needed for them to feel empowered, motivated, cared for, and caring, feelings that will allow them to become truly effective learners. The physical environment must provide for large and small groupings as well as room for individuals to learn. The environment should designate spaces for a variety of materials and content at a range of ability levels. It should use color, sound, and texture to support the learning process. While integrative education can take place without the support of the responsive learning environment, the use of such an environment will make the job of the teacher and the learner much easier, more efficient, and far more effective.

STRATEGIES FOR DEVELOPING CONTENT

The determination of what content will be used is a concern of educators, students, parents, and the larger community. In this day it is not easy to select content that will be basic to everyone's education because in most disciplines information is burgeoning at a pace that even our advanced technology cannot keep up with. Just when a theory seems to be gaining validation, new information requires a new theory be developed, and a new set of problems appears. It is also difficult to find solutions by staying within disciplines or by calling upon expertise from any one content area, as real world problems are increasingly demanding multidisciplinary study. Single disciplines no longer define a problem; understanding our world requires a view that considers the interdependence and interrelationship of all knowledge. The need is for far more multidisciplinarity in content areas than the schools are prepared to offer. With the help of the strategies given in the sections to follow, it is hoped that curriculum can be planned that will include these concerns, meet the unique needs of gifted learners, and by providing the flexibility for individualizing, result in challenging and complex learning experiences.

When giftedness is shown in the content area, it will be important to assess the level of skill the student has already mastered. Gifted learners are commonly 2 to 8 years ahead of their chronological age peers. Once assessed, the students should participate in individual conferences, acquainting them with their own profile of strength areas and the scope and sequence that is followed in those areas, allowing them to see the skills for which they are now ready and the possible future goals for which they might plan.

The needs of the gifted are not deficit needs, but rather needs for challenge in specific areas of strength. Just providing more of the same level of content will not fulfill this need; we must find ways to accelerate and enrich the concepts and processes in each content area of strength. The taxonomy developed by Bloom (1956) will allow us to assess our curricular planning and its appropriateness to the gifted student's profile. Generally, our main goal should be to go beyond mastery of standard content processes to develop with these students a greater understanding of the concepts underlying the content discipline. In both mathematics and science, we often find the computational and rational applications emphasized exclusively, so that the excitement found by the practicing mathematician or scientist is missing. Firing the imagination and creative ability of gifted students requires inclusion of the intuitive aspects of math and science. Only in this way can we help students view such subjects as dynamic, with real problems yet to be solved. These, after all, are the students who will contribute most to the expanding fields and disciplines. We must present them with an expanding, potentially limitless world view.

Curriculum Compacting

Renzulli (1977) has developed forms and procedures that make the pretesting and posttesting of content much easier and lead into a way of making more appropriate use of a gifted student's time. The curriculum compacting system was designed to provide evidence for those needing it regarding a student's mastery of the skills and concepts required in the regular curriculum. Once the skill or concept has been learned it becomes wasteful to have the student keep reviewing the information or skill again and again. "Curriculum compacting has three major objectives: (1) to create a more challenging learning environment, (2) to guarantee proficiency in the basic curriculum and (3) to 'buy time' for more appropriate enrichment and/or acceleration activities" (Renzulli & Reis, 1986, p. 232). An important part of the services provided by the Enrichment Triad Model (Chapter 7), curriculum compacting is a valuable tool to be used with any curriculum plan as an aid in individualizing the content area.

Another approach to implementing differentiated curriculum is suggested by Tannenbaum (cited in Morgan, Tennant, & Gold, 1980). After assessing the peak areas or gifted needs of your students, develop a grid with all of the content areas on one side and possible ways to modify the content across the top (see Figure 8.1). Possible modifications could include telescoping, that is, accelerating the content; expanding basic skills to include skills to produce as well as consume knowledge; prescribed augmentation, that is, modification directly related to the discipline; teacher-designed augmentation—finding new solutions, ways of mastering more complex, abstract ideas; and out-of-school augmentation, which could include mentors, field experiences, etc. In addition, it is hoped that with what you now know you will include integrative experiences.

Language Arts

Expressing oneself and communicating one's ideas to others are among the most basic of our sets of skills. These are also the skills gifted children often develop first, enabling us to identify their advancing intellect. Linguists tell us that they can already predict potential language problems by 3 months of age. Not only can early

---

Possible Modifications

Content Areas	Telescope	Expand Basic Skills	Prescribed Augmentation	Teacher-Designed Augmentation	Out-of-School Augmentation
Language Arts					
Science					
Mathematics					
Social Sciences					
Arts					
Supplementary Content 1, Depending on Areas of Giftedness					
Supplement 2					
Supplement 3					

Figure 8.1 Content Adjustment Chart.

communication be used to predict future language skills, but early exposure to language skills, especially allowing the child to read, may actually trigger the development of high levels of intelligence.

Gifted ability in language arts is one of the easiest areas of ability to discover. Children with high ability in this area often use complex sentence structures before 2 years of age. Their conceptual development is reflected in the questions and observations they make and the vocabulary they use at this age. Their memory for events seems unusual, and they have a growing body of information they enjoy sharing even before the age of 3.

As an example, a 22-month-old child was talking on the phone to her grandmother and when asked what she was doing said,

"I'm playing with my chalkboard."
"You are?," was the response.
"Yes. I played with it yesterday too."
"Really," commented the surprised grandmother upon which the child replied,
"Don't you remember? You gave it to me for my happy birthday last Wednesday."

Other characteristics from the list in Chapter 2 can be seen emerging early.

Reading

Often gifted children will come to school reading significantly beyond their age peers. Care must be taken, however, that the scope of material presented is difficult enough to tap the extent of this growth. "Top" reading groups may still be far below the gifted reader's capability. As we saw in Chapter 3 many children have ability, but they may not be given the opportunity to show just how capable they are.

A survey was conducted by Mangieri and Madigan (1984) to find out what schools are doing in the area of reading instruction for gifted learners. Five findings were reported as having statistical significance:

1 The major focus of reading programs for gifted learners is enrichment.
2 Teacher recommendation was the major identification tool.
3 The same basal series that was used with the nongifted was used with the gifted reader.
4 The regular classroom teachers were responsible for the majority of the instruction and no staff development was available to upgrade their skills in this area.
5 A high degree of communication was reported between the school and the parents of the gifted students.

As we look at some of the strategies we might use to differentiate instruction, we should know what provisions most schools are making.

Brown and Rogan (1983) make an interesting point that, just as you would not expect Olympic-bound athletes to get by on their own, gifted readers are in the greatest need of brilliant coaching or, in this case, special and intensive reading instruction. By keeping these children in the regular basal series, insisting that they adhere to the regular reading program, follow-up, and skill-builder activities, we often frustrate them. This can destroy their belief in school as an interesting, exciting place and in learning and books as the wonderful experiences they thought they were. These researchers point to age-in-grade grouping and the reluctance to provide acceleration or experiences outside of the regular classroom as obstacles to appropriate programming for gifted readers. Allowing young children to read widely, creatively, critically, and with an excellent and motivated teacher is suggested as part of the solution to providing more appropriate language arts instruction.

Savage (1983) suggests solving the basal problem by the use of reading guides. To be used at any level, including high school, a reading guide is an individual assignment sheet that includes a set of questions and activities that structure a reading lesson. Such a structure allows for creativity, student input on activities and evaluation, and more complex and challenging assignments.

Writing

From her work on improving writing through the use of imagery in the classroom, Hess (1987) has found these commonalities:

1 Details and descriptions are vivid.
2 Hints of characters' moods and emotions are present.
3 Choice of words is more evocative than informative, thus creating a clear mental picture in the reader's mind's eye.
4 Stories contain events and scenes that are believable even when imaginary.
5 Individual interpretations are as unique as the writers creating them. (p. 18)

Imagery. As an example of the use of imagery with the teaching of grammar, try the following exercise: Ask the students to close their eyes and imagine that they are on a hill in summer, lying on their backs and watching the clouds floating by in a blue sky. A biplane comes into view and begins to do some skywriting. It is writing their names. After completing the name, describe how the plane continues writing five words describing them around their names. When the last descriptive word is completed, bring them slowly back into the room and ask them to write the words on a piece of paper. Now ask the students to turn to their neighbor and write five words on their paper describing the neighbor. Give the students a few minutes to share the descriptions they are willing to share with their neighbor, then ask them to close their eyes.

Ask them to see themselves doing something they would feel comfortable doing right then in front of their neighbor. When they have done this, ask them to open their eyes and do what they saw themselves doing, taking turns with their partner. Now ask them to write on their paper five words describing how their partner did whatever he or she did, not what the partner did, but how the partner did it. Write words on the board given to you by the class: one list of words describing themselves or their partners, another list describing how their partners did the action requested. Now explain the differences between the lists and introduce the categories of adjectives and adverbs. This is an interesting way to present grammar and you will find that a high level of understanding and retention follows.

Mind Maps.   Mind maps, developed by Buzan (1983), allow students to use both hemispheric specializations to support and to improve their information processing and retention. In addition to many clues that might improve reading skill, memory, and other school skills, Buzan offers a strategy for note taking that he refers to as mind maps. Designed to give students an alternative to the traditional linear mode of organizing information, mind maps ask students to use the multidimensional and pattern-making capabilities of their brains to organize and record information. Because the brain works primarily with key concepts in an interlinked and integrated manner, Buzan suggests that notes and word relations should be structured in a way that shows these interrelationships as easily as possible. To record information most efficiently Buzan suggests that "one should start from the centre or main idea and branch out as dictated by the individual ideas and general form of the central theme" (p. 91). Buzan gives the following suggestions for creating a mind map:

1 Print words in capital letters. Printed words are more photographic, more immediate, and more comprehensive when the information is read back.
2 Print words on lines and connect lines to other lines. This gives the mind map a basic structure.
3 Print words in units. This leaves each word to be joined to other thoughts and allows note taking to be more free and flexible.
4 Print the ideas freely and with no concern for order. More will be captured in the mind map when you allow your mind to recall every-thing as quickly and as freely as possible. Final order will evolve from the map itself.

The importance of the ideas is clearly indicated when main ideas are in the center and the less important ideas are at the edge, making links between concepts immediately recognizable. New information can easily be added, and recall and review are both more effective and more quickly completed.

Figures 8.2 and 8.3 show the results of first a mind map, and then a linear outline for a speech I gave recently. The mind map was a great help to me during

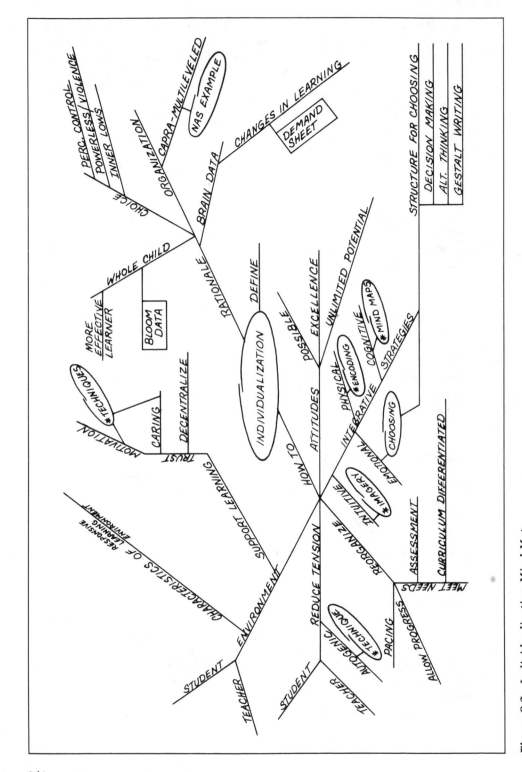

Figure 8.2 *Individualization Mind Map.*
Source: Clark (1986, p. 156).

Overview and goals

Definition of individualization

Highly structured, complex, decentralized
Environment supports learning
  characteristics of responsive learning environment
Allows variation in pace, level, grouping
Meets each learner's needs
Participation and involvement encouraged
Bloom study

Rational for

Brain-compatible learning
  Brain data
  Demand Sheet
  NAS experience—Multilevel administration, cross age
Perceived control: teacher and student
  Inner locus/lessons with rewards
  Powerlessness main cause of stress, violence
Actualize more potential, more motivation, higher level of learning
Important to all children

How to develop

Environment—responsive, trusting, complex, highly structured, flexible
Reduce tension—Autogenic exercise
Organize for—progress, meeting needs, continuous assessment
Develop shared responsibility—
  Scope and sequence
  Choice and perceived control
  Alternative thinking, decision making
  Self-assessment and evaluation
Develop effective learners—brain compatible
  Integrative Education Model
    Cognitive, affective, physical, intuitive

Results for students

Importance of attitude

Change is possible
Potential is unlimited, each student has a unique contribution to make
We can be more effective and efficient
It begins with YOU

Figure 8.3 *Personalizing Education: Using Individualization: A Linear Outline of Mind Map.*
Source: Clark (1986, p. 157)

the planning stage, while the outline aided the organization of my delivery. This exemplifies my belief that the ideal learning process would make available strategies that use both brain specializations and allow students to choose which strategy works best for them. We must present students with the opportunity to strengthen both the linear, rational and the spatial, gestalt thinking processes and then allow them to choose which process to use. With this strategy we will truly empower the student cognitively and allow for optimal learning.

Bibliotherapy

The term *bibliotherapy* refers to the strategy of using books and other reading materials as tools to aid children in solving their problems, whether personal or educational. The strategy has been used to help develop a more positive self-concept, to change attitudes and values, and to promote mental and emotional health. The use of this technique with gifted children has special advantages. It takes some of their strength areas, e.g., their ability to conceptualize, to generalize, and to abstract, and allows them to use these strengths to support areas of need and personal growth. To begin such a program, the needs of the children to be served must be assessed. Then assistance should be sought for appropriate books to provide solutions for identified problems. A selection of appropriate alternatives should be made available. You may want to establish a file of such books as you discover them. Follow-up activities and discussions are an important part of such a program. For resources you may want to consider the Frasier and McCannon (1981) selection of books covering personal, social, and educational/vocational problems.

Other Activities in the Language Arts

A Project on Propaganda and Advertising. Students learn the basic techniques of propaganda and then analyze grocery and department store displays, newspaper ads, and television commercials for evidence of propaganda.

Meet the Author. After reading and discussing the works of authors, the class could invite these authors to teach a seminar on writing with a group of interested students.

Integrative Lesson 8.1 shows how the reading of a new story can become an integrative lesson while expanding the children's vocabulary (Clark, 1986, p. 195).

Integrative Lesson 8.1   A Personal Word List

Purpose: Shown in Figure on next page (following the reading of a new story)
Time involved: 15 to 20 minutes
Materials: Chalkboard
Organization preferred: Total group
Teacher role: Facilitator

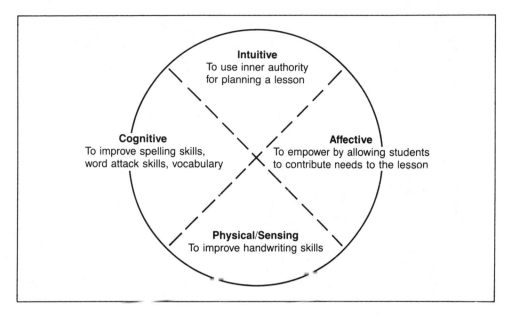

Procedure:

    1 Ask students to find any new or difficult to remember words from the new story that was just read.

    2 Ask them to gently close their eyes and see three new or difficult words inside their head. "Now open your eyes and let's put them on the board."

    3 The teacher writes words on the board as children call them out.

    4 The teacher then says, "Notice how you feel about each of these words. If some of them are new or difficult for you you can borrow them from the person who gave them to us. They can be added to the words on your list."

    5 Ask the children to choose one word from their lists; have one child at a time act out a word for the others to guess.

Other Possibilities: To add interest and challenge to written and oral presentations, the gifted student could be encouraged to become a/an

- African historian
- Alumni detective
- Animal advisor
- Animator
- Bilingual pal
- Class curator
- Class interviewer
- Class publisher
- Exchange ambassador
- Game manufacturer
- Holiday historian
- Language etymologist
- Philatelist
- Political cartoonist
- Resource cart organizer
- Test modernizer
- Unusual fact researcher
- Weather forecaster.

The list never ends.

The outdoor classroom on a learning expedition is naturally multidisciplinary.

Science

More than any other area science has had an explosion of knowledge to assimilate. And more than any other area this knowledge has affected the daily lives of us all. Understanding science concepts allows us to understand our world, indeed our inner and outer universe. Gifted children are intensely curious about the questions of science long before they can understand the structure of the discipline. How can we keep that interest alive? How can we encourage the wonder and awe that the study of our physical and biological worlds creates as these bright children continue through school? Whether or not a career in science is chosen, lifelong learning in this area is necessary if we are to make informed decisions about our future. And for those who choose to pursue their life's work in this area, how can we help them to be humane and caring in the new worlds they are about to discover? From the very beginning science must be an integrative, multidisciplinary search. The following exercises will give us some ways of reaching these goals.

The School and the Gifted Individual

Inquiry

Rationale: To aid students to become independent in their thinking requires the development of many skills (making careful observations, asking good questions, alternative thinking, comparing, discovering relevant data, summarizing, and generalizing from data, to name a few). Inquiry sessions give students practice in these skills.

Time involved: 45 minutes to an hour

Material needed: Films, filmstrips, or materials to set up a dissonant event

Organizational pattern: The classroom must have resources, trust between students and teacher, and a sense of freedom for inquiry. The group should be 7 to 10 students, depending on age—the younger, the smaller the group.

Teaching function: The facilitator must have the ability to inquire; create classroom conditions that are accepting; clarify; probe for data, intent, prediction, and statements of theory; and be silent. (Teacher silence is critical in allowing students to think through the problem.)

Procedure: The facilitator sets up a dissonant event, on either film or tape, or by demonstration. For example, a film depicts two men sitting in a restaurant at identical tables placed next to each other. Both tables are set with exactly the same type of cloth and service. The waiter serves soup to the first man, then to the second. He notices a spot on the tablecloth at one table. Although the man is eating his soup, the waiter takes a hold of the edge of the tablecloth farthest from the diner and removes it in one motion without disturbing the man or the service at all. The other diner watches, is amazed, and decides to try the same thing at his table. He takes hold of the tablecloth on his table, just as the waiter did; but when removing the cloth, he causes all of the service to fall on the floor. This provides the focus for the inquiry. The students must now try to explain the event they observed and theorize about why the objects or systems functioned as they did.

The rules:
1 Students must ask questions that can be answered "yes" or "no."
2 Students, when recognized by the facilitator, may ask questions until they wish to yield. They indicate this by declaring that they "pass."
3 The facilitator does not answer statements of theories or questions attempting to gain approval for a theory (whether the facilitator accepts the theory or not).
4 Any student may test a theory at any time.
5 During inquiry, students are not allowed to discuss among themselves unless they call for a conference. This may be done at any time.
6 Inquirers may consult resources in the room at any time.

The inquiry continues until all theories are satisfactory to their originators. The facilitator then debriefs the session, helping the students to become aware of the processes they were using, what questions provided useful data, and how they might gain more information next time.

Other dissonant events:
1 A glass filled with water and a glass filled with alcohol look the same. Put an ice cube in each and different things happen. In this case only show the demonstration. Do not volunteer information on the contents of the glasses.
2 See the resource book with the *Inquiry Development Program* (1966).

Integrative Lesson 8.2 shows an example of a science lesson developed by Tobias Manzanares.

Integrative Lesson 8.2   ***The Heart and the Human Circulatory System***
Purpose:

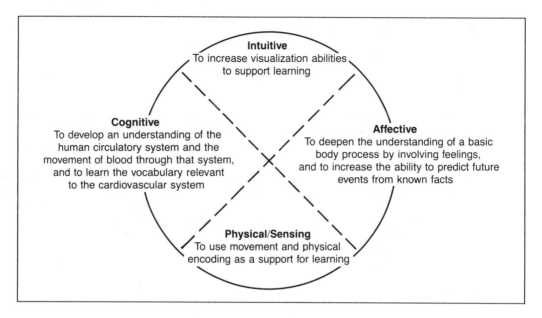

Time involved: One 50-minute class period
Materials needed: 30 red and 30 blue cards or pieces of construction paper, movable classroom furniture
Organization preferred: Total class with teacher in open space in classroom
Teacher role: Information giver, facilitator
Procedure:

1 Ask the students to draw the diagram of the circulatory system (see Figure 8.4).
2 Ask the students to visualize the room as being a human body with the desks arranged in the center of the room to represent the four-chambered heart. Ask for volunteers to represent the brain, the lungs, and the digestive tract. Direct them to their appropriate places in the room (body).
3 Distribute one red and one blue card to each of the remaining students. They are now red blood cells. When they reach the lungs and become oxygenated they are to hold up the red card until they reach an organ using oxygen, where they will lower their red card and raise their blue card representing deoxyge-

nated blood. The blue card will be held overhead until they reach the lungs to be recharged with oxygen.

4 With the red card in their right hand and the blue card in their left have students begin a walk-through of the cycle using the following sequence: right atrium, right ventricle, pulmonary artery, lungs, pulmonary veins, left atrium, left ventricle, aorta, upper body (brain) or lower body (digestive tract), superior vena cava or inferior vena cava, right atrium. This completes the cycle and begins the next trip.

5 Ask for a student volunteer to retrace the 10 sequential steps (assist the student as necessary).

6 Instruct the remaining students to fall in line behind the student leader to begin the first cycle. As the student red blood cells pass remind the students representing the lungs to raise their right hands (red cards); as the students pass those representing the brain or intestine remind them to lower the red cards and raise the blue cards. Instruct the student red blood cells to name out loud each of the 10 structures as they pass these locations in the room.

7 Stop the cycle. ***HEART ATTACK!!***

8 At this point the brain can control the pace of circulation and the group can play with the various ideas affecting the speed of circulation (running, sleeping, yawning, meditating, watching a scary movie, etc.). Ask for volunteers to replace the students representing the brain, lungs, and intestines so those students can go through the process.

9 Stop the process again and ask how long the students think it will take to go through one complete cycle. Record the guesses on the board and time one cycle. Ask the class to see if they can improve the time while still verbally indicating the name of the structure they are passing. On your mark—get set—go!

10 After the class has returned the room to its usual order discuss the entire procedure and how it feels to learn in this way.

Other Science Activities

Weather Prediction. By keeping records and consulting past records of weather and climatic conditions, students can use the laws of probability to predict the weather.

Planning and Developing a Planetarium. By careful study of known astronomical data, gifted students can design and build models of the planetary system that can be used for programs they conduct.

The Future and the Laser. Experts work with students in their laboratory, sharing ideas for future uses of the laser.

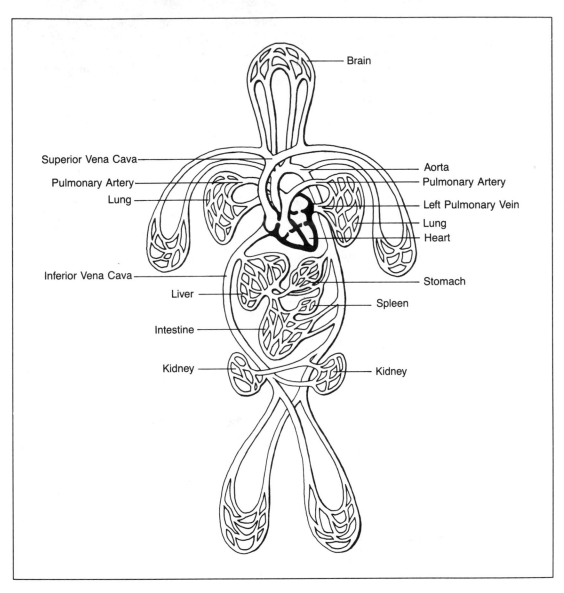

Figure 8.4 *The Heart and Circulatory System*

The School and the Gifted Individual

Mathematics

Ages ago the mathematicians were also mystics, e.g., Pythagoras, and even more recently important mathematicians and physicists, e.g., Einstein, who communicated in math symbols wrote about the solutions to mathematical problems that they found in images. Today schools treat the study of math as though there is no mystery, no insight, no wonderful visions involved. For those few who have inspired teachers who themselves value the beauty of math their enthusiasm keeps this sterile teaching area alive. For others, especially gifted girls, math is only computational rather than conceptual, only analytic, seldom visual, and almost always fraught with anxiety. In this section you will find some ways to play with math.

The Wind Rose

This exercise is taken from a lesson by Marina Krause (1973). This is a story of the most effective means of shrinking space yet invented by humans, mapping. It is about mathematics, exploration, and art. We are going to construct a wind rose.

You may have seen the beautifully colored geometric, flower-like design on charts and maps and thought of it only as a compass of sorts. Were you aware that the wind rose can be found on maps long before 1500? They first appeared on the sailing charts of early Mediterranean pilots. For the sailor the usual 4 directions on a map were not enough. Winds came from many directions, and the rose of the wind charted those directions for the sailors. Using a circle early mariners charted 8 principal winds: north, south, east, west, northeast, southeast, southwest, and northwest. The 4 points between north, south, east, and west were still not enough, and 8 half-winds were added to the circle, bringing the number of points to 16. Then 16 more points, marking the quarter-winds, were added bringing the total charted to 32. Direction-finding lines radiated from the wind rose's 32 points. These lines aided the sailor in traveling to a distant point. Vivid colors were used so that on a dimly lit ship, bobbing around on the sea, the chart could be read more easily. By following the 11 steps in Figure 8.6 you can construct your own wind rose. An example of one designed by an ancient mapmaker is shown in Figure 8.5. It represents his idea of beauty; yours may show your idea.

Directions for the step-by-step construction of the wind rose are shown in Figure 8.6, steps A through K. (Although the angles involved in the drawing of the wind rose can be measured with a protractor, a neater and more accurate design can be made using only a ruler and a compass. Only two geometric constructions are used, the construction of a line perpendicular to a line at a point on the line [Step 1] and the bisection of an angle [Steps 3, 5, 7, and 10]. Construction lines and arcs can be erased when the wind rose is completed.)

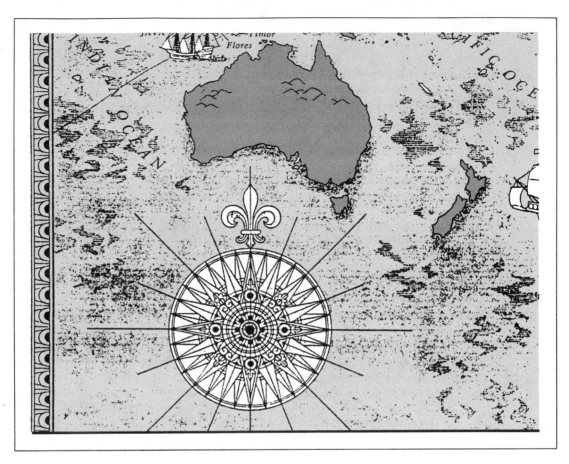

Figure 8.5 *An Ancient Map with a Wind Rose*

Figure 8.6 *Step by step construction of the wind rose.* →

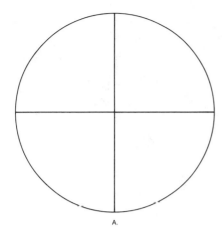

A.

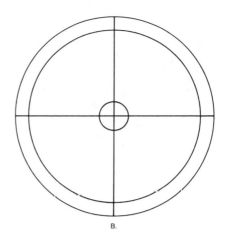

B.

1 Draw a circle. Then divide the circle into 4 equal parts. Draw a diameter of the circle. Draw a second diameter perpendicular to the first diameter as shown in Figure A, the divided circle.

2 Using the center of the original circle as a center, draw a circle with a radius a little less than the radius of the original circle. With the same center, draw a circle with a small radius. (See Figure B.)

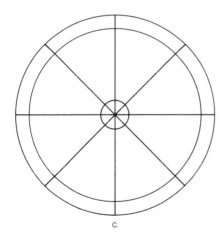

C.

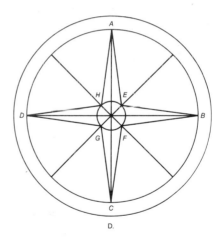

D.

3 Next, each of the 4 parts is halved. Bisect the angles formed by the 2 diameters and draw the diameters on the angle bisectors. (See Figure C.)

4 The first 4 points of the wind rose are made by drawing line segments from the 4 points on the second circle (A, B, C, D) to the 4 points on the third circle (E, F, G, H). The first 4 points of the wind rose are the points marking the north, east, south, and west winds. (See Figure D.)

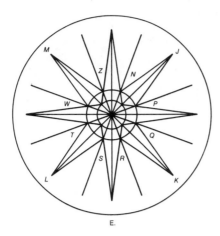

E.

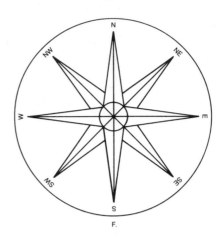

F.

5 Each of the 8 parts of the circle is halved again. (Bisect each of the 8 angles and draw the diameters on the angle bisectors.) Using the center of the original circle as the center, draw a circle with a radius of 14 mm. The second set of 4 points of the wind rose is made by drawing the line segments from the 4 points *J*, *K*, *L*, and *M* to the 8 points *N*, *P*, *Q*, *R*, *S*, *T*, *W*, and *Z*. (See Figure *E*.)

6 Next, the 8 principal winds are named. (See Figure *F*.)

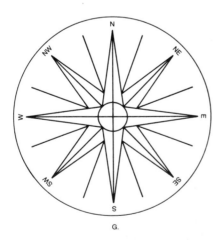

G.

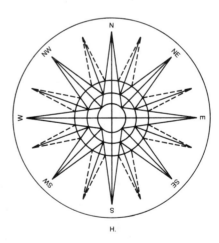

H.

7 Each part is halved again to locate the diameters on which the points marking the 8 half-winds are to be located. (See Figure *G*.)

8 To draw the points marking the half-winds, draw another circle using the same center and a radius of 20 mm that contains the points *N*, *P*, *Q*, *R*, *S*, *T*, *W*, and *Z* as shown in Figure 8.10. Draw the segments indicated by the dotted lines as shown in Figure *H*.

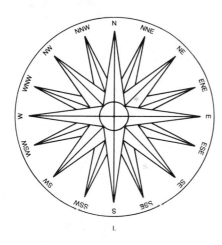

I.

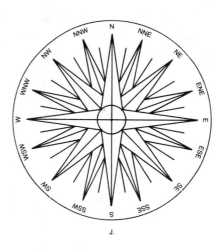

J.

9 The names of the 8 half-winds are added to the design. (See Figure *I.*)

10 Each of the 16 parts is halved. (See Figure *J.*)

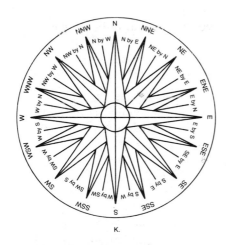

K.

11 The 16 additional points are the quarter-winds, and they can be named. The wind rose now has 32 points in all. A fleur-de-lis may replace *N,* if desired, as shown on Figure *K.*

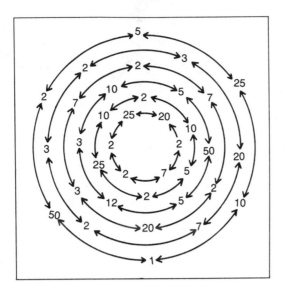

Figure 8.7   Maze.

Brain Games

1 Mazes Amaze!!!

Nearly half a century ago, a maze similar to the one in Figure 8.7 stirred considerable interest at the World's Fair. A person entered the maze upon purchasing a ticket. The ticket was punched with the numbers of the gates that the person passed through in attempting to get to the center. In the center of the maze was a small building with the number 138 over the entrance. Anyone holding a card with 6 numbers (1 for each gate) that added up to 138 won a prize. See if you can figure a winning route through the gates to the center. Only 6 gates can be used, and the total must be 138.

Example: If a person went through the gates which have the numbers of 25, 20, 1, 50, 10, and 2, the total would be 108. Too bad. Can you do it? (Loomis, 1977)

2 The idea is to connect A with A, B with B, and C with C in Figure 8.8 so that no lines cross each other. Lines must stay inside the big rectangle, and they may not go through the small rectangles in which the letters have been placed. (Loomis, 1977)

3 Can you split 100 into 4 parts so that when you add 4 to 1 part, you get the same answer as when you multiply 4 by another part, or subtract 4 from another part, or divide the last part by 4?

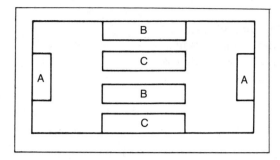

Figure 8.8 *Connect the Boxes.*

4 Can you put the digits in for the letters in the following statement so
that the addition makes sense in numbers too? All the *o's* must be
replaced by the same digit, all the *n's* by the same digit, and so on.

<table>
<tr><td>*Easy*</td><td>one</td><td>*Difficult*</td><td>forty</td></tr>
<tr><td></td><td>+one</td><td></td><td>ten</td></tr>
<tr><td></td><td>two</td><td></td><td>+ten</td></tr>
<tr><td></td><td></td><td></td><td>sixty</td></tr>
</table>

5 In the city of Roundsville (which is in the country of Rouny-go-Round),
all numbers are written in Roundian. In Figure 8.9, A shows us how the
number 48 looks; 845 is written as in B. See if you can figure out what C
means. Could you write the number 42,065? (Loomis, 1977)

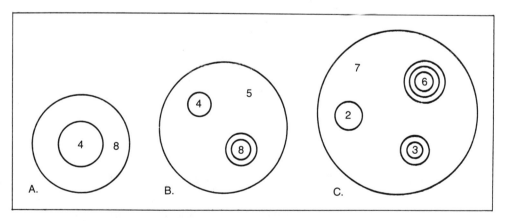

Figure 8.9 *Roundian Numbers.*

Answers

1 One answer is to go through the
gates which have these numbers in
them: 50, 20, 20, 3, 25, 20. Another is
50, 2, 1, 50, 10, 15.

2

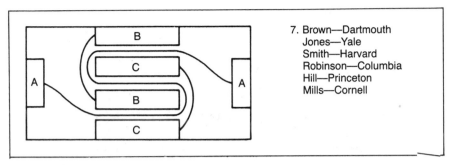

7. Brown—Dartmouth
   Jones—Yale
   Smith—Harvard
   Robinson—Columbia
   Hill—Princeton
   Mills—Cornell

Figure 8.10   Solution to Connect the Boxes.

3 The 4 parts include 64, 20, 12, 4.

4

271	and	432	29786
271	and	432	850
542		864	850
			31486

5 C. 6,327

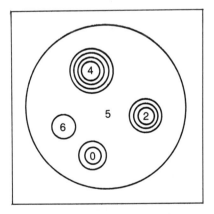

Figure 8.11   The Number 42,065 in Roundian.

Integrative Lesson 8.3 provides an example of a math lesson developed from a
lesson designed by Heide Kalmar (Clark, 1986, pp. 201–202).

Integrative Lesson 8.3 *Measuring, Estimating, Graphing*
Purpose:

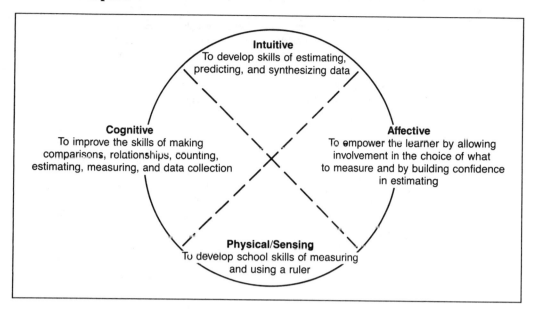

Time involved: 20 to 30 minutes
Materials needed: 10 to 20 "feet" (cardboard cutouts of feet exactly 12″ long); rulers; paste; small containers which hold 1, 2, 3, and 4 cups; containers holding 4 to 6 ounces; rice, cornmeal; gravel; water; paper; crayons; 10″ x 24″ piece of cardboard; 1″ x 10″ strips of construction paper in 2 colors; clothespins with names of children printed on them; tape to protect edges of board
Organization preferred: Small group of children and teacher around a table
Teacher role: Demonstrator, facilitator
Procedure:

Measurement

1 Ask children to choose objects or areas they would like to measure. Show the children a "foot" and ask them to estimate how many feet they think will be in their chosen object or area.
2 Give the children each a "foot" and allow them to measure their chosen object or area.
3 Ask the children to draw their object or area and write the number of "feet" they found it to be.
4 Encourage the children to measure with other things like hands, books, pencils, etc., e.g., "How many books high is the door?"
5 Ask, "How many things did you find that were _____ feet long? How close to your guess was the measurement? Which things are longer? Shorter? The same?"

Estimating

1 Ask the children to predict how many cups can be filled from each container. Have the children write their predictions on a piece of paper in front of the containers.

2 Have the children experiment and check their estimates.

3 Discuss how close the prediction came to the actual measurement. "What did you find? Which container filled the most cups? Is that what you thought would happen? Which containers are largest? Smallest? The same?"

4 "How did you feel when you had more cups than you predicted you would? When you had fewer? When you came very close?"

Graphing

1 Ask the children to decide what they would like to find out about the people in the class, e.g., their favorite fruit, animals, and colors. Explain that they will survey the class to get that information.

2 Have the children decide on two possible choices that the person surveyed could make, e.g., "Is your favorite color red or blue?" Have them draw or color a picture to represent each category and clip each picture to opposite sides of the cardboard chart.

3 Have the children predict which color will get the most votes.

4 With a clothespin representing each person in the room have the children conduct their survey and place the clothespins on the appropriate sides of the chart.

5 Ask the children to summarize their data. "What did you find out? How many children did you ask? What color was chosen most? What does that mean? Which color do you like best? How do you feel about the class choice?"

Evaluation: Ask another question about preferences and have the children suggest how they could find out. Allow them to try their suggestion.

Social Sciences

By its very nature the area of the social sciences is multidisciplinary. It is the study of systems past and present, human and political. As we combine this area with science, math, and the language arts, powerful concepts about our world emerge. Again we must be aware of the need to conceptualize, to bring past, present, and future into the overall conceptualization and to reach for the larger themes. A few approaches follow:

A Classroom Inquiry Problem

The following classroom inquiry problem was developed for a social studies unit on Africa. It was designed for fourth graders. The objective is for the children to bring forth their geographic and climatic knowledge about Africa to discover if they can apply this knowledge in a situation that appears unrelated to their study of Africa.

Problem setting: Pretend the year is 2088 and you and your spaceship crew are on a 100-year outer space mission. You have all just awakened from your solar sleep 3 weeks prior to your reentry into the Earth's atmosphere and scheduled touchdown. You discover that your radio works, but you can't communicate with the National Aeronautics and Space Administration (NASA). The lines are dead. You are worried about why NASA doesn't answer, but also you are worried about coordinating landing plans and instruments. Your spaceship has a manual on landing without NASA's help, but it has never been done that you know of. To complicate matters, 2 days before reentry you hit a terrific solar storm. Many of your instruments malfunction. Bravely, you and your crew prepare to land on Earth.

Miraculously, the landing was perfect. The crew is safe and alive. However, when you open the door of the spaceship, you realize you are not at the NASA landing strip in Nevada.

All your instruments that tell latitude and longitude, etc., broke during the storm. You must discover . . .

Focus setting: "Where on Earth you are!"

Structuring: You instruct your crew to make a list of the things they see around them to help decide where they have landed. They agree to meet back at the ship in an hour to compare data.

I am going to tell you what was on the list briefly. It is your job to ask me more specific questions about the items listed so that later you can give opinions about where they are, from the information I have given and you have asked about.

The list:

1 Landed on flat ground.
2 Miles in the distance emerald green looking mountains.
3 A small river running (20 feet wide) 1/2 mile from spaceship.
4 Several large hawks circling above area from time to time.
5 Temperature about 85°F—sunny.
6 A clump of trees near ship that look stunted but have leaves on them; another group of trees that look as if they were planted with their roots in the air instead of having leaves on their tops.
7 The soil is rocky, but there is a lot of scrubby green plant life.
8 Snakes sighted.
9 Down by the river doglike paw marks.
10 A group of small apelike creatures seen in rocky hills one and one-half miles from spaceship—probably baboons.
11 Biggest find of all—houses sighted; constructed of materials found in area.
12 People seen high up in hills through binoculars tending sheep.

Accepting, clarifying: By asking more questions about the list I've read, you should be able to give an idea as to what:

1 Country they landed in.
2 Time of year it is.
3 Time of day.
4 Type of life the inhabitants are living.

Inquiry session process debriefing: Through the debriefing period, the students may be helped to see their processes as less or more powerful and to find ways of improving their skills.

The preceding inquiry problem is in the format of the original inquiry session. Many modifications have been devised, and the strategy has been used for problem solving in science, social science, class discipline, and other subjects. Students can also be given opportunities to work on separate inquiry skills, such as asking good questions and finding irrelevant data, in short skill-development sessions. Through inquiry, students can become aware that truth still remains to be discovered.

An Integrative History Lesson

Ask the students to close their eyes and with soft, relaxing music playing guide them back in time to the period being studied. Give the students several minutes just to listen to the music and look around in this time frame. Then ask, "What do you see? Who is there? Are there people? What are they like? What are they doing, wearing, living in? Are there animals? Plants? What do you see, smell, hear?"

After several minutes, bring them gradually back to the room. Ask them to turn to one or two friends and discuss what they saw. Ask the group to record their experiences. Now introduce original materials, books, and journals from that period. Ask the students to compare and contrast their records with those from that period. Finally introduce the organization provided by the text you are using and allow them to note how all three sources compare. You will find the students much more interested in the material and more understanding of the reality experienced by those living in that time period.

Geography

Integrative Lesson 8.4 presents an example of a geography lesson developed in part from a lesson by Beverly Galyean (Clark, 1986, pp. 199–200).

Integrative Lesson 8.4 *California (Your State's Name)*
Purpose:

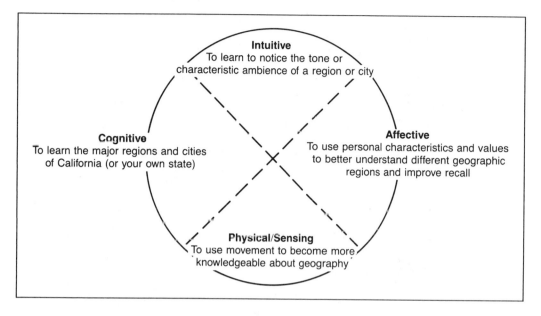

Time involved: 30 to 40 minutes
Materials needed: A large floor map of a state, Values Guide Statements (Galyean, 1976) (Figure 8.12)
Organization preferred: Total group, small groups, individual
Teacher role: Facilitator
Procedure:

1 Ask students to read the section of the text that discusses cities and regions of California.
2 Write the names of California cities on slips of paper and put them in a bag, then ask the students to draw several slips from the bag (the number depends on the time allowed for this activity). When it is their turn, the children move one at a time to the floor map and walk from their home city to the city on their slip of paper (e.g., if they live in Los Angeles and they have drawn Fresno they must find both on the map and walk from LA to Fresno).
3 When each arrives at the destination, ask the class to share all they can remember about the city and the region in which the student now stands.
4 After most of the cities and regions have been described, ask the students to fill out the Values Guide Statements (Galyean, 1976) (see Figure 8.12).
5 After the students have filled out their individual guides have them form small groups to discuss their results.

```
I am a person who is
                    likes
                    wants
                    hopes for
                    believes in
                    loves
                    dreams about

_____(City)_____   is most like me because  _____.

____(Region)____   is most like me because  _____.

Example: I am a person who is free and easy
                    who likes water
                    who wants lots of space
                    who hopes for lots of natural environment
                    who believes in love and peace
                    who loves people
                    who dreams about a home on the beach

_____Eureka_____  is most like me because  it is open, small, has people who know

each other well, and is by the beach.
```

Figure 8.12 *Values Guide Statements*
Source: Galyean (1976).

6 As part of the small group discussion ask the students to predict what will happen to "their" city and region in the next 10 years.

7 Discuss in a total group.

Evaluation: The improved understanding and recall will be apparent on any test or evaluation procedure.

Other Social Science Activities

City Redevelopment Project. With outside consultative help, students can plan solutions for some of the city problems and present their ideas to appropriate government bodies.

Foreign Exchange. Students in this country exchange with students in other countries for study.

Land and Mountain Measurement.   Instruction and field trips with a licensed land surveyor give students a new view of math, geology, and land use planning and development.

Academic areas such as mathematics, science, and social studies (including psychology, sociology, anthropology, economics, etc.) can be made exciting and appropriate for gifted learners by use of integrative experiences, use of the community, and outside experts. Encouraging research, survey, and field study techniques can make each discipline dynamic. It is the larger concepts, peopled by real participants, not just the involvement with the facts, that stimulates and challenges gifted learners. Allowing students to develop their own curriculum after they have been given conceptual frameworks such as Bloom's (1956) taxonomy is a good way to assure that they will be able to pursue their own interests, as well as those the teacher feels are necessary.

Visual and Performing Arts

To develop abilities in the visual and performing arts the strategies must be specific to the art skill being developed and should be planned and implemented by an accomplished artist. While all children would benefit from exposure to enrichment in this area, only those teachers with advanced skills will be able to guide a student who shows giftedness through artistic ability.

While children who show their giftedness through expression in the visual arts are difficult to detect at the elementary level, such identification is important if the proper encouragement is to occur. A strategy suggested by Chetelat (1981) to use for nurturing gifted artists within the classroom is the station learning experience, in which a child can investigate visual arts concepts with an emphasis on exploring in a more individual, independent, and accelerated manner. One such station devised by Chetelat contained three 18" x 24" wooden panels containing on each side reproductions of drawings and paintings of landscapes by great artists, statements concerning advanced concepts to be read and studied, and art history books. One panel contained a landscape by Van Gogh, the other side a landscape by Cezanne. The directions read,

> Look at landscape drawings by Van Gogh and Cezanne to discover ways that the artist used line to represent surface qualities found in nature. Use oil pastels to create a drawing of scenes in your community. Use line direction to emphasize contours of observed surfaces and use line to create textures and patterns on the surfaces of various objects in your drawing. (p. 156)

Chetelat found his students enthusiastic about the station learning experience and advises that, when supervised by an art specialist, such an experience can be an effective way of providing for gifted artists within the classroom.

Some art educators believe that the most important thing a teacher can do for artistically gifted children is to encourage them to maintain a sketchbook (Szekely, 1982). Such a book can serve to record observations, try out new ideas, develop technical skills, facilitate fanciful play, and most of all provide the growing artist with a place of privacy and freedom that has neither time pressures nor continuity. It is important that the sketchbook be chosen and retained by the artist as personal property. If there is to be an assigned format, it should be in a different book, one to be shared. Encouraging your students to keep their own sketchbooks is encouraging them to be their own art educators, encouraging the freedom, independence, and personal commitment of the accomplished artist.

To help children move from the consumer role in the arts to a creator role and to aid in the identification of those who are most able, programs must be developed to give experiences and understanding of how artistic products are created. An interdisciplinary thematic model, Arts from the Inside Out, including all areas of the arts, was designed by Cohen (1981). The program focused the first year on opera and included visiting artists, singers, and production personnel; visits to the orchestra, to cast rehearsals, and to performances behind the scenes; tours; workshops; and in-class projects. The children designed and built sets and props and worked on stage lighting. Some took parts in productions at theaters in the area. All learned first hand about every aspect of opera production. Arts from the Inside Out was an example of what is possible when children, artists, and teachers work cooperatively together.

Mary Hunter Wolf, long a leader in arts for the gifted, suggests that unusual talent can be uncovered by the use of exercises aimed at

- Learning how to enter and share a learning community.
- Exploring and sharpening individual powers of concentration.
- Learning to own, release, and actualize one's imagination.
- Developing and sharpening environmental awareness.

For an interesting exploration of abstract form Kaplan (1976) suggests several activities to help students gain an awareness of shape, form, and transformation, which he believes will be useful in fostering personal expression in art.

1 Ask children to sketch from memory a room in their house using only shapes, circles, squares, rectangles, and triangles in various combinations. They are to include all the details that they can remember, e.g., light switches and locks. Take the drawings home and check them out; what did they forget? Draw those in with a different color. Note if one shape seems to dominate. Discuss sketches in class.

2 Draw another site, e.g., schoolroom or playground, but from observation and increase the shapes the children can use by including cubes, cones, spheres, and cylinders. Use these drawings to introduce cubist art.

3 Place an object in front of the class and have students come up and demonstrate visually a new use for it. Nonverbal sounds can be used but no words. The class tries to guess what the new object is from the clues given.

4 Ask students to assume 25 of the most extraordinary and/or peculiar shapes they can with their bodies. Ask them to concentrate on their own explorations, not on other people's ideas. Have them choose their favorite body shapes to share with the class.

As a result of using such exercises, gifted students will discover (1) how to use themselves more effectively as learning instruments, (2) the use of different learning styles and strategies to accomplish different tasks, and (3) their own special interests and talents (Wolf, 1981). Many of these types of strategies can be found in the section on developing process later in this chapter.

A specialized curriculum will not, in the view of Passow (1981), develop poets, musicians, etc., but should "activate and motivate the commitment and the development of the competencies and affective behaviors required for nurturing such talents" (p. 6).

Academics and the Arts

When we speak of *multidisciplinarity,* we usually refer to the study of the relationships among the academic subjects. It is time to include the arts in this integration. I do not mean just as a follow-up enrichment activity but as a full partner in the enterprise of learning. On several occasions I have had this art-academic role brought to my attention: from students, from readings, and most powerfully, from events. At a conference for educators interested in serving gifted learners I had an opportunity to see a performance of a group of students from the Los Angeles County High School for the Performing Arts. The performance piece they had selected was entitled "Metamorphosis" and told the story in drama, chant, dance, and song of an adolescent's transformation from a self-conscious, confused teenager to a resolute, self-confident, independent young adult. It was well written and magnificently performed. At the end it occurred to me that this was indeed a powerful learning experience for the audience, as it was not possible to be present at this event and not be changed, in attitude, in point of view, or, at the very least, be put in touch with one's own past. From this experience I realized that the arts could have a dynamic place in the transmission of academic knowledge. Such a performance would make immigration, probabilities, change, just to mention a few possible topics, all far more meaningful and, therefore, more understandable.

Inclusion of such experiences in our academic teaching would be more effective than lecture and would carry understanding to the level of change in the learner.

And now a biochemist, Robert Root-Bernstein (cited in Ferguson, 1985), proposes much the same idea:

> It's time the contributions of the fine arts to science and technology are recognized and used. . . . (With them) we can provide tools for educating the eye of the mind more fully, or we can (continue) to send students into the world blinkered or blind. It all depends on what kind of science we want to foster. (p. 1)

Root-Bernstein sees the creative process as the unifier of art and science. He believes that the arts embody rational techniques that can be used as organizers for information. Perhaps we really do have two paths to cognitive processing. And, perhaps, as some are now suggesting, by acquainting ourselves with the structure and underlying principles of each specialization we will come to a unified thinking process of great power. Perhaps nonverbal forms of thought, especially visual thinking, are more important to scientists than verbal forms—Root-Bernstein think so. Perhaps scientific and artistic problem solving involve a similar process —physicists Murray Gell-Mann, Victor Weisskopf, and Robert Wilson think so. Perhaps mathematics and music do have parallel and similar complex systems sharing the same rules and patterns—mathematician Ralph Abraham thinks so (cited in Ferguson, 1985). Perhaps as Root-Bernstein postulates, "The ability to translate *between* modes of intelligence may be a key" (p. 2). Or it just might be that by the integration of these processes we can develop the power of which each of the academicians is speaking. The next section of this chapter will be devoted to strategies in each major area of processing in the brain. As we learn to use each area and then to join them integratively, the Integrative Education Model introduced in Chapter 7 will become a reality and the power we spoke of will become available to ourselves and our students.

STRATEGIES FOR DEVELOPING PROCESS: COGNITIVE, AFFECTIVE, PHYSICAL, AND INTUITIVE

The selection of processes to teach is a most important part of curriculum planning. The strategies to develop processes are discussed in this section in the four major categories of the Integrative Education Model: cognitive, affective, physical/sensing, and intuitive. Though we discuss each of these processes separately, no one of them should be used in isolation. It is in the integration of the brain functions that the real power of the brain is available to us. Remember, we are biologically structured to integrate function. To focus on only one of the major areas in our planning is to lose the advantage we have for effective and efficient learning.

Strategies for Cognitive Development

The processes that are most often a part of any differentiated plan are those of productive or critical thinking, research skills, and learning-to-learn skills. Occasionally the skills of technology are also included. These cognitive processes are important and when used with the other three areas of process will aid gifted students in fulfilling their learning potential. We have identified some of the cognitive models for developing differentiated curriculum; let us now look at some of the strategies.

Cognition will be the most familiar area of brain function for both teachers and students alike. What may not be as familiar is the way in which this area of function can be strengthened by integrating both the rational, linear and the spatial, gestalt processes, making learning available through both verbal and visual modes. Additional power results when these processes are combined with the other brain functions such as physical / sensing, affect, and intuition. While the activities suggested here focus on cognitive development, the other functions will be seen to be integrated into this focus, providing accelerated learning, higher retention, and a more complex understanding. All of the strategies that follow can be adapted for use at the elementary or secondary levels.

Messing Around

Rationale: In all inquiry, there must be a period of time when the inquirer simply encounters the materials within the environment. Suchman (1961, 1962) believes that one of the primary functions of a teacher is to provide for these encounters. Such exploration is structured only by the properties of the materials and the experiences of the learner. During this activity, the learner begins to wonder, hypothesize, and experiment with ideas.

Time required: Large blocks of uninterrupted time

Material needed: Numerous components related to a specific principle, e.g., principle—electricity; components—batteries, cells, wire, light bulbs, circuit breakers, etc. Or you can use all material in a specific setting, such as tide pools and beach items. Books and equipment for research should be available.

Organizational pattern: Freedom of movement; working singly, in teams, or in self-evolving small groups

Teaching function: Provider, resource person, facilitator

Procedure: After setting up guidelines for movement, care of materials, and group structure, allow students to explore materials freely.

Evaluation: You may ask students to collect data on their observations, hypotheses, and conclusions throughout the experience (clipboards are good for mobile data collection) or have a group sharing at the end of the experience.

Synectics

Rationale: Another approach to integrating the cognitive function with other functions of the brain is synectics, a strategy developed by W.J.J. Gordon (1961). The assumptions underlying this strategy are that learning is a combination of focusing, connection making, and application and that "to learn, students must respond to subject matter by focusing on important points, internalizing those points, expressing their comprehension, and sometimes creatively applying what they have learned. Effective internalization takes place when students connect the subject matter to something they already know about" (Gordon & Poze, 1980, p. 147).

Time involved: Variable

Material needed: Specific to the subject or demonstration

Organizational pattern: Large or small groups

Teaching function: Introducing terms and ideas, facilitating discovery, analyzing problems or ideas, and useful metaphors to express the paradox found in the problem or idea, and the communication of the solutions

Procedure: The ways these assumptions are realized in the curriculum or the problem-solving situation follow several steps and utilize analogy and metaphor as tools for learning. The first step is to discover within the concept to be learned or problem to be solved the paradox that exists at the core. For an example, Gordon shows that the concept of symbiosis has the paradox of double weakness, or that needs when taken together make for strength. Next, the student is asked to develop an analogy for the paradox. Gordon states that the very use of a connective analogy lends clarity and sophistication to expression of the concept. Later personal analogies are constructed by the students to clarify the concept further. This strategy allows children to work at their level of ability and can be used with a heterogeneously grouped class. Gifted students will produce creative extensions of the process, resulting from connection-making processes that were subliminal, which become conscious, explicit, and within their control.

Evaluation: Use of the synectic techniques in solving other problems.

Decision Making, Alternative Thinking

Rationale: Gifted students will function in society as change agents, innovators, and reconstructionists. It is believed that societal problem solvers will come from this group. By being exposed to many ways of viewing problems, students may find better solutions. Give students experiences that allow them

- To become aware of bias in thinking, the difference between belief and fact.
- To see that each conflicting viewpoint may be valid.
- To see the importance of sources of information.
- To experience the importance of cooperation and consensus in group action.
- To seek many alternatives before deciding on solutions.

If teachers want to help students make decisions on their own, they must present them with only the alternatives for which they can understand the consequences. If students cannot understand, they are not really making a choice. By beginning there and gradually increasing the number and complexity of the alternatives, students will gain confidence in their abilities and become better decision makers (Jellison & Harvey, 1976).

Decision by Consensus

Time involved: Approximately 1 hour
Material needed: Instructions (Figure 8.13), group summary and scoring sheets for each student (Figure 8.14)
Organizational pattern: Groups of 5 to 7, flexible grouping, responsive environment
Teaching function: Modeling, encouraging student decision making in educational matters, facilitation of group exercises
Procedure: This is an exercise in group decision making. Your group is to employ the method of *group consensus* in reaching its decision. This means that the prediction for each of the 15 survival items *must* be agreed upon by each group member before it becomes a part of the group decision. Consensus is difficult to reach. Therefore, not every ranking will meet everyone's *complete* approval. Try as a group to make each ranking one with which all group members can at least partially agree. Here are some guides to use in reaching consensus:

1 Avoid arguing for your own individual judgments. Approach the task on the basis of logic.
2 Avoid changing your mind only in order to reach agreement and avoid conflict. Support only solutions with which you are able to agree somewhat, at least.
3 Avoid "conflict-reducing" techniques such as majority vote, averaging, or trading in reaching decision.
4 View differences of opinion as helpful rather than as hindering in decision making.

On the Group Summary Sheet (Figure 8.14), place the individual ranking made by each group member using Figure 8.13. Take as much time as you need in reaching your group decision.

Scoring instruction for decision by consensus: The prediction is that the group product will be more accurate than the average for the individuals. The lower the score, the more accurate. A score of "0" is a perfect score.

Individual score: Individuals can score their own sheets. As you read aloud to the group the correct rank for each item (Figure 8.15), they simply take the difference between their rank and the correct rank on that item and write it down. Do this for each item and add up these differences—*disregard* "+" and "−".

Instructions: You are a member of a space crew originally scheduled to rendezvous with a mother ship on the lighted surface of the moon. Due to mechanical difficulties, however, your ship was forced to land at a spot some 200 miles from the rendezvous point. During reentry and landing, much of the equipment aboard was damaged and, since survival depends on reaching the mother ship, the most critical items available must be chosen for the 200-mile trip. Below are listed the 15 items intact and undamaged after landing. Your task is to rank order them in terms of their importance for your crew in allowing them to reach the rendezvous point. Place the number 1 by the most important item, the number 2 by the second most important, and so on through number 15, the least important.

Box of matches   _____

Food concentrate   _____

50 ft of nylon rope   _____

Parachute silk   _____

Portable heating unit   _____

Two .45 calibre pistols   _____

One case dehydrated Pet milk   _____

Two 100-lb tanks of oxygen   _____

Stellar map (of moon's constellations)   _____

Life raft   _____

Magnetic compass   _____

Signal flares   _____

First aid kit containing injection needles   _____

Solar-powered FM receiver-transmitter   _____

5 gallons of water   _____

Figure 8.13   A Group Consensus Problem.

To get the average for all individuals, divide the sum of the individual scores by the number of individuals in the group. Compute the group score in the same way you computed each of the individual scores. If our hypothesis is correct, the group score will be lower than the average for all individuals.

	1	2	3	4	5	6	7	8	9	10	11	Group Prediction
				Individual Predictions								
Box of matches												
Food concentrate												
50 ft of nylon rope												
Parachute silk												
Portable heating unit												
Two .45 calibre pistols												
One case dehydrated Pet milk												
Two 100-lb tanks of oxygen												
Stellar map (of moon's constellations)												
Life raft												
Magnetic compass												
Signal flares												
First aid kit with injection needles												
Solar-powered FM receiver-transmitter												
5 gallons of water												

Figure 8.14 Group Summary Sheet.

You are a member of a space crew originally scheduled to rendezvous with a mother ship on the lighted surface of the moon. Due to mechanical difficulties, however, your ship was forced to land at a spot some 200 miles from the rendezvous point. During reentry and landing, much of the equipment aboard was damaged and, since survival depends on reaching the mother ship, the most critical items available must be chosen for the 200-mile trip. Below are listed the 15 items left intact and undamaged after landing. Your task is to rank order them in terms of their importance for your crew in allowing them to reach the rendezvous point. Place the number 1 by the most important item, the number 2 by the second most important, and so on through number 15, the least important.

Little or no use on moon	15	Box of matches
Supply daily food required	4	Food concentrate
Useful in tying injured together, help in climbing	6	50 ft of nylon rope
Shelter against sun's rays	8	Parachute silk
Useful only on moon's dark side	13	Portable heating unit
Self-propulsion devices could be made from them	11	Two .45 calibre pistols
Food, mixed with water for drinking	12	One case dehydrated Pet milk
Fills respiration requirement	1	Two 100-lb tanks of oxygen
A principal means of finding directions	3	Stellar map
CO_2 bottles for self-propulsion across chasms, etc.	9	Life raft
Probably no magnetic poles; useless	14	Magnetic compass
Distress call when line of sight possible	10	Signal flares
Oral pills or injection medicine valuable	7	First aid kit with injection needles
Distress signal transmitter, possible communication with mother ship	5	Solar-powered FM receiver-transmitter
Replenishes loss from sweating, etc.	2	5 gallons of water

Figure 8.15 Key to Group Consensus Problem

The School and the Gifted Individual

Possible questions for the group:

1 Did the group really go by consensus? Or did we gloss over conflicts?
2 Did the group stay on the intellectual or task aspects or did we stop to examine our process to see how we could work more effectively?
3 How satisfied were we with the way the group worked? How efficient were we?

1 _____ 9

very poor   excellent

4 How satisfied are you (as members) with the group?
5 How much influence did you feel you had as an individual on the group decision?
6 Did the group listen to you? Ignore you?
7 Did you stay involved in the exercise or did you give up?
8 In what ways could you change or improve your interaction with others?

Evaluation: Debrief and discuss the NASA solutions with the class. Discuss the process of consensus.

The material in Figures 8.13 to 8.15 was developed by NASA for use in classrooms. By contacting the Educational Programs Officer at your nearest regional NASA Center, you can receive information on a variety of other educational programs and workshops available to teachers. New programs are made available as new technology is developed.

Simulation

While simulation develops cognitive abilities and understanding, it does so by the use of affective involvement. Simulation is the process of exploring a problem or idea by simulating, i.e., recreating the events within the classroom. It requires active participation on the part of the learner. The outcomes are decided by this participation. It has the advantages of

- Bringing out a high degree of motivation.
- Leading the learner to inquiry and research.
- Using the skills of decision making, communication, persuasion, and resource allocation.
- Integrating curriculum areas.
- Developing a deeper level of understanding.
- Changing attitudes.
- Enhancing personal growth.

My only caution is in regard to the heavy emotional loading that often occurs. Although you may tell the students that they are simulating events, gaming, and role playing, a well-structured simulation may be so real that students will need help leaving their roles and looking at the process skills and information they have gained. For these reasons, you must debrief the sessions thoroughly.

Among the several types of simulations are board games, such as chess and Stocks and Bonds (3M Company). Paper and pencil exercises can also be designed as simulations. Environmental simulations can be accomplished by use of media equipment (e.g., geographical experiences or trips through body systems).

"Real life" simulations have the most impact (e.g., crises at the United Nations, power status of socioeconomic classes, or the signing of the Declaration of Independence). While a number of companies develop and sell simulations, teachers and students can also structure and run them. The following resources will aid you in developing simulations of your own: Boocock and Schild (1968); Seidner (1976); Sisk's *Teaching Gifted Children;* Taylor and Walford (1972); and Zuckerman and Horn (1973).

Metacognition

Metacognition is the conscious knowledge of one's cognitive processes and capabilities that allow one to monitor, regulate, and evaluate one's own cognition (Flavell, 1979). By use of the process a student can become a more efficient and flexible learner. Borkowski (1985) sees metacognition as important in academic achievement because it promotes strategic, thoughtful performance. With the knowledge that intelligence involves complex internal processes rather than only unidimensional, observable behaviors, Carr and Borkowski (1987) contend that the ability to diverge from the concrete and the obvious is an indicator of intelligence. They believe that explicit training of metacognitive skills may enhance academic achievement, intelligence, and creative problem solving.

Instrumental Enrichment

A somewhat similar view of the learning process is embodied in the work of Israeli psychologist Reuven Feuerstein (1978). His theory includes the following theoretical aspects:

1 *Structural Cognitive Modifiability.* Feuerstein (1978) describes this concept as "the unique capacity of human beings to change or modify the structure of their cognitive functioning in order to adapt to changing demands of life situations" (p. 1.1). Cognitive changes can be considered structural when they are self-perpetuating, of an autonomous and self-regulatory nature, and when they show permanence. Human beings are open systems, accessible to change throughout their lives.

2 *Mediated Learning Experiences (MLE).* Although much is learned through direct experience, most of the structural changes that occur in human cognition are the result of MLE. Characteristically these experiences are intentional, have the quality of transcendence, have meaning for the learner, mediate behavior, and mediate a feeling of competence.

3 *Learning Potential.* Almost everyone has a great deal more capacity for thought and intelligent behavior than is often exhibited. Assessing this potential requires a dynamic assessment of the learning process rather than a sampling of previously learned material, e.g., instead of asking "How much does a person know?" the question becomes "How can the person learn?"

Feuerstein's learning process moves the student from passive dependence to autonomous, independent learning. This along with the underlying assumptions of Instrumental Enrichment make this model a valuable one for introducing complexity and cognitive challenges. The training which accompanies the use of material developed by Feuerstein includes attention to the students' feeling and attitudes, and to relating the information to real-life circumstances. The following paragraph from a gifted fifth-grade student provides an example of this model's outcome.

Instrumental Enrichment and Space

Instrumental Enrichment has taught me to think and recall instead of being impulsive. The instrument dealing with space has shown me how to think vividly and pictorially instead of at a more concrete and symbolic level. Now I use different strategies and use cues and deferred judgement which helps me in life, such as in baseball and math. Now I hypothesize more than I've ever done. I put myself in a position that could happen and think of alternatives. I've learned to internalize. Instrumental Enrichment and Space have probably changed my life from an impulsive person to a *kid with a flowering mind.* (Chang Weisberg, 1984)

Learning Styles

Griggs and Dunn (1984) report increasing support for the positive relationship between improvement in student academic achievement, attitudes, and behavior and accommodation of the student's learning style preferences in the classroom. Gifted learners as a group seem to show evidence of having learning style preferences. Gifted elementary school children show high tactile and kinesthetic and low auditory preferences; gifted junior high school students show similar patterns. Gifted students prefer little structure, independence, and flexibility in learning; are highly persistent and self-motivated; and resist conformity.

Studies comparing the learning styles of the gifted to nongifted learners (Price et al., 1981) indicate that elementary and secondary gifted learners prefer less supervision in the learning setting; manipulative and active, real-life experiences to lectures, discussions, and tapes; and more small group, individual, and self-designed instructional opportunities.

Finding out the learning styles of our students, either by use of an assessment tool, e.g., The Learning Style Inventory, or by observation, gives us assurance that we are allowing access to the necessary variety of styles and experiences in the classroom.

As we consider ways to use more of our brain's capabilities for the learning process, we must be very aware that each of us has all the learning styles or modalities available to us. I believe it would be unfortunate if we were to assess our students as to their preferred style or modality and then restrict them to that style. Research has shown that when people were encouraged to develop a mental area they had previously considered weak, this development, rather than detracting from other areas, seemed to produce a synergetic effect in which all areas of mental performance improved (Buzan, 1983).

Group Exploration: Jigsaw Groups or Cooperative Learning

Rationale: Often by discussing with others and sharing interests, students can become more aware of different ideas and areas. It is also possible to set up situations where exploration as a group creates more data and excitement (such as demonstrations, group movement, group energy exchanges; these have more impact when more people participate).

Time involved: Variable

Material needed: Specific to the demonstration or often to the students

Organizational pattern: Large group, with the possibility of breaking into smaller groups and then returning to large group discussion

Teaching function: Group facilitator, demonstrator, occasional discussion leader; can be assumed by classroom teacher or student

Procedures: Jigsaw groups are small, independent learning groups where students cooperatively teach each other. If there is a single topic chosen, each student learns a portion of the material and then teaches that portion to the other group members while learning the remainder of the material from them. This procedure gives students differing points of view, a vested interest in and practice with open communication, and the development of interpersonal relations. Evaluation is on material learned and is done individually by examination or by other mutually agreed-upon method. Research on this strategy has shown that it has positive interpersonal effects; cooperative groups perform better than competitive ones; students learn more than when in competition; attitudes toward school improve; there is a substantial improvement in the performance of minorities; and even in heterogeneously grouped classrooms, high-ability students benefit (Blaney et al., 1976; Dunn & Goldman, 1966; Durrell et al., 1959; Lucker et al., 1976; Yuker, 1955).

Speakers

Rationale: By bringing experts from a variety of areas into a class, you give the students not only the chance to hear and ask questions, but also the opportunity to be exposed to fields of study through the enthusiasm of people actively engaged in creating and using that kind of knowledge.

Time involved: Variable; weekly, to several times a year

Material needed: Dynamic people, knowledgeable in their field

Organizational pattern: While these presentations can be made to the total group, it is often more successful to announce the speaker's subject in advance and invite interested students to sign up. The presentation is conducted in the discussion area of the room, and students who have no interest can work in other areas.

Teaching function: Organizer, provider of related resource material for preparation and follow-up

Procedure: Dependent on the speaker

Evaluation: Optional, may serve as one of many resource experiences.

Field Trips and Visitations

Rationale: A great deal of the world cannot be re-created inside a classroom. Students can learn naturally, in integrated ways in the setting of the specific events. For example, a trip to an island can provide experiences in math (arranging the trip, transportation, expenses, meals, etc.); science (climate, geology, astronomy, land and sea flora and fauna, navigation, food preservation and preparation, tide data, etc.); language (journal writing, communication with planning groups, letters to authorities requesting permission, etc.); social science (government jurisdiction and involvement, economics, ecology, etc.); and interpersonal relations. All of these and more have great built-in motivation.

Time involved: Variable; one day, a series of visits, or a week-long journey

Material needed: Transportation and financing; if camping, all necessary gear

Organizational pattern: Adult-to-child ratio according to age and destination

Teaching function: Pretrip planning and facilitation of arrangements; organization of trip; group leader and facilitator during trip; posttrip follow-up

Procedure: This will depend on the goals of the trip and should be decided in cooperation with the students and the parents. Parents can take students to museums, concerts, and other places either during or after school hours. Torrance (1968a) calls such provisions "time-outs." He believes strongly in such leave taking. Encouraging parents to become involved in school activities is important for both home and school. The students always benefit from this type of cooperation. Investigate the rules applying to field trips and parental responsibilities and rights. You may have options you didn't know you had. Just because it hasn't been done, doesn't mean it can't be.

Evaluation: Journals; projects, films, and slides.

Research Skills

Gifted students need a way to get to information and ideas far sooner than more typical learners. They must be able to move efficiently on their own into areas not yet explored. They need to become familiar with the skills of historical research, descriptive research, and experimental research as tools for future learning and thinking. Torrance and Myers (1962) report such a project as highly successful.

Other Possibilities

Many other possibilities exist for integrating cognition with the other brain functions:

Academic Core Classes.   In small groups, or individually, gifted students could take a particular period, concept, person, or object and, using it as a central theme, investigate the history, art and music, and social, cultural, economic, etc., conditions surrounding the core subject. By actually "living" through the creation of this person, object, period, or concept, the student will understand and appreciate inquiry far more.

Seminar Program.   A seminar program offers pupil assessment and individualized planning, open curriculum guides, and a variety of resource people. This program combines the use of independent study, advanced coursework, advanced placement in colleges, and special seminars for gifted students on an individual basis (Martinson, Hermanson, & Banks, 1972).

Executive High School Internships.   This national internship program for high school juniors and seniors allows them to serve, for a full semester, on sabbatical from regular classes, as interns to business executives and managers, government commissioners and administrators, newspaper editors, television producers and directors, hospital administrators, judges and attorneys, and directors of social service agencies and civic associations. In addition to Monday through Thursday placement, the students attend a Friday seminar on management, administration, and decision making. The program is managed by a local coordinator trained by the national parent organization, Executive High School Internships of America, located in New York City (Hirsch, 1976).

Publishing.   Gifted students should be encouraged to publish their work, either in established journals and magazines or in school- or class-produced publications.

Editing for publication teaches far more grammar, punctuation, and spelling than skill drilling and sentence diagramming.

Resident Expert.   Encourage all gifted students to become resident experts in the one area in which they are most interested. Call upon their expertise; let them help you and others in the school with problems in their area of knowledge.

Conceptual Frameworks and Systems.   Be sure to expose gifted students to conceptual frameworks that you use to organize your thinking (e.g., Bloom, 1956). Encourage their participation in new problems—yours, theirs, the school's, and the community's—by the development of systems or conceptual frameworks. Be sure there is a way for the students to share their creations. Example: A group of fifth- and sixth-grade students were studying the land use in their area. They obtained advice from architects, city planners, and engineers who paid regular visits to their classroom. After several months, one group devised a plan for development that excited them. Their teacher arranged for them to present their plan, with maps and graphs, to the County Planning Board. Later, the students were notified that a portion of their plan had been adopted. They received a commendation from the county for their work.

High School, Junior College, or University Placement.   In many areas, high schools, junior colleges, and universities are making classes available to upper elementary gifted students. Some allow participation in regular classes, some in specially designed classes. In some cases, parents organize after-school and weekend classes. These classes have saved many bored youngsters from giving up on school as a place to learn.

Strategies for the Feeling or Affective Function

As we have seen, the brain makes special use of feelings or emotions in the learning process. When learning becomes separated from human values, the persons involved are alienated from each other and from themselves. Emotions are the gateway-triggering mechanism for higher cognitive function.

Strategies for affective development must be well integrated into the students' daily activities. Before using any of the activities that follow, the teacher must feel comfortable with them. Of all the areas, success of the strategies in the affective or feeling area depends most on the attitude and development of the teacher.

The ideas presented are not only useful for gifted students, but may be used in heterogeneous groupings. However, as in the cognitive area, the needs of the gifted are different—more intense, with more information on emotions to process, of broader concerns, etc. The gifted need opportunities to work with their intellectual peers in groups and, on other occasions, with groups of varying ages and abilities. Because these techniques concern human beings, there is no limit on the ages of the students participating. It will be necessary for teachers to adapt the presentation to their own particular group, whether it is at the elementary level or at the secondary level.

It has been said that all major decisions are made at a feeling level. As we saw in Chapter 7, Krathwohl and his committee (1964) have organized affective learning into a taxonomy. This taxonomy and the material the committee developed for it may help you in organizing an affective curriculum for your students. Tomer (1981) suggests using the taxonomy as an organizer for developing a curriculum in the area of interpersonal communication.

Some activities that help students become aware of their emotional life follow. Be sure to take time to discuss these feelings with the students in an accepting manner. Often students are led to believe that some feelings are "wrong" or "bad." Help them to know that feelings just are. Once we recognize we have certain feelings, then we can decide what we want to do about the way they affect us and others. Try these activities:

1 For a day or a week list every incident and/or person that makes you angry (or happy, or scared, etc.). Discuss the list.
2 Do something nice for someone each day for a week. Tell how you felt doing it, when they knew, and when they didn't know that you had done it. List your feelings. Discuss what you found out.
3 When you feel especially angry (or happy, or anxious, etc.), write down where in your body you felt it (throat, head, stomach). Discuss.
4 Have children role play different situations while wearing glasses depicting various emotions. Find out how the situation would be different if you were angry, happy, felt cared for, were lonely, etc. Discuss differences in perception.

Valuing

As individual guides to living, values evolve and mature as experiences evolve and people mature through them. The concern is not with the particular value outcomes of any person's experience, but rather with the process used to develop values. It is important that our values work effectively and lead us to a satisfying, actualizing life. In this way, we form the moral character discussed by Kohlberg (1964, 1972) (see Chapter 4).

Valuing begins with the awareness of what values we now hold. Helping students to clarify their own values and to be aware of the values of others is the first step. First, encourage discussion of open-ended problems and positions on controversial issues. The next step provides knowledge of the process of decision making, knowing that each person is free to choose. The effects of expectations, responsibilities, and consequences must become a part of the information available to students.

Once their values have been affirmed, students need the opportunity to transform them into action, to experience them as an acknowledged part of their life. Change will come only from an examination of their own values and the way these values work for them.

There are a number of resources on valuing available that will give you help in this area of your planning (Arnspiger et al., n.d.; Casteel & Stahl, 1975; Drews & Lepson, 1971; Elder, 1972; Harmin, 1973; Paulsen, 1974; Raths, Harmin, & Simon, 1966; Simon, Howe, & Kirschenbaum, 1972; Simon, Kirschenbaum, & Fuhrmann, 1972).

Gifted students have need for some strategies that take their growing independence into consideration. They need more cooperative than authoritative guidance as they get older. Here is an idea for doing that:

Complaining Dyads. Students work with a partner and are instructed to take turns sharing all the unfair or misunderstood occasions they have experienced that day (or week). They are to be active listeners as their partner shares. This may not produce solutions for their problems, but it has a very calming effect and unloads a lot of the frustration and hostility.

For resources on strategies for awareness, see Brooks (1974), Dinkmeyer (1969), Freed (1971), James & Jongeward (1973), Palomares (1972), Samples (1970), Schrank (1972), Sonntag (1972), and Stevens (1971).

Developing Open Communication

Communication between unique human beings arises as some kind of miracle. Open communication clearly conveys what is being felt and gives clear information to both giver and receiver. To achieve these goals, students must be aware of their real feelings and find a way to communicate them clearly. They must also be aware of how active listening affects the communication. To get the feeling and the words to match, the nonverbal and the verbal to convey the same message, is not easy. Students need lots of practice in meaningful situations with the chance to analyze what happened and try again. These activities are examples of techniques that will help.

Ways of Sharing Me.   Have students select a partner. Sit in front of the partner and talk about 5 minutes. Share information about yourselves—who you are. Listen as your partner shares, and notice how this feels. After 5 minutes, close your eyes and remember the conversation. Notice how you feel about this person, what you know about the person, and what you think the person knows about you. Is that what you want your partner to know? Ask the partner to open his or her eyes and find another partner. Again they share themselves, but this time sit back-to-back, not looking, as they talk. After 5 minutes, ask them to close their eyes again and review the questions asked before. Compare how this situation was different (better, worse, etc.) from the first situation. Again, select a new partner; face each other and share without talking. Gesture or give any nonverbal clues. After 5 minutes, again close

A trust circle provides a feeling of belonging and caring.

eyes, review, and compare with the other two situations. With a new partner, sit facing, no talking, no looking; only hands can be used for communication. After 5 minutes, review and compare. Discuss the entire experience. What kinds of information did you get? Was it different for the different ways? Which way was hardest, easiest? Whom do you feel you know better?

I'm Not Listening. Partners face each other; one role plays an active nonlistener. One partner is to talk about something important to him or her, while the other partner does anything to indicate that he or she is not listening. The nonlistener may do anything except leave the room. After 5 minutes, switch roles. This is very powerful, so use only one-to-one dyads and watch the time. You may want to tell the students that this is going to be difficult, but to be effective, they must play their parts the best they can. Discuss feelings.

Backoff Space. On some issues students and teachers, as well as parents, often find that they hold different perceptions and different values. For some students this can create crisis situations. Often teachers and parents are not prepared for gifted students who do not share their view and who challenge their ideas and values. The parent or teacher may consider such differences as disrespectful or as a challenge to their authority. For teachers and parents who want to develop increasing understanding instead of alienation between themselves and the student, backoff space can be a useful tool. The teachers (or parents) first share with the students their own weaknesses or moods and discuss how the students can know when this is happening. For example, some days teachers are especially tired or are experiencing low energy, and they do not want to deal with a lot of extra problems—this is picked up by students through body posture and facial expressions. A teacher may be annoyed with a student's manner and not be able to listen further to complaints or "good" reasons and excuses—the student observes this from the tight lips and abrupt manner.

Once the teacher or parent and the students have discussed their own foibles, they agree to allow space for the other person and open communication of problems with dignity and caring—an understanding that when I'm not doing well you will give me space and I will do the same for you. When confrontations occur, both parties are committed to discuss, in private, the situation as they see it and to listen to the other person. Open communication respects the feelings of both parties and clarifies the situation. If both parties can arrive at a mutual agreement at that time, they do; if not, both agree to back off, and each gives the other time to cool off. Later discussion may prove more fruitful. The entire class shares this agreement for open communication and backoff space so that anyone can use it when needed and, at a point of confrontation, the other class members will be aware of the need to allow such a use of time by the teacher and the student. It is important for everyone to agree to participate with a high level of regard and for the technique not to be used punitively.

Assertion Training.   Older students especially need assertion training. In the past, men and women have been caught between two exclusive ways of behaving —aggressiveness for men, passivity for women. To reverse these roles courted criticism and often rejection. For many people, neither stance was satisfying. With the identification of assertion as a possible alternative for both men and women, communication can become more effective. *Assertion* is defined as communication that allows people to state their feelings and ideas clearly so that they may be considered in any decision making, and they take full responsibility for their decisions. While assertion does not promise that you always get your way, it does allow for open discussion, compromise, and far better understanding and relationships than the domineering, demanding role of the aggressive or the manipulative, martyr role of the passive.

One of the best ways to familiarize your students with the consequences of assertion, aggressiveness, and passivity is to set up open-ended situations and have the students in small groups (four to five) role play the various positions as they try to resolve the dilemma. You will find Alberti and Emmons (1970) and Phelps and Austin (1975) helpful in suggesting different techniques in assertion training.

Family Sculptures.   As students begin to seek independence and consider establishing their own family units, they will need help in understanding the effects of family structures. They must understand how expectations they place on others control themselves as well as the others and how responsibility functions (you can't give it; you can allow someone to take yours; you can't take it; others can allow you to take theirs). Satir has developed some powerful techniques for clarifying these two understandings. Her book *Peoplemaking* (1972) describes them and gives very useful information from her research with growth-producing family structures. I especially recommend the family sculptures technique. Your students physically assume positions portraying the common family structures. This statuelike positioning provides many insights into the dynamics of the relationships and their consequences. For some further resources for strategies in open communication, see Beier (1974), Clark (1974), Geldard (1968), Sisk (1975a), and Stevens (1971).

Group Interaction

Students who have explored their concept of self and their interaction with others are now ready to function effectively in a group. These skills of group interaction can make student participation in a group more productive and more satisfying.

Inner-Outer Circle. Students select partners whose function will be to observe their participation in group discussion. One of the partners joins others in a circle. The observing partners position themselves where they can see their partner's face. The teacher gives the discussion group a topic that is controversial and/or meaningful to them. Observers are asked to watch their partners for any use of listening skills, responses, initiating activity, nonverbal communication, etc., that inhibits or facilitates the group discussion. After 15 minutes, ask the discussants to join their partners for suggestions and observations of their participation in the group. Encourage the observers to give helpful suggestions also. After about 10 minutes, ask the partners to change roles and give the new group a discussion topic. Repeat the process.

Developing Self-Esteem

To develop a positive view of ourselves, we must be given opportunities to experience ourself as a positive, loving person who is cared about and thought well of by others. The following strategies give students those opportunities. The time involved depends on the group response; however, it is important not to hurry such activities. The teaching function is to facilitate the establishment of a climate of trust, acceptance, and caring. No materials are needed unless specified, and the organizational pattern is a small group, or at least a close, interactive group.

Mural. Have students build a mural of things they like about themselves. The mural can consist of cutouts from magazines or objects and can be put together individually or as a class.

Surprise Package

Purpose: To put all members of the class in touch with their happy feelings.
Time Involved: 15 minutes (or until each child has a chance to share if you choose)
Materials needed: None
Organization preferred: Total class seated in a circle
Teacher role: Facilitator
Procedure: Invite children to sit in a circle. Say to them, "Close your eyes and imagine a box in the middle of the circle. . . . It can be any size, any shape, or any color. . . . Put a surprise in the box that will make you happy . . . something or someone that will make

you feel very happy when you open the box. . . . Now wrap the box in the prettiest way you can imagine. . . ."

Have the children open their eyes and take turns describing their box and let other children guess what is in their box. After several guesses ask the child to (pretend) open the box and show everyone what is in it. Other children now take turns describing their boxes.

You may wish to have only a few open their boxes at one sitting and do this again later.

Integrative Lesson 8.5 gives an example of a self-knowledge lesson on the body (Clark, 1986, p. 198).

Integrative Lesson 8.5 *Inner and Outer Space*

Purpose:

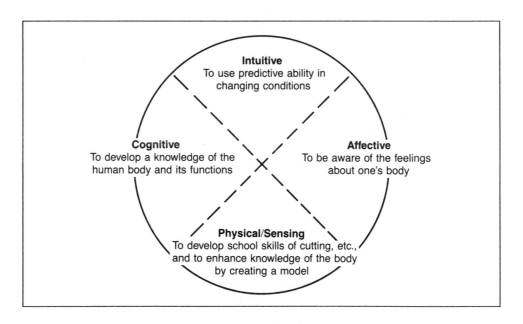

Time involved: 20 to 30 minutes
Materials needed: Butcher paper in a large roll, scissors, colored markers, crayons, paste
Organization preferred: Small group or individual activity
Teacher role: Demonstrator, facilitator

Procedure:

1 Invite children to cut a piece of butcher paper large enough for them to lie on. Ask them to estimate the size.
2 Ask the children to lie down on their piece of butcher paper. Trace around their body or allow a partner to do so. Encourage them to lie in any action position they feel good about.
3 Ask the children to cut out their figure and then trace and cut another piece of paper exactly like the first. Attach the two figures at the top of the head.
4 Have the children look into a mirror to help them draw their likeness on one of the papers. They may wish to draw in clothing with their crayons.
5 Now ask the children to close their eyes and imagine the inside of their bodies. Take a fantasy journey through the body, describing the location, shape, and function of each part of the body and its organs.
6 Invite the students to take colored paper or to color paper and cut out organs, such as the heart, the lungs, the stomach, etc. Ask them to place them inside the body by lifting up the outside paper image and attaching the organs to the second paper figure.
7 Ask the students, "What makes your chest move? Where does the air you breathe go? Can you feel your heart? What does it do? Why is it important? Where does the food go? What does the brain do?" etc.
8 Hang finished life-size figures around the classroom.

Evaluation: Knowledge of the body can now be tested or shown by filling in paper drawing of human body.

Here are some resources for strategies for building self-esteem: Briggs (1970), G. Brown (1971), Brown, Yeomans, and Grizzard (1975), Canfield and Wells (1976), Krippner and Blickenstaff (1970), Purkey (1970), Samples and Wohlford (1973), Satir (1972), Sonntag (1967), and Vogel (1974).

Strategies for Physical Integration

In addition to cognitive and affective development, gifted students must be given opportunities to integrate their minds with their physical bodies. In the past, schools have required the development of the physical body only as a separate entity. This development yields far more when integrated with the other functions.

Far back in recorded history humans talked of the need for balance in their lives. The ebb and flow of human energy has been central to many belief systems—the Yin/Yang of ancient China, the Ka of the ancient Egyptians, the Chi of the Eastern Indians, the Kaa of the American Indians, the Mana of the Hawaiians, and the circadian and biorhythm cycles of the Westerner. We are all affected by the differing amounts of energy available in our lives and by what inhibits or facilitates our energy supply. Researchers such as Selye (1956) and Pelletier (1977) present much information on how stress reduces our energy and on ways to move into energy-producing modes instead. Feldenkrais (1972), Gallwey (1974), Leonard (1975), Masters and Houston (1978), Schutz (1976), and Spino (1976), to name but a few, show us ways to integrate the mind and body, thereby promoting increased function and energy for all human systems. As important as this more total view of the human being is to all people, it is even more essential for the gifted person. It has been already noted that high levels of anxiety reduce access to higher brain functions (Hart, 1981), interrupt the natural flow of information and processing between the hemispheres (Wittrock, 1980a), and inhibit prefrontal cortex functions (Goodman, 1978). If we are to allow students the best education possible then we must teach tension-reducing techniques to help prevent excessive stress.

Stress is an unavoidable consequence of the challenges of living. As Albrecht (1979) states, "The great defining characteristic of this period—the first three-quarters of the twentieth-century—have been change, impermanence, disruption, newness and obsolescence, and a sense of acceleration in almost every perceptible aspect of American society" (p. 2). Stress is inevitable in such a climate, and the need to keep stress within manageable limits has been recognized by psychologists and medical professionals alike.

Selye (1956, 1979) emphasizes that one form of stress, *eustress*, results from achievement, triumph, and exhilaration. Only when stress becomes *distress*, producing a sense of loss of security and adequacy, does it become dangerous to health and well-being. From Selye's seminal work came the discovery that stress produces chemicals within the brain that shut down the system and, over time, create permanent damage. Although the body reacts to protect the system, prolonged or frequent use of this reaction will in fact wear the system out.

Capra (1982) identifies stress as "an imbalance of the organism in response to environmental influences" (p. 324). He believes that some stress is an essential part of living. Only as temporary stress becomes prolonged can it become harmful. Stress then affects the body's immune system and plays a significant role in the development of many illnesses.

Stress can affect learning even when the imbalance is not this severe. Hunt (1982) suggests that under stress we forget things we know well. He explains that part of the reason is that "the stressful input takes up most of the mind's conscious equipment and so impedes the retrieval of information from long term memory" (p. 89).

Of interest to the educator is the finding that " . . . a person's higher level mental faculties are substantially impaired by extreme stress and that they function more effectively when he is comparatively calm and not highly aroused" (Albrecht, 1979, p. 75). For that reason Albrecht and others believe that "one of the most important survival skills for human beings in twentieth-century America is a *neurological skill*—the ability to physically relax, unwind, and demobilize the body for long enough periods to allow it to recuperate and repair itself" (p. 79). Should anyone believe that the concern over stress is that of but a few researchers, there is an International Institute of Stress that claimed in 1979 to have in its library more than 120,000 publications on stress (Selye, 1979).

Several researchers suggest that instead of trying to avoid stress altogether the real key is to balance our life-styles: balanced amounts of work and play, challenge and ease, stress and relaxation, companionship and solitude (Leonard, 1975, 1978; Pelletier, 1977; Selye, 1956).

Early in school, the usual physical education curriculum can become boring to gifted youngsters. For many, body coordination does not keep pace with their accelerated mental development, thereby frustrating their expectations of performance. The patience required to drill and practice assures average youngsters of adequate physical performance in games and competitive activities. Youngsters more accustomed to moving rapidly through new ideas and challenges often lack that patience. When their physical performance falls short of the standards they set for themselves, when their opportunities for improvement come from repetitive activity, they often choose other alternatives, such as becoming ball monitors, judges, or umpires. They even seek excuses from doctors for such problems as asthma or they find leadership or teaching roles that allow them to use their cognitive ability to advantage.

It is not physical movement, but rather the traditional competitive system that creates the problem. Given the opportunity to structure their own physical education class, a group of gifted junior high school students turned to tennis, track events, and various mind/body integrating activities such as Yoga, T'ai-chi Ch'uan, and Aikido with enthusiasm.

Prior to the involvement in physical education classes in school, most gifted children have no problem integrating physical and mental development. A rich fantasy life creates many opportunities for young gifted children to be physically active. They could use this same ability to continue their integrative development. In some schools and in professional sports, the use of fantasy has gained acceptance and is profitably used. Hendricks and Roberts (1977, p. 28) define *fantasy* as "the use of the natural ability of mental imagery to enhance performance or personal growth." They point out that the U.S. Olympic ski team, professional baseball and football teams, and highly successful track and field competitors have psychologists instruct them to use fantasy for improving performance. The tennis instruction methods of Gallwey (1974) exemplify how imagining or fantasizing correct performance actually changes the physical performance.

Dolle and Bardot (1979) reported confirmation of the importance of physical exercise on cognitive development as a result of their study exploring the influence of physical activity on mastery of cognitive structures in male and female adolescents (11-year-olds). They made over six times as much progress as did the controls, who also lacked the depth of understanding shown by the experimental group. The use of judo served as an integrative strategy in teaching the laws of physics.

Physical Relaxation

Even the most everyday tasks—driving, teaching, working around the house, or simply walking down the street—involve staying attentive, watchful, and alert. Some of your muscles are ready for action, the capillaries constricted to slow down circulation of the blood. The cells in those muscles are producing energy, available nutriment is being used up, and toxic wastes are being excreted by the cells. To receive the full benefit of a steady flow of blood the cells in and around the constricted muscle need to go through their full cycle of tension, release of energy, and relaxation. Unless they complete the cycle, those cells end up being under-nourished and even drugged by the toxins that build up around them. The problem is that many muscles do not complete the cycle but rather operate at "ready" much of the time. This causes the entire body to be in a constant state of tension, making the body more prone to disease.

The first step we must take is to begin to pay closer attention to the physical sensations of our own body. By becoming sensitive to and intimately familiar with the signals from our body it is possible to prevent stress from becoming *distress*.

There are many strategies and forms of relaxation that can be employed to develop the skill of physically reducing tension. We will look at some of those forms and detail a few strategies to use in the classroom.

Progressive Relaxation.   Progressive relaxation (Jacobson, 1957) is probably the simplest form of relaxation and involves sitting or lying in a comfortable position with your eyes closed. Concentrate on various muscles in your body, relaxing them one at a time. A systematic sequence is suggested; try starting at the top of the head and progressing to the feet, releasing each of the muscle groups in turn. Imagery may enhance the process, e.g., imagining each area is gradually turning to jelly or sinking into the floor.

Autogenic Training.   This relaxation technique from the concept *autogenic,* meaning self-generating, originated in Germany over 30 years ago (Schultz & Luthe, 1959) and involves the use of tension and release, imagery, and mental concentration. A simple way to experience this form of relaxation is to make a fist with your right hand. As you squeeze your fist shut, push your arm away from your body. Continue pushing and squeezing until you feel discomfort in your arm, then quickly release all tension and allow your arm to hang beside your body. Notice how your hand and arm feel. Be aware that you can relax them even more. Allow your hand and arm to relax more deeply. Notice how that feels. Allow your hand to feel very heavy (it may even begin to feel a little warm). You could relax even more; however, bring your hand and arm back to their normal states by gently moving your fingers and arm. Notice the difference between your right hand and arm and

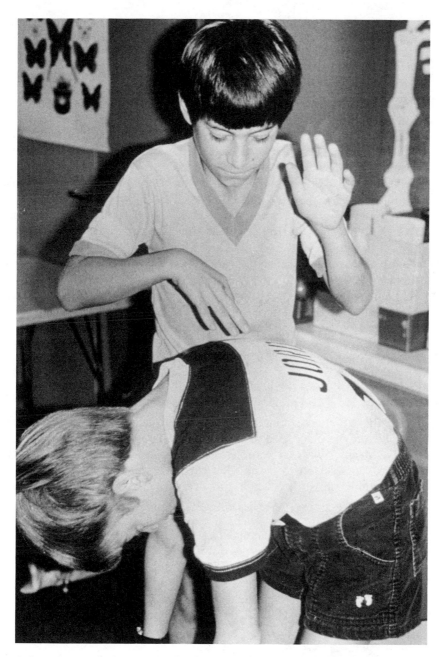

Relaxation techniques are the first step to optimizing learning.

the left hand and arm you have not relaxed. To avoid muscle imbalance use the same procedure on the left hand and arm. You can use this tension-relaxation procedure on muscles throughout your body.

Rethinking, Thought Stopping, and Mental Diversion. These are mental techniques used for creating physical relaxation (Albrecht, 1979). Rethinking involves recognizing negative or nonproductive thoughts and substituting them with positive, constructive ones. When you say to yourself, "This is terrible!" rethink, "This is just the way it is now. Let's see what I can do about it." If you find yourself thinking, "He is acting so stupid I can't stand it!" rethink, "I'm really uncomfortable with the way he is handling this. How shall I deal with him?"

Thought stopping is precisely that: When you find yourself having thoughts that are uselessly depressing or critical try to hear in your mind the shouted word "Stop!" Substitute a new and more productive train of thought. This is one way to recognize negative feelings that only add to your tension and reduce your effectiveness.

Mental diversion is the process of consciously choosing to focus your mind on positive thoughts instead of negative ones. When you are anxious about an event or decision and have already done all you can to assure its outcome, begin thinking about a positive topic. Unless you replace one topic with another your mind will continue to hold on to the anxiety already produced.

Mental Rehearsal. Allow your mind to move through anxiety-producing events prior to the actual confrontation. Visualize each step and each detail of the coming event. Picture the place, people, and possible happenings. See yourself carrying out the task, dealing with any problems or obstacles that arise, and bringing it to a successful completion. Work out alternative ways of handling the event so that you will maximize flexibility when the event occurs. By carefully rehearsing the situation in your mind you can reduce the anxiety you feel and prepare yourself to give your best effort.

Students feel most anxious when faced with an examination. Anxiety interferes with the learning process not only by reducing the amount that can be learned but also by blocking the retrieval of information previously learned. The following exercise is a more detailed account of a guided imagery activity to prepare for testing. High school biology teacher Toby Manzanares uses this mental rehearsal to help his students lower their anxiety prior to an examination.

Procedure: Give the following directions to the class just before an examination. Allow plenty of time for them to react to your instructions. Never rush this exercise; give the students the benefit of approaching an examination with their minds clear and ready. "I need you to take five cleansing breaths. . . . Inhale quietly through your nose. . . . Exhale quietly through your mouth. . . . Each time you exhale imagine that you are blowing tension out of your body. . . . Allow your eyes to close gently. . . . Feel your body soften as the tension leaves your muscles. . . . Allow any sounds that come into the classroom to float through your consciousness and back out again; you need not hold onto any of these sounds. . . . Again, take another deep cleansing breath. . . . And relax. . . . This is a special time for you to find your center. . . . Imagine that you are lying on a hilltop and watching clouds gently drift across a vivid blue sky. . . . Feel the breeze blow through your hair. . . . Feel its coolness. . . . Watch as the clouds move into different shapes. . . . Notice how relaxed your body is . . . and how comfortable you feel. . . . Imagine yourself as you take the exam. . . . Notice the look of confidence on your face, a look that reflects the confidence in your ability to remember. . . . Everything that you've ever heard is permanently recorded year after year in your brain. . . . The more relaxed you can become the more you can remember and the greater the access to your incredible memory. . . . Notice the smile on your face as you mark the correct answers on your answer sheet, and notice how comfortable your body feels. . . . When you're ready, return to the classroom and open your eyes. . . . Remain relaxed and notice how you feel. . . . You are now in a better mental state to perform well on your exam . . . Remember that smile of confidence as you begin. If you feel tension building, close your eyes for a moment, take a few cleansing breaths, and blow out the tension as you exhale."

Basic Body Relaxation.   It is useful to experience physical relaxation. While autogenics and progressive relaxation both have a particular methodology, they use the basic concept of awareness of tension followed by relaxation. This process can be used throughout the body.

Begin basic body relaxation by asking students to sit or lie down comfortably. Use your own words for these ideas: "Close your eyes and get in touch with your breathing. Just notice; do not try to change your breathing. Allow it to happen. We each have our own rhythm of breathing. You will find that, as you notice, your breathing will begin to deepen, to become slower; soon you will be breathing with your whole body. . . . Now I am going to ask you to focus on some of the muscles throughout your body that may be holding tension. A muscle is supposed to tense, act, and relax. Sometimes all the tension is not released. Focus on the muscle across your forehead, just above your eyebrows and just below your hairline. This muscle may feel tight. As you breathe in, let air go into that area, and as your breathe out, let the tension out. . . . Now focus on your jaw muscles."

Continue talking your students through other muscles such as the muscles on either side of the neck, the shoulder muscles, the back muscles, down the legs, down the arms, letting all the tension flow out. Ask them to again be in touch with their breathing. Tell them that you will soon ask them to come back to their place in the room. Allow time for them to adjust. You might ask them to imagine what the room looked like when they closed their eyes, then imagine themselves back in the room. Tell them that when they are ready, they may open their eyes and return to the room. Allow time for them to come back. They may want to share their experience.

For very young children, use this method:

Materials needed: One small, limp rag doll; recording of slow, quiet music.
Organization: Children sit on the floor around the teacher.
Procedure:

1 Hold the rag doll with both hands and show the children how limp it is. Shake it gently and call attention to the way its head, legs, and arms hang loosely.
2 Have children shake their hands and arms and let them hang limply. Do the same with their heads and bodies.
3 Play the record, and have children move around the room as if they were rag dolls.
4 Have children lie down. Go around to each one, lifting his or her arms and legs and letting them drop gently, saying, "Feel like a rag doll. Make your arms and legs heavy and floppy."

In a study with gifted children using progressive muscle relaxation and electromyogram (EMG) biofeedback, Roome and Romney (1985) found that both treatment groups showed a significant reduction in anxiety and a shift toward internal locus of control as compared with the untreated, control group. Neither treatment was shown to be more effective than the other. Roome and Romney (1985) conclude that relaxation training should be considered a routine part of the education of gifted children, especially those who are underachieving, because of the evidence that it facilitates the production of cognitive-emotional states where reality testing is suspended and personal insight, creation of ideas, and inspiration are more likely to occur.

These resources provide further information on physical relaxation: Bernstein and Borkover (1975), Hendricks and Roberts (1977), Hendricks and Wills (1975), Jacobson (1957), Pelletier (1977), Samuels and Bennett (1973), and Schultz and Luthe (1959).

Centering

The gifted can use another approach called *centering*. Useful not only for physical endeavors, but equally effective for intellectual and emotional balance, centering means the ability to relax, focus energy, and move with one's own natural rhythm. Nearly all human activity improves when one moves or acts from a centered position, as opposed to a fragmented or tense manner. Centering allows the integration of mind and body that results in synergistic thinking. It is exciting to have the feeling of being fully available, of discovering that solutions exist for problems you were not consciously processing. The concept of *centering* means combining the mind and body in such a way that we have total accessibility to our functioning. We become integrated, focused, and calm. Energy is readily available, and tasks are accomplished with grace and ease. We flow with nature and events. Centering nurtures.

If you were to draw a line from the top of your head to your toes, intersecting that line half way would put you at the gravity center of your body. It is here that the Chi or Ki of Eastern belief is found. From here we seek balance, peace, and concentration. By focusing at this point we can be physically centered, and from here we begin the centering process.

Next we relax and allow our awareness to move to this point in our physical body. From this point, we can use the ability of imagery now used by so many professional athletes. It is also from this center that we can begin the processes of healing, meditation, and other emotional and intuitive integrative techniques.

The *Centering Book* (Hendricks & Wills, 1975) and the *Second Centering Book* (Hendricks & Roberts, 1977) present activities and a rationale for developing our ability to center. One technique to show how being centered affects our movement is a game students of any age enjoy.

Standoff. Stand facing a partner. You should be close enough that your hands can touch each other's shoulders. Now bend your arms in front of you with your palms facing your partner. Your hands will be touching your partner's. Center yourself standing with your feet comfortably apart, knees slightly bent. You should feel heavy below your waist and light above. Without moving your feet, use your hands in forward or backward thrusts to unbalance or bring your partner out of center. Your partner will do the same to you. The first one who must step forward or back to maintain balance loses that round. One clue: When your partners thrust forward, give way, allowing them to come fully forward. Often this lack of confrontation will pull your partner out of center. If you both remain centered, you have a standoff. When this happens, it feels very much like a ballet. It's better than winning.

Don't view standoff as a game of strength, but as a game of centering and balance. This requires concentration. You will find out more about what unbalances you as you play with different partners. What you discover will apply not only to this game, but may tell you something about how you function in life.

Sensory Awareness

Sensory awareness is important in expanding the abilities of people. We are able to think or feel only about those objects or ideas brought into our awareness. We know gifted individuals have a heightened ability to use their senses. The following exercises will help them continue their growth in this important area. They require no materials unless specified and an organizational pattern of flexible grouping in a large, open area of the room. The teacher directs the activity and joins in when needed for correct numbers or when desired. Evaluation consists of a discussion of the students' experiences.

Visual Awareness

Rationale: The sense of sight is our first and most powerful interpreter of our environment. It provides a shortcut for our concept processing and feedback for our personal and social development. The next two sensory exercises are designed to aid in developing visual awareness.

Do you see a change?

Time involved: twenty minutes, approximately.
Procedure: Have students wander around the room in any direction. Ask them to stop and face the person closest to them. (Be sure everyone has a partner.) Ask them to look carefully at the person they are facing. After a few moments, ask the students to turn their back to their partner and change three things about their appearance (clothing, jewelry, hair, etc.). When all are ready, ask them to turn and face their partner and look for three things they have changed. If after a while any of the changes remains undiscovered, ask everyone to reveal their changes to their partner. Have all readjust their appearance and repeat from the beginning, finding new partners at least two more times.

Visual follow-the-leader

Time involved: 15 to 20 minutes
Procedure: Have the group form a circle standing. Ask for three volunteers to step outside where they cannot hear or see the group. After the volunteers have left, explain to the group that they will follow a leader from their place in the circle. However, it is important that they do not look at the leader, but get their clues from others. Only a few should be actually looking at the leader. Ask for a volunteer leader; then, after the group has started, bring in one of the volunteers from outside the room. They must now find the leader visually. Repeat for each volunteer, with new leaders each time.

Tactile and Kinesthetic Awareness

Rationale: Simon (1974) has found that children are prohibited from touching each other or adults so early that, as we grow up, we have a problem he calls "skin hunger." Because of our human needs for tactile stimulation and to reduce our alienation from

---

The School and the Gifted Individual

each other, Simon suggests that we find safe ways to allow people to explore their tactile and kinesthetic senses. These next two exercises will aid in developing an awareness of these senses.

Whose hands?

Time involved: 20 minutes

Procedure: Divide the class in half. Form partners facing each other, standing in two concentric circles. Ask the students in the outside circle to remove all watches, bracelets, and rings, putting them in a safe place. Students on the inside of the circle now close their eyes and put their hands out in front of them with their palms up. Ask them not to open their eyes until you say so. Ask all students in the outside circle to go to any person except their partner and place their hands in the hands of that person. The inside circle students, still with eyes closed, are directed to feel the hands of the person in front of them. After several moments, ask the outside circle to go back to their partner. When all are in the original position, ask the students in the inside circle to open their eyes. The outside circle is now directed to extend their hands, and those on the inside are to locate the person they were facing by feeling the hands of those in the outside circle. After a while, help those who have not yet found their "hands" partner to do so. Now reverse roles and try it again.

Massage train   (Simon, 1974)

Time involved: 5 to 7 minutes

Procedure: Have students stand, facing counterclockwise in a single circle. Ask them to stand close enough to place their hands easily on the shoulders of the person in front of them and tell them to massage shoulders. End after a few minutes by slowly withdrawing hands from shoulders. Have everyone turn around and do this again to the person who just did it to them. Be sure to join in on this one.

Auditory Awareness

Rationale: Sight is such a powerful mediator of our experience that we do not develop our capacity to use our hearing as we should. Listening activities such as the following two help to develop more of these abilities and increase our auditory awareness.

Listen without labeling

Time involved: 5 minutes

Procedure: After explaining our amazing hearing ability, ask the students to close their eyes and listen to the inside of themselves. Have them start by swallowing and follow that sound inside their bodies. Without labeling, what do they hear? After a while of listening inside, ask that they listen outside of themselves to sounds inside the room, then outside the room (the halls, room upstairs, the road by the school, etc.), and finally stretch to hear as far away as possible. Reverse the process, ending inside the room. Discuss what surprises they had.

Taped mysteries

Time involved: Ongoing
Procedure: Tape familiar sounds around the house or school. Place cassette and recorder in an interest center with a listening post. Allow students to listen and try to identify sounds. Let students make their own sound mystery tapes to share with the rest of the class.

Awareness of Taste and Smell

Rationale: Again sight overrides the senses of taste and smell in interesting ways. By shutting out sight, familiar things become an adventure. Try this exercise to develop an awareness of taste and smell.

Tasty-turvy

Time involved: 20 minutes
Materials needed: Cheese, breads (white, rye, wheat), and apples cut into pieces
Procedure: Have students form groups of two or three. Give each group an assortment of cheese, apple, and bread pieces. One student closes his or her eyes and is fed by the others. Sometimes request that the students hold their noses during feeding. Ask students to experiment with different combinations of food (apple with cheese, bread with apple, etc.). After 10 to 15 minutes, discuss the experience. Be sure every person has an opportunity to be fed.

Mixing the Senses   To synergize the senses, try this exercise.

Have a sense-in

Procedure: Students are invited to taste, smell, and feel all kinds of food and nonfood items, sometimes with sight, sometimes without, in a sense-in. They are required to use their senses to solve mysteries at different centers, such as salt in a sugar bowl sitting on a C&H sugar advertisement—use sight and feel and smell; cold mashed potatoes colored purple sitting in a snow cone cup with a small wooden spoon—use taste, sight, feel, and smell. The students can put together great centers once they understand the concept.

Movement and Physical Encoding

When dancers listen to music their minds very often choreograph the music and they "see" dancers moving with each passage they hear. After experiences with physical encoding students report that they can "see" ideas physically represented or encoded even when they have not participated in actual movement. Young learners learn through physical activity; it seems curious that such activity is by design denied as a support system soon after the learner enters school. Except in a few disciplines—music, physics, chemistry, and art—learning strategies that promote movement and the physical/sensing function disappear from the school. The following exercises are excellent examples of practical, effective techniques to help students grasp ideas and abstract concepts they might otherwise have problems understanding.

Fractionated Groups

Purpose: To understand the concept of fractions
Time involved: 15 minutes
Material needed: None
Preferred classroom structure: Students standing with enough space for them to move into and out of small groups
Teaching function: Group leader
Procedure: Ask for volunteers to form a small group (four to six students), then ask another student to use the group to show one-half of the group; one-third of it, one-fourth of it, etc.

Now ask all the students to form groups of various sizes of their choice. Have them add, subtract, multiply, and divide fraction problems using their group, then ask them to work problems with mixed fractions by using their group and other groups.

Example: A group has six members. They are to find one-half of the group. The group must divide themselves in half. A group of five members will notice the difficulty and the need to have a remainder.

Example: Groups are asked to add one-half and one-third. They must first find one-half of one group and one-third of another and then add them together.

Be sure to discuss each problem with the entire class after a group demonstrates a solution. A guided imagery exercise in which the students imagine groups moving could be the next step. This activity precedes pencil and paper work.

Clock Math. This exercise was developed and successfully implemented by Christine Cenci at LaMerced Elementary School, Montebello, California.

Purpose: To develop the concept of time and the use of a clock to tell time
Time involved: 5 to 10 minutes
Material needed: None
Preferred classroom structure: Students standing with enough space for them to move around
Teaching function: Director/facilitator
Procedure: Ask children to use their arms (and/or legs) to show 3:00, 6:00, 4:30, etc.
Variation: The body can also be used to show geometric shapes.

Strategies for Intuitive Development

The least known and yet the most powerful area of human brain function, intuition is probably the area that promises the most for the continuance and fulfillment of humankind. All other areas of the brain provide support for and are supported by this area of function. As each area evolves to higher levels, more of the intuitive and creative functions become available (Goodman, 1978; MacLean, 1978; Restak, 1979).

A strange paradox exists in this area of function. According to neurobiologists the prefrontal cortex is the most uniquely human area of the brain. It is species specific, that is, humans share this area of the brain with no other life form. The functions of this area, however, are those that are least discussed by researchers, least recognized by educators, and most ridiculed by otherwise intelligent, thoughtful people. One thing is certain: This area of the brain function is seldom discussed without some kind of emotional response.

The prefrontal cortex's functions seem to include planning, insight, empathy, introspection, and other bases for intuitive thought (MacLean, 1978). It is engaged in firming up intention, deciding on action, and regulating our most complex behaviors (Restak, 1979). The prefrontal cortex is, in fact, the area that energizes and regulates all other parts: It houses our purpose.

The prefrontal lobes of the cortex play a critical role in high-level intellectual and emotional operations, curiously probing for and monitoring input, analyzing and synthesizing incoming information, excluding the irrelevant, and then referring the new information to memory. Later these areas reconstruct from scraps whole and relevant memories, taking the outward leap of hunches and fantasy, guessing and postulating, carrying the mind into the future, making plans, shaping strategies for goals, forecasting, and then making readjustments to fit new perceptions and new goals. Emotionally they will provide empathy and cues to sociability, the basis for a communal spirit, and a moral sense (Loye, 1983).

Goodman (1978) more specifically places the following functions in the area of the prefrontal cortex, which he believes fully develops between ages 12 and 16. Luria (1973) puts maturation of this area between the ages of 4 and 7.

Those most responsible for changing our culture (Plato, Newton, da Vinci, Einstein, etc.); important poets, musicians, and artists (Keats, Mozart, Monet, etc.); philosophers, mathematicians, psychologists, and educators (Phythagoras, Tesla, Jung, etc.); and modern scientists (Bohm, Prigogine, Pribram, etc.) all wrote about the use of intuition in their great discoveries and creative contributions. Although these abilities were highly valued by these eminent contributors to our culture, schools do nothing to enhance them but rather ignore or actually inhibit their use.

The business community, a group whose organizations and techniques are so often used as models for making schools more efficient and effective, now shows an interest in intuition, especially the type of intuitive ability that allows prediction and forecasting. This interest is reflected in the increasing number of articles being written by and for the business community regarding the importance of the hunch in making executive decisions and the correlation between success in business and intuitive ability. Screening tests are now available to help those hiring at the executive level to know just what prospective candidate for an executive position ranks highest in intuitive ability (Goldberg, 1983; Loye, 1983).

Stories of those who have used the intuitive hunch successfully are fast becoming a part of the literature of success in business (Dean, Mihalasky, Ostrander, & Schroeder, 1974). Ray Kroc was advised by his staff, his board, and all those he consulted not to buy a small hamburger chain he was considering purchasing. He had a nagging hunch that he could not dismiss and after several days of personal introspection called his lawyer and ordered him to buy McDonald's. As he said later, "I felt in my funny bone it was a sure thing" (Goldberg, 1983).

Agor (cited in Ferguson, 1986b) contends that top executives have an integrated style and can function both intuitively and analytically. He believes that intuition is crucial in areas such as marketing, intelligence work, sales, and emergency-care nursing. His work leads him to the conclusion that people can ground and fine-tune their intuition simply by noticing the function more and more.

Cognitive psychologist Arthur Reber (cited in Guillen, 1984) has found that people who intuit their way through subtle tasks actually have a competitive edge over those who consciously try to think their way through. He finds this true of complicated tasks in reading, writing, composing music, and inventing scientific theories. In actual practice a synthesis of the two modes of learning—analyzing and intuiting—is preferable over use of just one or the other.

The intuitive process seems to be highly synthetic and dynamic, drawing from and integrating all other brain functions. This integrative characteristic allows the intuitive process to be compared with creativity. It is my belief that these two terms may be referring to the same human ability; the processes are quite similar regardless of which term you choose to use. The integration of all of our human functions—thinking, feeling, and sensing—releases intuition, as well as creativity. Restricting any one of these functions restricts intuition, and again creativity. Intuition requires synthesis of all functioning as well as a spark from another dimension; so does creativity. Creative and intuitive processes seem to be expressions of the highest level of human intelligence. While this discussion will focus on the intuitive process, I ask you to note the similarity to discussions of the concept of creativity. Creativity may be, in fact, a part of the intuitive process.

Defining Intuition

Different investigators find different ways of viewing and defining intuition. As we have become aware in previous discussions of the Integrative Education Model (Chapter 7), Jung (1933) referred to intuition as one of the four basic human functions. Bruner (1960) discussed intuition as an important part of the education process and encouraged its training. Expanding on the work of Loye (1983), and for the purposes of our discussion and the development of implementation strategies, I like to think of intuition as occurring on at least three levels: rational, predictive, and transformational.

Rational Intuition.   While this may seem to be a contradiction of terms, rational intuition expresses a level of intuitive behavior that realigns known information in such a way that new insights emerge. We intuit the next step to take in solving a problem, evaluating alternatives, diagnosing a treatment, or resolving a personal crisis. Though we know the facts, we see them in a new light, put them together in a new way, or infer from the past the direction to be taken. This area of intuition relies heavily on the highly synthetic characteristic of the intuition process. By combining all our consciously known information with information we once processed but we no longer consciously have available, new alignments and new patterns seem to emerge.

Predictive Intuition.   The predictive level enlarges upon the processes of the rational level by including new information into existing patterns or sequences. Predictive intuition includes the ability to complete unfinished pictures, see a gestalt from little information, and gain accurate insights not previously available with the given information. This level also builds on the first level by including unknown or only suspected information into the synthesis process. This is the level of the hunch, the "best guess," and the perception of the whole picture when only the parts can be seen by others. Here an unconscious impression or information of some seemingly unknown source becomes an important part of the new patterns formed, the insights, or the profound conclusions. An individual may arrive at a solution to a problem while remaining unaware of the process involved. For some this process is called *creativity* (Goldberg, 1983).

This type of intuitive process is responsible for many breakthrough discoveries. The "Aha!" experience that comes after perhaps months or years of extensive preparation and that appears when the person is relaxed or involved in an entirely different task is a part of this level of intuition. The experience is euphoric, the solution suddenly absolutely clear. At this level the brain perceives matters with a holistic, gestalt awareness rather than in the linear, sequential mode.

This level of intuition is responsible for the forecasting of trends and the intuitive leap so valued in business, diplomacy, science, economics, and personal life decisions. Loye (1983) believes that the very best forecasting is done by those who can access all four functions: thinking, feeling, sensing, and intuiting.

Transformational Intuition. This third level of intuitive processing, transformational intuition, is the most fascinating and the most awesome. When operating on this transformational level, a person seems to be using a different kind of sensing that "picks up information through a means that has defied scientific understanding" (Loye, 1983, p. 52). Those who have received information at this level often report that ideas came to them suddenly, unbidden or in a dream, or that what they wrote came through them as if from an outside source. Brier and Tyminski (1970) concluded that such abilities may be common to us all, but for most it is a very weak signal usually missed due to the noise of everyday living.

Goldberg calls this *operative intuition* and finds that it subtly guides, "sometimes with declarative force, sometimes with gentle grace" (Goldberg, 1983, p. 54).

Another way that this level of intuition may appear is as a coincidence, or what Jung calls *synchronicity*. These are happenings where events that have no apparent causal connection occur in such a way as to give meaning or significant impact. You seem to be at the right place at the right time, or you think of someone and very soon that person appears.

Finally, this level of intuition can be experienced as transcendence. This level can be observed within the brain as a change in the rate of coherence or the correlation between brain waves from separate regions of the brain. This coherence seems to be at its highest during transcendence (Goldberg, 1983). This highest form of knowing occurs when one knows and knows totally the universe, the self, and the connection between. Maslow (1971) began to explore this way of knowing just prior to his death, and his final work predicted that psychology would become more involved in the transpersonal and in transcendence. Eastern mystics seek this elevated state of knowledge as do the religious of all faiths. Variously known as enlightenment, illumination, ecstasy, or by other similar terms, this form of intuition is the ultimate experience, the drawing together of all other forms of intuitive process.

Although a single definition of the intuitive process would be difficult, it is possible to show several common characteristics, as identified by Bruner, 1960; Capra, 1982; Goldberg, 1983; Loye, 1983; and Luria, 1973. Intuition at all levels seems to be

1 A highly synthetic and dynamic process that integrates all other brain functions.
2 Most accessible when one is in a relaxed state of mind and body.
3 Inhibited by fear, tension, and stress. The harder we try to grasp it the less available it becomes. It is the first area of brain function to drop out when anxiety becomes too high.
4 Difficult to communicate in a rational, linear mode, and is often symbolic in nature. Vocabulary for expressing intuitive experiences is limited.
5 Free of the need to see the world in dichotomies, but is a merging of opposites. Wrong answers are often the best way to learn the correct information. The view of reality includes unity and separation together, self as a part of the world and at the same time apart from the world.
6 A natural process that can be encouraged and developed, and that seems to improve with use.
7 Productive of insights, creative products and solutions, and affective actions.
8 Usually following and based on an accumulation of skill or knowledge.
9 Complementary to analytical thinking.
10 Instantaneously knowing, complete, and often spontaneous.

Using Intuition

Intuition can be quite fascinating to discuss, but of what value is it in the classroom? Again let us look at history for some possible reasons to include intuitive process skills in our concern for optimal learning. Goldberg (1983) shares the following insights on using intuition:

> In the original manuscript describing his sun-centered cosmos, Copernicus mentioned the possibility that planetary motion might be elliptical rather than circular. He crossed it out. History credits the discovery of Johannes Kepler, who also had turned his back on the idea for three years before accepting it. "Why should I mince my words?" Kepler wrote. "The truth of Nature, which I had rejected and chased away, returned by stealth through the back door, disguising itself to be accepted. Ah, what a foolish bird I have been!" Kepler finally opened the door to elliptical motion, but, in turn, he closed it to universal gravitation, leaving that gem for Newton.
>
> When you find yourself leaning away from an intuitive idea, you may be acting like a "foolish bird." (pp. 195–196)

The physicist Capra (1975) tells us that rational knowing is useless if not accompanied and enhanced by intuitive knowing, equating intuition with new creative insights. Many of those working to include intuition in the classroom believe that the ability to concentrate with unusual clarity on complex tasks is a result of the intuitive function.

Gifted students have been found to be predominantly intuitive in their processing of information and use a high degree of feeling in decision making (Hanson, Silver, & Strong, 1984). The preferences most commonly shown were

- For generating possibilities beyond what is present, obvious, or known
- For generating ideas rather than putting them into action
- For their own way of doing things
- For being patient with complicated details
- For working best in bursts of energy powered by enthusiasm
- For comfort with open-ended tasks
- For desiring to achieve important solutions to long-range and important social problems
- For working continuously when interest is aroused
- For learning new skills even if not put to use.

Intuition is always available to us. Huxley (1962) believed that intuitive ability could be developed and viewed cognition as a conscious, active power and intuition as a complementary, receptive power. "Both kinds of training," he wrote, "are absolutely indispensable. If you neglect either you'll never grow into a fully human being" (p. 255).

Fostering Intuition

Bruner (1960), Galin (1976), Goldberg (1983), Loye (1983), and Raudsepp (1980) have identified the following conditions for fostering intuition:

- A relaxed state
- Silence
- Focused attention
- A receptive, nonjudgmental attitude
- An ability to synthesize all brain functions
- Novelty and variety in the environment
- A teacher who
  —values and encourages intuitive processes
  —provides opportunities for educated guessing, hypothesis setting, probability testing
  —is comfortable with mistakes, both the students' and personal
  —emphasizes personal discovery over memorization of facts
  —models intuitive behavior.

These same researchers note that other conditions stifle intuition:

- Focusing on mistakes instead of successes
- Avoiding change, seeking control and predictability
- Adhering rigidly to rules and set procedures
- Anticipating disasters instead of miracles
- Taking ourselves, our work, and our problems too seriously
- Relying heavily on analytic procedures.

Clark (1977) gives three basic steps for developing our intuitive abilities: Quiet the mind, focus attention, and use a receptive attitude. These simple steps cannot be developed unless teachers regularly allow time for them, practice them, and value the outcomes. This is not a one-time-only exercise or strategy.

The intuitive process seems to be triggered by a number of practices or skills that can be incorporated into the curriculum, allowing students to release more of their intuition and to become more creative. Students can expect to make impressive gains in the areas of cognition, self-concept, and social-emotional development by using intuition-incorporating strategies. Among the cognitive gains are accelerated learning, higher levels of retention and recall, and higher interest in content. Other areas will show improvement in how competent the student feels, pleasure derived from learning, interpersonal relations, and teacher-student rapport (Bordan & Schuster, 1976; Galyean, 1977–80; Gaylean, 1978–81; Lozanov, 1977; Prichard & Taylor, 1980; Samples, 1975).

Tension Reduction

Nervousness, fear, and tension block even learned knowledge; the first step to releasing intuitive ability is to reduce tension (Assagioli, 1973; Roberts & Clark, 1976). Teaching techniques that reduce tension allow more interaction between the cortical hemispheres and better integration of their specializations. The resulting relaxation allows students to gain access to higher centers of the brain/mind system and to produce biochemical support for the learning process (Hart, 1978; Restak, 1979).

To begin, have the students sit quietly and comfortably. Ask them to relax and allow their minds to be very quiet. Be sure to explain that this is difficult, so that they won't be disappointed with themselves if they are not totally successful the first time. When a thought comes into their minds, ask them to allow it to be surrounded by a soft cloud and drift away. Try this for 3 to 5 minutes at first, gradually building up the skill to 10-minute periods. When this is possible for them, ask them to become quiet in their minds and then "see" a large screen inside their eyelids. Have them put a square on the screen, then a circle, now a triangle. In the triangle place numbers one at a time. Do this with several numbers. Now, on a blank screen, allow a picture to emerge. After a while ask them to open their eyes and share this picture by talking with a partner, drawing a picture, writing about it, and so on. This technique and variations of it will begin to develop powers of intuition. Its purpose is to develop the skills by quieting the mind, focusing the attention, and being receptive.

At home, parents can begin by valuing and trusting their own intuition. How many times have you known, really known, how you wanted to do something, but, for whatever reason, allowed yourself to do it another, possibly more "sensible," way only to discover later that your original idea would have proved far more workable? Trusting ourselves to know what is best for us is not easy. We often allow outside pressures to influence any use we might make of this type of knowledge. Begin by demonstrating the usefulness of your knowing as often as you can allow. Listen to yourself and act on that information more often. Then observe and discover your children's inner rhythms and ideas. Children are less out of touch with intuition than adults. They do not have to work as hard to regain their intuitive power. Find ways to draw out their ideas and show that you respect and value them. The inhibition of this ability begins when children find it ridiculed or devalued by those important to them.

As in other integrative work, we begin with relaxation and tension reduction. Use any of the relaxation techniques suggested earlier in this chapter.

Imagery, Fantasy, and Visualization

Important components in developing intuitive ability are imagery, fantasy, and visualization. Noted scientists Faraday, Galton, and Einstein have reported solving scientific problems in visual images and only afterwards translating their thoughts into words (Hunt, 1982).

> In a famous instance of this, Einstein, unable to reconcile his special theory of relativity with Newtonian physics, pictured a box falling freely down a very long shaft; inside it, an occupant took coins and keys out of his pocket and let them go. The objects, Einstein saw, remained in midair, alongside him, because they were falling at the same rate as he—a situation temporarily identical with being in space, beyond any gravitational field. From this visual construct, Einstein was able to sense some of those seemingly contradictory relationships about movement and rest, acceleration and gravity, that he later put into mathematical and verbal form in his general theory of relativity. (p. 215)

Singer (1976) believes that the foundation for serenity and purpose in our lives may lie in fantasy. He found that those who have trouble using fantasy to enrich their lives or to substitute for aggression have serious problems. Children whose games are lacking in fantasy have trouble recalling facts and integrating events. In adolescence these children are dependent on the external environment and may engage in antisocial, delinquent, and aggressive acts as a result of their inability to internalize humanistic attitudes. As adults their problems increase and "their inner experiences seem less insistent than even the most irrelevant physical fact of their immediate environment'' (Singer, 1976, p. 34). Alcoholism, obesity, and drug abuse may be the consequences of such an impoverished inner life.

Nurturing the growth of fantasy is easy. Using sound effects and voice changes while reading to children, allowing them to make up plays, to finish open-ended stories, and to play pretending games all provide opportunities for such development. A climate that encourages the sharing of fantasies will allow those fantasies to become the basis for books, reports, poems, and journals.

Fantasy journeys also can be helpful and can provide understanding not available from factual reading. A high school teacher reported using fantasy as a tool for teaching history. After relaxing, the students were asked to go back in their imagination to the 1860s. They were told to see, taste, smell, and hear all that they could. After a time the students were returned to the present and asked to write down everything they could remember. After compiling all the experiences into a class journal the students were told to validate as much as they could by using library resources, texts, journals, and diaries written during that period. The results were an exciting learning experience that will long be remembered by the students. Using this same technique electronics teachers can send their students as electrons through an entire circuit, and science teachers can guide their students who imagine themselves to be red blood cells through the circulatory system.

The use of inner visualization is growing in therapeutic settings. Evidence suggests that changes in perception, attitude, behavior, and even physiology can be made by visualization procedures (Goldberg, 1983). Hunt (1982) reports that a recent study revealed greater success with a recall exercise when a group of university students were told to visualize the room in which they had originally learned the words. Visualization allowed them to equal the recall of those who were tested in the original room. Students tested in a different room without visualizing were less successful.

Meier (cited in Ferguson, 1984) found that college students using mental imagery performed 12% better on immediate recall and 26% better on long-term retention than did those students not using it. He commented,

> We all possess the world's finest multi-sensory teaching machine right inside our own heads. . . . We need to give mental imagery the same attention we are giving to sophisticated, computer-driven audiovisual learning devices. (p. 3)

Kosslyn (1985) reports on research that shows several successful uses of imagery: (1) as a substitute for actual practice in performing some activity; (2) as a stand-in for perceptual stimulation, producing effects such as those evoked when subjects actually view a stimulus; and (3) as a part of an individual's reasoning skills. It seems that imagery is not a single ability, rather an integration of many abilities.

Imagery represents the process of creating and intellectual problem solving as much as any other abstract process encouraged by schools. Roodin (1983) suggests the use of imagery in helping children to remember. By establishing vivid images of the items that are to be recalled, the ability to remember is heightened. He asks us to consider that imagery is not restricted to the visual mode alone, but can stimulate sound, taste, smell, and touch. We are reading of more and more musicians, artists, and athletes who make good use of such images. Roodin comments that,

> Regardless of the domain, imagery appears useful in the creative process and is, in fact, a major component of flexibility in thinking. . . . In fact, imagery has been reported to provide greater flexibility than verbal techniques in a variety of problem-solving situations. (p. 6)

Imagery can serve the adolscent well as thoughts of future goals and careers begin to be explored. Gifted adolescents are especially able to project the future and to evaluate the emotional satisfactions, personal identity, and specialized roles a career may involve. Such a tool must become more available in the classroom. The next exercises use mental imagery in three different subject areas.

Spelling.   Ask the students to gently close their eyes, then ask them to see in their mind's eye something to write on: a chalkboard, a piece of paper, sand, etc. Ask them to write (or print if younger children are involved) each word as you spell it. Ask them to visualize each word clearly. Ask them to gently open their eyes and look at each word as you have written it and compare it with their own image. Later have them see their imagined list of words again. Remind them to check their list image when they are spelling each word as you check for retention.

Math.   To teach concepts such as diameter, radius, and circumference ask students to close their eyes and visualize a large round swimming pool. Ask them to swim around the edge of the pool; they are now swimming around the circumference of the pool. Ask them to swim from the side to the middle of the pool; they are now swimming the radius of the pool. Ask them to swim back to the edge and then swim directly from one side of the pool to the other; they are now swimming the diameter of the pool. Ask the students to gently open their eyes and draw each way they just swam. Write the words on the board and ask them to use them in describing the route they swam.

Composition.   Galyean (1983) reports that very original and creative compositions can be elicited from students by using their own internal images. For example, ask the students to write about "Things I Like at School" and "Things That Bother Me at School." Begin the lesson by asking the students to close their eyes and imagine themselves as photographers taking pictures of things they like and don't like around the school. After they have had sufficient time to "see" several photos for each topic ask them to draw and write about their topics using the pictures they just "took" with their mind camera. Galyean finds that this intuitive beginning helps students to succeed in their writing.

I'm sure you can think of a myriad of other exercises using these techniques in the classroom. If you want to read more about imagery, fantasy journeys, and visualization, refer to Ahsen (1973), Bagley and Hess (1982), Castillo (1974), DeMille (1973), Galyean (1983), Hendricks and Roberts (1977), Hess (1987), Hills and Rozman (1978), Morris (1976), Rozman (1976), Samples (1976, 1977), Singer (1975), and Vaughan (1979).

Alternative Ways of Knowing and Futuristics

Good decision making and the development of intelligence are highly dependent on our ability to produce and evaluate alternatives. Probability guessing is an activity that brings the intuitive function into the learning process.

For example, when the Westward Movement is the topic of study the teacher might ask the students to consider the following: What if France had not been willing to sell the Louisiana Territory? What if there had been twice as many Indians living on the Plains? What if gold had not been discovered in California and Colorado? This kind of "what if" questioning can lead to some interesting discussions and motivate students to learn more. Once students feel safe in the environment provided and know that you value and encourage their intuitive ability, you will learn a great deal from them about intuitive functioning. As with all other human abilities intuition becomes better with use.

Student-generated scenarios forecasting future events are another natural result of alternative thinking. The field of futuristics, the study of alternative futures (Kauffman, 1976), is rich in the use of intuitive processing. There is no one future, rather we have the opportunity to collectively create among a number of possibilities.

The intuitive skill of forecasting is important in the development of future scenarios. Lahe (1985) points out that both futuristics and gifted education emphasize higher level thinking skills, creativity, learning outside of the classroom, enrichment, and affective needs, all of which make the classroom for the gifted a good place for this type of program. At the very least futurists believe that from the activities involved in looking at alternative futures, gifted children will develop a positive image of the future. This could be very important to how the future will take shape.

The following exercise in alternative ways of knowing has been used with students from preschool age to graduate level. All find it an amazing experience, assuring them that they have a great deal of intuitive ability. Lady Bug gives them an opportunity to notice how the intuitive process feels and allows them to stretch their ability further. When Chris Cenci first originated the exercise, she used a stuffed toy lady bug with her preschool students as the object they were to "find." Older students have used cookies, flowers, or crackers with excellent results.

Lady Bug

Purpose: To allow the students to experience a way of knowing other than the rational and to give them concrete experiences with some of the intuitive processes

Time involved: 20 to 30 minutes, perhaps longer if the students have a lot of interest in their experience and want to talk or write about it

Materials needed: A stuffed animal (e.g., lady bug); cookies, crackers, or flowers (each person involved should be given two cookies or crackers if these are to be used as the object)

Organizational pattern: Total class or small group activity

Teaching role: Director and guide throughout the activity, facilitator of follow-up discussions

Procedure: When the students are seated in a circle or semicircle pass around a stuffed toy. Ask the students to observe it carefully. Ask the students to look at the color of the object, to feel the texture, experience the smell, the feel (for cookies and crackers, the taste). If you are using cookies or crackers invite the students to eat one now. Now take the object and place it where the students cannot see it, preferably in a different room or outside. Once the object is out of sight ask the students to close their eyes and remember all they can about the lady bug: how it felt, how it looked, how it smelled (and tasted). Ask the students to become the lady bug. Then say, "The lady bug is no longer in this room. Can you imagine where it is? Is it in a place that is light or dark? Hot or cold? Is it over something or under something? What colors are around it? Is there anything else you are aware of around the lady bug that I have not thought to ask you?"

Ask the students to open their eyes and record all that they can about the where-abouts of the lady bug. Ask the questions again, this time tallying the answers on the board to see if today "we are mostly on target or off target." Invite the students to follow you or the person who hid the lady bug and see just where it is. When they return ask them to refer to their papers. Discuss what details they visualized that had been validated by their observation. Do not collect the papers; they may or may not choose to show them to you. There are no right or wrong answers, only observations that are on or off target for the day. Remind them that as with any other skill intuitive ability can be improved with use.

Some amazing on-target experiences with this exercise include students who have "seen" patterns on the sofa next to the cookies, the color and shape of the drying rack on which the cookies were placed, the crystal glasses on shelves alongside the cookies, and a chicken wire divider in a storage room close to where the cookies were hidden. What moved me most, however, was an experience during one of the discussions after the exercise.

A group of high school students had been participating and as we were discussing their experiences I asked if any of them had had similar experiences. Several of the students shared events they considered to be similar, times when they knew something before it happened, dreams that seemed to be precognitive, etc. A young student in a wheelchair raised her hand to speak and when the group turned their attention to her she said quietly, "I just want to thank you for sharing those experiences with me." She sat perfectly still for a moment and with a catch in her voice continued, "I have had things like this happen to me all my life, but I thought I was weird, an alien or something, so I never told anyone. I just continued to feel that I was so different that I didn't fit in anywhere. Now all of you are saying that you have had these experiences too. I'm not so weird, and for the first time I feel like a part of things, I feel that I belong. Thank you." It was obvious that she was about to cry. Everyone was very quiet. We were all affected by the understanding and affection in the room. If allowing students to own part of themselves and letting them feel like they belong is the only thing that ever results from these kinds of exercises I consider them well worth the time and tremendously important.

Telepathy Targets.

Now let's look at a telepathy exercise developed by Hendricks and Roberts (1977). Its purpose is to improve the receptive ability of the students.

Before a telepathy session, choose or ask students to bring in pictures to be used for targets. They should choose emotionally stimulating pictures that bring out strong reactions. Ask one student to act as a sender and seat him or her where the class cannot be seen. The sender selects a target picture and uses the following procedure:

Procedure: "The activities on this card will help you send your picture to the rest of the class. You may do these in any order you wish. As you do these, keep the class in mind too."

1 Looking at the whole picture, what do you feel? Make that feeling stronger, if you can.
2 Pretend you are actually in the picture and can move around in it. In your mind, point out things to the class.
3 Imagine you are touching, tasting, or using your other senses on the objects in the picture.
4 If the picture shows something to do, imagine you are doing it with the rest of the class.
5 On a piece of paper, draw some of the things in the picture.
6 Can you think of something else to do? (p. 171)

Have the class relax and begin to write down or draw ideas as they come to them. After a while, tell them to finish any idea they now have, then call in the sender and show the target picture. The sender may discuss what he or she did to help send the target to the class.

Strategies to Develop Creative Ability

In our discussion of creative behavior in Chapter 2 we looked at the concept holistically and examined a model that used the four brain functions, synthesizing them as the highest expression of giftedness. Strategies and conditions favoring development of each aspect should allow teachers and parents to provide better for creative individuals and encourage more complete and balanced experiences to developing their creative behavior.

Strategies for Developing the Rational Aspects of Creativity

Creative Thinking Skills. Originality, fluency, flexibility, and elaboration can be increased by using the following activities suggested by Rob Russell. Although they were used at the junior high level, they can be adapted to elementary or secondary situations.

1 Give as many reasons as possible why . . . people wear clothes; x loves y but marries z; an elephant hunter meets an elephant in the jungle but doesn't shoot it.
2 Cut a pie into eight pieces with only three cuts
3 What would it feel like to be a . . . misspelled wurd, last snow flake, trash can?
4 List all the things that come in twos.
5 List all the things that are . . . solid, flexible, colored . . . white, soft, edible. . . .
6 List all the attributes of . . . a banana, a belt, a window, an idea.
7 How could you use a vacuum cleaner to hold up a bank . . . a paper plate to stop a robbery?
8 What number . . . belongs to you, is you, is a mommy, is happy, is sad?
9 What are some unusual uses for a . . . tin can, newspaper (remember, be creative, not just practical)?
10 How could you improve a . . . bike, shoe, skate, coat, telephone . . . ?
11 What would an elephant wish to be? A teacher? A school? A spider?
12 Given a stimulus word, try to come up with a word that has an unusual connection to the first.
13 Given two distantly related words, supply a third word that is related to the first two.
14 List as many possibilities as you can.
15 Show children a picture of a situation.
   a Have them ask all the questions they can about it (questions should be of the type that can't be answered just by looking at the picture).
   b Have the students infer all the consequences of the situation.
   c Have the students infer all the causes of the situation.
16 What would happen if . . . a person could become invisible at will, a hole were bored through the earth, the language of birds and animals could be understood by us, the days were twice as long, a person (or all people) could live forever, shadows suddenly came alive . . . ?

17 Give students an answer and have them come up with as many problems as they can that have that solution.

18 Solve Mother Hubbard's problem.

19 What happened when the cow jumped over the moon?

20 Visualize this: . . . hard . . . red . . . snow . . . falling in one-half-inch cubes . . . playing music.

21 Visualize an animal. Pick out its outstanding characteristic. Get with two other students and make up a composite animal combining the characteristic of each of your animals. Draw a picture of it, give it a name, and write a story to explain why your animal did not make it onto the ark.

22 Finish the picture in Figure 8.16. What can you make?

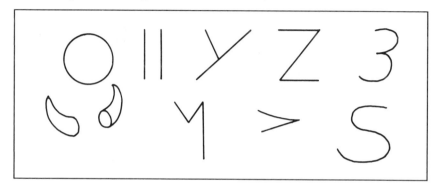

Figure 8.16 Incomplete Pictures.

Brainstorming

Rationale: A greater fluency of ideas is believed to produce ideas of higher quality. This strategy allows groups to explore ideas without judgment or censure. All ideas receive acceptance and consideration. Unusual ideas or takeoffs from ideas already suggested are encouraged.

Time involved: 15 to 30 minutes. The session may last as long as the group continues to offer ideas. Follow-up activities may take another 30 minutes or could lead to a longer project.

Material needed: None

Organizational pattern: Small group with a facilitator

Teaching function: The teacher may serve as the group facilitator.

Procedure: A focus for the group shall be given and the rules of brainstorming stated:

1 No criticism is allowed; all ideas are accepted.

2 Make your ideas as unusual as possible; give as many as you can.

3 Build on ideas you get from others.

4 Do no evaluation until the session is over.

The facilitator lists all ideas on the board with no comment. Only after the 15- to 30-minute time period are the ideas discussed. The teacher may then help the group evaluate the ideas against a criterion for selection that they must devise. The ideas may serve as the basis for further development by individuals.

Evaluation: The more ideas, the better. Be sure to use the ideas for a purpose; the outcomes should seem meaningful to the students. If you use real problems, they will have more meaning.

Trash Archeology

Purpose: To have students use creative thinking skills in an interesting way
Procedure: Have students collect wastebaskets from at least three locations in the school at the end of the day. Treat the trash basket as an archeological dig and reconstruct the events throughout the day in that location, noting approximate times, events, possible antecedents, and outcomes, based on materials deposited in the trash basket.(Be sure that the people whose baskets are to be explored have given their permission. Some trash could be classified and reveal top secrets.)

Interest Centers

Rationale: Gifted students need opportunities to explore areas of their interest and become aware of areas not known to them. By establishing centers built around specific disciplines, and by covering, at various times, numerous areas of basic knowledge, both can be accomplished.
Time involved: Ongoing, large blocks of time
Material needed: The centers should be open ended and exciting, and they should provide understandings of how people in that field contribute to society; for example, an archeology center would incorporate instructions on organizing a dig, journals or books from famous digs, how the findings have changed our view of history, what experiences archeologists have, information on nearby sites now being excavated or worth excavation, films, tapes, etc.
Organizational pattern: Open structure with simultaneous activity, freedom of movement, field trips available.
Teaching function: Organize centers or help students organize centers; resource person.
Procedure: Students work at centers singly, in teams, or in small groups. The center provides the procedure to follow.
Evaluation: Journals, projects, oral reports, conferences. In some cases, you may wish to have the student explore several interest centers without evaluation.

Other ideas for developing rational aspects of creativity can be found in Bruner and Dow (1967), Clymer and Wardeberg (1971), Covington, Crutchfield, and Davies (1967), Feldhusen, Treffinger, and Pine (1975), Gagné (1965), Gordon (1961), Hendrickson and Torrance (1960, 1961), Hopkins and Shapiro (1969), Kresse (1968), Myers and Torrance (1965), Parnes (1967), and Renzulli (1973b).

Strategies for Developing the Feeling Aspects of Creativity

Who Are You?

Purpose: To get in touch with the uniqueness of the persons they are

Procedure: Have students write the answer to the question, "Who are You?" nine times on a piece of paper that only they will see. Either the teacher may repeat the question nine times, or the student can be given a paper with the question at the top. After the students have written the nine responses, ask them to look at each response carefully and cross off any such that, if they could not be that, they would still be themselves. Give students time to share any of their responses they wish with the group.

Experiencing the Now

Purpose: To focus on awareness of the moment and to help students enrich their perception of themselves and their environment

Procedure: Students form dyads and are instructed to converse with their partner about anything they wish as long as they do not refer to the past or the future. All of their focus must be on the present. After 5 to 10 minutes, discuss the experience with the group.

How Do You Feel?

Purpose: To have students discover how congruent their feelings and expression of feelings are for each of them, to notice in what ways they protect themselves and how their feelings about the opinions and observation by others affect them.

Procedure: Have students face a partner. They are not to talk, just to observe their partner while their partner observes them. Now ask them to close their eyes and notice how they are feeling . . . about themselves . . . about their partner. Now they open their eyes and again observe the partner. Ask them to discover anything they can about this partner. Is the person nervous? Open? Friendly? etc. Now ask them to close their eyes and again be in touch with their feelings about the experience. Once more observe the partner and try to communicate a particular idea or feeling nonverbally. Ask them to write down what they know about this person. After a while allow the partners to discuss with each other the observations and any of the written list they wish, sharing their feelings about the experience. Discuss the experience with the group.

Growth Groups.

Not a single strategy, but a type of organized group that can nurture and support self-actualization, a growth group has the same characteristics and goals as those needed in the feeling aspect of creativity: individuality, well-integrated people, focus on higher levels of Maslow's needs hierarchy, openness, ability to change, confidence, and sense of acceptance that allows and tolerates experimentation with new ideas, and responsiveness (Holleran & Holleran, 1976).

Any of the strategies for self-concept development and self-actualization would help in developing this aspect of creativity.

Strategies for Developing the Physical Sensing Aspect of Creativity

Creative Writing Pry-Mer

Purpose: To give students a way to experience their own creative ability, especially those who don't think they have any.

Procedure: As a way of getting creative writing started, write the following categories across the top of the blackboard: Characters—Goals—Obstacles—Results. Ask the students to help you list 10 items under each category, e.g.,

CHARACTER	GOALS	OBSTACLES	RESULTS
1 Wonder Woman	**1** Wealth	**1** Fire	**1** A big bang
2 Abraham Lincoln	**2** Moon flight	**2** Stupidity	**2** Elected President

When you have 10 in each category, ask the students to take their own telephone number, drop the first three digits, and, using the last four digits, match the sequence to the numbers of the items in each of the four categories (e.g., for the phone number 448-1121 the items would be Wonder Woman, wealth, stupidity, a big bang). They are now to write whatever story comes to their mind using their items. Have those who want to, share with the class.

Creative Learning Centers.

The visual, auditory, and kinesthetic-tactile are just some of the senses that can be developed in learning centers. You might also want various arts and craft centers, writing centers, and so on (see Figure 8.17).

Other Creative Activities.

Make a famous sculpture using junk, and do the following:

1 Add a Texture. From magazines, cloth scraps, rubbings, think of words to describe these textures.
2 Squirt the Shirt! Use rubber bands or string to tie knots in your T-shirt. Squirt different colors of dye into the tied area. Allow dyes to soak into the shirt. Remove ties, unfold, hang to dry.
3 Puppet Parade! Take two soup bowls and cut one in half. Staple together. Create your own puppet, using paint, material scraps, colored paper, clay.
4 Drop-a-Dot Original. Cover the entire construction paper with water, using a brush. Load the brush with one watercolor and squeeze the color off onto the paper. Repeat with three more colors. Dry. List the different things you see in your design.

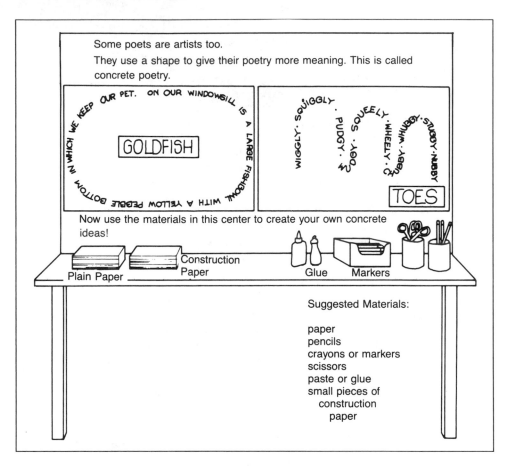

Figure 8.17   Creative Learning Center.

Other Ideas for Developing Creative Talent.

Maynard (1970) suggests these ideas:

1   Arrange for children who are especially interested in one area of talent to watch, or better yet, work with an accomplished amateur or professional in that area.
2   Record the songs, poems, and stories that express a child's spontaneous response to life.
3   Provide lots and lots of materials to work with; avoid art materials that inhibit the child's imagination by imposing adult stereotypes of the way the world is supposed to be.
4   Let students help decorate the classroom.
5   Have students make and mail out greeting cards.

Also investigate Orff-Schulwerk as a way to bring out musical creativity.

Figure 8.18 *Thinking Space Relaxation Corner.*

Strategies for Developing Creativity Through Higher Levels of Consciousness

Movie Moods.

One of the hardest things to do is to get students to let go of their habitual ways of viewing the world so that they can perceive freshly and creatively. This exercise is a great mood setter, and it works with any age group over third grade. Select three films of approximately the same length. Try to get films with action or natural settings. Set up the films in your room so that you can run them all at the same time but separately on one wall. Have students face this wall, either in chairs or lying on the rug. Select one sound track or a tape of music about the same length as the films. Turn off the other sound tracks and show the films all at once. You will be amazed at how much interrelationship the films have with each other and with the sound track. Afterwards, discuss with the students what they saw during the presentation. Be accepting of all comments. Now proceed to creative activities. You will find a very effective mood has been established. This exercise gives students a chance to let go of their usual way of perceiving.

Coherence Corner

Materials needed: Tape recorder; tapes of natural sounds, tranquil or classical music, or relaxation exercises; listening post (see Figure 8.18).
Procedure: Direct students to sit or lie down comfortably, take 10 to 15 minutes just to relax and imagine or meditate. Return to studies renewed.

You will find other strategies for developing the feeling area of creativity in Hendricks and Roberts (1977), McConnell (1971), Osborn (1957), and Otto and Mann (1971).

Many professional educators will need to change their attitudes and practices if intuition is to become a valued part of the curriculum. In a study of teacher attitudes toward students who exhibit characteristics of creativity, all cultures sampled punished children who were considered intuitive thinkers, emotionally sensitive, and/or who were unwilling to accept matters as traditionally presented (Dettmer, 1981). Rockenstein (1985), in her development of a taxonomy for the intuitive domain, comments, "Teachers know very well how to train students to prepare and verify. But if incubation is prevented, and illumination is blocked, there may well be little of worth to verify" (p. 94).

Wescott (1968), Raudsepp (1980), Krippner (1983), and Goldberg (1983) view the following characteristics as indicative of intuitive thinkers. Most intuitive thinkers

- Accept and trust the intuitive process.
- Are unconventional and willing to take risks.
- Are confident, secure, and independent.
- Think holistically.
- Enjoy abstract thinking.
- Focus on outcomes, the long-term view.
- Are frequently involved in art, drama, and/or music.
- Read enthusiastically.
- Tolerate ambiguity and change and are flexible.
- Are playful, whimsical, and enjoy humor and informality.

If ever a society needed the wisdom and inspiration of intuitive people, it is ours. A growing awareness of the contribution of intuitive and integrative processes in our lives is now taking place. More and more eminent figures can be heard openly alluding to the part such experiences play in their growth and in their achievements. Pete Rose, during an interview just after he had broken Ty Cobb's batting record, admitted that he was very excited but that "It was only when I looked up and saw my dad and Ty Cobb standing just above me smiling that it got me and I started crying." When in a televised interview Barbra Streisand was asked why she demands perfection in all things, she explained that she just sees things differently, as though they are complete, perfectly finished; she will not settle for less. The business world is not the only area interested in developing the intuitive potential, and it will be up to teachers to find ways to expand and enhance this valuable resource. Integrative education can help in this search.

DEVELOPING THE PRODUCT

According to Kaplan (1986), the product can be used both to verify that learning has taken place and as a tool within the learning process. The following formats were developed to allow the teacher to plan in such a way that a wide range of content, processes, and products would be a part of the planning of all lessons. By changing the formats to meet your particular needs and style of planning, you may find them useful as you individualize the programs for your students.

Formats for Planning Differentiated, Individualized, and Integrative Curriculum

The Teacher's Planning Sheet for Integrative Lessons (Figure 8.19) presents a structure or format that can be used over and over to help plan for integrative learning regardless of the subject or content. The sheet serves as a reminder to include all human functions and also allows more effectiveness with less time involved. You can see at a glance what you want the students to learn, what brain functions you will be using in that learning, and the strategies you will use to include them. The five integrative lessons presented in this chapter use this format, as do many of the other exercises and activities.

The section that outlines the Purpose of the lesson or unit is divided into the four areas of the Integrative Education Model. Not all lessons or units will be planned to meet goals in all four areas; however, by organizing the purposes in this way the amount of class time spent on each area of growth becomes apparent.

The Time Involved and Materials Needed sections allow for preplanning to aid in the efficiency and effectiveness of the lesson or unit. The section Organization Preferred allows preparation for the preferred structure for the classroom and grouping of students. The Teacher Role suggests the level of instruction or facilitation the teacher may want to assume for the lesson or unit to be most successful. The Procedure section gives step-by-step directions for implementation and includes strategies that will be used to create optimal learning. Finally, Evaluation of the lesson or unit will depend on the purposes stated; whatever procedure is designed for evaluation should collect data that directly assesses the level of attainment of these purposes.

The Student's Integrative Education Planning Sheet (Figure 8.20) is one way of presenting curriculum choices to help students become more responsible for

---

```
┌─────────────────────────────────────────────────────────────────────┐
│ Purpose:                        Planning Sheet                        │
│ Cognitive                              Intuitive                       │
│ ─────────────────────────────────────┼──────────────────────────────│
│                                        │                               │
│ Physical/Sensing                       │ Affective                     │
│ ───────────────────────────────────────────────────────────────────│
│ Time involved:                                                        │
│ Materials needed:                                                     │
│ Organization preferred:                                              │
│ Teacher role:                                                         │
│ Procedure:                                                            │
│ 1.                                                                    │
│ 2.                                                                    │
│ 3.                                                                    │
│ 4.                                                                    │
│ 5.                                                                    │
│ 6.                                                                    │
│ 7.                                                                    │
└─────────────────────────────────────────────────────────────────────┘
```

Figure 8.19   *Teacher's Planning Sheet for Integrative Lessons.*

their own learning. Allowing students to participate in the learning process at the planning level makes them feel far more empowered.

In the upper left corner you will find *Nonnegotiable. This tells students that whatever is on a line with an asterisk is not a negotiable item and must become a part of their plan of study. Under the heading Content/Skills, the teacher lists all of the content or skills involved in the lesson being taught, with nonnegotiables listed first. The teacher may then list a number of other areas of content or skills that could be studied but that are not required. For example, in a lesson on Westward Movement of the United States, the nonnegotiable content might be the geography of the Westward Movement, the dates involved, and the major events leading to this movement. Other areas of content that might be interesting to study but which would not be required could include the economic climate of the times, the role of women, or the affect of the discovery of gold in California. Students use the box on the right of the teacher's listing of content or skills to list the content or skill choices they wish to put in their study plan.

Under Ways to Learn you will note four subcategories: cognitive, affective, physical, and intuitive. Using the Westward Movement example some of the activities that might appear under the cognitive subcategory could be "Read the text pp. 22 to 115," "Read and report on four sources other than your text," or "Collect a series of maps showing the Westward Movement." The text reading would be preceded by an asterisk, indicating required reading. The affective area might have suggestions such as, "Participate in a class simulation of the Westward

Figure 8.20   *Student's Integrative Education Planning Sheet* →

*Nonnegotiable Content/Skills

Your Choice	Ways to Learn	Your Choice	Products	Evaluation Criteria	Your Choice
* ___	*Cognitive ___	*Choose at least one from each ___	* ___	___	* ___
* ___	*Affective ___	___	* ___	___	* ___
* ___	*Physical ___	Other: ___	___	___	Other: ___
Other: ___	*Intuitive ___		___	___	

Your Plan:

Content/Skills	Ways to Learn	Products	Evaluation
	Cog.		
	Aff.		
	Phys.		
	Int.		

Time Line

Task					Dates				

Movement," "Prepare a monologue revealing the feelings of a Plains Indian as the land of these people began to be invaded by the pioneers," or "Read the open-ended vignettes about life in the covered wagons and discuss with one or two classmates the possible resolutions to the problems posed." The physical category would include, "Develop a salt and flour map of the territories explored during the Westward Movement," "Collect and display items for a museum on this historical period," or "Build a model of a covered wagon." The intuitive area might read, "Participate in a class fantasy trip back in time to the days of the movement West," "Write a short essay on what would have changed if there had been no mountains in the West," or "Can you imagine the outcome if there had been thousands more Indians in the West?" Again the students choose those ways to learn that they prefer, writing them in the spaces to the right of the teacher's list. Students are required to list one activity from each subcategory.

The Products section lists suggested outcomes and the criteria the teacher will use to evaluate them. Using the same Westward Movement example some products might be "An examination," "A filmstrip of life in the West," or "A study center on Women of the West," asterisks again communicating which products are nonnegotiable. Students are free to add ideas agreeable to the teacher to any of the sections. (In Chapter 9 an expanded integrative lesson, Westward Movement, is presented.)

The Time Line in the lower right-hand corner of Figure 8.20 allows both the student and the teacher to project the deadline dates for different areas of study.

At the lower left of the sheet is a shortened version of the student planning sections. After students have used this type of planning sheet for a while they know the kind of items the teacher will accept and can design their own study plan with only nonnegotiables necessary from the teacher. The students can develop this shortened plan, allowing them to feel involved in the learning experience in a very meaningful way. Such experiences add to the responsible behavior teachers wish to build.

In this chapter we have looked at examples of strategies appropriate to meeting the needs of gifted learners in grades K–12. The strategies develop concepts that are important to every age group, although many of the strategies will need to be adapted to fit your students. In view of the importance of differentiating and individualizing curriculum for gifted learners, some of the skills and methods needed for such development in the classroom have been discussed. The discussion in the Responsive Learning Environment section provided an optimal, individualized setting for the presentation of strategies. Following the Grid (Kaplan, 1986) from Chapter 7 on curriculum models, the strategies were organized by content, process, and product. Within the Strategies for Developing Content section, strategies were introduced to support differentiation of curriculum in language arts, science, mathematics, social sciences, and visual and performing arts. In the Strategies for Developing Process section, the processes of the Integrative Education Model—cognitive, affective, physical, and intuitive—were used to categorize strategies in the process area of the Grid. This extension of the

Integrative Education Model introduced in Chapter 7 furthers our ability to optimize learning. Products were seen to be the natural extension of these strategies and can be quite varied. The forms given are examples of ways the variation and planning for differentiated curriculum can proceed.

Questions Often Asked

1. Why is individualized instruction so important for gifted learners?

It is important for all learners; however, learners with special needs find it essential. Gifted students are so different from each other, as well as from less able students, that they do not fit into any norms. They do not achieve at high levels in all of the content areas. It then becomes important to know just where they are and allow them to move from there.

2. How can I find time to build trust in a 45-minute period in secondary school?

The 45-minute block is a difficult time frame for any kind of learning. You may wish to spend a bit more time on trust activities at the beginning of the year with the notion that once trust is built it seems to carry its own momentum. Of course it must be maintained, but once a week for an opening (10 minutes) or a closing (5 to 15 minutes) should help. Using relaxation often and empowering language daily will also help maintain trust in the room. The payoff in real learning is worth the time you give.

3. Which type of classroom is more effective for learning, the teacher-centered or the student-centered classroom?

Neither. A balance of both teacher and student decision making is the most effective. That is why the Shared Responsibility Model is such an important part of the responsive learning environment. There are some things that must be your responsibility and you must make the decisions about, just as there are some things the students should be allowed to make decisions about. A balance where everyone feels that they are participating is the most effective for learning.

4. Can I use curriculum compacting if I am not using the Enrichment Triad Model?

Yes, curriculum compacting is an important concept. Curriculum scope and sequence have long been available to teachers who pretest and posttest students to place them at their appropriate levels of difficulty in the content areas. Renzulli (1977) has developed that concept into a packaged program that is most helpful for the procedures it provides. Any strategies from any model are tools to use as you, the professional, need them.

5. If a teacher is not "enthusiastic" about math and only follows the textbook what can she do?

No one is great at everything. That is why it is so helpful to team with those who have other interests and skills. If you choose not to team teach you may wish to take a workshop or two from a very enthusiastic math specialist. Mentors can be of help here, parents, professionals, or older students with high levels of ability in math. None of us will be really enthusiastic about everything so we must be able to facilitate getting the child to someone who is. By using the integrative approach to teaching math as described in this chapter, you may find that you become enthusiastic.

6. Don't you have to have some degree of anxiety or stress in the classroom to keep students motivated?

There are two types of stress according to Selye (1956, 1979): eustress and distress. Eustress is inevitable and can be motivating, while overstress and the destructive aspects of distress are preventable or at least can be minimized most of the time. The research on learning indicates that relaxed-alert brains/minds function best both for initial learning and for retrieval of information. High levels of thought, creativity, and other intuitive processes require conditions of low tension to at least be available to us.

7. How can we use imagery and intuitive processes in the classroom without upsetting the administration or the parents? Won't they think something strange is going on?

It is most important that you invite the parents to a meeting to explain your purpose and the expected outcomes before you begin working with any new strategies. The meeting should be conducted professionally, and you should explain how brain research provides the biological basis for the changes you plan to make. By involving the parents and the administration from the beginning, you will assure them that you have the same goals for the children as they do. Your belief in its importance will communicate that importance to others.

9. Secondary Schools and the Gifted Adolescent

Presented in the chapter for the reader are

- An overview of adolescence as a transition period for the gifted learner.
- A discussion of current programs available and possible structures for the gifted in secondary schools.
- An overview of a plan and a step-by-step procedure for a beginning activity for individualizing the secondary experience.
- Suggestions for integrating learning in the secondary setting.

> *Intelligence can come only when there is freedom—freedom to think, to observe, to question.*
>
> —KRISHNAMURTI

THE GIFTED ADOLESCENT

Adolescence is a particularly challenging period of growth. The following goals are often mentioned as the focus during this phase of life:

- Achievement of independence
- Discovery of identity as a person
- Establishment of personal values and philosophy, both personal and social
- Development of self-guidance, self-motivation, and self-esteem
- Awareness of needs of others and how the self can contribute to meeting those needs
- Exploration and acceptance of sexuality
- Acknowledgment of intellectual power
- Acquisition of life maintenance, career, and self-actualization skills
- Development of meaningful interpersonal relationships
- Exploration of reality structures by use of personal experiences.

Our society seems to be organized to ignore and often actively inhibit the physical, mental, and emotional transitions from child to adult. In some cultures the transition is supported by ritual or is allowed to occur naturally as a useful phase of life. But in cultures such as ours, achieving any meaningful place in the society must be delayed. Training for one's life work is continued well beyond puberty, and control of one's life is denied until well into the productive and creative phase of early adulthood. For many adolescents such practices have forced the creation of subcultures of teenagers with values, morals, and life-styles that seek to depart from the accepted values and traditions of the established culture. Keniston (1975) suggests that many of the problems of this period are the result of the conflict in the youths' feelings of who they are and what society wants them to be. Many try to transform themselves, with resulting periods of introspection, drug use, and experimentation with various identities and roles. A teenager's future may be radically altered by the ways in which identity and meaning are sought during this transition period.

The gifted, the creative, and the talented adolescent may be better equipped in many ways to meet the biological and psychological challenges of this period.

Their ability to conceptualize, to see alternatives, to seek out diverse patterns and relationships, to delay closure (which allows them a higher degree of tolerance for ambiguity), and to express themselves in fulfilling ways will serve them well during this period of constant and often threatening change. But these very qualities that can lead to competence and power can bring to gifted, creative, and talented youth some unique problems.

There are few role models of their own age to emulate, and they seldom find peer guides, which can result in a feeling of isolation. Existing guidelines for the average teenager are often not applicable to their needs. For example, the question of overload: How much is too much extracurricular activity or attempted academic coursework? Often there is a lack of challenge, no chance to push to their limits, to make mistakes, to learn to cope. Because they do so many things well how much exploring should they do? In how many areas? When should they begin to focus? Make career choices? Specialize?

Gifted girls are especially vulnerable during this period. Society gives adolescent girls mixed messages. More than ever before, they are urged to contribute their abilities and talents to society. More careers are open for their choosing, and higher levels within those careers are beginning to accept women. At the same time, the belief in male superiority still exists in many professions and sex role stereotyping still affects socialization and development at home and at school. Sex role differences are so evident by junior high years that girls begin a decline in achievement from the advantaged position they showed in elementary school (Maccoby & Jacklin, 1974). Fox (1981) tells us that these years are critical. If characteristics such as assertiveness, independence, leadership, and analytic and critical thinking are viewed by parents, teachers, and peers as masculine, the gifted girl will be forced to choose between being gifted and being feminine. Such a choice should never have to be made.

Adolescence may be the most frustrating time for youth and those who care about them, but it is also the best time for encouraging self-initiative, independence, and the growth of the creative mind. This period of reconstruction can be the beginning of personal excellence.

The Physical Transition

Not since the fetal period and the first 2 years of life has the human body had as much change occurring to its physical structure so quickly. The development of sex organs and new hormonal balances add to the bewildering array of physical change to which the youth must adjust. Unlike during the period of infancy these changes occur with the full awareness of the young person who can observe with both joy and frustration the whole complex process (Craig, 1980).

Male high school students who show their giftedness in visual and performing arts have been found to differ significantly from average male students in their

An exciting alternative to traditional physical education.

attitudes toward physical activity (Confessore & Confessore, 1981). Whereas the average youth prefers physical activities having a strong element of daring or requiring him to take chances, the talented youth prefers more aesthetic experiences, those that use the body as an instrument of expression. This is similar to the preference shown by the gifted female population, and is the activity least preferred by the average males. It was suggested that the affinity of males for aesthetic experiences as a way to show their giftedness in the arts may cause others to view them as effeminate and that their low preference for any cathartic physical activity should be viewed seriously as a clue to further study of the problem of suicide and emotional disturbance among this population.

Often gifted students have been accelerated and now find themselves with a physically more mature peer group. This can result in more pronounced feelings of difference for gifted youth and they may retreat still further into activities of a cognitive nature. It is at this period that the proclivity for the separation of the activities of the mind and body is most evident, and unless opportunities are provided for integration, a neglect and avoidance of physical pursuits may occur. By use of the gifted student's verbal and rational strength, an understanding of the dramatic changes that are occurring can be achieved and the need to integrate mind and body can be addressed. The following provisions will aid in this transition:

- Experiences designed to heighten and clarify sensory awareness
- Experiences designed to promote awareness of the student's own body and the creation of a positive body image
- Experiences and information to heighten awareness of the pleasures of having a healthy body, and of the means for health maintenance and growth
- Information and opportunities for inquiry into the clarification of physical responses to emotions
- Instruction and practice in techniques of relaxation and tension reduction
- Opportunities for self-expression through movement, pantomime, dance, etc.
- Opportunities to develop individual physical competence and experience the satisfaction of physical activity in ways chosen by the student from a wide range of structured and nonstructured, competitive, cooperative, and individual processes
- Exposure to and opportunities to learn one of the disciplines devoted to mind/body integration (Yoga, T'ai-chi Ch'uan, etc.)
- Support for and assistance in making the care and development of one's own body a part of an individual life-style
- Opportunities to examine the implications of current social and political policies for the health of people in the community.

The Intellectual Transition

For most adolescents, the intellectual transition marks the beginning of what Piaget calls *formal operational thought.* Most youth now become capable of reasoning with alternative hypotheses, entertaining the possible and the probable in addition to the real and the concrete. While as many as 20 percent of the students of this age will not show a capability for this expansion of awareness, judgment, and insight (Neimark, 1975), the gifted student has been performing many such tasks for years and is now faced with an intolerable amount of repetition and conceptual stagnation.

It is quite common for schools to use the middle-school grades to review and reintroduce concepts developed in the later elementary years. For gifted youth who have been allowed to accelerate according to their needs and ability, such repetition is regressive. Even for those who have not had such opportunities the repetition of known concepts can create boredom and indifference to classroom achievement. The organization of most middle schools makes personalized instruction, which was found to be highly beneficial for the gifted student during the elementary years, difficult to continue. The student is now faced with discrete time blocks and segregated subject matter as most middle schools begin the practice of educational departmentalization.

The incidence of underachievement rises during this time. Boredom with school offerings, the need to challenge parental and teacher-related values, and the desire for group acceptance combine to create the denial of academic ability. Girls, especially, will succumb to the conformity needs of this period.

Learning styles are also different between cognitively and academically gifted junior high school students and other students on at least five variables. Gifted students are less teacher motivated and more self-motivated; more persistent; prefer some sound to quiet during concentrated study; prefer visual, tactile, or kinesthetic to auditory modes of learning; and prefer to learn alone (Griggs & Price, 1980). These suggestions can alleviate many of these problems:

1 Develop an academic core within the departmentalized setting where three periods may be combined with a team of two or three teachers. Gifted students can then be brought together for more appropriate instruction. Within such a core, flexible grouping can occur. Permitting able students to group for instruction at their level of need is far superior to the tracking plan employed by many middle-school and senior high school administrators, for it recognizes that the gifted student is not gifted in every subject, allows for appropriate curricular modifications, and permits the advantages of mental peer interaction. Through the elective period choices, such a structure also allows broader exposure to students whose abilities may be in less academic areas.

2 Use mentors to provide for the acceleration and depth of interest of gifted learners. Such specialized instructors can be found among the retired community, among parents, and within the business community of any city or town.

3 Use the resources of neighboring senior high schools, junior colleges, and universities. Many universities have special provisions for middle-grade students during summers in the regular courses where credits can be accumulated on an official university transcript. Some institutions of higher education offer specially designed programs to middle-school talented and able learners in selected disciplines throughout the academic year.

When planning curriculum experiences, note that some researchers have found that educators need to be more aware of the cognitive processing differences between males and females. For example, Weiner and Robinson (1986) found not only that adolescent males have higher mathematical reasoning ability than females, but also that this ability is the single best predictor of their mathematical achievement. For adolescent females, verbal reasoning ability was the best predictor. For females learning mathematics, textbooks should place more emphasis on the conceptual approach rather than the usual approach of deriving equations with gaps in the logical process. Teaching alternative cognitive styles also helps. Both female and male gifted students need the following:

- Exposure to the environment and the culture, including aesthetic, economic, political, educational, and social aspects
- Exposure to, and opportunities to work with, peers, adults, and other students with expertise in the student's interest areas
- Advanced and/or unusual subject matter
- Experience in identifying data needs, establishing data organization, and data collection
- Opportunities to communicate and exchange ideas, information, and opinions in a variety of ways
- Instruction in developing original applications of knowledge and understandings, including hypothesizing and hypothesis testing
- Opportunities to examine and/or alter existing patterns physically and mentally
- Opportunities to identify and clarify standards of comparison and evaluation
- Instruction in, and opportunities to develop, data evaluation and decision-making skills
- Opportunities to evaluate personal choices in terms of available data, individual needs and goals, and choice consequences
- Opportunities to apply these ideas to real world situations.

Social-Emotional Transitions

Acceptance, belonging, and self-esteem are the areas of critical concern to the maturing adolescent. Up to this point in time, modeling, guidance, rewards, and punishments have been used to give the young person an external value structure. During adolescence most young people are attempting to develop a personal value structure, their own moral system.

Giftedness gives special advantages and disadvantages to this process. While all adolescents can be characterized as intense and show rapid fluctuations in emotion and widely ranging mood swings (partly a result of biochemical changes that are occurring), the gifted confound this behavior by interspersing periods of unusual maturity and marvelous insight.

Bright adolescents appear to develop autonomy and time perspective faster than their average counterparts. And for gifted students who have in the past been threatening to teachers, a new assertion of independence during this period may result in verbal or sometimes even physical confrontation. Teachers least equipped to deal with this situation are those who see their role as one of authority that must be preserved. Those teachers who are successful in guiding the gifted adolescent can admit their own inadequacies and meet the gifted student as a person, for they care more about understanding problems or miscommunications than about being in charge.

The more typical adolescent admires those who are athletic or socially gregarious. If academic success is to be given approval by their peers, the gifted boy must be athletically able, often an impossible task for the student who is younger and less developed than his classmates. For both boys and girls good grades must be earned with seeming ease, for studious habits are often looked upon with suspicion and are often penalized. For girls intelligence is seen as too aggressive, too masculine; for boys, too feminine. These perceptions cause internal conflicts in the gifted.

Adolescents are on an emotional roller coaster too. After in-depth study of the lives of teenagers of today, Csikszentmihalyi and Larson (1987) conclude that the typical teenager comes down from extreme happiness or up from deep sadness within 45 minutes, in contrast to an adult whose happy/sad "fluxuations" can take several hours. They get the most satisfaction from meeting challenges that fit their developing skills and provide them with meaningful rewards. They like to develop new levels of expertise and accomplishment, and their success stimulates them to search for fresh challenges, slightly harder but within reach. It is this pattern of growing ability that helps make the transition between the impulsive, egocentric activities of childhood and the world of adults. Guidance is needed so that appropriate challenges are found and made available.

Too many teenagers use their time seeking challenges in aimless activities with friends or escape through television. Such short-term pleasures deny them the personal fulfillment of more productive activity. Csikszentmihalyi and Larson (1987) suggest that adults provide models of how to choose among goals, how to persevere with patience, and how to recognize challenges and enjoy meeting them. With adult guidance adolescents can find productive ways to achieve control over their lives and responsibility for their experiences.

Without guidance high levels of cognitive ability can be used to meet the youth's needs in ways that will prove to be socially destructive. Manipulation of others to gain personal goals is a skill too often found in these very able youngsters. Often the intense desire to know, to follow up on concepts, to pursue ideas will result in a social insensitivity that can lead to rejection and isolation. Often large gaps between intellectual, physical, and emotional growth will need sorting out with adult help. It is important that nonjudgmental, open communication exist between teacher and student. Schools need to develop more expedient ways for the gifted to contact counselors and advisors. Too often, the intermediate and secondary systems with their departmentalization, administrative hierarchies, and large plants make immediate personal contact almost impossible. By the time a counseling session has been scheduled, with the proper hall passes and classroom permission secured, the student has given up on seeking help through the system. Overburdened counselors may be available only to disruptive or acting-out students. Gifted students complain that the counselor only relates to them for class scheduling or college preparation information. Some schools do recognize the problem; they set aside one day a week for counseling gifted students or run small counseling groups. Some have even developed a crisis contact system available to the gifted as well as to other students.

An interesting framework for viewing problems encountered by gifted adolescents has been proposed by Manaster and Powell (1983). Divided into three categories, the problems that may confront gifted adolescents include being

1 *Out of Stage.* These are the multitalented youngsters who may be intellectually bored because they are reacting to and dealing with concepts and goals far beyond the reach of those around them. They may be so focused on success and perfectionism that they are out of touch with their immediate environment and the meanings and potential satisfactions that may be there for them.
2 *Out of Phase.* Youngsters who are aware of their differences and because of their unusual abilities or interests have become alienated and distant from or without a peer group. Often they seem to have a deficiency in social skills.
3 *Out of Sync.* These adolescents may be out of stage, out of phase, or both and feel their differences in ways that they determine that they do not, should not, or cannot fit in. Such feelings of difference could be viewed by these youngsters as positive or negative. They show insecurity, anxiety, and low self-concept.

This attempt to conceptualize a framework for looking at problems commonly found among gifted adolescents is offered so that teachers, researchers, and gifted children themselves can get a better perspective on possible maladjustments that can occur within this population. A plea is made that all of us view "the gifted as average with gifts, not as superior with faults" (p. 73).

Gifted students can be helped to enjoy their differences, their uniqueness. They need to develop skills of individual competition, group cooperation, and trust. They need opportunities to work with students who are their intellectual peers and those with a variety of abilities. They can be taught to value their intellectual power and to use it to deal effectively with their emotions and their values. These are the students who can entertain new constructs of reality and who can envision more productive, higher levels of development for all humankind. Suggestions for working with their emotional and social transition might include these:

- Opportunities to identify and name one's own emotions, perceptual filters, and defense systems and those of others
- Opportunities to expand and to clarify awareness of the physical, social, and emotional environment
- Experiences and instruction in attitudes of receptivity and suspended judgment
- Opportunities and support for actively seeking ideas and feelings from others
- Opportunities and instruction in constructing, clarifying, and expressing personal values
- Opportunities to clarify short-term goals and examine them in relation to personal values and to achievability
- Support for making personal values the foundation for career choice
- Opportunities to develop effective community membership by participating in activities with a variety of groups, examining roles in groups and the effect of those roles, practicing open communication, examining their own functioning within groups, and improving that function
- Opportunities to develop skills with group process including leadership skills and use of power
- Opportunities to develop commitment to groups and to larger community, including goals of humankind.

Intuitive Transitions

Gifted youth have an early concern and interest in intuitive knowing. They need opportunities to converse meaningfully with philosophers and others who share their interest. Such inquiry can be made through independent study, with mentors, through group experiences led by guest experts, and through class discussions. It is important for gifted adolescents to be open to experiences in this area so that they

Sharing with intellectual peers is important for gifted adolescents.

may recognize their own intuitive energy and ability and how it contributes to their cognitive and emotional growth. They need guidance in becoming familiar with, analyzing, and evaluating such phenomena and should be provided with both the historical approach and the current body/mind data. As this dimension of creativity seems to be available to everyone but is to be found more active in the gifted and talented populations, guidance in evaluating appropriate uses of this type of creative effort should be available. The intuitive function is involved in initiating or insightful acts and in creative activity. It is an area that promises much for the fulfillment of humankind.

Peers in the school climate influence learning; in the case of creative students, their peer interactions do not seem to facilitate creative growth.

During adolescence classrooms must provide a safe place, but not overly limit risktaking and reaching beyond known paths. It is now that teachers become consultants and guides, and their past positions as authority figures and decision makers must be transformed. Knowing how to support without taking over, how to present consequences without removing choices, and how to provide structure without limiting are some of the challenges faced by teachers of adolescents. For teachers of more sensitive gifted, talented, and creative adolescents, the challenge is even greater, and the significance of their success affects all of history.

PROGRAMS FOR THE GIFTED IN SECONDARY SCHOOLS

Often those who plan the gifted program in the district concentrate on the elementary school structure and curriculum. Part of the reason for such omission of secondary levels can be found in the greater flexibility available in the elementary structure and time organization. Many of the needs created by the characteristics found among gifted learners—e.g., need for continuity, interdisciplinary content, delay of closure, flexible grouping to take advantage of peak learning areas, depth and diversity of interest, alternative learning styles and creative expression—can be more easily met in the elementary school organization. Other reasons are the limitations of the secondary structure in time given to each class and to each student because of the large number of students who must be served each day by each teacher and the limited interaction between faculty of the various disciplines. Though there are ways all of these problems can be resolved to provide appropriate programs for gifted learners, the largest barrier is the perception that program modification for gifted students is unnecessary in secondary schools. The assumption is that in a departmentalized setting students can choose programs that will meet their needs from the variety of courses offered. There may even be special honors classes available from which the gifted student can choose.

One often used practice that needs to be examined is the establishment of one or two advanced classes into which all gifted students are tracked regardless of their needs and abilities. Many high schools use special mathematics or science classes for this purpose. Such classes comprise the entire gifted program, and if students do not do well in mathematics or science, their identification as gifted comes under suspicion. We must offer the widest range of qualitatively different experiences we can devise, for this population is the most diverse in ability. Therefore, neither tracking systems nor a few special classes comprise a complete program that can meet the needs of gifted learners.

Therefore, neither tracking systems nor a few special classes comprise a complete program that can meet the needs of gifted learners.

Silverman (1980) points out that while elementary gifted students may have relatively little involvement in the identification and planning procedures used in their program, secondary gifted students should be involved in both. In addition to more generally used identification procedures, she suggests the use of subject area examinations, preferably college-level assessments; independent study proposals designed by the students; auditions and interviews; and self-nomination and self-selection.

PROGRAMS FOUND IN SECONDARY SCHOOLS

Certain traits found in gifted adolescents should define the programs planned at the secondary level; they are intellectualism, style, reflection, altruism, and idealism. As we look at the programs now found in secondary settings it will be well to see if such characteristics can be included.

The Advanced Placement Program

Available at approximately 20% of the secondary schools in the nation is the Advanced Placement (AP) Program, a program of college-level courses and examinations sponsored by the College Entrance Examination Board in New York City. Usually planned for a full year, AP can take the form of an honors class, an advanced course, a tutorial, or an independent study. Such experiences are intended to be challenging, giving greater opportunity for individual progress and accomplishment. They often require more work, take more time, and go into greater depth than the usual high school course. AP examinations are given each year in the spring and result in credit or advanced placement in participating colleges and universities. In many universities a full year of college credit can be earned by AP work.

The International Baccalaureate Program

Originating in Geneva, Switzerland, this program also demands a high level of subject mastery. The program is comprised of a 2-year program outline, although it is quite flexible and a school is permitted to write its own program on the basis of the strengths and interests of the students involved. The resulting diploma is recognized by the major European universities, and many American universities allow full college credit.

The secondary learning experience can be exciting, differentiated, and individualized.

Academic Core Classes

The time limits of classes in schools organized by subjects can be alleviated and the multidisciplinarity of subjects enhanced by the use of a core class organization. This approach allows two or three secondary teachers to block out multiple periods, usually two or three each day, during which flexible grouping and a cross-subject focus can be utilized. The usual student/faculty ratio is maintained, but space is provided for the two or three groups that were formerly separate classes to meet as one group, with the two or three teachers forming an instructional team. The remainder of the students' schedules are as before, with electives chosen by the normal scheduling procedure.

Group Seminars

Another possibility for programming at the secondary level is the use of independently planned group seminars. An example of this type of structure for meeting the needs of gifted students at the secondary level is the Teacher/Advisor Model. Students are allowed to ask any faculty member to serve as their gifted advisor. They then sign up for one period of gifted program time and arrange with their advisor how this period will be used. This is a highly individualized model wherein the gifted students may do directed independent study, cooperatively design seminars with their advisor to be conducted by either the student or the advisor, and/or take regular classes. Having a small area set aside as a gifted center helps to make this a socially, as well as academically, successful modification. Teacher acceptance of this plan is unusually high, and it provides for a wide choice of curriculum.

College and University Classes

Classes on college and university campuses are used successfully by many secondary schools. The assessment for such placement is the responsibility of the school district where the student is enrolled. This is frequently overlooked in programs that have limited offerings. Not all gifted students can benefit by attendance in such classes. Such a provision should not constitute the entire gifted program at the secondary level for all gifted students in that district. Placing students in advanced classes should be only part of a secondary gifted program.

Governor's Schools

Special schools have been successfully implemented at the secondary level. Notable has been the success of the various Governor's Schools. Several states are providing the experience of a Governor's School for their gifted and talented learners. In some states the funding for all aspects of the program except transportation is provided by a combination of state and private resources. Most of the programs are located on university campuses for full utilization of campus facilities. In some cases students are taught by university faculty. Many of the teachers are from secondary schools and are carefully selected. Student/teacher ratios are kept low. In most programs, grades are not awarded and university credit is not granted for completion of these programs.

The programs vary in length from 4 to 6 weeks and are in session mostly in the summer. They offer enrichment and acceleration in a variety of subject areas with different programs focusing on different areas. The students in some programs are as young as sixth graders, while in others the participation is limited to high school juniors and seniors. All participants are chosen from very carefully developed criteria (Karnes & Pearce, 1981).

One exception to the above profile is the new Governor's School in North Carolina, opened in September, 1980. It was the first public residential high school for highly able students in science and math. The school offers a full range of courses for eleventh and twelfth graders but emphasizes expanded course offerings in science and mathematics. Full costs of education and living expenses are provided by the state (Selby, 1980).

School-Within-a-School

Somewhat like a combination of core curriculum and special schools, the school-within-a-school approach allows gifted students to meet in a more flexible, integrated setting for their entire educational experience but utilizes the regular school facility and resources. Physically the students are located in a wing of the school or in bungalows on school grounds. As a separate unit they can pursue a curriculum that is accelerated and uses processes at a higher level of complexity than the regular secondary classroom can provide. Such a setting allows for more community and field experiences and flexibility of grouping without interrupting the overall school schedule. Many districts find such provisions especially attractive for the highly gifted or as a solution to low-achieving gifted groups, as the cost is little more than offering another section of a regular class.

Minicourses

What would happen if all secondary teachers could teach only what they wanted to teach and the students were allowed to learn just what they wanted to learn? This was the question that started an interesting minicourse structure at a high school in the Los Angeles area. A group of teachers came together to find out. After securing permission to use a 6-week time block, each teacher listed courses he or she most wanted to teach and how many weeks they would require. These were then scheduled under traditional categories such as history, biology, language, science, etc., with a descriptive, often creative title. Not surprisingly, most teachers found that their favorite themes fell within the area in which they were credentialed to teach. The students were then given the list of minicourses and allowed to choose their favorites. As much as possible, first choices were honored with second choices used only when classes became too full. Classes that were not chosen were dropped. These minicourses comprised only a part of each student's schedule and were fitted into the more traditional class schedule with other periods run as usual.

The results were exciting! The students and the teachers were highly motivated; the classes became far more creative, better attended, and more productive. The next time minicourses were being scheduled, nearly twice as many faculty wanted to participate and students who had previously not wished to participate in the gifted program requested permission to sign up. The experiment might have eventually encompassed the entire school had there not been a change in administration, with a resulting return to more traditional and "manageable" scheduling procedures.

In addition to these special types of programs and useful in conjunction with them are the program models for gifted secondary learners discussed in Chapter 5. Refer again to the Autonomous Learner Model (Betts, 1985), the Secondary Triad Model (Reis & Renzulli, 1986), and the Purdue Secondary Model for Gifted and Talented Youth (Feldhusen & Robinson, 1986) for suggestions for your program planning. Radical acceleration as exemplified by the SMPY program, mentor programs, and programs for independent study, all discussed in Chapter 5, can be successfully implemented at the secondary level. At the very least, two interested teachers can combine their blocks of time and their students to create a laboratory setting where individualization, flexible grouping, and some cross-grading and interdisciplinary learning can occur. In addition to the provisions described, other options might include

- Summer university courses, institutes, or programs for gifted learners
- Curriculum acceleration and early graduation through competency testing and fast-paced materials
- Flexible scheduling (less regular class attendance)
- Interdisciplinary courses or themes
- Community-based career education and internships
- Special-topic courses
- Exchange student programs
- Special study centers
- Private schools for the gifted.

SPECIAL PROBLEMS IN EVALUATING PROGRAMS FOR THE GIFTED IN SECONDARY SCHOOLS

One source of evaluation of gifted programs in intermediate and high schools is the students themselves. Raspberry (1976) quotes a gifted student who left his junior high school because the environment

> Was not conducive to academic achievement. . . . In order to gain acceptance by the student body, one had to give some visible deference to either athletics, "partying" or some form of rebellious activity. Those who excelled academically had to prove that they were "all right." The studious males ran the risk of being called "sissy." The studious females were definitely considered square. . . . Students make the difference, for students set the mood of the campus. (pp. 36, 38)

In a 1958 study, Thistlewaite reports that 45% of the gifted students surveyed found their secondary programs either inadequate or having specific defects. My experiences with secondary programs for the gifted in the past 10 years tell me that this percentage is still valid, perhaps even higher today. To make a videotape series at our university exploring the feelings of gifted youths toward their programs, we selected gifted students from diverse racial, cultural, and socioeconomic backgrounds. The students most commonly complained that they were never challenged to use their abilities. They were often given more work, but usually of the same type used with typical learners. Even in situations where they were grouped with other gifted students for a small part of their program, they felt that the programs remained the same; only the people were different. Occasionally teachers worked with them to set up interesting educational experiences from which they could learn. These were the exceptions, however, and they expressed the belief that most of their teachers found them threatening and resented any special provisions made on their behalf.

The groups had suggestions for improving the situation. Most felt that a more open, flexible approach would have benefited them. One young woman, who experienced an individualized program for a couple of years in a language arts class, told of how much progress everyone had made and how interesting it was. "But the next year we had to go back into basic texts with our new teacher. We could use equipment like the controlled reader, but they set it at 400 words a minute and wouldn't let us change it. We were already reading 800 words per minute, but they didn't care. They said for our grade level, that was where we were supposed to be," she told us. One boy wanted to branch out and combine music, his first love, with math, history, and language. He suggested that such interdisciplinary study would be natural and would lead on and on to more exciting learning. He had just been dropped from the xx track classes (highly gifted) for gifted students because he felt the work was too boring and refused to do it. He was finding the x track (gifted) just as bad. All of these students expressed great appreciation for teachers who treated them like people and seemed to care how they felt. The students most pleased with their program came from an intermediate school where they were grouped together for three of their six periods in a cross-graded (fifth through eighth grade), open structure. Their two-teacher team used the responsive learning environment model and taught them all of their basic subjects. They were allowed to choose electives for the remaining periods from classes throughout the school. These students expressed none of the boredom and dissatisfaction of the others we interviewed.

Rice and Banks (1967) interviewed another group of junior and senior high school students regarding their opinions and recommendations for changes in their program. The findings will be given in some detail, for they are typical of comments found throughout the literature, in my work with gifted youth, and of teachers and coordinators with whom I have been in contact through our teacher training program.

In answer to a question on designing their own curriculum, the students wanted courses that would allow them to work at their own individual level of ability. They wanted more freedom in course selection and more flexibility in grade level placement. They divided their preference for the subjects offered equally among the sciences, mathematics, fine arts, foreign languages, and social sciences, with the request that the curriculum be culturally enriched and diversified. Students at the junior high school level requested interdisciplinary seminars. The students also asked that they be allowed to pursue courses in more depth, and that advanced placement and equivalency testing be made available.

In response to a question on opportunity for creative expression, the students requested more independence to create what they wanted instead of producing only what the school wanted. Girls expressed a greater need for more freedom of choice and creative outlets than did boys. In discussions of grouping, nearly all students favored some opportunity to learn with other gifted students; the highly gifted unanimously favored completely separate education. Students favored acceleration on a subject-by-subject basis, although they did not see it as taking the place of individualization. They gave preparation for formal education, emphasis on the use of the intellect, and promotion of social development and maturity as the top-priority purposes for high school education.

In another survey of gifted 14- to 18-year-olds in an affluent community in Los Angeles County (Stark, 1972), students gave the highest priority for their high school goals as preparation for finding a career that would be interesting to them, being able to decide what vocation to follow, and being able to discover what special abilities they had. They felt their high school should teach more classes on how to live in the world. These students were interested in a career that would provide them with self-worth rather than high pay or security, and they preferred a job that would allow them to work with people rather than with data or things. They felt their greatest problem at school was overcoming boredom, and they wanted the chance to participate in a group that could discuss personal problems with an understanding adult. They desired an advanced program in which they could work alongside a professional in the actual environment. They believed that teachers could help them learn if the teachers were more interested in them as individuals. Although the population and the questionnaires differed from those of the Rice and Banks (1967) study, the ideas expressed by the students are surprisingly similar.

Students have not been the only ones to criticize the secondary programs for gifted students. In a 4-year follow-up study of gifted students in high school programs, Meeker (1968) found through measures of creativity, leadership, motor skills, grades, intelligence, and achievement that potentially brilliant achievers have been lost as a consequence of inadequate attention during the secondary school years. She blamed expectations and traditional departmentalized practices.

A study (Tremaine, 1979) comparing the attitudes, accomplishments, and achievements of gifted high school students participating in a gifted program with gifted high school students who did not participate reported the following results: The gifted students

- Earned higher GPAs.
- Took more advanced classes.
- Scored higher on SAT testing.
- Won significantly more scholarships and awards.
- Planned to attend a four-year university in far greater numbers.
- Expressed more positive attitudes toward school after graduation.

- Were involved and spent more time in school activities.
- Evaluated their teachers higher.
- Enjoyed as many friends.

Tremaine feels that the contention that gifted programs result in snobbery, indifference, conceit, or any other negative quality cannot be validated by these data. In fact, they indicate that gifted programs in the secondary school make significant positive differences and are well worth the development and implementation effort.

By synthesizing the developmental theories as they apply to gifted adolescents, Leroux (1986) has been able to offer some suggestions to teachers to aid them in their work with these youngsters. The following list is but an excerpt:

1 Set exams that require creative, imaginative, and open-ended solutions.
2 Ask open-ended questions which encourage risk and tolerate ambiguity.
3 Consciously remove fear of failure and competitive elements in the teaching process.
4 Expect quality but not perfection from highly able students.
5 Encourage symbolic expression in the widest possible integration of sensory experiences.
6 Use peer counseling to discuss emotions, sexual roles, social relations, and self-worth.
7 Have students establish their own code of rules for behavior.
8 Have students set goals for personal achievement in a subject.
9 Develop a community service module for independent study.
10 Conduct philosophy seminars to discuss principles of justice and moral reasoning.
11 Have students and faculty participate jointly in decision-making.
12 Plan group activities which build awareness of personal skills and social responsibility. (pp. 74–76)

Many of these activities were suggested as part of the Responsive Learning Environment (Chapter 8) and further validate the concern for developing responsibility by sharing responsibility and empowering the student. There are four times as many suggestions made by Leroux that you may find helpful as you seek ways to optimize the learning in your classroom.

In a review of literature on creativity in gifted adolescents, Milgram (1984) found that people recognized as creative seem to be characterized by a common core of distinct personality characteristics. Perhaps more importantly, this core of personality characteristics is remarkably similar between children and adolescents who score high on creativity tests and adults of recognized real-world creativity. It also appears that creative behavior is fairly constant over time. With these factors in mind we are advised by Milgram to use self-report questionnaires of past creative activity as perhaps the best available predictor of future performance and to include these in any battery of tests given for program and curricular decisions.

USING INTEGRATIVE EDUCATION IN THE SECONDARY CURRICULUM

All of the characteristics and needs of the gifted discussed in Chapter 8 are applicable to secondary as well as elementary students. Therefore, there remains the same need for differentiating and individualizing the curriculum. If anything, differentiation is more needed during adolescence, for it is during this period that the gifted pursue their independence and separate identity from their parents and their childhood values—sorting, testing, and validating their competence.

The philosophy of learning and teaching is also equivalent, as advances in brain/mind research make the same demands for change on the secondary teacher as they make on the elementary teacher. While the theories of cognitive development and the curricular models that attempt to facilitate them are important at the secondary level, the necessity of including and integrating other functions of feeling, intuition, and physical sensing are as critical to optimal learning and development in the secondary as they were at any other point in the growth of the gifted learner.

The secondary teacher is asked to look again at Chapter 7, with a view to adapting and translating the models and suggestions to fit his or her gifted learners. The description of the Integrative Education Model and its use of brain/mind research in the classroom does not change, nor does the environment in which it can best be implemented, whether at the elementary or at the secondary level. What does change is the way the implementation looks. Just as a decentralized laboratory setting in language arts looks different from this type of environment in science, so the individualized setting looks different when a school has a core curriculum or a six-period day. The look may be different, but the same rules apply.

Individualizing the secondary experience for students is within reach of teachers even in the traditional departmentalized setting with 35 students per period and at least 175 different students every day.

The following is an overview of a plan and a step-by-step procedure for a beginning activity for individualizing that has been successful in a senior high school where the teacher who uses it, Toby Manzanares, averages 170 students each 8-hour day with some days bringing over 200 students to his classroom. He begins the individualizing process the first week of the new semester. The process will last the entire year and will be modified, improving as the students give input. One advantage secondary teachers have is the ability of their students to assume a partnership role in individualizing their learning. When given the opportunity, students can share the responsibility. Figures 9.1 and 9.2 support this process.

Period: _____   Name: _____

PERSONAL INVENTORY BY INTERVIEW

1. If you could go anywhere in the world, where would you go and why would you go there?_____

2. Who is the person you admire the most and why?_____

_____

3. What is your favorite book?_____

4. What is your favorite song?_____

5. Are you extreme, liberal, conservative, or otherwise?_____

6. What is your favorite sport (as a participant)?_____

7. What is your favorite sport (as a spectator)?_____

8. What is your favorite pastime?_____

9. What is your favorite class and why?_____

10. What is your favorite animal and why?_____

11. What would you do with $115,000?_____

12. What is the funniest thing that ever happened to you?_____

13. What is the greatest thing that has ever happened to you?_____

14. What is the strangest thing that has ever happened to you?_____

_____

15. What are your special talents?_____

16. What makes you unique?_____

17. Additional questions:_____

_____

Figure 9.1 *Inventory Sheet.*

448

DATA SHEET 1—INDIVIDUAL INVENTORY

1. Name:_____

Notes and Observations:_____

_____

2. Name:_____

Notes and Observations:_____

_____

3. Name:_____

Notes and Observations:_____

_____

4. Name:_____

Notes and Observations:_____

_____

5. Name:_____

Notes and Observations:_____

_____

6. Name:_____

Notes and Observations:_____

_____

7. Name:_____

Notes and Observations:_____

_____

Figure 9.2 Data Sheet.

The Individual Inventory

Step 1 The class participates in a lecture/discussion of an educational concept that operates from the premise that, "Each individual in this room has knowledge, that once shared will be valuable to the teacher-learner and just as importantly, to each student as a learner-teacher."

Step 2 The class is asked to consider things of value that can be shared with the group. (A typical comment at this point is, "Like what?", which leads nicely to the introduction of the inventory sheet.)

Step 3 The inventory sheet is examined and the questions discussed [see Figure 9.1]. Students are instructed to scan the room looking for people they don't know. Students are instructed to stand up and select one of these unknown students for a partner. At this point the teacher may add, "Should any of you have a concern about not being picked as a partner, then be the first to move to make a selection."

Step 4 The teacher helps the few students remaining form dyads and works with the last student should there be an odd number present.

Step 5 Instructions for the dyads are:

    a Write your partner's name in the space provided on the inventory sheet.

    b Interview your partner using the questions on the sheet and note your partner's answers as you go. Take turns answering questions as you work down the sheet. At the end of 10 minutes, you will introduce your partner to the class and your partner will introduce you sharing with the group two or three unique qualities you've discovered about each other.

Step 6 Instructions to the class before the sharing session: "On your data sheet [see Figure 9.2] record the name of the person being introduced and one of the unique qualities he or she possesses. Also record at least one observation of your own as you attend to the person being introduced."

Step 7 The teacher now invites a dyad to begin by introducing each other.

Step 8 As students introduce each other, the teacher can record relevant personal data for each individual on the reverse side of the class roster. By the end of the session you will have the beginnings of a data bank on each student. In addition, the teacher can collect the papers from the group and will then have 34 student perceptions of each individual in the room. (Developed by Tobias Manzanares, Schurr High School, Montebello, California, 1986)

Manzanares feels that the process of individualizing your classroom begins with getting to know each of your students as a unique individual. He believes that as he comes to know his students over the semester, he learns from each of them what they care about, what they are interested in, their strengths, what they want to improve, and where they want to go in life. He pays careful attention to what they tell him and uses these data to connect the content of the course to the individual student in a meaningful way. By the end of the semester, he has gotten to know most of his students well. He believes his life is richer for knowing them, and they benefit from knowing each other. The entire learning experience becomes more personal.

Later in the course Manzanares continues the individualization process with

Customized Term Projects and Learning Expeditions. (For a step-by-step plan and support material for the Learning Expedition see Chapter 4, pp. 85–108 in *Optimizing Learning,* Clark, 1986.) Manzanares believes that with the attitude that it is possible to individualize the secondary classroom, the reality can be achieved step by step. Empowering learners gives them greater skill at making choices. Planning a curriculum with choices available individualizes the classroom as students learn to personally select more meaningful learning activities.

Another approach to more meaningful learning experiences in a secondary classroom is offered by Subotnik (1984) for those involved in social studies. Brainstorming, attribute listing, morphological synthesis, reverse historical chronology, webbing, consequence charts, and guided fantasy are some of the strategies she suggests and explains. She believes that through these approaches students learn to make alternative choices and have opportunities to be playful, witty, adventurous, idealistic, and reflective. Subotnik believes that to be useful to the future gifted adult the learning experiences should be sophisticated and multifaceted, and should encourage various forms of expression and the generation of new ideas and products.

The secondary teacher is also asked to review the strategies given in Chapter 8 to illustrate the four major brain functions, again with an eye to adapting them when needed and re-creating them for the specific groups of learners. All of the strategies given have been used in some form with students from preschool through graduate school. The results have been most exciting! The elements of integrative education are not limited to any age group. However giftedness is expressed, the strategies given are useful.

Because the secondary schools are presently structured in a departmental format, strategies for integrative learning will be made within that format. Feel free to extend, expand, and invent, for the examples given are only suggestive of what might be done.

It is at the secondary level that real concern begins to be felt by gifted learners, their parents, and their teachers for academic performance. This is the point in an academic career when future opportunities may be facilitated or closed, depending upon the student's performance. Testing is often the measure of that performance, and ways to improve a student's ability to perform on such tests may be quite interesting to that student.

We have seen in Chapter 8 that relaxation is an important tool in optimizing learning. Not only will reduced tension allow more information to be processed more quickly, it will also allow the retrieval of more information more accurately. In a conversation with a secondary teacher regarding the use of relaxation in the classroom, I was told about a student who seemed to the teacher to be extremely able, but who, however, almost always received low grades on written tests. The teacher began using guided fantasies prior to the administration of tests and found the students far less tense and the quality of the answers much improved. For the girl who had tested consistently low, the results were grades that went from C and D to grades of A and B. The teacher now teaches relaxation skills regularly and encourages the students to use such skills before any testing in which they must be involved. He tells the students that he cannot guarantee results, but that it has worked remarkably well for many students. He also informs them that the army is using similar techniques in their training programs. In addition to guided fantasy (see pp. 407–409 in Chapter 8), the teacher informs me that during a test a break for the Massage Train (found on p. 397 in Chapter 8) revitalizes the students and aids their performance.

Using Integrative Education in Secondary Science Teaching

The following lesson has been successfully implemented by Tobias Manzanares in his high school biology class.

Integrative Lesson 9.1 *Phagocytosis*

Purpose: To develop an understanding of the body's immune system through an integrative activity, and to reinforce the terminology used in the unit on the circulatory system
Time involved: One 50-minute class period
Materials needed: Handout of a drawing of the process of phagocytosis; classroom or outdoor area representing the human body

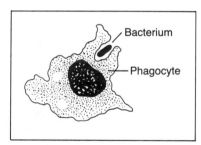

Figure 9.3 Phagocytosis.

Procedure:

1 Students should record in their notebooks the diagram showing phagocytosis (Figure 9.3) and should note the following:
   a Many white blood cells are capable of phagocytizing, or eating, large numbers of invading microorganisms.
   b Specialized cells in the liquid-filled spaces of your tissues are also capable of phagocytizing invading organisms, and are most effective in the specific region of a skin wound.
   c If the infection moves into the body from the region of entrance, phagocytic cells residing in the lymph nodes will ingest the invaders. Additional phago-

cytic cells are found in the liver and spleen, should the infection reach the blood stream.

2 Share with the class, so that everyone will be able to participate as either a part of a white blood cell or as a triad member representing an invading cell. Ask for volunteers to make three triads. Members of these triads can decide whether to be a virus or a bacterium.

3 The remainder of the class links arms to form a closed circle representing a white blood cell. This group selects a member to act as the nucleus.

4 Instruct the invading triads to leave the room momentarily and when they return to remember that they are invading the body (the room) through a wound, scratch, or any other method they may choose to describe. (Example: *Giardia lambia* is a protozoan that enters the body through contaminated drinking water.)

5 Instruct the remaining group (white blood cells) that they are charged with the responsibility of protecting the body by ingesting and thus destroying the invading organisms.

6 As the invading triads (arms linked) enter the room (body), instruct them to move at the speed of a microorganism (very slowly). Instruct the nucleus of the white blood cell to direct the action of the cell in the very best style and wisdom of a nucleus.

7 Allow 3 to 5 minutes for the phagocyte to phagocytize. As an invading triad is ingested, instruct them to become part of the larger phagocyte by linking arms with that group.

8 Stop the activity momentarily (after ingestion) to have the group focus on their feelings by asking the following questions . . . To the phagocyte: "How did you feel as you attacked and ingested an invader? Did you have a sense of power? Did you feel a sense of responsibility? Success?" To the invading triads: "Did you feel a sense of exclusion relative to the bigger group? Did you feel differently after becoming part of the larger cell? What kinds of feelings were experienced upon penetration of the body?"

9 Have the class return to their seats and write a metaphor about their immune system.

10 Conduct the following guided imagery to raise the students' awareness of their ability to assist their body's immune system, using imagery.

"Allow your eyes to close gently . . . take five cleansing breaths, breathing quietly in through your nose and out through your mouth. . . . Become aware of your skin as a protective barrier completely surrounding your body. . . . Imagine yourself beginning to shrink in size until you are microscopic in dimension. . . . Imagine that you are a white blood cell floating down an endless river within your body. . . . Notice the body organs and structures from this new perspective, from the inside. . . .

"Become aware of the millions of other phagocytes who like you are charged with the responsibility of protecting the body from invading organisms. . . . Notice the enormous feeling of well-being that comes from being part of such an enormous and powerful group. . . . Become aware of a small number of cancer cells that have invaded the body and notice the immediate response of the phagocytes now mobilizing to destroy these invaders completely. . . . Notice the scene of the invasion as the cancer cells are rendered harmless by the action of these powerful phagocytes. . . . Notice the healthy color and glow return to the tissues in this scene as you and the other white blood cells move on in your protective responsibilities. . . . Begin now to grow larger and larger until you fill the physical frame of your body. . . . When you're ready, you may open your eyes and form triads to share your experiences during this imaging session."

Evaluation: The evaluation of this activity can be done with any of evaluative tools you would normally use. Manzanares has found that the students understand more clearly and will retain the information longer than with the usual teaching approaches.

Using Integrative Education in Secondary Social Science

The content of the following exercise was suggested by Ella Schroeder while a teacher at Krantz Junior High School, El Monte, California.

Integrative Lesson 9.2 *American History—The Westward Movement*

Purpose: To conceptualize and develop a better understanding of the life and the problems facing the native tribes of the American West and the migrating settlers during the westward movement

Time involved: One 50-minute period or broken up into several periods if more research is desired

Materials needed: Original journals or diaries of the time period written by those involved in the settlement of the American West, newspapers of that period, and all first-hand data and artifacts from the historical period under investigation that can be obtained. If possible, a native American could be invited to speak to the group during this unit of study. Books written about this period of Western history should be made available. Student journals and tape recorders are optional.

Procedure:

1 Briefly describe the setting and time period to be introduced, the American Westward Movement.

2 Ask the students to get comfortable in their seats and gently close their eyes. Instruct them as follows: "Breathe deeply and slowly allow your body to relax. . . . Let all the tension flow out of your body. . . . Relax. . . . With each breath, you are allowing your body to become lighter, to expand, to slowly become all of the air in the room. . . . Gently let yourself rise slowly above your desk . . . above the room . . . rising gently, slowly above the school . . . . Imagine that you are now slowly moving through time and you are going backward about 10 years . . . 50 years . . . 100 years . . . back to the time when the tribes of native Americans still lived in the Western United States. . . . You are now over the area of the United States that was the home of these tribes. . . . Look down. . . . What do you see? . . . What is happening? . . . What are the people who live here doing? . . . How do they live? . . . What do they eat? . . . What are they wearing? . . . What do they do for fun? . . . Become one of the native people. . . . What are you doing?

Look out over the land. . . . You can see wagons moving slowly toward this spot. . . . How do you feel? . . . What are you concerned about? . . . What do you do? . . . Slowly rise above the tribal encampment. . . . Move toward the wagons of the settlers. . . . What are they doing? . . . Become one of the settlers. . . . How do you feel? . . . What are you concerned about? . . . What do you do? . . . Let yourself slowly rise above the wagons again. . . . Let yourself drift forward in time . . . slowly allow yourself to drift back into this room. . . . Notice how you feel here in this room and when you are ready, slowly, gradually open your eyes and return to the group. . . . When you are ready, open your eyes and choose two other people to share your experience."

3 Ask the students to share in triads, recording their experiences in their journals, in a group journal, or on the tape recorder (if one has been provided).

4 Ask the members of each triad to use the original materials in the room to expand and authenticate their experiences. Use the other materials for comparison and record similarities and differences in all the sources.

5 Ask each triad to prepare a product relating their experiences and research to be shared with the class.

6 Ask for one triad to volunteer as the class historian and assemble the records or products of each triad into a class journal or display.

7 Ask each triad to share their most interesting information in whatever way they choose, allowing five minutes per triad (or whatever time is available).

8 Discuss with the total class the types of problems they felt each group might have, how they felt as a member of each group, and what solutions they felt each group might have tried. Discuss how their ideas related to the historical records. Which solutions might have had the best results? How does this situation seem to reflect events happening today? What are the similarities and the differences? Ask the students to take one emerging issue in today's world and develop possible solutions, either independently or with their triad, for presentation later in the week.

Evaluation: From the journals and position papers, the depth of understanding of the period will be evident. Use any evaluation tools you would normally choose.

Extension: If more than one time period is used, the students can be asked to role play a confrontation between the two groups and discuss the outcomes and consequences of the confrontation.

Using Integrative Education in Secondary Language Teaching

A project conducted in the Los Angeles City Schools by Galyean (1976, 1977–1980, 1978–1981) for teaching foreign language to seventh- through eleventh-grade students included guided imagery, movement and art, fantasy, poetry, drama, music, and values clarification. Many of the curricular ideas used in the project can be found in the references cited.

Examples

When they are practicing tenses of verbs, have students close their eyes, breathe deeply, and take an imaginary journey to a significant event in their past. When they have explored the event, have them open their eyes, draw the event, and write about the experience in the foreign language they are practicing.

When they are learning the verb *to love,* have students close their eyes and imagine themselves with five people they love. Have them tell each person why they are loved and then return, make a drawing of each person, and caption each with words from the foreign language.

Although we have discussed examples from only three of the possible academic areas found in the secondary school, all areas can be enhanced by the use of integrative education techniques.

In this chapter we have extended our concern for the education of gifted children into the adolescent years and specified programs and problems unique to the education of these students. While examples of integrative lessons presented to secondary gifted students have been given, those particularly interested in this population are asked to review Chapters 7 and 8 and to adapt the integrative techniques to their classrooms. Do not allow the few examples given to limit the possibilities for your students. We are all creating new ways to include cognitive, affective, intuitive, and physical sensing functioning in all of the disciplines we teach. That is, of course, the joy of teaching.

Questions Often Asked

1. There has been concern about junior high school students being in a period that the brain is between growth spurts. Should junior high programs reflect this by offering only review and no new material?

The ideas about brain growth occurring in cycles are interesting theories that bear watching; however, even if they are accurate, each person will have a somewhat different time cycle. Those who will be most different will be the gifted students. One of the problems we are now having in this age population is the school's reintroduction of information gifted students have already covered in elementary school. There needs to be more articulation between elementary programs, junior high programs, and senior high programs. It would be far better to individually assess the students using pretesting and posttesting, functional assessment, and individual conferences to find out what they need to learn instead of generalizing about cycles of learning that may or may not be occurring.

2. Should high school teachers be concerned with process when they are really more responsible for teaching specialized content?

It is important that students be introduced to and learn the most content and as many skills as they can during high school, and that is exactly why process is so important. All of the information in Chapter 8 under process planning allows the teacher to present content and skill development in the most effective and efficient ways possible. Empowering the student by using processes that integrate all of the brain functions, using a variety of materials and methods of teaching, and individualizing instruction assures a higher level of motivation, attention, rate of acquisition, and longer retention. Without concern for the process we are using we will only be covering content; the students will not necessarily be learning it. You need not choose between process and content; they are interdependent and both are important.

3. Individualization, flexible grouping, multidisciplinary teaching, responsive environments—these all sound good, but how can we do any of these with only 40 minutes per class?

A 40-minute time block is very difficult to work with. You might want to try to find another teacher or two who want to team for at least part of the day. That would allow you to put two or three time blocks together, teach in a multidisciplinary way (if the other teacher were from a different discipline), and use flexible grouping. Even in a single time block you can get closer to these ideas if you create an environment that is supportive and more like a learning lab. If neither of these is possible you then must become very creative to include as much as you can from the research information that results in optimal learning much as Manzanares does on pp. 448–451. You have identified one of the greatest barriers to making the secondary system more effective, the short blocks of time in which the teachers and students try to operate.

4. Aren't advanced placement and honors classes enough to meet the needs of the gifted?

They are one way of providing for content needs when they are organized and taught with the needs of the students in mind. However, they do not meet all the other needs noted in Chapter 7 and this chapter and suffer from the same lack of continuity, articulation, limited time, etc. that we have seen in other discussions of the secondary structure. AP and honors classes should be only a part of an overall plan for the secondary program for gifted and talented students.

Secondary Schools and the Gifted Adolescent

10. Areas of Concern in Gifted Education

This chapter presents discussions and information regarding

- Labeling gifted learners.
- Grading and its effect on gifted learners.
- Underachieving gifted students.
- Disadvantaged gifted students.
- Culturally diverse gifted students.
- Handicapped gifted learners.
- Gifted females.
- Career education for the gifted.
- Developing leadership ability.

Children are not things to be molded, but people to be unfolded.

—ANONYMOUS

The purpose of this chapter is to discuss and disseminate information on several areas within gifted education that have presented special problems. This chapter presents some suggestions for solutions and reports from programs that have been successful in remedying similar situations in their settings. This information should lead to a clearer understanding of the nature of the problems. Mostly, in confronting issues that have not been successfully handled, we raise questions that only show our awareness that the problems exist. However, these can also be helpful, for as soon as we become aware of a problem, as soon as we can state a question clearly, we have begun the process that will lead us to its solution.

Here, then, is a discussion of concerns with labeling and grading gifted learners; underachieving, disadvantaged, culturally diverse, and handicapped gifted students; gifted females; career education for the gifted; and leadership ability of the gifted.

You are sitting outside the principal's office waiting for the time of a previously arranged meeting to discuss the gifted program at her school. You begin to be aware of voices rising in volume inside. As the door opens, you hear clearly an angry, almost threatening statement, "Well, just what do you intend to do about it? You told me he was gifted!" The principal quietly comments, notices you, smiles, and finishes the conversation with the woman; still a little annoyed, the woman leaves. After joining the principal in her office, you learn that several weeks before, the woman's child had been identified for the gifted program. The parent had always wanted to be musician and now felt that, if the child were gifted, he could become an accomplished violinist in no time. After 3 weeks, with the child totally uninterested in violin, the parent became very frustrated and when, finally, the violin teacher informed her that it would be best to stop the lessons, the parent came to the principal demanding that something be done.

LABELING GIFTED LEARNERS

Labeling students results in a change in parent and teacher expectations, as well as in the self-concept of the child. Often calls come to California State University, Los Angeles (CSULA) from parents who have just received a note from school that their child has been identified as gifted. The comment usually is "He (or she) was such a nice child. What do I do now?" Sometimes parents feel suddenly inadequate to guide their child's development once they know their child is "gifted." Sometimes the label results in very unreal expectations.

In high schools, labeling a student as gifted can result in placement in every high track class, whether the student is advanced in that particular discipline or not.

An interesting, although frustrating, experience occurred at CSULA when we began a General Honors Program for students in their first 2 years who had shown a great deal of academic potential in high school. Immediately some professors began shifting their course presentation and requirements leaving out the basic information and requiring synthesis of graduate-level work. Those who did became very disappointed and angry at the students; they complained loudly against the program, all because of their expectations of "honors" students. Talking with them about student need or potential ability made no impression.

Labels create expectations. When using labels such as *gifted* or *honors,* we must be very clear to state the precise meaning of the term, what it is and what it is not. Parents deserve more than an announcement of a new label for their child. We should arrange parent meetings to explain and answer questions regarding the concept of giftedness and its development at home and at school. We should communicate the meaning of giftedness and describe how the school experience will be different for the child after identification. Sending out additional information outlining ways the home can be involved in the further growth of the student would help.

The gifted student also needs to know what is meant by the label *gifted.* In Chapter 1 there is information that all gifted children should be aware of, understand, and be allowed to investigate. The lesson on understanding giftedness at the end of Chapter 1 should be an important part of every gifted program. This course structure has been used for children from early elementary through high school and is always one of their favorite topics.

Guskin, Zimmerman, Okolo, and Peng (1986) from a questionnaire survey of over 300 gifted students between the ages of 9 to 15 found the following attitudes toward giftedness expressed:

> The findings suggest that these students, who are above average to superior in abilities or talent but not necessarily outstanding, have highly favorable views of themselves and of academically gifted and artistically talented students more generally. They believe that giftedness can be attained by hard work and that gifted and talented students are not very different from others; they perceive others as treating them either no differently than others or more favorably. Only a minority report negative reactions from peers. (p. 64)

In regard to the impact of labeling, several researchers have begun to look at the effect of the identification of one family member on the rest of the family. Cornell (1983) reports that the label generally is received by the family as positive with the child given more status. The question was raised, however, that one effect of the labeling may be disruption, as siblings of gifted learners were reported to be less well adjusted both emotionally and socially than their counterparts in families without identified gifted siblings. Colangelo and Bower (1987) also believe that parents need to be concerned, for their review of the literature on the effects of identifying one family member as gifted shows a trend toward adjustment problems for the nongifted siblings. Their study, however, indicates that over the long term such effects may not remain so negative. Instead it seems to be the gifted student that perceives the negative effects on the family, real or imagined. While students so labeled enjoyed participating in the gifted program, they felt that neither their siblings nor the family as a whole had a positive attitude toward their label. Colangelo and Bower suggest that attention be given to youngsters at the time they are labeled to prevent disruption within the family or even perceived disruption.

After an extensive review of the literature in the area of labeling and its impact on the gifted, Robinson (1986) comments on the complexity of the issues stating, "We desperately need multivariate studies which investigate gifted children, their school mates, teachers, siblings, and parents simultaneously" (p. 12). Some of her recommendations for research include needs for

- Longitudinal or cross-sectional labeling studies to investigate the effects over time
- Self-concept studies to investigate the effects of labeling on gifted children and their peers
- Studies to investigate how teachers form their expectations of gifted children
- Labeling studies to simultaneously investigate the effects of labeling on gifted children, their school mates, siblings, parents, and teachers.

When a school establishes a program for gifted learners, it should include inservice training for the entire faculty and staff regarding the meaning of giftedness and the importance of the new program. For the child's welfare and the success of the program, the school must work as a unit, and all of the personnel must see how the program will fit within the goals and structure of the school. Without such information, misunderstandings, hostility, and unnecessary obstructionism will be focused on the program, the responsible teacher, and the gifted child. As we saw earlier, teachers, administrators, and counselors often have very negative attitudes toward gifted students in most schools. Yet, by planning a program around the students' needs and purposefully communicating information on the program and giftedness in general, we can influence these attitudes to become favorable, even supportive.

If we label children *gifted* to improve their educational experience, then we have an obligation to keep the negative aspects of labeling from becoming the major effect.

You attend a commencement program at a local high school. The senior class valedictorian, a lovely young woman, gives a pleasant, but not very insightful address. As the scholarships from local service organizations are announced, you notice that the students you know well from the Honors and Advanced Placement classes receive only a few awards. After the ceremony, you inquire of one of the students about the identity of the valedictorian, someone you had not known before. "Oh, she's a home economics major," you are told. "Her grade point average was higher than any of ours because we took all those accelerated classes." To your dismay, you discover this is also the reason the gifted students did not receive more of the service club special awards and scholarship money.

GRADING GIFTED LEARNERS

To understand the problems in grading encountered by gifted students, we must first understand the problems inherent in the practice of grading itself. The picture of grading began as our society moved toward the goal of mass education. When it became impossible for school personnel to know each student and that student's ability, a system was devised to give a symbol, the grade, for each student's achievement. Individual ability disappeared into a more manageable, numerically manipulable representation of academic ability. Grades have been an integral part of schooling, indeed the major part, for more than half a century. Now it is difficult to conceive of schools functioning without them. Grading does not, however, contribute to the learning process and in many ways inhibits and impedes learning. Whatever reasons are given for continuing to use grading, it must be recognized as a force external to the student. These reasons are given for using grades (not evaluations, but grades):

1 They provide a convenient communication of the student's academic progress to parents, administrators, other teachers, and the student.
2 They provide motivation for performance.
3 They help the school gain the cooperation of the parents in pursuing educational goals.
4 They establish an overall academic pattern of the student for other teachers, counselors, and administrators.
5 They establish data for educational research.

Grades Have No Inherent Stable Meaning and Are Low in Reliability

Grades are usually based on tests, observations, and performance as rated by the teacher. Tests are almost always subjectively constructed by the teacher, even when they are given and scored in an objective manner. Few teachers take the time needed or have learned the skills necessary to construct valid tests. Although observations made over time provide far more data than test scores, many teachers have not developed adequate observational skills; the observations they make are partly influenced by such things as their personal feelings about the student and the student's behavior, appearance, status, previous academic record, label, and so on (LaBenne & Greene, 1969; Reichstein & Pipkin, 1968; Rothney, 1955).

Teachers differ significantly in their interpretations of grades and in the standards they use. Even the philosophy of grading varies from teacher to teacher: Some believe grades should show student effort; others grade on how much success a student has had in meeting a goal set by the teacher and student in consultation; still others grade against an outside goal set up for the entire class or grade level. Many teachers grade according to a distribution dictated by the statistical representation of a normal population ("grading on the curve"). Although statisticians will quickly point out that the size of most classes makes the use of the curve technique totally inappropriate, it is, nevertheless, quite commonly used, especially in secondary and higher educational systems. Even with adaptations, this method of grading can be very unfair to the students and result in arbitrary and capricious grades (LaBenne & Greene, 1969; Pressey, 1925).

Researchers pointed out this variation in interpretation and its effect on grading in a number of studies where teachers from different classes, in some cases from different schools, were asked to grade the same papers. The range of grades on a single paper was extreme. Some more defensive teachers blamed the results on the material used, and they believed that the outcome would be different if papers and examinations from the more precise disciplines of math and science were used. If anything, the range in grades was even greater in the math and science studies. Even when graders have received intensive training to ensure reliability, they disagree significantly. Such things as fatigue, personal values, neatness, organization, and showing or not showing calculations all influence grading. Over a 2-month period, teachers have been found to be inconsistent in re-marking the same paper. And so it seems that variability in marks is not a function of the subject, but rather of the grader. While looking at what grades mean, we should mention that some teachers even use testing and test grades for punishment, e.g., the "pop quiz" to punish those who might not have studied (Dexter, 1935; Edwards, 1956; Rosenthal & Jacobsen, 1969; Starch, 1913; Starch & Elliott, 1912; Temple University, 1968; Tiegs, 1952).

Grades Do Not Predict Success in Careers, in Living, or in Level of Ability

Numerous studies continue to show little or no correlation between grades received in high school or college and future success in the world of work. There is only moderate correlation between test scores and grades with long-range academic performance and none with postacademic performance. Even in professions highly dependent on skills (e.g., engineering, teaching, physics) there is little relationship between grades and later success. The type of schools attended, the number of years of education, and the people studied under and with all seem to have more correlation with success. The only predictive ability grades seem to have is on the basis of entry screening, where the grade point average (GPA) is used for hiring, placement, or further study; but beyond this use as a screen, little correlation with job performance has been found. It has been pointed out that the GPA is an average or mean figure that flattens any high levels of achievement, leaving outstanding abilities hidden in some cases (Chansky, 1964; Drews, 1972; Hoyt, 1965; Lavin, 1965; Martin & Pacheres, 1962; Pallett, 1965; Wright, 1965).

For Most Students, Grades Do Not Motivate Learning

For a few successful students, grades provide the external motivation toward greater effort and achievement. A student who has experienced success repeatedly may be moved to perform for grades. Even with these students, we run the risk of lessening their intrinsic motivation and creating a reward situation that makes learning only a means, not a fulfilling or exciting pursuit in its own right. For less successful students, grades serve only to demean and debilitate their self-concept further. The research shows that downgraded students continue to fail.

Perrone and Male (1981) comment from their experience in interviews with high-achieving students that they "frequently dislike doing assignments and perceive a good grade not as recognition for what was produced but rather as payment for having endured such a painful or dull experience. Good grades may in fact lead good students to resent formal learning, while poor grades combined with a dislike of the learning task may lead poor achievers to abhor formal learning" (pp. 69–70). Both those who are failing and others whose performance is mediocre will sometimes resort to failure-avoiding strategies such as false effort, academic cheating, or acting out in class to gain peer approval (Covington & Beary, 1976).

Intellectual ability may not be the determiner for the categorization of students that grading creates. Under the threat of grades, bright students balk at venturing into the unknown or trying any area in which they are not sure they will succeed. Boredom, irrelevant assignments, repetition, meaningless or unrealistic subject matter, and lack of opportunity to build skills all contribute to low grades. Grades have been shown to be poor indicators of student learning. Short-term memorization, cheating, and other coping strategies result directly from grading practices; learning does not (Bowers, 1964; Chansky, 1962; Fala, 1968; Knowlton & Hamerlyneck, 1967; LaBenne & Greene, 1969). Researchers (Bidwell, 1973; Covington & Beary, 1976) have found that the excessive reliance on extrinsic rewards, the atmosphere of continual evaluation, and the fact that standards for success or failure are set by someone rather than the student result in a breakdown in commitment and in self-regulated learning. When performance is exchanged for grades, many high achievers learn shortcuts to achievement rewards and learn to regard out-of-class learning as unrewarding (Doyle, 1978). Maehr and Stallings (1972) provide evidence that continuing motivation may be directly affected by the nature of evaluation procedures. They found that external evaluation, even though used to maintain or increase performance in the classroom, does so at the expense of negative effects on continued motivation.

Evaluation Without Grades Is Facilitating to the Learning Process

Allowing students the knowledge of their strengths and weaknesses while giving them support and opportunities to develop their skills is important to learning. Providing an environment where mistakes are valued as learning experiences promotes exploration and increases areas of knowledge. Reducing anxiety promotes long-term retention and higher quantities of knowledge gained. Evaluation, a continuous process, can use many sources for data collection. In evaluating, the teacher is the facilitator who helps the students discover their strengths and weaknesses and their interests and abilities, and who guides their growth toward greater fulfillment of their potential.

> The question is not how many of the "right" things the student remembered, what the student did to the subject, or how well he compared with others. It is rather how well did the student do in the things the teacher and student agreed were important, what the subject did to the student, and how he compared to his own goals and objectives. (LaBenne & Greene, 1969, p. 87)

Gifted students have special problems with grading practices. When placed in homogeneously grouped classes, they earned significantly lower grades than when placed in heterogeneously grouped classes, although there were no differences between the groups on standardized achievement tests. These grades become a part of their permanent record, with notations about honors classes or special sections seldom made (Chansky, 1964; Hausdorff & Farr, 1965).

Gifted students in pullout classes often encounter grading practices that penalize them for missing class sessions while they attend their special class. One junior high student related that his math teacher not only held him responsible for material covered during the classes he missed, although he was working on second-year algebra in his gifted class, but would explain assignments for the week and how he wanted them done while the student was out of the room. When he returned and asked for the information, the teacher said, "You're gifted. Figure it out." One of the reasons for the criticism by gifted students and their parents of special classes and honor programs is the inequitable grading.

As evidenced in our vignette, students in high schools find scholarships, honors at graduation, and even membership in honor societies based on their GPA. I have, on several occasions, noted the frustration of gifted students passed over for special awards because of their attendance in the honors classes. In an attempt to correct the situation, some schools have adopted a grading policy that requires accelerated classes to give all students A's, or in some cases A's and B's. This becomes threatening to some teachers; and those who pride themselves in being "tough" will likely circumvent the rule by unreasonable assignments or pressure on students to transfer from their classes. It is important that accelerated classes be taught only by teachers who do not feel threatened by bright students.

Parents have often been the cause of schools keeping or reverting to grading practices. In many schools, we find teachers and administrators pleased by the conference method of evaluating. Although it is often more work, many teachers feel it more clearly reflects the student's achievements and is far more diagnostic in nature. However, they complain that the parents insist on knowing how their children compare to other children, rather than what their strengths and weaknesses are; what grade they received, rather than in what areas they should be guided.

In a survey taken of parents and teachers by the California Association for the Gifted, the following questions produced some interesting answers:

1 What grading practices are used in honors classes in your district or your school?

In one district program no grades were given; 70% used a normal curve or traditional grading with several parents complaining that grades are used as motivators and require more work to obtain than the same grade in a regular class; and 30% make special provisions such as narrative reporting with grades, counseling during day-to-day evaluation, and detailed reporting of data from projects used for grades.

2 Do you feel that grading practices are a major consideration in whether students enroll in these classes?

More than half of the teachers and parents answering believed this to be a factor.

3 If you feel grading practices penalize gifted students or discourage involvement in honors classes, what provisions are being made to remedy the situation?

In half the cases it was reported that either the local parent group or the individual parent recommended a change to the local School Board, with no results. Others had made no attempt to change the policy.

4 What would you recommend be done locally or statewide to alter grading procedures?

Some suggestions offered were self-evaluation, grading on an individualized basis, conferencing, no grades in honors classes, weighted grades for honors classes, inservicing for parents and teachers on grading practices and policies, use of more comments, and special notation of honors courses on the transcript.

Grades are quickly read, easy-to-manipulate symbols. In our ever growing school system, they provide a quick way to categorize and group children. However, grades are also unfair, misleading, meaningless in most cases, and damaging to the self-concept of both the bright and the less bright child. They create pressures and anxieties for both the teacher and the students. They neither motivate nor contribute to learning. They communicate information on a par with chance estimates; at best, what they say is neither explicit nor constructive. But for many parents and teachers alike, grades are the most important part of the school's responsibility.

Syphers (1972) tells of a teacher who wanted a different use to be made of the students' work and devised a way for students to do their own diagnoses. She displayed a checklist of common weaknesses and had the students organize and file sets of their papers. At regularly designated times, the students examined their papers to discover which mistakes they repeatedly made and why (due to carelessness, haste, lack of skill, misreading directions, etc.). She found that self-diagnosis created involvement on the part of the students in their own improvement and did not impose the stifling effects of grading. It also saved her a great deal of time. Even when you must ultimately record a grade, self-evaluation can be an important part of the process. It is possible to evaluate constructively and, if learning is our goal, the effort is really worth it.

I would like you to meet Rich. Rich attends a large integrated high school where the majority of students come from middle-class families. The school is in the suburbs of a large city. He is athletic, good looking, and always well dressed and well groomed. His family has fairly traditional values and aspirations of achievement for their children. Rich, the third of five children, has an older brother and sister who were both high academic achievers. His father was a grade school dropout, but has worked his way from a dock loader to an office job with the firm. His mother was a high school graduate, and her family is from a decidedly higher social stratum than her husband's.

Although Rich has been identified as a gifted learner, he does not belong to the group of school leaders and achievers who determine school activities. Instead, he has chosen a peer group of underachievers like himself among whom he is considered a leader.

Rich is known to be very good at sports and is probably one of the best tennis players in his school, although he refuses to try out for the school tennis team.

Rich has been placed in advanced classes, although he maintains about a C average. His teachers often comment that he is not living up to his capability. Part of the reason for his low grades is his habit of putting off all assignments to the last minute and then doing only enough to get by. He is a good reader, has an exceptional vocabulary, and reads extensively in books unrelated to his school subjects. When Rich "tunes in" to a class, rarely, he can pull an A without any problem. But that is only when he gets excited about the class or the subject, as when he got into government last year and became so involved with politics, political systems, and strategies that he spent hours before and after school questioning the teacher about everything he knew. He ended up being picked to attend a model government conference in the state capital last summer, but now, with his new classes, he has "tuned out" again.

Although Rich is outgoing and open with his peers, he is extremely nervous and uncomfortable around authority figures, such as teachers. He lacks confidence in himself and is not very self-accepting. Once he was allowed to contract cooperatively with his teacher for a project in which he felt he would be interested. He set unrealistically high standards for himself, even though the teacher insisted that she would settle for far less. He procrastinated for weeks and then gave up the entire project saying, "If I can't do a good job on something, I just won't do it."

In trying to understand Rich and help him with his underachieving pattern, one of his teachers met with Rich and his family several times in his home. Although his father expressed the desire for Rich to attend college, he seemed to have a very negative attitude toward education. His father was very insistent on his son's strict obedience to the rules, seeing each act of compliance as a minor victory for himself and a defeat for his son. There was an obvious emotional gap between the father and son. Rich's father seemed to express only two attitudes toward him, indifference or hostility. He seemed totally incapable of responding to any of Rich's achievements, no matter how excellent. The teacher's effort to discuss the accomplishments Rich had made in the government class were met with stony silence. It seemed as if there were actually a competition between the two, wherein the father hid his fear of losing behind demands for perfection and a refusal to recognize perfection should his son approach it. Thus, for Rich to attempt any new task meant risking almost certain reaffirmation of his inabilities, his self-believed worthlessness, and that would be even more traumatic should his efforts actually produce less than average grades or results. To fail became the one thing Rich could not allow. To quote Rich, "If I can't do a good job on something, I just won't do it."

UNDERACHIEVING GIFTED STUDENTS

Underachievement in gifted children is one of the most baffling, most frustrating problems a parent or teacher can face. You can see the child's possibilities, occasionally you're given a glimpse of the brilliance, but then it's gone, replaced by a wall of apathy or seeming unconcern. But all of this may be just a facade, for the underachiever may be even more frustrated than we are.

At least two types of underachievers have been designated. Those who underachieve only on occasion, as when a particularly difficult home problem erupts or a clash occurs with one particular teacher, are referred to as *situational underachievers.* They generally cause little real concern beyond getting help with the immediate problem.

Then there is the *chronic underachiever,* whose pattern recurs again and again, presenting a problem particularly resistant to remediation. In discussing this type of underachiever, keep in mind that the literature cautions us to be sure the underachievement is not of organic origin, by running the proper diagnostic tests for physical problems. If these measures do not indicate causation, then there are other places to look.

Lowther (1962) suggests that the term *underachiever* should be dropped as a label, for it is an inadequate and deceptively simple explanation of a very complex process. He suggests that it might be more useful to refer to *high, average,* or *low achievers,* for we would then need no explanatory implications, nor would our concern rest on any presumed ability-achievement relationship. Thorndike (1963a) feels that there is no such thing as underachievement, because what is implied is a standard of expected achievement, and it would be more accurate to discuss this phenomenon as overprediction. In light of the complexity of the problem and what we now understand to be additional problems for the student caused by labeling, Lowther's suggestion should be kept in mind. There is, however, a growing body of data regarding the underachievement problem that we should consider.

We define here the underachieving gifted student as someone who has shown exceptional performance on a measure of intelligence and who, nevertheless, does not perform as well as expected for students of the same age on school-related tasks. To show evidence of low performance, either achievement test scores or grades assigned by teachers could be used. Pippert and Archer (1963) reported that, when identifying by only comparing IQ with grades, they found 21 underachieving students, but when comparing IQ with achievement tests, they found 19 underachievers in their population. Most important was the fact that only 2 of the 40 children were found in both comparison groups!

While this is a limited definition of *gifted underachievement,* we cannot in good conscience use the "not performing up to capability" definition when we have no measures of capacity, innate or otherwise. The measure of achievement on intelligence tests and the evidence of performance on school-related tasks should show a considerable amount of discrepancy. Underachievement becomes especially evident when you observe a student over time and find a noticeable pattern —when you see the special moments, the brilliance. To use any other criterion would create an unmanageable number of underachievers that would certainly include most of the gifted population, as they are so rarely challenged to use their ability. Whitmore (1980) reports that with this definition we may have from 15 to 50% underachievers among the gifted population, though she feels that if the scores of all gifted students on individual aptitude tests were compared with their level of performance, we might find as many as 70% underachieving.

In a larger sense, everyone of us is underachieving, as we continue to use less than one-tenth of our brain's potential. Therefore, while we surely expect more of gifted third-grade students than we do of typical third-grade students, those who do not at least perform at an average level will be designated as *underachieving.*

Characteristics of Underachievers

You've met Rich. What about other underachievers? What are they like? The traits or characteristics of underachievers have been reported in many studies, although no one student would be expected to have all or even more than a few traits from this compilation. To complicate our identification of these children further, it has been noted that such children may be aggressive and act out their frustration by seeking attention negatively or they may withdraw and quietly allow their talents to waste away (Whitmore, 1980).

Misbehavior may be a way some underachieving gifted students attempt to prove that they are not so smart. They may also use it to cope with a lack of social comfort and competence with age peers and/or inappropriate curriculum and instruction in the regular classroom. Focusing on prevention, Delisle, Whitmore, and Ambrose (1987) remind us that,

> Gifted students generally do not develop behavior problems when they are: (a) placed with a teacher who enjoys teaching gifted children and learning with them; (b) afforded frequent opportunities to learn with intellectual peers; (c) actively engaged in learning that is appropriately complex, challenging, and meaningful; and (d) provided guidance in how to understand and cope with their giftedness in society. (p. 38)

The following is a compilation of characteristics identified among underachievers (Bachtold, 1969; Combs, 1964; Gallagher, 1964; Gowan, 1957; Karnes et al., 1961; Kurtz & Swenson, 1951; Morgan, 1952; Morrow & Wilson, 1961; O'Shea, 1970; Pearlman, 1952; Perkins, 1965; Raph, Goldberg, & Passow, 1966; Roberts, 1960; Rust & Ryan, 1953; Shaw, 1964; Shaw & Black, 1960; Shaw & McCuen, 1960; Terman & Oden, 1947; Walsh, 1956; Wellington & Wellington, 1965; Whitmore, 1980):

1 A finding repeated in most studies is the low self-concept of underachievers. They are negative in their evaluations of themselves. Their feelings of inferiority may be demonstrated by distrust, indifference, lack of concern, and even hostility toward others. They believe no one likes them.
2 They often feel rejected by their family; they feel that their parents are dissatisfied with them.
3 Because of a feeling of helplessness, they may take no responsibility for their actions, externalizing conflict and problems.
4 They may show marked hostility toward adult authority figures and general distrust of adults.
5 They may have an autonomous focus, resistant to influence from teacher or parent.
6 They may feel victimized.
7 They often do not like school or their teachers and choose companions who also have negative attitudes toward school.
8 They may seem rebellious.
9 Weak motivation for academic achievement has been noted, and they may lack academic skills.
10 They tend to have poor study habits, do less homework, frequently nap when trying to study, and leave more of their work incomplete.

11 They are less intellectually adaptive.

12 They are less persistent, less assertive, and show high levels of with-drawal in classroom situations.

13 They hold lower leadership status and are less popular with their peers.

14 They are often less mature than achievers (e.g., lack self-discipline, procrastinate, show unwillingness to complete tasks deemed unpleas-ant, have high distractibility, act highly impulsively, and are unwilling to face unpleasant realities).

15 They often show poor personal adjustment and express feelings of being restricted in their actions.

16 They may not have any hobbies, interests, or activities that could occupy their spare time.

17 They are often test phobic and have poor test results.

18 They tend to have lower aspirations than achievers and do not have a clear idea of vocational goals.

19 They are not able to think of or plan future goals.

20 They tend to state their goals very late and often choose goals that are not in line with their major interests or abilities. Often the goals they adopt have been set for them.

21 In choosing a career, they show preferences for manual activities, business, sales occupations, or anything with a strong persuasive trend, over more socially concerned or professional occupations.

Causes for Underachievement

While reasons for underachievement are quite complex and must be individually assessed for each learner, some definite patterns of causation have been reported and seem to occur with great frequency.

The Personality of the Child

Whitmore (1980) has done a most thorough job of bringing together the findings that aid us in understanding the gifted underachiever. Though she admits that the research findings available at this time would indicate that the personality of underachievers as described by the listed traits is certainly strongly involved in the problem of why they underachieve, she believes that such traits are only a part of the reason. There are, Whitmore states, internal pressures that influence the behaviors we observe, such as the gifted person's need for perfectionism, supersen-sitivity, and deficiency in social skills. There are, however, also external factors that may be equally at fault in creating this problem. From outside sources may come society's pressure to isolate one who is different, even if that difference would be beneficial to the group, and the pressure of societal expectations, which intensify the problems of the perfectionism and sensitivity found within the gifted learner. To all of these we may too often add the lack of appropriate educational provisions, which include inappropriate curriculum, a counterproductive instructional style and philosophy of the teacher, and the punitive social climate created by classroom peers.

Whitmore writes of the vulnerability that these pressures, both internal and external, create for the gifted learner and how the very characteristics typical of their high level of intelligence make it easy for them to feel rejected and valueless. She reports that parents and teachers often admit that children who learn quickly and think creatively tend to make them feel uncomfortable and that the child's endless questioning and verbalization cause them to feel irritated.

There is some indication that underachievement is a different problem for girls than for boys. Shaw and McCuen (1960) investigated patterns of underachievement of gifted students in eleventh and twelfth grades. They found that male underachievers began getting lower grades than achievers in first grade; underachievement became significant by third grade and more apparent each following year. Female underachievers exceeded achievers in first through fifth grade and began their decline in sixth grade. The difference became most apparent in grade nine. For both groups, the data demonstrate that the problem of underachievement worsens each year between third and twelfth grades. Barrett (1957) found evidence of underachievement at least as early as fifth grade and found that low achievers consistently did poorly on tests of numerical and abstract reasoning. Some of my students have found that these scores are good predictors of success with disadvantaged populations.

Pierce and Bowman (1960) found that girls respond to dominant parents by achieving, while boys require freedom to achieve and are inhibited by authoritarian control. Roberts (1960) found underachieving girls to be more lacking in self-confidence, more suggestible, impulsive, and vacillating, and showing a greater external locus of control. Underachieving boys were more demanding, headstrong, rebellious, undependable, impatient, and indecisive. Bachtold (1969) found that underachieving girls in the fifth grade lacked self-confidence, were more excitable, and showed less self-control. Boys demonstrated less emotional stability, seriousness, and sensitivity.

In all the studies reported, the incidence of underachievement in males was at least twice that found in females. Whitmore (1980) reported that 90% of all referrals for placement in the Underachieving Gifted Program in Cupertino, California, were male. It has been suggested that this results from the different expectations and opportunities provided by our society for females. Some gifted students, especially adolescent girls, feel that they risk unpopularity if they reveal their high academic ability. In many high school settings, academic achievement is not valued, and conformity is the yardstick of success.

Another cause of underachievement unique to gifted learners stems from their varied and numerous interests. They may, without proper guidance, extend their interests in too many areas, engage in too many activities, and be unable to set appropriate priorities. It is possible for gifted students to get involved in so many things that they do nothing well.

The Home and/or Parents

The literature indicates that the causes for underachievement can be found in the personality of the gifted child, in the home, and/or in the interaction between the children and the parents (Bricklin & Bricklin, 1967; Daniel, 1960; Kimball, 1953; McGillivray, 1964; Morrow & Wilson, 1961; Pierce & Bowman, 1960; Raph et al., 1966; Shaw & Black, 1960; Wellington & Wellington, 1965). The families of underachievers differ in many ways from families of achieving students.

In families of high-achieving students, often

1 Parents are more interested in their children.
2 The fathers are important life influences.
3 Mothers are more responsible and independent.
4 Parents have higher educational aspirations for their children.
5 Parents are better educated.
6 Families are smaller.
7 The student is often the first born or only child.

In families of underachieving students, often

1 The student is more dependent on the mother.
2 The father is rejecting and domineering and gives little warmth or affection.
3 The relationship between father and daughter or father and son is negative or nonexistent.
4 Parents set unrealistic goals for students, and the students imagine that they are only as valuable or "good" as their accomplishments.
5 Parents allow achievement to go unrewarded.
6 The students identify less with their parents.
7 There are deep social and emotional problems in the family.
8 Parents are less active and less supportive of students.
9 The student's achievements present a threat to the parents and their adult superiority.
10 Parents are less sharing of ideas, affection, trust, or approval.
11 Parents are more restrictive and severe in their punishment.

In some cases, the entire neighborhood devalues education and has caused some researchers to observe that low-achieving, low-socioeconomic students seem to fail not because of an initial lack of motivation to learn, but because basic learning processes learned in their own communities are not contiguous with those required for academic success (Bricklin & Bricklin, 1967; E. Brown, 1971; Fine; 1967; Kimball, 1953).

Coleman et al. (1966), Gallagher (1964), and Kurtz and Swenson (1951) all found the causes for underachievement different with the disadvantaged and culturally diverse gifted student. They found that when underachievement occurs,

1 The subculture does not support academic achievement.
2 Academic activity is seen as "sissy" for boys and too aggressive for girls; the subculture supports sex role stereotypes.
3 Low aspirations for career goals center on mechanical or survival skills.
4 Educational goals arc nonexistent.

The School

One source of underachievement mentioned less frequently than the home, although still of major importance, is that of the actual school situation. Whitmore (1980) suggests the schools may be not only a principal cause, but one that is most likely to yield to remediation. By changing the unproductive patterns traditionally found in all too many classrooms, we may prevent a large amount of the underachievement that we now observe. She states,

> Regardless of the extent to which innate personality characteristics may contribute to the development of the underachiever's problems, it seems much more useful for educators to examine how the environment might contribute to the child's difficulty and thereby be modified to help eliminate the problem.
>
> The actual causes of underachievement are a mixture of the student's characteristics . . . and a social environment that does not meet the personal needs of the child. Factors of the social environment that can contribute to the development of negative attitudes and underachieving behavior include external pressures of unrealistic expectations; emphasis on conformity and convergent thinking; a lack of rewards or the existence of social penalties for creativity and initiative; rigidity and inflexibility; excessive competition and criticism; and personally unrewarding curriculum and required activities. (pp. 190–191)

Predominant in this causal cluster is the incompetent or insecure teacher. Evans (1965) has grouped the behaviors of teachers known to contribute to underachievement into the following types of teachers, who

• Must maintain superiority in the field of knowledge.
• Impose unrealistic goals and standards (the perfectionist).
• Use threats, ridicule, warnings, and ultimatums and rarely show warmth or acceptance; are cold and impersonal.
• Are too easy; do not present a challenge.
• Have predictable, routine schedules and do not present a stimulating environment.

Bricklin and Bricklin (1967) and Fine (1967) also found poor teaching to be a major cause of underachievement in gifted students.

Closely related is the problem of poor work habits so many gifted students face upon meeting academic challenges (i.e., entering universities). After many years of learning in nonstimulating environments with little academic involvement, these students are required to perform with excellence. They find they do not have the basic knowledge, the academic tools or processes, or the habits of sustained inquiry to aid them. This problem may account for some of the large number of dropouts among gifted learners. Of the top 10% in the high school graduating class, it has been estimated that at least 27% did not continue their education. Of those who did, 70% lived in communities where attitudes toward college attendance were favorable. Of the boys, 85% continued, but only 64% of the girls did so (Kimball, 1953; Wright & Jung, 1959). Cassel and Coleman (1962) reported that only 7 to 10% of the students capable of college work actually attended. Douglass (1969) estimates that, of the 7.5 million dropouts in this decade, 10% (750,000) will have IQs in the top one-fourth of the population.

Remediation/Prevention

The earlier remediation for underachievement starts, the more effective it is; however, most reports on remediation look at secondary students. The availability of counseling at that level (which has been seen as a major intervention strategy) tries to rationalize this focus. Many of the projects yield disappointments both in the amount of change effected and in the time the change remained evident. Intervention during the elementary years, involving the entire family in a group counseling mode, has had the most and longest lasting impact (Bricklin & Bricklin, 1967; Fine, 1967; Gallagher, 1975; Satir, 1972; Shaw & Black, 1960; Shaw & McCuen, 1960; Shouksmith & Taylor, 1964).

Group counseling as an intervention strategy has been reported as successful in a number of studies. Adolescent gifted students who participated in group counseling made greater gains in reducing inappropriate behavior and raising grade point averages and in standardized achievement tests than uncounseled students (Broedel, 1958). In another study, underachieving high school gifted students who participated in either individual or group counseling over a semester improved slightly in grades; the students in group counseling showed the most favorable results. A third group, after a one-time-only pep talk about bringing up their grades, fell below the performance of the noncounseled control group. Unfortunately, parents and teachers too often use this very form of intervention just as unsuccessfully (Baymur & Patterson, 1960).

Underachievers (eighth grade) improved in interpersonal relationships with peers, siblings, and parents and in acceptance of self in a group counseling situation that met twice a week for 8 weeks. No improvement was made in academic performance or self-concept (Ohlsen & Proff, 1960). However, in a longer term study, researchers obtained positive results with preadolescent underachievers and their parents: Eight of twelve were no longer underachievers in less than a year (Shouksmith & Taylor, 1964).

Other forms of counseling have also been studied. Researchers found that individual counseling improved the scholastic achievement of highly able underachieving students over noncounseled highly able underachieving students at the college level (freshmen). Effects seemed to have persisted into the next semester (Ewing & Gilbert, 1967). Perkins and Wicas (1971) reported that when counselors worked with bright underachieving ninth-grade boys alone, mothers alone, and mothers and sons simultaneously, all groups showed improvements in GPA. In a study reported by Mallison (1972), intermediate gifted underachievers attended individual counseling, human relations, or academic groups for 6 months. Groups in human relations and academic groups improved academically, but the human relations group also improved in personal and social adjustment and maintained their gains in the follow-up testing, while the academic group did not.

Shaw and Black (1960) reported the results of a study using a family counseling model that was quite successful. At the first several sessions, underachieving students met with parents of other underachieving students to enable them to express themselves openly. The parents expressed their views for half the period, the students the other half. After several sessions, the students then met with their own parents for the remainder of the program.

In addition to counseling, some studies have investigated curricular and classroom organizational changes. In a 3-year program at the high school level, value was found in grouping underachievers with other gifted students and placing them with a supportive teacher. Goldberg (1959) emphasized the importance of the teacher in the success of the project. She felt that, before any program could be implemented, an adequate educational, psychological, and social diagnosis of each underachieving student was essential. At the end of the study, Goldberg drew the following conclusions:

1 Academic underachievement appears to be a symptom of a variety of more basic personal and social problems.
2 Underachieving students who improved were able to identify with a teacher who was consistently supportive and interested in them. The teacher helped them acquire necessary skills missed earlier.
3 It was more effective to separate teaching and guidance functions (because of grading).
4 Grouping underachievers together alone is unwise, although Whitmore's data indicate that such grouping is quite productive. Grouping in regular classroom by subject is not recommended.

Karnes, McCoy, Zehrbok, Wollershein, and Clarizio (1963) similarly found that underachieving gifted pupils enrolled in homogeneously grouped gifted classes made greater gains in academics, creativity, and perceived acceptance by peers than underachieving gifted enrolled in heterogeneously grouped classes.

Purkey (1969) reported on Project Self-Discovery, a program designed to promote social and personal development among bright, underachieving students. There were 12 chapters of reading and writing exercises dealing with interpersonal relations, self-confidence, individual differences, feelings, and self-discipline. While the material was designed for use with groups or in independent study, it is believed that a group guidance format would bring about more significant differences than when used for an independent study, correspondence-style format. Another program, the Great Cities School Improvement Program, used such aids as team teaching, parents in classrooms, different media, home visitation, and workshops for teachers and parents.

The children in Whitmore's (1980) program identified the following elements of their previous classroom environments that they believed contributed significantly to the development of their underachievement:

- Lack of genuine respect for each individual
- A competitive social climate
- Inflexibility and rigidity
- Stress on external evaluation
- The failure syndrome and criticism predominating
- Adult/teacher control
- An unrewarding curriculum. (pp. 192–193)

Whitmore believes that chronic underachievement by gifted students can be prevented by educational programs that allow these students to meet their needs. She also feels that early patterns of underachievement can be reversed through special education in elementary school. In her book she gives a detailed account of how effective classrooms can be developed. The similarity of these to the responsive, integrative environments we have discussed in Chapters 7 and 8 is striking.

Better than any form of remediation is prevention; however, as we have already seen, appropriate opportunities are not always provided for the gifted. Whitmore (1986) reminds us that, "Adults have a tendency to demand that a child be disciplined to work diligently even if the task is unrewarding" (p. 67). Even when the child is willing to spend the effort, the reward may be an assignment of more work that is equally unstimulating, typically unchallenging, and largely unsatisfying. When these conditions continue and the child begins to show lack of motivation we may be able to use some of Whitmore's suggestions, keeping in mind that the sooner we interrupt the pattern, the better.

1 Clearly assess the problem and, to the extent possible, the causes. Observe the child in a variety of settings, e.g., in the home, at school, and among intellectual peers, to discover what motivates and is interesting to the child.

2 Communicate your observations with the child, hypothesizing the problem behavior and the cause as you observe it. Share your understanding of the problem using your own personal experiences, and invite the child to share his or her perceptions of the problem. Only if the child sees the situation as personally unsatisfactory or there is discomfort with present conditions will the desire for change be forthcoming. The child must desire change before the third step can occur.

3 Develop a partnership with the child and include the parent or teacher if possible. Actively seek solutions to the perceived problem by problem solving together.

Whitmore advises that it is important for the parent to develop a sense of partnership with school personnel. Wherever the problem exists it can best be solved if all members of the team are working together. "The caring adult's role is to provide encouragement, guidance, affirming support and unconditional acceptance" (p. 69).

Rimm (1986) offers similar steps for reversing underachievement, but adds a few more. In the assessment phase Rimm suggests both formal and informal methods, supplying both instruments and forms to support the process. Her next step is also communication of the assessment. Rimm, like Whitmore, contends that the remediation is improved when parents, teachers, and students work together so the assessment is reported in a conference with information shared among all parties.

At this point the next step, Changing Expectations, is involved acknowledging that, unless all concerned change their expectations and recognize the improvements, old habits will continue. Rimm supplies formats to support this phase as well. Another new step, Identification, follows and uses the process of the child imitating an adult role model to support the child's new efforts. The following step, Correction of Deficiencies, focuses on any gaps in skill development the child may have that limit achievement.

The final step involves modifications, and Rimm gives us three choices for our selection, depending on whether the child is diagnosed as dependent, dominant conforming, or dominant nonconforming. Though Rimm does not promise a panacea, she believes that this approach is well worth the effort involved and cites the successes it has had for numerous other underachieving children in her professional experience.

In 1973 Martinson warned that gifted children placed in regular classrooms may regress to the achievement level of their classmates, may develop discipline problems as a result of boredom, and/or may withdraw to their own interests. She pointed out that there was evidence that students in the highest range of intellectual ability may have the greatest difficulty with adjustment in the regular classroom.

Both Whitmore (1980) and Pirozzo (1982) support the emphasis on a nonthreatening classroom environment where these children can engage in an

---

extensive period of self-discovery. What seems to be indicated by these data is more special-class placement, especially for the gifted underachiever. It may turn out to be, as Whitmore suggests, the least restrictive environment for the gifted child.

From the projects, the investigations, and the observations of teachers and parents, come the following suggestions for those who are concerned about the gifted underachiever.

If you are a parent,

1 Provide an intellectually stimulating, curiosity-producing atmosphere in your home.
2 Establish a close, mutually respectful relationship with your child.
3 Become a role model of behavior you desire your child to have.
4 Be interested in your child's activities at home and at school.
5 Do not compare siblings; each child is unique.
6 Help your child establish effective time priorities.
7 Guide your children toward goals of their interest; do not set goals for them.
8 Make your demands and rules reasonable and mutual.
9 Show your affection, trust, and approval.
10 Support your child; get involved.

If you are a teacher or a counselor,

1 Value achievements of high-ability students.
2 Assess each student regularly, beginning in elementary school; know your students' profiles.
3 Provide opportunities for students to build their self-concept.
4 Create a learning environment: open, accepting, warm, intellectually challenging.
5 Give the underachiever an opportunity to focus on an area of ability (e.g., music, art, athletics).
6 Be available when help is needed; be sure to have conferences periodically about personal as well as academic matters.
7 Arrange group sessions with peers and with family.
8 Look for ways to meet individual needs (e.g., a place to study, tutorial help).
9 Involve parents in school activities.
10 Offer college and vocational guidance early.
11 If more than 15% of the gifted in your school are seriously underachieving, look carefully at your program.

Jerry had just moved into the neighborhood. This was the ninth move the family had made since Jerry started school 5 years ago. Jerry's father had just started another new job and the family had moved to join him, hoping that this time there would be enough money so that his mother wouldn't have to worry so much. There really wasn't much involved in moving as there weren't many things to move, a few dishes and pans, some blankets and clothes, his few books his mother had given him, his little sister's toys, and the family TV set. His father always rented furnished houses and although the furniture was far from new and there never was much of it, it never had to be moved.

The school Jerry now attends has a gifted class, and by the second week he was there, Jerry was invited to attend this special class. For the first time he found other children who were interested in a lot of the same things he liked; he could talk to them just as he talked to his mother. He had an unlimited number of books he could read, as there were shelves filled with books right in the classroom. He began work-

ing on a special project with another boy in his gifted class and began to find that he really liked his new school.

Although there was no space to study at home and the sound of the TV made what room there was difficult for any concentration, Jerry could go to his class early and stay late and often work at his friend's house. After only 6 months Jerry mastered skills far beyond his grade level and began exploring a lot of areas he had never even thought about. His teacher was really interested in his progress and shared her pleasure with his mother.

One day when Jerry was coming home he saw a rent-a-trailer in front of the house, and his father was loading their things into it. Jerry ran to find out what was happening. "We're leaving this dump. I'm going to the desert to work. A guy told me there was a lot of good jobs there. We don't have to tell no one. I don't care if we do owe rent. It'll serve that jerk right for charging us so much on this dump. Come on, Jerry, get it in gear. We'll be in the desert by morning."

DISADVANTAGED GIFTED STUDENTS

First, we must clearly delineate the population we call *disadvantaged gifted students*. The terms *disadvantaged* and *culturally diverse* have often been used interchangeably in program reports, informational articles, and research reports. This practice is very misleading. While some children who are disadvantaged are also culturally diverse, many are not. And while some culturally diverse students are disadvantaged, again, many are not. In this discussion *disadvantaged* will mean being reared by poor, lower-class parents out of the economic (instead of cultural) mainstream. This population seems characterized more by poverty than by cultural difference. In referring to *culturally diverse learners* we speak of any student (such as Rosa; see p. 486) whose rearing is more typical of a culture that differs significantly in values and attitudes from the dominant culture. These students have unique problems even when not reared in conditions of poverty.

A major problem encountered in providing for gifted students among the disadvantaged is the attitude, shared by teachers and parents alike, that giftedness could not exist in lower-class populations. Such attitudes make identification very difficult. We have seen in Chapter 3 that the nurture of intellectual ability depends more on child-rearing patterns and attitudes than on social class or financial condition. For parents living in poverty, development of such facilitating conditions is not easy, but it is certainly not impossible. Because we have become aware of a gradual decline with age in measured intelligence among lower-class students, several projects in infant development have sent teachers into lower-class homes to teach parents how to use existing materials and resources to nurture their children. Such projects have met with success and important sibling carry-over. Many more projects have brought high-risk children out of their downward cycle through preschool group intervention programs (see Chapter 3).

Left to the educational opportunities available at existing schools in lower-class areas, data show that the longer the children are in these schools, the further behind they become in achievement. Substandard performance is expected. Even if disadvantaged students begin school with relatively few problems, and their reading achievement is at grade level in the early grades, these students fall increasingly behind national reading norms. Although arithmetic achievement stays closer to national norms, these scores also fall as the student moves through the school system. Intelligence test scores go down in proportion to the time spent in school. Average drops of as much as 20 points in measured intelligence have been reported as disadvantaged students move through the grades (Coleman et al., 1966; Passow, Goldberg, & Tannenbaum, 1967; Pressman, 1969; Sexton, 1961). The fact is that, until recently, few gifted students have emerged from this population because in part no one thought to look.

Characteristics of the Disadvantaged Gifted

Our first task is to make parents, teachers, principals, and boards of education aware that the gifted can be found in lower-class homes. Then we must know how to identify them. In Chapter 6 we reviewed the problems and alternative possibilities for identifying these gifted learners. Some traits of disadvantaged gifted learners that help with their identification (Baldwin, 1973; Farrell, 1973; McMillin, 1975; Torrance, 1964b), where testing often fails, are observations of the following:

- High mathematical abilities
- Alertness, curiosity
- Independence of action
- Initiative, eagerness to do new things
- Fluency in nonverbal communication
- Imagination in thinking
- Flexibility in approach to problems
- Learning quickly through experience
- Retaining and using ideas and information well
- Showing a desire to learn in daily work

- Originality and creativity in thinking
- Responding well to visual media
- Leadership ability in peer group
- Responsible social behavior
- Varied interests
- Ability to generalize learning to other areas and to show relationships among apparently unrelated ideas
- Resourcefulness, ability to solve problems by ingenious methods
- Entrepreneurial ability, readily making money on various projects or activities
- Imaginative story telling, language rich in imagery
- Mature sense of humor
- Responsiveness to the concrete.

Once identified as gifted, these disadvantaged learners may be grouped with more advantaged gifted students. Such grouping will aid them in many ways, but only if the teacher is aware that the needs of these learners may be quite different. It is unfair to expect lower-class gifted children to be like middle- and upper-class gifted children

Some characteristics have been found to differentiate lower-class gifted students from the more advantaged students. Frierson (1965) showed that differences in attitudes and interests exist, although he found no evidence of physical or personality differences. In interests and activities, upper-status gifted differed from lower-status gifted in the quantity and quality of their reading, in their awareness of parental aspirations for college attendance, in their positive attitudes toward school, and in their lower preference for competitive team sports. However, the personality patterns and interests of upper- and lower-status gifted children were more similar than were the personality patterns and interests of lower-status gifted and average children. Frierson also found that lower-class children, placed in a special program based on their giftedness by the second grade, differed markedly in achievement, attitudes, and aspirations from other lower-class gifted children by the time they reached the upper grades.

Houston (Goodall, 1972) found that, when asked to repeat a story to another child who then repeats the story to the teacher, black lower-class children do not score as well on accuracy as do middle-class white and black children. The lower-class children did score higher than the others on embellishing the story, which, it was pointed out, would not give them high scores on intelligence tests.

Family Patterns

Rohrer and Edmonson (1960) suggest some important differences in family structures and values between lower- and middle-class families that put the learner at a disadvantage. They have identified four major family patterns: Middle Class, Matriarchy, Gang, and Nuclear.

Middle-Class families hold values that view education as an important aspect of life. When lower-class families identify with this group and become upwardly mobile, these values take precedence over earlier religious, family, or political affiliations. However, if the pattern of Matriarchy, mother and daughter aligned against the world, is adhered to, there is a strong female dependency and male alienation that is not conducive to intellectual growth or independent thinking. The equivalent male pattern, the Gang, fosters aggressive independence, group secrecy and loyalty, and exaggerated masculinity. As educational achievement is seen by the gang as a feminine characteristic, alignment with such a pattern inhibits intellectual development. The Nuclear family, as defined in the study, does develop respect for parenthood, reliable employment, and family support. However, it is also characterized by suspicion and distrust of the outside world. Education is favored so long as it supports the unity of the family. If, as often is the case in higher education, discovery of different ideas and values brings the possibility of a different world view to the student, education may then be rejected. Any of these last three patterns would be antithetical to gifted development.

In a project conducted in the Los Angeles city schools to differentiate disadvantaged gifted learners from the regularly identified gifted learners (Arnold, 1974), the following classroom behaviors were noted among separate-criteria (disadvantaged) gifted. These students (1) exhibit greater dependence on the teacher for direction, which reduces their ability for self-directed activity; (2) reason in a more step-by-step process; and (3) appear to have more patience in dealing with tasks not easily resolved. The study also noted that parental involvement appeared to decrease from highly gifted, to regularly gifted, to special-criteria gifted.

Learning Differences

Sisk (1973) states that the most serious deficiencies for this type of child are in cognitive functioning (e.g., the ability to observe and state sequences of events, to perceive cause and effect relationships, and to categorize); language skills (e.g., limited vocabularies and nonstandard grammar); and reading. She states, "The variations in responses are due in part to the individual's motivation and in part to the availability of adequate adult mediators who can help the child develop concepts with which to interpret his environment" (p. 5). These deficits may result in classroom behavior we seldom associate with gifted students: negative attitudes toward school, toward teachers, and toward their own achievement; inability to focus on long-term goals; and the use of violence in resolving problems. Baldwin (1973) notes that disadvantaged gifted students have seldom been exposed to books and magazines at home and have been "starved for verbal encounters" (p. 11). She also notes that, as with most underachievers, disadvantaged gifted students exhibit an external locus of control.

Riessman (1962) reports differences in learning style, which include spatial —not temporal; physical—not aural; content centered—not form centered; and inductive—not deductive. You can begin to see how difficult it would be to plan for only characteristically gifted children when disadvantaged children are also in the program.

Intervention

As we have seen in Chapter 3, intellectual development is an important part of infant and early childhood education. For those children who could begin this actualization process only to have it limited or interrupted, intervention should occur as early as possible. However, most programs for the gifted, not to mention the disadvantaged gifted, do not begin until the middle elementary grades. There are a number of programs aimed at improving language skills in the disadvantaged population that would have a direct bearing on the giftedness of the student (e.g., McConnell, Horton, and Smith, 1969, whose preschool program for the disadvantaged showed significant gains; Deutsch and Deutsch, 1968; and Schaefer and Aaronson, 1972). Other experimental projects, classes, and schools have focused on changing the language-deficit problem, as well as other gaps in the education of the disadvantaged gifted. They come and go, usually not because of lack of success, but for lack of funding.

The literature contains many suggestions to consider when planning and implementing services for the disadvantaged gifted. Renzulli (1973c) believes that there are two major factors to consider, the characteristics of the teacher and the relevancy of the curriculum. Teachers must enjoy working with these children and experience real personal satisfaction with their achievements and growth for the program to be successful. The curriculum must be involved with the immediate lives of the students. Renzulli defines relevant curriculum as "a set of experiences which deal with topics and issues that youngsters would talk about if given a free choice" (p. 443). When structured properly, these issues can be used to teach all the process skills and content information, while eliciting far more motivation and interest. Douglass (1969) points to four essential elements to include:

- Greater flexibility in organization of the educational system, allowing for small learning groups and individualized instruction
- An earlier start toward intervention in the limitations to intellectual development and socialization
- Early apprenticeship so that lower-class children can experience types of work other than the low paid, hard, demeaning work often engaged in by their parents
- A more open, free, public, and universal educational system.

Edmonds (1980) believes that schools can be developed to overcome the limitations of impoverished family environments. He and his Harvard colleagues have identified five elements as the key to urban, low-socioeconomic-area school success. A school's leadership, its instructional emphasis and overall climate, how teachers imply what they expect, and how administrators use standardized testing results all affect student achievement. After conducting a needs assessment of the school, the Edmonds project provided help to bring it into positive alignment with the five elements for success. Through this procedure he improved the quality of many inner-city New York schools.

In addition to her work in identifying the culturally diverse gifted learner (Baldwin, 1980), Baldwin (1975) outlines programs and strategies necessary for the success of disadvantaged gifted learners. While many ideas are the same as those one would use to instruct advantaged gifted learners, a larger emphasis is given to the use of the community and models from the community as learning guides, to organized experience programs, and to creative teaching strategies. Unusual talents must be encouraged as the minds of these special learners are encouraged to expand.

Torrance (1977) has suggested the following approaches to programs for the gifted, which would make them more viable in meeting the needs of the disadvantaged gifted:

1 The curriculum should be designed to include the particular strengths of these students.
2 Unreasonable economic demands should be avoided.
3 Opportunities to help this group of children cope with and grow out of feelings of alienation must be provided.
4 Resources for study and information gathering must be made accessible.
5 The classroom should be organized to allow a lot of small group and team learning.
6 Mentors or sponsors should be developed.

By including the strengths and special needs of the disadvantaged in our curricular planning we can assure these children a better chance to grow with their giftedness.

Rosa is a lovely, dark haired girl who has lived with her Mexican-American family in the *barrio* all of her life. Her parents were raised in Mexico and came to Southern California to find a higher standard of living. They hold the traditional values of their culture and have found adapting to American values difficult. Throughout her high school career, Rosa has noticeably grown into a first rate student—curious, intelligent, constantly pursuing ideas and problems to ferret out original and creative solutions. She totally enjoys her scholastic ability. Rosa is quiet, poised, and self-confident. Her family provides her with strength and love and values her as a woman of their culture.

At the beginning of her senior year, the

gifted coordinator suggested that she apply for scholarships to major universities throughout the country. She wrote to Stanford, Harvard, Yale, UC at Berkeley, and Columbia. When she received her scholarship offer from Stanford, everyone at school was excited. Then, when Harvard, Yale, and Berkeley also offered excellent scholarships, the entire faculty and all her friends were ecstatic. They all were anxious to see which one she would choose. What a fantastic opportunity! But then the gifted coordinator got the word. Rosa's father refused to allow her to go to college, any college. It was not right for women to be away from home unless they were married, and her place was with her family. Besides, what did she need a college degree for? She must start her family soon. Women had no business running around getting ideas put in their heads. The gifted coordinator talked to Rosa's father, and the principal and the family priest talked to him, but to no avail.

Then one day in May, Rosa came to school very disturbed and asked to see the gifted coordinator and one of her favorite teachers. As they sat down together, Rosa quietly, almost in whispers, with sadness brimming in her eyes and spilling softly down her cheeks, said that her father had issued an ultimatum. If she persisted in her foolishness of wanting to go to college, she would no longer be considered his daughter. She would have to move out of the house and never come back. Her beloved family would no longer claim her. He would forbid her mother, her brothers and sisters, even her grandmother and other relatives, to contact her or to receive her ever again. As far as the family would be concerned, she would not exist.

Rosa now sat looking very small as she lowered her head, and the momentary pause gave the others a chance to take in the finality and enormity of what she had said. Before anyone else could speak, she said, "I will leave this weekend." Now everyone spoke at once. Graduation was still a month away, the scholarships would not begin for 3 months after that. Where would she go; how would she live? Rosa sat looking very lost. Although she had thought of the questions herself, she had not worked out any answers. She only knew she had to be free to make her own choice. She had to decide for herself what her life was to be. To do that, she must leave home this weekend. The teacher, her own daughter in her mind, spoke first. "You will come live with me until you decide." And so it was that Rosa, who loved her family and loved the marvelous ability of her mind, was forced to give up one to have the other. Whether her father could be persuaded or time might change his resolve was known only to the future. For now, her loss was almost too great to bear.

CULTURALLY DIVERSE GIFTED LEARNERS

Our educational system often penalizes children who are raised with significantly different values and attitudes from those found in the dominant culture. Subcultures can create conditions for their members that can be as limiting as those discussed for the disadvantaged. If you add to cultural differences circumstances of poverty, the growing child risks alienation and very limited intellectual development. For example, it has been shown that unfavorable socialization experiences, unequal school opportunities, and obvious occupational discrimination all work together to lower the motivation and achievement of black children, especially boys, no matter how gifted they are. They attend school less regularly, they drop out in greater numbers, and their talents are more often lost (Bloom, Davis, & Hess, 1965; Dreger & Miller, 1960; Pettigrew, 1964).

However, in some subcultures, the reverse is true. Where the subculture's values and attitudes approximate those of the dominant culture, development is often facilitated. Cultural group support may enable the child to reach outstanding achievement.

Giftedness at the highest level can be found in every subcultural, racial, or ethnic group. However, the incidence of giftedness does differ from group to group. This difference results from differing values, attitudes, and opportunities. Groups also differ on other measures: those of cooperation, of production of certain kinds of talent, of spiritual leadership, and so on. What is valued in the culture is produced by the culture. In some instances the overlay of the problems of poverty makes it difficult to assess potential achievement in certain subcultures.

In subcultures that give the school the total responsibility for the education of their children and for the provision of models of adult achievement, painful disappointments cannot be avoided. The problems, and therefore the solutions, seem to lie partly with the family and its representation of the subculture, partly with the dominant society expressed through the people of the mainstream culture, and partly with the school as a translator of the dominant society's values and attitudes.

The United States has taken some pride, in the past, in being a "melting pot" for all nationalities and ethnic and racial groups, and as a haven for all religions. Our laws become more and more protective of rights to ensure the equality of diverse groups. And yet the attitudes of the people within the groups are not always so open or so free. Often people are thought of as inferior, when actually they are only different. We have a long way to go to reach our goal of valuing each individual for his or her uniqueness. And yet the dream is there, and that, after all, is a very important part.

Cultural Differences in Attitudes and Skills

What responsibilities to that dream do the families within the subcultures have? The attitudes and skills for thinking and learning are established in the family, a base that forms the future of the children. The information is generalized and oversimplified regarding the contributions various subcultures make to the educational development of their children; yet it can show us trends that may help us as parents and teachers to be more aware of the preparation we make for these children. The data in Table 10.1 came from studies of culturally diverse gifted children and may not be applicable to those who, in addition to their cultural difference, must deal with the limitations of poverty.

Every subculture and ethnic group instills both advantages and limiting attitudes in their children before they enter the school situation. The same can be said for every family from every area of the country, regardless of the culture. Families who want to help their children become all they can be need to be aware of any limiting practices in order to reduce them as much as possible. There is no reason to weaken the ties the child has with the culture. With awareness of what facilitates and what inhibits growth, families can find a way to strengthen the positive attitudes and abilities.

Strengths in some cultures could improve the functioning of others. For example, the achievement orientation of the Jewish culture combined with the cooperative spirit of the Mexican-American culture would enrich both groups. The possibilities are fantastic when we let go of the view of superior or inferior groups and notice that we are all just different.

Culturally diverse gifted children differ in many respects, but they do hold certain mental traits in common (Gallagher & Kinney, 1974):

- The ability to manipulate some symbol system held valuable in the subculture meaningfully
- The ability to think logically, given appropriate data
- The ability to use stored knowledge to solve problems
- The ability to reason by analogy
- The ability to extend or extrapolate knowledge to new situations or unique applications.

In a well-documented discussion of culturally related differences in cognitive styles, De Leon (1983) presents a thoughtful rationale for the lack of success Mexican-American students have with current identification procedures resulting in their underrepresentation in gifted programs. Through a review of the literature De Leon makes a number of interesting observations. It seems clear that certain ethnic groups have cognitive styles that are distinct from those of other groups. These style preferences result from socialization practices, culture, and the ecology of the group's environment. The cognitive style from which children operate affects their view of themselves in relationship to others and their sense of being a separate self (which is associated with field independence) or not being separate (which is associated with field dependence). A sense of separateness or field independence results in reduced reliance on external sources of guidance and an ability to break up an organized perceptual field, whereas field dependence results in heavy reliance on external guidance, acceptance of the prevailing field, and inability to separate an item from its context.

Mexican-American children have consistently been shown to be more field dependent than Anglo children, and family socialization practices that do not encourage autonomy are seen as the main reason (De Leon, 1983). In other words, the traditional Mexican culture, attitudes, and values related to family cohesiveness have been associated with the lack of development of a separate sense of identity.

Table 10.1 *Facilitating and Limiting Culturally Supported Attitudes and Abilities*

Subculture or Ethnic Group	Facilitating Culturally Supported Attitudes and Abilities Children Often Bring to the Learning Situation	Limiting Culturally Supported Attitudes and Abilities Children Often Bring to the Learning Situation
Japanese, Chinese, and other Asians (Coleman et al., 1966; Kitano, 1975; Klineberg, 1944)	Ability to listen, to follow directions Attitudes favoring education Respect for teachers and others Attitude toward discipline as guidance Serious and caring attitude toward their own development Tend to test at, or above, the norm on all tests of intelligence High achievement motivation Family unity, very supportive of child's achievement	Attitudes unfavorable to participation in discussion groups Little experience with independent thinking Strong valuing of conformity, which inhibits creative activity or divergent thinking Quiet manner, which may foster unrealistic expectations and inappropriate assessments Attitude of perfectionism, making using mistakes as learning experiences quite difficult Sex role differentiation —male more desirable and dominant sex Critical self-concept
Jewish (Adler, 1964; Barbe, 1953; Brill, 1956; Garrett, 1929; Hollingworth, 1942; Stodtbeck, 1958; Sumption, 1941; Terman & Oden, 1947; Witty, 1930)	Tendency to test high on all tests of intelligence, often registering very high scores Attitudes favoring education, personal improvement Very high achievement orientation Experience with independent thinking, abstract thinking, and problem solving Confidence, good self-concept Exposure to many ideas and content areas Highly verbal Belief that the world is orderly and can be rationally controlled Expectation that each child will leave home and achieve own contributing unit	Often overly competitive Perfectionist attitude that causes tension and frustration in learning new material Pressure to achieve from family sometimes excessive, especially with males

	Strengths	Problems
	Preference for individual rather than family credit for achievement Trend toward equality in family structure	Limited experience with varied or extended language patterns Sex role stereotyping—sexes have defined roles, twice as many girls are identified gifted as boys, more black women employed than men Lower-class blacks have problems that are typical of disadvantaged populations. Such problems are not a result of cultural values.
Black (Barbe, 1953; Gallagher, 1975; Garrett, 1947; Jenkins, 1950; Klineberg, 1944; Lawrie, 1969; Luckey, 1925; Miles, 1954)	Experience with independent action Self-sufficiency Imagination and humor Physical action oriented Middle-class blacks accept as valid the values and attitudes of dominant society's middle class.	
Mexican-American (Bernal, 1973; Aragon & Marquez, 1975)	Attitudes of cooperation Attitudes favoring education through high school Supportive family, community Affectionate, demonstrative parental relationship Unusual maturity and responsibility for their age Experience with giving advice and judgments in disputes, planning strategies, etc. Eagerness to try out new ideas Ability to initiate and maintain meaningful transactions with adults Facility for learning second language	Language of dominant culture often unfamiliar Attitudes depreciating education for family after high school; higher education seen as unrealistic, especially for women Attitudes that differ on basic time, space reality; may cause misunderstandings Attitudes against competition make it difficult to succeed in some more traditional classrooms Sex role stereotyping—each sex expected to adhere to defined role Lack of experience with values of other cultures Emphasis on family over achievement and life goals of children

Field-dependent children are as proficient in concept attainment as field independents, but they express themselves differently in these ways:

Field dependents

- Are superior in the incidental learning of social stimuli
- Are affected more by negative reinforcement
- Prefer a spectator approach
- Do better on verbal tasks of intelligence tests than on analytic
- Learn materials more easily that have human, social content and that are characterized by fantasy and humor
- Are sensitive to the opinions of others
- Perform better when authority figures express confidence in their ability
- Are more cooperative.

Field independents

- Prefer discovery learning
- Do best on analytic tasks
- Learn material that is inanimate and impersonal more easily
- Are not greatly affected in their performance by opinions of others
- Are more competitive.

De Leon concludes that, "The only difference between the two modes of functioning lies in the type of information each processes most effectively and the situation which aids in the processing" (p. 174). He cautions that unless we change our concept of giftedness, the ways in which we identify, and the focus of our activities for learning to include other cognitive styles, we will never discover other modes of interacting that can be as valuable as our current dominant mode.

Remediation

More evidence for reexamination of the program content as experienced by Anglos and Mexican-Americans can be seen in the study reported by Weaver (1983). The study examined the performance patterns of both groups of gifted students in a 2-year program teaching critical thinking skills. While there was significant improvement of both groups, the Anglos' growth was far greater in the same material. Although Weaver looks at many influencing factors, she suggests that both the identification procedures and the design of the curriculum need to be questioned for appropriateness for both groups.

In her discussion of the issues concerning all American minority populations these are related to the gifted and talented among them, Baldwin (1985) notes that the literature available on minorities has been focused more on deficits than on strengths. Her discussion of three basic themes—defining the population, setting goals for their education, and determining the most effective instructional system and evaluating the process and products of that system—is based on three assumptions:

1 Giftedness exists in all human groups, and this giftedness does not manifest itself in a manner that can be genetically ascribed to that group. Culture and environment play important roles in a person's developing a penchant for certain activities and skills, but highly developed specific behaviors associated with a particular group do not provide the basis for assuming that these represent the innate capacities of the group.
2 Techniques other than usual standardized tests can be used to identify the gifted.
3 Behaviors that may be unique or special to a cultural group can serve as accurate indicators of high-level capacity to conceptualize and organize phenomena. (p. 226)

A helpful part of Baldwin's discussion is the identification of factors that may influence the functioning level of minority children. She believes that such factors will be found more frequently in lower classes than in middle classes. Here are some of the factors she mentions:

1 Parents who cannot speak English and thus cannot converse with their children may be unable to foster English language skills.
2 A home environment that lacks toys and other playthings may not stimulate cognitive and developmental skills.
3 A lack of conversation in the home may deny children the opportunity to listen to the discussion of topics and learn the art of participating in dialogue.
4 The type of discipline given by parents may not encourage children to develop an inner locus of control, which may lead to a lack of self-motivation and problem-solving skills. (p. 238)

The other factors mentioned are equally valuable to educators designing useful strategies for identifying or working with minority gifted children. Baldwin concludes that,

Planners for gifted minorities should be concerned with these unique elements: positive attitudes toward cultural differences; an awareness of cultural and ethnic history and traditions; the availability of resources related to minorities (including books and media as well as human resources); how flexible an organization is in accommodating programs for gifted minorities; and high levels of knowledge of behavioral manifestations of conceptual capacity. (p. 246)

Choosing Teachers

Schools face the problem of deciding who is best qualified to teach gifted culturally diverse learners. Often we hear requests for teachers who understand intimately and deeply the culture of a particular group. At the same time, the same people often demand integrated classrooms, while expressing a need for cultural pluralism and exposure to the values of the dominant culture. Such demands place teachers in an impossible position. Few people have the experience or information to understand the values and attitudes of the dominant culture and even one additional subculture intimately. If we select a teacher for an integrated class because of upbringing in one subculture or ethnic group, how will the teacher relate to others in the class from other subcultures or to those from the dominant culture?

Wouldn't it be better to select teachers on the basis of their self-image, interest, concern, openness, desire to work with culturally diverse children, and teaching skills? Focusing on the qualities that create student success in a classroom seems a far better rationale for teacher selection than race or ethnic membership. Raising the awareness of all teachers and parents of the different needs of children from diverse cultural backgrounds should concern every teacher training and inservice education program. To have cultural diversity available in a classroom, why not have teams of culturally different teachers? The children can then truly benefit from seeing and experiencing a model interface of cultures. Think what both teachers and learners could gain from such experiences. The possibilities are unlimited.

Probably the most important and certainly the most far-reaching unsettled questions were asked at one of the first conferences for studying the problems of culturally diverse gifted children (Gallagher & Kinney, 1974): Does our society really want cultural pluralism, or are we going to continue to insist on cultural assimilation? How do we plan to handle self-determinism and democratic ideals in the mode that we choose for our answer? What are the universal values, the common causes of all humanity? How can we reach the goals of human unity and love while still holding on to our own identities as culturally diverse beings?

These questions have no easy answers, and yet we must discuss them as parents, as teachers, as students, among ourselves, and all together. Many of the great thinkers, philosophers, and religious leaders have told of a unity for humankind that is like the waters of a river flowing into the cosmic oceans, mingling, coming together, and yet still maintaining their own essence and uniqueness. Perhaps the answer is not a choice, but an acceptance of reality as a oneness, a blending of dichotomies, with cohesion and separation available at the same time.

Parents, counselors, and teachers who wish to work successfully with culturally diverse gifted learners will find help from the suggestions offered by Frasier (1979) and Colangelo and Zaffrann (1981):

1 Use mentors to tutor culturally diverse students.
2 Help them to develop questioning, introspective attitudes.
3 Help them to understand and explore the problems they may face as they become upwardly mobile, as they try to align their cultural values

with those of the dominant culture, as they try to develop their own individuality and establish their personal and cultural identity.

4 Help them to cope with peer pressures not to succeed, when they exist.

5 Help them to remediate any areas of skill that are lacking, especially limited language skills.

6 Give them opportunities to explore a variety of career options.

In response to the limiting conditions some cultures impose on their children seen in Table 10.1, I would add these suggestions:

1 Help them to deal with excessive pressures to succeed.

2 Help them to learn to value all persons, regardless of cultural or sexual identity.

3 Give them opportunities to share their ideas, attitudes, and values.

4 Help them to learn of the strengths of each culture and the unity of all people.

Mike sat staring off into space, munching on a stick of high protein that was given in his class as a "reinforcer." He was seated at a desk alone, or as alone as you can be with 15 students, 2 teachers, and 3 teacher aides. The room was arranged so that each student was comparatively isolated, sometimes achieving this with the use of cardboard dividers between the desks. Rock music played in the background. This was a special class, and Mike had been sent here at the first of the year—7 months, 4 days, and 2 hours ago. He was selected because he was educationally handicapped, "passive-aggressive," the psychologist had said. He supposed he was; he sure wouldn't do the work in those dumb junior high classes, partly because the teachers were so "stupid" and partly because he'd already done all that stuff, for about 3 years running. Once, he remembered, in third grade there was this neat teacher who had let them all make a movie about a story by Shakespeare and had let some of the kids use her trig book for their math lessons. That was his best year, Mike thought.

"What are you doing, Mike?" came a voice close by. "Huh! Oh, nothin'," Mike re-sponded. "Well, it will be checkup time in 5 minutes and I don't see much student behavior going on." Mike grunted at the teacher, shifted his slouch to a forward lean and picked up his pencil. The "task" before him, the completion of which would show "student behavior," was a work page out of a seventh-grade workbook on basic science. Oh, they had taken it out of the book and clipped off the identifiers so that Mike, an eighth grader, wouldn't know it was baby work, but he knew. "Boy, they must think I'm really stupid," he groused, looking over the low-level questions on the page. But he didn't bother to put in the answers; instead he reached over to a plant near his desk and deposited his protein stick wrapper in its pot.

"Take that out of there, Mike," came the voice again. "It's ok," Mike answered, "It's really an ash tray." Actually it was. Last month one of the "creativity projects" was to take a bunch of old ashtrays the teacher brought in and papier-mâché them into pots for these new plants. Of course Mike realized he was stretching a bit, but he was right. "I said take it out, now." Mike did and then made an elaborate and very grand passage to the wastebasket and back to deposit the wrapper. It took fully 3 of the remaining

---

minutes before "checkup time." On the way back, Mike managed very cleverly to start a fight between two other boys, who each thought the other responsible for the jabs and bumps they received. Mike looked the soul of innocence. One quickly executed swipe of his pencil completely dislocated the mast of a model ship the boy two tables back was assembling; then he slid back into his seat.

A little bell rang, checkup time was announced, and the teachers and aides hurried through the room giving check marks on cards presented by the students to redeem later that day for protein sticks, puzzles, and other prizes. One of the aides approached Mike, who now was sitting straight, feet on the floor, the perfect model of the attentive student. "You get one check for following directions," referring, Mike supposed, to his wastebasket trip, "and one check for behaving like a student." Mike wasn't sure how she arrived at that assessment. "But Mike, I can't give you a check for work completed. You have another half hour now before lunch to finish your task." As she moved away, Mike slid back down into his seat, eyes glassy, staring off into space, and quietly began munching on another protein stick.

Oh yes, they all knew Mike tested around 165 IQ, but the gifted class wouldn't take him until he learned to behave like a student. In the regular class he was too disruptive and never accomplished anything, so here he was and they were going to have him complete his work successfully if it killed them.

HANDICAPPED GIFTED LEARNERS

Gifted learners appear in every population of handicapped students with the obvious exceptions of the mentally retarded and severely developmentally disabled. Special classes for the deaf, the blind, the emotionally disturbed, the orthopedically handicapped, and the learning handicapped very often have among their students children who are also gifted. Mauser (1980) found that 2.3% of the learning-disabled children he tested in Illinois fell into the gifted range. A 1979 U.S. Office of Gifted and Talented Fact Sheet estimated that close to 300,000 children in the United States are both gifted and handicapped. Whitmore (1981) suggests that the figure may be as high as 540,000.

Until recently, little concern has been felt for these gifted children beyond the remediation of their handicapping condition. Children who are gifted and handicapped have need for special educational programming that can remediate any deficits in learning caused by their disability, accommodate the learning experience to minimize the impact of the disability (the condition with which the child was born) and any handicap (the degree to which the disability is allowed to interfere with the child's growth and function) it has created, provide opportunities for development of their special abilities, and challenge them to fuller utilization of their potential. Unfortunately, gifted programs often refuse to handle the handicapped gifted learner.

The focus of special education teachers is often on the remediation needed by the child because of the presence of a disability. In a project developed by Eisenberg (1981) for the New York City schools, one of the outcomes was the realization of the teachers of the handicapped that their children could be extremely able. The belief had been that if the child were gifted, he/she would not be in a class for the handicapped. Their expectations had to be reassessed. Karnes (1979) believes that special education teachers focus on the weakness and deficits of the handicapped because of their training and because they have little or no exposure to gifted education.

In a report of the Retrieval and Acceleration of Promising Young Handicapped and Talented (RAPYHT) Program for young gifted/talented handicapped children, Karnes, Schwedel, and Lewis (1983) show how early identification and programming for the young gifted/talented handicapped child has "paid off." Even with the success of the program she believes even more gains would have been made if inservice training had been available to help elementary teachers program more appropriately for the children. She recommends that such training be conducted for all regular teachers and all special teachers of handicapped classes. She further sees the need for parents of the young gifted/talented handicapped to become effective advocates for their children. It must be noted that the RAPYHT Program provided the young gifted/talented children that it served with skills, attitudes, and habits that are reflected in above-average school progress during their elementary school attendance and should be viewed as a model for more progress to be established in the future.

Overcoming Teacher Attitudes

The inservice training that Karnes is seeking is needed even at the awareness level in light of the results of a study on teacher attitude toward handicapped gifted children (Minner, Prater, Bloodworth, & Walker, 1987), in which 68 public school teachers were randomly assigned to one of three groups and given vignettes briefly describing a gifted child. The descriptions were exactly the same except that one-third were labeled learning disabled, one-third were labeled physically handicapped, and one-third were nonlabeled. The teachers were asked, based on the information they were given, to make a decision regarding the referral of each child for a gifted class. There were essentially no differences in the referrals made from the nonlabeled or the physically handicapped groups; however, the label of learning disability had a negative effect upon the teachers' recommendations. Because this is the largest of the handicapped populations and has within it a large number of handicapped gifted children, it is hoped that efforts will be made to better inform teachers of the nature of learning disabilities, thereby ameliorating some of the negative feelings evidenced by this study. Educators working with the gifted seldom understand the handicapped. Teachers who are well trained and who are given adequate support will determine how much of the gifted potential each gifted handicapped learner will be allowed to meet. It has been suggested that such teachers develop the following competencies (Hegeman, 1981):

- Knowledge of student abilities and disabilities and how these individual differences affect learning
- Competence in methods of disability-related skills development and compensation
- Adaptive strategies necessary for curricular modifications
- Proficient and judicious use of devices, aids, technological equipment, and other resources and support services
- Awareness of the psychological and counseling needs of the gifted handicapped student
- Attitudes of cooperation with concerned staff, since teamwork is a necessary part of educational services for gifted handicapped students
- Careful attention to the development of the students' social skills and relationships with both normal and disabled peers
- Good interpersonal relations with parents, providing information, advice, and support
- Realistic expectations in regard to both gifts and disabilities.

Identification and Program Provision

Identification of the handicapped gifted learner will follow many of the same procedures of screening and multiple data collection that produce the best results in the gifted population. There are, however, some special considerations created by the disability that must be made to alleviate the masking of the ability. Pendarvis and Grossi (1980) present detailed procedures specific to each disability area, which should prove quite helpful.

Strategies and programs developed for the handicapped have tended to assume cognitive limits and often fail to provide opportunities for self-directed learning, creative self-expression, and exploration of the sciences and the arts—all of which are areas critical to programming for gifted learners (Whitmore, 1981). More collaboration between the teachers of the handicapped and the teachers of the gifted will be needed if the goals of both programs are to be made available to the handicapped gifted learner. Maker (1977) brought together some interesting data that can serve as a basis for such planning. She found that different disability groups differ in intellectual capacity, cognitive development, and self-concept.

The blind and visually impaired seem to be capable of the same ability levels as the sighted, but attain their maximum levels later. These students often show deficits in meaningful verbal memory. Maker interviewed some gifted visually handicapped people. Their suggestions included a desire for involvement in less protective, more integrated educational environments and more opportunities to explore the environment using their other, more operable senses. Maker noted a slower rate of development and difficulty dealing with abstractions among the deaf. Her deaf interviewees praised special separate schools. Learning disabled and emotionally disturbed students have diverse problems that reflect the wide array of characteristics under these designations. Problems of attention, perception, and ability to evaluate adequately were the most commonly found. For the physically handicapped, unless the condition is also related to mental retardation, the rate and type of cognitive processing would be comparable to the range of a normal population.

Maker examined the special problems that people who are both handicapped and gifted have in developing a positive self-concept. When the low self-esteem that develops around the disabling condition is combined with the often unrealistic expectations of the gifted learner, a level of dissonance between real and ideal self that adds greatly to the handicapped person's inability to relate and succeed can occur.

This initial drawing together of material showing some of the problems of the handicapped gifted in an educational system that often responds to categories instead of the individual learners has many excellent suggestions for the home and the school. In addition, Maker's book discusses programs for handicapped gifted and talented children and has a very useful section on organizations, agencies, and other resources. While Maker herself claims to raise more questions than she answers, her book, *Providing Programs for the Gifted Handicapped*, provides a valuable resource for those interested in this developing area of gifted education.

There has been growing attention given to the learning-disabled (LD) gifted student in recent years. The increasing number of books and journal articles provide resources previously unavailable to teachers to meet the special needs of this population. It is interesting to note that many of the articles and studies discuss the inability of the remediation model used in special education to meet the gifted needs of these students. An example of such a discussion can be found in Baum's article (1984). She shows through case studies the debilitating outcomes for three LD gifted students when appropriate educational experiences are not provided. Her suggestion is to provide an enrichment experience in addition to the remedial work, contending that the intervention strategies of special education and the modifications necessary for development of high potential cannot successfully be provided in the same setting.

In most special education settings now in existence her points are well taken: Approaches to remediation and enrichment are traditionally in opposition to each other in form and content; most remediation is provided through noncontextual learning, which is focused on isolated basic skills; and the interests and strengths of students are often misused in remedial settings. But does this model of remediation as it is now used in special education provide the best approach for even learning-disabled students, not to mention gifted learning-disabled students? Perhaps a program using many of the elements of the Responsive Learning Environment as described in Chapter 8 could incorporate both needs, with integrative learning empowering the learner to grow in both need areas. Baum brings up important issues that must be considered as we seek answers to serving our LD gifted students. That the kind of in-school/out-of-school dichotomy of behavior—in-school filled with frustration, anger, and failure; out-of-school filled with creative, self-motivated, fullfilling activity—described by her exists for these students is of serious concern.

It seems increasingly possible that LD gifted students either may be identified only for the LD class with the giftedness masked by the learning disability or may be using giftedness to compensate for the learning disability so successfully that both go undetected and the student continues functioning at or near grade level. Suter and Wolf (1987), in discussing this issue, suggest that teachers look for performance characterized by considerable variability across tasks, low motivation and task completion, impaired long- and short-term memory, visual or auditory processing difficulty, poor self-concept, high levels of self-criticism, withdrawal or aggression, short attention span, difficulty following directions, and poor peer relations.

Rather than placing these children in traditionally organized regular classrooms, gifted programs, or remedial resource rooms, Suter and Wolf suggest formation of a class for students with dual exceptionalities. This would allow the kind of ongoing support such children need and would provide the multidimensional approach that is necessary to develop both areas of need.

> Successful programming for gifted/LD children must be based on individual needs of each child and the setting in which services are provided. Important components include instruction in compensation strategies, exposure to higher level concepts and materials, and a counseling program for students and parents. (p. 235)

Two books that have focused on gifted LD children allow in-depth study of this area of growing concern: *Learning-Disabled/Gifted Children* (Fox, Brody, & Tobin, 1983) and *Teaching the Gifted/Learning Disabled Child* (Daniels, 1983). Both offer valuable insights on characteristics, identification, programming, and counseling for this diverse and challenging population.

Whitmore and Maker (1985) see the emegence of a new field of education of handicapped gifted students. They see the field engaged in the development of five major goals:

- Increasing the accuracy of the identification and diagnostic process
- Increasing the amount of research-and-development activity directed toward expanding the body of knowledge and instructional technology
- Implementing the necessary major changes in the preparation of service personnel
- Increasing the sense of shared responsibility for the total development of gifted/disabled children among professionals and parents
- Preparing gifted/disabled students for lifelong satisfaction in careers and self-selected avocations.

Their book, *Intellectual Giftedness in Disabled Persons* (1985), pursues these goals and presents a more in-depth look at the major disability areas seen from the perspective of the dual exceptionality giftedness. Case studies, discussions of issues, and specific guidelines and recommendations make the book a valuable resource.

Those who work with the gifted need to become aware of what can be and is being done to promote services for the handicapped gifted learner so that their educational experience can work not only toward keeping the disability from becoming handicapping, but also toward actualizing the high potential of these students. The following are some indicators of progress in this direction (Karnes, 1979; Karnes & Bertschi, 1978; Karnes, Schwedel, & Lewis, 1983):

- Efforts to increase public awareness of the needs of gifted handicapped learners, to bring them to the attention of local and state educational agencies, and to support advocacy in their behalf
- Development of programs such as the New York City Program for Special Gifted Children in which regular and special educators work together to nominate, identify, and counsel students in special education who have exhibited above-average to superior ability and to find appropriate placement for them, often within gifted classes
- National conferences devoted to the problems of the handicapped gifted
- More generic training for special education teachers so that they will be able to identify and plan for the gifted in their disability populations
- Implementation of mainstream placement and the concurrent inservice in special education of general education teachers, making them more aware of the needs of gifted learners
- Strong advocacy for gifted education from organizations whose historical role has been primarily associated with the handicapped, such as The Council of Exceptional Children
- Sponsorship of national conferences for the study of problems of the gifted by such groups, such as a conference on culturally diverse gifted conducted by the Foundation for Exceptional Children
- The establishment in institutions of higher learning of programs to train leadership and teaching personnel in gifted education within the Departments of Special Education
- Specialized graduate programs in the area of gifted handicapped, such as the one preparing teachers at the University of Denver
- The existence and work of the Committee for the Gifted Handicapped of the Association for the Gifted in the Council for Exceptional Children
- Programs for young gifted handicapped learners that explore early intervention, identification procedures, and programming strategies, such as the RAPYHT Program conducted at Chapel Hill, North Carolina.

For those interested in further reading in the area of the gifted handicapped learner, an excellent bibliography prepared by Dr. Elinor Katz, University of Denver, Denver, Colorado, should be of help to you.

The concern for gifted handicapped learners gives educators an opportunity to appreciate the value of working in an interdependent, cooperative, collaborative style, for these children can be served in no other way. The skills of the regular classroom teacher, the special educator, the educator of the gifted, the parent, the counselor/psychologist, the administrator, and the researcher are needed if these children are to actualize their potential abilities.

Jane stood at the board between Tommy and her best friend Doris. As the teacher pronounced each word, they wrote it on the board, carefully covering their work until everyone was finished. When all the chalk was returned to the chalk tray, the teacher spelled the word so that they could check their own work. Doris had missed two already, and this time Tommy misspelled the word. Jane noticed that the two of them nodded to each other and, although she wasn't sure, she felt that they were excluding her. Four more words, and Doris missed another one. Tommy missed the next one. Now it was obvious that she was being excluded as Doris and Tommy exchanged gestures and looks of "I know how you feel" and "Jane thinks she's so smart." Jane felt really uncomfortable. She really liked Doris and Tommy; Why did they have to act like that? There were only two words left on the test when Jane decided that they would like her better if she missed some words, too.

"Receive," said the teacher.

Jane carefully wrote *r-e-c-i-e-v-e.* Not too obvious, she thought. It wouldn't help if they thought she missed on purpose. Everyone stood back. Tommy spelled it just as she did. When the teacher read the right answer, Tommy noticed hers was wrong and grinned at her encouragingly. She felt much better.

"Commitment," said the teacher.

C-o-m-m-i-t-t-m-e-n-t wrote Jane. Tommy got this one right. Both he and Doris looked sympathetically at Jane. Jane felt even better.

"For those who have 100% on their test today," the teacher was saying, "I've got a special treat. The rest of you take out paper and pencil and write the words you missed correctly 100 times." The teacher took the "good students" in tow, and off they went down the hall. Jane wanted to go too. After all, she knew those words. She wanted to tell Miss Jennings why she missed them, but that was silly. She'd never understand. After everyone left, Tommy and Doris began talking to her; she was obviously in their favor now. She thought a moment about the treat and wondered what it was, but as she heard comments around the room about the "smarty alecks," and the "prissy britches" who had just left, and as she looked again at her friends happily chatting with her included, she thought it was really worth it.

GIFTED FEMALES

Only recently has there been interest and effort spent on understanding the problems encountered by the gifted female in our society. The January 1977 supplement of the *National/State Leadership Training Institute Bulletin* featured attitudes of the past toward gifted women. Let us look at profiles of some of those noted.

After 29 American medical schools rejected her, *Elizabeth Blackwell* (b. 1821) was accepted by New York's Geneva College because the student body voted in the "hen-medic" as a lark. She graduated at the head of the class. Barred from

---

The School and the Gifted Individual

Gifted females must be given opportunities and support for traditional male activities.

practicing in city hospitals, she opened a one-room dispensary in a New York slum that became the New York Infirmary for Women and Children.

Because "her presence would distract the male students," *Belva Lockwood* (b. 1830) was refused admittance to law school for 2 years. When she did complete the course, she had to petition the school's honorary president, U.S. President Ulysses S. Grant, to get her diploma. When denied access to federal courts to try cases, she persuaded Congress to pass a special bill. In 1879 she became the first woman to practice law before the U.S. Supreme Court.

Founder of ecology as a science, with specialties in water pollution, home economics, and consumer rights, *Ellen Swallow Richards* (b. 1842) was the first woman graduate of the Massachusetts Institute of Technology. Also the first female faculty member at MIT, she was denied a doctorate by the narrow policies of the school. Smith College made her an honorary Doctor of Science at the age of 69, just 1 year before her death.

One would like to think the experiences of these women are now considered ridiculous and that they simply couldn't happen today; however, a special issue of

Time in 1972 published this advice: "If a woman wishes to become a college president, she is advised to become a nun" (p. 91). This was in response to the statistic given that only 1% of college presidents are women, and almost all of them are nuns. The same issue reported that, of all PhDs granted, only 13% go to women. The situation hasn't gotten much better. Reis (1987) reports that only 26% of the positions in higher education faculties in the United States are filled by women.

While the percentage of doctorates awarded to women has increased dramatically during the past decade, unemployment rates for women with PhDs are two to five times higher than for men with PhDs. Women who get an academic job are likely to be assigned a lower rank and salary than their male counterparts. These data provided the basis for a study of the bias in hiring in academia conducted by Geis and colleagues at the University of Delaware (cited in McLeod, 1984). Identical résumés using a male or female name were sent to university department heads. Male names earned the rank of associate professor, while the same information from female applicants received the lower ranking of assistant professor. Geis states that studies of actual rankings of men and women show the same discrepancy. Salaries of male faculty members exceed those of women by 15% even when rank, tenure, publications, and type of institution are equivalent. These women now become the role models for later academic women, as did a friend of mine who completed a doctorate at a well-known university. She received her diploma, which announced to the world that Mr.___ had completed *his* work . . . , etc. She returned the diploma for more appropriate wording.

Although one would like to think the current interest in women's rights and equality of opportunity would be reflected in the career data, the status of women actually declined between 1950 and 1970. In the 1940s women held 45% of all professional and technical jobs, but in 1970 the percentage dropped to 40% (Theodore, 1971). Dowling reported in 1981 that two-thirds of working women were earning less than $10,000 a year; half were in jobs with no pensions; and 80% occupied menial or semiskilled jobs. Reis reports that in 1986 women were found to earn, on the average, the same as high school dropouts. They comprise 71% of the elderly poor, with one out of four women facing the prospect of poverty in her old age.

While IQ bears a fairly close relationship to accomplishment among men, it bears essentially no relationship among women, with two-thirds of the women with IQs of 170 or above occupied as housewives or office workers. Many take jobs as backups to men in power, receiving neither the credit nor the responsibility for their contributions (Dowling, 1981). More than one-third of all candidates for MBA degrees are women, but only 5% of the executives in the top 50 American companies are women (*Time,* July 12, 1982). In technical and professional fields the representation of gifted and talented women has actually experienced a decline since the early 1900s (Hollinger & Fleming, 1984).

One of the barriers to gifted women's becoming more involved in nontraditional careers is their lack of mathematics preparation. A study of 1,324 children in grades 2 through 12 found no significant differences between boys and girls in reported enjoyment of mathematics (Ernest, 1976). However, Ernest (1980) acknowledges that when mathematics becomes an optional course of study in high school, few girls enroll. Luchins and Luchins (1980) may have some of the reasons. They report that interviews of 350 female members of the Association for Women in Mathematics and a smaller number of male mathematicians produced some interesting differences in career encouragement and discouragement received by them. Three times as many women reported being discouraged by teachers or advisers than did men, with the most marked discouragement occurring at the graduate level. The women mathematicians experienced all the stereotypic behaviors and comments we have noted earlier. They were told that boys do not like or are afraid of girls who are smart. They found that boys were given more support; less was expected of them as girls; they were advised to go into more traditional fields; their competence was questioned; and they had a problem being taken seriously.

When the female mathematicians applied for jobs, they encountered fewer offers, lower salary, and less advancement potential than equally or less qualified males. The women in this study had some suggestions for change if women are to be encouraged to pursue mathematics as a career:

1 Increase emphasis on precollege mathematics education for girls.
2 Teachers, counselors, and parents should encourage, not discourage, interest.
3 Treat girls as equal to boys in this area of study.
4 Provide female role models.
5 Provide awareness of career opportunities.
6 Change the conception of mathematics as a masculine domain.
7 Stress intuitive-re-creational mathematics throughout school to dispel fear of the subject.

Rekdal (1984) showed that less than 12% of women entering the University of California system today have the high school math prerequisites that would allow them to participate in 80% of the majors offered by that system. According to Rekdal gifted females do not pursue math even when they express levels of interest in math and perform as well as males. Hollinger (1985) adds to this dilemma by noting that this attitude continues through adolescence even though the females are aware of their abilities as shown by their descriptions of their math skills, which Hollinger found to be accurate.

Even in professions that are dominated by women, such as education, men comprise 80% of all elementary school principals, 96% of all junior high principals, and 99.9% of all school superintendents. Of all classroom teachers, 70% are women, yet for the same job, they make an average of $3,000 a year less than their male colleagues (*Time,* July 12, 1982). Data reported in 1987 show virtually no gains in these statistics (Reis, 1987). Furthermore, schools of education are fairly equally staffed except for their departments of educational administration, which are often totally staffed with male professors. From the enrollment figures in these departments, it seems that they accept as students an almost all-male population.

The famous Terman study of gifted children becoming adults followed the progress of only the men for information on careers because not enough women were expected to become professionals to make collection of data from them necessary. Later, when the women were not restricted from reports, it was found that 11% of the women were working in a professional job, while 45% of the men were so engaged. Although 70% of both men and women graduated from college, 13.8% of the men (compared to only 4% of the women) had taken a doctorate. Of the men, 47.7% earned over $10,000 a year, while only 6% of the women did so. The median earnings for the men were $9,640; and $4,875 for the women (Terman & Oden, 1959).

Kerr (1985a) points to another interesting finding in the Terman and Oden (1959) data. As a group, the participants lost an average of 9 IQ points during adolescence, but the loss for the females was five times larger than for the males. The females scored 13 IQ points lower; the males fewer than 3 IQ points lower. Interestingly the grades for both groups continued to be high. Could a sudden dramatic genetic change have occurred? Were the tests significantly altered? Kerr suggests that the females may possibly have decided not to try on the IQ test or that the label *gifted* may, during adolescence, have become unacceptable. They may have decided to begin denying their giftedness.

The importance of helping young gifted women pursue career goals can be seen in the reports from women who were part of the Terman study and who are now in their 70s (Holahan, 1984). The majority of our gifted girls of today will be members of the work force tomorrow, and these data clearly make opportunities to enhance their choice of careers necessary.

In the Terman study, some data appeared that raised questions about the loss of contributions of the gifted and talented women to society. Seven of the most talented writers in Terman's gifted group of children were girls, yet practically all the eminent adult writers were men. Carroll (1940) observed a similar contradiction in a follow-through study of artistic ability. While nearly all the eminent artists were men, the gifted girls, as a group, had been superior to the boys in artistic ability.

Why does this happen? If females have outstanding ability at one point in their lives, why not at another? To understand, we must look at society's expectations for women, the type of encouragement that is given, and the consequences of achievement for women.

Barriers to Equity

At Home

In our dominant culture, and even more intensely in many subcultures, girl babies have an entirely different experience as a member of the family and the larger community than do boys. There is evidence that one of the most consistent determinants of parental expectations, perceptions, and organizers of behavior is the sex of their infant. This difference in expectation is evident even before the child is born. Parents prefer male offspring across a wide variety of cultures (Arnold et al., 1975; Poffenberger & Poffenberger, 1973). Hoffman (1977) found that in the United States there was a 2:1 preference for boys over girls. Among men the preference was 4:1. Couples are more likely to continue having children just to get a boy. Boys have a larger number of different toys and twice as many toys as do girls (Rheingold & Cook, 1975). The colors and the volume of sound surrounding them, the type of material used to clothe them, the toys given to them, the activities they are allowed to engage in, as well as the way they participate, are all very different.

From the beginning, girls are taught to be passive, accepting, nurturing. They are expected to enjoy quieter games and activities and not to take risks. They receive these messages from many places and many people in our society. Mothers encourage daughters to stay close by, to work with them. They buy irons and ironing boards, miniature kitchens, doll houses, tiny brooms, and baby dolls with cradles and bathinettes for them so they can imitate and learn the woman's role. Little boys are discouraged from playing with these "sissy" toys and, even when dolls are included for boys, they are "GI Joe" dolls or stuffed animals.

You can guess the sex of a baby just by walking into the nursery of most middle-class or upper-class homes. The wallpaper, the mobiles, the choice of pictures and colors differ for boys and girls. The babies also receive different treatment within the nursery. Researchers have discovered that fathers and mothers both turn boy infants out toward the world and push them; little girls more often get hugged up close, face-to-face (Serbin & O'Leary, 1975).

Rubin, Provenzano, and Luria (1974) report interesting results from a study where parents were asked to describe their newborn first child within the first 24 hours. The infants were nearly identical in length and weight and all were healthy. The parents were given a list of opposite words and asked to choose ones that best described their infant. They believed the baby to be better coordinated, more alert, more attentive, bigger, and stronger if it was a boy. If a girl, the description included softer, finer featured, littler, and less attentive. Though the descriptions contradict the fact that physiologically girls are less vulnerable, nonetheless the stereotype held in every case.

In spite of their greater sturdiness and developmental maturity, female babies are handled less vigorously than are boy babies (Hoffman, 1972). The caregiver responds differently to crying from boys than from girls. Because they are comforted less and their crying is less often attended to, boy babies learn to become their own emotional caregiver, while girls learn to rely on others to meet their needs. Because her cries are often met with anxiety and concern, a girl learns to doubt her own competence.

This is the point at which parents begin inculcating their small daughters with the idea that so far as risktaking and the evaluation of their own safety are concerned, they should not trust themselves (Dowling, 1981, p. 109). Risktaking, self-trust, and independence are necessary to the development of high levels of intelligence. Studies show that bright girls consistently underestimate their own ability. The brighter the girl, the less expectation she has for intellectual success (Crandall, Katlovsky, & Preston, 1962).

At School

As children enter school, more subtle, and some not so subtle, clues inculcate their role expectation. Preschool teachers reinforce the same types of behavior noted in the home. Little girls are allowed to stay near and are patted and spoken to quietly, while little boys are given directions for independent activity and sent on their way. Boys get more attention when they actively misbehave, and the teacher is more active in controlling them.

Boys actually learn more than girls because the teacher explains how things work and encourages them to try out toys and materials. Little girls are shown passively, as the teacher usually does the manipulation. Boys can explore and get involved in games and activities that are considered too rough for girls and from which, as girls, they are protected (Serbin & O'Leary, 1975).

In my childhood, I distinctly recall my father's aversion to my involvement in tree climbing. Our neighborhood was predominantly male, so my playmates were all tree climbers. There were dire consequences, both natural, as when I fell, and inflicted, as when I got caught, for my participation in this activity. Although I did not always escape undetected, I must admit that I was the best tree climber in the neighborhood. I could not only go higher, probably because I weighed less, but I also mastered the chicken house, the garage, and the neighbor's grape arbor. I never did think prohibiting me, while letting all those boys climb without any discouragement, was really fair. They didn't worry at all about getting caught.

Bardwick and Douvan (1971) theorize that little boys learn to cope with stress and switch to an independent mode by the age of 2, while girls are actually kept from learning to cope by having stress-related situations mediated to the point of overprotection. The result is that passivity and a dependent orientation toward adults appear consistently in girls into adulthood (Dowling, 1981).

Serbin and O'Leary (1975) discovered that girls' actions have far less effect on their environment than do the actions of boys. The kind of help each receives, encouraging action for boys, passivity for girls, also seems to influence the development of their spatial and analytic reasoning. Boys learn to manipulate the environment openly, whereas girls must sit passively by and watch, manipulating covertly, out of frustration.

The preprimers and beginning readers given to school children express this same attitude. Recently, a student of mine surveyed the preprimers and beginning readers adopted for use in California schools to look for sexist materials. The results were amazing. She converted the especially biased pages into slides, and for over 20 minutes our class watched page after page build a stereotype of females that was demeaning, unrelentingly insipid, and totally incompetent. We watched Jane and

Mother make lemonade to take out to Dick and Mike, who were building a neat doghouse. We saw Mother get ready to go on a shopping trip and put on earrings that did not match, an act that was discovered by Dick and Father with the comment, "Silly, silly Mother." At each crisis, we found we had to wait with Mother and Jane until Father came home to solve the problem. The final blow came when my student showed a slide of a page of occupations Dick was considering when he grew up. There were six columns of small print covering the page with a wide range of possible jobs. The next page was for Jane and showed the choices available to her. There were three very short columns with very large print. The first column read, "Nurse, Teacher, Mother, Secretary." The two other columns were equally imaginative.

Guttentag (1975) found that, by age 5, most children are already sexists. They are convinced that boys are strong and fine and can do all sorts of interesting jobs, but that girls are weak and silly and best kept at home. By the fifth grade, it didn't matter for boys whether their mother was a homemaker or a doctor; the peer group pressures and media influences outweighed the example they got at home. Girls were not affected the same way. They responded to a course given in the fifth grade on sex roles by accepting the idea that women can enter a wide variety of jobs and combine work and family. The course also resulted in an increase in self-esteem for the older girls. Boys only expressed traditional opinions more freely.

We know that gifted children tend to develop more quickly than more typical children, and we find that gifted girls usually develop even more quickly in the first few years. Connelly (1977) points out that this may cause devastating loneliness for sensitive girls of high potential. This loneliness may persist through their adult lives or lead to an eventual disconnect between their actual lives and their untapped abilities. When, as youths, these girls try to show their ability, they are accused of being bossy, unfeminine, and show-offs, so they tend to withdraw. Gifted girls are often considered aloof, conceited, and totally self-sufficient, and others do not feel comfortable with them. For this reason they may go through life with very few friends (Connelly, 1977). Average-ability classmates and teachers who have not had a course in gifted education perceive gifted girls more negatively than they do gifted boys (Solano, 1977).

Add to this the observation that gifted girls more resemble gifted boys than nongifted girls on tests of interest, personality, and values. They demonstrate stronger academic and career interests and may be far more adversely affected by conflicts between their goals and the traditional role expectations of females in the society (Fox, 1977).

Other comparisons have been made. Gifted girls who reject traditional feminine sex-typed behaviors have higher intellectual ability than those who accept the feminine stereotype (Kagan & Freeman, 1963), although there is reason to believe that gifted girls are not less interested in traditional feminine fields, but exhibit more interest in traditionally masculine domains (Fox, Pasternak, & Peiser, 1976). In addition to the usual cognitive differences between gifted and nongifted females, the gifted can be distinguished by their more dominant career orientation, higher mathematical aptitudes and interests, less traditional sex role orientation, and greater need to achieve (Wolleat, 1979).

To check if the sexism observed in the classroom in the 1970s had disappeared, the Sadkers (1985) did a study in more than one-hundred elementary classrooms and found that, unfortunately, it has not. Among their findings were these:

1 If a boy calls out in class, he gets the teacher's attention, whereas a girl calling out is told to raise her hand. Support for this observation comes from data reported by Bouman (1986) that response opportunities given to males are at a ratio of from 9:1 to 4:1 better than those given to girls.
2 Teachers praise boys more than girls.
3 Teachers give boys more academic help than girls.
4 Boys' comments are accepted more than those of girls.
5 Boys dominate classroom communication by a ratio of 3:1.
6 Teachers give boys dynamic, precise, and effective responses; girls receive bland, diffuse reactions.

On a positive note the researchers found that these patterns can be eliminated. After only 4 days of training to establish equity in classroom interactions, not only were the teachers able to eliminate the patterns, they improved their overall teaching effectiveness as well.

As early as junior high school the career expectations of gifted males and females differ, with 98% of the males and only 46% of the females expecting to have a full-time career; many of the females expected to be involved in careers only until they married or had children, or only part-time, or with interruptions to have children (Fox, Tobin, & Brody, 1981). Up to 94% of a group of very gifted females wanted to have careers; however, 71% of these females either did not plan to work or planned to work only part-time.

Garrison, Stronge, and Smith (1986) point out how society helps to establish these mixed expectations by expressing attitudes that give mixed messages: Women should fill a supportive nurturing role, but they are expected to assertively develop their own talent; girls are rewarded by teachers and parents for good grades and high school performance, but society as expressed in media, in books and textbooks, and through peer groups relays the message that intellectual pursuits are unfeminine. With these mixed expectations and few role models of successful women to follow, it is easy for gifted females to become confused about how to pursue a truly satisfying future. These researchers suggest some goals and strategies for career programs for gifted females:

1 Information should be presented which dispels the myth of a forced choice between career and family and the myth of irreversible life planning.
2 Males as well as females should be counseled about the redistribution of family responsibilities when this is a desirable solution.

3 Experiences should be provided which help girls develop their autonomy, self-esteem, self-confidence, tolerance for ambiguity, willingness to compete, and assertiveness.

4 Information and role models should be provided which illustrate a variety of possible satisfying lifestyles.

5 Gifted girls should be encouraged to engage in appropriate career planning and be taught how to incorporate interruptions and delays for childraising into their career plans. (p. 120)

In Society

The literature on need achievement should give us some clues as to why females start out so well, only to achieve in very small numbers. It should; however, it does not for the simple reason that, in the impressive and theoretically consistent body of data about the achievement motive, women have been left out altogether (Horner, 1969). In the few studies that include women, the results were so contradictory or confusing that they omitted women from future consideration. The *need to achieve* has been defined as an internalized standard of excellence, motivating the individual to do well in any achievement oriented situation involving intelligence and leadership ability. We do know that women get higher test-anxiety scores than men, probably because a female who is motivated to achieve directly contradicts the role expectation of feminity. Horner states, "A bright woman is caught in a double bind. In testing and other achievement-oriented situations she worries not only about failure, but also about success" (p. 38). The solution for most women is to inhibit achievement motivation. Horner (1968) has done research on what she has termed the *motive to avoid success*. The results are most interesting:

1 Success inhibits social life for females; it enhances social life for males.
2 Women will fully explore their intellectual potential only when they do not need to compete.
3 Women block achievement even more when in competition with men.
4 Society holds the belief that it isn't ladylike to be too intellectual.
5 Most men treat the intelligent woman with distrustful tolerance at best, and outright prejudice at worst, if she pursues a career.

She found that the women in her study also equate intellectual achievement with loss of femininity and respond to success in one of three ways, by (1) showing anxiety about becoming unpopular, unmarriageable, and lonely; (2) feeling guilt and despair and doubting their femininity or normality; and (3) denying the possibility that a mere woman can be successful.

Horner's original studies began in 1964, and in the 1970s she again looked at these issues, using as her population the "liberated" young women of the new women's movement era. She found an even higher portion of women showing fear of success, coping poorly or avoiding competition, and lowering their career expectations. The negative attitudes expressed by females had increased from 65%

in 1964 to 88.2% in 1970 (Horner, 1972). This fear of success has been shown to intensify as girls move from seventh to tenth grade (Lavach & Lanier, 1975).

IQ can be found to correlate positively to boys' expectation for success and negatively to the success expectations of girls (Walberg, 1969). Girls seem to believe that if they succeed, it is luck; if they fail, it is their fault. Boys reverse this view for their successes and failures. It has been shown that teachers have contributed significantly to these views (Dweck et al., 1978). In the study, whenever a girl's work was evaluated negatively, it was always pointed out that the failure resulted from intellectual inadequacy; however, the feedback the boys received attributed failures to nonintellectual aspects of their performance, to their efforts or motivation. D. Rogers (1969) noted that achievement orientation is thought to prove maladaptive for girls because "highly motivated girls may never quite resign themselves to the routines of domestic life" (pp. 251–252). They could also create stress for their husbands by forcing them to fill the achievement needs they left unfilled, he says.

In the intellectual realm, Maccoby (1966) found that any differences persisting until high school show females ahead of males on intellectual tasks. However, in high school females begin to fall behind in some areas, and beyond high school their productivity and accomplishments drop off rapidly.

Noting the continuing lack of adult creative productivity in females, and the prevailing attitudes that continue to support this occurrence, Reis (1987) draws our attention to attitudes held by the female that may be contributing to self-sabotage. Gifted women often believe that they must excel in every role they play and they must play every role assigned. High energy is expended by such women to simultaneously maintain their femininity; succeed as a wife; have an outstanding career; be a perfect parent; have an attractive body; and run a beautiful, well-managed home. Reis believes that it is important to teach gifted girls that it is impossible to be perfect in everything they do and that choices about careers, marriage, and children will have to be made. This perfection complex causes women not only to set impossible goals but to continually strive to achieve at ever higher levels. The self-sabotage continues to work as bright young women attribute their success to factors other than their own efforts and see their outward image of success as undeserved or accidental. Bright men on the the other hand attribute their success to their own efforts.

Reis (1987) asks that research be done to help alleviate some of these problems and specifies these major areas needing research: (1) identification of the degree that cultural, societal, and environmental factors impact upon the educational experiences of female students and how the impact, if negative, can be controlled; (2) identification of the internal barriers experienced by females that might have an impact on their ability to realize their potential; and (3) longitudinal/developmental studies of both females and males. Our further efforts, says Reis, should concentrate on treatments for the problems that have been identified by prior research.

Hollinger and Fleming (1984) believe that the well-documented fear of success so often demonstrated by women may be playing a part in this phenomenon of self-sabotage and is even more prevalent in gifted women than in the nongifted as the possibility of success is greater. The general androgeny of giftedness also plays an important role as the characteristics of the gifted are more aligned with male interests than female, which creates problems during adolescence, as does the gifted students' intense commitment to work and their sense of mission (Kerr, 1985b). Kerr believes that some of these problems can be developed as strengths if there is strong emotional support and recognition of individuality and inner worth. Kerr suggests several activities that teachers might provide to increase the likelihood of gifted women moving into male-dominated professions and careers: exposure to biographies of women in diverse fields, counseling females into advanced math and science courses, and providing opportunities for the females to visualize their lives 10 years in the future.

Expectations of society also enter into career decisions. To resolve the home/career conflict, women may choose to delay their education or the pursuit of appropriate career placement until after the family's needs have been mostly met and the children are less dependent, which has them beginning their career at an older age. Or they may choose an occupation, such as teaching or nursing, that is more compatible with the approved female role. These careers also meet the need of availability in most localities, as the primary decision of where the family will live will usually be the man's choice. If a more male-dominated career is chosen, the woman may work only part time and choose specializations more compatible with the female role expectations (Wolleat, 1979).

The National/State Leadership Training Institute on the Gifted and the Talented, January, 1977, supplement on gifted females states,

> With the objective of ending sex discrimination in American education, Title IX, which is part of the Education Amendment of 1972, became effective July 21, 1975. The approximately 16,000 public school systems and 2,700 post-secondary institutions affected were urged to consider Title IX as an opportunity to ensure equal opportunity in education. (p. 2)

My involvement with the implementation of Title IX provisions tells me that attitudes are changing; however, the awareness of the need for change is still very low.

Even after breaking the barrier of college admittance, women who earn baccalaureate degrees are less than half as likely as men to earn a graduate degree, despite the fact that, on the average, they have better undergraduate records (Jencks & Riesman, 1968). Nearly half of all bachelor's and master's degrees, approximately one-fourth of the professional degrees in medicine and law, and 14% of the doctorates awarded in 1979 went to women. The doctorates earned were primarily in the fields of home economics, foreign languages, and library science. There was, however, an increase in doctorates earned even in more nontraditional fields such as law and medicine (National Center for Education Statistics, 1979). In the 1980–81 school year the Association of American Medical Colleges reports that

26% of the total enrollment was comprised of women, a record. However, no woman yet heads a medical school; only 10% of the nation's physicians are women; and women trail far behind in admission to training programs in surgery, ophthalmology, allergies, and ear, nose, and throat specializations. If they specialize at all, women are expected to be in pediatrics, psychiatry, radiology, anesthesia, or pathology (Squires, 1981).

Another type of discrimination exists for those women in the sciences. Candace Pert was denied a Lasker Award for her research on brain peptide-opiate relationships, with the award given to a man. Jocelyn Bell failed to receive the Nobel prize for her discovery of pulsars; the award went to the professor for whom she worked at the time of her discovery (Cleaveland, 1979).

With such family and educational experience in a culture that "characterizes women as inconsistent, emotionally unstable, lacking in a strong superego, weaker, nurturant rather than productive, intuitive rather than intelligent and—if they are at all normal—suited to the home and family. . . . If she knows her place (the home) she is really a quite loveable, loving creature, happy and childlike" (Weisstein, 1969, p. 58), what about the gifted woman's career?

Joesting (1970) relates a story of a young preteen who attempted to get a paper route only to be refused on the grounds that "there are too many job hazards for girls." Joesting believes that vocational counseling should begin at the junior high school level, because it is there that gifted girls begin to be "shuttled" into stereotypic jobs (nurse instead of doctor, legal secretary instead of lawyer, etc.)

As with achievement motivation research, career development theory is derived almost entirely from research on males (Mattheis, 1974). D. Rogers (1969) finds that general society and individual families spend less money and effort to provide girls with the adequate education required for good jobs.

As we have seen from Chapter 1, differences in ability between men and women may be rooted in biological differences that are established in the brain during prenatal life, shown in later differences in brain organization, and enhanced by hormones throughout the life span (Levy, 1980). How the sexes differ genetically in the way their brain develops, how the outside environment modifies this development, and how much we as parents and educators can affect the development of brain organization are questions now being asked and studied by those in the neurosciences. The next 10 years will be most interesting as these questions begin to be answered. Some of the differences were summarized by Block (Nova, 1980) into seven major areas:

1 *Aggression.* Males are far more aggressive, as expressed in play, in fighting behavior, in preference for more adventurous and aggressive films and stories, and in greater competition.
2 *Activity.* Males play outside more, more actively, with more variety, and they find it harder to stay still.
3 *Curiosity and exploratory behavior.* Males want to know how things work and they engage in more exploratory activities than females.

4 *Impulsivity.* Males find it more difficult to resist temptation, distractions, risktaking, and becoming involved in dangerous situations.

5 *Importance of social relationships.* Females are more nurturant from an early age and express concern for the welfare of the group, cooperate and compromise more, and are more empathic. Females have fewer, but more intimate, intense relationships.

6 *Self-concept.* Males view themselves as more powerful and having more control over events in the world, and they believe that they make a difference. They see themselves as more effective, more ambitious, more assertive, and more able to make things happen.

7 *Achievement-related behaviors.* Males expect to do better than females and set higher levels of aspiration for themselves. Females tend to underestimate their performances and are less confident. Males blame failure on external circumstances and take credit for their successes. Females reverse this view.

Kerr (1985a) summarized previously conducted research to develop a profile of gifted females. Here are her key points:

Regarding younger gifted girls,

1 Many gifted girls were superior physically, had more social knowledge, and were better adjusted than were average girls.

2 In their interests, gifted girls were more like gifted boys than they were like average girls.

3 Highly gifted girls were often second-born females.

4 Highly gifted girls were often loners without much need for recognition.

5 Gifted girls were interested in fulfilling needs for self-esteem through school and club achievements. (pp. 91–92)

Regarding adolescent females,

1 Gifted girls' IQ scores dropped in adolescence perhaps as they began to perceive their own giftedness as undesirable.

2 Gifted girls were likely to continue to have higher academic achievement than gifted boys exhibited until college, when a reversal took place.

3 Gifted girls maintained a high involvement in extracurricular and social activities during adolescence.

4 Highly gifted girls often did not receive recognition for their achievements.

5 Highly gifted girls attended less prestigious colleges than did highly gifted boys, and this fact seemed to lead to lower status careers. (p. 103)

Regarding gifted women,

1 Gifted women's academic and vocational achievement compared to that of gifted men continues to decline throughout adulthood.

2 Salaries of gifted women are much lower than those of gifted men in occupations at the same level.

3 Gifted women engaged in income-producing work are more satisfied with their lives than are those who are not engaged in income-producing work.

4 Highly gifted men's income has averaged almost twice that of highly gifted women.

5 Integrators are more satisfied with their careers than are single-career women and are as satisified with their families as are homemakers.

6 Mental stability and the support of others is crucial to successful integration of career and family. (pp. 121–122)

From her concern for the negative effects that these profiles show, Kerr has developed guidelines for parents and teachers that follow gifted girls from preschool through their emergence as gifted women in the workplace. These suggestions for changing the limiting conditions into enhancing conditions for the lives of gifted females are quite valuable.

From these summaries, it is evident that these differences in expectations and results, whether caused primarily by biological differences, environmental differences, or an interaction of both, do not favor independent, successful achievement for females.

What Can Be Done?

There may be a change occurring in what Burns (1983) calls the "silent message" of sex differences. Although her study showed that stereotypes still exist among parents of gifted—as expressed by their preferences for male children to have "fundamentally male" characteristics and females to have "fundamentally female" characteristics—the gifted youngsters showed far more androgyny, incorporating the most positive behaviors and attributes of each sex.

A study on teacher attitude toward the gifted female student has also found a change of attitude in the educational setting (Cooley, Chauvin, & Karnes, 1984). The results of a survey administered to teachers of gifted students showed that male teachers still had a tendency to view female students in a more traditional manner than did female teachers, characterizing them as more emotional, high strung, and gullible and less imaginative, curious, inventive, and individualistic. However, these same teachers were able to envision female students in occupations and professions that were previously closed to women and were supportive of them in their choice of traditionally male courses. While both female and male teachers need to change their perceptions in some areas to be more equitable, progress can be seen. In looking at educational progress for gifted girls, Higham and Navarre (1984) see the following areas as in need of differential treatment:

- In awareness programs for parents where sex differences and the influence of the parents' beliefs and actions on the achievement and career patterns of their daughters need to be explored
- In educational and career counseling where the underrepresentation of

gifted girls in science, mathematics, and other male-dominated courses can be discussed and broader career choices for females can be made known

- In the selection of role models and mentors from nontraditional and interesting careers
- In secondary and higher education where gifted females may find advantages in single-sex classes or schools.

Higham and Navarre do not feel that the issues of sex differences in measures of achievement, in learning and teaching styles, in behavior, and in selection of courses of study and career are currently being adequately addressed by the schools.

Grau (1985) writes of eight psychosocial barriers to the career achievement of gifted girls:

- The psychological construct of femininity being inconsistent with achievement
- Women's self-sabotage
- The socialized need for affiliation
- Female reliance on external sources of control and praise
- The motherhood mandate
- The home and hearth mandate
- Male or female labeling of occupations and professions
- Lack of nontraditional female role models.

Grau's suggestions for dealing with these barriers to free the achievement possibilities include becoming well read about these issues, understanding the barriers, and being prepared to deal with them. Support groups and available role models would also aid in meeting these needs.

There are few studies of women, much less of gifted women. Connelly (1977) has the following comments on some areas that might be researched and developed:

- Teaching women how to establish their credentials
- Teaching how to cope with anger
- Teaching to use power effectively, assertiveness
- Investigating networking, a source of peer contacts, for women, since the "old boy" tie seems to be a fact of life among men
- Help with personal development and self-actualization even when the woman is not meeting society's role expectations for females.

Wolleat (1979) suggests that a counseling program should be designed to ensure gifted females with both personal and academic resources so that they may develop their abilities more fully. Such a program should include

---

- Deliberate psychological education, including examination of forces that facilitate and inhibit their achievement
- Dual (male/female) career-decision making, which has the family at the center
- An all-female career day
- Mentors, successful role models
- Support groups
- Support for self-concept development, nontraditional interests, coping with success.

Callahan (1980) suggests that the curriculum could do the following:

1 Provide activities that require females to practice visual-spatial problem solving from a young age.
2 Provide role models of gifted women engaging in successful problem-solving activities.
3 Provide activities that teach gifted girls the impact they can have on their own destinies, i.e., help them develop an internal locus of control.
4 Provide opportunities for gifted females to interact with successful, attractive feminine role models in a variety of professions.
5 Provide activities that encourage women to establish their own personal goals.
6 Set equivalent standards and criteria for reinforcement for males and females. (p. 20)

Fox (1977) concludes that there are five major areas of concern for future research and program planning that become evident from the existing evidence on sex differences. By investigation of these areas, both gifted boys and gifted girls will benefit:

- Sex role stereotypes
- Homogeneous grouping
- Acceleration of learning and appropriate content for the gifted
- Need for early identification and planning
- Counseling for gifted learners.

It doesn't seem that the secure, self-sufficient, successful, self-actualizing gifted woman is commonly found in and supported by our society. Groth (1975) observes that the pattern for men's success is a straight, conventional one, encouraged by society. Women's pattern is far more complicated, when even success can bring failure.

The interview with the group of highly gifted high school seniors was being videotaped for use in a teacher education class. They had covered most of the usual issues when the interviewer asked, "What do you plan to do when you graduate? What do you think you want to do with your life?" A couple of students mentioned college, although they weren't sure why. It just seemed to be the expected next step. A very pretty young woman spoke up, "I don't know, the way school is and everything. I'm really not interested in anything we've done. There's such pressure to fit into a mold, especially for women, you know. I just don't know. Maybe I'll travel a year and write. I still like to write, not in English class, but for myself. But right now I just want to get away from school, it's such a drag. I really feel dull and bored."

When you looked at her pretty, young face, so serious, so tired looking, so depressed, you really had to wonder what had disillusioned her, "turned her off" so completely. The group was quiet then, and you could tell they knew what she was feeling. They all wondered what was next, and no one seemed happy about the prospects.

CAREER EDUCATION FOR THE GIFTED

Some of the problems encountered by gifted women pursuing careers and some possible solutions have been discussed. The general area of career education for the gifted has drawn the attention of educators, researchers, and government agencies since the National Invitational Seminars on Career Education for Gifted and Talented Students convened at the University of Maryland on October 15, 1972. Hoyt and Hebeler (1974) reported the contributions of this and a subsequent conference. The following discussion summarizes some of these contributions. Although we can find a variety of definitions and objectives for career education in the schools, most definitions include these factors:

- Availability of information and experience on the world of work to all students from K–14 and beyond if desired
- Provision of occupational skills and related knowledge and skills
- Development of attitudes conducive to occupational responsibility
- Development of personal and interpersonal skills, valuing, and communication and decision-making skills
- Awareness of consumer issues and consumer rights
- Relevancy of school studies to preparation for gainful and satisfying employment.

It has been pointed out that career education is not intended to displace liberal arts curricula, but rather to strengthen the student's motivation for pursuing such education. While some fear that overemphasis on vocational training may subvert the broader goals of education, the belief expressed by those espousing career education is that education that does not contain future goals for the learners becomes irrelevant. It is true that career education and career guidance should be available to all students. What is not true is that all students should be presented with the same options, asked to process the same information, or proceed through the same decision-making steps (Herr & Watanabe, 1979). There must be individualized programming and resources available. All students may experience some of these concerns regarding their career choices (Hoyt & Hebeler, 1974):

1 Worker alienation is widespread as a result of
   a The fragmentation and repetitive nature of some jobs
   b The number of unskilled workers in an increasingly complex job market
   c Rapid change in skills required
   d Inflexibility of systems and people who are not equipped for change.
2 Current life expectancy and rapidly changing demands of society make several occupations in a lifetime an increasing reality.
3 Relationships between education and the occupational society are increasing.
4 Students also show evidence of alienation to their school curricula.
5 Fragmentation and repetition can be seen in school organization and are partially responsible for worker alienation among teachers, counselors, and school administrators.

Gifted and talented students, in addition, may encounter the following problems in establishing their careers (Hoyt & Hebeler, 1974; Herr & Watanabe, 1979; Rodenstein, Pfleger, & Colangelo, 1977; Willings, 1986):

1 They find conventional career search programs boring and trivial.
2 They possess multiple talents and interests that complicate career choices and tend to make career search a painful process of focusing on one talent area and rejecting other areas.
3 Many become frustrated with the study of science.
4 Many are not motivated to succeed but rather to avoid failure at all costs.
5 High expectations of parents, teachers, themselves, and society operate as pressures and restrict their choice.
6 The length of training for most professional careers preferred by many gifted students is long, requiring an early vocational decision and long-term commitment. Newland (1976) states that the "brighter the individual, the later his decision regarding the specific area of commitment should be made" (p. 146).
7 The gifted regard their career as a life-style: They tend to regard their work as a means of self-expression and build a life-style around it, becoming consumed by work-related activities.
8 Social isolation results from interests that are too different from those of their peers.

9 There is a lack of adult role models who have the intelligence or creative ability of the gifted student in the area of interest.

10 Problems faced by women seeking careers in our society are of special concern to nearly all gifted females.

To aid in understanding a commitment to career education, Hoyt and Hebeler (1974) give the following definitions to clarify what have been felt to be misconceptions in this field:

- *Work*—the conscious effort aimed at producing benefits for one's self and/or for others
- *Career*—the totality of work that one does in his or her lifetime
- *Education*—the totality of formal, informal, and incidental processes through which an individual learns
- *Vocation*—one's primary work role at any given point in time
- *Occupation*—one's primary work role in the world of paid employment
- *Leisure*—activities that an individual pursues when not engaged in his or her vocation
- *Career education*—the total effort of public education and the community to help all individuals become familiar with the values of a work-oriented society, to integrate those values into their personal value systems, and to implement those values in their lives in such a way that work becomes possible, meaningful, and satisfying to each individual. (pp. 43–46)

Suggested Programs

Feldhusen and Kolloff (1979) suggest a three-stage model of career education that includes instructional activities to enhance and develop creative thinking, problem-solving skills, project abilities, exploratory reading, and independent learning capacity. The model provides a framework for instructional planning for gifted learners. Stage 1 focuses on basic thinking skills and is characterized by short span activities. Stage 2 introduces creative thinking and problem-solving strategies that stress the process of fact finding, problem finding, idea finding, solution finding, and acceptance finding. While guidance is still provided by the teacher, the student is involved in implementing the problem-solving process. It is at this stage that the child begins self-study and is guided toward self-understanding. At Stage 3 the student gets guidance and encouragement from the teacher, but independently proceeds to research and complete a project. Gifted learners will not be content to be given the factual data, nor merely to observe someone involved in a career that interests them. The mentor relationship is encouraged by Feldhusen and Kolloff (1979) to provide a role model and a guide for meaningful career exploration. From printed materials and visiting professionals, the gifted child can begin to explore career possibilities. Career mentors provide the next step in career exploration, with an in-depth involvement on site, an example of third level exploration. The

Purdue three-stage model can be used in a regular classroom, in a resource room, or in a special class.

Delisle (1984) presents a career education program based on the acronym BIASED. The program for gifted adolescents incorporates these concepts:

B—*Basic information* about currently available career options and possible future choices based upon employment projections.

I—*Introspection* regarding the personal comforts and disadvantages of selected careers.

A—*Adaptation* to particular occupations through active involvement in the workaday lives of professionals.

SE—*Selection* of a career path based on knowledge and insights gained by completing various portions of the above activities.

D—*Direction* to students who are not yet ready to select a career path or area of professional training.

Willings (1986) offers a seven-module program, Enriched Career Search, that can be offered as a two-year program with one class meeting each week, two two-week programs held in two consecutive summers, or a three-week program for teachers and counselors that includes training in administering the program. The programs are available in English and Spanish.

Module 1 *Your Career and You:* The students explore the theory that in work people are seeking to satisfy two drives—the drive "to be somebody" and the drive "to do something worthwhile." Other issues are discussed, e.g., moving from fantasy to reality, money in the context of overall satisfaction, etc.

Module 2 *Self-Evaluation:* Students gain wider insights into themselves by writing and evaluating exercises exploring their career choices to date.

Module 3 *Job Study:* Students are introduced to the various aspects of job study—the hidden factors, the key and complementary skills, physical skills, job features, requirements for entry, problems of training, difficulties and distastes, and sources of rewards.

Module 4 *The Adult World:* Students participate in simulations of various situations.

Module 5 *Group Roles:* The students discover the various roles needed by each group.

Module 6 *Ethical Considerations in Work:* The codes of ethics of various professionals are discussed, and guidelines are offered on how the students can analyze their personal reactions to ethical situations and, from their reactions, arrive at their personal code of ethics. Willings feels that no one can or should tell a student what is right and good.

Module 7 *Career Strategies and Strategies for Creative Growth.*

Including values clarification in the study of careers is also a concern of other researchers (Garrison, Stronge, & Smith, 1986; Kerr, 1986). Identifying the aspects of a career that are personally important is an outcome of the study of values that is a great advantage to the gifted student (Garrison, Stronge, & Smith, 1986). Kerr (1986) believes career education must be a search for meaning not a search for a job. She points out that clarifying values and goalsetting based on values has caused honors students to change not only their career goals, but the way they determine those goals. The frequent occurrence of early eminence among very bright gifted adolescents makes finding a mentor a crucial step in their career development, especially for women. Mentors not only provide role models, they can support, encourage, and facilitate professional socialization and access to advanced training, says Kerr. An additional phase drawn to our attention by Kerr is the maintenance of productivity. Counselors and those teaching career education can find helpful ideas in Kerr's work.

Moore (1979) believes that the main purpose of career education is to provide gifted students with skills and attitudes necessary for "changing with change," including these:

- Basic academic skills
- Decision making, job seeking, and job holding skills
- Good work habits. (p. 20)

More specifically related to gifted and talented students are these:

- Exploration skills to assist with all other future career decisions
- Skills for developing occupations
- Abilities to cope with a number of different and/or interrelated occupational skills
- The ability to move freely between occupations with the least amount of resistance and restrictions. (p. 20)

In a survey of teachers of the gifted, career counselors, principals, and college professors in Illinois (Ford & Ellis, 1979), the most frequently mentioned practices were the use of community resource persons, field trips, and guidance and counseling. Abraham (1976) suggests that competent counseling can direct individuals into new fields that they might not have considered, encourage delaying a decision until major possibilities are known, and help the student to understand parental pressures and to facilitate scholarship opportunities.

Career education for the disadvantaged gifted is an area needing special attention according to the work of Dunham and Russo (1983). Some of the trends evident in careers today are especially difficult for gifted students from low-socioeconomic homes, e.g., career changes, rising college costs, and less support available for college tuition. This research team suggests providing a program of career education that includes realistic job opportunities consonant with the potential of disadvantaged students, that envisions a broad horizon and avoids limited or short-sighted goals, and that provides opportunities for adults to (1) serve as role models in the students' own community and (2) work closely with the career education program.

There is evidence that the results of career education programs for gifted and talented are worth the effort. In a post-high school follow-up of participants and nonparticipants of a career education program for gifted and talented, the students were asked which high school experiences had the greatest impact on them. Among the experiences, the career education program received 53.33%, extracurricular activities received 33.3%, and a regular course was selected by only one student. Neither participants nor nonparticipants mentioned advanced courses, enrichment activities, or the school counseling program (Colson, 1980). To optimize a career education program, Hoyt and Hebeler (1974) suggest the following guidelines:

1 Career education programs should begin, as should other programs for gifted learners, with consideration of their special needs and characteristics.
2 Decision-making skills should be included.
3 Provisions must include actual involvement in the community and the world of work.
4 Care should be taken to discover and enrich the talented students' career potentials as well as those of the gifted.

Torrance (1976) suggests that gifted students need to learn about the future: "We need to help them invent alternative futures, evaluate these alternative futures, improve these alternatives and make choices about them that will make a difference in the kind of world we shall have" (p. 143).

Futurists describe shifts in our occupational focus from agricultural to industrial to service (Little, 1973). Resources were located primarily in the land, and the dominant figure in society was the landowner. The focus then moved to business, and the businessperson became the dominant figure. Now scientists and researchers assume a major role, as the focus shifts to knowledge and technology (Bell, 1972). Maruyama (1975) optimistically identifies the following positive changes in emphasis that society is making: from competition to interdependence, from efficiency to esthetics and ethics, from conquering nature to living in harmony with nature. Many believe the future will require more cooperation, more recycling and conservation, more creativity, and more interdependence.

We must be careful that the career education does not focus on careers that may become obsolete by the time our students move into the world of work. We must be sensitive to shifts in the needs of this area and focus our efforts on such future preparatory issues as comfort with change; access to information; skills of creative thinking, problem solving, and forecasting; effective communication, personal competence, and self-esteem; and the background needed to understand modern humans and their environment.

Singer (1974) finds that the student's image of the future influences the achievement of that student in the present. If the belief in the future is a positive one, if the student can envision personal success, academic achievement will be high and school will have meaning for that student. When the future focus is weak or negative, poor achievement, maladaptive behavior, and dropping out of school may result. The study of futures can be intriguing to gifted students and can impact their career choices. (See Chapter 8, pp. 410–412, and Chapter 12.)

Activities to Develop Awareness of Career Possibilities

The following activities can be done in the class or suggested by the career counseling center:

1 Ask students to bring to class the "Help Wanted" section of their newspaper. In small groups, compile the following information:
   a Identify the kinds of job opportunities that now exist.
   b What differences are there in job opportunities for men and for women?
   c What kinds of qualifications and training are required?
   d Discuss.
2 Watch for job roles on television during 1 week and note the different jobs presented.
   By whom are they filled (e.g., men, women, older, younger, minorities, etc.)? What kinds of qualifications do you notice the job holders having?
3 Write a list of job categories on the board (e.g., Agricultural, Business, Banking, Body and Fender, Computing, Data Processing, Clerical, Craftsman, Dental, Drafting, Electronics, Engineering, Firefighting, Florists, Graphic Arts, Health, Home Economics, Hotel/Restaurant, Law Enforcement, Repairperson).
   Ask students to write down as many names of people who fit in these categories as they can in 3 minutes. Now ask them to go over their lists to see how many are men, women, minorities, etc.
   Discuss.
4 Have students list all advertised positions that interest them personally. Then have them list unadvertised job titles in those interests that describe more specifically what they want to do. These lists can be used by the teacher or counselor to discuss further academic training needed to fill those positions.
5 Using a current issue of a newspaper, working in small groups, list societal problems that are not yet solved. Discuss possible solutions and what jobs these solutions might create. What jobs might no longer exist if the problems are solved? Discuss the group's findings with the class.

DEVELOPING LEADERSHIP ABILITY

Although the literature presents no agreement on the best approach for leadership training, or even on what constitutes leadership, we shall discuss it as a set of skills that enable a group to reach its goals to maintain itself with mutual satisfaction, and to adapt to environmental change; and that allow individuals within the group to attain self-fulfillment. By this definition, leadership skills are mostly interpersonal and include flexibility, openness, and ability to organize. Leadership requires self-esteem, high values, and mature emotional development. Knowledge of group process and communication techniques strengthens the effectiveness of leadership. The characteristics found commonly among gifted children can, if given opportunities to develop, enhance any leadership role. In this context, the strategies presented in the affective domain will be of great benefit. Some of these characteristics are common in successful leaders (Judkins, n.d.):

- Above-average intelligence
- Skills of decision making
- Ability to deal with abstract concepts, future planning, time constraints
- A sense of purpose, direction
- Flexibility, adaptability
- Loyalty, responsibility
- Self-confidence, knowledge of self
- Perseverance
- Tolerance, patience with people
- Enthusiasm
- Ability to express ideas in oral or written form clearly.

Opportunities to enhance any of these characteristics would be an important part of your leadership training program.

Leadership development is an important focus for staff training in business and industry, in government, in universities, and in the military. The commitment to addressing the skills involved in leadership has increased the attention the educational community has paid to this area, and research projects and articles have become more numerous. Among the additions to the literature is the 1987 Yearbook for the Association for Supervision and Curriculum Development entitled, *Leadership: Examining the Elusive* (Sheive & Schoenheit, 1987). While the attention is now focused on leadership at the adult level, more is becoming known about the development of these skills at earlier ages.

Leadership has been found to have its beginnings in the patterns being established in very young children. Montagner (cited in Pines, 1984) observes that parents of children who become leaders communicate with their children a great deal; they use mimicry, gestures, and words; and they stoop down to the children's level to talk with them. They ask their children what they want to do, listen to what their children say, and pay attention to any spontaneous behavior. They do not threaten or use aggressive behavior toward their children, nor are they overprotective. Montagner finds that their behavior is consistently stable.

One example of a current educational project in leadership is the Leadership Studies Program, developed by Karnes, Meriweather, and D'Llio (1987). This is an individualized, diagnostic-prescriptive program that has been found effective in increasing the identified skills of leadership. It incorporates the Leadership Skill Inventory for assessing skills identified from the literature as important to the development of leadership. The inventory is comprised of nine factors: fundamentals of leadership, written communication skills, speech communication skills, values clarification, decision-making skills, group dynamics skills, problem-solving skills, personal development skills, and planning skills. The Leadership Skill Inventory is self-rated and self-scored, allowing the student to determine skills already acquired and those needing to be learned. Appropriate activities from the *Learning Skill Inventory Activities Manual* can then be offered to develop the weaknesses the student has identified. The activities may be individually developed or be conducted through group discussions or simulations with the teacher and the student becoming partners in the learning process. The pre and post data showed that all of the nine factors contribute to the effectiveness of this program.

Leadership needs are often thought to be met by nominating class officers. That is only one type of leadership. It will be important for the gifted to become more involved in a system of evolving group leadership. When groups are encouraged to problem solve by using the skills and special abilities of all of the group members, gifted students will learn another, possibly more valuable, way of leading, that of sharing the leadership function. To learn more about developing leadership, see Arnold (1976), Csoka (1974), Cunningham and Gephart (1973), Fiedler (1967, 1971), Fleisham and Hunt (1973), Gibb (1969), Gowan and Demos (1962), Isaacs (1973), *Leadership: A Survey of Literature* (1976), Sheive & Schoenheit (1987), Stogbill (1974), Stogbill and Coons (1957), and Yamamoto (1975).

In this chapter, we have briefly explored nine problems currently being researched in gifted education: labeling, grading practices, underachievement, disadvantaged gifted, culturally diverse gifted, handicapped gifted, gifted females, career education for the gifted, and developing leadership ability. The intent was to create an awareness of the problems in the hope that such awareness might foster increased efforts toward solutions, both in the home and at school.

Questions Often Asked

1. What is the biggest problem with labeling a child gifted?
Would it be better to call gifted children by another word?

The word *gifted* does give an unfortunate connotation to the group of children who bear that label. People often think that they were given a gift, that is, they did nothing to earn their ability or talent. In our society we are suspicious of anyone who gets something for nothing, and we think that if they didn't earn what they have they probably do not deserve to have it. Certainly they should not have more. This line of thinking has been responsible for a lot of misunderstanding about gifted children. However, giving them a different label would still not solve the problems labeling causes. We have this label now so perhaps the best we can do is to be sure everyone, including the gifted child, understands what we mean by it.

2. If you have to give grades, how can you do it with the least problem for the student?

Developing a procedure that involves the student in planning and evaluation makes a big difference in the effect grading can have. Student contracts, criteria for evaluation (sometimes developed by the student), and student conferences to work with the teacher on turning the work done into a respresentative grade are some ways to alleviate the problems of grading.

3. Why is there concern about grading anyway? We are certainly evaluated in the real world.

Evaluation is not the problem, grading is. There are many ways to evaluate a process or product that can be very constructive for the student. As you can see from the discussion in this chapter the research shows nothing constructive about grading practices.

4. If gifted students are underachieving is it better to place them with other underachieving gifted students in a special class or keep them with the regular class where they will have better role models?

Actually the students could have the advantage of both a special class for part of their work and placement in a regular class for work they are better able to do. The concept of mainstreaming asks that we consider the least restrictive environment. Each student will have a different cluster of needs, and the decision as to placement must take into account his or her needs, what the special class provides, and what can be provided by the regular class. The students' individual programs will dictate where and how often they are placed for the best advantage. The teacher's skills, the parents' wishes, and the school's resources all must be considered in this decision. Don't forget to assess the children's feelings and information on possible choices; these could be very valuable and allow them to participate in their own learning.

5. If a child is bored with school, doesn't want to do the work, and really doesn't even want to be there what can the parents do?

It is very important that you ask for a team meeting with the teacher, yourselves, and the child. Try to find out what everyone thinks is happening and what might happen. Offer to help with whatever plan the teacher feels will help, and if possible offer the child several choices of ways to change the situation. At the very least get the child's perspective and be sure the child understands the expectations and the consequences for doing or not doing what is planned. Above all, don't just let it go on thinking it will pass. Learning patterns are formed in this way that can lead to underachievement patterns that will be hard to break later. What may only be a misunderstanding or lack of information now could be a difficult problem later.

6. Do culturally diverse students require a separate curriculum?

If the instruction is individualized and the curriculum is differentiated, a separate curriculum would not be necessary. What will be important, however, is that the teacher and others involved in gifted programs where culturally diversity exists hold positive attitudes toward cultural differences and have an awareness of cultural and ethnic history and traditions, that there are lots of resources related to diverse populations available, and that the program be flexible and responsive to each child's needs.

11. Teachers of the Gifted at School and at Home

This chapter presents material concerning teachers of the gifted at school, those who support their work, and parents, who are the teachers of the gifted at home. The chapter covers

- The abilities, values, and characteristics necessary to be an effective teacher of the gifted learners at school.
- Presenting gifted education to classroom teachers, administrators, and parents through university programs and other inservice opportunities.
- The need for support systems, when establishing effective gifted education and for a teacher's unique teaching style within the school system.
- Other personnel within the school system, such as administrators and counselors, and their role in gifted programs.
- The need for establishing parent organizations.
- Inservice experiences for parents of gifted learners.
- The importance of parents as resources.
- Living with gifted children.

No man can reveal to you aught but that which already lies half asleep in the dawning of your knowledge.

The teacher . . . gives not of his wisdom but rather of his faith and his lovingness.

If he is indeed wise he does not bid you enter the house of his wisdom, but rather leads you to the threshold of your own mind.

—KAHLIL GIBRAN

Some years ago at a conference sponsored by the American Educational Research Association, David Aspy presented the results of a research project on factors differentiating effective teachers from less effective ones. I was most impressed to hear that one factor counts far more than any other, the teacher's self-concept. The high self-esteem of a teacher, Aspy related, correlates with student success in the classroom; no other factor shows such a significant correlation (Aspy, 1969). On the same panel, William Brookover stated that the teacher's attitude toward self and others is more important to classroom success than techniques, practices, and materials, and that accepting one's self made one more accepting of others (Brookover, 1969). When he suggested that the development of self-concept might be more important in teacher education than methodology, I was truly amazed.

It was not that I had difficulty in integrating such data into my view of reality, for my experience in working with teachers supported everything they said. What was amazing was, and still is, that if this is true, why are there no selection criteria, no courses in the teacher training institutions, and no qualifications in the hiring practices of school districts that relate to this critical factor? Since that time, our institution has developed coursework for generating positive teacher self-concept, and a few other institutions and districts have become concerned with this issue in teacher preparation. It remains a low priority for most, however, and still does not influence screening, teacher selection, or hiring practices to any great degree. In part, we can understand, for there is a lack of acceptable standardized instruments to measure a person's self-concept. Academic achievement scores and grade point averages are still considered "safer" and are more acceptable in the educational decision-making process. Measureability has been a controlling factor for a long time now.

Almost everyone agrees that the teacher has the most significant influence on a learning environment. Many factors influence the learning of a student, but within the classroom situation, the teacher is of critical importance. In a survey of people working in gifted programs, Renzulli (1968) found that they ranked the teacher highest as a factor critical to the success of the programs. They considered both selection and training of teachers as major issues. Anderson and Kennedy (1932) long ago stated that the mental attitude of the teacher most influenced the atmosphere of the classroom. Gallagher, Aschner, and Jenne (1967) found intellectual productivity in school directly related to the teacher's style, expectations, and response patterns. Webb (1971) believes that his data show that the way teachers behave, not what they know, is the most important issue in the transmission of the teaching-learning exchange. It seems apparent that those who wish to provide optimal learning situations for gifted students will be concerned about the characteristics, values, self-concepts, and training of the teachers who implement gifted programs.

Surprisingly, only 20 states have any requirements beyond the regular teaching credentials for teachers of the gifted. Even worse, few institutions, districts, or state departments of education provide preservice or inservice experiences in gifted education. The National/State Leadership Training Institute on Gifted and Talented has made one of the most impactful contributions in this area. By setting up summer institutes and national conferences, they have begun to make people in every state aware of this critical training need and have provided models and expertise for changing what was a desolate picture. Much still remains to be done, for we already know that attitudes of teachers, counselors, and administrators change favorably toward the gifted when they have participated in some gifted education. If we are ever to provide opportunities that will allow gifted children to develop their potential, we must have sensitive, knowledgeable teachers both at school and in the home.

As we begin our discussion of teachers of the gifted, we will consider a recent case brought to adjudication for the purpose of deciding if a school board had the right during a period of declining enrollment to retain a 5-year teacher trained to work with gifted learners over a tenured senior classroom teacher who did not have special training (Renzulli, 1985). The ruling was that even though special certification was not required by the state the school board did not violate collective bargaining agreements by retaining the specially prepared teacher over the senior teacher. This ruling establishes a precedent that other teachers and school boards may wish to consider. Renzulli suggests that several issues from this case be carefully noted for future consideration:

1 Job descriptions used in announcements of positions for gifted specialists should include explicit statements regarding training requirements and types of teaching skills involved.
2 Descriptive statements regarding the special program should be maintained.
3 The program model and the teacher's competencies necessary to implement the model should be specified.
4 Careful documentation of all program activities must be made.

The ruling in this case supports the position that teachers of the gifted do need special training and are qualified to be considered educational specialists.

TEACHERS OF THE GIFTED: AT SCHOOL

Abilities, Values, and Characteristics

Few educational decisions have as much influence on the gifted program as teacher selection. If we believe the lists of characteristics offered by researchers and writers in this field, we would need to find a person who is so outstanding and exemplary that few gifted programs could exist. Some believe that the teachers of gifted students must be brilliant and highly gifted to keep ahead of their students. Others want them learned and wise, with extraordinary insights and a depth of understanding of their subject or field that comes with years of living and teaching. Some would require the teacher to be an accomplished counselor, a profound philosopher, and an active community leader.

After reading the lists, one has the impression that only a Shakespearean sonnet could do them justice. At the least, those employed to select such a teacher must be totally overwhelmed. To complicate matters, there are teachers who have only a few of the characteristics commonly listed who are exciting and productive in the classroom; others have many of the characteristics, but they are cold, arrogant boors who communicate little of value to their students. To compile the ideal profile, we should look at the traits that seem not just desirable, but most essential. We can find clues to effective characteristics and attitudes from those who work in gifted programs, from researchers, and from the students themselves.

One especially significant body of data derives from projects developed by Arthur Combs (1969; Combs et al., 1974) that resulted in an innovative teacher education program at the University of Florida (Wass et al., 1974). Validation for Combs's work also has come from Usher and Hanke (1971) at the University of Northern Colorado and from numerous doctoral studies. These studies concluded by identifying the differences between effective and ineffective teachers (Combs, 1969):

Effective teachers have a general frame of reference that emphasizes

- The internal rather than the external
- Concern with people rather than things
- Meaning rather than facts or events
- The value of authenticity
- Immediacy in causation of behavior
- A phenomenological or perceptual orientation rather than a behavioristic one.

Effective teachers tend to perceive other people and their behavior as

---

- Able rather than unable
- Friendly rather than unfriendly
- Worthy rather than unworthy
- Internally rather than externally motivated
- Dependable rather than undependable
- Helpful rather than hindering.

Effective teachers tend to perceive themselves as

- With people rather than apart from people
- Able rather than unable
- Dependable rather than undependable
- Worthy rather than unworthy
- Wanted rather than unwanted.

Effective teachers tend to perceive the teaching task as

- Freeing rather than controlling
- Larger rather than smaller
- Revealing rather than concealing
- Involved rather than uninvolved
- Encouraging process rather than achieving goals.

Another clue comes from Iannon and Carline (1971) in their conclusion that teachers who have qualities of spontaneity, acceptance, creativity, and self-realization can most effectively help develop human potential. Aspy (1969) concurs in his request for accepting, supportive, facilitating teachers. Flanders (1960) adds the need for teachers to have the ability to provide several support and organizational structures for students and to be sensitive as to when their use is appropriate.

Aspy and Roebuck (1972) investigated the relationship between teachers' classroom behavior and students' level of cognitive functioning. They found that teachers whose students attained cognitive levels beyond memory and recognition provided significantly higher levels of positive regard than those whose students stayed at that level. Only the levels of positive regard were significantly different between groups of teachers. Positive regard is directly facilitative of higher cognitive functioning within the instructional situation, these researchers concluded.

Insecure, insensitive, sarcastic teachers not only do not facilitate learning, they have a marked negative effect on the quality and quantity learned, as well as on the student's self-esteem (Aspy, 1969; Webb, 1971).

Promoting (and Inhibiting) Characteristics of Effective/Affective Teachers

Another way to look at facilitating learning is to specify the results we wish to obtain and the teacher behaviors and attitudes that have been shown to achieve these results best. The following compilation reported by Gordon (Welch, Richards, & Richards, 1973) uses the research of Amidon and Flanders (1961), Anderson and Brewer (1946), Brown (1968), Ober (1970), Severy and Davis (1971), and Soar (1970):

To promote growth of the inquiring mind,

1 Involve the pupil in incomplete situations.
2 Lead the pupil to a question or problem that puzzles.
3 Ask the kind of question that is not readily answerable by a study of the "lesson."
4 Permit the pupil to suggest additional or alternative answers.
5 Encourage the pupil to hypothesize about the unknown or untested.
6 Entertain even wild or far-out suggestions by pupils.
7 Ask the pupil to support answers or opinions by providing evidence.
8 Provide material and time for the pupil to develop ideas.
9 Ask "How would you predict?" questions.
10 Make "If, then" statements.

To promote growth of self-respect,

1 Move freely among the pupils.
2 Engage in positive redirection, attend to pupils closely, give individual attention.
3 Praise, smile, laugh, nod, show authentic feelings.
4 Admit errors openly.
5 Listen to each pupil's opinion.
6 Use group discussion to allow feelings to be expressed, to solve problems.
7 Have the pupils write stories about self.
8 Take time for activities in developing self-esteem.
9 Tell the pupils about their work.
10 Plan and evaluate cooperatively.

To inhibit growth of self-respect,

1 Humiliate pupils as a form of control.
2 Punish pupils for showing anger.
3 Require pupils to line up.

4 Require pupils to work only on specific instructions from the teacher.
5 Ignore pupils.

To promote growth in respect for others,

1 Ask pupils to help others.
2 Help pupils to solve problems of disturbing others.
3 Ask the class to discuss differences in people.
4 Discuss controversial issues with the class.
5 Ask the class about how they think others might feel.
6 Use value clarification techniques.
7 Encourage social interchange and cooperation.

To promote growth of sense of competence, aiding self-esteem,

1 Have pupils find their own information.
2 Provide the time and opportunity for pupils to use special aids, language aids, tape recorders, learning centers, etc.
3 Tell the pupils when they have done a good job.
4 Allow pupils space to display their own work.
5 Give alternative ways of working when a pupil shows a lack of interest or frustration.
6 Keep a record of work accomplished (visibly and cooperatively).
7 Give fewer directions, less criticism, less lecturing; encourage participation.

To promote growth of the sense of responsibility for one's own conduct,

1 Have pupils make their own analysis of subject matter.
2 Have pupils find detailed facts and information on their own.
3 Have pupils work independently on what concerns them.
4 Encourage self-discipline on the part of the pupil.
5 Withhold judgment on pupil's behavior or work.
6 Encourage the pupil to put his or her ideas to a test.
7 Evaluate the work of different pupils by different standards, cooperatively.
8 Use self-evaluation.

To inhibit growth of the sense of responsibility,

1 Allow no discussion.
2 Make all the rules and decisions.
3 Tell pupils to raise their hands, wait their turn, and stay in their seats.
4 Help pupils only when they raise their hands for help.

To promote growth of the sense of commitment, encourage pupils to engage in the following behaviors with peers and others:

1 Showing concern.
2 Advising, suggesting, or interpreting.
3 Comforting or reassuring.
4 Fixing something.
5 Protecting, warning, defending.
6 Getting help for somebody else, helping another accomplish a task, or helping out in distress.
7 Offering needed help.

Students also provide a source of information on effective teaching strategies, attitudes, and characteristics. Schaefer (1970) found that the creative high school girls in his sample specified the following traits as indicative of outstanding teachers they had had:

- Enthusiasm for subject taught, ability to make a subject come alive
- Personal interest in the student and belief in his/her ability
- Sincerity and honesty, especially in acknowledging personal mistakes or information gaps
- A good listener who encourages students to express themselves
- Likeable, warm, kind, concerned.

Johnson (1976) asked 1,800 students 5 to 18 years old, from kindergarten through high school in the Philadelphia area, to answer two sets of questions. One set asked what made a teacher good and what teachers did to help them learn; the other questioned what teachers did that made it hard to learn. A partial summary will show a surprising consistency with the other data we have previously mentioned. Johnson tells us that the children pointed to nearly the same teacher behaviors whether they were young or older, high or low achieving, from economically deprived or from affluent areas. These teacher traits helped them learn:

- Paying attention to their needs; listening to them
- Understanding their problems; communicating
- Sharing their successes; making them feel important
- Treating them openly, fairly, and with respect
- Having a sense of humor and pleasant nature; being real and authentic.

Overall, the affective qualities were more important to the students than the cognitive traits, and the personal, human qualities outweighed concerns with methods, materials, and curriculum. They found it hard to learn from teachers who

- Yelled at them, embarrassing them.
- Made unreasonable demands.
- Used physical restraint and punishment, "many commonly used management devices" (e.g., staying in at recess or after school, writing as punishment, standing in the corner, hitting or slapping).
- Acted condescending; as one student put it, "They talk down to you even if you're taller."
- Acted "real phony."

The above practices distinguish effective teachers in regular educational settings. They should be the basis for choosing teachers who will and will not work with the gifted.

Certain specific qualities also have been shown to make good teachers of the gifted. Some writers suggest that we specify characteristics of teachers according to what is effective with different types of gifted children (e.g., disadvantaged, underachieving, creative). They advise different selection and training depending on the subgroup involved. In my experience, this would not only be impractical and needlessly restrictive, but a disadvantage for both the teacher and the program. Few programs are so specialized that such subgrouping would be feasible. In most groups of gifted children, all subgroups are duly represented.

A possible exception might be in the area of the visual and performing arts. As we have seen, this is an area that requires a level of accomplishment, unreached by many of us, to make the role of teacher of use to the student who shows giftedness in this area. As one student so wisely observed, "Every teacher is different; his or her talents, skills and interests vary. To be most beneficial, the teacher should perceive not only the needs of the individual student, but his or her own capability to fill those needs" (Dubner, 1980).

A major study (Bishop, 1968) used student selection of the "most successful" teachers of high school gifted programs, results of teacher and student questionnaires, teacher interviews, teacher academic records, and testing scores. Bishop offers the following conclusions: while not differing in sex, marital status, type of undergraduate institution attended, highest degree held, course work preparation, and extent of association with professional organizations, the teachers judged effective by intellectually gifted, high achieving students did differ from teachers not so identified. Effective teachers

- Were more mature, experienced teachers.
- Were mentally superior.
- Pursued intellectual avocations.
- Had high achievement needs.
- Pursued intellectual growth.
- Showed more favorable attitudes toward students, were sensitive and empathetic.

- Were more student centered in their teaching approach.
- Assumed a more systematic, orderly, and businesslike classroom approach.
- Were more stimulating, imaginative, well-grounded, and enthusiastic toward the subject and teaching.
- Supported special educational provisions for gifted students.

In a study by Kathnelson and Colley (1982) students 6 to 16 years of age, in a special project for gifted and highly able learners, were asked to record descriptions of what they would like an ideal teacher to do as a teacher and as a person. The results showed the following student responses regarding desirable characteristics:

Items mentioned 50% of the time

- Someone who understands them
- Someone who has a sense of humor
- Someone who can make learning fun
- Someone who is cheerful.

Items mentioned 30% of the time

- Someone who supports and respects them
- Someone who is intelligent
- Someone who is patient
- Someone who is firm with them
- Someone who is flexible.

Items mentioned occasionally (5 to 10% of the time)

- Someone who knows the subject
- Someone who explains things carefully
- Someone who is skilled in group processes.

The teachers and parents chose "knowledge of nature and need of gifted," "skill in developing self-concept," and "skills in integrating the cognitive, affective, sensory and intuitive abilities" as top priorities in their ranking of professional competencies for the teachers of gifted. They listed "understands, accepts, respects, trusts and likes self"; "supports, respects, trusts and is sensitive to others"; and "is open to new ideas, flexible" as the top priorities for personal attributes. The project was a summer school that used the Integrative Education Model (see Chapter 7) as its philosophical and instructional base, so the emphasis among parents choosing the school and faculty teaching at the school would be on goals associated with this educational approach.

Through the use of observations, interviews, and search of the literature a study (Story, 1985) was conducted to discover the behavioral characteristics necessary for successful teaching of the gifted. Phase 1 involved interviews with leaders in the field of education of the gifted and revealed four types of characteristics seen as necessary for teachers of the gifted: professional commitment, skills in facilitating learning, knowledge both in general subject areas and in the theory of education of the gifted, and personality factors. Phase 2 produced six categories of behaviors that were obtained from the observations of teachers in the field:

1 Teachers of the gifted provide for positive and close physical relationships that support learning for gifted children.
2 The quality and quantity of verbal interaction is a key factor in successful teaching of gifted children.
3 Teachers of the gifted are flexible with their use of time scheduling according to students' needs.
4 Teachers of the gifted are process oriented, with children's creative productivity the ultimate goal.
5 Teachers of the gifted provide or suggest appropriate environmental supports based upon children's independent study interests.
6 The teacher of the gifted displays "gifted behavior" as brought to bear upon his or her professional responsibilities.

The results of the interviews, observations, and search of the literature suggest that it is the above-average, creative, and task-committed teacher that can learn the roles necessary for teaching gifted children. The researcher believes that the list of behaviors resulting from this study can serve as a guideline for administrators hiring new staff and evaluating current staff in programs for the gifted.

In a study by Dorhout (1983) of the preferences of gifted elementary and secondary students and their teachers' perceptions of their preferences for teacher behaviors, it was found that elementary gifted students and their teachers showed no significant differences. However, significant differences were seen between what secondary students preferred in teacher behavior and what their teachers thought they preferred. Both elementary and secondary gifted students showed a strong preference for items on the Preferred Instructor Characteristics Scale (PICS) that expressed personal-social behaviors such as "I prefer a teacher who: (a) covers all the material, (b) treats us as mature people," with (b) of course being the personal-social item. Teachers of the elementary gifted accurately predicted that their students would show this preference for personal-social behaviors and even went a bit further to that end of the scale in their responses. Secondary school teachers, however, predicted that their gifted students would prefer cognitive-intellectual attributes, which was in fact not the case. The researcher suggests, in light of these findings, that those responsible for teaching gifted students on the secondary level undergo staff orientation and training regarding preferred teacher attributes shown by the students. He contends that the discrepancy shown may be creating an atmosphere in the classroom that is not optimally conducive to learning.

Another study that turned out to be supportive of the personal-social characteristics as preferred for teacher behavior by gifted students was conducted by Maddux, Samples-Lachmann, & Cummings (1985). Gifted students in seventh, eighth, and ninth grades showed a significant preference for personal-social characteristics over cognitive or classroom-management variables. Of interest was the observation that the higher IQ group valued cognitive variables more than the lower IQ group and that this pattern more resembled an Israeli study than the other results derived from this study. The top items in each of the categories are also of interest: For personal-social—friendly, confidence in students, and sense of humor; for cognitive—knowledge of the subject taught, imaginative, and teaches useful information; for classroom management—allows open class discussion, treats me as an adult, and teaches in an organized way. The researchers feel that this study may have some tentative implications for preservice and inservice teacher education in gifted and talented education.

Lindsey (1980) presents us with a synthesis of what is known to be preferred in the personal characteristics and teaching behaviors of those who are successful in their work with gifted learners:

Personal characteristics
- Understands, accepts, respects, trusts, and likes self; has outstanding ego strength
- Is sensitive to others, less concerned with self; supports, respects, trusts others
- Is above average intellectually; exhibits an intellectual style of conceptualizing, generalizing, creating, initiating, relating, organizing, imagining
- Is flexible, open to new ideas
- Has intellectual interests, literary and cultural
- Desires to learn, increase knowledge; has high achievement needs
- Is enthusiastic
- Is intuitive, perceptive
- Is committed to excellence
- Feels responsible for own behavior and consequences.

Personal-professional predispositions
- To guide rather than to coerce or pressure
- To be democratic rather than autocratic
- To focus on process as well as product
- To be innovative and experimental rather than conforming
- To use problem-solving procedures rather than jump to unfounded conclusions
- To seek involvement of others in discovery rather than give out answers.

Teaching behaviors

- Develops a flexible, individualized program
- Creates a warm, safe, and permissive atmosphere
- Provides feedback
- Uses varied strategies
- Respects personal self-images and enhances positive ones; respects personal values
- Respects creativity and imagination
- Stimulates higher-order mental processes
- Respects individuality and personal integrity. (pp. 13, 14)

Whitmore (1980) believes that the most critical factor in developing appropriate educational experiences for gifted children is the teachers involved. She would want the teacher of the gifted to be, in part, a person who models the traits and life-style of a scholar, challenges the student to think at higher levels, and stimulates interest and independent pursuits; and to be compatible with the need for flexibility, increasing self-direction, reduction of pressure, and opportunities for self-expression. Such a person must have superior organization skills; enjoy energetic, inquiring minds; and understand the needs of gifted children.

The above qualities do make good teachers, and students prefer them. Some of the characteristics may even be unique preferences of gifted students. We cannot be sure which are desirable for all students and which are necessary for only the gifted. It is my belief that there are specific abilities, attainable by many teachers, that are necessary if they are to provide effective programs for gifted learners. For example, a teacher does not need to be highly intelligent to work effectively with the gifted learner, but that teacher should definitely value intelligence, understand its implications, and know how to nurture it. Not all teachers will have or will desire to acquire the abilities listed here, but it is possible for many to do so. Teachers for gifted programs should be selected on the basis of such abilities. Specifically, teachers must develop these abilities if they are to be effective with gifted learners:

1 They must have a knowledge and understanding of the cognitive, social, and emotional characteristics, needs, and problems found in gifted students as a result of their atypical mental development.
2 They must be able to develop a flexible, individualized, differentiated curriculum appropriate to meeting the individual gifted pupil's needs and nurturing group interaction.
3 They must be able to create an environment in which the gifted can use their strengths, explore their personal and interpersonal development, risk new areas of thought and action, feel challenged, and actually be more of who they are.
4 They must be able to teach the gifted learner the skills of higher level cognitive thinking, integration of mind and body, self-actualization, intuitive development, and self-evaluation.

5 They must know how to nurture creativity in all its aspects of thinking, feeling, intuiting, and expressing talent through products.

6 They must be able to encourage in gifted learners a sense of social awareness and commitment to humanity and to their environment, and a respect for the worth and dignity of others.

7 They must relate well to colleagues and parents of gifted learners and conduct professional meetings for their benefit.

To develop such traits requires an uncommon amount of ability to

- Empathize and inspire
- Tolerate ambiguity; be open, flexible, and innovative
- Share enthusiasm, a love of learning, and a joy of living
- Be authentic, congruent, and humane as a deep personal commitment
- Be alert, knowledgeable, and informed
- Value intelligence, intuition, diversity, and uniqueness in self and others
- Value change, growth, and self-actualization for self and others.

The research of the following persons supports the need for these abilities: Baldwin (1977); Bishop (1968); Drews (1972); Freehill (1975); Gallagher, Aschner, and Jenne (1967); Lyon (1975); Newland (1976); C. Rogers (1969); Rogge (1970); Strang (1960); Ward (1961); and Wilson (1958).

Knowing the traits that, when present, prevent teachers from encouraging the development we are seeking in gifted students is also important. Torrance (Gowan, Demos, & Torrance, 1967) found the following characteristics present among teachers who could not apply one or more accepting, supporting principles used in his study:

> . . . authoritarian, defensive, dominated by time, insensitive to their pupils' intellectual and emotional needs, lacking in energy, pre-occupied with their information giving functions, intellectually inert, disinterested in promoting initiative and self-reliance in their pupils, pre-occupied with disciplinary matters, and unwilling to give much of themselves in the teaching-learning compact. (p. 162)

Frasier and Carland (1980) felt that it was also important to understand the relationship that exists between regular classroom teachers and teachers of the gifted. From a survey of a national sample of teachers and program directors, they discovered that some of the factors viewed as important in the development of a positive relationship were having strong administrative support; communicating goals and objectives of the gifted program, the selection procedures, and the student's performance in the program; and provision for inservice for all teachers. Factors judged least important were that teachers of the gifted have the same number of students as the teacher of the regular classroom and that the teacher of the gifted work along with the regular classroom teacher in developing appropriate curricula. As these relationships have a lot to do with how well the gifted program can be implemented and the amount of success that can be achieved by gifted students, these factors could be valuable clues to all who wish to serve gifted learners.

To discover what teachers believed to be the most supportive behaviors teachers of the gifted could provide to classroom teachers, Wyatt (1982) distributed questionnaires at a state conference for those interested in working with gifted and talented students. The behaviors felt to be most helpful were

- Communication on a regular basis, including seeking ideas and information, using teacher expertise, and joint planning
- Provisions of classroom materials, including enrichment of the environment and centers
- Education about gifted/talented pupils and programs
- Working in the classroom, including demonstrations and team teaching showing differentiated instruction, independent study skills, and higher level thinking.

Elizabeth Drews (1976) reminded us,

The teacher's task is to inspire and release. . . . The teachers who have the greatest appeal to the gifted are those who combine two characteristics. First of all, they must know a great deal, and their knowledge should extend to the far reaches of their subjects. (Those who are themselves excited learners can communicate this feeling to their students.) Second, they must have a superlative ability to relate to others. For the gifted as well as for all students, the creative teacher is one who has faith in young people and loves students, who is cooperative and kind, who is democratic and considerate. Such teachers act on the belief that all human beings are naturally good and have transcendent potentiality. With such values and guidance, the student can make the most fundamental decisions—choices of life-style and world view—as well as the minute-to-minute choices of which most people actually remain unaware. . . .

Let us all recognize that gifted children have great insights from the beginning and that our task as teachers is the Socratic one of leading out the creative and letting them be where, as Rousseau, Wordsworth, and Thoreau divined, they can discover what in truth they already know. (p. 28)

TEACHER EDUCATION AND CERTIFICATION

The seven specific abilities of teachers necessary for effectively working with gifted students (pp. 543–544) provide a base of competency toward which teacher educators can instruct and state agencies can certify. Basing a teacher education program, either preservice or inservice, on the seven competencies ensures that those who acquire such education have at least the basic requirements for providing quality programs for gifted learners. There is no way to ensure success in classrooms; however, opportunities can be provided for teachers to gain an awareness and an experiential background in these areas that have been shown to increase their effectiveness in gifted programs. There are many ways for teachers to gain these competencies, from district-sponsored workshops and conferences to an intensive involvement in a university teacher education program leading to a credential or a graduate degree. This discussion details two of the many models that could be used and, in addition, briefly looks at some other alternatives.

College and University Programs: Preservice and Inservice

At least 140 colleges and universities in more than 40 states currently offer some type of program to teachers wishing to specialize in the teaching of the gifted learner (Hultgren, 1981). The programs may offer only one or two courses periodically or there may be an entire multicourse program leading to a degree and/or credential in the gifted specialization, with the MA degree programs the most commonly found. Several surveys have indicated that many courses offered do not lead to degrees or credentials, are nearly all at the graduate level of study, and require the candidate to have a teaching credential and some previous teaching experience (Lindsey, 1980).

According to data reported by Parker and Karnes (1984), 13 colleges and 88 universities in 38 states and the District of Columbia offer programs which culminate in one or more graduate degrees in education of the gifted. All offer at least one master's degree option, 20 offer educational specialist degrees, and 37 offer the doctor of education and/or doctor of philosophy degrees. A listing of these programs can be found in their article.

While it seems that more universities and colleges are developing programs addressing the needs of teachers of the gifted, there are some further concerns that must be addressed. In a survey of practitioners in the field, a list of areas not adequately addressed by the university programs they attended emerged. Included in this list were leadership skills, counseling for the gifted, career options for gifted, cultural differences, educational technological developments, the needs of underachievers, and parent/community relations and resources. The university personnel surveyed also were concerned about the lack of opportunities in many of the areas. One of the highest rated deficiencies on preparation programs was the lack of supervised practicum experience. At both the teaching and administrative levels, opportunities for practicum experience were seen to be inadequate or missing in far too many programs (Hultgren, 1981).

State-mandated certification is favored by a large percentage of both university program directors and practitioners (Hultgren, 1981). Of the state consultants reporting (40), 70% favored certification requirements. Those not favoring such requirements cited lack of established teacher competencies and the limited number of college and university teacher education programs. Some practitioners

Teacher education can be a challenging, exciting experience.

feel that such a mandate would cause inconvenience to them due to the need to add more requirements, especially in areas where programs in education of the gifted are largely unavailable. Administrators are often concerned about a loss of autonomy should such requirements become law. However, most educators feel that the advantages of having well-trained professionals far outweigh the disadvantages (Hultgren, 1981).

In 1981 a set of professional standards for training programs in gifted education were recommended jointly by a special task force on teacher education from The Association for the Gifted (TAG) and a committee on professional training from the National Association for Gifted Children (NAGC) (Seeley, 1981). The task force and committee specified these purposes for such standards:

1 In gifted/talented child education—Establishing standards encourages the continued growth of our field. Standards provide a basis for communication and reciprocity among programs, and for continued dialogue relative to the nature of training in our evolving field. Providing an impetus for continued improvement of professional programs would also promote the advancement of the field.

---

2 For institutions—Adopting standards for approved programs performs a crucial function on this level: ensuring a minimum university commitment to professional training. By "institutionalizing" programs, we are eliminating much of the "patched on" quality which is unfortunately beginning to characterize many higher education programs. Institutionalization and program approval move us closer to permanence.

3 In training programs—It is not the purpose of standards to guarantee that graduates have mastered particular skills. However, professional standards would ensure that trainees at various levels have been exposed to essential information in theoretical and applied contexts. (pp. 165, 166)

The task force and committee recommended seven standards:

I Admission and Selection Criteria—The institution should publish specific criteria for admission to programs at each degree level. These criteria should include cognitive and affective evidence obtained from multiple sources and should be congruent with stated program philosophy and goals.

II Curriculum and Competence Areas—Training programs should establish a coherent, comprehensive and discernible curriculum that addresses the major areas of gifted education as well as related studies. The curriculum should address theory, practice, and research in each of these areas.

III Degree Programs—Degree programs with a major emphasis in gifted education should be offered only at the graduate level and should be differentiated from each other appropriate to level (i.e., master's, specialist, doctoral).

IV Faculty for Graduate Programs—Faculty members with major teaching responsibilities in graduate programs should hold the doctorate with advanced study in gifted child education, or have competence in the field as demonstrated by significant research, writing or leadership in gifted education. Faculty members who conduct the advanced programs should be engaged in scholarly activity that supports their specialization in the field, and have experience which relates directly to gifted/talented child education.

V Administrative Structure: Staffing—The faculty for advanced programs should include at least one full-time doctoral-level person who holds an appropriate degree or has demonstrated competence, and at least three persons who hold the doctorate in fields which directly support the degree programs.

VI Administrative Structure: Evaluation—The program's mission and course offerings should be reviewed regularly. The results of this evaluation should be used in program modification and improvement efforts. Systematic opportunities should be provided for student and faculty input into program administration, review and planning.

VII Resources and Facilities—Institutions that offer graduate programs in gifted education should assure adequate human and material resources and facilities to implement their prescribed course of study. (pp. 166–168)

The adoption of such standards will allow the specialization of gifted education to build from a base of excellence and professional quality.

The Environment

Lindsey (1980), in reviewing studies of institutions in which student values show the most change during their university years, found that these characteristics were shared commonly:

> Relationships between students and faculty were close; it was expected that ideas would be questioned, differences of opinion would be examined, and persons would be held accountable for their decisions; the instructional strategies emphasized dialogue, discussion, debate, and inquiry. (p. 27)

In our university, it was determined that, to facilitate human learning, a more flexible, more nurturing environment would be needed for the teacher/learners in the gifted education program. It would be far easier, went the thinking, to teach appropriate education for gifted learners if it matched the type of education that the teacher/learners experienced during their program. With this in mind, a plan was developed to equip one room in the university instructional unit with carpet, tables, floor pillows, comfortable furniture, listening posts, and other media equipment necessary for establishing learning centers. The walls were painted a warm color, and attractive posters were hung. Later, an additional room was similarly equipped. With this physical environment available, in addition to on-site environments within elementary and secondary schools, the teacher/learners could experience how a responsive learning environment operates by learning in one.

An important part of the climate of any teacher education environment is the ability and attitude of the teacher educator. Those who teach teachers must themselves possess the attributes, knowledge, and skills essential for optimizing learning and developing individual potential. The program should allow all who participate to learn in a structure and with the teaching and evaluation strategies they are being asked to create. Those processes we value in gifted education must be modeled in the university classroom. The characteristics and competencies appropriate for a teacher of the gifted must be evident in the teacher of that teacher.

The Course Work

Although the number and regularity of offerings vary, according to surveys (Zettel, 1979; Hultgren, 1981) the overall content of courses on education of the gifted is similar in most institutions involved in gifted education programs. Most commonly offered is a course that explores the education and psychology of the gifted individual; introduces the concept of giftedness; and includes definition, identification, characteristics, etiology, and nurture. Many institutions also offer a course in methods and curriculum for teaching gifted learners. Other areas that may be found as part of programs leading to degrees or credentials in education of the gifted are measurement and testing, leadership principles and practices, affective development, creative behavior, classroom management, advanced studies, research methods, and administrative provisions. Practicum experiences are rated as essential by both practitioners and university trainers; yet 37% of universities offering programs in gifted education offer no practicum experiences in teaching the gifted learner and 76% offer no administrative practicum (Hultgren, 1981). In the same sample, 61% of the practitioners assessed had no practicum in teaching and 80% had no administrative practicum, although one-third engaged in administration of gifted programs. Universities offering higher degrees rather than just occasional course work offered more practicum experience.

We have seen that attitudes of teachers are influenced favorably toward gifted learners if they have had even one course in education of the gifted (Weiner & O'Shea, 1963). It has also been noted that the major part of the educational experience of most gifted students is planned and implemented by the regular classroom teacher, and yet we find information regarding gifted learners and their needs rare in the general offerings for teachers. Most of the courses with information on understanding giftedness are offered at the graduate level and to students taking them in pursuit of a higher degree in this area of specialization.

Competency-Based Programs

Programs that list competencies or skills to be developed by perspective teachers have several advantages: the competency approach is systematic, it is process oriented, and it is designed by and communicated to those in the particular setting. To develop a competency-based program for training teachers of the gifted Lindsey (1980) suggests four basic steps:

Step 1 Define the knowledge, skills, and attitudes to be achieved. Each university will have a list particularly meaningful to them. In Hultgren's study (1981) 24 competencies were selected and among them the following were considered most essential:

- Knowledge of nature and needs of gifted
- Skill in promoting higher cognitive thinking abilities and questioning techniques
- Ability to develop methods and materials for the gifted
- Knowledge of affective/psychological needs of the gifted
- Skill in facilitating independent research and study skills
- Ability to develop creative problem solving
- Skill in individualizing teaching techniques
- Knowledge of approaches to extend and enrich subject areas
- Ability to teach a group of gifted students (a supervised experience).

Our university has developed competencies based upon the seven abilities necessary for effective teaching with gifted children (listed on pp. 543–544). Lindsey (1980) suggests that we consider at least three areas in which competencies should be developed: what a teacher needs to be, to know, and to be able to do. The unifying theme is the development of the wholeness of the person.

Step 2 Design alternative strategies for helping different students achieve the listed competencies. Just as we believe the best way for gifted children to reach their potential is through educational programs that are individualized with varied opportunities, so too should teacher preparation programs be planned to allow each teacher to identify and meet his or her own needs and interests appropriately.

Step 3 Evaluate the degree to which the competencies are met, allowing for a variety of evaluative procedures. Evaluation is not synonymous with examination, and it has been my experience that far more learning and change occur when a variety of data—such as student projects, papers, journals, observations, case studies, task sheets, book and journal reviews, media productions—provides the means for evaluation.

Step 4 Feedback the results into all elements of the system. Finally, Lindsey (1980) suggests these questions as a guide for assessing the quality of each teacher education program:

1 Are the goals of the program made explicit?
2 Are the opportunities the program provides for students consistent with the stated goals?
3 Is the program dynamic rather than static?
4 Are those who design and operate the program effective models?
5 Are those who have a stake in the program significantly involved in its designing, implementation, and evaluation?
6 Are adequate resources available and productivity used?
7 Does the institutional environment stimulate expectancies and achievement?
8 Does the program provide continuity between practice and theory?
9 Does the program provide both social and independent experience? (pp. 43–45)

A national survey of teacher competencies for the education of gifted and talented children was conducted during the spring of 1978 (Seeley, 1979). The respondents, representing universities and colleges, principals, and teachers, ranked the following competencies in order of perceived importance with little disagreement between groups. Competencies considered most important were higher cognitive teaching and questioning, curriculum modification strategies, special curriculum development strategies, diagnostic prescriptive teaching skills, and student counseling strategies. As the purpose of the study was the establishment of a teacher certification regulation, the data were summarized into the following recommendations:

1 Teachers specifically assigned to teach gifted and talented children should hold a master's degree in the field.
2 State certification and endorsement standards should be mandatory, with provisions for a permissive phase-in until sufficient qualified professionals are available.
3 Information concerning gifted and talented children should be a part of every teacher's training.
4 One to two years of successful teaching experience should be required of teachers before assignment to gifted and talented special programs.
5 Teachers of gifted and talented children should have a strong content area emphasis in their background.
6 Teachers should have a variety of special competencies for teaching gifted children. (p. 13)

Five major components that contribute to teacher training were identified by Joyce and Showers (1982) in their review of the literature in this area. These components should be considered in the planning of any teacher training program or inservice for teachers:

- Presentation of theory or description of skill or strategy
- Modeling or demonstration of skills or models of teaching
- Practice in simulated and classroom settings
- Structured and open-ended feedback about performance
- Coaching for application or transfer of skills to the classroom.

It is important to note that the components do not, in their analysis, work in isolation, but must be combined for effectiveness.

Although inservice of teachers has been conducted by university faculties for years, one recent outcome of the educational reform legislation in many states has been the opportunity for universities to expand the structures and delivery systems of teacher inservice to include more effective models. One form this has taken has been the establishment of university/district cooperative partnerships. At California State University, Los Angeles, this has allowed for more off-campus courses, planned specifically for particular school faculties, to be taught directly on school sites. The modeling, demonstration, and follow-up support can be far more meaningful in the on-site setting. For special populations such as the gifted learner, such on-site partnerships can involve large numbers of school faculty not before available and can improve instruction throughout the school program.

Monaco and Georgiades (1986) suggest that university teacher training could be improved by using researchable problems gleaned directly from the teachers in a format that incorporates basic principles of teacher preparation. They have chosen to illustrate these principles, which were taken from guidelines prepared by the

National/State Leadership Training Institute for Gifted/Talented (Curry & Sato, 1984): Training is reinforced and extended through appropriate material; training strives to meet the specific needs of participants; and training is problem and product oriented. Monaco and Georgiades (1986) describe problem-solving situations, results, and conclusions based on real teacher problems.

Other types of inservice provided by universities have been summer institutes, conferences and workshops, demonstration classes, and consulting services. More cooperation between university faculties, district teachers and administrators, and state consultants and directors can only enhance the implementation of quality programs. In most states cooperation is still sorely needed.

Other Forms of Inservice

A number of other inservice models have been used in addition to those provided by the universities. Among them have been district or state sponsored conferences or workshops, regional service centers, and district or regional consortiums. In planning inservice experiences, the same competencies that can be found in more extensive credential and degree programs offered by universities should serve as a basis.

One statewide format for inservice that has evolved over two decades with increasing effectiveness can be found in Illinois (Van Tassel-Baska, 1986b). Having begun as gifted program demonstration centers, the current Area Service Centers now include services in computers, math, science, and reading in addition to service in gifted education. This format allows for pooling of strength and resources from many areas in the service of each. The mission of the Area Service Centers includes these goals:

1 Provide technical assistance for inservice training to local districts, enhance participation of new and continuing local education agencies (LEAs) in the gifted education reimbursement program, achieve comprehensive articulated program development and improvement, and assist in evaluation and longitudinal data collection.
2 Assist the State Board of Education in processing and approving LEA reimbursement applications, and in monitoring and evaluating programs.
3 Assist local districts in identifying students and establishing programs for low-incidence highly gifted students.
4 Disseminate information.
5 Participate in planning and conducting annual state-wide gifted education conferences.
6 Assist the Illinois State Board of Education in its implementation of rules, policies, and practices.

Over the long history of this program several generalizable ideas for assuring the effectiveness of inservice have been noted:

1 Real needs as well as perceived needs must be included. Those planning inservice experiences must assess them in order to determine what is needed to improve the program as well as what teachers want from inservice.
2 Inservice should follow a developmental model. The needs will be different depending on the level of knowledge and experience with gifted programming a district has, and the inservice experiences should build upon this growing expertise.
3 Training should be targeted toward specific outcomes for individuals and groups. This type of attention to specific needs has proven more effective than the wider service to large numbers of teachers.
4 Follow-up observation and monitoring are critical to the effectiveness of the inservice.
5 Techniques and ideas for continuing staff development are important for those involved.

These suggestions should add to the effectiveness of any inservice planning and its ability to effect change.

An inservice project developed and implemented to enhance the creative and critical thinking of students was reported by Schlichter (1986). The project, known as the Talents Unlimited Inservice Education Model, was based on the multiple-talent approach to teaching developed by C. Taylor (1967) and followed the major components identified by Joyce and Showers (1982). The overall goal of the Talents Unlimited project was to help teachers gain and maintain the necessary knowledge, skills, and attitudes for successfully implementing the multiple-talent approach to teaching in their classrooms. This was done by training teachers in the recognition and nurturing of students' multiple thinking abilities; the development of materials to support the integration of the thinking processes into the regular curricula; and the enhancement of student performance in academic achievement, creative thinking, and self-concept. Although the project was initially developed with regular heterogeneously grouped classrooms, later implementation in gifted settings showed its usefulness with this population.

An important outcome of well-planned and well-implemented inservice programs is the increase in the teacher's perception of competence. In a study by Adkins and Harty (1984) these feelings of competence had interesting results for gifted programs. Through longitudinal measures taken over 19 months, the researchers found that "appropriate, consistent, and timely inservice preparation can provide school staff with the capacity to better monitor and evaluate the degree to which the needs of gifted students are met in a school system" (p. 40). They found further that growing feelings of competence and confidence in applying concepts of gifted education lead teachers to support homogeneous-ability classes or groups, releasing pupils to special classes, increased interest in improving gifted education, and promoting quality education for gifted students. Another interesting finding was that, for some teachers, increased knowledge and understanding of the gifted resulted in less enthusiasm and interest in teaching the gifted learner as they discovered that truly differentiated curriculum required more work and more challenging learning experiences. Both results can only strengthen the quality of education available to gifted learners.

A survey (Tomlinson, 1986) of teacher responses to techniques used in inservice and staff development workshops resulted in information that could be of benefit to those planning such experiences for teachers. Of most benefit were the group participation and hands-on experiences; lectures used alone were perceived as least beneficial. Consultants should be prepared to make whatever information they share immediately applicable to the teaching situation. Whenever possible, grouping of participants should be by teaching areas, disciplines, and grade levels for maximum benefit. While it is not suggested that inservice present material relating only to the desires and perceived needs of participants, it is considered helpful to know what those perceptions are.

Weiss and Gallagher (1986) present TARGET, a needs-assessment approach to gifted education inservice that proved to be successful; data from this approach also proved to be useful to others planning such a program. A needs assessment showed the areas in which the teachers perceived they had a need and the areas in which they believed they had knowledge. A training module was designed with these data in mind in combination with five other areas of focus derived from the literature:

1 A variety of learning activities and strategies should be used to reach the program goals.
2 Inservice goals associated with the acquisition of new skills and behavior need trial experience with feedback and discussion.
3 Demonstration and practice with new techniques and strategies contribute to the teacher's comprehension.
4 Content of inservice programs should be specifically related to and directly applicable to the teachers' situations.
5 Incentives are important and should be predetermined.

Time was allowed between sessions for teachers to try some activities related to these areas. The results of trying these new ideas in class were discussed at the beginning of each session. Benefits seem to have been gained by the sharing of such information.

At the end of the inservice teachers were asked to identify specific examples of their use of learning from the inservice. A follow-up was conducted a month later, and the results of the inservice were perceived as positive, with the continued use of the materials and strategies still evident. The elements of this inservice may be of benefit to others who have the responsibility for planning gifted inservice.

Most district conferences and inservice workshops have one abiding weakness: their overemphasis on strategies and "how to do its." Teachers need to be aware of effective techniques to use with gifted children; however, if they are never exposed to a deeper understanding of the needs and problems of these children, they will never learn to generate activities appropriate to themselves and to the atypical learners with whom they work daily. What does one do after having attended the workshop on "101 Creative Activities for Gifted Learners" on the 102nd day? Our teachers deserve better than the dependency and confusion that result from total reliance on these workshops and conferences.

Of course, the opposite is also true. Inservice programs that give nothing but theoretical background with little or no participation can result in little or no change in the classroom. Inservice for classroom teachers should be offered in a total context of theory and practice, designed not only to teach strategies, but to show in what way the strategies meet the needs of gifted learners. Teachers of the gifted must themselves understand the nature of these learners and the needs they have. The information presented at inservice sessions is too often only at the knowledge level and it is left to the teacher to find ways to take the information and turn it into something useful in the classroom. While there may be great enthusiasm for the ideas, actual strategies for incorporating them in a school program as well as fiscal or moral support for such incorporation are too often missing.

In most teaching and learning models currently discussed in staff inservice there seems to be an external set of procedures or criteria that is inflexible. The procedures presented for improving the classroom and teaching have been determined to be what is needed, and the teacher has no input into that structure. It is important to identify the components of effective teaching and learning, to give examples of best practices, and to demonstrate these in the classroom, but it must then be possible for teachers to develop that information into a model that works for them, to add to it, to take from it, with their students' and their own personalities reflected in what is to become the procedure for that particular school. It is most important to have the teachers and the administrators become a community of learners. Imposing models, ideas, and strategies on teachers renders them powerless. If we do not want teachers to do this to their students, we must not do it to the teachers. They must be empowered if they are to empower.

From the experience I have had with university/district inservice I would like to suggest nine steps to effective staff development:

1 Develop trust and the perception of control with and among the teachers and administrators.

2 Focus on the teachers' needs. Meaningful staff development that creates change in the classroom will not happen in just one session; it will unlikely happen in a series of sessions unless the teachers and their needs are the focus.

3 Expose teachers to many possibilities of what can be learned to improve teaching and learning and then let them choose those they want, while

encouraging them to add their own ideas to those suggested. It is unproductive to simply ask teachers what they need from their inservice program. That would be like asking those coming into a new country what they would like to see when they do not even know what is available. One of the first steps in any inservice program must be the development of an awareness on the part of the teachers of the full range of what can be learned to optimize learning and teaching.

4 Help the teachers become aware of what they are already doing that works, and allow time and a structure for them to share their successes. A consultant or a team of colleagues, in consultation with each teacher, should observe the classroom to identify the behaviors that do work and those that don't that they want to change. Successful inservice education must include the involvement of the learner.

5 Conduct a needs assessment. Once teachers become aware of the new research and strategies for improving learning and teaching, and have looked at their own strengths, a needs assessment should be made of what they now wish to learn.

6 Plan the content and procedures for the inservice program. This decision making can now be shared with teachers.

7 Include classroom support. Inservice education can begin to change teacher behaviors only if there is actual support in the classroom either from the person who is directing the inservice or when such support is planned into the program. Inservice programs can provide support for change in the classroom through the inclusion of demonstration teaching, videotaped examples of teacher behavior to be used by the teacher and other faculty if desired, and continuing consultations when requested. It is one thing to give information; it is quite another thing to actually show how that information can function in the classroom and be there to support its use.

8 Keep in mind the importance of providing continuity, meeting specific identified needs, and presenting practical implications and strategies for all new ideas. Inservice education should use and exemplify what we know are good learning procedures.

9 Facilitate continuing self-evaluation and the development of effective teaching. At the end of the project there should exist a community of learners among the faculty that will encourage continued self-growth.

This is exactly the pattern that we find most effective in the classroom itself. Students are made aware of a scope and sequence so they know what is possible for them to learn, and they are provided an assessment so that they know what skills they already have developed and which ones are needed. They are given a variety of strategies and methods among which they can choose and are supported during the learning process. They are then given the opportunity to see how the new skill or information fits into their own lives, with self-evaluation encouraged. Much is known about how to optimize learning. This knowledge and these practices should be part of all inservice programs if we are really going to make learning to teach more effective.

For descriptions of other programs that may be helpful in your planning, see Gear (1974), Maker (1975), Renzulli (1973a), and Sisk (1975b).

SUPPORT SYSTEMS: ADMINISTRATION AND COUNSELING

The teacher of the gifted, especially if she or he is creative, innovative, effective, and successful, will quite likely find some unexpected consequences of that success. Many of our more traditional schools resist change and reward conformity. In such a system, the person who deviates, who does not follow the usual procedures, is neither valued nor supported and, in many cases, is not even tolerated easily. Many subtle pressures maintain the system as it is and discourage new ideas. For example, teachers who innovate more open structuring may find that they are left to eat alone in the teachers' lunchroom. Teachers who start new programs find their students reprimanded for being outside of class and disturbing others, even when such activities were part of the classroom program and were being carried out in the agreed-on manner. When such a teacher requests help, other teachers may refuse or point out that, if the "rules" were being followed, they wouldn't need "so much help." Any deviation from the value structure of some teachers may be met with censure, backbiting, and unpleasant confrontations.

I believe that innovating teachers should present the changes as inoffensively as possible, remain aware of any imposition their practices may have on others, and keep from becoming defensive and retaliatory in behavior. Teachers who are not part of the regular faculty, but hired as special teachers, have an even more difficult problem. You must be aware that your very presence says to some teachers "I am here to do what you can't. I'm a special teacher." For some, that is very threatening. You will need to focus on establishing good interpersonal communications with the entire faculty. And no matter how caring you are, it may not work.

Such experiences can certainly take the joy out of teaching and create loneliness, frustration, and even the inclination to give up ideas you have shown to be effective. Some teachers leave the profession rather than have such dissension become part of their everyday lives.

Other solutions besides conforming or quitting exist. You can establish a support system and use it. It is neither weak nor unworthy to need support in your attempt to create an effective learning situation for your students. Support systems can be built in many ways:

1 Watch for those teachers who are interested in what you are doing, invite them into your room, share your materials and ideas, ask them for their opinions, share.

2 Be sure to take every opportunity to let the entire faculty know they are welcome at any time to visit, participate, share ideas, or have their children work with yours.

3 Discuss what you are doing with the principal and other administrators. Keep administration informed and invite their participation. But be careful of making presentations before the entire faculty. Many may be there only because they were required to attend and will view the proceeding as a put-down of what they are doing. Unexpected attacks may follow such a presentation, no matter how good it is.

4 Include parents whenever possible. If they are informed, they will provide tremendous support. Parents have the power to establish or close a program. Make sure they know your goals and are involved in their implementation.

5 Custodians and office clerks can provide invaluable support. They have knowledge about systems and how to make them work that can never be learned from those "in charge."

6 Attend workshops, conferences, and university classes that present training in the areas of your interest and in innovative approaches. Meet others, exchange phone numbers, and then call them when you need sympathetic, understanding discussions. Near the end of each class I teach, we discuss the problem of support. The students exchange addresses and phone numbers so that they know there are always knowledgeable, caring people out there, should they need them.

Don't minimize the need for support systems. Many people cannot handle change. Once you accept that fact and know that it really isn't you, it's just the institutional apathy in your way, you can then go about your job of providing the best education you know how to gifted children. They, after all, will be your best support system. Purposefully include in your life supportive, nurturing people. Whatever you do, don't quit. We need you.

Administrative Support

Administrative support is as important to success as a well-chosen teacher. We often find that such support is withheld only because of lack of information. The coordinator must stay in close touch with the school principal, the superintendent, and the members of the school board. Don't wait until they have questions or you have a problem; prepare a package of information to leave with them, make an appointment, and present the program to them in detail. These are some areas you must be sure to cover:

- Who the gifted are and why they need special programs
- The types of program experiences you have, or would like to plan

- What your program offers that is not already being provided
- How it will be staffed, scheduled, and equipped
- What it will cost, and how it will be paid for
- How it will be evaluated
- How your program will benefit the entire school or district
- Ways in which parents will be involved
- How the persons or groups to whom you are speaking are needed, and the role they will play in the success of the program.

Finally, find out what they want from the program, and be prepared to answer any questions they may have.

Involve the administrative personnel in your program planning and evaluation as much as possible. Several years ago, one of my students took over the coordinator role of a district near Los Angeles. Not only was very little happening in gifted education within this district, but a great deal of negative feeling pervaded the area from experiences with previous programs for the gifted. The new coordinator used her first year to gain the administration's confidence, change attitudes, and establish support for the structure she was developing. She carefully assessed the needs of each principal, the superintendent, and the school board members.

At times, she called me to discuss a particularly untractable or negative stance she had confronted. The university offered a 6-week course in the evening to parents, teachers, and administrators at a site in their district on education of the gifted. In the spring, the coordinator arranged a 3-day retreat conference. Using teams and facilitators, those attending planned the district program. She involved all levels of the educational structure. The participants had time to discuss problems and correct misunderstandings. By beginning this way, the program had excellent results. The program has continued to build and is now one of the strongest, most effective gifted programs in the state. You may wish to look at the possibilities of a similar cooperative effort for your district. Informed, involved administration makes quality education for gifted learners possible. Be sure to give your administration the opportunity to become informed and involved.

In recent years administration in many areas—business, industry, education —has begun to change from hierarchical systems to participatory management systems, from paternal to shared decision making. Those involved in gifted education find this move to be especially significant. This is what we are trying to teach our students: skills of creative, alternative thinking, good decision making, sharing of responsibility, communication, and cooperation. We want our students to feel safety, belonging, motivation, commitment, responsibility, and autonomy. The old hierarchical, parental administrative system cannot provide these outcomes for teachers or students; the shared decision making of participatory management can. There are trade-offs that teachers, students, parents, and administrators must recognize and agree to: decision making will be slower, faculty will have an increased demand made on their time, compromise will be essential, and willingness to expeditiously change decisions and structures that aren't working will be necessary. The growing body of literature in this area shows that the quantity and quality of achievement improve as the ownership and identification with actions taken increase. The guiding principle of this new management system is that those affected by the decisions have the right to participate in making those decisions; the more the decision affects any individuals the more they should be involved in the process.

Changing administrative structures is not an easy task. Not only must the administrator be willing to share the power, but the faculty, the students, and the parents must develop the skills to accept and use the power effectively. Teacher training institutions must include these skills in their programs for both administrators and teachers. Teachers must include such skills in parent training and in the structure and curriculum of the classroom. Parents must be willing to include and model these concepts in the home. Roeper (1986), Jensen (1986), and Dart (1986), all writing in a recent issue of *Roeper Review,* give us some guidance as to how they in their respective schools have accomplished this change. You can also find detailed directions for such a system outlined in *Optimizing Learning* (Clark, 1986). Many resources are available to us from the literature of systems theory, business management, and educational administration. We must begin the process of change for there is so much to do and so much to gain.

Counselors and Psychologists as Support Personnel

Most gifted students, especially in secondary programs, perceive the counselor as a program scheduler. Sometimes they experience the counselor as a tester or evaluator. Unfortunately, gifted learners are too often given this limited view of the educational staff member who could provide them with a valuable, even in some instances, critical service.

A number of years ago, my own son in junior high had for several semesters complained about his dull, repetitive math class. I became aware that, if something were not done, his interest in math, previously a true fascination, would be completely gone. I phoned the school counselor to arrange an appointment to discuss the problem. After identifying myself and the problem as I perceived it, I asked for consultation time. "I don't recall any problem we have had," said the counselor, "Let me pull his file." After a pause, he returned to the phone to assure me that there was no problem and an appointment would not be necessary.

I repeated my perception of the problem, assuring him that I realized that my son was not a behavior problem, but that I felt he did need help. I suggested that I would be agreeable to let him attend math classes at the nearby high school if that were considered feasible, but in any case, I would like an opportunity to explore the issue. "Well, we don't use acceleration. Our policy is against it except in rare cases. We have lots of students here as smart as your son. I don't see any purpose in a conference. He is not a problem, is doing excellent work, and his file shows that he is well-adjusted. I'll call you if we see any problem in the future." End of conversation. I was not at all assertive at that point in my life and was unsure of the value of pursuing the matter further. My son did drop his math interest and, although he might have done so in any case, I will always wonder. My work over the years that followed convinces me that gifted children who are not "problems" very often get little, if any help from school counselors.

When a counselor or guidance staff member becomes involved in the program for gifted learners, the results and benefits are very exciting, not only to the gifted students, but to their teachers and parents as well. Borgers and Treffinger (1979) admonish counselors to consider three basics to any effective counseling program: (1) counselors must be sensitive to any internal or external force that limits individual potential; (2) to meet such individual needs, they must provide a variety of services; and (3) they need to be "developmental and proactive rather than remedial and reactive" (p. 240).

A counselor can provide students with preventive and informational consultation, crisis intervention, and ongoing process or self-discovery counseling. Rather than wait for a problem to occur, the counselor should inform gifted students of such things as graduation needs, career counseling, and alternative choices for future planning (e.g., whether to go on to college immediately or work or travel for a year first). The counselor has access to resources that are not known to the student, the teacher, or the parents.

Gifted students have many problems to which they could find their own solution if given just a little help from an effective counselor. Gowan and Demos (1964) found that gifted students at all levels, elementary through secondary, profit greatly by having a counselor available as soon as problems arise. The same observation is true of gifted university undergraduates. Rothney and Koopman (1958) believe gifted students can be very independent in counseling situations and can evaluate information with their counselor very effectively. Moore (1980) states that gifted students profit more from counseling than their more average classmates. Vargiu (1971) sums up by saying,

> With relatively little help gifted students can learn to become more in touch with all their personality aspects and develop them further, in a balanced, harmonious and effective way. They can be helped to solve their inner conflicts, and to coordinate and integrate their personality through discovery of a stable center of identity and awareness from which to function in the world. (p. 2)

Gifted students and those who work with them (Gowan & Demos, 1964; Newland, 1976; Rothney & Koopman, 1958; Zaffrann & Colangelo, 1977) most often mention the students' need to

- Discuss what is happening to them in their classroom, in their program, and in their personal lives.
- Find ways to communicate effectively with their teachers and parents.
- Discuss questions of identity, roles, relationships, and self-concept.
- Discover their special abilities and vocational choices, selecting from an overwhelming number of interests and abilities.
- Develop study habits, overcome underachievement patterns.
- Develop effective self-expression and communication.
- Develop personal standards of conduct; discuss frustration over discrepancy between ideals or intellectual conception of performance and physical ability to realize a performance level that is high enough to meet their expectations.

Immediacy of contact is the major element of crisis intervention counseling that must be available. Many students complain that, when they want to get help from a school counselor, the procedure is so cumbersome and time consuming that they seldom persevere. In her work, Newman (1967) emphasizes the necessity for available and continuing support of the counseling staff. She favors on the spot, as opposed to scheduled, seminars for staff consultations. Extending this approach to students could create some scheduling problems. However, the present situation in many schools must be looked at carefully to make some decisions regarding priorities of services. If gifted students benefit so much from crisis intervention counseling, they must be able to get it.

Counselors should provide a third service for gifted students: process, or personal growth, consultation. Some programs use small counseling groups that meet weekly for support and discussion of personal problems. The adult counselor facilitates but also encourages students to give their ideas. Group members assist in clarifying problems and presenting solutions. Even if they cannot agree on a solution, having the opportunity to discuss the problem with sympathetic listeners often helps them to alleviate the crisis, allowing the student to try alternative ideas for coping. Such a group can serve as a peer counselor training experience at the same time. Often, a group session is more beneficial to the student than an individual session.

In addition to problem solution, a growth group structured as a learning experience can provide a safe place for gifted students to explore areas of communication, self-concept, assertion, and other strategies to facilitate personal and interpersonal growth. Gifted students will be able to interact with other students who have many of the same problems and are more of a peer group than students found at their grade level. Teachers trained and experienced in guidance procedures may provide these functions. Whether through a counselor or a teacher, this type of guidance must be available to the gifted throughout their academic careers. Sanborn (1979) declares the need for counseling and guidance activities to be designed "to help children learn about their own qualities and to attempt to relate these qualities to opportunities open to them both in the present and in the future" (p. 159). In turn, the counselor must make use of this knowledge to help the school better understand the student so that more appropriate and meaningful educational opportunities can be planned.

The Counseling and Personnel Services Clearinghouse (1982) suggests that counselors coordinate a system-wide needs assessment with gifted learners to determine counseling program goals unique to their population. Although every group of gifted learners differs, these problems and issues are often found:

1 Positive self-concept may be difficult to maintain because of excessive self-criticism and sensitivity to criticism from others. Gifted students may experience a split self-concept because of the conflict between superior ability and the need to be "one of the gang."

2 Great frustration may occur in gifted students with subjects or situations they cannot handle. They are unaccustomed to this experience and think they should know all the answers. As a result, they may not know how to ask for help when they need it.

3 Greater sensitivity and perceptiveness may result in acute negative responses to lack of genuineness, warmth and understanding, or to an uncomfortable situation.

4 Values and attitudes are likely to be divergent, different from the "norm." This can make it difficult for them to find true peers. It can also complicate career/vocational choices and pursuits.

5 Gifted students are not necessarily aware of their own abilities. They may not have had the opportunity to do truly outstanding work because they have not been fully challenged in the classroom. Both academic and career/vocational decisions can be seriously misguided.

6 Gifted students may have intense single interests and fail to apply themselves in other areas of school and social life. They may have poor and inefficient study habits.

7 Gifted girls often face socialization conflicts and lack good role models. Personal and social problems can result, as well as underachievement in school and career/vocation.

8 Gifted cultural and racial minorities may lack family support, appropriate role models, and social/economic access to particular careers or vocations.

9 The wider interests and multiple superior abilities of gifted students often require a broader range of career areas for exploration and selection. (p. 2)

For the teacher of the gifted, the counselor may provide help in identification and with assessment profiles. A helpful consulting service would make suggestions for placement and how to meet needs best. A counselor could train teachers to use strategies and procedures they might otherwise not know. Teachers often encounter problems that require professional guidance; they should be able to seek the help of their colleagues. Often such mutual support between teacher and counselor is missing or is turned into a competitive situation, each needing to show the other that he or she is more effective. In such situations, everyone loses. Each member of the team in a gifted program has valuable skills. No one needs to use rank or professional one-upmanship to prove the importance of one's service; each function is critical.

For the parents of gifted learners, the counselor can provide information, understanding, and guidance. In crisis situations, a counselor can set up one of the most effective approaches ever developed for finding solutions to family problems, the family therapy group. So many student problems can be solved only when all the family members are aware of their responsibility for the problem and the need the student has for their support. Family therapy groups have been extremely productive.

When districts choose not to have a full-time coordinator, the counselor must take on coordinating tasks as well. A number of counseling approaches have worked well with gifted students. Gowan and Demos (1964) found a preference for a less directive approach.

Buescher (1987) offers a curriculum model that can be used to proactively counsel and support the growth of young gifted adolescents. He suggests that use of such a specialized curriculum reflects several important principles that both the counselors and teachers must hold: (1) Effective guidance and counseling occur at a proactive, preventative stage rather than a reactive, intervention stage; (2) the expectations of others, teachers, parents, and peers, coupled with the extraordinary self-expectations, can immobilize gifted adolescents; and (3) the multipotentialities and intensity of a gifted adolescent can provide keen insight into the dynamics of adjustment the student is using. Buescher provides three stages of support in the model: perceiving, ideating, and presenting. Although he feels the perception of new information is a step often emphasized in the learning process, he believes that research shows the other steps must follow if a concept is to be gained or a behavior affected and changed. There are several ways the counseling curriculum can be implemented: within a course in personal growth and adjustment or literature and writing, or as the content focus for a monthly series of special topical seminars. The model is also suggested for training teachers, counselors, and parents of gifted adolescents.

Among the resources available on guiding gifted students is a book originating from the professional psychological community (Webb, Meckstroth, & Tolan, 1982). Its goal is to serve as a practical source of information on gifted learners for parents and teachers. Through the awards and national acclaim the book has received, it has brought a new focus on gifted children and their emotional and social needs from the psychological community. The larger community of parents has also become more aware of these needs through the conferences and a national network originated by the book's authors. Starting from concern for a single family's efforts to understand the unbearable emotional stress with which their gifted adolescent was unable to cope, Webb, Meckstroth, and Tolan share their perceptions of the problems and their ideas for guiding children of this extraordinarily sensitive population.

TEACHERS OF THE GIFTED:
AT HOME—PARENTS

The beginning of this book emphasized how important parents are to actualizing the giftedness of each child. Throughout the book we have seen how parents and the home play a significant part in every phase of a child's growth and influence the outcome of every educational decision. I am firmly convinced that the home is the true cradle of eminence. Whatever we find in our world that we would like to change, we must begin at the starting place with parenting. Some have tried to show that other influences are equally or even more important; however, they have yet to account for the powerful effects of motivation, self-image, and attitudes toward self and others—the factors that find their definition in the home.

What a parent is, even before conceiving the child, profoundly influences the child's physical, emotional, social, intuitive, and cognitive abilities. What a parent does, all of the decisions and actions the parent makes, follow directly from who and what the parent is. Our society would never think of allowing damage and misuse to happen to our highways, our food, our financial arrangements, even our political and professional institutions; yet we refuse to interfere in the gross misuse of our children. If we were to care for our children, all of our children, in ways we already know, we would abundantly increase the population of children who could actualize their potential to the degree we now designate as *gifted*. Giftedness may be more "normal" than the behaviors and abilities we now call typical.

The teacher in the home begins the process of human actualization, maintains and supports it, and allows this unique essence to become known while continually nourishing it with love. Anything less is unthinkable. There is no one way to nurture. As parents, we grow as the child grows; we make mistakes. Not all of our actions are the finest, nor even always what we know we are capable of, but rather than feel guilt, we feel joy in our learning. We try again, and we do better at our next chance. There are times when we feel inadequate to the task, frustrated by our inabilities, by our lack of patience and energy.

We need to continue to value our own growth, to challenge ourselves in each area of our functioning to be more of who we are. We must find more ways to allow our growing children their own uniqueness, not limited by our perception of the world, but free to teach us their views. And between us, we should continually nurture and value love for ourselves, for each other, and for that part of us that exists in all things. If we do all this, we have done enough, for it is incomparable. With this great respect and appreciation for parenting, the section of this book that deals with our present world comes to an end. As it began with concern for parenting, it is fitting that it should end with parenting.

Organizing for Cooperation

As children move into the school system, with their environment and their opportunities no longer as closely controlled by the home, parents often begin to feel powerless. They may be unaware that they have ways to influence what is happening to their child. When confronted with a situation that they know is not appropriate or that could even be damaging to their child's welfare, they may react as I did when my son was in need—trust that the school knows best and do nothing. Some parents of gifted children (fewer, I'm sure, than their public image suggests) attempt to change what is happening by complaining, attacking those they feel to be responsible, and creating only enough conflict and pressure to make everyone defensive.

There is a better way. Fortunately, both parents and school personnel want what is best for the child—at least, what they perceive to be best. The most effective way to change or correct a bad situation is not by direct confrontation, in most instances, but by an organized, knowledgeable, cooperative effort. If there must be winners and losers, too often the child is one of the losers, no matter who wins.

The first step is to organize, even before a problem crops up. Join with other parents of gifted children in your school or your district. Such organizations have accomplished many goals. As your child finds the school experience different than others find it, you as parents will find your experience with your child differs from the more typical parental experiences. Review the characteristics and unusual needs your gifted child has as a result of heightened mental ability, and you will begin to understand why your role as a parent is also unusual. It helps to meet with other parents who are experiencing themselves and their children in ways similar to yours. When a group of parents of gifted children organizes, they find such understanding, and even relief, in their sharing of common concerns and experiences.

Once your group begins to meet, you will easily find people willing to share information on educating gifted children. They can inform you of what is known about giftedness, the identification procedures used in your district, the gifted program in which your child participates, and answers to many questions you will have. They will tell you of many alternatives and possibilities for providing quality education both at home and at school. You will now be in a position to help change inadequate or unfair practices in your schools. Many teachers, administrators, and school board members are anxious to make changes, try more challenging programs, or end detrimental practices. However, they do not want to go against the wishes of the community. It is, after all, your school; these are your children.

As a group, you should present informed support for the practices you prefer for your children, not only showing what is wrong, but presenting other alternatives. By suggesting positive changes, you will be far more able to resolve the problems. If no one needs to defend, each can spend that energy constructing. Organize first, then become informed. With so many resources (e.g., people, books, classes, conferences) available, becoming informed will not be difficult. I have found that most people who are committed to gifted education are very interesting and generous. You may find learning about giftedness more fascinating than you thought.

One note of caution: Gifted children often have gifted parents who exhibit all the same characteristics and who have some of the same independent, divergent natures. Organizing such groups may take a bit of doing; diverse opinions must be expected and allowed. For information on how others have organized groups of parents of gifted children write to the ERIC Clearinghouse on Handicapped and Gifted Children, Council for Exceptional Children, 1920 Association Drive, Reston, Virginia 22091. The same group publishes two very useful handbooks (Delp & Martinson, 1974; Kaufmann, 1976) that can be obtained at minimal cost. Two other very useful books that you will find helpful are by Hall and Skinner (1980) and the American Association for Gifted Children (1980) and were written for the Perspectives on Gifted and Talented Education project directed by Abraham Tannenbaum.

Often groups of parents of gifted provide out-of-school experiences for their children when changes do not occur in the schools as fast as they had hoped. A parent group in California, the Gifted Children's Association, offers an extensive curriculum after school and on Saturdays. They house their program on junior college campuses, charge a small tuition to cover the cost of hiring professors and teachers, print and distribute the schedule of offerings, and handle fees and registration. Their brochures would rival any college extension program.

Informed groups can also schedule field trips to enrich the learning of their children. Many educational trips that single families would not find accessible are available to groups. Factories; museums; dress rehearsals of concerts, plays, and ballets; tours of industries, professional groups, and businesses; archeological digs; and historical events can all be experienced by your group. The possibilities are limitless, but be careful not to spend all your energy outside of the school system, with none left for changing what is happening to your child all day, 5 days a week.

Parent Inservice

It is equally important for teachers in the home to understand the needs of gifted children and how to meet these needs as it is for teachers in the schools. I have often given 5- to 8-week parent inservice courses that help parents better understand the problems of the school, the program, and their gifted children. Among other things, we discuss alternative programs and strategies to use both at home and at school to build self-concept and open communication and to develop all four areas of functioning: thinking, feeling, sensing, and intuiting. I will outline the sessions here so that you might know what we do as you consider inservicing the parents of the gifted in your organization. The gifted coordinator will often provide such a course or hire someone to present it. If not, you may wish to bring your resources together, using your parent organization as the coordinating or planning group. We use the following five sessions:

1 Understanding Giftedness—Who are the gifted? How do you nurture giftedness?
2 Emotional and Social Development of the Gifted—Developing self-esteem, values, and creativity

3 Meeting the Needs of the Gifted—Program alternatives, differential curriculum, learning and challenges, integrating all four areas of learning, and evaluation

4 Effective Teachers at Home and at School—The nurturing home, growth, families, communication, the teacher in the classroom as a part of the learning community

5 What Can You Do Now?—Planning with the school, student-parent-teacher interaction, legislative possibilities and provisions, becoming active in your community for gifted education.

Parents as Resources

Parents can cooperate with the schools in providing quality education for their gifted learners in many ways. One way is to offer their services as teachers. If the classroom is individualized and/or organized into centers, a parent can create and implement a center for a given period of time. For example, in a school near our campus, a kindergarten teacher assesses the interests, occupations, and abilities of the parents of the children in her class each year. She invites them to share something they are especially good at with a small group of children in a learning center for 3 days. She has had language centers, construction centers, baking centers, black history centers, Cinco de Mayo centers, and numerous others. The parents are much more involved in the classroom, provide many other needed services, and enrich the learning experience for everyone. Often parents will be comfortable sharing with a few children, even when they would never consider "teaching" the entire class.

Parents can also provide materials, help with construction when changing the classroom environment, run individualized learning labs in subjects such as reading or math, and provide transportation, additional supervision sources, and arrangements for field trips. Some parents enjoy organizing other parents to make all of the above suggestions possible. It is important that teachers ask for the help they need and not waste parental talent on busy work. Parents can make important contributions to classroom learning if both teacher and parents take the responsibility to initiate and carry out such involvement.

At the very least, parents should be involved in planning and evaluation conferences with their child and the teacher. Each of these persons has something unique to contribute to the data needed for good educational decision making. Such involvement is at the heart of the Integrative Education Model discussed in Chapter 7.

Parents can make a significant impact in the area of legislation. Most of the provisions for special education at the state and federal levels have been enacted because of the efforts of groups of parents. Parents must stay informed about bills and legislative action and let their elected representatives know what they want. Government officials are asked to resolve many problems. It is very easy for them to feel that the needs of gifted students, if they know of them at all, have very low priority. Teachers and other school personnel cannot influence the boards of education, the state superintendents, the governors, and the legislators with anywhere near the effectiveness that parents can. In sheer numbers, parents have the advantage. You as parents truly have the power in our school systems. Be aware of it. Use it for the benefit of your children.

I have found the following suggestions useful as a parent and as a teacher. Many of them came from other parents or from students, and some my children taught me. If you live with gifted children,

1. Create open communication that is available from birth on. Set aside a special time for each child to have you to him/herself, to be interested in her/him alone, to be listened to nonjudgmentally, to share ideas. Don't wait for problems or decision-making times. I personally used the time I tucked each child in bed, sitting down each evening for 10 to 30 minutes, with all our attention available to each other. Also try the family council described in Chapter 4.

2. Do what you like doing and include the child, as well as doing things in which the child is interested.

3. Permit the children their own individuality, and enjoy them for who they are, not what you would like them to be.

4. Respect your child and allow the child as much dignity as you would a friend.

5. Allow your children to make lots of decisions, and consult them on issues affecting them whenever you believe they can understand the consequences.

6. Don't confuse the IQ with the child; the child is much more.

7. Help the child understand and deal with his or her belonging and conformity needs. Often, especially for girls, the pressure is very great; they must feel it's really all right to be different.

8. Help children with their need for perfectionism and what that does to their self-image. Serve as an example of how hard it is to accept your own mistakes, and show them how you keep trying. Let them feel your acceptance of them as people. Help them set realistic standards and do not hold everyone up to them.

9. Arrange back-to-nature times and quiet together and apart times; value reflection and daydreaming.

10. Help your child set time and energy priorities. Too often the world is so exciting for these children that they seem to need to do everything at once.

11. Help them appreciate individual differences, both in themselves and in others.

12 Instruct by your actions more than your words. If you want your child to be an avid reader, you will probably need to be one. Other interests develop this way, too.

13 Don't insist that every project have closure before other things can happen. Often, what the child wanted or needed to learn from an experience occurs before the project is "finished." Sometimes other fascinating areas just have to be explored before the project can be finished properly. Otherwise, you may end up with a few finished projects and a turned-off child.

14 Be careful about supporting teachers when they are doing stupid things (e.g., a homework assignment of 50 problems all on a concept that your child mastered 2 years ago, or the insisting, under threat of low grades, on completion of an overnight project even when your child is playing in a special concert that evening). You should plan a conference with the teacher and be sure the situation is understood. If the teacher remains unreasonable, you have a right to discuss your perception with the principal. There is little value in obedience at any cost.

15 Provide a safe place. At times, your child will find being different very difficult. Neither the teacher nor the child's friends will always understand, and your child will need a place where it is safe to be who he or she is.

16 Enjoy living with your child! Your life together will be a great adventure! Children are not comparable, so value each for what each offers. As parents, we are truly blessed to be able to become so intimately involved with such marvelous people, our children.

In this chapter, we have discussed abilities, values, attitudes, and characteristics of effective teachers of the gifted at home and at school. The teacher is the most significant influence on the learning environment at school. We have identified general differences between effective and ineffective teachers. In addition, we have looked at the abilities every teacher of gifted learners should develop. To develop them, both preservice and inservice teacher education must be provided. For classroom teachers to become more effective, especially in situations requiring change and innovation, they will need to establish a support system. Among suggestions to aid in such development, we looked at the possible contributions of administrators, counselors, and guidance personnel. However, the gifted program must be made known to them and provision for their services planned if they are to be used properly.

The parents of the gifted (their teachers at home) were encouraged to organize, to become informed, and to work cooperatively with school personnel to provide the best possible education for their children. We looked at some of the services parents can provide and suggested ways to live effectively with the gifted.

As we began the book by showing the importance of parenting, so we bring the current information in the book to an end by recognizing parents as the most valuable teachers of the gifted.

Questions Often Asked

1. Should teachers of the gifted be gifted themselves?

While it is not necessary for teachers of the gifted to meet the criteria for giftedness, it is important that they be bright, enthusiastic about learning, and understanding of the differences a high level of intelligence brings to the student. It is always preferable to have personal experiences to draw from in helping gifted students meet the problems they will face; however, none of us ever has quite the same problems to solve. Openness, caring, and personal commitment mean a lot to the students, and the processes of thinking must be ones you are experiencing if you are to lead someone else into these skills. Curiosity will be important as it leads to expertise that can be shared in various content areas. A teacher of the gifted may not be gifted, but should be intelligent at an above-average level and still growing in exciting ways.

2. The data indicate that the personal-social characteristics of teachers are of most concern to gifted students, yet the criteria for certification of teachers are all cognitive. How can we meet both needs?

Cognitive skills are the most easily measured; however, it is possible for teacher training institutions to include personal-social competencies into their programs. District personnel can also look for and even specify in the job description personal-social characteristics of the type the gifted students request. It is important that university programs and district personnel value these characteristics so that they will find many ways to facilitate teachers who have them.

3. What can you do if your principal doesn't believe in "gifted education"?

A lot of different ideas have been tried. One teacher sent her principal short articles on a regular basis that showed the advantages of gifted programs to the students and to the school. She then requested a conference with the principal to present her plan for an adjunct program that would benefit the students. From that beginning she showed how such programs were important to the school and gradually got more adequate programming into the regular schedule. Sometimes parent requests will make a difference. Sometimes it is necessary to work directly with the school board members who share your interests; sometimes it takes legislative mandates. One teacher I knew did all he could, then took administrative courses while trying to make changes that he could, and finally got his own school where he developed a strong gifted program. Another teacher I know asked for a transfer to a school that was more supportive of her interests.

4. If a number of the faculty want to engage in a more shared decision-making model but the principal doesn't, can anything be done?

You might try collectively discussing the idea with the principal in a cooperative mode sharing all the advantages of the new model. If you have a plan of how it might happen and the advantages to the school, parents, and students, and to the goals for which the principal is most responsible, you could be successful. Most people who hold to the hierarchical model do so because it is the only one they understand and feel comfortable with, or they fear they will not get the results they must have with the new model. You should show the principal the advantages and a plan for a clear transition.

5. What if the principal wants to use a participatory management style, but the teachers are unwilling to become involved?

Again, it will be necessary to be sure the teachers understand the advantages to the school, to the students, and especially to themselves and their success as teachers. If the teachers are getting along with what they are doing it is hard for them to understand why they should change, and you need to show them what change can do. Also, there must be a plan that makes the change easy and productive. The teachers must feel supported as the change occurs. It has been my experience that once most teachers experience shared decision making they do not want to go back to being told what to do in the parental structure of the hierarchical model.

6. Our counselors have full case loads for scheduling and placement. How can our gifted students get any personal counseling services?

Counseling issues can be built into the curriculum, or special seminars can be developed on a regular weekly basis. Counselors can be invited to group sessions to teach their skills to teachers, parents, and/or students or to present special topic sessions within the classes. Peer counselors can be trained and scheduled for groups. Because personal counseling is an important goal, creative ways must be found to meet it.

7. If parents want to help but no one from the school asks them, what can they do?

Decide what services you would be willing to provide and then offer your services. Often the need is there but no one has the time to organize to get help. It would be of great service if under the teacher's direction you could organize a group of parents to provide support services.

12. The Amazing Possibilities Ahead

This chapter introduces the reader to some of the future influences on gifted education, which include

- Ideas of physicists and philosophers on reality, and our connectedness.
- Developments in brain research that are expanding our concept of who we are and what we can become.
- Better understanding of our growing self, especially as shown in the use of biofeedback and superlearning techniques.
- The link between integrative education and transpersonal learning.
- Parapsychology and psi research, and their relationship to our understanding of our intuitive abilities.
- The importance of future studies in our search for optimal realities for each of us.

We are living in a most interesting and exciting time. As each year passes, more astounding discoveries are being made. More amazing thoughts are being discussed. More beliefs are being jiggled. The results are an overwhelming excitement, a constant rethinking of old structures, dramatic reassessment and realignment of who we are, why we are, and where we are. If I had lived during the Renaissance, I could not have felt more excited about the changes appearing in every facet of life. Though I'm sure that that period was very special and the people then would have found themselves in awe of their circumstances, they should be here now!

What we will share in this chapter will only touch on some of the contributing events, and much of what we will discuss will be only theories, best guesses, clues to what lies ahead. But already what can be seen tells us that we are not just looking at how we may better use the resources we now have, both human and material; we are redefining our reality, our meaning, and our connection to the universe. We may find ourselves not only a wondrous part of the creation, but an intimate part of the creating.

THE UNIFYING: EXPERIENCING OUR CONNECTEDNESS

As we explore the new areas of scientific thought that affect us as guides to the intellect of ourselves and others, we must first give up the need for dichotomies. It no longer seems possible to believe one truth or one view; the operable word has become *and.* This can be seen in so many places and is being seen by so many of our best minds. In physics it is now necessary to believe that everything is both waves and particles. In human understanding we are asked to reconcile two paths, the rational, empirical path of science and the inner path of the intuition and imagination. Each of us is asked to see himself or herself as being and becoming. Even our classrooms are places of the integration of polarities of knowing. Without a need for right/wrong, true/false, we are free to examine a few of these bigger, more wonderfully outrageous ideas and those who ask us to entertain them.

Of course, the person who is responsible for much of the change in our view of reality and for the subsequent amazing directions in which inquiry has proceeded is Albert Einstein, called by some the greatest physicist since Newton. As we again look, with Zukav's (1979) help, at the principles upon which Einstein built his special theory of relativity, we can begin to see just how important and far reaching his visions were. The principle of the constancy of the velocity of light is the first foundation stone of the theory. The speed of light is invariably 186,000 miles per second. This was the first contradiction to common sense. Second, he posited that all the laws of nature are exactly identical in all frames of reference, moving uniformly relative to each other. The outcomes of these two principles are that a moving object appears to contract in the direction of motion as its velocity increases, and the mass of a moving object increases as the velocity of the object increases. There is no such thing as space and time as separate dimensions, there is only space-time, a continuum. From this continuum theory reality is four-dimensional and everything that now seems to unfold before us with the passing of time already exists—past, present, and future. The last aspect of Einstein's special theory of relativity that Zukav asks us to consider is the revelation that mass is a form of energy, and that energy has mass ($E = MC^2$). Energy and mass are different forms of the same thing and, like space and time, they are not separate entities but rather mass-energy. Zukav comments,

> One of the most profound by products of the general theory of relativity is the discovery that gravitational "force", which we had so long taken to be a real and independently existing thing, is actually our mental creation. There is no such thing in the real world. (p. 206)

This is the basis and the beginning of the speculations regarding the connected-ness of the universe we live in now being explored by physicists, systems theorists, neurobiologists, psychologists, and others who look beyond.

Zukav summarizes this new look at reality in his statement:

> "Reality" is what we take to be true. What we take to be true is what we believe. What we believe is based upon what we look for. What we look for depends upon what we think. What we think depends upon what we believe. What we believe determines what we take to be true. What we take to be true is our reality. (p. 328)

Leshan and Margenau (1982) give us another idea to ponder in their suggestion that different areas of experience may have their own set of guiding principles, one set incomplete or meaningless when used to explain a different set of experiences. Instead of one reality there indeed may be many:

> Science today, both in physics and in the social sciences, has brought us to the point where we must face the fact that if we wish to proceed on the scientific path and attempt to make our data lawful, we simply cannot have only one set of principles about how reality works. We need to allow for a number of alternate realities. (p. 21)

Reporting on a recent conference of physicists Jonas (1986) comments,

In the experiments they described, a single particle can apparently exist in two places at the same time, an experimenter can apparently influence the behavior of a particle not only in the present but also in the past, and there appear to be indissoluble links between certain pairs of particles even when the particles are separated by room-size distances and are flying away from each other at the speed of light. (p. 11)

Some of the participants observed that the experimental evidence in quantum mechanics suggests that we have a role in creating the universe.

Astronomers are exploring the edge of the universe and finding such interesting phenomena as quasars energized by black holes that may mark the boundaries of the cosmos (Overbye, 1982). To help understand these phenomena other scientists (Oppenheimer, 1984) are attempting to detect and measure gravitational waves, one of the crucial tenets of Einstein's general theory of relativity. These waves, carried by the still hypothetical particles called gravitons, occur when an object changes its shape or redistributes its mass. Showing their existence would help scientists understand gravity and many of its phenomena such as black holes.

Davies (1984) asks us to go a step farther when he theorizes that each of us may throughout our bodies carry 11 dimensions of space. Some of the world's leading physicists are currently exploring the implications and consequences of multidimensional space. They believe that the only way we can make sense of the subatomic world is in the context of a multidimensional universe. Such phenomena as gravity, nuclear energy, and electromagnetic forces may be manifestations of these dimensions of hyperspace.

The fourth dimension of this hyperspace is under current investigation in such diverse fields as medicine, weather prediction, sociology, and oceanography (Segal, 1984). Computer graphics have made the visual exploration of this dimension possible. Quantum physicists have discovered results from experiments that cannot be explained by the usual notions of speed and communication so are theorizing a universe shot through with passageways, possibly running through black holes, that allow shortcut communication at speeds greater than light taking place in a fourth dimension. According to Segal, "In all, it is entirely possible that we Earthlings are now on the verge of transcending the limited three-dimensional environment that has traditionally programmed and confined our thinking" (p. 69).

Even more thought provoking is Segal's contention that the view of the world that most people consider obvious and natural may be incorrect. These views have been accepted without proof and now hold a place of accepted truth: (1) realism—regularities in observed phenomena are caused by some physical reality whose existence is independent of human observers; (2) inductive reasoning—this is a valid mode of reasoning that can be applied freely, allowing conclusions to be drawn from consistent observations; and (3) Einstein separability—no influence of any kind can propagate faster than the speed of light. In light of the results of new experimentation in quantum mechanics these realistic theories are being seen as almost certainly in error.

Bohm (1980) asks that we cease to think of reality as made up of independent fragments:

> The notion that all these fragments are separately existent is evidently an illusion, and this illusion cannot do other than lead to endless conflict and confusion. Indeed, the attempt to live according to the notion that the fragments are really separate is, in essence, what has led to the growing series of extremely urgent crises that is confronting us today. (pp. 1, 2)

Fritjof Capra (1982), a physicist at the Lawrence Berkeley Radiation Laboratory, expands on these ideas and finds in his pursuit of the atomic and subatomic world that the universe is interdependent and involved in cyclical change. He believes that the seemingly separate objects we have thought to exist in our world are in reality patterns in an inseparable cosmic process, which are intrinsically dynamic, continually changing into one another, holistic, and ecological. Capra sees this view of reality affecting all forms of social organizations and institutions.

A part of the "way the world is" has been the idea that entropy exists, that is, all of the matter and energy in the universe is gradually being reduced to an ultimate state of inert uniformity. Now we are asked to see such events not as a reduction in organization, but as a catalyst of complexity or increasing order. Ilya Prigogine (1980), a Belgian chemist and Nobel Prize winner, believes that everything is alive and these living systems periodically become so disrupted by disharmony that they appear to fall apart. What is really happening is that the turbulence has led to a transition, a movement toward a higher level of organization. The more the turbulence, the more complex will be the restructuring; the more complex a structure becomes, the more often it will go into apparent disharmony. The part I like best is that a seemingly small number or critical mass can create enough disharmony that even huge systems and institutions will be forced to change.

Think what that can mean to those involved in gifted education at every level. A small creative and committed group of educators can indeed have an effect on even such a large system as the institution of education in today's society. Prigogine speaks of examples such as biological systems, black holes, chemical reactions, brains, cultures, and social arrangements all being similarly affected. He calls such systems "dissipative structures," and because such structures cannot accommodate entropic disorder beyond a critical point, they suddenly reconfigure themselves into more highly ordered systems that can accommodate the increased entropy. In such a view, all systems become open to fluctuation and to innovation. With such a view, there can be no prediction other than the constant movement toward higher being.

One of the complex systems that is affected by Prigogine's theory is the human brain. To add to the theory of "dissipative structures," we now have two very impressive thinkers asking us to see it also as a hologram. A hologram, you remember, can reconstruct a three-dimensional picture from a process involving interference waves of light and can reconstruct such a picture from any fragment of its surface. The brain is considered such an instrument by David Bohm (1980), an English physicist and mathematician and a protégé of Albert Einstein, and by Karl Pribram (1977), a neurophysiologist and respected researcher from Stanford University. Together they conclude that not only is the brain a hologram, but it interprets for us in a holographic way the larger hologram, the universe. This means that the brain is far more complex than we now imagine and that it operates in dimensions as yet unknown, possibly beyond time and space. Our brains construct "concrete" reality by interpreting frequencies from other dimensions, allowing us to feel at home in whatever level we can understand. "We were beginning to find in our laboratories that the brain was actually responding to vibrations," commented Pribram (cited by Tarrytown Group, 1982, p. 13).

Notions of common sense, inductive reasoning, and speed of light as an upper limit of information transfer may also be changing. Bernard d'Espagnet (1979), a French physicist, has reported some interesting findings that support Pribram's view of vibrations and Capra's sense of an inseparable, holistic universe. His research is showing a mysterious linkage between the properties of subatomic particles separated by a considerable distance. His data seem to imply that all objects constitute an indivisible whole. He believes that the concept of an independently existing reality is remote from everyday experience.

Physicist Geoffrey Chew (Ferguson, 1982d) states that physics is "evolving beyond attempts to isolate phenomena, reproduce experimental results and make clear distinctions between separate aspects of the world. Viewing the universe as a collection of pieces is no longer tolerable" (p. 1).

This linking, this indivisibility affects the way we view learning. According to a new theory by Rupert Sheldrake (Sheldrake, 1981), these invisible organizing fields create a "morphic resonance" that affects an entire species:

> Whenever one member of a species learns a new behavior, the causative field for the species is changed. These fields have no energy, but are causative because they serve as blueprints for form and behavior. For example, if a human being learns to do a task that no other person has ever done before, humans everywhere else in the world should be able to learn the task more easily, in the absence of any known type of physical connection or communication. (p. 749)

Such a theory again supports the idea of a holographic reality.

While more centered on the brain as the mediating system, the theory proposed by William Gray, a Massachusetts psychiatrist, also has important implications for human learning. "Feelings may be the organizers of the mind and personality. Finely tuned emotions may form the basis of all we know" (Ferguson, 1982a, p. 1). According to this new theory, feelings form the underlying structure of thought, with emotion serving as the key to memory, recognition, and generation of new ideas. Gray believes that humans are more intelligent than other species because they have a richer supply of emotional nuances available to them. This results from the larger human forebrain and the more extensive connections between the frontal lobe and the limbic system. Gray says,

> I had important confirmation in Einstein's repeated statement that ideas come to him first in the form of vague and diffuse bodily sensations that gradually refined themselves into exact and reproduceable feeling-tones. Only when this process was completed could Einstein mathematically define the new concept. (p. 1)

Paul LaViolette (Ferguson, 1982a), a systems theorist, combined Prigogine's theory and Gray's theory to explain how the brain physically processes new ideas. "Mental events—sensations, perceptions, feelings, emotions—are encoded and processed by the brain as if they were AM/FM neuroelectric waveforms" (p. 1). The encoded waveforms are then amplified into thoughts while they recycle between the limbic and cortical systems. A higher degree of intelligence then means a higher degree of caring.

According to Gray and LaViolette, the brain uses feelings to structure information. Abstract information may be so hard to recall because it is cut off from feelings. Often, even after a decade of exploration of affective or feeling education, the cognitive or rational learning mode is most highly valued. The irony is that the efficiency of learning is prevented by ignoring feelings. Integration of emotion and cognition is far more efficient, more easily and rapidly dealt with, contends Gray.

One of the leaders in gifted education, John C. Gowan, had during the past decade been exploring the area of creativity in a way that opened for him areas to be explored beyond those usually assigned to this field of inquiry. While some have been satisfied to limit their inquiry to the realm of creative problem solving and creative thinking, Gowan discussed and theorized in areas he referred to as those of increasing order. This seems to indicate a tie to Prigogine's theory of the ever increasing complexity of higher levels of organization, or, if you will, increasing order. Gowan wrote of the operations of these levels of increasing order and attempted to describe, organize, and map this new territory (Gowan, 1980). With his help and that of others such as those found in this chapter, we may indeed, as Gowan suggested, "illuminate the Divinity which resides in each of us and make it blossom like a rose" (p. xv).

A very special person who took this idea of a holographic universe one step further and through delightful analogies has left us with quite a lot to think about was Itzhak Bentov. Having been with him only once, I was very surprised by the loss I felt and continue to feel at his death in the DC-10 crash in Chicago in 1979. I suppose this is the mark of a master teacher, for he was truly that. He could take very abstract and difficult concepts and with humor help me to understand many levels of meaning. I continue to read his books (Bentov, 1977, 1982) and continue to wonder and to learn. He seems to tickle the mind with his comments, for example,

Everything in the entire universe, including our bodies, is made of this cosmic substance. We contain atoms from the most distant galaxies and are thus connected to the whole universe. (1982, p. 5)

The universe is a hologram or interference pattern in which all parts are interconnected, containing information about each other and thus about the entire universe. . . . Each individual human consciousness is part of that hologram; therefore, by projecting one's consciousness into the Universal Mind in a heightened state of awareness, one can obtain knowledge about the whole universe. . . . It also follows that the thoughts of all human beings are interconnected, affecting each other and in turn affecting the entire universe. Whatever one thinks or does becomes part of the universal hologram. (1982, p. 6)

In short, consciousness in a vibratory state manifests as our familiar matter, from which the different forms that we see around us are made. The table, the flowers, the scent of the flowers, and our bodies are all made of rapidly vibrating consciousness. (1982, p. 11)

If we take a chicken egg and attach electrodes to the two ends, we discover that it reflects the structure of the universe. . . . Every seed in nature, whether plant or animal, has a similar current running along its axis, creating an electromagnetic field around the seed. (1982, pp. 31, 32)

I suggest, therefore that our brain is not the *source* of thought but a thought *amplifier*. As we have seen, it takes a tiny impulse, magnifies it for us, and only then does it become a thought. It appears that the thought does not originate within the brain; rather, the brain picks up the tiny impulses implanted there. . . . (1977, p. 86)

Margaret Mead was concerned about global interdependence and an emerging world culture (Houston, 1977a). She believed that we have now reached an age when the planet must be mutually shared. We are, she felt, on the brink of a planetary integration that will provide "opportunities for human and cultural potentiation of a scale and depth never known before" (p. 58). However, such wholeness would need to be seen in a framework of preserving human differences and individual uniqueness. In such a vision, the smallest actions of each of us affect the reality of us all. Although this view may seem impossibly optimistic, Mead assures us that "what seemed impossible to accomplish yesterday is a shared activity of thousands tomorrow" (p. 58). It requires only the development of the ideas.

Life-styles and belief systems change, dichotomies no longer exist, and time and space have another dimension. Reality is seen as an outward projection of internal thoughts, feelings, and expectations. Energy is the connector, the center, the basis of all matter, and consciousness forms reality. It is this progression that we make available as we present opportunities to our students that allow the integration of body and mind. As science continues to validate this interconnected view of reality, Western pragmatists will join Eastern mystics, and all humans will benèfit. Human potential, as yet unknown, will have the chance to develop.

Teilhard de Chardin (1959) predicted that the future of consciousness is to become more complex, more inclusive. He too believed that we are evolving toward a harmonious interrelationship, a single entity, one that will not diminish all of its parts but enhance our individuality, making each of us more truly what we are. He spoke of love as the elemental energy drawing the whole toward its culmination and fulfillment. This vision has been shared by philosophers and educators throughout the ages.

While all of the foregoing are just theories, I remind you that theories are all we have in constructing our reality and ordering our thoughts. They are the best explanations their originators have for what is happening. Observations and "facts" are also theories that we accept and have decided to use to help us understand our world and ourselves in it. It may be, as Bentov said, that "we are all part of this great hologram called Creation which is everybody else's SELF. . . . You create your own reality. It's all a cosmic play, and there is nothing but *you*!" (1982, p. 85).

What does all of this mean to us as educators of the gifted? From Bentov (1977), Bohm (1980), Capra (1982), Dossey (1982), Hunt (1982), Leshan and Margenau (1982), Loye (1983), Prigogine and Stengers (1984), Wilber (1982), Zukav (1979), and others it is possible to learn

- About issues that must be shared with the bright minds we teach.
- That content is only meaningful as it aids the knowledge of recurrence, as it keeps the individual from having to rethink the past.
- That our primary mission is to provide the climate for insight and exploration of insight. Knowledge without freedom to go beyond is useless.
- That energy must be raised if insight is to occur. Energy is now being wasted on fear, resistance, and sameness. If there is fear within one person that person will be weakened; if one person brings negative energy into the classroom the body of the class will be weakened; to the school, the body of the school will be weakened.
- That we are not separate dots with a space between; we are a line where separate dots form the line.

BRAIN RESEARCH: EXTENDING THE LEARNING ABOUT OURSELVES

Within the past few years, technology has been vastly improving our ability to understand how our brain functions, leading to a better understanding of how we, as human beings, learn. Curiously the more we are discovering, the more we can validate the ancient wisdoms that have come to us from Chinese, Hindu, Egyptian, and other age-old teachings.

One example is the work of the Japanese inventor, Hiroshi Motoyama, who has designed the Apparatus for Measuring the Functioning of the Meridians and Corresponding Internal Organs (AMI). The AMI can distinguish disorders of organs and specific disease tendencies. Used by the government in Japan to screen employees during a required medical exam, the AMI tests have indicated that energy flowing in and out of the meridians can interact with the meridian energy of other persons. This energy does not travel through the nervous system. Instead it is conducted electrolytically via connective tissue emitting signals near the surface of the body. The energy points correspond to the locations of the Hindu *chakras,* or energy centers, and the Chinese acupuncture meridians. It is most interesting to find validation for the often experienced notion that each human energy field influences others in its vicinity. Motoyama's work was reported in the *Brain/Mind Bulletin* (Ferguson, 1981b).

Another interesting view of how we function is coming from the use of the magnetoencephalogram (MEG), which has allowed researchers to map the brain at work. This instrument is giving researchers a clearer understanding of the link between higher mental processes (such as understanding the meaning of words) and underlying brain activity. The MEG works by detecting the extremely small magnetic fields associated with the movement of ions into and out of the brain cells. The MEG has the advantage of needing only to be placed next to the head without touching it and is relatively impervious to signals from anywhere other than precisely where it is focused. The MEG permits the detailing of the intricacies of the brain at work, while minimizing interference with its natural activity (Zimmerman, 1982).

Another exciting new technological breakthrough is the invention of the nuclear magnetic resonance (NMR) scanner, literally a new kind of window to the interior of the brain and the entire body. Previously used diagnostic tools, such as the computerized axial tomography (CAT) scanner and the positron emission tomography (PET) scanner, have involved the use of ionizing radiation that can be injurious to the patient and to the operator. The NMR requires no X-rays or other harmful material, as it works by use of harmless magnets and a radio-frequency energy about a billion times weaker than that of visible light. By sensing the exchange of atoms between molecules in chemical reactions, NMR can literally watch physiological processes in action, including the brain and its natural rhythms (Wingerson, 1982a).

Brain research is also opening up new fields of inquiry that already ask us to stretch, or in some cases change, our belief systems about how we function. Chronopsychology is the mind/body study involving daily (circadian) and other temporal cycles and the effects of biological rhythms on physical, cognitive, and emotional aspects of human behavior. Results of research in this new field have shown us these things about ourselves:

1 Short-term memory is less effective in the afternoon, as long-term memory improves.
2 Reading speed declines during the day; comprehension increases.
3 Birth most commonly occurs at 4 a.m., death at 6 a.m.

4 Activity phases of most circadian rhythms peak in early afternoon, rest phases shortly after midnight.

5 Levels of hormones change; mood swings, cell division, pulse rate, blood pressure, body temperature all fluctuate.

Circadian timetables influence learning, effectiveness of medication, immune responses, and susceptibility to disease. The recorded fluctuations in intellectual performance over the day are sufficiently great to account for the difference between an A, B, or C grade on tests (Ferguson, 1981a).

The possibility of learning to strengthen the immune system of the body mentally has received validation from the experiments of Ader and Cohen of the University of Rochester in New York (Wingerson, 1982b). Their work, along with that of others throughout the United States and Canada, has opened a new field of investigation in how the brain affects the ability of the immune system to fight off disease, psychoneuroimmunology.

According to a number of researchers there is mounting evidence from the field of psychoneuroimmunology that organic diseases are linked to the attitudes, beliefs, and relationships one has and to one's position in the social world. Ornstein and Sobel (1987) believe that a primary function of the brain is health maintenance. This may be carried out by numerous connections between the nervous system and the immune system allowing the mind to influence resistance or susceptibility to disease. In addition, the biochemicals of the brain may induce a response from the cells of the immune system. They report that the combination of high expectation and poor performance can be reflected in increased susceptibility to infectious disease. In an effort to remedy this Ornstein and Sobel discuss the results when visualization and hypnosis were introduced. Younger people seemed to benefit the most and showed an increase in the responsiveness of their immune systems. Relaxation was also investigated, and it was found that relaxation training can enhance cellular immune function.

There are many indications that a stable, secure connection to the larger society versus loneliness and isolation improves resistance to disease and increases life expectancy (Diamond, 1986; Ornstein & Sobel, 1987). Although findings seem speculative regarding the linking of the brain/mind and the health of the individual, innumerable researchers in countries all over the world are investigating these connections and the results are well worth watching.

David Loye (1982) tells us that individuals with balanced brain hemisphere dominance apparently are better predictors than persons with strong dominance in a single hemisphere. Acting as the executive, the frontal lobes monitor differences of right and left brain input, then decide what is the true composite nature of the future and how it is to be lived.

It seems that the information regarding the prefrontal cortex is not exactly new (Goodman, 1978). In the early 1960s those involved in lobotomy treatments had already begun to notice functions lost when this area of the brain was no longer available to a person. It was from these data that Halstead (cited in Goodman, 1978) posited the theory of two separate modes of intelligence: psychometric intelligence, located in the posterior regions of the brain, the mode measured by the intelligence tests; and biological intelligence, located in the frontal lobe regions, the mode related to higher functional activity underlying foresight, self-regulation, and social sense. It is interesting to note that after lobotomy the measured intelligence is not lessened; instead, in some cases it has been shown to increase. The loss has been in the blunting of emotional responsiveness and the lowering of moral standards. It is the difference between the impulsive, willful child and the sensitive, altruistic adult—characteristics that intelligence tests do not tap.

Also from this work the forebrain was associated with foresight, insight, and imagining and thinking about the personal future. Added support has come from Soviet researchers (Luria, 1973) who have identified the prefrontal cortex as associated with integrative, holistic, creative abilities that include contributions from both hemispheres. As Goodman (1978) comments,

> More creative, holistic and integrative, the future intelligent human can maintain drive toward completion, experience intellectual ecstasy and invent new systems —including new systems of thought and consciousness. But first we must move beyond the underdeveloped 12-year-old mind. (p. 49)

Once the educational community lets go of the fiction of separate right and left brains, the integrative nature of the brain will allow us to begin producing effective and efficient learning. As Levy (1985) comments,

> To the extent that regions are differentiated in the brain, they must integrate their activities. Indeed, it is precisely that integration that gives rise to behavior and mental processes greater than and different from each region's special contribution. (p. 43)

With this integration of function we may ultimately develop our creative and intuitive processes. Levy points out that no evidence exists that even suggests that either process is the sole property of the right hemisphere of the brain. She believes that they almost certainly depend on an intimate collaboration between hemispheres.

Other interesting findings in brain research include these:

1 Male sex hormones (androgens) may affect the ability to visualize and manipulate objects mentally, key components of mathematical skills widely considered to be more innate to males than females (Hier & Crowley, 1982).

2 Mature nervous systems form new synapses in response to changes in the environment, intense muscle activity, variations in hormone levels, and prolonged drug treatment (Cottman & Nieto-Sampedro, 1982).

3 The stream of consciousness is activated when 100 million synapses are

simultaneously engaged in quantum interactions. This type of information begins to provide a physical definition of consciousness. There is even the possibility that translocation, the transporting of oneself instantly to a new location, may be possible, as there is such a precedent in the quantum effect known as *tunneling* (Ferguson, 1982b).

4 Memory drugs, experimentally used to improve performance on memory tasks, have been found to give results significantly higher than chance. Originating in Belgium, piracetam has been researched in Europe for over 5 years and is in test status in the United States. It has been found effective in improving the recall of students and in treating disorders of senility. Researchers believe its effectiveness results from its ability to aid integrative activities in the brain (Ferguson, 1977b).

FURTHER POSSIBILITIES IN HUMAN LEARNING: SUPERLEARNING

Certain elements, independently used, have positively affected learning and have been reported in the educational literature during the past decade:

- The critical influence of teachers and their personalities
- The importance of supportive, responsive, stimulating environments
- The reduction of tension and anxiety in the learning interaction
- The need for a variety of approaches
- The need for a change of pace in the presentation of material.

In Bulgaria, a teacher/researcher by the name of Georgi Lozanov (1977) has been putting such information together and has, through numerous experiments, developed a system he calls *Suggestopedia* that not only accelerates the learning process, but dramatically increases the retention factor. Lozanov bases the Suggestopedia system on three principles: joy and the absence of tension, oneness of the conscious and unconscious, and suggestive interaction.

To assure the first principle, a relaxed ambience is developed using tension reduction and relaxation techniques. Any practice that would produce anxiety, stress, fear of failure, or humiliation for the learner must be discontinued. The student is encouraged to view learning as a pleasant activity, one he or she will enjoy, with results easily obtainable. The second principle is developed by the use of music (generally classical) chosen for this purpose. Dramatic skits and psychodrama may also be used to heighten the awareness of wholeness or oneness. Lozanov (1977) states,

> Oneness of the conscious and the unconscious (or totality) requires that the learning process be so organized that it uses not only the reactions and the conscious functions of the learner's personality, but also his unconscious authority. . . . It raises consciousness in the wider sense of behavior and motivation to a higher level. (p. 3)

The third principle can be met only by a sensitive, nonthreatening, caring teacher. The part the teacher plays and the attitude emanating from this instructor-supporter-facilitator are critical.

The Suggestopedia system of accelerated learning has produced some impressive results: Students show significant improvement in memory; they cover material, which under former educational methodology and situations took over a year to learn, in 2 to 3 months with a higher level of retention. Recent research shows that Suggestopedia can be used in every discipline, for the students benefit by feelings of harmony, restfulness, pleasant emotions, and the calling forth and combining of all the mental, physical, and psychic reserves. Racle (1977) reports that this type of instruction is not only "many times more efficacious" than other teaching methods, but "much more humane and much less burdensome for the studying individual" (p. 2).

As reported by Eggers (1984), Suggestopedia includes a number of methodological differences from the traditional approaches:

- Use of the arts such as music, drawing, and theatrical presentations in establishing a creative, emotionally stimulating environment
- A tension-free environment
- Real communication situations where natural language is created
- The belief that the learning task is easy and self-confidence in success
- The instructor's awareness of the suggestive factor such as body language, dress, intonation, facial expressions, and the classroom environment
- Credibility of the instructor
- The delayed correction technique.

Eggers feels that the main point to remember is that, by reducing negative suggestive factors and increasing positive ones, far more powerful learning can take place.

Bancroft (1982) found in the United States that three elements of Suggestopedia were essential to the success of the acceleration and retention: (1) an attractive and pleasant classroom, (2) a teacher with a dynamic personality, and (3) a state of relaxed alertness in the students. While much of the program does not translate literally to the American educational system, these elements can be replicated and are components found in the Responsive Learning Environment described in Chapter 8.

Many countries, including the United States, and also the United Nations Educational Service (UNESCO), are interested and involved in research of the possibilities of accelerated learning. Conferences, workshops, pamphlets, and journal articles have begun to disperse information about this exciting new practice. To learn more, you may contact the Society for Suggestive-Accelerative Learning and Teaching, Inc., 2740 Richmond Ave., Des Moines, Iowa 50317. Here are some other thoughts toward optimizing learning:

1 Relaxed concentration facilitates learning; performance equals potential minus self-interference (Gallwey, 1974).

2 Human beings experience numerous states of waking consciousness without full awareness of the potentials and abilities unique to each state. Educators must be about the business of teaching this awareness (Roberts, 1982).

3 Individual biases toward attending to or ignoring stimuli can be measured soon after birth. Infants at high risk, related to differences in reading ability, for example, can be diagnosed in time to remediate their problem (Ferguson, 1981a).

4 Computerized video games may have major implications for the future of learning. Eventually they may be directed by brainwave biofeedback. They are highly interactive and provide immediate response. Games are now being developed to feature realistic simulation experiences that reward original, creative thinking (Adkins, 1982).

5 Synchronization of the hemispheres may allow greater intuitive learning. Such synchronization may be self-taught by the use of biofeedback instrumentation (Millay, 1981a).

Biofeedback is proving to be a valuable tool for optimizing learning. Although it has long been recognized that nearly all organs and parts of the human body generate electrical current, only after the discovery of biofeedback techniques did we find that this electrical activity is within our control. And more than just an internal generation is possible.

Dr. Elmer Green, founder of the Biofeedback and Psychophysiology Center at Menninger Foundation, tells us that biofeedback uses an approach to self-regulation in human beings that means getting immediate, ongoing information about one's own biological processes or conditions, e.g., heart action, temperature, brain-wave activity, blood pressure, or muscle tension, and using the information to change and control voluntarily the specific process or response being monitored. He suggests that you must visualize what you want the body to do, tell it to do it, and then relax and let it happen. The biofeedback instrument only allows you to observe the change. The process does nothing to the person; rather it is a tool for releasing that person's potential (Pew, 1979).

During biofeedback, the electrical energy of the body is turned into a source of electrical power. It seems that only a fraction of the electrical power we develop as our bodies function is actually used. Most of this energy emanates from the body and dissipates into the environment around us. Some researchers have tapped this source of electrical energy and made its existence dramatically real by using body energy to light displays, power sound devices, and even run electric trains (Brown, 1974). Brown feels that staggering amounts of energy are untapped and wasted constantly because we have not yet learned how to harness this never-ending master resource. She envisions using bioenergy as a source of electrical energy to run computers and other powered devices or as a sophisticated communications system.

Discovery of the techniques of biofeedback has provided us with important information and insights into the functioning of our human system. Biofeedback techniques can be as simple as looking into a mirror or as complex as the monitoring of sophisticated electronic devices. Any object or material that provides information about the body's systems can be called a biofeedback device. Biofeedback is important to education because it can give us information on how our biosystem functions and on abilities about which we have been previously unaware. Already many psychologists and educators are finding a multitude of uses for this tool. Kamiya, Haight, and Jampolsky (1975) use biofeedback to remove learning blocks, but not to manipulate or gain control of behavior, calling this process "personal biology." Reportedly, it has had much effect on student self-image and on improvements in focus of attention, emotional stability, communications, and reading skills. There have also been reports of reduction in anxiety and hyperactive behavior in students (French, 1978). These reports show that biofeedback has been used in a college physiology course, as part of the training of student nurses, and with the developmentally disabled, all with results showing significant gains in learning. "Feedback display systems have evolved from clicks, beeps and flashing red lights into multi-dimensional color video and concert quality musical tones. Children can affect the race of turtles across a video screen by

Watching yourself think using biofeedback is a tool for today and tomorrow.

increasing their production of alpha brainwaves (French, 1978, p. 2). Relaxation exercises learned in biofeedback training helped University of Wisconsin football players to cut their injuries and win more games; they improved from a 60% win record to a 90% win record after training (Pew, 1979).

Mulholland (1973) believes there is tremendous potential for biofeedback in education, but that there exists a pronounced communication gap between the two areas. He believes educators could use biofeedback in at least three ways: (1) to enhance self-awareness, self-exploration, and self-control; (2) to accentuate processes conducive to learning and to diminish those that impede learning; and (3) to strengthen a specific skill. The attending process could be facilitated by self-regulating biofeedback units, ensuring better attention during learning. Learning could also be facilitated by training students to be more in control of their emotional states, for we know that emotions have as much effect on learning as attention. With biofeedback training, students could become aware of the physiological states associated with pleasant feelings and train themselves to use such states to reduce states of anxiety, fear, or anger that tend to impede learning. By intelligent and creative application of current research in biofeedback, Mulholland believes that the educational community will achieve a major professional advance.

Students can participate in researching these new body data. By bringing resources and practitioners to class, you can open this fascinating area for your students. Once they understand the concept, they will find methods and materials in common use from which they can gain more biofeedback information. For more biofeedback information, see Brown (1974); DiCara (1970); Lang (1970); Shapiro, Tursky, Gershon, and Stern (1969); Stearn (1976); and Taylor and Bongar (1976).

Brown (1974) believes that with biofeedback we now have a way to observe different types of learning. She sees biofeedback as an important step toward the realization of the truly integrated, responsible learner:

> Physical and mental attitudes more suitable for learning could be learned more readily as well as improvement of their attention span by their own volition. Feedback could initiate in Western education something that it has lacked since the time of Plato—a holistic education, an education of mind and body together so that finally the student might truly be educated in terms of that ancient but futuristic motto: mens sana in corpore sano. (p. 388)

A true education of mind and body now seems available. In 1981, Frank Farley, then President of the American Educational Research Association, in his address to the conference said,

> Education in the year 2000 will be radically altered by emerging conceptions of what the brain can do and what we can do to the brain. Discoveries in brain research demand many radical changes.

Some of those changes we have discussed; some are yet ahead to amaze us.

INTEGRATIVE EDUCATION: CREATING TRANSPERSONAL LEARNING

As we discovered in Chapters 7 and 8, there is a way to use the elements from these new approaches and the implications of the brain research in the classroom. It is called *integrative education.* Barzakov (Ferguson, 1982c) reports from his work that all things in the environment, including colors, sounds, textures, rhythms, shapes, objects, other persons, and the appearance and syntax of a text, are significant in the learning process. We optimize the learning process when emotional, physical, mental, and intuitive energies are presented harmoniously. The mind does not perceive just bits and pieces, but is constantly weaving a large pattern from our experiences. "If you feed the brain properly, there is practically nothing it isn't capable of learning" (p. 1), states Barzakov. He believes that our best learning and performance come from the hidden teacher/artist within each of us. This inner teacher is one of the basic elements of the integrative approach (see Chapter 8).

Abraham Maslow, mentioned in Chapter 4, developed a hierarchy of human needs that has much to say to educators. At the highest level, level 5, Maslow placed self-actualization. Subsequent writing, just prior to his death in 1970, showed his thinking regarding a higher, sixth level that would go beyond self-actualization into a state he referred to as *transcendence.* This would be the level of interconnectedness, the state of oneness with the universe that would include and use all of human functioning at its highest actualization. Writers, psychologists, and philosophers since Maslow's death have developed the basis for a new psychology, called *transpersonal,* that builds on his work on self-actualization and includes the concept of transcendence. This concern in psychology has begun to touch education. With the same values and concerns, the area of integrative education has begun to take root. The thoughts of East and West are coming together in a climate of acceptance.

Coming together can be seen as the central theme of this book, the model on which its structure is based, a coalescing of thinking, feeling, sensing, and intuiting functions. While approaches may differ, those involved in integrative education are seeking to unite the logical with the mystical, the analytical with the intuitive. As transpersonal psychology seeks a more inclusive vision of human reality, including areas of human experience not yet explored, integrative education attempts to translate this vision into the realization of more and more aspects of human potential. The results will be a greater connectedness within and among people, a greater sense of wholeness, of purpose, of inner direction, and of outer responsible caring.

As integrative education becomes more accepted and practiced, we will find more curricula that include relaxation and development of integrative abilities. Guided fantasies and dreams, recognition and use of altered states of consciousness, and centering activities will develop more of our intuitive abilities. As this chapter suggests, there are new possibilities for expanding even those areas of human learning we have always been using. All this and more lie ahead as we seek to bring all of our knowledge, feelings, talents, and creativity into the classroom in the service of actualizing and transcending. Integrative education promises this, and it is also the message of this book.

PARAPSYCHOLOGY, PSI, AND OUR INTUITIVE AWARENESS

There was a time when information about fields of energy surrounding the body, out-of-body experiences, healing energy, the influence of magnetic energy from outside this planet, and the results of unexplained human abilities was labeled as fraudulent, unnatural, absurd, or worse. Some still choose not to believe such phenomena exist. But for several decades such information has been under scientific investigation. The findings of psi research have begun to coalesce with the research findings of the hard sciences. For those who must have physical proof to believe in the existence of such phenomena, their need is now being met. All of these inquiries are fascinating and surely add to or modify our view of reality, making any phase of this research valuable content for the education of human beings. In this brief discussion, we will mention only a few of the directions parapsychology and psi research are taking to extend the abilities available to humans.

Psi is defined as the acquisition of information by means other than the known senses or a reasonable inference based on sensory experience, and/or the effecting of change in the environment by means other than the known biophysical ones (George, 1981). Views of the American scientist Tiller (Ferguson, 1973) on characteristics of psychoenergetic phenomena are not compatible with the more limited laws of conventional science. He reports that the energy fields seem to be different, that there is a level of substance that is dominantly magnetic with an organizing, rather than disorganizing, tendency as temperature increases. At the physical level, he notes a hologram of energy that acts as a force envelope around the organized substances. He, too, comments on the interconnectedness between all things in the universe.

Krippner (Chance, 1973) has conducted experimental work on telepathy, precognition, dreams, and out-of-body experiences, and other psi phenomena. He is convinced that all these occurrences are available and evident in all human beings and can be explained by natural biological and physical forces. Understanding them requires only that we take a more holistic view of the universe. He feels we can no longer continue to hold onto a simplistic cause-and-effect notion of human behavior. He believes that while scientific methodology must change, our basic understanding of nature will only be enhanced. He expresses the belief that altered states of consciousness, psychic phenomena, and many types of creativity will be found to be closely linked to right-brain function.

Interest in healing energy is creating a plethora of books and conferences on the subject. University of California at Los Angeles researcher Thelma Moss has used Kirlian photography to capture some provocative pictures of the actual energy that healers send (Mishlove, 1975). Her work follows years of Kirlian study by Russian scientists (Ostrander & Schroeder, 1970). Krieger (1976) of New York University discovered that hemoglobin levels of patients could be changed positively by the therapeutic touch of nurses trained to "touch with the intent to heal" (p. 2). She feels the discovery is highly significant, as hemoglobin can be considered a valid index of the body's basic metabolism. She taught this procedure to 32 RNs with results that had a probability of chance occurrence of only 1 in 1,000. Frank (1977) of Johns Hopkins has commented to his colleagues in a speech that, although he is convinced that healing power does exist, it can never be evaluated clearly enough for full acceptance by Western scientists.

Kraft (O'Connell, 1976) feels that the intuitive and the psychic are the same thing and are part of the consciousness of all humans. Among others who have made similar observations, Mishlove (1975) notes Carl Jung, Jerome Bruner, Albert Einstein, Isaac Newton, Pythagoras, Plato, and Goethe.

Businessmen such as Ray Kroc (McDonald's) and David Mahoney (Chair, Norton Simon), in the tradition of J. P. Morgan and Cornelius Vanderbilt, take great pride in their intuitive "hunches." Chief executives of some of the largest corporations in our nation make their corporate decisions on more than feasibility studies, risk-reward ratios, and cost analysis figures. A measurable correlation has been shown to exist between the company's profitability and the boss's precognitive ability. While often depicted as a wholly analytical creature, in reality, says Mintzberg of McGill University's Faculty of Management, the corporate executive is a holistic, intuitive thinker constantly relying on hunches to cope with problems far too complex for rational analysis. There is even a company, Williams Inference Service of New York, that sells educated hunches or "disciplined intuition" to major corporations (Rowan, 1979).

Agor (1983) believes that managers of the future will face increasingly complex situations in which they will need to make decisions on less than complete data. They also will be involved in increasing demands for participation in the decision-making processes. He believes that these managers will need to rely less on the traditional authority patterns of decision making and more on their intuitive judgment to handle these changes. With so many factors to consider, the synthetic nature of the intuitive process has been shown to be far more productive than the analytic, linear style of traditional managers. In testing over 2,000 managers across the United States in business, government, education, military, and health, Agor has found that the top managers in every organization rated significantly higher than middle- and lower-level managers in their use of intuitive ability. He suggests three rules to improve intuition: Believe in it; practice it; and create a supportive environment in which intuitive skills are valued. The business community seems far ahead of education in the use and valuing of this important human function.

Kasatkin, a Russian doctor who has spent his life studying the value of dreams for diagnosis and treatment of illness, believes he has clear evidence that dreams inform us of our upcoming illness while we sleep. Different illnesses show defined brain patterns and produce recurrent and typical dreams that begin to repeat a month or more before the illness can be diagnosed any other way. He states,

> One has to remember that the sensitivity of the outer layer of the brain is very high, much higher than that of any other part of the brain. I call it the dream band. It is a thick skin around the brain, with about sixteen million nerve cells. We have found that the pain centers inside the brain do not pick up deviations as quickly as the cells on the outer layer. Its more sensitive cells monitor what is happening in your mind and body and react to the minutest deviation from normal conditions. The danger then is registered in these outer layers. It becomes a vivid dream as you sleep, indirectly issuing an early warning of coming illness. Different areas of the "dream band" handle specific illnesses. (cited in Gris & Dick, 1978, p. 317)

Vilenskaya of the Bio-Information Department of the Popov Group, Moscow's parapsychology center, has reported an investigation of "optical sensitivity of the human skin to record images, both by direct contact and at a distance" (Gris & Dick, 1978). Experiments have demonstrated that with proper training students can be taught to identify the color and form of images by touch or near-touch, identify hidden objects, and pinpoint magnetic fields. Results of this training have been noted to be 60 to 90% accurate. The process is referred to as *Dermo-Optical Perception* (DOP). This is seen as a great benefit to the blind, and further experiments are involved in teaching the blind to read using these techniques. Chinese paranormal research is also involved in exploring these techniques (Krippner, 1981).

A 1981 report to Congress urged a serious assessment of psi research in the United States. The report cited over 150 areas of potential study. Among them were

- Medicine—advancing the use of mind-initiated cures
- Business—applying psychic ability to executive decision making
- Investigation—detecting emotional imprints of past events that provide clues for archaeological and detective work
- Defense—exploiting the obvious implications of one's ability to identify distant sites and affect sensitive instruments or other humans
- Weather modification, earthquake prediction, and nutrition.

In 1983 Senator Pell and others from Congress publicly asked the Congressional Research Service to report on the status of parapsychological research (Holden, 1983). Called the *Research Into 'psi' Phenomena: Current Status and Trends of Congressional Concern,* the report discusses the potential educational, military, anticrime, and health applications of psychic phenomena. However, the report acknowledges, less than $500,000 a year is supporting such research, and that is

Technology is a natural ally of gifted learners.

from private sources. In contrast, the Soviet Union spends tens of millions of dollars yearly.

While parapsychology and psi research are in themselves fascinating, their real value lies, in part, in their ability to point out inadequacies in our current belief systems. This type of information, and even the development of these types of abilities, provide one more link in the exploration of human potential.

STUDYING THE FUTURE: CREATING AN OPTIMAL REALITY

Throughout history there have been those people and those moments that have brought dramatic change to all who followed. Today it is becoming increasingly evident that such times are occurring with greater frequency, and the need for gifted people to bring vision to these times is of foremost concern. How can we who are most concerned with the nurture of gifted people help provide the experiences and the tools, the attitudes and the commitment they will need to optimize our future? That is the mission of a group of educators who are increasing in number and organizational strength each year. Their academic discipline is most commonly called *Future Studies* and deals with the process of change, alternative thinking, choice, self-concept, values, and the development of optimistic images of the future. A futurist must deal comfortably with uncertainties, open-ended situations, and vastly divergent possibilities. Cornish (1977), a futurist with the World Future Society, believes it imperative that we study the future in order that we may

- Forecast crises so that they may be averted.
- Assist in deciding the future we want.
- Be prepared to live in a changing world.
- Discover a format for working together cooperatively.
- Contribute to and participate in the furtherance of science and thought.
- Encourage more creativity.
- Increase the motivation to learn.
- Provide for the development of a well-balanced and integrated personal value structure and philosophy of life.
- Provide a means for recreation and fun.

In underscoring our need to include the study of the future, Goodlad (Silvernail, 1980) states,

> Other generations believed that they had the luxury of preparing their children to live in a society similar to their own. Ours is the first generation to have achieved the Socratic wisdom of knowing that we do not know the world in which our children will live. (p. 17)

Undoubtedly all children will need the attitudes, skills, and information that would result from the future studies curricula, but for the gifted there are some special benefits and some special responsibilities involved. One of the most obvious reasons for the involvement in gifted education comes from the needs and characteristics of the gifted themselves. The interdisciplinary nature will appeal to children who think in diverse ways and who see unusual relationships. The higher levels of thinking will meet needs these children do not often find met in their educational experiences. The challenge of delving into unknown areas will appeal to the gifted of all ages, and the support for self-actualization, creative thinking, and value exploration will further the search for higher values that is characteristic in so many gifted individuals. It seems that the correlation between the needs of the gifted and the goals of the future studies programs is significant and meaningful.

The curriculum of future studies can be quite varied. Silvernail (1980) suggests that a futuristic curriculum contain the following components:

- Basic skills, both the traditional 3 *R*'s and new skills such as skill in humanistic processes, cross-disciplinary understandings, computer language, research skills, anticipatory skills of seeing relationships and taking action on evaluated data, skills based on cross-cultural and multiethnic insights, and change skills
- Study of the future that would include examination of the past and emerging issues and developing creative plans for action
- Self-concept
- Self-actualization, the exploration and planning for personal futures
- Valuing.

In a study reported by Wooddell, Fletcher, and Dixon (1982), the curriculum was organized around three aims or areas of competency to be developed in the students: (1) a futures perspective that involved the "recognition and valuing of an interest in the future and a concern for how actions and decisions can affect individual and collective futures"; (2) self-actualization, as described by Maslow (1954); and (3) "futuring competencies, involving those abilities to locate, process and evaluate information, to make decisions, to solve problems and systematically to consider alternative futures" (Wooddell et al., 1982, p. 26). The content for the program was eclectic and covered a wide range of subjects. In this study the gifted groups showed higher scores on all the instruments given and even the gifted in the control group outscored the nongifted in the experimental group receiving the future studies curriculum. The gifted in the experimental group outperformed the control group on measures of self-actualization and inner locus of control, with the control group showing actual declines in this area. Gifted students had a significantly higher futures perspective than the nongifted, but it was noted that the gains made by the nongifted in the experimental group, having started the program at a lower level, were greater.

A program in future studies that began operation during the early 1970s and now involves over 75,000 gifted students in grades 4 through 12 throughout the United States is Torrance's Future Problem Solving Program (Torrance et al., 1980; Torrance, 1981). The program consists of a year-long curriculum project and a local, state, and national interscholastic team and individual competition. Its goal is to provide experiences that will allow gifted students to make a constructive difference in the future through development of creative problem-solving skills; through skills of teamwork, cooperation, and communication; through an international sense; and through enlarging, enriching more accurate images of the future. The program has established statewide and national networks of interaction of students and teachers interested in future studies and in affecting the world of the future. For more information, write to Future Problem Solving Program, Nebraska Department of Education, Lincoln, Nebraska 68508.

The methods and materials developed for future studies curricula are exciting and guaranteed to motivate students of all ages. Here are some examples:

1 Future System's Innovative Learning Series (Kauffman, 1976): Its games and exercises involve the student in consequences and side effects of various actions, future problem finding, seeing the total or holistic view, alternative thinking, and in seeing and evaluating interrelationships.

2 The Future Wheel and the Cross Impact Matrix (Bleedorn, 1976): Involving exercises on thinking processes, these are two usable techniques for bringing futuristic perspectives and processes into K–12 classrooms.

3 Scenarios (Torrance et al. 1980): Students develop scenarios by studying the available information about a problem, selecting an alternative, and then imagining what might result as a consequence of following that alternative. This technique is commonly used by futurists in military and government agencies to create national and international policies. Scenario writing can be used in every subject area and can be clearly related to real-life situations.

4 Films, audiotapes, games, and simulations: *World Future Society Catalog, 1979* is a catalog compiled by the World Future Society, which lists valuable resources for future studies curricula. Examples of games listed:

   a *Space Future,* a game involving missions into space that stresses the cooperative approach to solving problems and settling other planets

   b *Earth Game,* another cooperative game that involves the students in problems of the planet

   c *Future Shock,* a game of the effects of rapid change in our lives.

Torrance (1981) summarizes the importance of future studies in the gifted curriculum:

> Perhaps the most important challenge in educating gifted, talented, and creative students for the future is to help them acquire a positive image of the future —especially a positive image of their own future careers. Positive images of the future seem to have a powerful and magnetic force. Our future images draw on us and energize us. They give us the courage and will to take important initiatives to "make a difference" in the future. (pp. 45–46)

In this chapter we have looked briefly at some exciting possibilities on the horizon. The almost unbelievable ideas of the physicists and philosophers blend views of reality that change our relationship to each other and to our universe and speak to us of the unlimited potential of which we are an integral part. As we seek to optimize the use of that potential it becomes critical to look more closely and more knowledgeably at the human brain, how it works, and the part it plays in the creation of our reality. As brain researchers explore this inner world we find more and more links to our total connectedness.

If we are to develop the human brain/mind system optimally, we must understand our own development, beginning prior to our birth, proceeding through the important periods of early learning, and climaxing in the efficient and effective use of the total brain/mind system we are calling *integrative education,* a lifelong way to actualize our transpersonal self. Biofeedback, computers, and techniques of Suggestopedia are but some of the techniques that can enhance this actualization.

Psi research continues to be an area of fascination as it continues to extend the range of human ability and empower each of us beyond the limits by which we believed we were bound. Studying the future can bring the excitement of all we have discussed in this chapter directly into the classroom, where the gifted among us can learn the skills, develop the attitudes, and find the freedom so necessary to dreaming the dreams, seeing the visions, and translating them into a future where all humankind can realize their place in the universe.

Giftedness is, for now, a way of speaking about and defining a few who are intellectually able. When we have integrated our focus, changed and extended our view of reality, and established the underlying connectedness of each to all, we will then have a new meaning of giftedness. The gifted, the talented, and the creative will then be merged, and we will truly be *GROWING UP GIFTED: DEVELOPING THE POTENTIAL OF CHILDREN AT HOME AND AT SCHOOL.*

Questions Often Asked

1. Why is it important to discuss theories about reality in the education of gifted learners?

There are several reasons such discussions are important. They allow bright minds to be challenged by the thoughts and questions of innovative philosophers and scientists. Such discussions clearly show that there are no "facts," only theories, and allow the students to stretch into unknown areas. They show that there are alternative solutions for every problem and encourage the development of problem-solving and evaluation skills in the context of "real world" situations. Information of this kind affects all of us and is relevant, timely, and truly fascinating. Gifted students are the ones that have the ability to ponder these kinds of abstract and profound ideas.

2. Do the ideas about connectedness and unified energy have anything to do with curriculum for the gifted learner?

While these ideas affect all learners, the gifted are the ones who will be most attracted to the conceptual frameworks and theoretical constructs involved. The ideas of connectedness and unified energy actually can change the way we see ourselves, the curriculum, and our place in the larger community. If you believe that your actions affect everyone else and all other energy, this concept of self is much different than one that involves no responsibility or individual power and supports the notion that what you do just does not matter. A curriculum built from the belief in connectedness and unity will be far more multidisciplinary and interrelated than one that is structured to teach discrete disciplines. A world view is important to education of the gifted, and these ideas support such a view.

3. If concepts such as gravity, entropy, inductive reasoning, cause and effect, and the constancy of the speed of light are being challenged, what can we teach that's right?

These theories are not wrong; they are just limited in the way they can be used and in the understandings they provide. Seeing them as universal absolutes has been the problem. As we explore multidimensional reality we will challenge a lot of traditionally accepted theories, and that is exactly the type of experience with which the gifted student must feel comfortable. We need to help the students give up the need for right and wrong facts. Our teaching and evaluation of knowledge must be involved with best theories and most powerful ideas that can always be challenged and changed as new and more accurate information or ideas come along.

4. Can we really use altered states of consciousness in the classroom? What will the parents say?

Any ideas or methods that are used in the classroom should first be presented to the parents for their information and reaction. Brain research provides a good biological base for the use of strategies for learning that include altered states of consciousness, but the parents must understand exactly what the data base is and how you plan to use it. The phrase *altered states of consciousness* may sound too strange, so you need to be sure it is understood or use other terminology that better communicates what you intend to do. Sleep is an altered state of consciousness; daydreaming is an altered state of consciousness; tension induces an altered state of consciousness, as do television, sunbathing, and roller coasters. These are familiar terms and do not seem threatening, whereas the phrase *altered states of consciousness* may not be familiar and may sound quite threatening. While learning in the classroom can most certainly benefit from the use of many different states of consciousness, the concept and strategies must be understood so that everyone involved may benefit.

5. Why spend time predicting the future when it probably will not turn out the way we predict?

It is the process of predicting that is so valuable for students. The knowledge of trends, the skills of decision making and forecasting, and the insights that develop from examining the factors that play a part in shaping the future all give students important understandings regarding their own lives and the role they play in what the future can be. If we are to believe the physicists, the view we have of the future actually sends energy into creating it. Helping the students to see a future they want, a positive, exciting future, will go a long way toward achieving such a future.

REFERENCES

Abraham, W. (1976). Counseling the gifted. *Focus on Guidance, 9*(1), 1–12.

Adkins, D., & Harty, H. (1984). Longitudinal view of teacher-leaders' reactions toward gifted education. *Roeper Review, 7*(1), 36–40.

Adkins, L. (1982). Video games could revolutionize the way we learn and teach. *Brain/Mind Bulletin, 7*(12), 2.

Adler, M. (1964). Ethnology of a group of gifted children. *Gifted Child Quarterly, 5,* 40–41.

Agor, W. (1983). Tomorrow's intuitive leaders. *The Futurist, 17* (4), 49–53.

Ahsen, A. (1973). *Eidetic behavior.* Yonkers-on-Hudson, NY: Eidetic.

Ainsworth, M. (1974). Individual differences in strange situation behavior of one-year-olds. In H. Schaffer (Ed.), *Origins of human relations.* New York: Academic Press.

Alberti, R., & Emmons, M. (1970). *Your perfect right: A guide to assertive behavior.* San Luis Obispo, CA: Impact.

Albrecht, K. (1979). *Stress and the manager.* Englewood Cliffs, NJ: Prentice-Hall.

Alexander, P., & Skinner, M. (1980). The effects of early entrance on subsequent social and academic development: A follow-up study. *Journal for the Education of the Gifted, 3*(3), 147–150.

Alexander, R. (1981). An historical perspective on the gifted and talented in art. *Studies in Art Education, 22*(2), 38–48.

Allen, G., Giat, L., & Cherney, R. (1974). Locus of control, test anxiety and student performance in a personalised instruction course. *Journal of Educational Psychology, 66,* 968–973.

Allen, R. W. (1968). Grouping through learning centers. *Childhood Education, 45,* 200–203.

Allport, G. (1955). *Becoming.* New Haven, CT: Yale University Press.

Alvino, J., McDonnel, R., & Richert, S. (1981). National survey of identification practices in gifted and talented education. *Exceptional Children,* October, *48*(2), 124–132.

Amabile, T. (1986). The personality of creativity. *Creative Living, 15*(3), 12–16.

American Association for Gifted Children. (1980). *Reaching out, advocacy for the gifted and talented.* New York: Teachers College Press.

Amidon, E., & Flanders, N. (1961). The effects of direct and indirect teacher influence on dependent-prone students learning geometry. *Journal of Educational Psychology, 52,* 286–291.

Anderson, H. H. (1959). Creativity as personality development. In. H. H. Anderson (Ed.), *Creativity and its cultivation.* New York: Harper & Row.

Anderson, H. H. (1968). On the meaning of creativity. In F. Williams (Ed.), *Creativity at home and in school.* St. Paul, MN: Macalester Creativity Project.

Anderson, H. H., & Anderson, G. (1965). A cross-national study of children: A study of creativity and mental health. In I. J. Gordon (Ed.), *Human development.* Chicago: Scott, Foresman.

Anderson, H. H., & Brewer, J. E. (1946). *Effects of teacher dominative and integrative contacts on children's classroom behavior* (Studies for Teachers' Classroom Personalities II). Palo Alto, CA: Stanford University Press.

Anderson, K. (Ed.). (1960). *Research on the academically talented student.* Washington, DC: National Education Association.

Anderson, L. (1981). *Assessing affective characteristics in the schools.* Boston: Allyn & Bacon.

Anderson, M. (1962). The relations of psi to creativity. *Journal of Parapsychology, 26,* 277–292.

Anderson, V. V., & Kennedy, W. M. (1932). *Psychiatry in education.* New York: Harper.

Andrews, E. G. (1960). The development of imagination in the preschool child. *University of Iowa Studies of Character, 3*(4), 1–64.

Andrews, F. (1975). Social and psychological factors which influence the creative process. In I. Taylor, & J. Getzels (Eds.), *Perspectives in creativity.* Chicago: Aldine, 117–145.

Andrews, G., & Debus, R. (1978). Persistence and the causal perception of failure: Modifying cognitive attributions. *Journal of Educational Psychology, 70,* 154–166.

Aragon, J., & Marquez, L. (1975). Spanish-speaking component. In J. Miley, I. Sato, W. Luché, P. Weaver, J. Curry, & R. Ponce (Compilers), *Promising practices: Teaching the disadvantaged gifted.* Ventura, CA: Ventura County Superintendent of Schools.

Arlin, M., & Whitley, T. (1978). Perceptions of self-managed learning opportunities and academic locus of control: A causal interpretation. *Journal of Educational Psychology, 70,* 988–992.

Armitage, S. (1980). Newborns can learn to call for mother's voice and prefer it. *Brain/Mind Bulletin, 5*(17), 1.

Arnold, A. (Ed.) (1974). *Programs for gifted: Research abstracts 1973–1974.* Los Angeles, CA: Los Angeles City Unified School District.

Arnold, A. (Chair). (1976). *Leadership: A survey of literature.* Los Angeles, CA: Los Angeles Unified School District, Instructional Planning Division.

Arnold, R., Bulatao, R., Buripakdi, C., Chin, B., Fawcett, J., Iritani, T., Lee, S., & Wu, T. (1975). *The value of children: Introduction and comparative analysis* (Vol. 1). Honolulu: East-West Population Institute.

Arnspiger, V., Rucker, W., Brill, J., & Blanchette, Z. (n.d.). *Human values series.* Austin, TX: Steck-Vaughn.

Asimov, I. (1965). *The human brain.* Boston: Houghton Mifflin, 1965.

Aspy, D. (1969, February). *Self theory in the classroom*. Paper presented at the annual meeting of the American Educational Research Association, Los Angeles, CA.

Aspy, D., & Bahler, J. (1975). The effect of teacher's inferred self concept upon student achievement. *Journal of Educational Research, 68,* 386–389.

Aspy, D., & Roebuck, F. (1972). An investigation of the relationship between student levels of cognitive functioning and the teacher's classroom behavior. *Journal of Educational Research, 65*(8), 365–368.

Assagioli, R. (1973). *The act of will.* New York: Viking.

Ausubel, D. P. (1967). Cognitive structure: Learning to read. *Education, 87,* 544–548.

Bachtold, L. (1968). Interpersonal values of gifted junior high school students. *Psychology in the Schools, 5,* 368–370.

Bachtold, L. (1969). Personality differences among high ability underachievers. *Journal of Educational Research, 63,* 16–18.

Backman, M. (1972). Patterns of mental abilities: Ethnic, socioeconomic, and sex differences. *American Educational Research Journal, 9,* 1–12.

Bagley, M. T., & Hess, K. K. (1982). *200 ways of using imagery in the classroom.* Woodcliff Lake, NJ: New Dimensions of the 80s.

Baldwin, A. (1973, March). *Identifying the disadvantaged.* Paper presented at the First National Conference on the Disadvantaged Gifted, Ventura, CA.

Baldwin, A. (1975). Instructional planning for gifted disadvantaged children. In B. Boston (Ed.), *Gifted and talented: Developing elementary and secondary school programs.* Reston, VA: Council for Exceptional Children.

Baldwin, A. (1977). Seven keys in program planning for gifted and talented. *Roeper City and County School Parent Communication, 2,* 3–6.

Baldwin, A. (1980, April). *The Baldwin Identification Matrix, its development and use in programs for the gifted child.* Paper presented at the Convention of the Council for Exceptional Children, Philadelphia, PA.

Baldwin, A. (1985). Programs for the gifted and talented: Issues concerning minority populations. In F. Horowitz & M. O'Brien (Eds.), *The Gifted and Talented Developmental Perspectives.* Washington, DC: American Psychological Association.

Bancroft, J. (1982). Suggestopedia, sophrology and the traditional foreign language class. *Foreign Language Annals, 15*(5), 373–379.

Barbe, W. (1953). *A follow-up study of graduates of special classes for gifted children.* Unpublished doctoral dissertation, Northwestern University, Evanston, IL.

Barbe, W. (1954). Differentiated guidance for the gifted. *Education, 74,* 306–311.

Barbe, W. (1955). Evaluation of special classes for gifted. *Exceptional Children, 22,* 60–62.

Barbe, W. (1964). *One in a thousand—A comparative study of moderately and highly gifted elementary school children.* Columbus, OH: Ohio State Department of Education.

Barbe, W. (1965). *Psychology and education of the gifted.* New York: Appleton-Century-Crofts.

Barbe, W., & Renzulli, J. (Eds.). (1975). *Psychology and education of the gifted* (2nd ed.). New York: Irvington Publishing.

Bardwick, J., & Douvan, E. (1971). Ambivalence: The socialization of women. In V. Gornick & B. Moran (Eds.), *Woman in sexist society.* New York: Basic Books.

Barnett, M., & Kaiser, D. (1978). The relationship between intellectual-achievement responsibility attributions and performance. *Child Study Journal, 8,* 209–215.

Barrett, H. (1957). The intensive study of thirty-two gifted children. *Personnel and Guidance Journal, 36,* 192–194.

Barron, F. (1969). *Creative person and creative process.* New York: Holt, Rinehart & Winston.

Bar-Tal, D., Kfir, D., Bar-Zohar, Y., & Chen, M. (1980). The relationship between locus of control and academic achievement, anxiety, and level of aspiration. *British Journal of Educational Psychology, 50,* 53–60.

Baum, S. (1984). Meeting the needs of learning disabled gifted students. *Roeper Review, 7*(1), 16–19.

Bayley, N. (1955). On the growth of intelligence. *American Psychologist, 10,* 805–818.

Bayley, N. (1968). Behavioral correlates of mental growth: Birth to thirty-six years. *American Psychologist, 23,* 1–17.

Bayley, N., & Schaefer, E. S. (1964). Correlations of maternal and child behaviors with the development of mental abilities: Data from the Berkeley Growth Study. *Monographs of the Society for Research in Child Development, 29* (6, Whole No. 97).

Baymur, F., & Patterson, C. (1960). Three methods of assisting underachieving high school students. *Journal of Counseling Psychology, 7,* 83–90.

Beach, D. (1977). *Reaching teenagers: Learning centers for the secondary classroom.* Santa Monica, CA: Goodyear.

Beadle, M. (1970). *A child's mind.* Garden City, NY: Doubleday.

Beck, J. (1967). *How to raise a brighter child.* New York: Trident.

Becker, W. (1964). Consequences of different kinds of parental discipline. In L. Hoffman & M. Hoffman (Eds.), *Review of child development research* (Vol. 1). New York: Russell Sage Foundation.

Beckwith, C. (1971). Relationships between attributes of mothers and their infants' I.Q. scores. *Child Development, 42,* 1083–1097.

Beechhold, H. (1971). *The creative classroom: Teaching without textbooks.* New York: Charles Scribner's Sons.

Beier, E. (1974). Nonverbal communication—How we send emotional messages. *Psychology Today, 8*(5), 53–56.

Bell, D. (1972). *The coming of post-industrial society: A venture in social forecasting.* New York: Basic Books.

Bennett, G., Seashore, H., & Wesman, A. (1963). *Differential aptitude tests.* New York: Psychological Corporation.

Bentov, I. (1977). *Stalking the wild pendulum: On the mechanics of consciousness.* New York: E. P. Dutton.

Bentov, I., with Bentov, M. (1982). *A cosmic book: On the mechanics of creation.* New York: E. P. Dutton.

Berliner, D. (1979). Tempus educare. In P. Peterson and H. Walberg (Eds.), *Research on teaching: Concepts, findings, and implications.* Berkeley, CA: McCutchan, 120–135.

Bernal, E. (1973, March). *Mexican American perceptions of child giftedness in three Texas communities.* Paper presented at the First National Conference on the Disadvantaged Gifted. Ventura, CA.

Bernal, E. (1978). The identification of gifted Chicano children. In A. Baldwin, G. Gear, & L. Lucito (Eds.), *Educational planning for the gifted.* Reston, VA: Council for Exceptional Children.

Bernstein, D., & Borkover, T. (1975). *Progressive relaxation training: A manual for the helping professions.* Champaign, IL: Research Press.

Bessell, H., & Palomares, U. (1970). *Methods in human development, theory manual* (1970 rev.). San Diego, CA: Human Development Training Institute.

Betts, G. (1985). *The autonomous learner model.* Greeley, CO: Autonomous Learning Publications Specialists.

Bidwell, C. (1973). The social psychology of teaching. In R. Travers (Ed.), *Second handbook of research on teaching.* Chicago: Rand McNally.

Bills, R. (1978). *Sex, race, and developmental differences in self-concept variables as shown by the index of adjustment and values.* Paper presented at the Self-Concept Symposium, Boston, MA.

Binet, A. (1969). The education of intelligence. In P. Torrance & W. White (Eds.), *Issues and advances in educational psychology.* Itasca, IL: F. E. Peacock.

Binet, A., & Simon, T. (1973). *The development of intelligence in children (the Binet-Simon Scale)* (E. Kite, Trans.). New York: Arno Press. (Original work published, 1916).

Birch, H., & Gussow, J. (1970). *Disadvantaged children.* New York: Harcourt, Brace & World.

Birnbaum, M. (1977). Educational problems of rural education for the gifted. In B. Johnson (Ed.), *Ideas for urban/rural gifted/talented.* Ventura, CA.: Office of the Ventura County Superintendent of Schools, National/State Leadership Training Institute on the Gifted/Talented.

Birns, B., & Golden, M. (1972). Prediction of intellectual performance at three years from infant test and personality measures. *Merrill-Palmer Quarterly, 18,* 53–58.

Bish, C., & Fliegler, L. (1959). Summary of research on the academically talented student. *Review of Educational Research, 39,* 408–450.

Bishop, W. (1968). Successful teachers of the gifted. *Exceptional Children, 34,* 317–325.

Blakemore, C. (1974). Developmental factors in the formation of feature extracting neurons. In F. O. Schmidt & F. G. Warden (Eds.), *The neurosciences: Third study program.* Cambridge, MA: MIT Press, 31–41.

Blancher-Dixon, J., & Turnbull, A. (1978). A pre-school program for gifted-handicapped children. *Journal for the Education of the Gifted, 1*(2), 15–22.

Blaney, N., Stephan, C., Rosenfield, D., Aronson, E., & Sikes, J. (1976). *Interdependence in the classroom: A field study.* Unpublished manuscript, University of Texas at Austin.

Bleedhorn, B. (1976). Future studies for the gifted. *Gifted Child Quarterly, 20,* 490–496.

Bloom, B. (Ed.). (1956). *Taxonomy of educational objectives. Handbook I: Cognitive domain.* New York, David McKay.

Bloom, B. (1964). *Stability and change in human characteristics.* New York: John Wiley & Sons.

Bloom, B. (1982). The role of gifts and markers in the development of talent. *Exceptional Children, 48*(6), 510–522.

Bloom, B., Davis, A., & Hess, R. (1965). *Compensatory education for cultural deprivation.* New York: Holt, Rinehart & Winston.

Bloom, B., & Sosniak, L. (1981). Talent development vs. schooling. *Educational Leadership, 39*(2), 86–94.

Bodmer, W., & Cavalli-Sforza, L. (1970). Intelligence and race. *Scientific American, 223*(4), 19–29.

Boehm, L. (1962). The development of conscience: A comparison of American children of different mental and socioeconomic levels. *Child Development, 33,* 575–590.

Bogen, J. (1975). Some educational aspects of hemispheric specialization. *UCLA Educator, 17*(2), 24–32.

Bohm, D. (1980). *Wholeness and the implicate order.* Boston: Routledge & Kegan.

Boocock, S., & Schild, E. (1968). *Simulation games in learning.* Beverly Hills, CA: Sage.

Bordan, R., & Schuster, D. (1976). The effects of suggestion, synchronized breathing and orchestrated music on the acquisition and retention of Spanish words. *SALT Journal, 1*(1), 27–40.

Bordie, J. (1970). Language tests and linguistically different learners: The sad state of the art. *Elementary English, 47,* 814–828.

Borg, W. (1964). *An evaluation of ability grouping* (U.S. Department of Health, Education and Welfare, Office of Education, Cooperative Research Project No. 577). Logan, UT: Utah State University.

Borgers, S., & Treffinger, D. (1979). Creative talent: Implications for counselors. In N. Colangelo & R. Zaffrann (Eds.), *New voices in counseling the gifted.* Dubuque, IA: Kendall/Hunt.

Borkowski, J. (1985). Signs of intelligence: Strategy generalization and metacognition. In S. Yussen (Ed.), *The development of reflection in children.* New York: Academic Press.

Borland, J. (1978). Teacher identification of the gifted: A new look. *Journal for the Education of the Gifted, 2*(1), 22–32.

Borland, J. (1986). IQ tests: Throwing out the bathwater, saving the baby. *Roeper Review, 8*(3), 163–167.

Bortner, M. (Ed.). (1979). *Cognitive growth and development—Essays in honor of Herbert G. Birch.* New York: Brunner/Mazel.

Bouman, L. (1986). Gender expectations and student achievement in math. *The Calculator, 27*(1), 1,3.

Bower, R., Broughton, J., & Moore, M. (1970). Assessment of intention in sensorimotor infants. *Nature, 228,* 679–681.

Bowers, W. (1964). *Student dishonesty and its control in college.* New York: Bureau of Applied Behavioral Science.

Bowles, N., & Hynds, F. (1978). *Psi search.* San Francisco: Harper & Row.

Bradley, R., & Caldwell, B. (1976). Early home environment and changes in mental test performance in children from 6 to 30 months. *Developmental Psychology, 12,* 93–97.

Braga, J. L. (1969). Analysis and evaluation of early admission to school for mentally advanced children. *Journal of Educational Research, 63,* 103–106.

Braga, J. (1971). Early admission: Opinion vs. evidence. *The Elementary School Journal, 72,* 35–46.

Branscomb, A. (Chair). (1980, May). *Commerce Technical Advisory Board recommendations on learning environments for innovation* (Report of the CTAB to Jordan J. Baruch, Assistant Secretary for Productivity, Technology and Innovation). Washington, DC: U.S. Department of Commerce.

Brazelton, T. B., & Als, H. (1979). Four early stages in the development of mother-infant interaction. *Psychoanalytic Study of the Child, 34,* 349–369.

Breidenstine, A. (1936). The educational achievement of pupils in differentiated and undifferentiated groups. *Journal of Experimental Education, 5,* 91–135.

Bremer, J., & Bremer, A. (1972). *Open education: A beginning.* New York: Holt, Rinehart & Winston.

Bricklin, B., & Bricklin, P. (1967). *Bright child—poor grades: The psychology of underachievement.* New York: Delacorte.

Bridgman, A. (1986). Preschool pressure, later difficulties linked in study. *Education Weekly, 5*(30), 1, 15.

Brier, C., & Tyminski, W. (1970). PSI applications: Parts I and II. *Journal of Parapsychology, 34,* 1–36.

Brierley, J. (1976). *The growing brain.* Windsor, Great Britain: NFER.

Briggs, D. (1970). *Your child's self-esteem: The key to his life.* Garden City, NY: Doubleday.

Brill, M. (1956). Studies of Jewish and non-Jewish intelligence. *Journal of Educational Psychology, 47,* 302–309.

Brill, M. (1982, November 12). *Los Angeles Times.*

Broedel, J. (1958). *A study of the effect of group counseling on the academic performance and mental health of underachieving gifted adolescents.* Ann Arbor, MI: University of Michigan Press.

Brookover, W. (1969, February). *Self and school achievement.* Paper presented at the annual meeting of the American Educational Research Association, Los Angeles, CA.

Brookover, W., LePere, J., Hamachek, D., Thomas, S., & Erickson, E. (1965). *Self-concept of ability and school achievement* (Vol. 11) (USOE Cooperative Research Report, Project No. 1636). East Lansing: Michigan State University.

Brooks, C. (1974). *Sensory awareness.* New York: Viking.

Brown, B. (1968). *The experimental mind in education.* New York: Harper & Row.

Brown, B. (1974). *New mind, new body. Biofeedback: New directions for the mind.* New York: Harper & Row.

Brown, C., & Rogan, J. (1983). Reading and young gifted children. *Roeper Review, 5*(3), 6–9.

Brown, F. (1971, February). *Underachievement—A case of inefficient cognitive processing.* Address to the American Educational Research Association, New York.

Brown, G. (1971). *Human teaching for human learning: An introduction to confluent education.* New York: Viking.

Brown, G., Yeomans, T., & Grizzard, L. (1975). *The live classroom: Innovations through confluent education and Gestalt.* New York: Viking.

Bruch, C. (1971). Modification of procedures for identification of the disadvantaged gifted. *Gifted Child Quarterly, 15*(4), 267–272.

Bruner, J. (1960). *The process of education.* Cambridge, MA: Harvard University Press.

Bruner, J. (1964). The course of cognitive growth. *American Psychologist, 19,* 1–15.

Bruner, J. (1968). *Toward a theory of instruction.* New York: W. W. Norton.

Bruner, J. (1973). Organization of early skilled action. *Child Development, 44,* 1–11.

Bruner, J., & Dow, P. (1967). *Man: A course of study; a description of an elementary social studies curriculum.* Cambridge, MA: Education Development Center.

Bryden, M. (1970). Laterality effects in dichotic listening: Relations with handedness and reading ability in children. *Neuropsychologia, 8,* 443–450.

Bucke, R. (1929). *Cosmic consciousness* (6th ed.). New York: E. P. Dutton.

Buell, S., & Coleman, P. (1981). Quantitative evidence for selective dendritic growth in normal human aging but not in senile dementia. *Brain Research, 214*(1), 23–41.

Buescher, T. (1987). Counseling gifted adolescents: A curriculum model for students, parents, and professionals. *Gifted Child Quarterly, 31*(2), 90–94.

Bull, B., & Wittrock, M. (1973). Imagery in the learning of verbal definitions. *British Journal of Educational Psychology, 43,* 289–293.

Burns, F. (1983). Sex differences—A silent message? A comparison study of parents' assessment and junior high school student's self-assessment of learning strengths and interests. *Journal for the Education of the Gifted, 6*(3), 195–212.

Buros, O. (Ed.). (1959). *Mental measurement yearbook* (Vols. 1 & 2, 5th ed.). Highland Park, NJ: Gryphon.

Buros, O. (Ed.). (1965). *Mental measurement yearbook* (Vols. 1 & 2, 6th ed.). Highland Park, NJ: Gryphon.

Buros, O. (Ed.). (1972). *Mental measurement yearbook* (Vols. 1 & 2, 7th ed.). Highland Park, NJ: Gryphon.

Business Week. (1985, September 30). Are you creative?

Buzan, T. (1983). *Use both sides of your brain.* New York: E. P. Dutton.

Callahan, C. (1980). The gifted girl: An anomaly? *Roeper Review, 2*(3), 16–20.

Callaway, W. R. (1969). A holistic conception of creativity and its relationship to intelligence. *Gifted Child Quarterly, 13,* 237–241.

Callaway, W. R. (1970). Modes of biological adaptation and their role in intellectual development. *The Galton Institute Monograph Series, 1*(1), 1–34.

Calsyn, R. (1973). *The causal relationship between self-esteem, a locus of control and achievement: A cross-lagged panel analysis.* Unpublished doctoral dissertation, Northwestern University, Evanston, IL.

Cancro, R. (Ed.). (1971). *Intelligence: Genetic and environmental influences.* New York: Grune & Stratton.

Canfield, J. (1987, February). *Self esteem and the gifted child.* Paper presented at 25th Annual Conference for the California Association for the Gifted, Los Angeles.

Canfield, J., & Wells, H. (1976). *100 ways to enhance self-concept in the classroom.* Englewood Cliffs, NJ: Prentice-Hall.

Capra, F. (1975). *The Tao of physics.* Berkeley, CA: Shambhala.

Capra, F. (1982). *The turning point: Science, society, and the rising culture.* New York: Simon and Schuster.

Carew, J. (1976, April). *Environmental stimulation: A longitudinal observational study of how people influence the young child's intellectual development in his everyday environment.* Paper presented at the annual meeting of the American Educational Research Association, San Francisco, CA.

Carr, M., & Borkowski, J. (1987). Metamemory in gifted children. *Gifted Child Quarterly, 31*(1), 40–44.

Carroll, H. (1940). *Genius in the making.* New York: McGraw-Hill.

Cass-Beggs, B. (1978). *Your baby needs music—A music sound book for babies up to two years old.* New York: St. Martin's Press.

Cassel, R., & Coleman, J. (1962). A critical examination of the school dropout, reluctant leader, and abler non-college student problem. *NEA Secondary School Principal's Bulletin, 46,* 60–65.

Cassel, R., & Haddox, G. (1959). Comparative study of leadership test scores for gifted and typical high school students. *Psychological Report, 5,* 713–717.

Castaneda, C. (1972). *Journey to Ixtlan: The lessons of Don Juan.* New York: Simon & Schuster.

Casteel, J., & Stahl, R. (1975). *Value clarification in the classroom: A primer.* Pacific Palisades, CA: Goodyear.

Castillo, G. (1974). *Left-handed teaching.* New York: Praeger.

Cattell, R. (1949). *The culture-free intelligence test.* Champaign, IL: Institute for Personality Assessment and Testing.

Cattell, R. (1971). The structure of intelligence in relation to the nature-nurture controversy. In R. Cancro (Ed.), *Intelligence genetic and environmental influences.* New York: Grune & Stratton.

Cenci, C. (1980, Summer). *Lady Bug* (An activity developed for the New Age School). Los Angeles.

Chall, J., & Mirsky, A. (Eds.). (1978). *Education and the brain: The seventy-seventh yearbook of the National Society for the Study of Education,* Part II. Chicago: University of Chicago Press.

Chance, P. (1973). Parapsychology is an idea whose time has come. *Psychology Today, 7,* 105–116.

Chance, P., & Fischman, J. (1987). The magic of childhood. *Psychology Today, 21*(5), 48–58.

Chansky, N. (1962, March). The x-ray of the school mark. *The Educational Forum,* 347–352.

Chansky, N. (1964). A note of the grade point average in research. *Educational and Psychological Measurement, 24,* 95–99.

Chess, S. (1971). Why some bright children have trouble in school. *Parents Magazine, 46,* 42–43; 85; 89–90.

Chetelat, F. (1981). Visual arts education for the gifted elementary level art student. *Gifted Child Quarterly, 25*(4), 154–158.

Childs, R. (1981). A comparison of the adaptive behavior of normal and gifted five and six year old children. *Roeper Review, 4*(2), 41–43.

Chomsky, N. (1966). *Cartesian linguistics.* New York: Harper & Row.

Christiansen, T., & Livermore, G. (1970). A comparison of Anglo American and Spanish American children on the WISC. *Journal of Social Psychology, 81,* 9–14.

Christianson, B. (1969). Learning centers that work. *Instructor, 79,* 135.

Chukovsky, K. (1966). *From two to five.* Berkeley: University of California Press.

Clark, B. (1983). *Growing up gifted* (2nd ed.). Columbus, OH: Charles E. Merrill.

Clark, B. (1986). *Optimizing learning: The integrative education model in the classroom.* Columbus, OH: Merrill.

Clark, B., & Kaplan, S. (1981). *Improving differentiated curricula for the gifted/talented.* Los Angeles: California Association for the Gifted.

Clark, F. (1977). Building intuition. In G. Hendricks & T. Roberts (Eds.), *The second centering book.* Englewood Cliffs, NJ: Prentice-Hall, 1977.

Clark, H. (1974). The power of positive speaking: It takes longer to understand no. *Psychology Today, 8*(4), 102–111.

Clarke Stewart, K. (1973). Interactions between mothers and their young children: Characteristics and consequences. *Monographs of Society for Research in Child Development, 38* (No. 153).

Cleaveland, M. (1979). Discrimination at all levels [Letter to the editor]. *Science News, 115*(16), 259.

Clymer, T., & Wardeberg, H. (1971). *Skills handbook: To turn a stone.* Lexington, MA: Ginn & Co.

Cohen, E. (1981). The arts from the inside out: Developing a performing arts curriculum. *G/C/T, 20,* 38–42.

Colangelo, N., & Bower, P. (1987). Labeling gifted youngsters: Long-term impact on families. *Gifted Child Quarterly, 31*(2), 75–78.

Colangelo, N., & Kelly, K. (1983). A study of student, parent, and teacher attitudes toward gifted programs and gifted students. *Gifted Child Quarterly, 27*(3), 107–110.

Colangelo, N., & Lafrenz, N. (1981). Counseling the culturally diverse gifted. *Gifted Child Quarterly, 25*(1), 27–30.

Colangelo, N., & Zaffrann, R. (1979). Special issues in counseling the gifted. *Counseling and Human Development, 11*(5), 1–12.

Cole, H. (1969). Process curricula and creativity development. *Journal of Creative Behavior, 3,* 243–259.

Coleman, J. (1960). The adolescent subculture and academic achievement. *American Journal of Sociology, 65,* 337–347.

Coleman, J. (1962). *The adolescent society.* New York: Free Press of Glencoe.

Coleman, J., Campbell, E., Hobson, C., McPartland, J., Mood, A., Weinfeld, F., & York, R. (1966). *Equality of educational opportunity.* Washington, DC: U.S. Government Printing Office.

Colson, S. (1980). The evaluation of a community-based career education program for gifted and talented students as an administrative model for an alternative program. *Gifted Child Quarterly, 24*(3), 101–106.

Colvin, S. (1915). What infant prodigies teach educators. *Illustrated World, 24,* 47–52.

Combs, A. W. (Ed.). (1962). *Perceiving, behaving, becoming* (Yearbook of the Association for Supervision and Curriculum Development). Washington, DC: National Education Association.

Combs, A. W. (1969). *Florida studies in the helping professions* (Social Science Monograph, No. 37). Gainesville: University of Florida Press.

Combs, A. W., Blume, R. A., Newan, A. J., & Wass, H. L. (1974). *The professional education of teachers: A perceptual view of teacher preparation* (2nd ed.). Boston: Allyn & Bacon.

Combs, A. W., & Snygg, D. (1959). *Individual behavior* (rev. ed.). New York: Harper & Row.

Combs, C. (1964). Perception of self and scholastic underachievement in the academically capable. *Personnel and Guidance Journal, 43,* 47–51.

Confessore, G., & Confessore, S. (1981). Attitudes toward physical activity among adolescents talented in the visual and performing arts. *Journal for the Education of the Gifted, 4*(3), 261–269.

Connelly, M. (1977). Gifted girls and gifted women. *Roeper City and County School Quarterly, 12,* 12–13.

Cooley, D., Chauvin, J., & Karnes, F. (1984). Gifted females: A comparison of attitudes by male and female teachers. *Roeper Review, 6*(3), 194–197.

Coopersmith, S. (1967). *The antecedents of self-esteem.* San Francisco: W. H. Freeman.

Coopersmith, S. (1975). *Developing motivation in young children.* San Francisco: Albion.

Cornell, D. (1983). Gifted children: The impact of positive labeling on the family system. *American Journal of Orthopsychiatry, 53,* 322–335.

Cornell, D., & Grossberg, I. (1987). Family environment and personality adjustment in gifted program children. *Gifted Child Quarterly, 31*(2), 59–64.

Cornish, E. (1977). *The study of the future.* Washington, DC: World Future Society.

Cottman, C., & Nieto-Sampedro, M. (1982). Brain function, synapse renewal and plasticity. *Annual Review of Psychology, 33,* 371–401.

Council for Exceptional Children. (1978). *The nation's commitment to the education of gifted and talented children and youth: Summary of findings from a 1977 survey of states and territories.* Reston, VA: Council for Exceptional Children.

Counseling and Personnel Services Clearinghouse. (1982, Winter). Counseling gifted students. *Highlights.* Ann Arbor, MI: University of Michigan.

Covington, M., & Beary, R. (1976). *Self-worth and school learning.* New York: Holt, Rinehart & Winston.

Covington, M., Crutchfield, R., & Davies, L. (1967). *Teacher's guide to the productive thinking program: General problem-solving* (16 self-instructional lessons). Berkeley, CA: Educational Innovations, Box 9248.

Cox, C. (1926). The early mental traits of three hundred geniuses. In L. Terman (Ed.), *Genetic studies of genius* (Vol. 2). Stanford, CA: Stanford University Press.

Cox, J., & Daniel, N. (1983, September/October). The role of the mentor. *G/C/T,* 1–8.

Cox, J., Daniel, N., & Boston, B. (1985). *Educating able learners: Programs and promising practices.* Austin, TX: University of Texas Press.

Craig, G. (1980). *Human development* (2nd ed.). Englewood Cliffs, NJ: Prentice-Hall.

Cramond, B., & Martin, C. (1987). Inservice and preservice teachers' attitudes toward the academically brilliant. *Gifted Child Quarterly, 31*(1), 15–19.

Crandall, V., Katkovsky, W., & Preston, A. (1962). Motivational and ability determinants of young children's intellectual achievement behaviors. *Child Development, 33,* 643–661.

Crutchfield, R. (1969). Nurturing the cognitive skills of productive thinking. In L. Rubin (Ed.), *Life skills in school and society.* Washington, DC: Association for Supervision and Curriculum Development, National Education Association.

Csikszentmihalyi, M., & Larson, R. (1987). *Being adolescent: Conflict and growth in the teenage years.* New York: Basic Books.

Csoka, L. (1974). A relationship between leader intelligence and leader rated effectiveness. *Journal of Applied Psychology, 59,* 43–47.

Cunningham, L., & Gephart, W. (Eds.). (1973). *Leadership—The science and the art today.* Itasca, IL: F. E. Peacock.

Curry, J., & Sato, I. (1984). Principles of educating teachers. *Quarterly Bulletin of the National/State Leadership Training Institute on the Gifted and Talented, 10*(2).

Damm, V. (1970). Creativity and intelligence: Research implications for equal emphasis in high school. *Exceptional Children, 36,* 565–569.

Daniel, R. (1960). Underachievement of superior and talented students. In B. Shertzer (Ed.), *Working with superior students.* Chicago: Scientific Research Associates.

Daniels, P. (1983). *Teaching the gifted/learning disabled child.* Rockville, MD: Aspen.

Dart, P. (1986). Effective collaborative administration: Concept and practice. *Roeper Review, 9*(1), 13–16.

Darwin, C. (1859). *On the origin of species.* London: Murray.

Das, J., Kirby, J., & Jarman, R. (1975). Simultaneous and successive syntheses: An alternate model for cognitive abilities. *Psychological Bulletin, 82,* 87–103.

Davies, A. (1965). The perceptual maze test in a normal population. *Perceptual and Motor Skills, 20,* 287–293.

Davies, P. (1984). The eleventh dimension. *Science Digest, 92*(1), 72, 105.

Davis, A., & Eells, K. (1953). *Davis-Eells games.* New York: Harcourt, Brace & World.

Davis, G. (1975). In frumious pursuit of the creative person. *Journal of Creative Behavior, 9,* 75–87.

Davis, G., Manske, M., & Train, A. (1967). *Training creative thinking.* Occasional paper No. 6. Madison, WI: Research and Development Center for Learning and Re-education, The University of Wisconsin.

Dean, D., Mihalasky, J., Ostrander, S., & Schroeder, L. (1974). *Executive ESP.* Englewood Cliffs, NJ: Prentice-Hall.

deCharms, R. (1976). *Enhancing motivation: Change in the classroom.* New York: Halsted.

deCharms, R. (1984). Motivation enhancement in education. In R. Ames & C. Ames (Eds.), *Student motivation* (pp. 275–310). New York: Plenum Press.

Deci, E. (1975). *Intrinsic motivation.* New York: Plenum Press.

Deci, E. (1985). The well-tempered classroom. *Psychology Today, 19*(3), 52–53.

De Leon, J. (1983). Cognitive style difference and the underrepresentation of Mexican Americans in programs for the gifted. *Journal for the Education of the Gifted, 6*(3), 167–177.

Delisle, J. (1984). The BIASED model of career education and guidance for gifted adolescents. *Journal for the Education of the Gifted, 8*(1), 95–106.

Delisle, J., Reis, S., & Gubbins, E. (1981). The revolving door identification and programming model. *Exceptional Children, 48*(2), 152–156.

Delisle, J., Whitmore, J., & Ambrose, R. (1987). Preventing discipline problems with gifted students. *Teaching Exceptional Children, 19*(4), 32–38.

Delp, J., & Martinson, R. (1974). *The gifted and talented: A handbook for parents.* Reston, VA: Council for Exceptional Children.

DeMille, R. (1973). *Put your mother on the ceiling.* New York: Viking.

Dennis, W. (1960). Causes of retardation among institutional children: Iran. *Journal of Genetic Psychology, 96,* 47–59.

Dennis, W., & Dennis, M. (1935). The effect of restricted practice upon the reaching, sitting and standing of two infants. *Journal of Genetic Psychology, 47,* 21–29.

Dennis, W., & Najarian, P. (1957). Infant development under environmental handicap. *Psychology Monograph, 71*(7, Whole No. 436), 1–13.

Desmond, M., Rudolph, A., & Phitaksphraiwan, P. (1966). The transitional care nursery: A mechanism of a preventive medicine. *Pediatric Clinics of North America, 13,* 651–668.

d'Espagnet, B. (1979). The quantum theory and reality. *Scientific American, 241*(5), 158–181.

Dettmer, P. (1981). Improving teacher attitudes toward characteristics of the creatively gifted. *Gifted Child Quarterly, 25*(1), 11–16.

Dettmer, P. (1985). Attitudes of school role groups toward learning needs of gifted students. *Roeper Review, 7*(4), 253–257.

Deutsch, C., & Deutsch, M. (1968). Brief reflections on the theory of early childhood enrichment programs. In R. Hess & R. Bear, *Early education.* New York: Aldine.

Dexter, E. (1935). The effect of fatigue or boredom on teacher's marks. *Journal of Educational Research, 28,* 664–667.

Diamond, M. (1986, February). *Brain research and its implications for education.* Speech presented at the 25th Annual Conference of the California Association for the Gifted, Los Angeles.

DiCara, L. (1970). *Biofeedback and self control.* Chicago: Aldine.

Dinkmeyer, D. (1969). *Developing understanding of self and others.* (A kit of materials). Circle Pines, MN: American Guidance Service.

Dirks, J., & Quarfoth, J. (1981). Selecting children for gifted classes: Choosing for breadth vs. choosing for depth. *Psychology in the Schools, 18*(4), 437–449.

Dobzhansky, T. (1964). *Heredity and the nature of man.* New York: New American Library.

Doherty, E., & Evans, L. (1981). Independent study process: They can think, can't they? *Journal for the Education of the Gifted, 4*(2), 106–111.

Doktor, R., & Bloom, D. (1977). Selective lateralization of cognitive style related to occupation as determined by EEG alpha asymmetry. *Psychophysiology, 14,* 385–392.

Dolle, J., & Bardot, A. (1977). Learning judo and cognitive development: Understanding the laws of physics through judo. *Psychologie Française, 24*(2), 97–109.

Doman, G. (1964). *How to teach your baby to read.* New York: Random House.

Domino, G. (1969). Maternal personality correlates of son's creativity. *Journal of Consulting and Clinical Psychology, 33,* 180–183.

Dorhout, A. (1983). Student and teacher perceptions of preferred teacher behaviors among the academically gifted. *Gifted Child Quarterly, 27*(3), 122–125.

Dossey, L. (1982). *Space, time & medicine.* Boulder, CO: Shambhala.

Douglass, J. (1969, April). *Strategies for maximizing the development of talent among the urban disadvantaged.* Paper presented at the annual meeting of the Council for Exceptional Children, Denver.

Dowling, C. (1981). *The Cinderella complex.* New York: Summit Books, Simon & Schuster.

Downing, J. (1973). *Dreams and nightmares.* New York: Harper & Row.

Doyle, W. (1978). Classroom tasks and student abilities. In P. P. Peterson & H. Walbert (Eds.), *Conceptions of teaching.* Berkeley, CA: McCutchan.

Dreger, R., & Miller, K. (1960). Comparative psychological studies of Negroes and whites in the United States. *Psychological Bulletin, 57,* 361–402.

Drevdahl, J. (1956). Factors of importance for creativity. *Journal of Clinical Psychology, 12,* 21–26.

Drews, E. M. (1963). The four faces of able adolescents. *Saturday Review, 46,* 68–71.

Drews, E. M. (1964, 1965, 1966). *The creative intellectual style in gifted adolescents* (Vols. 1, 2, & 3). E. Lansing, MI: Michigan State University.

Drews, E. M. (1972). *Learning together: How to foster creativity, self-fulfillment and social awareness in today's students and teachers.* Englewood Cliffs, NJ: Prentice-Hall.

Drews, E. M. (1976). Leading out and letting be. *Today's Education, 65,* 26–28.

Drews, E. M., & Knowlton, D. (1963). The being and becoming series for college-bound students. *Audiovisual Instruction, 8,* 29–32.

Drews, E. M., & Lepson, L. (1971). *Values and humanity.* New York: St. Martin's.

Dreyer, A., & Wells, M. (1966). Parental values, parental control in young children. *Journal of Marriage and Family, 28,* 83–88.

Dubner, F. (1980). Thirteen ways of looking at a gifted teacher. *Journal for the Education of the Gifted, 3*(3), 143–146.

Dubos, R. (1969). Biological individuality. *The Columbia Forum, 12*(1), 5–9.

Dubrowsky, W. (1968). Gifted children benefit from learning to be self-accepting. *Gifted Child Quarterly, 12,* 85–88.

Dunham, G., & Russo, T. (1983). Career education for the disadvantaged gifted: Some thoughts for educators. *Roeper Review, 5*(3), 26–28.

Dunn, B. (1969). *The effectiveness of teaching early reading skills to two-to-four-year-old children by television.* Unpublished doctoral dissertation, University of California, Los Angeles.

Dunn, L. (1973). *Exceptional children in the schools* (2nd ed.). New York: Holt, Rinehart & Winston.

Dunn, R., & Dunn., K. (1975). *Educator's self-teaching guide to individualizing instructional programs.* West Nyack, NY: Parker.

Dunn, R., & Goldman, M. (1966). Competition and noncompetition in relationship to satisfaction and feelings toward own-group and non-group members. *Journal of Social Psychology, 68,* 299–311.

Durden, W. (1980). The Johns Hopkins program for verbally gifted youth. *Roeper Review, 3*(2), 34–37.

Durden-Smith, J. (1980, October). Male and female—Why? *Quest,* 15–19; 93–98.

Durkin, D. (1966). *Children who read early.* New York: Teachers College Press.

Durrell, D., Scribner, H., McHugh, W., Manning, J., & Rockfort, G. (1959). Adapting instruction to the learning needs of children in the intermediate grades. *Journal of Education, 142,* 1–78.

Dweck, C., Davidson, W., Nelson, S., & Enna, B. (1978). Sex differences in learned helplessness. *Developmental Psychology, 14,* 268–276.

Dweck, C., & Goetz, T. (1978). Attributions and learned helplessness. In J. Harvey, W. Ickes, & R. Kidd (Eds.), *New directions in attribution research* (Vol. 2). Hillsdale, NJ: Erlbaum.

Eccles, J. (1973). *The understanding of the brain.* New York: McGraw-Hill.

Edmonds, R. (1980, November 12). Inner-city schools can be effective. *Report on Education Research.*

Education Consolidation and Improvement Act. (1981). Public Law 97–35.

Education for All Handicapped Children Act. (1975). Public Law 94–142.

Edwards, P. (1956). The use of essays in selection at 11 plus: Essay marking experiments: Shorter and longer essays. *British Journal of Educational Psychology, 26,* 128–136.

Eggers, P. (1984). Suggestopedia, an innovation in language learning. *Media & Methods, 21*(4), 16–19.

Eisenberg, D. (1981). Handicapped children can be gifted too, say educators. *Education of the Handicapped,* December.

Eisenman, R., & Schussel, N. (1970). Creativity, birth order and preference for symmetry. *Journal of Consulting Clinical Psychology, 34,* 275–280.

Elder, C. (1972). *Making value judgments: Decisions for today.* Columbus, OH: Charles E. Merrill.

Elkind, J. (1973). The gifted child with learning disabilities. *Gifted Child Quarterly, 17,* 96–97.

Ellinger, B. (1965). The home environment and the creative thinking abilities of children (Unpublished doctoral dissertation, Ohio State University, Columbus, OH, 1964). *Dissertation Abstracts International, 25*(6), 6308. (Order No. 65-3850)

Ellis, M., & Scholtz, G. (1978). *Activity and play of children.* Englewood Cliffs, NJ: Prentice-Hall.

Ellison, R., Abe, C., Fox, D., & Coray, K. (1976, Winter). Using biographical information in identifying artistic talent. *Gifted Child Quarterly, 20*(4), 402–413.

Emde, R., & Robinson, J. (1976). The first two months: Recent research in developmental psychobiology and the changing view of the newborn. In J. Noshpitz (Ed.), *Basic handbook of child psychiatry.* New York: Basic Books.

Engelmann, T., & Engelmann, S. (1966). *Give your child a superior mind.* New York: Simon & Schuster.

Epstein, H. (1978). Growth spurts during brain development: Implications for educational policy and practice. In J. Chall & A. Mirsky (Eds.), *Education and the brain, the seventy-seventh yearbook of the National Society for the Study of Education,* Part II (pp. 343–370). Chicago: University of Chicago Press.

Erikson, E. (1964). *Childhood and society* (rev. ed.). New York: Norton. (Original work published 1950)

Erikson, E. (1968). *Identity, youth and crisis.* New York: Norton.

Ernest, J. (1976). Mathematics and sex. *American Mathematical Monthly, 83*(8), 595–614.

Ernest, J. (1980). Is mathematics a sexist discipline? In L. Fox, L. Brody, & D. Tobin (Eds.),

Women and the mathematical mystique. Baltimore, MD: Johns Hopkins University Press.

Ertl, J. (1968). Intelligence testing by brain waves. *Mensa Bulletin, 110,* 3–6.

Evans, E. (1965). Pupil underachievement, Are we responsible? *Instructor, 75,* 25–42.

Ewing, T., & Gilbert, W. (1967). Controlled study of the effects of counseling on the scholastic achievements of students of superior ability. *Journal of Counseling Psychology, 14,* 235–239.

Fadiman, J. (1976). *The mind can do anything.* Talk presented to the Mind Can Do Anything Conference, San Rafael, CA.

Fala, M. (1968). *Dunce cages, hickory sticks and public evaluations: The structure of academic authoritarianism.* Madison, WI: The Teaching Assistant Association, University of Wisconsin.

Falbo, T., & Cooper, C. (1980). Young children's time and intellectual ability. *Journal of Genetic Psychology, 137*(2), 299–300.

Fantz, R. (1961). The origin of form perception. *Scientific American, 204,* 66–72.

Fantz, R. (1965). Visual perception from birth as shown by pattern selectivity. *New Issues in Infant Development, New York Academy of Sciences Annals, 118*(21), 793–814.

Faraday, A. (1972). *Dream power.* New York: Coward, McCann & Geoghegan.

Farrell, P. (1973). *Teacher involvement in identification.* Paper presented at the First National Conference on the Disadvantaged Gifted, Ventura, CA.

Fearn, L. (1976). Individual development: A process model in creativity. *Journal of Creative Behavior, 10,* 55–64.

Feldenkrais, M. (1949). *Body and mature behavior.* New York: International Universities Press.

Feldenkrais, M. (1972). *Awareness through movement.* New York: Harper & Row.

Feldhusen, J., Denny, T., & Condon, C. (1965). Anxiety, divergent thinking and achievement. *Journal of Educational Psychology, 56,* 40–45.

Feldhusen, J., & Klausmeier, H. (1962). Anxiety, intelligence and achievement in children of low, average and high intelligence. *Child Development, 33,* 403–407.

Feldhusen, J., & Kolloff, M. (1979). An approach to career education for the gifted. *Roeper Review, 2*(2), 13–16.

Feldhusen, J., & Kolloff, P. (1986). The Purdue three-stage enrichment model for gifted education at the elementary level. In J. Renzulli (Ed.), *Systems and models for developing programs for the gifted and talented.* Mansfield Center, CT: Creative Learning Press.

Feldhusen, J., & Robinson, A. (1986). Purdue secondary model for gifted and talented youth. In J. Renzulli (Ed.), *Systems and models for developing programs for the gifted and talented.* Mansfield Center, CT: Creative Learning Press.

Feldhusen, J., Treffinger, D., & Pine, P. (1975). *Teaching children how to think* (Teacher's ed.) (Technical Report No. NIE-G-74-0063). Washington, DC: National Institute of Education.

Feng, G., & Wilkerson, H. (1969). *T'ai-Chi: A way of centering and I Ching.* New York: Macmillan.

Ferguson, M. (1973). *The brain revolution.* New York: Taplinger.

Ferguson, M. (1977a). Bohm sees hologram as model for new description of reality. *Brain/Mind Bulletin, 2*(16), 2.

Ferguson, M. (1977b). Memory drug piracetam now being researched in U.S. *Brain/Mind Bulletin, 2*(16), 3.

Ferguson, M. (1977c). 'Mind mirror' EEG identifies states of awareness. *Brain/Mind Bulletin, 2*(30), 1–2.

Ferguson, M. (1981a). Chronopsychology links brain function to cycles. *Brain/Mind Bulletin, 7*(1), 1, 3.

Ferguson, M. (1981b). Electronic device reads acupuncture meridians. *Brain/Mind Bulletin, 7*(2), 1, 2.

Ferguson, M. (1982a). New theory: Feelings code, organize thinking. *Brain/Mind Bulletin, 7*(6), 1, 2.

Ferguson, M. (1982b). Subatomic physics may offer models for consciousness, psi. *Brain/Mind Bulletin, 7*(10), 1, 3.

Ferguson, M. (1982c). Optimalearning: Orchestrating best performance. *Brain/Mind Bulletin, 7*(8), 1, 2.

Ferguson, M. (1982d). The new reality: interacting approximations. *Brain/Mind Bulletin, 7*(10), 1, 2.

Ferguson, M. (1983). Jerre Levy: Human brain built to be challenged. *Brain/Mind Bulletin, 8*(9), 1.

Ferguson, M. (1984). Federally funded study shows imagery boosts learning, recall. *Brain/Mind Bulletin, 10*(2), 1,3.

Ferguson, M. (1985). Arts enhance scientific intelligence, study says. *Brain/Mind Bulletin, 10*(12), 1–2.

Ferguson, M. (1986a). Growing old can mean getting better, experts say. *Brain/Mind Bulletin, 12*(2), 1,2.

Ferguson, M. (1986b). Weston Agor on logic of intuitive decision-making. *Brain/Mind Bulletin, 12*(2), 1,3.

Feuerstein, R. (1978). *Learning potential assessment device.* Baltimore, MD: University Park Press.

Fiedler, F. (1967). *A theory of leadership effectiveness.* New York: McGraw-Hill.

Fiedler, F. (1971). Validation and extension of the contingency model of leadership effectiveness: A review of empirical findings. *Psychological Bulletin, 76,* 128–148.

Fincher, J. (Ed.). (1981). *The brain mystery of matter and mind.* (The Human Body Series). Washington, DC: U.S. News Books.

Findley, W., & Bryan, M. (1971). *Ability grouping 1970. Status, import, and alternatives.* Athens, GA: Center for Educational Improvement, University of Georgia.

Fine, B. (1964). *Stretching their minds.* New York: E. P. Dutton.

Fine, B. (1967). *Underachievers—How they can be helped.* New York: E. P. Dutton.

Fischer, D., Hunt, D., & Randhawa, B. (1978). Empirical validity of Ertl's brain-wave analyzer. *Educational and Psychological Measurement, 38*(4), 1017–1030.

Flanders, N. A. (1960). *Teacher influence—Pupil attitudes and achievement* (Final report, University of Minnesota Project No. 397). Washington, DC: U.S. Department of Health, Education and Welfare, Cooperative Research Program.

Flavell, J. (1979). Metacognition and cognitive monitoring: A new area of cognitive-developmental inquiry. *American Psychologist, 34,* 906–911.

Fleisham, E., & Hunt, J. (Eds.). (1973). *Current developments in the study of leadership.* Carbondale, IL: Southern Illinois University Press.

Flescher, I. (1963). Anxiety and achievement of intellectually gifted and creatively gifted children. *Journal of Psychology, 56,* 251–268.

Ford, B., & Ellis, J. (1979). Career education: A continuing need of Illinois gifted students. *Journal for the Education of the Gifted, 2*(3), 153–156.

Fowler, W. (1962a). Cognitive learning in infancy and early childhood. *Psychology Bulletin, 59,* 116–152.

Fowler, W. (1962b). Teaching a two-year-old to read: An experiment in early childhood learning. *Genetic Psychology Monograph, 66,* 181–283.

Fowler, W. (1963). The concept of the gifted child and the preschool years. *Gifted Child Quarterly, 7,* 102–105.

Fox, L. (1977). Sex differences: Implications for program planning for the academically gifted. In J. Stanley, W. George, & C. Solano (Eds.), *The gifted and the creative: A fifty-year perspective.* Baltimore, MD: Johns Hopkins University Press.

Fox, L. (1981). Instruction for the gifted: Some promising practices. *Journal for the Education of the Gifted, 4*(3), 246–254.

Fox, L., Brody, L., & Tobin, D. (Eds.) (1980). *Women and the mathematical mystique.* Baltimore, MD: Johns Hopkins University Press.

Fox, L., Brody, L., & Tobin, D. (1983). *Learning-disabled/gifted children.* Baltimore, MD: University Park Press.

Fox, L., Pasternak, S., & Peiser, N. (1976). Career-related interests of adolescent boys and girls. In D. Keating (Ed.), *Intellectual talent: Research and development.* Baltimore, MD: Johns Hopkins University Press.

Fox, L., Tobin, D., & Brody, L. (1981). Career development of gifted and talented women. *Journal of Career Education, 7,* 289–298.

Fox, L., & Turner, L. (1981). Gifted and creative females in the middle school years. *American Middle School Education, 4*(1), 17–23.

Frank, J. (1977). Talk to annual meeting of the National Institute for the Psychotherapies in New York, reported in *Brain/Mind Bulletin, 2*(15).

Frasier, M. (1979). Counseling the culturally diverse gifted. In N. Colangelo & R. Zaffrann (Eds.), *New voices in counseling the gifted.* Dubuque, IA: Kendall/Hunt.

Frasier, M. (1987). The identification of gifted black students: Developing new perspectives. *Journal for the Education of the Gifted, 10*(3), 155–180.

Frasier, M., & Carland, J. (1980). A study to identify key factors that affect the establishment of a positive relationship between teachers of the gifted and regular classroom teachers. *Journal for the Education of the Gifted, 3*(4), 225–227.

Frasier, M., & McCannon, C. (1981). Using bibliotherapy with gifted children. *Gifted Child Quarterly, 25*(2), 81–85.

Freed, A. (1971). *TA for kids.* Los Angeles: Jalmar.

Freed, A. (1973). *TA for tots.* Los Angeles: Jalmar.

Freehill, M. (1975). Teachers for the gifted. In B. Boston (Ed.), *A resource manual of information on educating the gifted and talented.* Reston, VA: Council for Exceptional Children.

Freehill, M. (1977). Foreword. In B. Johnson (Ed.), *Ideas for urban/rural gifted/talented.* Ventura, CA: Office of the Ventura County Superintendent of Schools, National/State Leadership Training Institute on the Gifted/Talented.

French, D. (1978). Microcomputers revolutionizing biofeedback; California school districts develop curricula. *Brain/Mind Bulletin, 4*(1), 2.

Friedman, P., Friedman, R., & Van Dyke, M. (1984). Identifying the leadership gifted: Self, peer, or teacher nominations? *Roeper Review, 7*(2), 91–94.

Frierson, E. (1965). Upper and lower status gifted children: A study of differences. *Exceptional Children, 32,* 83–90.

Fromm, E. (1959). The creative attitude. In H. H. Anderson (Ed.), *Creativity and its cultivation.* New York: Harper & Row.

Fund for the Advancement of Education. (1957). *They went to college early.* (Education Report No. 2). New York: Author.

Gagné, R. (1965). *The conditions of learning.* New York: Holt, Rinehart & Winston.

Galin, D. (1976). Educating both halves of the brain. *Childhood Education, 53*(1), 17–20.

Gallagher, J. (1958). Social status of children related to intelligence propinquity and social perception. *Elementary School Journal, 58,* 225–231.

Gallagher, J. (1964). *Teaching the gifted child.* Boston: Allyn & Bacon.

Gallagher, J. (1966). *Research summary on gifted child education.* Springfield, IL: Office of the Superintendent of Public Instruction.

Gallagher, J. (1975). *Teaching the gifted child* (2nd ed.). Boston: Allyn & Bacon.

Gallagher, J., Aschner, M., & Jenne, W. (1967). Productive thinking of gifted children in classroom interaction. *CEC Research Monograph Series B, B-5,* 1–103.

Gallagher, J., & Crowder, T. (1957). The adjustment of gifted children in the regular classroom. *Exceptional Children, 23,* 306–312; 317–319.

Gallagher, J., & Kinney, L. (Eds.). (1974). *Talent delayed—talent denied, the culturally different gifted child—A conference report.* Reston, VA: The Foundation for Exceptional Children.

Galloway, C. (1970). *Teaching is communication* (Bulletin No. 29). Washington, DC: Association for Student Teaching.

Gallwey, W. (1974). *The inner game of tennis.* New York: Random House.

Galton, F. (1869). *Hereditary genius: An inquiry into its laws and consequences.* London: Macmillan.

Galyean, B. (1976). *Language from within.* Los Angeles: Prism.

Galyean, B. (1977–1980). *The confluent teaching of foreign languages* (ESEA Title IV-C project year-end reports). Los Angeles, CA: Los Angeles City Unified Schools.

Galyean, B. (1978–1981). *A confluent language program for K–3, NES LES students* (ESEA Title IV-C project, year-end reports). Los Angeles: Los Angeles City Unified Schools.

Galyean, B. (1979). *The effects of guided imagery activities on various behaviors of one class of low achieving students* (Research paper). Los Angeles: Ken-Zel.

Galyean, B. (1983). *Mind sight.* Long Beach, CA: Center for Integrative Learning.

Gardner, H. (1983). *Frames of mind.* New York: Basic Books.

Gardner, J. (1971). *The development of object identity in the first six months of infancy.* Paper presented at the Biennial Meeting of the Society of Research in Child Development, Minneapolis, MN.

Garrett, H. (1929). Jews and others. *The Personnel Journal, 7,* 341–348.

Garrett, H. (1947). Negro-white differences in mental ability in the United States. *Scientific Monthly, 65,* 329–333.

Garrison, V., Stronge, J., & Smith, C. (1986). Are gifted girls encouraged to achieve their occupational potential? *Roeper Review, 9*(2), 101–104.

Gazzaniga, M. (1975). Review of the split brain. *UCLA Educator, 17*(2), 9–12.

Gear, G. (1974). *Teaching the talented program: A progress report.* Storrs, CT: University of Connecticut.

Gear, G. (1976). *Effects of the training program, Identification of the potentially gifted on teacher's accuracy in the identification of intellectually gifted children.* Unpublished doctoral dissertation, University of Connecticut, Storrs, CT.

Gear, G. (1978). Effects of training on teachers' accuracy in the identification of gifted children. *Gifted Child Quarterly, 22*(1), 90–97.

Geldard, F. (1968). Body English. *Psychology Today, 2*(7), 43–68.

George, L. (1981). A survey of research into the relationships between imagery and psi. *Journal of Parapsychology, 45,* 121–146.

Gesell, A., Halverson, H., Thompson, H., Ilg, F., Castner, B., Ames, L., & Amatruda, C. (1940). *The first five years of life: A guide to the study of the preschool child.* New York: Harper.

Getzels, J., & Jackson, F. (1961). Family environment and cognitive style: A study of the sources of highly intelligent and highly creative adolescents. *American Sociological Review, 26,* 351–359.

Getzels, J., & Jackson, F. (1962). *Creativity and intelligence.* New York: John Wiley & Sons.

Gibb, C. (1969). *Leadership: Selected readings.* Baltimore, MD: Penguin.

Gibb, J. (1961). *Defensive communication* (Research Reprint Series Number 12 of National Training Laboratories). Washington, DC.

Gifted and Talented Children's Act. (1978). Public Law 95–561.

Goertzel, V., & Goertzel, M. (1962). *Cradles of eminence.* Boston: Little Brown.

Gold, M. (1965). *Education of the intellectually gifted.* Columbus, OH: Charles E. Merrill.

Goldberg, M. (1959). A three year program at DeWitt Clinton High School to help bright underachievers. *High Points, 41,* 5–35.

Goldberg, M., Passow, A., Justman, J., & Hage, G. (1965). *The effects of ability grouping.* New York: Bureau of Publications, Columbia University.

Goldberg, P. (1983). *The intuitive edge.* Los Angeles: J. P. Tarcher.

Goldstein-Jackson, K. (1978). *Experiments with everyday objects; Science activities for children, parents, and teachers.* Englewood Cliffs, NJ: Prentice-Hall.

Goleman, D. (1976). A new computer test of the brain. *Psychology Today, 9*(12), 44–48.

Goodall, K. (1972). Tie line: Who's bright, two approaches. *Psychology Today, 5*(11), 24–26.

Goodman, D. (1978). Learning from lobotomy. *Human Behavior, 1,* 44–49.

Gordon, D. (1977). Children's beliefs in internal-external control and self-esteem as related to academic achievement. *Journal of Personality Assessment, 41,* 383–386.

Gordon, I. (1970). *Baby learning through baby play.* New York: St. Martin's.

Gordon, W. (1961). *Synectics: The development of creative capacity.* New York: Harper & Row.

Gordon, W., & Poze, T. (1980). SES Synectics and gifted education today. *Gifted Child Quarterly, 24*(4), 147–151.

Gorman, A. (1974). *Teachers and learners: The interactive process of education* (2nd ed.). Boston: Allyn & Bacon.

Gough, H. (1960). The adjective checklist as a personality assessment research technique. *Psychological Reports, 6,* 107–122.

Gould, S. J. (1981). *The mismeasure of man.* New York: Norton.

Gowan, J. C. (1957). Dynamics of the underachievement of gifted students. *Exceptional Children, 24,* 98–102.

Gowan, J. C. (1965). What makes a gifted child creative? *Gifted Child Quarterly, 9,* 3–6.

Gowan, J. C. (1972). *Development of the creative individual.* San Diego, CA: Robert R. Knapp.

Gowan, J. C. (1973, March). *The education of gifted youth.* Paper presented at the First National Conference on the Disadvantaged Gifted, Ventura, CA.

Gowan, J. C. (1974). *The development of the psychedelic individual.* Buffalo, NY: Creative Education Foundation.

Gowan, J. C. (1975). *Trance, art, and creativity.* Buffalo, NY: Creative Education Foundation.

Gowan, J. C. (1980). *Operations of increasing order.* Westlake Village, CA: Gowan.

Gowan, J. C. (1981). Introduction. In J. Gowan, J. Khatena, & E. P. Torrance (Eds.), *Creativity: Its educational implications* (2nd ed.). Dubuque, IA: Kendall/Hunt.

Gowan, J. C., & Demos, G. D. (1962). *How to enhance effective leadership.* Long Beach, CA: California State College.

Gowan, J. C., & Demos, G. D. (1964). *The education and guidance of the ablest.* Springfield, IL: Charles C. Thomas.

Gowan, J. C., Demos, G. D., & Torrance, E. P. (Eds.) (1967). *Creativity: Its educational implications.* New York: John Wiley & Sons.

Grace, H. A., & Booth, N. R. (1958). Is the gifted child a social isolate? *Peabody Journal of Education, 35,* 195–196.

Grant, W. V., & Lind, C. G. (1977). *Digest of education statistics* (1976 ed.). Washington, DC: U.S. Government Printing Office.

Granzin, K., & Granzin, W. (1969). Peer group choice as a device for screening intellectually gifted children. *Gifted Child Quarterly, 13*(3), 189–194.

Grau, P. N. (1985). Counseling the gifted girl. *Gifted Child Today, 38,* 8–11.

Greene, D. (1974). *Immediate and subsequent effects of differential reward systems on intrinsic motivation in public school classrooms.* Unpublished doctoral dissertation, Stanford University, Stanford, CA.

Grier, J., Counter, S., & Shearer, W. (1967). Prenatal auditory imprinting in chickens. *Science, 155,* 1692–1693.

Griffiths, R. (1945). *A study of imagination in early childhood and its function in mental development.* London: K. Paul, Trench, Trubner.

Griggs, S., & Dunn, R. (1984). Selected case studies of the learning style preferences of gifted students. *Gifted Child Quarterly, 28*(3), 115–119.

Griggs, S., & Price, G. (1980). A comparison between the learning styles of gifted versus average suburban junior high school students. *Roeper Review, 3*(1), 7–8.

Gris, H., & Dick, W. (1978). *The new Soviet psychic discoveries.* Englewood Cliffs, NJ: Prentice-Hall.

Groth, N. (1975). Success and creativity in male and female professors. *Gifted Child Quarterly, 19,* 328–335.

Guilford, J. P. (1956). The structure of intellect. *Psychological Bulletin, 53,* 267–293.

Guilford, J. P. (1959). Three faces of intellect. *American Psychology, 14,* 469–479.

Guilford, J. P. (1967). *The nature of human intelligence.* New York: McGraw-Hill.

Guilford, J. (1973). *Creativity tests for children.* Orange, CA: Sheridan Psychological Services.

Guillen, M. (1984). The intuitive edge. *Psychology Today, 18*(8), 68–69.

Gunther, B. (1966). *Sense relaxation below your mind.* New York: Collier Books.

Guskin, S., Zimmerman, E., Okolo, C., & Peng, C. (1986). Being labeled gifted or talented: Meanings and effects perceived by students in special programs. *Gifted Child Quarterly, 30*(2), 61–65.

Guttentag, M. (1975). *Undoing sex stereotypes.* New York: McGraw-Hill.

Hadley, D. (1969, April). *Effects of classroom anxiety on creativity.* Paper presented at a meeting of the Council of Exceptional Children, Denver.

Hagen, E. (1980). *Identification of the gifted.* New York: Teachers College Press.

Hagen, J., & Clark, B. (1977, July). *Unusual capacity-unusual needs.* Paper presented at the Second Conference of the World Council for Gifted, San Francisco, CA.

Haggard, E. (1957). Socialization, personality and academic achievement in gifted children. *School Review, 65,* 388–414.

Hall, E. (1984). What's a parent to do? PT conversation with Sandra Scarr. *Psychology Today, 18*(5), 58–63.

Hall, E., & Skinner, N. (1980). *Somewhere to turn: Strategies for parents of the gifted and talented.* New York: Teachers College Press.

Hallman, R. (1963). The commonness of creativity. *Educational Theory, 13,* 132–136.

Halpin, G., Payne, G., & Ellett, C. (1973). Biographical correlates of the creative personality: Gifted adolescents. *Exceptional Children, 39,* 652–653.

Handler, P. (Ed.). (1970). *Biology and the future of man.* New York: Oxford University Press.

Hanson, J. R., Silver, H., & Strong, R. (1984). *Roeper Review, 6*(3), 167–170.

Harmin, M. (1973). *Making sense of our lives.* A multimedia kit. Niles, IL: Argus Communications.

Harrington, D. (1980). Creativity, analogical thinking, and muscular metaphors. *Journal of Mental Imagery, 4*(2), 13–23.

Harris, T. (1967). *I'm OK: You're OK.* New York: Harper & Row.

Hart, L. (1975). *How the brain works.* New York: Basic Books.

Hart, L. (1978). The new "brain" concept of learning. *Phi Delta Kappan, 59*(6), 393–396.

Hart, L. (1981). Brain, language, and new concepts of learning. *Educational Leadership, 39,* 443–445.

Hassett, J., & Weisberg, A. (1972). *Open education: Alternative within our tradition.* Englewood Cliffs, NJ: Prentice-Hall.

Hausdorff, H., & Farr, S. (1965). The effects of grading practices on the marks of gifted sixth grade children. *Journal of Educational Research, 59,* 169–172.

Haynes, H., White, B., & Held, R. (1965). Visual accommodation in the human infant. *Science, 148,* 528–530.

Hayward, A. (1985). *Early learners.* Los Angeles: The Education Institute.

Hegeman, K. (1981). *A position paper on the education of gifted-handicapped children.* Paper presented to the Committee for the Gifted-Handicapped of the Association for the Gifted, Council for Exceptional Children, Reston, VA.

Heline, C. (1969). *Color and music in the new age.* Oceanside, CA: New Age Press.

Hendricks, G. (1979). *The family centering book: Awareness activities the whole family can do together.* Englewood Cliffs, NJ: Prentice-Hall.

Hendricks, G., & Fadiman, J. (1975). *Transpersonal education: A curriculum for feeling and being.* Englewood Cliffs, NJ: Prentice-Hall.

Hendricks, G., & Roberts, T. (1977). *The second centering book.* Englewood Cliffs, NJ: Prentice-Hall.

Hendricks, G., & Wills, R. (1975). *The centering book.* Englewood Cliffs, NJ: Prentice-Hall.

Hendrickson, P., & Torrance, E. (1960, 1961). *Just suppose* [Forms A & B]. Minneapolis, MN: Bureau of Educational Research, University of Minnesota.

Herr, E., & Watanabe, A. (1979). Counseling the gifted about career development. In N. Colangelo and R. Zaffrann (Eds.), *New voices in counseling the gifted.* Dubuque, IA: Kendall/Hunt.

Herrmann, N. (1981). The creative brain. *Training and Development Journal, 35* (10), 10–16.

Hess, K. (1987). *Enhancing writing through imagery.* New York: Trillium Press.

Hess, R., & Shipman, V. (1965). Early experience and the socialization of cognitive modes in children. *Child Development, 36*(2), 869–887.

Heyns, O. (1963). *Abdominal decompression: A monograph.* Johannesburg: Witwatersrand University Press.

Hier, D., & Crowley, W. (1982). Spatial ability in androgen-deficient men. *New England Journal of Medicine, 306*(20), 1202–1205.

Higham, S., & Navarre, J. (1984). Gifted adolescent females require differential treatment. *Journal for the Education of the Gifted, 8*(1), 43–58.

Hilliard, P. (1976). *Identifying gifted minority children through the use of non-verbal test.* Unpublished doctoral dissertation, Yeshiva University, New York.

Hills, C., & Rozman, D. (1978). *Exploring inner space.* Boulder Creek, CA: University of the Trees Press.

Hirsch, S. (1976). Executive high school internship a boon for the gifted and talented. *Teaching Exceptional Children, 9*(1), 22–23.

Hobson, J. (1979). High school performance of underage pupils initially admitted to kindergarten on the basis of physical and psychological examinations. In W. George, S. Cohn, & J. Stanley (Eds.), *Educating the gifted: Acceleration and enrichment.* Baltimore, MD: Johns Hopkins University Press.

Hoffman, L. (1972). Early childhood experiences and women's achievement motives. *Journal of Social Issues, 28,* 129–155.

Hoffman, L. (1977). Changes in family roles, socialization and sex differences. *American Psychologist, 32,* 644–658.

Hoffman, M., & Hoffman, L. (Eds.). (1964). *Review of child development research* (Vol. 1). New York: Russell Sage Foundation.

Hoffman, M., & Hoffman, L. (Eds.). (1966). *Review of child development research* (Vol. 2). New York: Russell Sage Foundation.

Holahan, C. K. (1984). The relationship between life goals at thirty and perceptions of goal attainment and life satisfaction at seventy for gifted men and women. *International Journal of Aging and Human Development, 20*(1), 21–31.

Holden, C. (1983). Parapsychology update. *Science, 222,* 4627.

Holland, J. (1959). Some limitations of teacher ratings as predictors of creativity. *Journal of Educational Psychology, 50,* 219–223.

Holland, J. (1961). Creative and academic performance among talented adolescents. *Journal of Educational Psychology, 52,* 136–147.

Holland, W. (1960). Language barrier as an educational problem of Spanish-speaking children. *Exceptional Children, 27,* 42–50.

Holleran, B., & Holleran, P. (1976). Creativity revisited: A new role for group dynamics. *Journal of Creative Behavior, 10,* 130–137.

Hollinger, C. L. (1985). Understanding the female adolescent's self perceptions of ability. *Journal for the Education of the Gifted, 9*(1), 59–80.

Hollinger, C. L., & Fleming, E. S. (1984). Internal barriers to the realization of potential: Correlates and interrelationships among gifted and talented female adolescents. *Gifted Child Quarterly, 28*(3), 135–139.

Hollingworth, L. (1926). *Gifted children.* New York: Macmillan.

Hollingworth, L. (1942). *Children above 180 IQ.* Yonkers-on-Hudson, NY: World Books.

Hopkins, L., & Shapiro, A. (1969). *Creative activities for the gifted child.* Palo Alto, CA: Fearon.

Hopson, J. (1984). A love affair with the brain: PT conversation with Marian Diamond. *Psychology Today, 18*(11), 62–73.

Horner, M. (1968). *Sex differences in achievement motivation and performance in competitive and noncompetitive situations.* Unpublished doctoral dissertation, University of Michigan, Ann Arbor.

Horner, M. (1969). Fail: Bright women. *Psychology Today, 3*(6), 36–38; 62.

Horner, M. (1972). Toward an understanding of achievement related conflicts in women. *Journal of Social Issues, 28,* 157–175.

Houston, J. (1977a). Margaret Mead at seventy-five. *Saturday Review, 6,* 58.

Houston, J. (1977b, August). *Re-seeding America.* Paper presented at the annual meeting of the American Humanistic Psychologists, Berkeley, CA.

Houston, S. (1972). [Reported in Tie Line]. *Psychology Today, 5*(11), 24–26.

Hoyt, K., & Hebeler, J. (Eds.). (1974). *Career education for gifted and talented students.* Salt Lake City, UT: Olympus.

Hoyt, P. (1965). *The relationship between college grades and adult achievement* (ACT Research Report No. 7). Iowa City, IA: American College Testing Program.

Hughes, H. (1969). The enhancement of creativity. *Journal of Creative Behavior, 3*(2), 73–83.

Hultgren, H. (1981). Competencies for teachers of the gifted (Doctoral dissertation, University of Denver). Ann Arbor, MI: UMI.

Hunt, J. McV. (1961). *Intelligence and experience.* New York: Ronald Press.

Hunt, J. McV., & Kirk, G. (1971). Social aspects of intelligence: Evidence and issues. In R. Cancro (Ed.), *Intelligence genetic and environmental influences.* New York: Grune & Stratton.

Hunt, M. (1982). *The universe within.* New York: Simon & Schuster.

Hunt, V. (1978). *A study of structural integration from neuromuscular, energy-field and emotional approaches.* Unpublished study from the Department of Kinesiology, University of California, Los Angeles, 1977. Reported by M. Ferguson, Electronic evidence of auras, chakras in UCLA study. *Brain/Mind Bulletin, 3*(9), 1–2.

Hutchinson, M. (1986). *Megabrain.* New York: Ballantine Books.

Huttunen, M., & Niskanen, P. (1978). Prenatal loss of father and psychiatric disorders. *Archives of General Psychiatry, 35,* 429–431.

Huxley, A. (1962). *Island.* New York: Harper & Row.

Iannon, R. V., & Carline, J. L. (1971). A humanistic approach to teacher education. *Journal of Teacher Education, 22,* 429–433.

Inquiry Development Program. (1966). Chicago, IL: Science Research Association.

Institute for Behavioral Research in Creativity. (1968). *Development of the alpha biographical inventory.* Salt Lake City, UT: Author.

Isaacs, A. (1973). Giftedness and leadership. *Gifted Child Quarterly, 17,* 103–112.

Isaacson, R. (1974). *The limbic system.* New York: Plenum Press.

Ismael, C. (1973). *The healing environment.* Millbrae, CA: Celestial Arts.

Jackson, N., Famiglietti, J., & Robinson, H. (1981, Winter). Kindergarten and first grade teachers' attitudes toward early entrants, intellectually advanced students and average students. *Journal for the Education of the Gifted, 4*(2), 132–142.

Jacobs, J. (1971). Effectiveness of teacher and parent identification of gifted children as a function of school level. *Psychology in the Schools, 8,* 140–142.

Jacobson, E. (1957). *You must relax.* New York: McGraw-Hill.

James, C. (1968). *Young lives at stake: The education of adolescents.* New York: Schocken Books.

James, M., & Jongeward, D. (1973). *Born to win.* Reading, MA: Addison-Wesley.

Jeffrey, W. (1980). The developing brain and child development. In M. Wittrock (Ed.), *The brain and psychology.* New York: Academic Press.

Jellison, J., & Harvey, J. (1976). Give me liberty: Why we like hard positive choices. *Psychology Today, 9*(10), 47–49.

Jencks, C., & Riesman, D. (1968). Where graduate schools fail. *Atlantic Monthly, 221,* 49–55.

Jenkins, M. (1950). Intellectually superior Negro youth: Problems and needs. *Journal of Negro Education, 19,* 322–332.

Jensen, A. (1969). How much can we boost IQ and scholastic achievement? *Harvard Educational Review, 39*(1), 1–24.

Jensen, A. (1974): The heritability of intelligence. In P. Rosenthal (Ed.), *Annual editions: Readings in human development.* Guilford, CT: Dushkin.

Jensen, A. (1986). Greater than the parts: Shared decision making. *Roeper Review, 9*(1), 10–13.

Jerison, H. (1977). Evolution of the brain. In M. Wittrock (Ed.), *The human brain.* Englewood Cliffs, NJ: Prentice-Hall.

Jersild, A. (1952). *In search of self.* New York: Bureau of Publications, Teachers College, Columbia University.

Joesting, J. (1970). Future problems of gifted girls. *Gifted Child Quarterly, 14,* 82–90.

John, E. (1971). Brain mechanisms of memory. In J. McGaugh (Ed)., *Psychobiology: Behavior from a biological perspective.* New York: Academic Press.

Johnson, B. (1962). *Ability, achievement and bilingualism: A comparative study involving Spanish-speaking and English-speaking children at the sixth grade level.* Unpublished doctoral dissertation, University of Maryland, Baltimore.

Johnson, B. (Ed.). (1977, January). [Gifted Female Suppl.] *National/State Leadership Training Institute on the Gifted and the Talented Bulletin.* Ventura, CA: Ventura County Superintendent of Schools.

Johnson, D. (1972). *Reaching out: Interpersonal effectiveness and self-actualization.* Englewood Cliffs, NJ: Prentice-Hall.

Johnson, G., & Kirk, S. (1950). Are mentally handicapped children segregated in regular grades? *Exceptional Children, 17,* 65–68.

Johnson, M. (1976). I think my teacher is a. . . . *Learning, 4,* 36–38.

Johnson, V. (1982, March). Myelin and maturation: A fresh look at Piaget. *The Science Teacher, 49,* 41–44.

Jonas, G. (1986). Observations: Reality anyone? *Science Digest, 94,* 11.

Jones, R. (1968). *Fantasy and feeling in education.* New York: New York University Press.

Jourard, S. (1964). *The transparent self: Self-disclosure and well-being.* Princeton, NJ: D. Van Nostrand.

Joyce, B., & Showers, B. (1982). The coaching of teaching. *Educational Leadership, 40*(1), 4–10.

Judkins, P., Jr. (n.d.). Certain criteria lead toward leadership. In *A new generation of leadership: Education for the gifted in leadership* (N/S-LTI-G/T Brief No. 4). Ventura, CA: Office of the Ventura County Superintendent of Schools.

Jung, C. (1933). *Psychological types.* New York: Harcourt.

Jung, C. (Ed.). (1964). *Man and his symbols.* New York: Dell.

Junior Great Books. Great Books Foundation, 400 E. Huron St, Chicago IL 60611.

Justman, J. (1953). Personal and social adjustment of intellectually gifted accelerants and non-accelerants in junior high schools. *School Review, 61,* 468–478.

Justman, J. (1954). Academic achievement of intellectually gifted accelerants and non-accelerants in junior high school. *School Review, 62,* 142–150.

Justman, J., & Wrightstone, J. (1956). Expressed attitudes of teachers towards special classes for intellectually gifted children. *Educational Administration and Supervision, 42,* 141–148.

Kagan, J. (1968). On cultural deprivation. In D. Glass (Ed.), *Environmental influences: Third of a series on biology and behavior.* New York: Rockefeller University Press and the Russell Sage Foundation.

Kagan, J. (1971). *Change and continuity in infancy.* New York: John Wiley & Sons.

Kagan, J., & Freeman, M. (1963). Relation of childhood intelligence, maternal behaviors, and social class to behavior during adolescence. *Child Development, 34,* 899–911.

Kagan, J., & Lewis, M. (1965). Studies of attention in the human infant. *Merrill-Palmer Quarterly, 11,* 95–127.

Kagan, J., & Moss, H. (1962). *Birth to maturity: A study in psychological development.* New York: John Wiley & Sons.

Kahl, D., & Gas, B. (1974). *Learning centers in the open classroom.* Encino, CA: International Center for Educational Development.

Kamiya, J., Haight, M., & Jampolsky, G. (1975). *A biofeedback study in high school.* Paper presented at a meeting of the Biofeedback Research Society in Monterey, CA.

Kanigher, H. (1977). *Everyday enrichment for gifted children at home and school.* Ventura, CA: Office of the Ventura County Superintendent of Schools.

Kaplan, D. (1976). Getting into shapes: Exploring abstract form in the classroom. *Learning, 4*(8), 68–71.

Kaplan, S. (1974). *Providing programs for the gifted and talented: A handbook.* Ventura, CA: Office of the Ventura County Superintendent of Schools.

Kaplan, S. (1986). The Grid: A model to construct differentiated curriculum for the gifted. In J. Renzulli (Ed.), *Systems and models for developing programs for the gifted and talented* (pp. 182–193). Mansfield Center, CT: Creative Learning Press.

Kaplan, S., Kaplan, J., Madsen, S., & Gould, B. (1975). *A young child experiences.* Pacific Palisades, CA: Goodyear.

Kaplan, S., Kaplan, J., Madsen, S., & Taylor, B. (1973). *Change for children.* Pacific Palisades, CA: Goodyear.

Karmel, B., & Maisel, E. (1975). A neuronal activity model for infant attention. In L. Cohen & P. Salapatek (Eds.), *Infant perception: From sensation to cognition: Basic visual processes* (Vol. 1). New York: Academic Press.

Karnes, F., & Collins, E. (1981). Teacher certification in the education of the gifted: An update. *Journal for the Education of the Gifted, 4*(2), 123–131.

Karnes, F., Meriweather, S., & D'Llio, V. (1987). The effectiveness of the leadership studies program. *Roeper Review, 9*(4), 238–241.

Karnes, F., & Parker, J. (1983). Teacher certification in gifted education: The state of the art and considerations for the future. *Roeper Review, 6*(1), 18–19.

Karnes, F., & Pearce, N. (1981). Governors' honors programs: A viable alternative for the gifted and talented. *G/C/T, 18,* 8–11.

Karnes, M. (1979). Young handicapped children can be gifted and talented. *Journal for the Education of the Gifted, 2*(3), 157–172.

Karnes, M., & Bertschi, J. (1978). Identifying and educating gifted/talented nonhandicapped and handicapped preschoolers. *Teaching Exceptional Children, 10*(4), 114–119.

Karnes, M., McCoy, G., Zehrbok, R., Wollershein, J., & Clarizio, H. (1963). The efficacy of two organizational plans for underachieving intellectually gifted children. *Exceptional Children, 29,* 438–446.

Karnes, M., McCoy, G., Zehrbok, R., Wollershein, J., Clarizio, H., Costin, C., & Stanley, L. (1961). *Factors associated with underachievement and overachievement of intellectually gifted children.* Champaign, IL: Champaign Community Unit Schools, Department of Special Services.

Karnes, M., & Shwedel, A. (1987). Differences in attitudes and practices between fathers of young gifted and fathers of young non-gifted children: A pilot study. *Gifted Child Quarterly, 31*(2), 79–82.

Karnes, M., Shwedel, A., & Lewis, G. (1983). Long-term effects of early programming for the gifted/talented handicapped. *Journal for the Education of the Gifted, 6*(4), 266–278.

Karnes, M., Shwedel, A., & Steinberg, D. (1984). Styles of parenting among parents of young gifted children. *Roeper Review, 6*(4), 232–235.

Kathnelson, A., & Colley, L. (1982). *Personal and professional characteristics valued in teachers of the gifted.* Paper presented at California State University, Los Angeles, CA.

Katz, I., Roberts, S., & Robinson, J. (1965). Effects of difficulty, race of administrator and instructions on Negro digit-symbol performance. *Journal of Personality and Social Psychology, 70,* 53–59.

Katz, I., Robinson, J., Epps, E., & Wally, P. (1964). Effects of race of experimenter and test vs. neutral instructions on expression of hostility in Negro boys. *Journal of Social Issues, 20;* 54–59.

Kauffman, D. (1976). *Teaching the future: A guide to future-oriented education.* Palm Springs, CA: ETC Publications.

Kaufman, A. (1984). K-ABC and giftedness. *Roeper Review, 7*(2), 83–88.

Kaufmann, F. (1976). *Your gifted child and you.* Reston, VA: Council for Exceptional Children.

Kavett, H., & Smith, W. (1980). Identification of gifted and talented students in the performing arts. *G/C/T, 14,* 18–20.

Kelley, T., Madden, R., Gardner, E., & Rudman, H. (1965). *Stanford Achievement Test.* New York: Harcourt, Brace, Jovanovich.

Keniston, K. (1975). Youth as a stage of life. In R. Havinghurst & P. Dreyer (Eds.), *Youth: 74th Yearbook of the NSSE.* Chicago: University of Chicago Press.

Kennell, J., Jerauld, R., Wolfe, H., Chesler, D., Kreger, N., McAlpine, W., Steffa, N., & Klaus, M. (1974). Maternal behavior one year after early and extended post-partum contact. *Developmental Medicine and Child Neurology, 16,* 172–179.

Kennell, J., & Klaus, M. (1979). Early mother-infant contact: Effects on the mother and the infant, *Bulletin of the Menninger Clinic, 43*(1), 69–78.

Kerr, B. (1985a). *Smart girls, gifted women.* Columbus, OH: Ohio Psychology Publishing Company.

Kerr, B. (1985b). Smart girls, gifted women: Special guidance concerns. *Roeper Review, 8*(1), 30–33.

Kerr, B. (1986). The career development of creatively gifted adults. In J. V. Miller & M. L.

Musgrove (Eds.), *Issues in Adult Career Counseling* (New Directions for Continuing Education, No. 32, pp. 59–69). San Francisco: Jossey-Bass.

Khatena, J. (1971). Some problems in the measurement of creative behavior. *Journal of Research and Development in Education, 4,* 71–80.

Khatena, J., & Torrance, E. P. (1976). *Khatena-Torrance creative perception inventory.* Chicago: Stoelting.

Killian, J., & Hughes, L. (1978). A comparison of short forms of the Intelligence Scale for Children—Revised in the screening of gifted referrals. *Gifted Child Quarterly, 22*(1), 111–115.

Kimball, B. (1953). Case studies in educational failure during adolescence. *American Journal of Orthopsychiatry, 23,* 406–415.

Kimura, D. (1967). Functional asymmetry of the brain in dichotic listening. *Cortex, 3,* 163–178.

Kimura, D. (1985). Male brain, female brain: The hidden difference. *Psychology Today, 19*(11), 50–58.

King, M. (1977). Biofeedback boosts students' self-concept. *Brain/Mind Bulletin, 2*(17), 1.

Kitano, H. (1975). Cultural diversity and the exceptional child. In J. Miley, I. Sato, W. Luché, P. Weaver, J. Curry, & R. Ponce (Eds.), *Promising practices: Teaching the disadvantaged gifted.* Ventura, CA: Ventura County Superintendent of Schools.

Klausmeier, H. (1971). Learning and human abilities. New York: Harper & Row.

Klineberg, O. (Ed.). (1944). *Characteristics of the American Negro.* New York: Harper & Brothers.

Kneller, G. (1965). *The art and science of creativity.* New York: Holt, Rinehart & Winston.

Knowlton, J., & Hamerlyneck, L. (1967). Perception of deviant behavior: A study of cheating. *Journal of Educational Psychology, 58,* 379–385.

Koestler, A. (1964). *The act of creation.* New York: Macmillan.

Koestler, A. (1968). *The ghost in the machine.* London: Hutchinson & Company.

Kohlberg, L. (1964). Development of moral character and moral ideology. In M. Hoffman & L. Hoffman (Eds.), *Review of child development research* (Vol. 1). New York: Russell Sage Foundation.

Kohlberg, L. (1972). Understanding the hidden curriculum. *Learning, 1*(2), 10–14.

Kohlberg, L. (1974). *First things: Social development: Grades 2 to 5.* New York: Guidance Associates.

Kohlberg, L. (1976a). *Relationships and values: Grades 7 to 9.* New York: Guidance Associates.

Kohlberg, L. (1976b). *Values in a democracy: Grades 9 to 12.* New York: Guidance Associates.

Kohlberg, L. (1977). *Universal values in America: Grades 9 to 12.* New York: Guidance Associates.

Kohn, A. (1986). How to succeed without even vying. *Psychology Today, 20*(9), 22–28.

Korner, A., & Grobstein, R. (1966). Visual alertness as related to soothing in neonates: Implications for maternal stimulation and early deprivation. *Child Development, 37,* 867–876.

Kosslyn, S. (1985). Stalking the mental image. *Psychology Today, 19* (5), 23–28.

Kough, J. (1960). Administrative provisions for the gifted. In B. Shertzer (Ed.), *Working with superior students.* Chicago: Science Research Association.

Kranz, B. (1978). *Multi-dimensional screening device for the identification of gifted/talented children.* Grand Forks, ND: Bureau of Educational Research and Services, University of North Dakota.

Krashen, S. (1975). The left hemisphere. *UCLA Educator, 17*(2), 17–23.

Krathwohl, D., Bloom, B., & Masia, B. (1964). *Taxonomy of educational objectives. Handbook II: Affective domain.* New York: David McKay.

Krause, M. (1973, May). Wind rose, the beautiful circle. *The Arithmetic Teacher,* 375–379.

Krech, D. (1969). Psychoneurobiochemeducation. *Phi Delta Kappan, L,* 370–375.

Krech, D. (1970). Don't use the kitchen sink approach to enrichment. *Today's Education, 59,* 30–32.

Kresse, F. (1968). *Materials and activities for teachers and children: A project to develop and evaluate multimedia kits for elementary schools* (Vols. 1 & 2) (Final Report, Project No. 5-0710). Washington, DC: U.S. Office of Education.

Krieger, D. (1976). Therapeutic touch affects hemoglobin. *Brain/Mind Bulletin, 1*(2), 2.

Krippner, S. (1967). The ten commandments that block creativity. *Gifted Child Quarterly, 11,* 144–151.

Krippner, S. (1968). Consciousness and the creative process. *Gifted Child Quarterly, 12*(3), 141–157.

Krippner, S. (1981). Parapsychologists make historic trip to investigate psi research in China. *Brain/Mind Bulletin, 6*(17), 2.

Krippner, S. (1983). A system approach to creativity based on Jungian topology. *Gifted Child Quarterly, 27*(2), 86–89.

Krippner, S., & Blickenstaff, R. (1970). The development of self-concept as part of an art workshop for the gifted. *Gifted Child Quarterly, 14*(3), 163–166.

Krishnamurti, J. (1964). *Think on these things.* New York: Harper & Row.

Kulik, C-L. C., & Kulik, J. A. (1982). Effects of ability grouping on secondary school students: A meta-analysis of evaluation findings. *American Educational Research Journal, 19,* 415–428.

Kulik, J. A., & Kulik, C-L. C. (1984). Effects of accelerated instruction on students. *Review of Educational Research, 54*(3), 409–425.

Kurtz, J., & Swenson, E. (1951). Factors related to overachievement and underachievement in schools. *School Review, 59,* 472–480.

Kurtzman, K. (1967). A study of school attitudes, peer acceptance, and personality of creative adolescents. *Exceptional Children, 34*(3), 157–162.

LaBenne, W., & Greene, B. (1969). *Educational implications of self-concept theory.* Pacific Palisades, CA: Goodyear Publishing.

Lahe, L. (1985). Sharing images of the future: Futuristics and gifted education. *Teaching Exceptional Children, 17*(3), 177–182.

Lamaze, F. (1970). *Painless childbirth: Psychoprophylactic method* (L. Celestin, Trans.). Chicago: Henry Regnery.

Landry, R. (1968). *Bilingualism and creative abilities.* Fargo, ND: North Dakota State University.

Lang, P. (1970). Autonomic control. *Psychology Today, 4*(5), 37–86.

Lao, R. (1970). Internal-external control and competent and innovative behavior among Negro college students. *Journal of Personal Social Psychology, 14,* 263–270.

Lavach, J., & Lanier, H. (1975). The motive to avoid success in 7th, 8th, 9th and 10th grade high-achieving girls. *Journal of Educational Research, 68,* 216–218.

Lavin, D. (1965). *The prediction of academic performances.* New York: Russell Sage Foundation.

Lawrie, J. (1969). Making it the hardest way. *Psychology Today, 3,* 29–31; 60.

Laycock, F., & Caylor, J. (1964). Physiques of gifted children and their less gifted siblings. *Child Development, 35,* 63–74.

Lazlow, A., & Nelson, P. (1974). Testing the gifted child in the elementary school. *Gifted Child Quarterly, 18,* 152–162.

Leadership: A survey of literature. (1976). Los Angeles: Los Angeles City Schools, Instructional Planning Division, Program for Gifted.

Leaverton, L., & Herzog, S. (1979). Adjustment of the gifted child. *Journal for the Education of the Gifted, 2*(3), 149–152.

LeBoyer, F. (1975). *Birth without violence.* New York: Random House.

Lehane, S. (1976). *Help your baby learn: 100 Piaget-based activities for the first two years of life.* Englewood Cliffs, NJ: Prentice-Hall.

Lehane, S. (1979). *The creative child, how to encourage the natural creativity of your preschooler.* Englewood Cliffs, NJ: Prentice-Hall.

Lehman, E., & Erdwins, C. (1981). The social and emotional adjustment of young, intellectually-gifted children. *Gifted Child Quarterly, 25*(3), 134–137.

Lehman, H. (1953). *Age and achievement* (American Philosophical Society Memoirs, Vol. 33). Princeton, NJ: Princeton University Press.

Leiter, R. (1951). The Leiter adult intelligence scale. *Psychological Service Center Journal, 3,* 185–236.

Lenneberg, E. (1967). *Biological foundations of language.* New York: John Wiley & Sons.

Leonard, G. (1975). *The ultimate athlete.* New York: Viking.

Leonard, G. (1978). *The silent pulse.* New York: E. P. Dutton.

Lepper, M., Greene, D., & Nisbett, R. (1973). Undermining children's intrinsic interest with extrinsic rewards. *Journal of Personality and Social Psychology, 28*(1), 129–137.

Lerner, G., & Libby, W. (1976). *Heredity, evolution, and society.* San Francisco: Freeman.

Leroux, J. (1986). Making theory real: Developmental theory and implications for education of gifted adolescents. *Roeper Review, 9*(2), 72–76.

Leshan, L., & Margenau, H. (1982). *Einstein's space and Van Gogh's sky.* New York: Macmillan.

Lessinger, L., & Martinson, R. (1961). The use of the California Psychological Inventory with gifted pupils. *Personnel and Guidance Journal, 39,* 572–575.

Levine, S. (1957). Infantile experience and resistance to physiological stress. *Science, 126,* 405.

Levine, S. (1960). Stimulation in infancy. *Scientific American, 202,* 80–86.

Levy, J. (1975). *The baby exercise book for the first fifteen months.* New York: Pantheon Books.

Levy, J. (1980). Cerebral asymmetry and the psychology of man. In M. Wittrock (Ed.), *The brain and psychology.* New York: Academic Press.

Levy, J. (1985). Right brain, left brain: Fact and fiction. *Psychology Today, 19*(5), 38–44.

Levy, J., & Reid, M. (1975). Work reported in right-hemisphere language function may exist only in split-brain subjects. *Brain/Mind Bulletin, 1*(2), 1.

Lewis, H. (1970). *Opening windows into the future.* Winston-Salem, NC: The Governor's School of North Carolina.

Lewis, M. (1972). State as an infant-environment interaction: An analysis of mother-infant behavior as a function of sex. *Merrill-Palmer Quarterly, 18,* 95–121.

Lewis, M., & Rosenblum, L. (1974). *The effect of the infant on its caregiver.* New York: Wiley.

Liberty, P., Jones, R., & McGurie, C. (1963). Age-mate perception of intelligence, creativity and achievement. *Perceptual Motor Skills, 16,* 194.

Lickona, T. (1977). How to encourage moral development. *Learning, 5*(7), 37–43.

Lightfoot, G. (1951). *Personality characteristics of bright and dull children* (Contributions to Education, No. 969). New York: Teachers College, Columbia University.

Lindsey, M. (1980). *Training teachers of the gifted and talented.* New York: Teachers College Press.

Linquist, E. F., & Hierony, A. N. (1979). *Iowa Tests of Basic Skills.* Boston: Houghton Mifflin.

Lipsitt, L., Mustaine, M., & Zeigler, B. (1976). Effects of experience on the behavior of the young infant. *Neuropadiatrie, 8,* 107–133.

Little, D. (1973). Post-industrial society and what it may mean. *The Futurist, 7,* 259–262.

Loeb, R., & Jay, G. (1987). Self-concept in gifted children: Differential impact in boys and girls. *Gifted Child Quarterly, 31*(1), 9–14.

Loomis, A. (1977). *Math is fun—Materials for task cards.* Montebello, CA: Montebello Unified School District.

Lorenz, K. (1969). Innate bases of learning. In K. Pribram (Ed.), *On the biology of learning.* New York: Harcourt, Brace & World.

Lowther, M. (1962). What is over- and under-achievement? *The University of Michigan School of Education Bulletin, 34,* 105–108.

Loye, D. (1982). People with balanced brains better forecasters. *Brain/Mind Bulletin, 7*(3), 1.

Loye, D. (1983). *The sphinx and the rainbow.* Boulder, CO: Shambhala.

Lozanov, G. (1977). A general theory of suggestion in the communications process and the activation of the total reserves of the learner's personality. *Suggestopaedia-Canada, 1,* 1–4.

Luchins, E., & Luchins, A. (1980). Female mathematicians: A contemporary appraisal. In L. Fox, L. Brody, & D. Tobin (Eds.), *Women and the mathematical mystique.* Baltimore, MD: Johns Hopkins University Press.

Lucito, L. (1964). Independence-conformity behavior as a function of intellect: Bright and dull children. *Exceptional Children, 31,* 5–13.

Lucker, G., Rosenfield, D., Sikes, J., & Aronson, E. (1976). Performance in the interdependent classroom: A field study. *American Educational Research Journal, 13*(2), 115–123.

Luckey, B. (1925). Racial differences in mental ability. *Scientific Monthly, 22,* 245–248.

Luria, A. R. (1973). *The working brain: An introduction to neuropsychology* (B. Haigh, Trans.). New York: Basic Books.

Lurie, T. (1978). *Conversations and constructions.* San Francisco: Journeys Into Language.

Lyon, H. (1975, September). *Realizing our potential.* Paper given at the First World Conference on Gifted Children, London, England.

Maccoby, E. (1966). *The development of sex differences.* Stanford, CA: Stanford University Press.

Maccoby, E., & Jacklin, C. (1974). *The psychology of sex differences.* Stanford, CA: Stanford University Press.

MacKinnon, D. (1964). The creativity of architects. In C. W. Taylor (Ed.), *Widening horizons in creativity.* New York: John Wiley & Sons.

MacKinnon, D. (1965). Personality and the realization of creative potential. *American Psychologist, 20,* 273–281.

MacLean, P. (1978). A mind of three minds: Educating the triune brain. In J. Chall & A. Mirsky (Eds.), *Education and the brain: The seventy-seventh yearbook of the National Society for the Study of Education,* Part I. Chicago, IL: University of Chicago Press.

Maddux, C., Samples-Lachmann, I., & Cummings, R. (1985). Preferences of gifted students for selected teacher characteristics. *Gifted Child Quarterly, 29*(4), 160–163.

Maehr, M., & Stallings, W. (1972). Freedom from external evaluation. *Child Development, 43,* 177–185.

Maggio, E. (1971). *Psychophysiology of learning and memory.* Springfield, IL: Charles C. Thomas.

Maker, J. (1975). *Training teacher for the gifted and talented: A comparison of models.* Reston, VA: Council for Exceptional Children.

Maker, J. (1977). *Providing programs for the gifted handicapped.* Reston, VA: Council for Exceptional Children.

Maker, J. (1986). Developing scope and sequence in curriculum. *Gifted Child Quarterly, 30*(4), 151–158.

Mallinson, T. (1972). *Gifted underachievers.* Toronto: Ontario Board of Education, Research Department.

Malone, C. (1974). *Identification of educationally deprived gifted kindergarten children.* Unpublished doctoral dissertation, United States International University, San Diego, CA.

Malone, C., & Moonan, W. (1975). Behavioral identification of gifted children. *Gifted Child Quarterly, 19*(4), 301–306.

Manaster, G., & Powell, P. (1983). A framework for understanding gifted adolescents' psychological maladjustment. *Roeper Review, 6*(2), 70–73.

Mangieri, J., & Madigan, F. (1984). Reading for gifted students: What schools are doing. *Roeper Review, 7*(2), 68–70.

Mann, H. (1957). How real are friendships of gifted and typical children in a program of partial segregation? *Exceptional Children, 23,* 199–201.

Marano, H. (1981). Biology is one key to the bonding of mothers and babies. *Smithsonian, 11*(11), 60–68.

Marland, S., Jr. (1972). *Education of the gifted and talented.* Report to the Congress of the United States by the U.S. Commissioner of Education. Washington, DC: U.S. Government Printing Office.

Martin, P. (1955). *Experiment in depth.* London: Routledge & Kegan Paul.

Martin, R., & Pacheres, J. (1962, February 24). Good scholars not always the best. *Business Week,* 77–78.

Martindale, C. (1975). What makes creative people different. *Psychology Today, 9*(2), 44–50.

Martinson, R. (1961). *Educational programs for gifted pupils.* Sacramento: California State Department of Education.

Martinson, R. (1972, March). Research on the gifted and talented: Its implications for education. In S. Marland, Jr., *Education of the Gifted and Talented.* Report to the Congress of the United States by the U.S. Commissioner of Education. Washington, DC: U.S. Government Printing Office.

Martinson, R. (1973). Children with superior cognitive abilities. In L. Dunn (Ed.), *Exceptional children in the schools.* New York: Holt, Rinehart & Winston.

Martinson, R. (1974, June). *The identification of the gifted and talented.* Ventura, CA: Office of the Ventura County Superintendent of Schools.

Martinson, R., Hermanson, D., & Banks, G. (1972). An independent study-seminar program for the gifted. *Exceptional Children, 35*(5), 421–426.

Martyn, K. (1957). *The social acceptance of gifted students.* Unpublished doctoral dissertation, Stanford University, Stanford, CA.

Maruyama, M. (1975). Post-industrial logic. In A. Spekke (Ed.), *The next 25 years: Crisis and opportunity*. Washington, DC: World Future Society.

Marzollo, J., & Lloyd, J. (1972). *Learning through play*. New York: Harper & Row.

Maslow, A. (1954). *Motivation and personality*. New York: Harper & Row.

Maslow, A. (1959). Creativity in self-actualizing people. In H. Anderson (Ed.), *Creativity and its cultivation*. New York: Harper & Row.

Maslow, A. (1962). *Toward a psychology of being*. New York: Van Nostrand.

Maslow, A. (1968). *Toward a psychology of being* (2nd ed.). New York: Van Nostrand Reinhold.

Maslow, A. (1971). *The farther reaches of human nature*. New York: Viking.

Mason, E. (1972). *Collaborative learning*. New York: Schocken Books.

Massialas, B., & Zevin, J. (1967). *Creative encounters in the classroom*. New York: John Wiley & Sons.

Masters, R., & Houston, J. (1972). *Mind games*. New York: Viking.

Masters, R., & Houston, J. (1978). *Listening to the body*. New York: Delacorte.

Matheny, K., & Edwards, C. (1974). Academic improvement through an experimental classroom management system. *Journal of School Psychology, 12*, 222–232.

Mattheis, D. (1974). Career education: What it is and what it seeks to accomplish. Paper presented at Career Education Conference, Edmund, OK, 1972. In K. Hoyt & J. Hebeler (Eds.), *Career education for gifted and talented students*. Salt Lake City, UT: Olympus Publishing.

Mauser, A. (1980). LD in gifted children. *ACLD Newsbriefs, 130*, 2.

May, R. (1953). *Man's search for himself*. New York: W. W. Norton.

May, R. (1959). The nature of creativity. In H. H. Anderson (Ed.), *Creativity and its cultivation*. New York: Harper & Row.

May, R. (1967). *Psychology and the human dilemma*. Princeton, NJ: D. Van Nostrand.

Maynard, F. (1970, January). How to raise a more creative child. *Woman's Day*, 33–68.

McCall, R. (1979). Qualitative transitions in behavioral development in the first two years of life. In M. Bornstein & W. Kessen (Eds.), *Psychological development from infancy: Image to intention*. New York: John Wiley & Sons.

McCandless, B. (1964). Relation of environmental factors to intellectual functioning. In H. Stevens & R. Heber (Eds.), *Mental retardation*. Chicago: University of Chicago Press.

McClelland, D. (1974). Do IQ tests measure intelligence? In P. Rosenthal (Ed.), *Annual editions: Readings in human development*. Guilford, CT: Dushkin.

McConnell, F., Horton, K., & Smith, B. (1969). Language development and cultural disadvantagement. *Exceptional Children, 35*, 597–606.

McConnell, R. (1971). *ESP: A curriculum guide*. New York: Simon & Schuster.

McGillivray, R. (1964). Differences in home background between high-achieving and low-achieving gifted children: A study of one hundred grade eight pupils in the City of Toronto Public Schools. *Ontario Journal of Educational Research, 6*, 99–106.

McGuinness, B., & Pribram, K. (1979). The origins of sensory bias in the development of gender differences in perception and cognition. In M. Bortner (Ed.), *Cognitive growth and development: Essays in honor of Herbert G. Birch*. New York: Brunner/Mazel.

McKenna, A. (1978). The role of the adult in infant speech. *Enfance, 1*, 5–12.

McLeod, B. (1984). Learning: Crosstalk. *Psychology Today, 18* (11), 14.

McMillin, D. (1975, May). *Separate criteria: An alternative for the identification of disadvantaged gifted*. Paper presented at the National Teacher Institute on Disadvantaged Gifted, Los Angeles.

McNeill, D. (1966). Developmental psycholinguistics. In F. Smith & G. Miller (Eds.), *The genesis of language*. Cambridge, MA: MIT Press.

Mead, M. (1954). The gifted child in the American culture today. *Journal of Teacher Education, 5*(3), 211–214.

Mednick, S., & Mednick, M. (1967). *Examiner's manual: Remote Associates Test*. Boston: Houghton Mifflin.

Meeker, M. (1968). Differential syndromes of giftedness and curriculum planning: A four year follow-up. *Journal of Special Education, 2*, 185–194.

Meeker, M. (1969). *The structure of intellect: Its use and interpretation*. Columbus, OH: Charles E. Merrill.

Meer, J. (1985). The light touch. *Psychology Today, 19*(9), 60–67.

Meltzoff, A., & Moore, M. (1977). Imitation of facial and manual gestures by human neonates. *Science, 198*, 75–78.

Mensch, I. (1950). Rorschach study of the gifted child. *Exceptional Children, 17*, 8–14.

Mercer, J., & Lewis, J. (1977). *Parent interview manual: System of multicultural pluralistic assessment*. New York: Psychological Corporation.

Mercer, J., & Lewis, J. (1978). Using the System of Multicultural Pluralistic Assessment (SOMPA) to identify the gifted minority child. In A. Baldwin, G. Gear, & L. Lucito (Eds.), *Educational planning for the gifted*. Reston, VA: Council for Exceptional Children.

Mercer, J., & Smith, J. (1972). *Subtest estimates of the WISC full scale IQs for children*. Rockville, MD: National Center for Health Statistics.

Miles, C. (1954). Gifted children. In L. Carmichael (Ed.), *Manual of child psychology*. New York: John Wiley & Sons, 1954.

Milgram, R. (1984). Creativity in gifted adolescents: A review. *Journal for the Education of the Gifted, 8*(1), 25–42.

Millay, J. (1981a). Bilateral synch: Key to intuition? *Brain/Mind Bulletin, 6*(9), 1, 3.

Millay, J. (1981b, June). [Talk given at the New Age School]. S. Pasadena, CA.

Miller, R. (1956). Social status and socio empathetic differences among mentally superior, mentally typical and mentally retarded children. *Exceptional Children, 23*, 114–119.

Mills, B. (1973). Attitudes of decision-making groups toward gifted children and public school programs for the gifted. Unpublished doctoral dissertation, UCLA, 1973. *Dissertation Abstracts International, 34*, 1739–1740.

Minner, S., Prater, G., Bloodworth, H., & Walker, S. (1987). Referral and placement recommendations of teachers toward gifted handicapped children. *Roeper Review, 9*(4), 247–249.

Mischel, W., & Baker, N. (1975). Cognitive appraisals and transformations in delay behavior. *Journal of Personality and Social Psychology, 31*, 254–261.

Mishlove, J. (1975). *The roots of consciousness. Psychic liberation through history, science, and experience*. New York: Random House.

Mitchell, B. (1982). An update on the state of gifted/talented education in the U.S. *Phi Delta Kappan, 64*(5), 357–358.

Mitchell, P., & Erickson, D. (1978). The education of gifted and talented children: A status report. *Exceptional Children, 45*(1), 12–16.

Moffit, A. (1971). Consonant cue perception by twenty-to-twenty-four-week-old infants. *Child Development, 42*, 717–731.

Mohs, M. (1982, September). I.Q.: New research shows that the Japanese outperform all others in intelligence tests. Are they really smarter? *Discover*, 18–24.

Monaco, T., & Georgiades, W. (1986). Preparing teachers of gifted students to solve problems. *Roeper Review, 9*(2), 85–87.

Moore, B. (1979). A model career education program for gifted disadvantaged students. *Roeper Review, 2*(2), 20–22.

Moore, G. D. (1980). Counseling the gifted child. *School Review, 68,* 63–70.

Moore, O. K. (1961). Orthographic symbols and the preschool child. In E. Torrance (Ed.), *Creativity.* Minneapolis, MN: University of Minnesota Press.

Moore, O. K. (1967). Personal letter to J. S. Chall. In J. S. Chall, *Learning to read: The great debate.* New York: McGraw-Hill.

Moore, T. (1967). Language and intelligence: A longitudinal study of the first eight years. Part 1. Patterns of development in boys and girls. *Human Development, 10,* 88–106.

Morgan, H. (1952). A psychometric comparison of achieving and nonachieving college students of high ability. *Journal of Consulting Psychology, 16,* 292–298.

Morgan, H., Tennant, C., & Gold, M. (1980). *Elementary and secondary level programs for the gifted and talented.* New York: Teachers College Press.

Morris, J. (1976). Meditation in the classroom. *Learning, 5*(4), 22–27.

Morris, V. (1966). *Existentialism in education.* New York: Harper & Row.

Morrison, A., & McIntyre, D. (1971). *Schools and socialization.* Baltimore, MD: Penguin.

Morrow, W., & Wilson, R. (1961). Family relations of bright high achieving and underachieving high school boys. *Child Development, 32,* 501–510.

Morse, W. (1964). Self-concept in the school setting. *Childhood Education, 41,* 195–198.

Moustakas, C. (1967). *Creativity and conformity.* New York: Van Nostrand Reinhold.

Mulholland, T. (1973). It's time to try hardware in the classroom. *Psychology Today, 7,* 103–104.

Munson, H. (1979). Moral thinking, can it be taught? *Psychology Today, 12*(9), 48–68; 92.

Murphy, J., Dauw, D., Horton, R., & Friedian, A. (1976). Self-actualization and creativity. *Journal of Creative Behavior, 10,* 39–44.

Murphy, L. (1972). Infants' play and cognitive development. In M. Piers (Ed.), *Play and development.* New York: W. W. Norton.

Myers, R. E., & Torrance, E. P. (1965). *Invitations to speaking and writing creatively.* Lexington, MA: Ginn & Company.

National Center for Education Statistics. (1979). *Degrees to women, 1979 update.* Washington, DC: Statistics Information Office.

National/State Leadership Training Institute on the Gifted and Talented. (1977, January). *Gifted female supplement.* Los Angeles: Author.

Nebes, R. (1975). Man's so-called "minor" hemisphere. *UCLA Educator, 17,* 13–16.

Neimark, E. (1975). Longitudinal development of formal operational thought. *Genetic Psychology Monograph, 91,* 175–225.

Nevin, D. (1977). Seven teenage math prodigies take off from Johns Hopkins on the way to advanced degrees. *Smithsonian, 8*(7), 76–82.

Newland, T. E. (1976). *The gifted in socioeducational perspective.* Englewood Cliffs, NJ: Prentice-Hall.

Newman, R. (1967). *Psychological consultation in the schools: A catalyst for learning.* New York: Basic Books.

Nichols, R. (1964). Parental attitudes of mothers of intelligent adolescents and creativity of their children. *Child Development, 35,* 1041–1049.

Nicol, G. (1985). The international baccalaureate. *Gifted Students Institute Quarterly, 10*(4), 4, 5.

Nova. (1980, September). *The pinks and the blues.* Broadcast by Public Broadcasting System.

Ober, R. (1970). Reciprocal category system. *Journal of Research and Development in Education, 4,* 34–51.

O'Connell, M. (1976). Intuitive and psychic identical, Kraft stresses at New York seminar. *Brain/Mind Bulletin, 1*(10), 2.

Ohlsen, M., & Proff, C. (1960). *The extent to which group counseling improves the academic and personal adjustment of underachieving, gifted adolescents* (Cooperative Research Project, No. 623). Washington, DC: U.S. Office of Education.

Ohnmacht, F. (1966). Achievement, anxiety, and creative thinking. *American Educational Research Journal, 3,* 131–138.

Olton, R. (1969). A self-instructional program for developing productive thinking skills in 5th & 6th grade children. *Journal of Creative Behavior, 3*(1), 16–25.

Oppenheimer, S. (1984). The search for gravitational waves. *Science Digest, 92*(3), 74–76.

Ornstein, R. (1972). *The psychology of consciousness.* San Francisco: W. H. Freeman.

Ornstein, R. (1973a). Right and left thinking. *Psychology Today, 6,* 87–92.

Ornstein, R. (Ed.). (1973b). *The nature of human consciousness.* New York: Viking.

Ornstein, R., & Sobel, D. (1987). The healing brain. *Psychology Today, 21*(3), 48–32.

Osborn, A. (1957). *Applied imagination.* New York: Scribner.

O'Shea, A. (1970). Low achievement syndrome among bright junior high school boys. *Journal of Educational Research, 63,* 257–262.

Ostrander, S., & Schroeder, L. (1970). *Psychic discoveries behind the iron curtain.* Englewood Cliffs, NJ: Prentice-Hall.

Ott, J. (1973). *Health and light: The effects of natural and artificial light on man and other living things.* Old Greenwich, NY: Devin-Adair.

Otto, H. (1973). *Group methods to actualize human potential.* Beverly Hills, CA: Holister Press.

Otto, H., & Mann, J. (Eds.). (1971). *Ways of growth: Approaches to expanding awareness.* New York: Pocket Books.

Overbye, D. (1982, December). Exploring the edge of the universe. *Discovery,* 22–28.

Owen, G., Fram, K., Garry, P., Lower, J., & Lubin, A. (1974). *A study of nutritional status of preschool children in the United States, 53,* Part II, Suppl. 597–646.

Owen, R. (1984). *Language development.* Columbus, OH: Charles E. Merrill.

Oyle, I. (1975). *The healing mind.* Millbrae, CA: Celestial Arts.

Painter, G. (1971). *Teach your baby.* New York: Simon & Schuster.

Pallett, J. (1965). *Definition and predictions of success in the business world.* Unpublished doctoral dissertation, University of Iowa, Iowa City, IA.

Palomares, U. (1972). *Magic circle.* La Mesa, CA: Human Development Training Institute.

Palomares, U., & Johnson, L. (1966). Evaluation of Mexican American pupils for EMR classes. *California Education, 3*(8), 27–29.

Parker, J., & Karnes, F. (1984). Graduate degree programs in the education of the gifted. *Journal for the Education of the Gifted, 7*(3), 205–217.

Parmelee, A., & Sigman, M. (1976). Development of visual behavior and neurological organization in pre-term and full-term infants. In A. Pick (Ed.), *Minnesota symposia on child psychology* (Vol. 10). Minneapolis, MN: University of Minnesota Press.

Parnes, S. (1963). Education and creativity. *Teachers College Record, 64,* 331–339.

Parnes, S. (1967). *Creative behavior guidebook.* New York: Charles Scribner's Sons.

Passow, A. (1980). *Education for gifted children and youth: An old issue—a new challenge.* Ventura, CA: Office of the Ventura County Superintendent of Schools.

Passow, A. (1981). The four curricula of the gifted and talented: Toward a total learning environment. *G/C/T, 20,* 2–7.

Passow, A., Goldberg, M., & Tannenbaum, A. (Eds.). (1967). *Education of the disadvantaged: A book of readings.* New York: Holt, Rinehart & Winston.

Paulsen, W. (1974). *Deciding for myself* [Multi-media kit]. Minneapolis, MN: Winston Press.

Payne, D., Halpin, W., Ellet, C., & Dale, J. (1971). General personality correlates of creative personality in academically and artistically gifted youth. *Journal of Special Education, 9,* 105–108.

Pearlman, S. (1952). *An investigation into the problems of academic underachievement among intellectually superior college students.* Unpublished doctoral dissertation, Columbia University, New York.

Pegnato, C., & Birch, J. (1959). Locating gifted children in junior high schools: A comparison of methods. *Exceptional Children, 25,* 300–304.

Pelletier, K. (1977). *Mind as healer, mind as slayer.* New York: Delacorte.

Pendarvis, E., & Grossi, J. (1980). Designing and operating programs for the gifted and talented handicapped. In J. Jordan & J. Grossi (Eds.), *An administrator's handbook on designing programs for the gifted and talented.* Reston, VA: Council for Exceptional Children.

Perkins, H. (1965). Classroom behavior and underachievement. *American Educational Research Journal, 2,* 172.

Perkins, J., & Wicas, E. (1971). Group counseling bright underachievers at 9 Florida high schools. *Gifted Child Quarterly, 18,* 273–278.

Perrone, P., & Male, R. (1981). *The developmental education and guidance of talented learners.* Rockville, MD: Aspen Publications.

Peterson, J. (1975). Extrasensory abilities of children, An ignored reality? *Learning, 4,* 10–14.

Pettigrew, T. A. (1964). *A profile of the Negro American.* Princeton, NJ: Van Nostrand.

Pew, T. (1979). Biofeedback seeks new medical uses for concept of yoga. *Smithsonian, 10*(9), 106–114.

Pflum, J., & Waterman, A. (1974). *Open education: For me?* Washington, DC: Acropolis Books.

Phares, E. (1975). *Locus of control in personality.* Morristown, NJ: General Learning Press.

Phelps, S., & Austin, N. (1975). *The assertive woman.* San Luis Obispo, CA: Impact.

Piaget, J. (1952). *The origins of intelligence in children* (M. Cook, Trans.). New York: International Universities. (Original work published, 1936).

Piaget, J. (1954). *The construction of reality in the child.* New York: Basic Books.

Piaget, J. (1965). *The moral judgment of the child* (M. Gabin, Trans.). New York: Free Press. (Original work published, 1932)

Pierce, J., & Bowman, P. (1960). Motivation patterns of high school students. *Cooperative Research Monograph No. 2: The Gifted Student* (OE-35016, pp. 33–66). Washington, DC: U.S. Office of Education.

Pietsch, P. (1981). *Shufflebrain.* Boston: Houghton Mifflin.

Pines, M. (1979a, September). A head start in the nursery. *Psychology Today, 13*(4), 56–68.

Pines, M. (1979b, June). Good Samaritans at age two? *Psychology Today, 13*(1), 66–77.

Pines, M. (1982, March 30). What produces great skills? Specific pattern is discerned [Science Time]. *New York Times*.

Pines, M. (1984). Children's winning ways, *Psychology Today, 18*(12), 58–65.

Pippert, R., & Archer, N. (1963). A comparison of two methods for classifying underachievers with respect to selected criteria. *Personnel and Guidance Journal, 41,* 788–791.

Pirozzo, R. (1982). Gifted underachievers. *Roeper Review, 4*(4), 18–21.

Pitts, M. (1986). Suggestions for administrators of rural schools about developing a gifted program. *Roeper Review, 9*(1), 24–25.

Pizzamiglio, L., & Cecchini, M. (1971). Development of the hemispheric dominance in children from 5 to 10 years of age and their relations with the development of cognitive processes. *Brain Research, 31,* 363–364.

Plowman, P., & Rice, J. (1967). *Final report: California Project Talent.* Sacramento: California Department of Public Instruction.

Podgoretskaya, N. (1979). A study of spontaneous logical thinking in adults. *Soviet Psychology, 17*(3), 70–84.

Poffenberger, T., & Poffenberger, S. (1973). The social psychology of fertility in a village in India. In J. Fawcett (Ed.), *Psychological perspectives on population.* New York: Basic Books.

Polland, B. (1975). *Feelings: Inside you and out loud, too.* Millbrae, CA: Celestial Arts.

Porteus, S. (1965). *Porteus maze test: Fifty years' application.* Palo Alto, CA: Pacific Books.

Powell, P., & Haden, T. (1984). The intellectual and psychosocial nature of extreme giftedness. *Roeper Review, 6*(3), 131–133.

Power, T., & Chapieski, L. (1986). *Developmental Psychology, 22*(2), 271–275.

Prescott, J. (1979). Alienation of affection. *Psychology Today, 13*(7), 124.

Pressey, S. (1925). Fundamental misconceptions involved in current marking systems. *School and Society, 21,* 736–738.

Pressey, S. (1955). Concerning the nature and nurture of genius. *Science, 31,* 123–129.

Pressey, S. (1964). The nature and nurture of genius. In J. French (Ed.), *Educating the gifted child.* New York: Holt, Rinehart & Winston.

Pressman, H. (1969). Schools to beat the system: Can we open the gates of the ghetto and let the children out? *Psychology Today, 2,* 58–63.

Pribram, K. (1971a). The brain. *Psychology Today, 5,* 44–48; 88–90.

Pribram, K. (1971b). *Languages of the brain: Experimental paradoxes and principles in neuropsychology.* Englewood Cliffs, NJ: Prentice-Hall.

Pribram, K. (1977). Primary reality may be frequency realm. *Brain/Mind Bulletin, 2,* 1–3.

Price, G., Dunn, K., Dunn, R., & Griggs, S. (1981). Studies in students' learning styles. *Roeper Review, 4*(2), 38–40.

Prichard, A., & Taylor, J. (1980). *Accelerating learning: The use of suggestion in the classroom.* Novato, CA: Academic Therapy Publications.

Prigogine, I. (1980). *From being to becoming.* San Francisco: Freeman.

Prigogine, I., & Stengers, I. (1984). *Order out of chaos.* New York: Bantam Books.

Provence, S., & Lipton, R. (1962). *Infants in institutions: A comparison of their development with family-reared infants during the first year of life.* New York: International Universities Press.

Purkey, W. (1966). Measured and professed personality characteristics of gifted high school students and analysis of their congruence. *Journal of Educational Research, 3,* 99–103.

Purkey, W. (1969). Project self discovery: Its effect on bright but underachieving high school students. *Gifted Child Quarterly, 13,* 242–246.

Purkey, W. (1970). *Self-concept and school achievement.* Englewood Cliffs, NJ: Prentice-Hall.

Racle, G. (1977). Documents: Research Institute of Suggestology, Sofia, Bulgaria, 1971. *Suggestopaedia-Canada, 2,* 1–3.

Radcliffe, S., & Hatch, W. (1961). *Advanced standing.* (New Dimensions in Higher Education, No. 8). Washington, DC: U.S. Government Printing Office.

Ramaseshan, P. (1957). *The social and emotional adjustment of the gifted.* Unpublished doctoral dissertation, University of Nebraska, Lincoln, NE.

Raph, J., Goldberg, M., & Passow, A. (1966). *Bright underachievers.* New York: Teachers College Press, Columbia University.

Raspberry, W. (1976). What about elitist high schools? *Today's Education, 65,* 36–39.

Raths, L., Harmin, M., & Simon, S. (1966). *Values and teaching.* Columbus, OH: Charles E. Merrill.

Raudsepp, E. (1980). Intuition: A neglected decision making tool. *Machine Design, 52,* 91–94.

Raven, J. (1947). *Raven's progressive matrices test.* London: H. K. Lewis.

Reichstein, K., & Pipkin, R. (1968). A study of academic justice. *The Law and Society Review, 2.* 259–276.

Reid, M. (1980). *Cerebral lateralization in children: An ontogenetic and organismic analysis.* Doctoral dissertation, University of Colorado, Boulder.

Reihart, R. (1970). *Selfawareness through group dynamics.* Dayton, OH: George A. Pflaum.

Reis, S. (1987). We can't change what we don't recognize: Understanding the special needs of gifted females. *Gifted Child Quarterly, 31*(2), 83–89.

Reis, S., & Renzulli, J. (1986). The secondary triad model. In J. Renzulli, *Systems and models for developing programs for the gifted and talented.* Mansfield Center, CT: Creative Learning Press.

Rekdal, C. K. (1984). Guiding the gifted female through being aware: The math connection. *G/C/T, 35,* 10–12.

Renzulli, J. (1968). Identifying key features in programs for the gifted. *Exceptional Children, 35,* 217–221.

Renzulli, J. (1973a). *Graduate study in special education of the gifted and talented.* Storrs, CT: University of Connecticut, Department of Educational Psychology. (Mimeographed)

Renzulli, J. (1973b). *New directions in creativity.* New York: Harper & Row.

Renzulli, J. (1973c). Talent potential in minority group students. *Exceptional Children, 39*(6), 437–444.

Renzulli, J. (1975a). Identifying key features in programs for the gifted. In W. Barbe & J. Renzulli (Eds.), *Psychology and education of the gifted.* New York: Irvington Publishing.

Renzulli, J. (1975b). *A guidebook for evaluating programs for the gifted and talented.* Ventura, CA: Office of the Ventura County Superintendent of Schools.

Renzulli, J. (1976). The enrichment triad model (Part I). *Gifted Child Quarterly, 20*(3), 303–326.

Renzulli, J. (1977). *The enrichment triad model: A guide for developing defensible programs for the gifted and talented.* Mansfield Center, CT: Creative Learning Press.

Renzulli, J. (1978). What makes giftedness? Reexamining a definition. *Phi Delta Kappan, 60,* 180–184, 261.

Renzulli, J. (1979a). *What makes giftedness: A Reexamination of the definition of the gifted and talented.* Ventura, CA: Office of the Ventura County Superintendent of Schools.

Renzulli, J. (Ed.). (1979b). *Sample instruments for the evaluation of programs for the gifted and talented.* Storrs, CT: Bureau of Educational Research.

Renzulli, J. (1985). Are teachers of the gifted specialists? A landmark decision on employment practices in special education for the gifted. *Gifted Child Quarterly, 29*(1), 24–28.

Renzulli, J., & Hartman, R. (1971). Scale for rating behavioral characteristics of superior students. *Exceptional Children, 38*(3), 243–248.

Renzulli, J., Hartman, R., & Callahan, C. (1971). Teacher identification of superior students. *Exceptional Children, 38*(3), 221–224.

Renzulli, J., & Reis, S. (1986). The enrichment triad/revolving door model: A schoolwide plan for the development of creative productivity. In J. Renzulli (Ed.), *Systems and models for developing programs for the gifted and talented.* Mansfield Center, CT: Creative Learning Press.

Renzulli, J., Reis, S., & Smith, L. (1981). *The revolving door identification model.* Mansfield Center, CT: Creative Learning Press.

Renzulli, J., & Ward, V. (1969). *Diagnostic and evaluative scales for differential education for the gifted.* Storrs, CT: University of Connecticut.

Restak, K. (1979). *The brain: The last frontier.* New York: Doubleday.

Restak, R. (1985). The human brain: Insights and puzzles. *Theory Into Practice, 24*(2), 91–94.

Restak, R. (1986). *The infant mind.* Garden City, NY: Doubleday.

Reynolds, M. (Ed.). (1962). *Early school admission for mentally advanced children.* Reston, VA: Council for Exceptional Children.

Rheingold, H., & Cook, K. (1975). The contents of boys' and girls' rooms as an index of parent behavior. *Child Development, 46,* 459–463.

Rhodes, M. (1961). An analysis of creativity. *Phi Delta Kappan, 42,* 305–310.

Rice, J., & Banks, G. (1967). Opinions of gifted students regarding secondary school programs. *Exceptional Children, 34*(4), 269–272.

Richert, S. (1985). Identification of gifted children in the United States: The need for pluralistic assessment. *Roeper Review, 8*(2), 68–72.

Riessman, F. (1962). *The culturally deprived child.* New York: Harper & Row.

Rimm, S. (1986). *Underachievement syndrome: Causes and cures.* Watertown, WI: Apple Publishing.

Rimm, S., & Davis, G. (1976). GIFT: An instrument for the identification of creativity. *Journal of Creative Behavior, 10*(3), 178–182.

Roberts, H. (1960). *Factors affecting the academic underachievement of bright high school students.* Unpublished doctoral dissertation, University of California, Los Angeles.

Roberts, J. (1973). *The education of oversoul # 7.* Englewood Cliffs, NJ: Prentice-Hall.

Roberts, J. (1974). *The nature of personal reality.* Englewood Cliffs, NJ: Prentice-Hall.

Roberts, T. (1982). Consciousness meets education at UC Berkeley. *Brain/Mind Bulletin, 7*(12), 1.

Roberts, T., & Clark, F. (1976). Transpersonal psychology in education. In G. Hendricks & J. Fadiman (Eds.). *Transpersonal education.* Englewood Cliffs, NJ: Prentice-Hall.

Robinson, A. (1986). Brave new directions: Needed research on the labeling of gifted children. *Gifted Child Quarterly, 30*(1), 11–14.

Rockenstein, Z. (1985). *A Taxonomy of educational objectives for the intuitive domain*. Unpublished doctoral dissertation. University of Georgia, Athens.

Rodenstein, J., Pfleger, L., & Colangelo, N. (1977). Career development of gifted women. *Gifted Child Quarterly, 21,* 340–358.

Roedell, W. (1984). Vulnerabilities of highly gifted children. *Roeper Review, 6*(3), 127–130.

Roedell, W. C., Jackson, N. E., & Robinson, H. B. (1980). *Gifted young children*. New York: Teachers College Press, Columbia University.

Roeper, A. (1986). Participatory vs hierarchical models for administration: The role of the principal. *Roeper Review, 9*(1), 4–10.

Rogers, C. (1959). Toward a theory of creativity. In H. H. Anderson (Ed.), *Creativity and its cultivation*. New York: Harper & Row.

Rogers, C. (1961). *On becoming a person*. Boston: Houghton Mifflin.

Rogers, C. (1969). *Freedom to learn*. Columbus, OH: Charles E. Merrill.

Rogers, D. (Ed.). (1969). *Issues in adolescent psychology*. New York: Appleton-Century Crofts.

Rogge, W. (1970, April). *IMPACT Session IV: Change: Risks, groups, processes*. Paper presented at the annual meeting of the Council of Exceptional Children, Chicago.

Rohrer, J., & Edmondson, M. (Eds.). (1960). *The eighth generation*. New York: Harper & Row.

Roome, J., & Romney, D. (1985). Reducing anxiety in gifted children by inducing relaxation. *Roeper Review, 7*(3), 177–179.

Rorvik, D., & Heyns, O. (1973). *Decompression babies*. New York: Dodd, Mead.

Rose, S. (1972). Environmental effects on brain and behavior. In K. Richardson and D. Spears (Eds.), *Race, culture and intelligence*. Baltimore, MD: Penguin.

Rosenberg, B., & Sutton-Smith, B. (1969). Sibling age spacing effects upon cognition. *Developmental Psychology, 1,* 661–668.

Rosenthal, R. (1968). *Pygmalion in the classroom: Teacher expectation and pupil's intellectual development*. New York: Holt, Rinehart & Winston.

Rosenthal, R., & Jacobsen, L. (1969). *Pygmalion in the classroom: Self-fulfilling prophecies and teacher expectations*. New York: Holt, Rinehart & Winston.

Rosenzweig, M. (1966). Environmental complexity, cerebral change and behavior. *American Psychologist, 21,* 321–332.

Rosenzweig, M. (1984). Experience, memory and the brain. *American Psychologist, 39*(4), 365–376.

Rothenberg, A. (1979). Creative contradictions. *Psychology Today, 13*(1), 55–62.

Rothney, J. (1955). *Evaluating and reporting pupil progress*. Washington, DC: National Educational Association.

Rothney, J., & Koopman, N. (1958). Guidance of the gifted. In N. Henry (Ed.), *Education of the gifted. Fifty-seventh yearbook* (Part II, National Society of Secondary Education). Chicago: University of Chicago Press.

Rowan, R. (1979). Those business hunches are more than blind faith. *Fortune, 99,* 110–114.

Rozman, D. (1976). *Meditation for children*. Millbrae, CA: Celestial Arts.

Rubenzer, R. (1979). Identification and evaluation procedures for gifted and talented programs. *Gifted Child Quarterly, 23*(2), 304–316.

Rubin, J., Provenzano, F., & Luria, Z. (1974). The eye of the beholder: Parents' views on sex of newborns. *American Journal of Orthopsychiatry, 44,* 512–519.

Rugg, H. (1963). *Images and imagination*. New York: Harper & Row.

Runions, T. (1980). The Mentor Academy Program: Educating the gifted/talented for the 80's. *Gifted Child Quarterly, 24*(4), 152–157.

Rust, J., & Lose, B. (1980). Screening for giftedness with the Slosson and the Scale for Rating Behavioral Characteristics of Superior Students. *Psychology in the Schools, 17*(4), 446–451.

Rust, R., & Ryan, F. (1953). The relationship of some Rorschach variables to academic behavior. *Journal of Personality, 21,* 441–456.

Rutherford, G. (1977, August). *An attitudinal survey of teachers toward gifted education.* Paper presented at California State University, Los Angeles, Department of Special Education.

Sadker, M., & Sadker, D. (1985). Sexism in the schoolroom of the '80s. *Psychology Today, 19*(3), 54–57.

Sagan, C. (1974). *Broca's brain*. New York: Random House.

Sagan, C. (1977). *The dragons of Eden*. New York: Random House.

Salk, L. (1973). The role of the heartbeat in the relations between mother and infant. *Scientific American, 288,* 24–29.

Samples, B. (1970). *Essence I & II* [Two classroom kits for awareness activities]. Reading, MA: Addison-Wesley.

Samples, B. (1975). Learning with the whole brain. *Human Behavior, 4,* 18–23.

Samples, B. (1976). *The metaphoric mind: A celebration of creative consciousness*. Reading, MA: Addison-Wesley.

Samples, B. (1977). Mind cycles and learning. *Phi Delta Kappan, 58,* 688–692.

Samples, B. (1987). *Openmind/wholemind*. Rolling Hills Estates, CA: Jalmar Press.

Samples, B., Charles, C., & Barnhart, D. (1977). *The wholeschool book: Teaching and learning late in the 20th century*. Reading, MA: Addison-Wesley.

Samples, B., & Wohlford, B. (1973). *Opening: A primer for self-actualization*. Reading, MA: Addison-Wesley.

Samuels, M., & Bennett, H. (1973). *The well body book*. New York: Random House.

Sanborn, M. (1979). Differential counseling needs of the gifted and talented. In N. Colangelo & R. Zaffrann (Eds.), *New voices in counseling the gifted*. Dubuque, IA: Kendall/Hunt.

Satir, V. (1972). *Peoplemaking*. Palo Alto, CA: Science & Behavior Books.

Sattler, J. (1970). Racial "experimenter effects" in experimentation, testing, interviewing, and psychotherapy. *Psychological Bulletin, 73*(2), 137–160.

Saunders, R. (1982). Art education for the gifted. *Roeper Review, 4*(3), 7–10.

Savage, J. (1983). Reading guides: Effective tools for teaching the gifted. *Roeper Review, 5*(3), 9–11.

Scarr-Salapatek, S. (1974a). Comment on individual and group differences in I.Q. In P. Rosenthal (Ed.), *Annual editions: Readings in human development*. Guilford, CT: Dushkin.

Scarr-Salapatek, S. (1974b, February). *Genetic determinants of infant development: An overstated case*. Paper presented to the Psycho-Biology Symposium: The Importance of Infancy, American Association for the Advancement of Science, San Francisco.

Schaefer, C. E. (1970). A psychological study of 10 exceptionally creative adolescent girls. *Exceptional Children, 36*(6), 431–441.

Schaefer, E., & Aaronson, M. (1972). Infant education pre-school project: Implementation and implications of a home tutoring program. In R. Parker (Ed.), *The pre-school in action: Exploring early childhood programs.* Boston: Allyn & Bacon.

Schaefer, E., & Marcus, M. (1973). Self-stimulation alters human sensory brain responses. *Science, 181,* 175–177.

Scheibel, M., & Scheibel, A. (1964). Some neural substrates of postnatal development. In M. Hoffman & L. Hoffman (Eds.), *Review of child development research* (Vol. 1.). New York: Russell Sage Foundation.

Schiff, M., Kaufman, A., & Kaufman, N. (1981). Scatter analysis of WISC-R profiles for learning disabled children with superior intelligence. *Journal of Learning Disabilities, 14,* 400–404.

Schlichter, C. (1986). Talents unlimited: An inservice education model for teaching thinking skills. *Gifted Child Quarterly, 30*(3), 119–123.

Schmuck, R., & Schmuck, P. (1971). *Group process in the classroom.* Dubuque, IA: William C. Brown.

School Staffing Survey 1969–70. Washington, DC: Department of Health, Education, and Welfare, U.S. Office of Education.

Schrank, J. (1972). *Teaching human beings: 101 subversive activities for the classroom.* Boston: Beacon Press.

Schulte, F. (1969). Excitation, inhibition, and impulsive conduction in spinal motoneurones of preterm, term and small-for-dates newborn infants. In R. J. Robinson (Ed.), *Brain and early behavior: Development in the fetus and infant* (pp. 87–109). New York: Academic Press.

Schultz, J., & Luthe, W. (1959). *Autogenic training: A psychophysiological approach to psychotherapy.* New York: Grune & Stratton.

Schutz, W. (1976). Education for the body. In G. Hendricks & J. Fadiman (Eds.), *Transpersonal education: A curriculum for feeling and being.* Englewood Cliffs, NJ: Prentice-Hall.

Schwartz, G., & Shapiro, D. (Eds.). (1976). *Consciousness and self-regulation* (Vol. 1). New York: Plenum.

Scientific American. (1979). *The brain.* San Francisco, CA: Freeman.

Scott, J. (1962). Critical period in behavioral development. *Science, 138* (3544), 949–953.

Seagoe, M. (1974). Some learning characteristics of gifted children. In R. Martinson, *The identification of the gifted and talented.* Ventura, CA: Office of the Ventura County Superintendent of Schools.

Sears, P., & Barbee, A. (1977). Career and life satisfactions among Terman's gifted women. In J. Stanley, W. George, & C. Solano (Eds.), *The gifted and the creative: A fifty-year perspective.* Baltimore, MD: Johns Hopkins University Press.

Seeley, K. (1979). Competencies for teachers of gifted and talented children. *Journal for the Education of the Gifted, 3*(1), 7–13.

Seeley, K. (1981). Professional standards for training programs in gifted education. *Journal for the Education of the Gifted, 4*(3), 165–168.

Segal, G., (1984). The fourth dimension. *Science Digest, 92*(1), 68–69.

Seidner, C. (1976). Teaching with simulations and games. In N. Gage (Ed.), *The psychology of teaching methods: The seventy-fifth yearbook of the National Society on the Study of Education* (pp. 217–251).

Selby, C. (1980). Science as the 'fourth R'—Basic and also beautiful. *Science Digest, 88*(3), 44–47.

Selye, H. (1956). *The stress of life.* New York: McGraw-Hill.

Selye, H. (1979). Foreward. In K. Albrecht, *Stress and the manager* (pp. v–vii). Englewood Cliffs, NJ: Prentice-Hall.

Serbin, L., & O'Leary, K. (1975). How nursery schools teach girls to shut up. *Psychology Today, 9,* 57–58; 102–103.

Sergent, J. (1982). The cerebral balance of power: Confrontation or cooperation? *Journal of Experimental Psychology: Human Perception and Performance, 8,* 1, 253–272.

Severy, L., & Davis, K. (1971). Helping behavior among normal and retarded children. *Child Development, 4,* 1017–1031.

Sexton, P. (1961). *Education and income.* New York: Viking.

Shapiro, D., Tursky, B., Gershon, E., & Stern, M. (1969). Effects of feedback and reinforcement on the control of human systolic blood pressure. *Science, 163,* 588–590.

Sharan, S. (1980). Cooperative learning in small groups: Recent methods and effects on achievement, attitudes, and ethnic relations. *Review of Educational Research, 50*(2), 241–271.

Shaw, M. (1964). Definition and identification of academic underachievers. In J. French (Ed.), *Educating the gifted* (rev. ed.). New York: Holt, Rinehart & Winston.

Shaw, M., & Black, D. (1960). The reaction to frustration of bright high school underachievers. *California Journal of Educational Research, 11,* 120–124.

Shaw, M., & McCuen, J. (1960). The onset of academic underachievement in bright children. *Journal of Educational Psychology, 51,* 103–108.

Sheive, L., & Schoenheit, M. (Eds.). (1987). *Leadership: Examining the elusive* (Association for Supervision and Curriculum Development 1987 Yearbook).

Sheldon, W., & Manolakes, G. (1954). Comparison of the Stanford-Binet, Revised Form L and the California Test of Mental Maturity (S-Form). *Journal of Educational Psychology, 45,* 499–504.

Sheldrake, R. (1981). A new science of life. *New Scientist, 90* (1256), 749, 766–768.

Shostrom, E. (1964). An inventory for the measurement of self-actualization. *Educational and Psychological Measurement, 24,* 207–218.

Shouksmith, G., & Taylor, J. (1964). The effect of counseling on the achievement of high ability pupils. *British Journal of Educational Psychology, 34,* 51–57.

Silberman, C. (1971). *Crisis in the classroom.* New York: Random House.

Silverman, L. (1980). Secondary programs for gifted students. *Journal for the Education of the Gifted, 4*(1), 30–42.

Silverman, L. (1986). Giftedness, intelligence and the new Stanford-Binet. *Roeper Review, 8*(3), 168–171.

Silvernail, D. (1980). Gifted education for the 80's and beyond: A futuristic curriculum model for the gifted child. *Roeper Review, 2*(4), 16–18.

Simon, S. (1974). Please touch! How to combat skin hunger in our schools, *Scholastic Teacher, 105,* 22–25.

Simon, S., Howe, L., & Kirschenbaum, H. (1972). *Values clarification.* New York: Hart Publishers.

Simon, S., Kirschenbaum, H., & Fuhrmann, B. (1972). *An introduction to values clarification.* New York: J. C. Penney.

Simonov, P. (1970). Emotions and creativity. *Psychology Today, 4*(3), 51–55, 77.

Simpson, R., & Martinson, R. (1961). *Educational programs for gifted pupils.* Sacramento, CA: California State Department of Education.

Singer, B. (1974). The future-focused role image. In A. Toffler (Ed.), *Learning for tomorrow.* New York: Vintage.

Singer, J. (1975). *The inner world of day dreaming.* New York: Harper & Row.

Singer, J. (1976). Fantasy: The foundation of serenity. *Psychology Today, 10*(2), 32–37.

Sisk, D. (n.d.) *Teaching gifted children* [Developed in conjunction with a Federal Grant from Title V, Section 505]. Project Director, James Turner, South Carolina. (Florida component)

Sisk, D. (1973, March). *Developing teacher mediators/teacher training for disadvantaged gifted.* Paper presented at the First National Conference on the Disadvantaged Gifted, Ventura, CA.

Sisk, D. (1975a). Communication skills for the gifted. *Gifted Child Quarterly, 19,* 66–68.

Sisk, D. (1975b). Teaching the gifted and talented teacher: A training model. *Gifted Child Quarterly, 19,* 81–88.

Sisk, D. (1987). *Creative teaching of the gifted.* New York: McGraw-Hill.

Skeels, H. (1966). Adult status of children with contrasting early life experiences. *Monographs of the Society for Research in Child Development, 31*(3).

Skeels, H., & Dye, H. (1959). A study of the effects of differential stimulation on mentally retarded children. *Proceedings of American Association on Mental Deficiency, 44,* 114–136.

Skeels, H., Updegraff, R., Wellman, B., & Williams, H. (1938). A study of environmental stimulation: An orphanage preschool project. *University of Iowa Studies in Child Welfare, 15*(4), 28, 264.

Skodak, M., & Skeels, H. (1949). A final follow-up study of one hundred adopted children. *Journal of Genetic Psychology, 74–75; 85–125.*

Slavkin, H. (1987, February). *Science in the 21st century.* Speech presented at the 25th Annual Conference of the California Association for the Gifted, Los Angeles.

Sluckin, W. (1965). *Imprinting and early learning.* Chicago, IL: Aldine.

Smith, R. (1965). *The relationship of creativity to social class.* (United States Office of Education Cooperative Research Project No. 2250). Pittsburgh, PA: University of Pittsburgh.

Soar, R. (1970). Research findings from systematic observation. *Journal of Research and Development in Education, 4,* 116–122.

Solano, C. (1977). Teacher and pupil stereotypes of gifted boys and girls. *Talents and Gifts. 19,* 4–8.

Sonntag, J. (1967). Sensitivity training with gifted children. *Gifted Child Quarterly, 13*(1), 51–57.

Sonntag, J. (1972). *Communications and relatedness: A curriculum guide for mentally gifted minors.* Sacramento, CA: California State Department of Education.

Sontag, L., Baker, C., & Nelson, V. (1958). Mental growth and personality development: A longitudinal study. *Monograph of Sociological Research in Child Development, 1958, 23* (2, Whole No. 68).

Special Projects Act. (1974). Public Law 93–380.

Spino, M. (1976). *Beyond jogging: The innerspaces of running.* Millbrae, CA: Celestial Arts.

Spolin, V. (1963). *Improvisations for the theatre.* Evanston, IL: Northwestern University Press.

Springer, S., & Deutsch, G. (1981). *Left brain, right brain.* San Francisco, CA: W. H. Freeman.

Squires, S. (1981, July 12). Subtle bias still limit them, black, women doctors say. *Los Angeles Times,* p. 10.

Sroufe, L. A. (1979). Socioemotional development. In J. Osofsky (Ed.), *Handbook of infant development.* New York: John Wiley & Sons.

Standing, E. (1966). *The Montessori revolution in education.* New York: Schocken.

Stanford study links parents' approach with children's grades. (1986, April 9). *Report on Education Research,* p. 3.

Stanley, J. (1979). The case for extreme educational acceleration of intellectually brilliant youths. In J. Gowan, J. Khatena, & E. P. Torrance (Eds.), *Educating the ablest. A book of readings* (2nd ed.). Itasca, IL: F. E. Peacock Publishers.

Stanley, J., Keating, D., & Fox, L. (Eds.). (1974). *Mathematical talent: Discovery, description, and development.* Baltimore, MD: Johns Hopkins University Press.

Starch, D. (1913). Reliability of grading work in mathematics. *School Review, 21,* 254–295.

Starch, D., & Elliott, E. (1912). Reliability of grading of high school work in English. *School Review, 20,* 442–457.

Stark, M. (1972). *Results of a questionnaire given to 152 high school gifted students.* Paper presented at California State University, Los Angeles.

State of the States: Gifted and Talented Education, 1986–87. (in press). Helena, MT: Council of State Directors of Programs for the Gifted.

Stearn, J. (1976). *The power of alpha thinking.* New York: William Morrow.

Steele, J. (1969). *Instructional climate in Illinois gifted classes.* Springfield, IL: Illinois State Office of the Superintendent of Public Instruction, Department of Program Planning for Gifted.

Stein, M. (1962). *Survey of the psychological literature in the area of creativity with a view toward needed research* (U.S. Office of Education Cooperative Research Project #E-3). New York: New York University.

Stephens, L. (1974). *The teacher's guide to open education.* New York: Holt, Rinehart & Winston.

Sternberg, R. (1981). A componential theory of intellectual giftedness. *Gifted Child Quarterly, 25*(2), 86–93.

Sternberg, R. (1985). *Beyond IQ: A triarchic theory of human intelligence.* Cambridge, MA: Cambridge University Press.

Sternberg, R. (1986). Identifying the gifted through IQ: Why a little bit of knowledge is a dangerous thing. *Roeper Review, 8*(3), 143–147.

Stevens, J. (1971). *Awareness: Exploring, experimenting, experiencing.* Moab, UT: Real People Press.

Stevenson, H., Hale, G., Klein, R., & Miller, L. (1968). Interrelations and correlates in children's learning and problem solving. *Monographs of the Society for Research in Child Development, 33.*

Stewart, E. (1981). Learning styles among gifted/talented students: Instructional technique preferences. *Exceptional Children, 48*(2), 134–138.

Stewart, K. (1969). Dream theory in Malaya. In C. Tart (Ed.), *Altered states of consciousness: Book of readings.* New York: John Wiley & Sons.

Stipek, D., & Weisz, J. (1981). Perceived personal control and academic achievement. *Review of Educational Research, 51*(1), 101–137.

Stodtbeck, F. (1958). Family interaction values and achievement. In D. McClelland (Ed.), *Talent and society*. Princeton, NJ: Van Nostrand Reinhold.

Stogbill, R. (1974). *Handbook of leadership: A survey of theory and research*. New York: Free Press.

Stogbill, R., & Coons, A. (Eds.). (1957). *Leader behavior; its description and measurement* (No. 88). Columbus, OH: Bureau of Business Research, Ohio State University.

Stollak, G. (1978). *Until we are six*. Huntington, NY: Academic Press.

Stone, L., Smith, H., & Murphy, L. (Eds.). (1973). *The competent infant: Research and commentary*. New York: Basic Books.

Story, C. (1985). Facilitator of learning: A micro-ethnographic study of the teacher of the gifted. *Gifted Child Quarterly, 29*(4), 155–159.

Stott, D. (1973). Follow-up study from birth of the effects of prenatal stresses. *Developmental Medicine and Child Neurology, 15*, 770–787.

Stott, D. (1977). Children in the womb: The effects of stress. *New Society, 40*, 329–331.

Strang, R. (1956). Gifted adolescents, Views of growing up. *Exceptional Children, 23*, 10–15, 20.

Strang, R. (1960). *Helping your gifted child*. New York: E. P. Dutton.

Struss, D. T., & Benson, D. F. (1984). Neuropsychological studies of the frontal lobes. *Psychological Bulletin, 95*(1), 3–28.

Subotnik, R. (1984). Emphasis on the creative dimension: Social studies curriculum modifications for gifted intermediate and secondary students. *Roeper Review, 7*(1), 7–10.

Suchman, J. R. (1961). Inquiry training: Building skills for autonomous discovery. *Merrill Palmer Quarterly of Behavior and Development, 7*, 147–169.

Suchman, J. R. (1962). *The elementary school training program in scientific inquiry*. Urbana, IL: University of Illinois Press.

Sumption, M. (1941). *Three hundred gifted children*. Yonkers-on-Hudson, NY: World Book.

Superka, D. (1974, November). Approaches to values education. *Science Education Consortium Newsletter*.

Suter, D., & Wolf, J. (1987). Issues in the identification and programming of the gifted/learning disabled child. *Journal for the Education of the Gifted, 10*(3), 227–237.

Sylwester, R. (1982a, September). A child's brain, Part I. *Instructor*, 90–96.

Sylwester, R. (1982b, October). A child's brain, Part II. *Instructor*, 64–67.

Syphers, D. (1972). *Gifted and talented children: Practical programming for teachers and principals*. Arlington, VA: Council for Exceptional Children.

Szekely, G. (1981). The artist and the child—A model program for the artistically gifted. *Gifted Child Quarterly, 25*(2), 67–72.

Szekely, G. (1982). Creative learning and teaching of the gifted through sketchbooks. *Roeper Review, 4*(3), 15–17.

Taba, H. (1966). *Teaching strategies and cognitive functioning in elementary school children* (U.S. Office of Education Cooperative Research Project #2404). San Francisco, CA: San Francisco State College.

Tannenbaum, A. (1962). *Adolescent attitudes toward academic brilliance*. New York: Bureau of Publications, Teachers College, Columbia University.

Tannenbaum, A. (1983). *Gifted children*. New York: Macmillan.

Tan-Willman, C., & Gutteridge, D. (1981). Creative thinking and moral reasoning of academically gifted secondary school adolescents. *Gifted Child Quarterly, 25*(4), 149–153.

Tarjan, G. (1970). Some thoughts on sociocultural retardation. In H. C. Haywood (Ed.), *Socio-cultural aspects of mental retardation*. New York: Appleton-Century-Crofts.

Tarrytown Group. (1982, May). Conclave in Bombay. *The Tarrytown Letter*, 1–3, 13.

Tayler, T. (1972). *Altered states of awareness: Readings from Scientific American*. San Francisco: W. H. Freeman.

Taylor, C. W. (Ed.). (1956). *Research conference on the identification of creative scientific talent*. Salt Lake City: University of Utah Press.

Taylor, C. W. (1959). Identifying the creative individual. In E. P. Torrance (Ed.), *Creativity: Proceedings of the second Minnesota conference on gifted children*. Minneapolis, MN: Center for Continuation Study.

Taylor, C. W. (1963). Clues to creative teaching: The creative process and education. *Instructor, 73*, 4–5.

Taylor, C. (1967). Questioning and creating: A model for curriculum reform. *Journal of Creative Behavior, 1*(1), 22–33.

Taylor, C. W., & Williams, F. E. (1966). *Instructional media and creativity*. New York: John Wiley & Sons.

Taylor, I. (1976). Psychological sources of creativity. *Journal of Creative Behavior, 10*, 193–202.

Taylor, J., & Walford, R. (1972). *Simulation in the classroom*. Baltimore, MD: Penguin Books.

Taylor, L., & Bongar, B. (1976). *Clinical applications in biofeedback therapy*. Los Angeles: Psychology Press.

Taylor, L., Tom, G., & Ayers, M. (1981). *Electromyometric biofeedback therapy*. Los Angeles: Biofeedback and Advanced Therapy Institute.

Teilhard de Chardin, P. (1959). *The divine milieu*. New York: Harper & Row.

Temple University. (1968). *Report of the college of education ad hoc committee on grading systems*. Philadelphia, PA: Author.

Terman, L. (1916). *The measurement of intelligence*. Boston: Houghton Mifflin.

Terman, L. (1925). Mental and physical traits of a thousand gifted children. In L. Terman (Ed.), *Genetic studies of genius* (Vol. I). Stanford, CA: Stanford University Press.

Terman, L. (1954). The discovery and encouragement of exceptional talent. *American Psychologist, 9*, 221–230.

Terman, L., & Oden, M. (1947). The gifted child grows up. In L. Terman (Ed.), *Genetic studies of genius* (Vol. IV). Stanford, CA: Stanford University Press.

Terman, L., & Oden, M. (1959). The gifted group at mid-life; thirty-five year's follow-up of the superior child. In L. Terman (Ed.), *Genetic studies of genius* (Vol. V). Stanford, CA: Stanford University Press.

Teyler, T. (1977). An introduction to the neurosciences. In M. Wittrock (Ed.), *The human brain*. Englewood Cliffs, NJ: Prentice-Hall.

Theodore, A. (1971). *The professional woman*. Cambridge, MA: Schenkman Publishing Company.

Thinking Caps: Materials for gifted: Cognitive, affective, psychomotor skills and activities. Box 7239, Phoenix, AZ 85011.

Thistlewaite, D. (1958). How the talented student evaluates his high school. *School Review, 66*, 164–168.

Thomas, A., Hertzig, I., & Fernandez, P. (1971). Examiner effect in IQ testing of Puerto Rican working-class children. *Measurement and Evaluation in Guidance, 4*(3), 172–175.

Thomas, J. (1980). Agency and achievement: Self-management and self-regard. *Review of Educational Research, 50*(2), 213–240.

Thompson, R., Berger, T., & Berry, S. (1980). An introduction to the anatomy, physiology, and chemistry of the brain. In M. Wittrock (Ed.), *The brain and psychology.* New York: Academic Press.

Thorndike, R. L. (1963a). *The concepts of over and underachievement.* New York: Bureau of Publications, Teachers College, Columbia University.

Thorndike, R. L. (1963b). The measurement of creativity. *Teachers College Record, 64,* 422–424.

Thorndike, R. L. (1975). Mr. Binet's test 70 years later. *Educational Researcher, 4*(5), 3–6.

Thorndike, & Hagern (1983). The Cognitive Abilities Tests.

Tiegs, E. (1952). Educational diagnosis. *Educational Bulletin* (No. 18). Monterey, CA: California Testing Bureau.

Time. (1972). *99,* 25–103.

Tomer, M. (1981). Human relations in education—A rationale for a curriculum in inter-personal skills for gifted students—grade K–12. *Gifted Child Quarterly, 25*(2), 94–97.

Tomlinson, S. (1986). A survey of participant expectations for inservice in education of the gifted. *Gifted Child Quarterly, 30*(3), 110–113.

Tonemah, S. (1987). Assessing American Indian gifted and talented students' abilities. *Journal for the Education of the Gifted, 10*(3), 181–194.

Torrance, E. P. (1960). *The Minnesota studies of creative thinking in the early school years.* (University of Minnesota Research Memorandum, No. 59–4). Minneapolis, MN: University of Minnesota, Bureau of Educational Research.

Torrance, E. P. (1962). *Guiding creative talent.* Englewood Cliffs, NJ: Prentice-Hall.

Torrance, E. P. (1963). *Education and the creative potential.* Minneapolis, MN: University of Minnesota Press.

Torrance, E. P. (1964a). Education and creativity. In C. W. Taylor (Ed.), *Creativity: Progress and potential.* New York: McGraw-Hill.

Torrance, E. P. (1964b). *Rewarding creative behavior.* Englewood Cliffs, NJ: Prentice-Hall.

Torrance, E. P. (1966). *Torrance Tests of Creative Thinking: Norms-technical manual.* Princeton, NJ: Personnel Press.

Torrance, E. P. (1968a). Creativity and its educational implications for the gifted. *Gifted Child Quarterly, 12*(2), 67–78.

Torrance, E. P. (1968b). A longitudinal examination of the fourth grade slump in creativity. *Gifted Child Quarterly, 12*(4), 195–199.

Torrance, E. P. (1969). Creative positives of disadvantaged children and youth. *Gifted Child Quarterly, 13*(2), 71–81.

Torrance, E. P. (1976). Future careers for gifted and talented students. *Gifted Child Quarterly, 20,* 142–156.

Torrance, E. P. (1977). Creatively gifted and disadvantaged gifted students. In J. Stanley, W. George, & C. Solano (Eds.), *The gifted and the creative: A fifty-year perspective.* Baltimore, MD: Johns Hopkins University Press.

Torrance, E. P. (1981). Cross-cultural studies of creative development in seven selected societies. In J. Gowan, J. Khatena, & E. P. Torrance (Eds.), *Creativity: Its educational implications* (2nd ed.) (pp. 89–97). Dubuque, IA: Kendall/Hunt.

Torrance, E. P., Blume, B., Maryanopolis, J., Murphey, F., & Rogers, J. (1980). *Teaching scenario writing.* Lincoln, NE: Future Problem Solving Program, Nebraska Department of Education.

Torrance, E. P., & Myers, R. (1962). Teaching gifted elementary pupils research concepts and skills. *Gifted Child Quarterly, 6,* 1–16.

Torrance, E. P., & Torrance, J. P. (1981). Educating gifted, talented and creative students for the future. *American Middle School Education, 4*(1), 39–46.

Treffinger, D. (1975). Teaching for self-directed learning: A priority for the gifted and talented. *Gifted Child Quarterly, 19*(1), 46–59.

Treffinger, D. (1986). Research on creativity. *Gifted Child Quarterly, 30*(1), 15–19.

Tremaine, C. (1979). Do gifted programs make a difference? *Gifted Child Quarterly, 23*(3), 500–517.

Trotter, R. (1971). Self-image. *Science News, 100,* 130–131.

Trowbridge, A. (1978). Evolution of triune brain consciousness. *Man-Environment Systems, 8*(3), 105–112.

Truesdell, B., & Newman, J. (1975). Can jr. highs make it with wide open spaces? *Learning, 4*(3), 74–77.

Tucker, R. (1986). Breaking through with your ideas. *Creative Living, 15*(3), 2–8.

Ubel, E. (1986, February 16). How science is learning to understand your brain. *Parade Magazine,* pp. 10–11.

Usher, R., & Hanke, J. (1971). Third force in psychology and college teacher effectiveness research at the University of Northern Colorado. *Colorado Journal of Educational Research, 10,* 2.

Uzgiris, I. C., & Hunt, J. McV. (1966). *An instrument for assessing infant psychological development* (Mimeograph paper). Urbana: University of Illinois, Psychological Department Laboratory.

Van Duyne, J., & D'Alonzo, B. (1976). Amount of verbal information and ear differences in 5- and 6-year-old boys and girls. *Perceptual and Motor Skills, 43,* 31–39.

Van Horn, M., & Hanson, R. (1975). *Leading creative participation.* Unpublished article.

Van Tassel, J. (1980). Evaluation of gifted programs. In J. Jordan & J. Grossi (Eds.), *An administrator's handbook on designing programs for the gifted and talented.* Reston, VA: Council for Exceptional Children.

Van Tassel-Baska, J. (1986a). Effective curriculum and instructional models for talented students. *Gifted Child Quarterly, 30*(4), 164–169.

Van Tassel-Baska, J. (1986b). Lessons from the history of teacher inservice in Illinois: Effective staff development in the education of gifted students. *Gifted Child Quarterly, 30*(3), 124–126.

Vare, J. (1979). Moral education for the gifted: A confluent model. *Gifted Child Quarterly, 23*(3), 487–499.

Vargiu, S. (1971). *Psychosynthesis case studies: Three gifted adolescents.* Redwood City, CA: Psychosynthesis Institute.

Vaughan, F. (1979). *Awakening intuition.* New York: Doubleday.

Vermilyea, J. (1981). Common sense in the identification of gifted and talented students who need alternative programming. *G/C/T, 16,* 11–14.

Vernon, P. (1979). *Intelligence: Heredity and environment.* San Francisco: Freeman.

Verny, T. (1981). *The secret life of the unborn child.* New York: Summit Books.

Vogel, J. (1974). Learning and self-esteem. *Learning, 2*(7), 68–72.

Voight, R. (1971). *Invitation to learning: The learning center handbook.* Washington, DC: Acropolis Books.

Vygotsky, L. (1962). *Thought and language* (E. Hanfmann & G. Vakar, Eds. and Trans.). New York: Wiley.

Vygotsky, L. (1974). The problem of age-periodization of child development (M. Zender & B. Zender, Trans.) *Human Development, 17,* 24–40.

Waber, D. (1977a). Biological substrates of field dependence: Implications of the sex difference. *Psychological Bulletin, 84,* 1076–1087.

Waber, D. (1977b). Sex differences in mental abilities, hemispheric lateralization and rate of physical growth at adolescence. *Developmental Psychology, 13,* 29–38.

Wachs, T. (1969, May). *The measurement of early intellectual functioning: Contributions from developmental psychology.* Paper presented at American Association on Mental Deficiency, San Francisco.

Wachs, T. (1976). Utilization of a Piagetian approach in the investigation of early experience effects: A research strategy and some illustrative data. *Merrill-Palmer Quarterly, 22,* 11–30.

Walberg, H. (1969). Physics, femininity, and creativity. *Developmental Psychology, 1,* 47–54.

Wallach, M., & Kogan, N. (1965). *Cognitive originality, physiognomic sensitivity and defensiveness in children.* Durham, NC: Duke University.

Wallas, G. (1926). *The art of thought.* London: C. A. Watts.

Walsh, A. (1956). *Self-concepts of bright boys with learning difficulties.* New York: Teachers College Press, Teachers College, Columbia University.

Wampler, M. (1973). *Music: A curriculum guide for mentally gifted minors.* Sacramento, CA: California State Department of Education.

Wang, M., & Stiles, B. (1976). An investigation of children's concept of self-responsibility for their school learning. *American Educational Research Journal, 13,* 159–179.

Ward, V. (1961). *Educating the gifted: An axiomatic approach.* Columbus, OH: Charles E. Merrill.

Wass, H., Blume, R., Combs, A., & Hedges, W. (1974). *Humanistic teacher education: An experiment in systematic curriculum innovation.* Fort Collins, CO: Shields.

Watson, G. (1957). Some personality differences in children related to strict or permissive parental discipline. *Journal of Psychology, 44,* 227–249.

Weaver, J. (1983). Performance patterns of two culturally different populations of identified gifted students on the Ross Test of Higher Cognitive Processes. *Journal for the Education of the Gifted, 6*(3), 178–194.

Webb, D. (1971). Teacher sensitivity: Affective impact on students. *Journal of Teacher Education, 22,* 455–459.

Webb, J., Meckstroth, E., & Tolan, S. (1982). *Guiding the gifted child.* Columbus, OH: Ohio Psychology Publishing Company.

Webb, R. (1974). Concrete and formal operations in very bright six to eleven year olds. *Human Development, 17,* 292–300.

Weiner, J. (1968). Attitudes of psychologists and psychometrists toward gifted children and programs for the gifted. *Exceptional Children, 34,* 354.

Weiner, J., & O'Shea, H. (1963). Attitudes of university faculty, administrators, teachers, supervisors, and university students toward the gifted. *Exceptional Children, 30*(4), 163–165.

Weiner, N., & Robinson, S. (1986). Cognitive abilities, personality and gender differences in math achievement of gifted adolescents. *Gifted Child Quarterly, 30*(2), 83–87.

Weinheimer, S. (1972, March). How to teach your child to think: A conversation with Jean Piaget, the "giant in the nursery." *Redbook*, 96–97, 118, 120.

Weinhold, B. (1976). Transpersonal communication in the classroom. In G. Hendricks & J. Fadiman (Eds.), *Transpersonal education*. Englewood Cliffs, NJ: Prentice-Hall.

Weinstein, G., & Fantini, M. (1970). *Toward humanistic education: A curriculum of affect*. New York: Praeger.

Weiss, M. (1972). *Free for baby and mother: An encyclopedia of things available to parent and child at no cost*. South Brunswick, NJ: A. S. Barnes.

Weiss, P., & Gallagher, J. (1980). The effects of personal experience on attitudes toward gifted education. *Journal for the Education of the Gifted, 3*(4), 194–197.

Weiss, P., & Gallagher, J. (1986). Project TARGET: A needs assessment approach to gifted education inservice. *Gifted Child Quarterly, 30*(3), 114–118.

Weisstein, N. (1969). Woman as nigger. *Psychology Today, 3*, 20–22, 58.

Welch, I., Richards, F., & Richards, A. (1973). *Educational accountability: A humanistic perspective*. Fort Collins, CO: Shields.

Wellington, C., & Wellington, J. (1965). *The underachiever: Challenges and guidelines*. Chicago: Rand McNally.

Wellman, B. (1940). Iowa studies on the effects of schooling. *Yearbook of the National Society on Studies in Education, 39*, 377–399.

Wescott, G., & Woodward, J. (1981). Locating the not so obvious gifted. *G/C/T, 20*, 11.

Wescott, M. (1968). *Toward a contemporary psychology of intuition*. New York: Holt, Rinehart & Winston.

White, B. (1975). *The first three years of life*. Englewood Cliffs, NJ: Prentice-Hall.

White, B., & Castle, P. (1964). Visual exploratory behavior following postnatal handling of human infants. *Perceptual and Motor Skills, 18*, 497–502.

White, B., & Watts, J. (1973). *Experience and environment* (Vol. I). Englewood Cliffs, NJ: Prentice-Hall.

White, M. (1970). The case of specifically designed education for the gifted. *Gifted Child Quarterly, 14*, 159–162.

Whitmore, J. (1980). *Giftedness, conflict, and underachievement*. Boston: Allyn & Bacon.

Whitmore, J. (1981). Gifted children with handicapping conditions: A new frontier. *Exceptional Children, 48*(2), 106–114.

Whitmore, J. (1986). Understanding a lack of motivation to excel. *Gifted Child Quarterly, 30*(2), 66–69.

Whitmore, J., & Maker, J. (1985). *Intellectual giftedness in disabled persons*. Rockville, MD: Aspen.

Wilber, K. (Ed.). (1982). *The holographic paradigm and other paradoxes*. Boulder, CO: Shambhala.

Williams, F. (Ed.). (1968). *Creativity at home and in school*. St. Paul, MN: Macalester Creativity Project.

Williams, F. (1979). Models for encouraging creativity in the classroom. In J. Gowan, J. Khatena, & E. P. Torrance (Eds.), *Educating the ablest, A book of readings*. Itasca, IL: F. E. Peacock Publishers.

Willings, D. (1986). Enriched career search. *Roeper Review, 9*(2), 95–100.

Wilson, F. T. (1958). The preparation of teachers for the education of gifted children. In B. Henry (Ed.), *Education for the gifted, 57th yearbook* (Part II). National Society for the Study of Education, Chicago: University of Chicago Press.

Wingerson, L. (1982a). A window on the body. *Discover, 3*(4), 85, 86, 88.

Wingerson, L. (1982b). Training the mind to heal. *Discover, 3*(5), 80–82, 85.

Witelson, S. (1976). Sex and the single hemisphere. *Science, 193,* 425–427.

Witters, L., & Vasa, S. (1981). Programming alternatives for educating the gifted in rural schools. *Roeper Review, 3*(4), 22–24.

Wittrock, M. (1980a). Learning and the brain. In M. Wittrock (Ed.), *The brain and psychology.* New York: Academic Press.

Wittrock, M. (Ed.) (1980b). *The brain and psychology.* New York: Academic Press.

Wittrock, M., Beatty, J., Bogen, J., Gazzaniga, M., Jerison, H., Krashen, S., Nebes, R., & Teyler, T. (1977). *The human brain.* Englewood Cliffs, NJ: Prentice-Hall.

Witty, P. (1930). A study of one hundred gifted children. *Bulletin of Education, 2*(7).

Witty, P. (1940). Some considerations in the education of gifted children. *Educational Administration and Supervision, 26,* 512–521.

Witty, P. (Ed.). (1951). *The gifted child.* Boston: Heath.

Wodtke, K. (1964). Some data on the reliability and validity of creative tests at the elementary school level. *Educational and Psychological Measurement, 24,* 399–408.

Wolf, M. (1981). The CTTE approach to innovative education. *Roeper Review, 4*(2), 33–34.

Wolleat, P. (1979). Guiding the career development of gifted females. In N. Colangelo & R. Zaffrann (Eds.), *New voices in counseling the gifted.* Dubuque, IA: Kendall/Hunt.

Wooddell, G., Fletcher, G., & Dixon, T. (1982). Futures study for the adolescent gifted: A curriculum evaluation. *Journal for the Education of the Gifted, 5*(1), 24–33.

Worcester, D. (1955). *The education of children above average mentality.* Lincoln, NE: University of Nebraska Press.

World Future Society. (1979). *World Future Society catalog* (4916 St. Elmo Ave. [Bethesda], Washington, DC 20014).

Wright, P. (1965). *Enrollment for advanced degrees* (E-5401-63, Circular No. 786). Washington, DC: Office of Education, U.S. Department of Health, Education and Welfare.

Wright, W., & Jung, C. (1959). Why capable school students do not continue their schooling. *Bulletin of the School of Education,* Indiana University, *35* (1).

Wyatt, F. (1982). Responsibility for gifted learners—A plea for the encouragement of classroom teacher support. *Gifted Child Quarterly, 26*(3), 140–143.

Yamamoto, J. (1975). *Leadership skill development syllabus.* Los Angeles. Los Angeles City Schools, Instructional Planning Division.

Yamamoto, K. (1964). Creative thinking: Some thoughts on research. *Exceptional Children, 30,* 403–410.

Yamamoto, K. (1965). Effects of restriction of range and test unreliability on correlation between measures of intelligence and creative thinking. *British Journal of Educational Psychology, 35,* 300–305.

Yarrow, L. (1968). Research in dimensions of early maternal care. *Merrill-Palmer Quarterly, 9,* 101–114.

Yarrow, L., Rubenstein, J., & Pedersen, F. (1973). *Infant and environment. Early cognitive and motivational development.* New York: Halsted.

Yarrow, L., Rubenstein, J., Pedersen, F., & Jankowski, J. (1972). Dimensions of early stimulation and their differential effects on infant development. *Merrill-Palmer Quarterly, 18,* 205–218.

Yuker, H. (1955). Group atmosphere and memory. *Journal of Abnormal and Social Psychology, 51,* 17–23.

Zaffrann, R., & Colangelo, N. (1977). Counseling with gifted and talented students. *Gifted Child Quarterly, 20,* 305–321.

Zettel, J. (1979). Gifted and talented education over a half decade of change. *Journal for the Education of the Gifted, 3*(1), 14–37.

Zimmerman, J. (1982). MEG gets inside your head. *Psychology Today, 16*(4), 100.

Zoccolotti, P., & Oltman, P. (1978). Field dependence and lateralization of verbal and configurational processing. *Cortex, 14,* 155–163.

Zuckerman, D., & Horn, R. (1973). *The guide to simulations/games for education and training.* Lexington, MA: Information Resources.

Zukav, G. (1979). *The dancing Wu Li masters: An overview of the new physics.* New York: William Morrow.

NAME INDEX

Abraham, R., 366
Abraham, W., 523
Adkins, D., 554
Adkins, L., 589
Agor, W., 401, 594
Ainsworth, M., 89
Alberti, R., 384
Albrecht, K., 388, 389
Allport, G., 141
Almada, P., 239
Alvino, J., 231, 232
Amabile, T., 52–53
Ambrose, R., 471
Amidon, E., 536
Anderson, H. H., 46, 56, 61, 536
Anderson, L., 245
Anderson, M., 65
Anderson, V. V., 533
Andrews, E. G., 67
Andrews, F., 70–71
Archer, N., 470
Arnold, A., 484
Aschner, M., 533
Aspy, D., 33, 141, 532, 535
Austin, N., 384
Ausubel, D. P., 75

Bachtold, L., 473

Bahler, J., 333
Baker, C., 21
Baldwin, A., 227, 234, 484, 486, 492–493
Bancroft, J., 588
Banks, G., 444, 445
Barbe, W. B., 136, 145, 224
Bardot, A., 389
Bardwick, J., 508
Barrett, H., 473
Barron, F., 71
Barzakov, 592
Baum, S., 499
Bayley, N., 21
Becker, W., 148
Beechhold, H., 270
Bell, J., 514
Bennett, G., 231
Bennett, H., 265
Benton, J., 218
Bentov, I., 581–582, 583
Bernal, E., 239
Bertschi, J., 243
Bessell, H., 262, 272
Betts, G., 191, 196, 204, 205
Binet, A., 16, 221
Birch, J., 153, 224, 228
Birnbaum, M., 211
Birns, B., 84

Bishop, W., 539–540
Black, D., 477
Blackwell, E., 502–503
Block, 514–515
Bloom, B., 19 20, 85, 120, 121, 212, 246, 254, 260, 282–285, 309, 334, 363
Bloom, D., 32
Boehm, L., 137
Bohm, D., 38, 579, 580
Boocock, S., 374
Bordie, J., 236
Borgers, S., 562
Borkowski, J., 374
Borland, J., 13, 224–225
Boston, B., 182–185, 194, 215
Bower, P., 462
Bower, R., 83
Bowles, N., 267–268
Bowman, P., 473
Branscomb, A., 180–181
Brazelton, T. B., 82
Brewer, J. E., 536
Bricklin, B., 476
Bricklin, P., 476
Bridgman, A., 114–115
Brier, C., 403
Brookover, W., 141, 532
Brown, B., 536, 589, 591

SUBJECT INDEX

Inquiry sessions, 345–346
Inservice teacher education,
    546–555
    effective, 555–558
Inservice training for parents,
    568–569
Instruction, explicit, 22
Instrumental enrichment,
    374–375
Integrated development,
    155–166
Integrative education, 107,
    218–219. *See also*
        Differentiated integrative
        curriculum
    brain functions and, 296–298
    components of, 299–302
    rationale of, 295–296
    results of, 303–304
    secondary school curriculum
        in, 447–457
    strategies of, 298
    transpersonal learning in,
        592–593
Integrative metaphoric mode,
    107
Integrity, despair, 150
Intellectual ability, 8
    development of from 2
        through 5 years, 101–110
*Intellectual Giftedness in
    Disabled Persons,* 500
Intellectual transition of
    adolescence, 432–433
Intelligence
    aging and, 20–21
    brain function in, 23–38
    capacity for, 21
    concept of, 8–12
    creativity and, 49–50
    definition of, 6, 221
    early development and, 19–21
    educability of, 17–18
    factors influencing growth of,
        7
    as fixed, 15–17
        challenge of, 17–19
    heritability of, 15–16
    historical views of, 15–23
    interactive view of, 9–12,
        17–23
    measuring of, 12–15. *See also*
        Intelligence quotient
        (IQ)
    modes of, 586
    neurobiological data on, 22
    as predetermined, 17
    rise in average, 21

seven types of, 22–23
survival and, 8
theoretical base for, 12
theories of, 15–23
triarchic concept of, 21–22
Intelligence quotient (IQ)
    early childhood development
        of, 20
    environment and, 10–11
    inconstancy of, 16–17, 20–22
    as inheritable, 9–10
    relationship to
        accomplishment in gifted
        females, 504
    sex differences in loss of, 506
    tests for, 12–15
        cultural bias of, 235–236
        culture free, 248–249
        experimenter effect in, 236
        to identify cognitively
            gifted, 221, 227–228
        popularity of, 16
        problems of for culturally
            diverse learners, 235–237
        scores for, 13–15
Interdisciplinary presentations,
    312
Interest centers, 415. *See also*
    Learning centers
International baccalaureate
    program, 439
Internships, 195–196, 379
Interpersonal intelligence, 22
Intimacy, isolation, 150
Intrapersonal intelligence, 22
Intrinsic motivation, 317–319
    creativity and, 52–53, 58
Intuition, 297–298
    creativity and, 65
    definition of, 402–404
    development and integration
        of, 302
    in integrative educional
        program, 267–270
    strategies for, 400–412
    disciplined, 594
    fostering, 405–406
    in gifted, 131*t*
    nurturing of, 163
    process of, 410–412
        in classroom, 426
        definition of, 404
    using, 404–405
Intuitive awareness, 593–596
Intuitive mind, 107–108
Intuitive transitions of
    adolescence, 436–438
Inventive metaphoric mode,

107–108
Iowa Tests of Basic Skills, 232
Isolation, 168–169, 173–174
    disease and, 585
    in traditional classroom, 315

Jewish culture, 489
Jigsaw groups, 376–377
Journal writing, 330–331*f*
Junior Great Books Program, 303
Junior high programs, 456
Justice, sense of, 164

Kaplan's Grid model, 276,
    279–282
Kaufman Assessment Battery for
    Children, 232
Kinesthetic awareness, 396–397
Kirlian photography, 594
Knowledge-acquisition
    processes, 22
    alternative, 410–412

Labeling, 460–463
    problems with, 527–528
Land surveying field trip, 363
Language
    development of, 101–103
    in early learning, 97*t*
    empowering, 300–301,
        321–322
    in preschool learning,
        113–114
Language Acquisition Device
    (LAD) period, 101–102,
    103
Language arts curriculum,
    335–337
    accelerated program of, 208
    activities in, 342–343
    bibliotherapy, 342
    reading, 337–338
    in secondary integrative
        curriculum, 455–456
    writing, 338–342
Leadership abilities, 271
    assessment of, 245
    characteristics of, 227, 526
    development of, 526–527
    identification of, 221
    testing for, 230, 232–233
Leadership Studies Program, 527
Learning
    active involvement of learner
        in, 39
    age and, 22–23